NEW PERSPECTIVES IN
ORGANIZATION RESEARCH

CONSISTING OF PAPERS FROM

A Conference on Research in Organizations
Sponsored by the U. S. Office of Naval Research
at Carnegie Institute of Technology
June 22–24, 1962

A Seminar on the Social Science of Organizations
Sponsored by the Ford Foundation
at the University of Pittsburgh
June 10–23, 1962

NEW PERSPECTIVES IN

ORGANIZATION RESEARCH

EDITED BY

W. W. Cooper, CARNEGIE INSTITUTE OF TECHNOLOGY

H. J. Leavitt, CARNEGIE INSTITUTE OF TECHNOLOGY

M. W. Shelly II, U. S. OFFICE OF NAVAL RESEARCH

JOHN WILEY & SONS, INC.

New York · London · Sydney

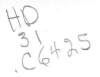

Contributors

WILLIAM W. COOPER, Graduate School of Industrial Administration, Carnegie Institute of Technology, Pittsburgh 13, Pennsylvania

HAROLD J. LEAVITT, Graduate School of Industrial Administration, Carnegie Institute of Technology, Pittsburgh 13, Pennsylvania

MAYNARD W. SHELLY II, Logistics and Mathematical Statistics Branch, U. S. Office of Naval Research, Washington 25, D. C.

JOHN H. HOAGLAND, Eppley Center, Michigan State University, East Lansing, Michigan

WILLIAM R. DILL, Graduate School of Industrial Administration, Carnegie Institute of Technology, Pittsburgh 13, Pennsylvania

VICTOR H. VROOM, Graduate School of Industrial Administration, Carnegie Institute of Technology, Pittsburgh 13, Pennsylvania

JOHN W. THIBAUT, Department of Psychology, University of North Carolina, Chapel Hill, North Carolina

BERNARD M. BASS, Graduate School of Business, University of Pittsburgh, Pittsburgh 13, Pennsylvania

RUTH LEEDS, Reed College, Portland, Oregon

DAVID MECHANIC, Department of Sociology, University of Wisconsin, Madison, Wisconsin

BRUCE J. BIDDLE, Social Psychology Laboratory, The University of Missouri, Columbia, Missouri

STANLEY H. UDY, JR., Department of Sociology, Yale University, New Haven, Connecticut

HARRISON WHITE, Department of Social Relations, Harvard University, Cambridge 38, Massachusetts

ABRAHAM CHARNES, Technological Institute, Northwestern University, Evanston, Illinois

ANDREW STEDRY, Massachusetts Institute of Technology, School of Industrial Management, Cambridge 39, Massachusetts

NEIL C. CHURCHILL, Graduate School of Industrial Administration, Carnegie Institute of Technology, Pittsburgh 13, Pennsylvania

RICHARD M. CYERT, Graduate School of Industrial Administration, Carnegie Institute of Technology, Pittsburgh 13, Pennsylvania

JAMES G. MARCH, Division of Social Sciences, University of California, Irvine, California

JAMES E. MC NULTY, Department of Industry, Wharton School, University of Pennsylvania, Philadelphia 4, Pennsylvania

THOMAS L. WHISLER, Graduate School of Business, University of Chicago, Chicago 37, Illinois

JAMES D. THOMPSON, School of Business, University of Indiana, Bloomington, Indiana

I. J. GOOD, Institute for Defense Analysis, Communications Research Division, Princeton, New Jersey

ANDREW WHINSTON, The Cowles Foundation, Yale University, New Haven, Connecticut

PRESENTLY AT: University of Virginia, Charlottesville, Virginia

MARTIN SHUBIK, IBM Corporation, Thomas J. Watson Research Center, Yorktown Heights, New York

PRESENTLY AT: The Cowles Foundation, Yale University, New Haven, Connecticut

RUTH M. DAVIS, Department of Defense, Research and Engineering, Pentagon, Washington 25, D. C.

GEORGE E. BRIGGS, Laboratory of Aviation Psychology, Department of Psychology, Ohio State University, Columbus, Ohio

MIHAJLO D. MESAROVIĆ, Systems Research Center, Case Institute of Technology, Cleveland 6, Ohio

C. FREMONT SPRAGUE III, Univac, Division of Sperry Rand Corporation, San Diego 6, California

JERRY L. SANDERS, Department of Systems Engineering, University of Arizona, Tucson, Arizona

SAUL B. SELLS, Institute of Behavioral Research and Department of Psychology, Texas Christian University, Fort Worth, Texas

JOSEPH E. MC GRATH, Department of Psychology, Group Effectiveness Research Laboratory, University of Illinois, Champaign, Illinois

Preface

The papers comprising the chapters in this volume are drawn from two sources: (1) From an Office of Naval Research Conference on Research in Organizations held at Carnegie Institute of Technology, June 22–24, 1962, and (2) from a Ford Foundation Seminar on the Social Science of Organizations held at the University of Pittsburgh, June 10–23, 1962. The Conference participants, by and large, were persons active in either the Management Sciences (including Operations Research) or the Behavioral Sciences (including Economics). The Seminar participants were drawn in pairs from designated universities, with one participant ordinarily coming from a school of business and the other from a social science department at the same university. The Conference and the Seminar were arranged so that the opening dates of the former could serve as terminating dates for the latter, and also so that some of the Seminar working papers could be included for presentation at the Conference. The organizers hoped thus to further a main seminar objective which was to initiate certain types of cross-disciplinary research on organizations that could then be continued and sustained, by further support if necessary, when the participants returned to their respective campuses.

The emphasis in the Conference was on new perspectives in organization research, at least in the sense of providing behavioral and management scientists with an opportunity to hear and evaluate each other's work. We tried to secure reports from persons who were known to have research already under way, thus avoiding an entirely programmatic approach to the Conference topics. On the other hand, we recognized that much of this research might exist only in a formative stage. Furthermore, the Conference was intended to encompass a wide variety of problems and approaches, so it did not seem advisable to restrict the presentations to reports of finished research results.

The chapters in this volume are organized into five categories: A short set describing the state of the art; a behavioral science set; an interdisciplinary set; a management science set; and a set oriented toward future research.

As W. R. Dill remarks in Chapter 3, research in organizations is generally "interdisciplinary." Nevertheless, it seemed desirable to use that term, as above, to distinguish one of the major sets into which these papers have been divided. This categorization should provide some guidance to readers of this volume. For instance, persons whose backgrounds are in sociology, psychology, or anthropology will perhaps find it easiest to read first the chapters in the behavioral science section. In the interdisciplinary chapters they may expect to find further behavioral science material, but now interlaced with management science and other approaches. Similar remarks apply to the division labeled "management science," but in either case the introductory-and-state-of-the-art sections might well be read first. Chapters from the other divisions deserve at least some sampling by all readers.

The classifications used are evidently very broad. They are certainly not mutually exclusive nor exhaustive. Moreover, our classification of a particular chapter does not always coincide with the designation that an author might have used.[1] The suggested sampling of chapters may thus help to guard against the editors' oversights while providing some flavor of the total volume. To aid the reader in his sampling, we have provided a rather detailed table of contents. This is also meant to serve in lieu of an index. For we concluded that no detailed index which we could prepare would be equally useful for this purpose.

This book does not purport to give a balanced assessment of the existing state of knowledge of organizational behavior. The emphasis here—as the title suggests—is on new perspectives, and even this emphasis is neither exhaustive nor completely successful. But it seems reasonable to suppose that much of our further progress will emanate from the two main groups represented in this volume: behavioral scientists, with a record of relatively recent but intense interest in organization theory and analysis; and management scientists, even more recently arrived upon the scene.

---

[1] Witness, for instance, the relegation of the papers by Whinston and Shubik (economists) into the management science division because (so it appeared to us) most readers would look there for the topics they treat or the modes of development they utilize.

Criticisms and reactions to the book will be welcomed and may be directed to the authors or the editors. Acknowledgment is due the U. S. Office of Naval Research for its sponsorship of the Conference and to the Ford Foundation for its sponsorship of the Seminar as well as for its grant of a faculty fellowship that freed one of the editors (Cooper) for the final work necessary on this volume. We are grateful to Dorothy M. Gilford, Luigi Petrullo, and Herbert A. Simon for their advice and help in planning this activity. Among the many other persons who assisted in the preparation of this book, we should especially single out Miss Barbara Barkovich, who administered the Conference and typed (and retyped) much of the text. Also, Mr. Trevor Sainsbury carefully reviewed the manuscripts, conducted correspondence with the authors, and prepared the bibliography which appears at the end of this volume.

W. W. Cooper
H. J. Leavitt
M. W. Shelly II

February 1964

Contents

PART FOUR   MANAGEMENT SCIENCE PERSPECTIVES, 349

29 *Organizational Design, 557*

R. M. CYERT AND J. G. MARCH

NEW PERSPECTIVES IN
ORGANIZATION RESEARCH

1

CHANGING PATTERNS OF
ORGANIZATION RESEARCH

W. W. Cooper, H. J. Leavitt, M. W. Shelly, II

. . . During the lifetime of most of today's leaders, the United States has covered the span from horses to space travel. This has not been achieved by retaining "buggy-whip" management philosophies. Indeed, industry has gone through a management revolution during this period. The refinement of skills, the replacement of skills by machinery, and the computerization of laborious engineering and office routines have markedly affected industrial processes and structures. In 1958, for the first time in the history of private industry in this country, white-collar workers outnumbered blue-collar workers, and the trend is continuing. Somewhat similarly in the military services, increasing complexity in weapons and equipment, caused largely by greater use of electronics and automation and approaching "push-button" warfare, has exerted pressures for more maintenance and support personnel behind the man behind the weapon. . . . But these forces which render obsolete traditional management methods also raise new problems in management of this country's most priceless resource—the human being.

The subtle changes in the status and standards of living of the American individual must be recognized and exploited, not ignored, in developing truly effective structures and processes of the future. The philosophical and psychological impact on human beings caused by space exploration; fantastic speeds; intricate, miniaturized equipment; and a greater degree of participation in technical effort and decision-making greatly influences the techniques which must be employed in attracting, training, motivating, and retaining the kind of civilians and military people the Department must have to perform its role on the defense team.

This statement, taken from a recent eight-volume report on U. S. Navy management [562],[1] points broadly to some large issues facing

---

[1] Numbers in brackets are keyed to the references which appear in the bibliography.

contemporary managers and administrators. In the face of such demands for innovation in management, what can we report about relevant ongoing scientific research?

This book contains reports of research and conceptual explorations by behavioral and management scientists about problems of organization design and management. In this introductory chapter we shall try to explicate the design of this volume and relate the sections and papers within sections to one another. The chapters immediately following this one—by Hoagland and by Dill—supply historical and current perspective to complete this introductory division of the book. Then follows, in sequence, a behavioral science division, an interdisciplinary division, and a management science division. The final division of the book consists of chapters which point up further issues and possible prospects and problems for future research.

As Hoagland and Dill suggest in Chapters 2 and 3 (which complete this first section), there is a history to research and reflection on organizations which has already reached into a variety of disciplines, and is growing vigorously. In these two chapters, the vigor of organizational research is apparent; but so, too, are the difficulties that have slowed progress in the field. One of the largest of these difficulties is "researcher isolation"—isolation from predecessors so that rediscoveries are often seen as new discoveries—and isolation within disciplines so that related journal articles (in unrelated journals) frequently pass in the night.

Perspectives from the Behavioral Sciences

One way to summarize the papers in this division of the book is to point to the increasing concern by behavioral scientists with the organization itself rather than only with individuals or with broad institutional problems. The papers in this division reflect this developing emphasis on organizational dynamics. Attention is directed toward management organizations as integrated—or disintegrating—systems, and attention is also directed toward analyses of relationships among individuals and groups rather than on the individuals themselves. Experimentation with gaming and other new approaches is also in evidence as an effort is made to interpret and reassess old problems like leadership, power, and status. Finally, a further twist and new perspective is obtained as some ideas from psychology, sociology, and anthropology are adjusted for their possible use in understanding the problems of managed organizations.

Chapter 4, by Leavitt, opens this division of the book by sketching the major variables of task, structure, technology, and people which are central for any behavioral science approach to organizations. Of course, these variables also provide a focus which is to be found in such "classical" writings as L. Gulick and L. Urwick's *Papers on the Science of Administration* [563]. On the other hand, a difference in emphasis is immediately noticeable if one compares Leavitt's discussion with those of Gulick, Urwick, Mooney, or Fayol as reported in [563]. Leavitt's emphasis on the interaction among these variables also distinguishes it from the approach of even more classical industrial psychology and carries with it an implicit call for research on better methods of analysis and implementation.[2]

One view of "people variables," i.e., these variables viewed from the standpoint of individual psychology, is next examined by Vroom in Chapter 5. In contrast to more classical attempts to apply the techniques of individual psychology to the problems of ongoing organizations (testing, selection, classification, training, etc.), the Chapter by Vroom should be regarded as one part of a larger program [3] designed to show that the behavior of individuals in organizations are instances of more general psychological laws. More generally, the avowed purpose of Vroom's program is to provide a bridge between psychology and organization theory so that each may contribute to and stimulate the other. These objectives are shared, of course, by Leavitt and others (see, e.g., Shelly, Chapter 20). Leavitt, however, proposes to make these contacts through social psychology. Vroom moves through individual psychology. He also modifies the emphasis which Leavitt accords to task, structure, and technology, relegating them to the background so that "people variable" can become the center of attention.

One purpose of research is to open new alternatives for possible exploitation. This is also one way to assess the value of a "new perspective" for research on organizations. The stimulus-response categorizations employed by Vroom might be considered as only a different phrasing of some of the job classification-personnel selection approaches. For example, he examines discrimination phenomena and asserts: "[One] . . . method is to keep the stimulus aspects of roles constant but to select role occupants who have proven capacities to make the relevant discriminations. . . ." On the other hand, this notion is immediately placed in a wider perspective when Vroom asserts, "another . . . method of doing this is to alter the character-

---

[2] For a brief but good history of industrial psychology in America, see L. W. Ferguson "The Development of Industrial Psychology," Chap. 2 in [189].
[3] See, e.g., V. H. Vroom [577] and also [579].

istics of stimuli which require different responses." [4] Also, Vroom suggests still further extensions when he observes the possible relevance of individual learning theory: "Insofar as the capacity to discriminate between stimuli can be modified by experience, it is possible for organizations to train individuals to make the discriminations required by their roles." This implicitly raises the possibility of an information strategy in which worse outcomes may perhaps be temporarily justified by a compensating improvement in performance (or reduced information cost) in the future. (This kind of possibility, at least as a learning or training device, appears to be pertinent to the command-control systems described by Ruth Davis, in Chapter 24, where the speed of electronic data processing, the number of variables available for display, etc., need to be matched against the likely capabilities of military commanders in these man-machine decision systems.)

Thibaut's Chapter 6 next considers some of the roles which people can occupy, along with some of the factors—information and belief or organization and technology—that cause them to assume these roles and act in particular ways. Leaders, and especially leaders at the top, are generally viewed as activists—men of action motivated by beliefs in ultimate right, justice, and the like. Thus, in his famous summary essay on political administration,[5] Machiavelli observes that:

It is not [sic] *unknown to me how many have been and are of the opinion that worldly events are so governed by fortune and by God, that men cannot by their prudence change them, and that on the contrary there is no remedy whatever, and for this they may judge it useless to toil much about them, but let things be ruled by chance.*

This problem of the activist relying on a "powerful external agency of control" is examined by Thibaut in Chapter 6. Machiavelli analyzed it by historical documentation on the deeds of "great men." [6] Thibaut's approach is via social psychology which he uses in conjunction with ideas from the theory of games. Thereby he brings organizational aspects of the problem into focus by means of coalition-payoff arrangements between a player (person) and an organization in the form of a game against nature (the environment). In contrast to

---

[4] The latter possibilities have already been exploited to some extent by A. Stedry who has added now a new category of "psychological" or "motivational cost" which can be considered for possible use alongside the more traditional categories of "opportunity" or "alternative" costs (economics) and "historical" costs (accounting). See [516] as well as the discussion in Chapter 13.

[5] *The Prince* [360], p. 91.

[6] See, e.g., *loc. cit.,* Chapter XV as well as [361] Chapter IX.

the usual mathematical characterizations of game theory, however, Thibaut's major focus is on social psychological variables. He considers the kinds of behavior which are likely to be exhibited in terms of "comparison level" constructs. By means of these constructs, Thibaut is able to extend the analysis of individual "learning" into a more general "adaptation" framework, in which the individual reacts both to his own perceptions of the experience of others and his own experience.

Any approach which is confined to social-psychological laboratory investigations is, of course, limited insofar as the study of "great" leaders (living and dead) are concerned. This approach however need not exclude recourse to other methods, e.g., historical research. Indeed, the question of innate greatness is itself a moot one for research, at least insofar as politics and administration are concerned. Machiavelli himself observes: [7]

That we cannot . . . change at will is due to two causes; the one is the impossibility of resisting the natural bent of our characters; and the other is the difficulty of persuading ourselves, after having been accustomed to success by a certain mode of proceeding, that any other can succeed as well. It is this that causes the varying success of a man; for the times change, but he does not change his mode of proceeding.

Evidently, however, there is some room for experimentation to counteract some of these tendencies toward the rigidity that can be imposed by a record of past success. Here, too, the concept of comparison levels offers at least one path where "learning from experience" can be utilized to produce part of a "set" toward flexibility, as well as the reverse.

Much has been said, but little has been done, in the way of utilizing gaming (as distinct from the theory of games) for research and teaching. The paper by Bass, Chapter 7, provides an example of some of these possibilities.[8] In this chapter the emphasis shifts from leadership at the top toward the study of interacting organizational devices for their possible bearing on the scalar principles of unity of command, and clear lines of authority.[9] For this purpose Bass uses gaming (competi-

---

[7] [361] *loc. cit.,* p. 443.

[8] Another use, in a less highly structured game, is reported in [478].

[9] That is, the emphasis here shifts from personnel at the entrepreneurial level, in the sense of Peter Drucker, to persons who are acting mainly in the role of manager-administrators. For further work directed towards lower echelon leadership problems see B. M. Bass and J. A. Vaughan [48]. See also the discussion of the leadership requirements at different organization levels in Chapter 13 of D. McGregor, *op. cit.* [380].

tive simulation) in order (*a*) to secure insight into organizational behavior and (*b*) to test certain kinds of generalizations. The first category of these POE (Production Organization Exercises) studies presents some data on the kinds of organizations (e.g., kinds of line-staff relations) which participants selected. Results from this type of investigation may be regarded as an extension of earlier findings by Guetzkow and Simon [242] in a simpler situation. A second category of POE studies some design proposals derived from recent social-psychological studies (notably those of Rensis Likert and his associates) [10] and compares their efficacy against certain commonly used types of formal organizations. This comparison is especially interesting because it supplies a perspective from which we can begin to see a basis for systematic progress as new organizational devices are developed from research in one context [11] and then altered or validated by reference to another research context, and so on.

Incipient attempts at strikes, picketing and unionization were all observed as "labor protests" in POE. In some cases "protest absorption" also appeared—as when, for instance, the agitators were promoted from labor to management positions.

Chapter 8, by Ruth Leeds, has "protest absorption" as its main concern. She also shifts attention from *utilitarian* types of organizations (e.g., a factory, a business firm) to ones which may be called *normative* in character (e.g., a church, an army). Finally, she moves from a laboratory into a historical-sociological context for material with which to illustrate her theoretical constructs and findings.

We distinguished earlier between "entrepreneurs" and "manager-administrators." It would be a mistake, however, to associate the former only with the topmost rung of an organization. We are reminded of this, as Leeds, in Chapter 8, analyzes the processes of protest absorption with special reference to the cases of St. Theresa and Claire Chennault. Charismatic leaders such as these may easily become heads of revolutionary movements even when motivated, initially, by overcommitment to their organizations. Part of the problem of management is to accommodate such persons to the parent organi-

---

[10] See Rensis Likert [350], pp. 181 ff. and observe that Bass (*a*) tests only the structural variables suggested by Likert and not his other variables such as quality of group, quality and nature of information and (*b*) modifies the portion of Likert's proposed structure which he does test.

[11] Of course this is not the first instance of an attempt to suggest organizational innovation from a basis of prior, or preparatory, research—as witness, for instance, F. W. Taylor's ideas on "functional foremanship" which also, presumably, were suggested by his researches.

zation while utilizing their innovative, or reformist, tendencies and energies. Leeds calls particular attention to the role of top manager and intermediary, e.g., the roles of Philip II, the Pope and Roosevelt, who either supported St. Theresa and Chennault, respectively, or else acted as arbitrators to mediate or circumvent the conservative opposition generally emanating from "middle managers."

Mechanic, in Chapter 9, carries such ideas a stage further. He analyzes the sources of power of lower participants even when the latter have neither leaders nor "enclaves" with which to identify. Of particular interest is the attitude of lower participants toward role structure and organizational control. As Mechanic asserts, "lower participants do not usually use the role structure of the organization to achieve control; rather they usually circumvent it, sabotage it, and manipulate it." [12]

A more precise description of the contents of Mechanic's paper is provided from the abstract which originally accompanied it:

This paper explores various factors that account for the power of secretaries, hospital attendants, prison inmates, and other lower participants within organizations. Power is seen as resulting from access to and control over persons, information, and instrumentalities. Among the various [factors] discussed affecting power are normative definitions, perception of legitimacy, exchange, and coalitions. Personal attributes related to power include commitment, effort, interest, willingness to use power, skills, and attractiveness. Finally, various attributes of social structure are discussed which also help to account for the power of lower participants. time spent in the organization, centrality of position, duality of power structures, and replaceability of persons.

The concept of "role" is important in social psychology as well as in sociology and anthropology.[13] It is, unfortunately, a term which is accorded different meanings by different authors. Hence it becomes worthwhile to attempt to clarify its possible meanings and modes of use. This task is essayed by Biddle in Chapter 10 where he tries to give the construct added sharpness by considering its utility for or-

---

[12] If space had permitted, we would also have found it interesting, to examine the ideas of power and authority which are implicit in Mechanic's discussion relative to more traditional constructs such as those of Mooney and Riley or Fayol. For a summary of these ideas see, e.g., L. Urwick "The Function of Administration" in Gulick and Urwick, *op. cit.* [563]. See also Glenn Gilman's effort [215] and H. Munsterburg [410] on the psychology of sub- and superordination.
[13] See, e.g., Ralph Linton [351] and [352]. A general discussion of different uses of this concept in the context of a study of managerial motivation (and "self theory") may be found in C. A. Hickman and M. H. Kuhn [269].

ganizational analysis. Using his extensive research into educational systems as background, Biddle proceeds to this development through systems which he refers to as "overt," "cognitive," and "official." These systems are accorded concrete realization in the form, respectively, of (i) "evident" or "observable acts" of an acting person or (ii) the mental processes which are presupposed for these actions and (iii) written codes or known rituals in terms of which the indicated actions are supposed to occur. Biddle does not stop with formal definitions and characterizations. Rather—as is also true in Mechanic's discussion—he draws pointed questions and propositions which are amenable to test. For example, he makes some assertions about possible absence of organizational purposes or goals, even in viable organizations, and challenges a voluminous literature which has insisted that purpose plus coordinated direction, are quintessential features of formal organizations. On the other hand, we might also note that his propositions are of a *ceteris paribus* variety—everything else held equal or constant. Hence, some care would be needed in testing their validity, and even more care would be needed to study effects of their joint variation with other factors, especially if we wished to apply them to problems of organizational design.[14]

Udy's Chapter 11 brings us into another realm—the realm of management practice in different cultures. Interest in comparative management has been intense, of late, partially because of the concern by labor economists about higher level manpower requirements in developed and developing countries. Harbison and Myers [252] have, for example, recently carried out a notable study on such issues. Because of their orientation, perhaps, they look at management as a *social class* or *elite;* an *economic resource* and a *system of authority.*

In Chapter 11 Udy approaches the same problem from another angle, by means of anthropological data. To understand how organizational arrangements are influenced by their environments, he studies nonindustrial, preindustrial or preliterate societies where no issues of industrialization and modernization, etc., intervene. In this "simpler" framework, using cross-cultural data, he examines the technological requirements for hunting, fishing, and agriculture in order to assess various modes of managerial organization and motivation that can be supplied. The focus is on rationality by reference to purpose, where purpose is judged in turn by reference to the activity being pursued,

---

[14] We shall shortly examine some of the methodological developments that bear on problems of multiple variable design.

as analyzed in the broader social context in which it occurs.[15] (In Biddle's terminology the analysis is in term of "overt" systems only; but the study is conducted in a broader and richer context than those which have been exclusively concerned with comparative management analyses relative to highly developed societies.)

Interdisciplinary Approaches

When summarizing papers in the behavioral science division, we observed some experimentation with newer techniques like gaming. We also observed how other received ideas from psychology, sociology, and anthropology were being adjusted for possible use in organization analysis *per se*. In the interdisciplinary division of this book, these tendencies became even more marked. Thus, for instance, extensive use of mathematics and electronic computer simulations become noticeably more prominent here. Furthermore, this research proceeds beyond straightforward attempts to apply already available methods and includes reports of research designed to extend the scope of these methods in order to make them more suitable for the analysis and solution of organization problems.

This kind of "methodological" research on computer simulation and mathematical models, as typical "management science" tools, provides one way of distinguishing the papers in this section. Another basis of distinction is provided by the fact that this division is concerned with more traditional characterizations of management problems and practices in areas like merger and divisionalization as well as in budgeting and accounting. Finally, a variety of ideas from economics as well as the other social and managerial sciences are here joined together in order to study problems like the relation of organization size to internal and external environmental situations as well as the uncertainties which can appear as causes or consequences of organization changes.

Sciences are sometimes classified by reference to their methodologies (e.g., laboratory sciences) as well as their subject matter (e.g., life sciences). The papers in this interdisciplinary division freely use the methodologies as well as the substantive findings of many different sciences. They also evidence considerable fluidity in their willingness to cross traditional boundaries and experiment with new ways of

---

[15] Particular attention should be called to the further discussion of rationality and bureaucracy, etc., given in Chapters 3 and 4, "Technology and Organization" and "Organization Structure and Society," in Udy [557].

studying organizations. Their attention to problems of "management" might seem to supply a common focus. Even here, however, some further qualification is needed since many of these studies evidence an eye toward possible extension of the underlying sciences as well.

This "interdisciplinary" division begins with a paper by Harrison White, Chapter 12, which uses a favorite management science technique, mathematics, to illuminate some important problems in anthropology. The importance of roles to organizational structure and analysis arose earlier in connection with Professor Biddle's chapter. Professor White adds significantly to this. What is specially interesting here is not merely the fact of increased power and manipulability which White demonstrates by applying his mathematics to kinship role analyses but also their possible use for discovering new types of relationships previously overlooked by anthropologists. Evidently, as White observes, these same mathematical devices can be employed to like ends in the analysis, for example, of existing and potential managerial relations.

Of course, there is room for innovation in mathematics as well as in management. Such innovation is suggested by White and also in the work of Charnes and Stedry reported in Chapter 13. Stedry's earlier work on motivational costs was almost necessarily confined to the study of aspiration level formation and behavior in a relatively simple one-goal, one-person task. Stedry has now joined forces with Charnes to experiment with some models and mathematical innovations which form a necessary prelude to more realistic and complex experiments. These elaborations are, in turn, needed before actual applications in large scale organizations can prudently be essayed. As a first step in this direction, then, Charnes and Stedry extend some of the mathematics which had previously been developed in operations research and elsewhere as an aid for functional *planning*. But still further mathematical innovation is likely to be required as their present studies in management *control* are extended to *operations* where planning and control must interact.[16]

The Charnes-Stedry paper may be viewed as a new approach to an old, familiar, and important instrument of management, viz., budgeting. The same is true for the study of audits discussed by Churchill and Cooper in Chapter 14. The approach is here pointed toward more than merely improving such instruments of management control for their customary applications. Thus instead of focusing on audits

---

[16] See preface and Chapter I in A. Charnes and W. W. Cooper [113] for further discussion of the terms planning, control and operations.

as a means for securing conformance to already prescribed policies and procedures, Churchill and Cooper are concerned to see how audit variables (including audit "anticipations") may be used to develop new modes of "automatic"—or "self"—management. The essential idea is to use auditing as a distinguishable form of "influence relation," and thereby provide an alternative to more traditional relations of supervision and subordination. In this connection we may note that part of the study is directed to analysis of audit effects produced when an auditor does not have any particular expertise in the task and its performance. "Accounting audits" are distinguished from "supervision audits" and studied for their respective effects on immediate "task performance" versus more remote "organization" desiderata and objectives. This still leaves untouched however, the question of multiple task performance and coordination in different parts of a complex organization, where, as previously noted,[17] further mathematical research and innovation will first be required.

In contrast to the Charnes-Stedry and Churchill-Cooper focus on particular managerial functions, we turn, in Bonini's Chapter 15, to the analysis of a total managerial system. The tool used is computer simulation and the study is modeled via materials drawn from known, readily available, parts of the management literature. The constructs are drawn from economics, psychology and accounting (as is typical in a behavioral-theory-of-the-firm type of study). The interaction of all of these is then examined via a series of decision centers, information centers and related rules of processing and presenting information to persons (with known properties) in a known organizational context. Finally all of the results are replicated (as can be done readily in such simulations) in a way that is ideally suited to the requirements of the statistical-experimental design which Bonini imposes on his work. Thus Bonini is able to study the effects of plans, controls, and personality factors; and then he is able to study, under known and given organizational interrelations, the resulting operations of his hypothetical firm. This perspective casts new light on a total situation previously susceptible only to piecemeal analysis.

The behavioral-theory-of-the-firm analysis supplied by Cyert and March, in Chapter 16, also rests on computer programs as, in their words, "the natural theoretical language" for describing the decision processes of organizations. Whereas Bonini's model is hypothetical, this is not true, in the same sense, for the results reported by Cyert

---

[17] See the preceding discussion of Chapter 13 by Charnes and Stedry. See also Chapter 22 by A. Whinston.

and March. Thus, in particular, they report on research which includes (1) an *in situ* simulation obtained as a result of studying the decision processes within a large retail department store; and (2) a simulation which was effected and tested against published data on two manufacturing firms. Reference to more detailed discussions (see [143]) will show that a variety of purposes were served by these studies. Here, however, the work is used chiefly to illuminate a preceding series of propositions—on conflict resolution, uncertainty avoidance, search, and organizational learning (or adaptation)—as ingredients for a theory of organizational decisions. Then, using the flow chart as a bridge back to the computer, Cyert and March proceed to sharpen these theoretical propositions and give them operational form by means of a general model, also coded for a computer, which can supply more detailed guidance for the construction of specific models. The latter, in turn, may be thought of as a part of a strategy for model syntheses which, in a sense, complements other such strategies. For instance certain kinds of operations research strategies revolve around a use of model "types" as more or less standard modules which can be combined to obtain a larger or more complex total model. That is, the "model type" approach generally proceeds to a construction of large nonstandard total models from the exactly known details of a set of smaller standard ones. By contrast, the Cyert and March framework can be used as a paradigm to represent the essential properties which any model of decision making in organizations will generally possess. Thus even though any particular model may depart in detail from the paradigm it will, in general, contain features of the latter. In this sense, then, the March-Cyert paradigm provides a start toward general theoretical constructs, whereas the model type approach is directed rather towards operational usage in specific practical applications.

In Chapter 17, McNulty studies changes in organization structure in response to risk or uncertainty. His studies are also, broadly speaking, in the tradition of behavioral-theory-of-the-firm analyses, in that he combines economic and other considerations in a way designed to lead to an extension or restatement of problem areas in economics and elsewhere. Traditionally, for instance, economic theorists have tried to explain what limits the size of firms by constructs like a "fixed factor of production" (e.g., the entrepreneur himself) or the principle of increasing risk (with increasing size and resource requirements).[18]

---

[18] See, e.g., N. Kaldor [303], pp. 69–70 and M. Kalecki [304], pp. 440–447. However, Edith Penrose [433] has attempted a reformulation to explain the *growth* of firms as well as limits to their *rate* of growth, e.g., by reference to organizational considerations.

These were usually treated, it seems fair to say, on the supposition that the basic organization of a typical firm did not undergo significant variation as its size was altered. By contrast, McNulty bypasses the question of size in order to examine the effects of risk (really *uncertainty*) [19] variation on organizational arrangements.

A knotty problem in organization theory concerns the development of satisfactory ways for describing and identifying "decentralization." If one supposes that centralization-decentralization can be represented on a continuum then a beginning might best be made, as Whisler does (Chapter 18), by experimenting with measures suited for such a continuum. This does not mean, of course, that one must restrict himself to a single numerical measure or index. Thus, after examining some of the known ambiguities of "concentration measures," which were devised for the study of income distribution in economics, Professor Whisler decides that graphic or tabular presentations of entire arrays are likely to be more informative. He then provides some provisional checks and further insights with an individual-company case study as well as by reference to industry (multicompany) compensation data.

The final chapter in this section of the book, Chapter 19 by Thompson, is also directed toward weaving together ideas on organizations and theoretical economics. Here, as in the case of McNulty, the problem of uncertainty is analyzed in a context of possible organizational responses. Now, however, a more detailed analysis of sources of uncertainty is undertaken. Thompson proceeds from the point of view of decision processes (or "strategies"). His focus is on intraorganizational arrangements for "uncertainty transfer." The latter, illuminated by a hypothetical example, is intended as a dynamic extension of what March and Simon [367] refer to as "uncertainty absorption" and, more especially, its "locus of absorption." We should note that these organizational responses may also be interpreted as tightenings and loosenings of organizational structures in response to uncertainty. Such changes are close to ideas of decentralization (or at least delegation) although, because they occur at "similar" organizational levels, they are not always thought of in these terms.

Management Science Perspectives

We have already remarked on some aspects of ongoing research in the methodology of mathematics and computers, for its possible bear-

---

[19] The distinction, as in game theory (see also Knight [318]), is between situations in which the probability distributions that apply are known (risk) or are themselves unknown (uncertainty).

ing on understanding and using organizations. Parts of this topic come even more to the fore in the next division of this book, "management science perspectives." The research in fields such as management science and operations research has often been motivated by attempts to expand mathematics or computer design and usage as well as by attempts to understand management problems and assist in their solution.

This attempt to expand the scope of science along methodological lines is completely consistent, of course, with the attempts to expand substantive disciplines like psychology, which, as we noted earlier, provided a motivation for some of the behavioral science research we reported. Of course, a distinction between methodology and substance cannot be sharply drawn here; thus some management science methodology can be used to illuminate other substantive disciplines (like economics) when it is studied in conjunction with substantive problems (like decentralized pricing) drawn from management. Similarly, it is unwise to draw sharp distinctions between management science and other disciplines, new or old, such as systems analysis or psychology. This, too, is illustrated by the papers which are included in this management science division of the book.

Chapter 20, by Maynard Shelly, serves to introduce this division. It can also be regarded as a kind of general summary and review of preceding material. Shelly is concerned with the intrinsic relation of the individual to the organization in models of organizational problems. He argues that an adequate analysis of many organizational problems, requires a model which can *simultaneously* consider both the characteristics of the individual in the organization and the characteristics of the organizational structure. In the terminology of a modern systems engineer, Shelly is examining the insides of the organizational "black box" without losing—in more classical terminology —the perspectives of an "holistic" [20] approach. The concept which ties the organization, O, together with the persons, P, of the organization is that of personal structure (PS). Personal structure relates the personal judgments of each individual to possible states of the environment, X. This gives rise to the idea of an "A-set" which is that set of states of the environment to which a given judgment is appli-

---

[20] This term appears to have originated with the South African scholar and statesman, Jan Christian Smuts, as derived from the Greek *holos* meaning "whole." See the discussion on pp. 4 ff. in A. G. Gruchy [237] where the discussion of American (institutionalist) economics is related to the "General Concept of Holism" in J. C. Smuts [509], pp. 85–117.

cable for a particular individual. Thus, if Φ represents the set of judgments that can be made by some individual P, then his personal structure, PS, is made to depend upon X, the organization states; Φ, the totality of all judgments available to him; and α, the subset of all valid mappings between X and Φ. Via this construction Shelly secures a representation for studying interactions between personal and organizational structures.[21] He then illustrates some of its potential applications to problems in role designation (and analysis), delegation, organization stability and change, and the information (including "information" on personal values) in terms of which judgments are compounded into decisions and, ultimately, into actions.

From one standpoint, Shelly's paper stands in a line of management science developments. It also stands in a line of development which goes back into the "field theory" approach of the psychologist, Kurt Lewin, and his successors in group dynamics. There are differences in point of view and research strategy, however, which might be noted. Thus, in contrast to Lewin,[22] Shelly's chapter emphasizes a somewhat different order in the use of empirical findings and model development by arguing (implicitly) that the phenomena of organizations are such that we cannot expect to accomplish much even in the way of identifying problems—hence in understanding or resolving them—without first having recourse to suitable modes of representation.

I. J. Good, in Chapter 21, from the traditions of statistical decision theory, answers a question raised by John Tukey [555] and develops (1) a way of identifying "decisions" and (2) a way of distinguishing between "decisions" and "conclusions." [23] The analysis is meant to accomplish something more than merely throwing light on certain deep and rather difficult problems in statistics. Whereas decision theory proper has been concerned with individual decision making, Good extends his ideas so that they are also pertinent for individuals operating in an organization. He thus moves toward further contacts with psychology: [24]

As a small contribution to the mathematics of the philosophy of psychology, a quantitative explication is offered for the change of mind, or rather the vari-

---

[21] Such "structures" are included in the states, X.

[22] See, e.g., his "Formulation and Progress in Psychology" in [344].

[23] The issue is connected with uses of statistics for making inferences testing hypotheses, etc., in science and management. See, e.g., R. A. Fisher [197] as well as Tukey [555.]

[24] Quoted from the abstract which Dr. Good supplied with his paper.

ation of mind, contained in a mental event, with respect to a class of acts. There is a discussion of the meanings of "decision" and "conclusion" and a brief reference to the relationship between decision and responsibility. My purpose throughout is clarification only, not application.

This last sentence (by Good) might also be applied to Whisler's approach to decentralization (Chapter 18). Good (like Whisler) effects his development by a quantitative analysis, although now the emphasis shifts to more purely mathematical ideas of "measure." Since many persons regard mathematics in a way which confines it to "quantitative" applications only, it may be well to note that the mathematics employed by Shelly—topology, formal logic—finds its main use in "qualitative" analyses. But the ideas of probability, etc., employed by Good are specimens of a measure-theoretic orientation in mathematics. Nor does this end the matter since evidently the quantitative and the qualitative may be combined in a variety of ways; and still other kinds of mathematics, e.g., the set theory which both Good and Shelly use, can be made to establish precise connections when wanted.[25] Finally, as the preceding discussion of computer usage —Bonini, Cyert, March, et al.—and empirical measure considerations (Whisler, et al.) has already indicated, there is no sharp boundary at which "mathematics" leaves off and other disciplines begin.[26]

. . . In a sense, but only in a sense, mathematics may be thought of as an abstract discipline concerned solely with the processes of formal reasoning. In a wider sense, however, such formal reasoning is an integral part of all disciplines—of all rational attempts at solving problems, drawing generalizations, seeking interrelations and extending the body of human knowledge. It is a mistake . . . to lay on this process artificial divisions simply because we have been accustomed to them by tradition or by administrative convenience [e.g., in university administration]. Whether receiving the formal designation of "mathematics" or whether a "mathematician" is formally present is a matter which is less important . . . than to recognize that this process of reasoning has been found to be an indispensable tool for progress and perfection in wide spheres of scientific activity and applications. . . .

Chapter 22, by Whinston, is illustrative of another aspect of this interplay. Notice, for instance, the meeting ground and common discourse which the languages of mathematics have supplied in the traditions of psychology, management and statistics. Notice also, as in the discussion of the Charnes and Stedry chapter, the need for further innovation as well as for fuller exploitation of recent mathematical

---

[25] The classic work by A. N. Kolmogorov [321] may be consulted on this.
[26] Quoted from A. Charnes [108].

developments. This is further illustrated in Whinston's paper. He employs recently developed mathematics, e.g., the Kuhn-Tucker theorem of nonlinear programming, to achieve a better understanding of certain ideas in the economic theory of prices. That theory had previously received extensive formulation and study by means of classical mathematical constructs. Whinston shifts the problem focus from inter-firm analyses of market behavior to intra-firm uses of prices as information guides for coordinating the decisions of individual managers in a decentralized entity and is thus able to move in the direction of exploring limitations as well as possible uses of prices for administrative purposes. This is done by reference to what Whinston calls "externalities." Externalities include, but are not restricted to, such classical economic problems as increasing returns to scale and they may be either external or internal to the organization. Thus, whereas classical economics (which had already identified some of these problems) generally proceeded on the assumptions that such problems, when present, could be handled by price-like devices (e.g., taxes and subsidies), Whinston is able to identify a wide class of externalities which cannot be satisfactorily handled in this manner [597]. Very naturally, then, he is led to examine "mixed systems." In such systems prices form only one part of an administrative totality. The mathematics which Whinston uses and the problems he is studying thus enable him to locate further information devices like redundancy which received no attention in classical economic discussions of pricing. Thus redundancy, as well as prices, is then seen to have important possibilities for transmitting information between different parts of an organization. A further examination of problems in administering mixed systems leads Whinston to some suggestions for more rational mechanisms by means of game theoretic constructs [27] wherein, *inter alia*, the idea of externalities provides one criterion for organizational design.

Whinston reports on his field inquiries as well as on his review of the literature in cost accounting. This field research helps to bring certain problems of practice into sharper focus, but since it is limited to two cases it cannot serve as a very wide base for inference. On the other hand, a general survey type of approach appears impossible at present if only because these problems have not yet been identified sufficiently well in the literature of accounting and management. But the importance—if not the universality—of these problems can hardly be denied. So here again we have another interesting illustration of

---

[27] See also M. Shubik [495]. A somewhat different approach in a more classical vein may be found in Hirschleifer [272].

what can be secured from an analytical approach to complex and subtle organizational phenomena. The abstract formulation and model development essayed by Whinston appears to have been a necessary first step for isolating problems which could then be discussed profitably with various business officials. Indeed, even the survey of cost-accounting literature could not easily have been undertaken without the insight and sharpening of issues that the preceding mathematical development supplied.

Shubik, an economist, has also been led to examine some of the newer mathematics, as found in the theory of games, for their possible bearing on problems of oligopoly ("competition among the few") which have been of concern to economists. This appears to be a promising course of inquiry if only because the methods and assumptions of classical economics have never yielded wholly satisfactory results. During the course of his investigations, however, Dr. Shubik found it necessary to achieve certain reorientations and extensions of standard constructs in the theory of games. See his Chapter 23, *infra*.

The desirability of progress in mathematical innovation has already been remarked upon. But such innovation need not have its source only in mathematics. For instance, mathematical research alone has not yet been able to supply a wholly satisfactory definition of "solution" for games in general. Hence, Shubik, along with others, has turned to gaming as a device for further study and insight. This, in turn, makes it useful to distinguish a new research activity called "experimental gaming" which proceeds under controlled laboratory conditions, as distinguished from other types of gaming, e.g., the classical military war games, which do not.[28]

In our earlier discussion on Bass' work (Chapter 7) we observed how experimental gaming was used to study various ways of organizing production. This was a main point of Bass' work. He made no effort to relate the results obtained to the mathematics of games or other related methodologies. Shubik, on the other hand, is very much concerned with the latter topic as he reports some of his reflections on games and gaming. Notice might also be given here—see Shubik's tabulations—to the interplay between the mathematics of game theory and the use of ideas from other disciplines. Thus, on the one hand, Shubik has used the theory of games as an analytical guide to his in-

---

[28] Other divisions appear to be emerging in the form of "gaming for training" (see, e.g., Vazsonyi [570]) and "nonexperimental gaming" for the purpose of securing knowledge (see, e.g. [47]). A general discussion may be found in Cohen, et al. [131].

quiries. On the other hand, he has not hesitated to extend the latter with ideas from economics, psychology, or other disciplines, in ways which can make the constructs of game theory more germane to a variety of problems which are, or should be, of concern for organization theorists.

The spirit of Shubik's inquiry can best be portrayed by quoting from the abstract that originally accompanied his paper:

The relationship between the formal theory of games and problems in experimental gaming is explored. Observations are made concerning the conceptual and experimental problems in the design of games which reflect uncertainty, various information conditions, and indeterminacy of the length of play. Fifteen different solution concepts are noted and some results of experimentation with games with no face-to-face communication are discussed.

The next three papers adopt a somewhat different approach. Here the systems viewpoint is emphasized and formal mathematics becomes only one part of a total system for manipulating and interpreting symbols. The paper by Ruth Davis, as we have already observed, is the result of a direct concern with actually functioning man-machine decision systems. Her discussion serves as an introduction to the papers that follow in this section.

Davis' Chapter 24 approach is part of a developing field of information engineering wherein analysis is directed to the problems of information systems and related hardware (and software) for human decision making. Since her problems arose in military command and control applications, she is naturally concerned with security aspects of the subject as well as the kind and quality of the information processed for decisions by the organization (as contrasted with its possible use by opposing or "hostile" organizations). Briggs, in Chapter 25, on the other hand, drops this concern with security; equating the terms "organization" and "system," he approaches the problem of information as one part of what he calls "human factor engineering." As a start toward a taxonomy of information-processing functions, he adopts some of the terminology of the information engineer to illuminate some underlying problems that a psychologist may encounter when he tries to adapt hardware designs to use by human beings in a complex system.

The paper by Mesarović, Sanders, and Sprague, Chapter 26, also maintains the spirit of a systems approach. Here the emphasis is on a *general* systems [29] approach. The term *general* may help to distinguish

---

[29] For example, in the sense of the general systems society. See, for instance [574].

this approach from others such as the ones used by Bonini et al., and discussed earlier as part of a systems analysis in the behavioral-theory-of-the-firm tradition. It is distinguished further by its almost exclusive use of computers and related engineering and analytical characterizations in which the goals of an organization are viewed as emerging from the interacting goals of individual units in various tiers of an organizational (systems) hierarchy. The analysis proceeds from the simple, e.g., $1l1g$ (one level, one goal), to the complex, e.g., $mlng$ (m levels, n goals), as well as from abstract (mathematical models) to concrete realizations which are designed to provide access to actual computer simulation runs.

Unlike the simulations of Bonini, these characterizations are not necessarily developed via the constructs of economics, accounting, etc. Rather they are designed to effectuate certain general "principles" which can be used either as guides (or axioms) for further model syntheses or as propositions which can be tested by further simulations. The ultimate objective is to secure empirical validation so that these principles can be used for understanding and even designing organizations. The emphasis, that is to say, is on a combination of computer simulations and heuristic and analytical guides which will ultimately lead to empirical validation and application, rather than the reverse.[30]

Perspectives for Further Future Research

Since almost all of the preceding papers are concerned with perspectives for future research, the title of this section may seem redundant. It seemed useful, nevertheless, to place these last three papers together here. They all draw upon a good deal of preceding work in order to delineate large problem areas that might be programmed for the future, and, inter alia, they also contain critical evaluations which bear on preceding work in the study of organizations.

Thus, Sells (Chapter 27) calls for, and outlines, a taxonomy of the variables, factors, and characteristics, which are important for guiding future research on organizations. This approach may be viewed as an alternative to other efforts to obtain a guiding concept by means of a more or less "simple" and universally applicable verbal definition. Notice that here, again, we may have to give up something of the

---

[30] This work, like that of Bonini (discussed in Chapter 15) is therefore to be distinguished from the "Industrial Dynamics" of Jay Forrester and his associates. See, e.g., Jay W. Forrester [200].

psychological comfort and aesthetic pleasure which a simple verbal definition may provide. This does not mean, however, that we must proceed in willy nilly fashion to such a taxonomy; nor is it the case that the taxonomy is to be used only as a convenient file for each of the admitted categories. Thus, for instance, we are to test for overlaps, lack of independence, etc., in the classifications and also to allow for manipulations to study the effects of interactions between factors in the various classifications and so on: [31]

A useful taxonomy should be a theoretical model which orders empirical observations and also permits predictions guiding new observations, based on the developed network of relationships. In its fullest development the taxonomic approach should conform to the general systems approach; in any case the two are compatible and perhaps the salient strengths of each may contribute to the goals of the other.[32]

The approach by McGrath (Chapter 28) is also taxonomic but its emphasis is different. So is its point of view. Sells' taxonomy is directed toward substantive problems, propositions, etc., while McGrath is concerned with methodology. Also, Sells directs his discussion toward a program for the future whereas McGrath is concerned with the problem of utilizing known methodologies in order to form a research strategy.

A question might be raised, of course, as to whether new methodologies might also be needed, but it is probably prudent to put such questions aside—as a matter of formal classification—until the issues can be sharpened by further progress in the methodological disciplines of science, technology and management.

The concluding chapter, which is Chapter 29, by Cyert and March, returns to a behavioral-theory-of-the-firm approach except that now a new direction for this research is indicated. In particular, a return is made to the grand problem of "organization design" that motivated the work of classical theorists. As might be expected, many of the concepts and methods which Cyert and March call into play differ from those that are commonly found in the classical literature. There is a difference in viewpoint, too. Traditional theorists tended to view science (or research) solely in the service of design, whereas Cyert and

---

[31] Quoted from Sells, Chapter 27. See also the discussion on taxonomy and theorizing in A. M. Rubenstein and C. J. Haberstroh [457], pp. 10–11.

[32] Observe also the relationships between this approach and the use of axiomatics as in J. H. Woodger [609] which attempts to axiomatize the three main fields of biology: embryology, genetics and taxonomy. For work by administrative theorists which is in this spirit see E. O. Stene [519] or A. Brown [86].

March also see the problems (and findings) of design in the service of organization theory viewed as a part of the total body of scientific knowledge.[33]

. . . There are two compelling reasons for proceeding with the study of organizational design without awaiting a complete tidying of the methodological mess. First, however incomplete and inaccurate the present models of organization may be, they seem to have both some validity and some possible relevance to design problems. The risks of using them for design purposes seem modest; the potential gains somewhat larger. Second, organization theory will develop faster if it is built on an engineering model of research as much as a "pure science" model. . . .

In support of these contentions one can call on the progress—in both models and methods—that has been effected by management scientists and operations research analysts by working on actual management problems. Something may also be said, as was already noted, on the progress which was made by classical writers who were concerned with actual problems of organization design. Finally, it is interesting to observe that the approach which Cyert and March here advocate departs from other "modern" approaches which have tended to introduce sharp distinctions between "descriptive" and "positive" approaches to organization research on one hand and "normative" or "prescriptive" approaches on the other. The latter distinctions, if rigidly maintained, can convey erroneous impressions and close off possibly fruitful avenues for the increase of knowledge. Hence, even at the expense of the clarity and comfort which such divisions have provided, it appears worthwhile to use work on the application of designs as one way to extend and strengthen the motivational basis of organizational research.

Conclusion

It is usual in economics (and elsewhere) to distinguish between the production and employment processes undertaken for income or profit and the consumption process in which the resulting satisfactions are achieved. However, such a view of the production process may not be wholly adequate when, as in the U. S., expanded levels of income and altered technological possibilities appear. The call for new methods of management is likely to become even more urgent as the U. S. continues toward a trillion-dollar-a-year economy. This call, in turn, is likely to require a continued acceleration in research on organizations to meet the needs for managerial innovation.

---

[33] Quoted from Cyert and March, Chapter 29.

The idea of "progress" came into being, according to J. B. Bury [92], some time subsequent to the sixteenth century. "It is one of those ideas, compounded of fact and fiction which have a special power for social action that can serve to bring about its own confirmation. Its appearance as an idea peculiar to the modern western world is associated with the growth of technology and the evolution of scientific research." [34] The idea of research directed toward the evolution of new forms of organization and management seems to be in this tradition and may also have this power. Of course, such ideas require confirmation, at least to some extent, if they are not to lose their force. They also require the stimulation of new ideas and new perspectives and it is toward these ends that the following papers are directed.

---

[34] See the introduction by Charles A. Beard in [92].

PART ONE

General perspectives

2

HISTORICAL ANTECEDENTS OF
ORGANIZATION RESEARCH

John H. Hoagland

Men have studied organization problems for centuries. Their research is an important part of the environment out of which today's ideas have evolved and it forms the foundation upon which tomorrow's will be built. Understanding the historical antecedents of organization research can help improve the results of current and future research. Reliance on distorted history, however, can cause unnecessary duplication of efforts and incorrect evaluation of research progress and it can delay or frustrate possible potential applications.

Unfortunately, there has been no comprehensive analysis of the history of organization research, and it is beyond the scope of this chapter to attempt one. So many interwoven threads of thought compose the fabric of this history that only a few can be followed herein. These are traced to demonstrate the potential of this history and to indicate some leads on often overlooked research so that others can follow them in their historical explorations.

In tracing threads of thought back through the centuries, it is evident that much research has been obscured by myths and fables. Some of these have been repeated so often that a folklore has evolved which has distorted the history of organization research. In this chapter some distortions are critically examined to reveal more clearly the actual threads of thought as they have been spun through the centuries.

Research Folklore

Most attempts at historical analysis of organization research have dealt predominately with twentieth-century events, because many writers have had the erroneous impression that such studies did not start until late in the nineteenth century.[1] This, however, is a distortion of facts. There were many who researched problems of work, organization, and management during earlier centuries, and this earlier research influenced much of what has occurred since the late nineteenth century. One primary cause of the resulting distortion seems traceable to a folklore which has developed around the work of Frederick W. Taylor, the so-called father of scientific management.[2] This folklore presents him as the originator of this type of research, and this has now come to be generally believed as a result (apparently) of mere repetition and inadequate attention to and dissemination of information on the preceding history of management research. In the following sections, we will examine some further evidence on these matters for the perspective that can thereby be secured for a fairer evaluation.

SCIENCE OF SHOVELING MYTH

An illustration of historical distortion is found in the research known as the science of shoveling. In the years prior to power equipment, many men were employed for the task of moving masses of materials by means of a spade or shovel. Since this was a relatively simple and common activity, researchers studied shoveling operations to analyze how they could be conducted most efficiently and effectively.

Since published research on the subject of shoveling has been available for centuries, it forms an interesting "case study" for examining how historical distortion may be brought about. Frederick W. Taylor wrote that, "the average man would question whether there is much of any science in the work of shoveling." [3] He also said he had "never met a single shovel contractor to whom it had even occurred that there was such a thing as the science of shoveling." [4] By way of contrast, Taylor described how he proceeded to study shoveling problems by "gradually varying the shovel load and having the conditions accompanying the work carefully observed for several weeks by men who were used to experimenting. . . ." [5]

This research reportedly was conducted at the Bethelehem Steel Company in the early 1890's to determine the best weight of a shovel

---

[1] [9], [39], [65], [96], [170], [194], [256], [289], [316], [350], [367], [438], [500], [514].

These numbers in brackets refer to the corresponding items indexed in the bibliography.

[2] [437].

[3] [538], p. 64.

[4] *Ibid.*, p. 65.

[5] *Ibid.*

load, the time to load a shovel, and "the time required to swing the shovel backward and then throw the load a given horizontal distance, accompanied by a given height." [6] These statements lent themselves to a distortion of the history of previous research on this topic. In fact, considerable publicity was given to these studies which were represented as the first of their type. They have now even been accorded the status of a first research (or scientific approach) to management, which, as such, provided the supposed original foundation for today's organization research.[7]

But now consider some of the preceding literature. William Stanley Jevons, a well-known economist and author of one of Taylor's college textbooks,[8] wrote:

Let us take such a simple kind of work as digging. A spade may be made of any size, and if the same number of strokes be made in the hour, the requisite exertion will vary nearly as the cube of the length of the blade. If the spade be small, the fatigue will be slight, but the work done will also be slight. A very large spade, on the other hand, will do a great quantity of work at each stroke, but the fatigue will be so great that the labourer cannot long continue at this work. Accordingly, a certain medium-sized spade is adopted, which does not overtax a labourer and prevent him doing a full day's work, but enables him to accomplish as much as possible. The size of the spade should depend partly upon the tenacity and weight of the material and partly upon the strength of the labourer. It may be observed that, in excavating stiff clay, navvies use a small strong spade; for ordinary garden purposes a larger spade is employed; for shovelling loose sand or coals a broad capacious shovel is

---

[6] [538], p. 67.

[7] See footnote 1.

There are also indications that Taylor based his work on earlier writings and then claimed undue credit for "his" accomplishments. For instance, in Taylor [538], p. 54, we find, "Our first step was to employ a young college graduate to look up all that had been written on the subject in English, German, and French."

For an example of the undue credit that Taylor was inclined to give himself, compare Taylor's testimony relative to Gilbreth and the facts. Refer to Taylor's *Testimony Before the Special House Committee,* as reproduced in [539], pp. 67 ff. See also records in Gilbreth Library at Purdue University, which include the letter from Calvin Yost, editor, *American Machinist,* to Margaret Ellen Hawley, April 6, 1927: "Taylor was extremely egotistical and frequently vindictive. He craved personal credit and admiration to an extreme degree. . . ." See also [539], pp. 184, 198 ff., pp. 208 ff.

As a readily verifiable example of misrepresentation, compare Taylor's story of his rise in Midvale Steel with the actual "inside track" which he had. Refer to Frederick W. Taylor [538], p. 48, and [136], pp. 61, 107, 117.

[8] *Annual Catalogue of the Stevens Institute of Technology,* Hoboken, New Jersey, 1883–1884, p. 13.

used; and a still larger instrument is employed for removing corn, malt, or any loose light powder.[9]

Earlier, in 1851, Charles Babbage, an acquaintance of Jevons, discussed the study of shoveling, which even then was known as "a familiar illustration." He wrote that, if one worker was

inferior even both in strength and activity, he might yet by means of his skill perform a greater quantity of work without fatigue.

He might have ascertained that a given weight of earth raised at each shovelfull, together with a certain number of shovelfulls per hour, would be more advantageous for his strength than any other such combination.

That a shovel of a certain weight, size, and form, would fatigue him less than those of a different construction.

That if its handle were two or three inches longer than he required, its additional weight would at the end of the day have been uselessly lifted many hundreds of times.

That if each spadeful of earth were lifted but an inch or two above the barrow, beyond what was necessary, a still greater waste of force would arise.[10]

The thread of thought about the science of shoveling can be traced still further into history, for Babbage knew about the work of Charles Augustus Coulomb [11] who wrote, in 1781, about timing various shoveling operations.[12] Coulomb's experiments, in turn, apparently were influenced by the 1699 writings of De la Hire,[13] whose work had resulted from an invitation for scholars to "study the operations done by the worker in his workshop, in order to help them do a better job," [14] an objective even of today's organization research.

De la Hire probably was influenced by some of the shoveling analyses found in the fifteenth-century notebooks of the renowned Leonardo da Vinci.[15] It is not known precisely when the thread of thought on such studies began, but historians have found that da Vinci copied many of his ideas from still earlier authors.[16] It is amply evi-

---

[9] [299] second edition, 1879, pp. 221–222.

[10] Charles Babbage [35], pp. 1–5.

[11] Babbage had a copy of Coulomb's studies in his library. See [512] item 48 under "Mechanics."

[12] Charles Augustus Coulomb [138], pp. 255–297.

[13] [161], pp. 153–162.

[14] *Ibid.*, p. 323.

[15] The author wishes to express his appreciation to Professor Henry G. Hodges for pointing out the work done by Leonardo da Vinci on shoveling. See, e.g. [566], pp. 317–320.

[16] An excellent collection of da Vinci's works and his sources of information can be found in the Elmer Belt Library of Vinciana, 1893 Wilshire Boulevard, Los

dent, however, that research on shoveling did originate long before the end of the nineteenth century and extends through many centuries.

OTHER MYTHS

Law of heavy laboring. Next we turn to the so-called "law of heavy laboring." In extolling his discovery of this law, Taylor said he had studied for many years before discovering it—a law which was "so simple in its nature that it is truly remarkable that it should not have been discovered and understood years before." [17] His law was "for each given pull or push on the man's arms, it is possible for the workman to be under load for only a definite percentage of the day." [18]

Actually, this supposedly remarkable law had been understood for years. Many earlier writers had discussed it. For example, in 1822, Christian stated it as "the first economically sound rule for the use of the force of the man consists in dispensing it in a period of time long enough to provide frequent periods of rest." [19]

Another myth in this folklore involves workmen carrying loads of pig iron. Previous research on workers carrying loads up inclined planes and flights of stairs was similar to the pig iron studies. Coulomb and others had written about such experiments in earlier centuries. [20] This earlier research was known about by such men as Dr. Robert Henry Thurston,[21] an internationally prominent educator who taught at Stevens Institute of Technology when Taylor studied there. [22]

Timing of operations. The timing of operations is another area which was researched long before the turn of the century. For example, in 1761, M. Perronet wrote about an analysis of the timing of operations, together with a description of production methods, tools, gauges, costs, profits, and other interesting information about mass production. [23] Perronet and other similar writers were outstanding scientists and mathematicians of their times. Among the subjects they studied were the amount of work a man can do in a day and what constitutes

Angeles, California. (Taylor may have actually known about some of da Vinci's work through the efforts of John Libe, a Stevens Institute of Technology graduate who established a da Vinci collection at Stevens Institute.)

[17] [538], p. 57.

[18] *Loc. cit.*

[19] *Vide* [273], p. 279.

[20] [273], pp. 74 ff.

[21] [547], pp. 53 ff.

[22] *Annual Catalogue of the Stevens Institute of Technology,* 1883–1884, *loc. cit.* See also [175], [546], and [274] reprinted in [275], pp. 24–25.

[23] [163].

a fair day's work—a type of research which is often believed not even to have been started until the turn of the twentieth century.

Interrelated character of studies and improvement of practice. Many of the pre-twentieth century studies were interrelated and were intended to be useful to industry and to the improvement of mankind. Thus, this too is not merely a modern tendency.[24] Some of the outstanding men who helped spin these threads of thoughts and weave the fabric of organization research were Bernoulli, Desaguliers,[25] Robinson, Buchanan,[26] Gerstner, Welcher, Nordwall,[27] Nicholson,[28] Emerson, Leslie, Hachette, Morisot, Hassenfratz, Navior, Amontons, Euler, Schulze,[29] and Sauveur.[30]

Recognizing Historical Distortions

In view of the current emphasis on organization research and in view of our preceding discussions, we might usefully record here some of the ways that these distortions of history have occurred. The use of a new term may be helpful, of course, but it can also introduce distortions when it results in camouflage that breaks an otherwise visible chain of research. For example, at the turn of the century the terms "efficiency" and "scientific management" received considerable emphasis. One book even used these terms in an effort to prove statistically the revolutionary growth of new concepts, but the author actually proved only an increased use of the words.[31] The underlying concepts had frequently appeared in earlier times under such terms as "commercial organization," [32] "animal strength," "prime movers," "industrial mechanics," and "natural philosophy." [33]

---

[24] See concluding portion of the Introduction and the concluding chapter, by Cyert and March, in this volume.

[25] Coulomb, *loc. cit.*

[26] [615], pp. 100–102.

[27] [160]. (The commencement of the first chapter translated from the German for the use of the author's friends in England), Vienna, 1834, pp. 15–45 (original published about 1831–1832).

[28] [422], first American from the second London edition, pp. 52 ff.

[29] [234], pp. 384–395.

[30] [81], p. 323.

[31] [170], *op. cit.*, pp. 20 ff.

[32] The term "commercial organization" was in relatively common use during the latter part of the nineteenth century. Interesting organization concepts and even an example of an organization chart can be found in [347].

[33] In pre-twentieth century literature, many concepts relative to organization research can be found in writings on natural philosophy. It is interesting to note

Claims to great originality or excessive and severe criticism of predecessors should also be treated with caution. It is surprising to observe the force that such claims can exert under suitable circumstances and the effect they can produce in discouraging or burying even careful work by contemporaries. For instance, at the turn of the century, there were numerous occasions when people spoke out against false claims of originality, but these protests were brushed aside. Critics were accused of being old-fashioned and relying on rule-of-thumb methods, and almost no attempt was made to give credit to previous research.

A closely related source of possible distortions is represented by the exaggerated claims that advocates of one or another approach may use. Claims to "scientific qualities" may have this character, and may even be used to promote a supposed need for "scientific" or "specialized" training which can become the basis of a cult commanding a special vocabulary as well as a common interest of its own. Consider, for instance, the claims to precision that were promoted by advocates of scientific management. Some people in the scientific management movement claimed such a degree of precision that it took years before many recognized its imperfections.

The formation of new professional societies is sometimes also undertaken to promote the interests of such cults, and, when this is the case, the resulting activities can result in obscuring the pursuit of truth in favor of other objectives. A good supply of literature and special conferences often aid in gaining academic acceptance of a trend. This may cause even respectable academic institutions to undertake the teaching and pursuit of questionable subjects. Academic acceptance gives credence to folklore and can perpetuate it for years; hence the university is a fair target for such movements when prosecuted with vigor. The 1911 Tuck School Conference on scientific management, for instance, gained considerable acceptance for scientific management folklore.[34] Harvard assisted by quickly following with a collection of writings promoting this same subject.[35] The early twentieth century was also a fruitful period for promotional books, magazine articles, and newspaper stories. Many of them made little contribution to new knowledge, but they did perpetuate historical inaccuracies.[36]

Of course, a folklore is more firmly established if there is a favor-

---

that such men as Dr. Thurston were professors of natural philosophy. See Durand [175], p. 44.

[34] [8].

[35] [96].

[36] See [1], [45], [62], [88], [94], [167].

ably biased biography of a leading figure. Copley's two-volume biography of Taylor became well known in the field, and its numerous inaccuracies helped to entrench that folklore.[37]

Some of the above characteristics can be found in other examples of historical distortion. As an illustration, those who write about automation largely ignore the fact that many similar problems were studied under such terms as "mechanization" and "technocracy." The writings of such men as Sir James Steuart [522] [38] have been overlooked, but in 1767 he analyzed the problems encountered when machines replace men. His solutions were not too different from some of those proposed today. Those interested in automation might also wish to compare the contents of the book *Automation,* in [166], with previous articles appearing in popular American magazines. It also is interesting to note that, although the author of this book supposedly originated the word "automation," this word is the title of an article published two years earlier—and it was reported to have been in use more than ten years earlier. (See [12], pp. 102–108.)

Historical Sources

A few of the places to turn for further leads on the historical antecedents of organization research are suggested in the following. The sources of men's ideas are so boundless that no effort is made to make these leads all-inclusive. These leads are merely suggestive as to the type of place where helpful information can sometimes be found about the historical antecedents of organization research.

LIBRARIES

Libraries, of course, constitute the major source of historical information. In addition to such well-known places as the Congressional and the New York Public Libraries, other specialized libraries may be useful. The William Freeman Myrick Goss Library of the History of Engineering, located at Purdue University, is outstanding in its field.[39] Also at Purdue University, the Gilbreth Library of Management contains valuable information. The Frederick Winslow Taylor Collection at the Stevens Institute of Technology is also useful.[40]

---

[37] [136], p. 127. For an indication of some of the gross errors in the biography of Taylor, see notes in Frank Gilbreth's personal copy in the Gilbreth Library, Purdue University.

[38] See I, pp. 119–124.   [40] [259].

[39] See [266].

Unfortunately, neither of these latter two collections is as complete as historians might wish.[41]

Some of the old encyclopedias contain helpful information about early research. Two of the many which I have found useful are the *Encyclopedia Metropolitana* and Diderot's *Encyclopedie*.[42] The latter contains excellent descriptions of French industry prior to the advent of the steam engine. (Some people may be surprised at how far advanced industry had progressed before the supposed beginning of the Industrial Revolution.)

In doing historical studies in these older encyclopedias, it should be remembered that sometimes the terms and phraseology under which a subject was catalogued differ from those used today, even though the basic ideas may be almost identical.

Proceedings and journals of professional and scientific societies contain useful historical information. Although many such societies were not established until the twentieth century, the forerunners of these societies did produce significant publications in prior centuries.[43] Too often, historians have lost track of a thread of thought because they traced it only to the formal origin of a society, overlooking the fact that usually a new society is the offshoot of a previous organization or activity.

The formation of the American Society of Mechanical Engineers illustrates how a new society can cause a thread of thought to be lost. Although some historically important papers were delivered at the early meetings of this society, few people have attempted to trace these ideas to earlier origins. I have, however, previously indicated how some of these ideas can be traced. Additional ideas may be traced through research on such men as the founder of the American Society of Mechanical Engineers, Dr. Robert Henry Thurston. He was first trained in the area of natural philosophy, and his organization concepts can be traced to this field of study through such books as *Natural Philosophy through the Eighteenth Century and Allied Topics* [44]

---

[41] See [273], pp. 322, 333, for further discussion.

[42] A good discussion of these sources may be found in [588], pp. 444–454.

[43] See [317] for instance. See also [357], [594], and [611].

[44] [188]. (Commemoration number to mark the 150th anniversary of the founding of the *Philosophical Magazine* in 1798.)

and *A Course of Lectures on Natural Philosophy and Mechanical Arts* [615].

Dr. Thurston was also closely associated with railroading activities, an important branch of civil engineering. Dr. Thurston probably was influenced by some of the earlier railroad writings of Henry Varnum Poor [45] and others. Poor's ideas are traceable to Dionysius Lardner,[46] who, in turn, was influenced by Charles Babbage.[47] As explained earlier, some of Babbage's ideas evolved from still earlier writers. Those interested in additional information on the historical antecedents of organization research in the railroad industry will find useful leads in the article "Early History of a Railway Organization." [48] Evidence indicates that many were concerned with organization problems in the railroad during the nineteenth century, and some of the earliest uses of organization analysis tools, such as organization charts, existed in this area.

MAGAZINES AND PERIODICALS

Some of the magazines and periodicals published in the nineteenth century are helpful in tracing threads of thought which supposedly did not begin until the end of that period. They include periodicals such as the following: *American Journal of Science; Annals of Philosophy, a Magazine of Chemistry, Minerology, Mechanics, Natural History, Agriculture, and the Arts; Cassier's Magazine, a Journal of Natural Philosophy, Chemistry, and the Arts; Edinburgh Journal of Science; The Engineer; Engineering Magazine; Engineering News;* and *Scientific American.*[49]

EDUCATIONAL INSTITUTIONS

The records of various educational institutions are another source of information about early organization research. The beginnings of industrial education, for example, go back as far as the sixteenth century; [50] and by the eighteenth century there were numerous people engaged in this activity in both Germany and France.

In 1824 a new phase of the industrial education movement spread through France, and within two years there were over 5000 people

---

[45] Alfred Dupont Chandler [103].
[46] Dionysius Lardner [330].
[47] [34].
[48] [296], pp. 153–179.
[49] Additional leads on useful American magazines may be found in such sources as [408].
[50] [16], pp. 518–523; see also [340], pp. 197 ff.

attending classes in 98 cities.[51] Some of the lectures of Baron Charles Dupin, a leader in that movement, contain ideas significant to organization research; see [273], pp. 375–394.

By 1850 there were over 100,000 people involved in the mechanics institutes in England.[52] These institutes were teaching scientific principles and their practical application to industry.[53] Such schools as L'Ecole Polytechnique, in Paris, offered opportunity for study of such problems as the amount of work a man could do in a day [54] and, also, courses on the construction of public works and the operations of mines.[55] Schools such as this might have been one of the sources of ideas for Henri Fayol's *Administration Industrielle et Generale.*[56]

In the United States, records of similar educational activities can be found in such sources as the *Journal of the Franklin Institute.*[57] The important influence of various university trends is revealed in Albion W. Small's article, "Fifty Years of Sociology in the United States" [506]. Reports of the Commissioner on Education also provide interesting information as to what was taught in this country.[58] An analysis of many of these earlier schools reveals that they had considerable influence on today's trends.

HISTORIES

Although a complete history of organization research is not available, this chapter has suggested how some threads of thought can be traced back through the centuries. Those who wish to follow the evolution of other ideas may find useful leads in publications such as the *Harvard Guide to American History* [90] and *Guide to Business History* [331]. A useful general background on sixteenth, seventeenth, and eighteenth century thought may be found in such works as those of A. Wolf.[59] The more current threads of thought are indicated in such books as the *Origin of Sociology* [60] and *Fifty Years Progress in Management.*[61] In addition, the Gulick and Urwick *Papers on the Science of Administration* [563] and Lepawsky's interesting book [340] may be useful to the organization researcher.

---

51 [174]; see II, title page and "Introduction."
52 [286], pp. vi ff.
53 Hudson [286], *op. cit.,* p. 56.
54 [300] (cinquième cahier), p. 18.
55 [300], *op. cit.* (onzième cahier), p. 375.
56 [186].

57 Wright, *op. cit.* [611].
58 [447], pp. 1861 ff.
59 [606] and [607].
60 Albion W. Small [507].
61 [17].

Conclusion

It is reasonable to suppose that the study of historical materials has more than intrinsic interest, and that the progress of research can be speeded by understanding the historical antecedents of organization research.[62] It is possible that attention has been diverted from this kind of research activity only because many people have not recognized the existence of any important pre-twentieth century research. As this may have resulted from the fact that the history of events has been distorted by myths, fables, and folklore, we can regard this chapter as an attempt to clarify the picture. In any event, this chapter illustrates how research threads of thought can be traced back through time to establish a better understanding of the historical environment out of which today's ideas have evolved. As a further aid in the latter direction, we have suggested some sources that are likely to prove useful in initiating a study of historical antecedents of contemporary organization research.

---

[62] This work extends back through many centuries, and the efforts of Plato and Aristotle, as discussed in R. P. McKeon (ed.) [381], pp. xv ff., are only the best known of such "classical" efforts. See e.g. [114] and [134]. For further work on military organizations, see Vegetius' "De Re Militari" as published in [570a], pp. 103 ff. There is also a distortion which arises from associating all such writings with Western (occidental) traditions only. This distortion may be readily corrected, however, by reference to "Art of War" by Sun Tzu, as reproduced on pp. 39 ff. in [530] (which antedates the work of Plato and Aristotle), or Ibn Khaldûn [315].

3

DESEGREGATION OR INTEGRATION? COMMENTS ABOUT CONTEMPORARY RESEARCH ON ORGANIZATIONS

William R. Dill

The dominant feature of contemporary research on organizations is its diversity. No brief survey can describe all that is being done. No theory of organization is comprehensive enough to subsume and order all that we have studied, and none is yet sacred enough to restrain or limit new kinds of research activity. Even March and Simon's theory [367], more comprehensive and more widely praised than most, is a limited statement of what research on organizations is about. Its own authors have already gone beyond it in important respects—March by his work with Cyert on a behavioral theory of the firm [143], and Simon by his work with Newell and others on the simulation of human learning and problem-solving behavior [419], [421].

Evidences of Diversity

As in other new and expanding fields of research, there is no union shop. Anyone can play. In this symposium alone, among 23 speakers, at least 8 kinds of backgrounds are represented: business and industrial administration, economics, mathematics, political science, psychology, social psychology, sociology, and statistics. Professionals in these fields have not always been known for an ability—or a willingness—to work together.

One quick and crude measure of the extent and nature of the diversity in contemporary research is to see in what journals it has been published. What do surveyors like V. A. Thompson [544], Blau and Scott [76], or March and Simon [367] include in their footnotes or bibliographies? What sources do the contributors to a symposium like Haire's *Modern Organization Theory* [247] acknowledge? Where do editors like Etzioni [184a], J. D. Thompson [542], and Rubenstein and Haberstroh [457] find selections for books of readings? From these seven books, all published since 1958, I made a tally of 600 journal citations summarized in Tables 1 and 2.[1]

The tally shows that anyone who aspires to master the literature about organizations must watch a very large number of journals. In 592 listings, many of which represent the same reference named in two or more books, more than 100 different journals and periodicals are mentioned. Haire's book alone, in 112 references, includes references to 46 journals; March and Simon, in the first 10 pages of a long bibliography, include references to 57. Even if we look only at the journals from which authors and editors draw most frequently and which, for any one book, account for half of the total references or selections, we get the list of eighteen journals presented in Table 2. These range from obvious choices like the *Administrative Science Quarterly* to "sleepers" like the *University of Iowa Studies in Child Welfare,* which is important because it published much of the research of Kurt Lewin and his associates.

The high variance among authors and editors in the sources which they use justifies Haire's comparing modern theorists and the organizations that they study to the blind men and the elephant of Indian folklore. In Haire [247], for example, only one-third of the journals mentioned are referred to by more than one author. Fewer than one-tenth are referred to by more than three authors, and only one (*Human Organization/Applied Anthropology*) is mentioned by more than half the participants in the symposium. Blau and Scott [76] and V. A.

---

[1] I should confess the crudeness of my methods by indicating for each book what I counted:

Blau and Scott: All journal references in the first 10 pages of a 40-page bibliography.

Etzioni: All selections which were taken from journals.

Haire: All footnotes to journals or end-of-chapter journal references.

March and Simon: All journal references in the first 10 pages of a 36-page bibliography.

Rubenstein and Haberstroh: All journal references in section introductions written by editors plus all selections taken from journals.

J. D. Thompson *et al.:* All selections which were taken from journals.

V. A. Thompson: All footnote references to journals (but unhappily without any check for duplicate references to the same article).

Table 1   Sources of Journal References in Current Books About Research on Organizations

Kinds of Journals	Blau and Scott [76] n = 131	Etzioni [184a] n = 18	Haire [247] n = 112	March and Simon [367] n = 193	Rubenstein and Haberstroh [457] n = 49	J. D. Thompson [542] n = 9	V. A. Thompson [544] n = 80
General behavioral and administrative science	14%	11%	10%	2%	4%	33%	8%
Social psychology	14	0	11	24	14	0	14
Other sociology	55	50	21	22	10	45	36
Other psychology	4	3	11	27	29	0	11
Psychiatry and medicine	1	0	2	1	0	0	5
Economics	2	11	4	8	0	0	1
Management science and operations research	2	0	6	1	12	11	0
General business	1	5	11	7	10	0	11
Political science and public administration	3	5	4	3	2	0	8
Anthropology	3	5	11	2	6	11	1
Other	2	6	9	3	12	0	5

Table 2   Journals Representing Half of the Total Journal References in Current Books About Research on Organizations

Journal	Blau and Scott [76]	Etzioni [184a]	Haire [247]	March and Simon [367]	Rubenstein and Haberstroh [457]	J. D. Thompson [542]	V. A. Thompson [544]
Amer. Sociol. Rev.	●	●	●	●		●	●
Administr. Sci. Qtly.	●	●	●			●	●
Jr. Abnormal and Social Psych.			●	●			●
Amer. Jr. Sociology	●			●	●		●
Human Organization			●				
Management Sci.			●	●	●		
Social Forces			●		●		
Behavioral Sci.							
Fortune							●
Human Relations				●			
Jr. Appl. Psych.					●		
Jr. Social Issues				●	●		
Occupational Psychology				●			
Psychol. Bull.					●		
Psychol. Rev.				●			
Rev. of Economics and Statistics		●					
Sociometry					●		
Univ. of Iowa Studies in Child Welfare							

Thompson [544], with a strong sociological bent, draw a third of their references from the *American Sociological Review* and the *American Journal of Sociology;* but March and Simon [367], with a broader perspective, take less than 15% from these two journals and draw much more heavily on psychological sources. Of the books of readings, Etzioni's [184a] and J. D. Thompson's [542] are primarily sociological in origin; but Rubenstein and Haberstroh's [457] draws more heavily from psychology, business, and operations research.

There is no professional organization that can attract the loyalties of all the varieties of men who are involved in contemporary organizational research. Of all the journals we have listed, none (including such new and interdisciplinary efforts as the *Administrative Science Quarterly* or *Management Science*) publishes a really broad range of materials on organizations.

IMPLICATIONS OF DIVERSITY

In its variety and lack of clear structure, contemporary research on organizations shares much with such other areas of science as operations research or biochemistry, where burgeoning investments of effort and funds and deliberate attempts to cross old disciplinary barriers also keep things in a state of flux. A good deal of the excitement in organizational studies today results because we have not settled basic questions about boundaries to the field, about approaches to theory and research method, and about claims and counterclaims from established traditions like sociology and from new entrepreneurial coalitions like the management sciences for control over future developments. Today is a time for desegregation—a time when our most important task may be to find ways to facilitate interaction among those interested in organization theory. It is a time for redefinition of relationships among research groups and research efforts.

Progress in Desegregation

In the rest of this chapter, let us first review the kinds of desegregation that have occurred and that are beginning to occur. Then let us ask what other developments are needed to bring about an integrated science of organizations.

COLLABORATION AMONG BEHAVIORAL SCIENTISTS

The most obvious progress in desegregation has been among the behavioral scientists interested in organizational processes. The coals of distrust and disdain which in the past have kept psychologists, sociologists, economists, and political scientists apart still flicker and occasionally burst into flames. Yet for increasing numbers of men from these disciplines the study of organizations—like the study of families or of international relations—has provided a focus for fruitful collaborative efforts.

Forceful early statements by men like Barnard [44] and Simon [500] pointed out that the processes of organizational behavior were not the province of sociology, psychology, or economics alone; but they had little research to draw on to prove their point. The dissolution of traditional boundaries really began to occur through the expansion of behavioral research of all kinds after World War II. Several things contributed to this expansion. First, each of the behavioral disciplines renewed efforts to broaden its boundaries. In social psychology, for example, men like Kurt Lewin [344] began to apply their theories and their research methods to the analysis of problems that had previously been left mostly to the attention of sociologists and anthropologists. Sociologists, in turn, began in greater numbers to run laboratory experiments on small groups as a means of satisfying their desire for better controls and more discriminating tests than they could obtain through field observations and surveys of social behavior. The increasingly strong empirical interests of both groups made it relatively easy to work together in the general area of social psychology without reference to overworked differences of "philosophy" between psychologists and sociologists. Equipment like tape recorders and methodological developments like new survey techniques, sociometry, and interaction process analysis helped both groups in their research.

An empirical tradition has been slower to develop in political science and economics, but some progress is being made. Economists are beginning to study how people define goals and expectations, how they make choices and decisions, and how they negotiate and bargain with one another. Political scientists have helped in the development of our understanding of attitude and value formation, of social influence processes, and of informal relationships within organizations.

One result of the proliferation of research efforts and the challenge of bringing diverse findings together has been the recent growth of theories with multidisciplinary origins. Argyris [22], for example, has combined propositions about developmental tendencies in human personality with propositions about the structure and dynamics of organizations to develop hypotheses about what organizational experience does to individuals and groups. Argyris's work blends ideas from clinical psychology and anthropology. March and Simon [367] draw more heavily from cognitively oriented studies for their theory of organizational behavior. Their approach is directly concerned with organizational problem-solving and decision-making procedures as well as with the personal adjustments of individuals and groups to an organization.

Homans has been more concerned with theories of small-group behavior than with theories of organization, but his two books nicely illustrate the differences between the old and the new. His first model of social behavior [282] stressed mainly sociological and anthropological research and dealt primarily with sociological constructs like sentiments, activity, and interaction. His most recent model [283] begins with a succinct statement of assumptions about how individuals perform. Based on the ideas of B. F. Skinner, a psychologist, and on ideas of cost and reward adapted from economics, Homans sets forth propositions about individuals—what motivates them and how they learn. He makes these propositions the basis for building his analysis of social behavior.

INSTITUTIONAL STUDIES WITH A BEHAVIORAL BASE

Although the increasing interaction among behavioral scientists represents the best developed trend toward desegregation in research on organizations, another trend deserves mention. It is the wave of fresh contacts between behavioral scientists, who tend to be interested in organizations simply as a general setting for the study of behavior, and institutional specialists, who are committed to understanding particular kinds of organizations (like a hospital) or specific organizational functions (like marketing). Books in fields like marketing and personnel management are beginning to go well beyond references to "behavior" in their subtitles and citations from the Hawthorne studies in the text. Increasing numbers now include detailed reviews of relevant findings in the behavioral sciences.

For a number of years, perhaps because real-world organizations hold the purse strings on research funds, behavioral scientists have taken cues from the problems of real-world organizations to design their experiments and field studies. Yet the reverse of this process is also important: the adaptation of behavioral scientists' methods by institutional specialists to study real-world processes more rigorously *in situ*. Some of this, of course, has been going on for a long time. There is an important tradition of field surveys and experiments on problems of personnel and industrial relations dating back past the Hawthorne studies; and behavioral studies of consumers' buying habits have been conducted for many years. The difference is that these studies are now beginning to be performed by men whose primary identification is with the institutional field rather than with one of the social sciences.

In marketing, for example, Kuehn [325, 204] has applied statistical learning models of the Bush-Mosteller-Estes variety to analyze questions like shifts in consumer brand preferences. In the field of managerial controls, Stedry [516] has applied basic notions about level of aspiration to the impact of budgets as a device for controlling performance. His research is an interesting mix: a firm basis in ideas derived from psychology, the extension of these ideas to formulate some normative models for the use of budgets, and the execution of a series of laboratory experiments to assess the validity of the normative models. Churchill [121] has tried much the same thing in his study of the effects of management audits on group performance.

Problems for the Future

To get greater scope in our research and theories, other trends toward desegregation need to be encouraged. I shall discuss several of these briefly.

NORMATIVE AND DESCRIPTIVE APPROACHES TO ORGANIZATIONAL RESEARCH

Relatively little progress has been made in breaking down barriers between essentially descriptive efforts to increase our understanding of how organizations work and essentially normative efforts to make organizations work better. Let us consider three kinds of normative approaches to organizational problems.

The first of these is the morally normative tradition, particularly in political science and public administration. For advocates of this approach, focus on what organizations do and how they operate is misdirected. They are more interested in asserting the goals toward which organizations should operate than in studying the means by which goals are set and achieved. The difference in approach shows clearly, for example, in a comparison of Snyder and Paige's analytical dissection of the decision to join battle with the Communists in Korea [510] with Batchelder's normative analysis [49] of the decision to produce and use the A-bomb.

The chances for a reasonable working relationship between descriptively oriented researchers and this group may be difficult. The latter do not seek empirical data to back their positions, and they have been known to attack people who urge an empirical approach for being "indifferent" to questions of value.

The second kind of normative orientation is seen in economics and in the newly developing fields of management science and operations research. Here attitudes seem to represent a greater confidence than most psychologists and sociologists have in the essential rationality of human behavior and a greater impatience than most psychologists and sociologists have with simply describing things as they are. Economists and operations research analysts are interested in things as they should be: they observe organizations and their environments in order to develop analytical models which will enable the organization to make more rational decisions. Their essential motivation may be to prove that they are smarter than managers.

The third orientation is that of some psychologists and sociologists who believe that from what we have learned about human behavior, we can prescribe more effective ways of organizing human effort. Skinner's *Walden Two* [505] is one of the more fanciful and more interesting efforts of this kind; and books by Likert [350] and McGregor [380] on the more prosaic problems of running a business firm also fall into the same category. Their arguments are more sophisticated, but their point of view is a first cousin to the views of the Utopians or the classical management theorists.

Desegregation of normative and descriptive interests is important to the progress of organizational research for two reasons. First of all, a great deal of the normative research on organizations does not rest on very valid assumptions about how the world works or about the extent to which the world will welcome new suggestions for organizing. Better models in economics and operations research and better judgments about basic questions of values and ethics in organizations will come from more adequate descriptions of what organizational systems are like and of what the effects of various kinds of shocks and disturbances to the system will be.

On the other hand, a great deal of our descriptive research is going to be wasted unless it takes better account of the directions in which the world is moving. Leavitt [336, 337] has pointed out that much of today's research on subjects like patterns of supervision has little significance for the kind of world that may exist tomorrow when computers and new analytic techniques for decision making are a much more conspicuous part of the management picture.

UNHUMAN ASPECTS OF ORGANIZATIONS

Another desirable kind of desegregation is that which will bring real interaction between those who see organizations as aggregations of people and those for whom the human element is relatively unimportant. The former are likely to work from two main assumptions: (1) that interactions among people are the only kind that an organization theorist needs to worry about and (2) that the interactions with others within an organization are a major focus of interest and motivation for people. The "unhuman" group is inclined to ignore people, sometimes because they do not believe that people are a very important variable in organizations, but perhaps more often because efforts to build human behavior into organizational models greatly complicate the task.

A glance at Tables 1 and 2 suggests that so far at least most researchers have treated organizations primarily as aggregations of people. Most studies are printed in journals of sociology or psychology. Yet particularly in modern industrial and military organizations, much behavior can be predicted without reference to the people involved simply by analyzing the machines, the information transmission devices, and the automatic decision and control systems that are used. There is a well-developed field, called human engineering, which deals with the interactions of individual men or small work crews with machines. There needs to be a comparable field for the total organization which will explore the important interactions between men and the machines that are their partners in the total functioning of the organization.

Even before computers and automatically controlled and self-regulating production systems, interactions with people on the job may not always have had as much to do with behavior as we have recently been inclined to believe. My secretary, for example, alleges that the behavior of her typewriter or the condition of the files she has to work from has a great deal to do with both her productivity and her morale.

Even if we restrict ourselves to the study of social interactions among people, it is important to pay more attention to interactions that occur outside the time reserved for organization-related activities. Dubin [171] and Remitz [446] have both presented evidence countering Mayo's argument that employment experiences are the major life interest for most people. The way in which an organization performs has much to do with the experiences of its members in family relationships, in bowling leagues, and in other forms of recreation and off-the-job experience.

COMPARATIVE STUDIES

Most of what we note as research on organizations today is very current and very American. But many of our basic ideas go back by various traditions to Europeans like Weber, Smith, Marshall, and Fayol. Some contemporary European research—notably that done at centers like the Tavistock Institute, the Social Sciences Research Centre in Edinburgh, or the Institute for Social Research in Oslo— has found its way into our surveys and summaries. A little has also been done by men like Abegglen [2] and Udy [557] [2] to study organizational behavior in nonwestern and noncontemporary settings. Yet it seems to be true that symposia on things as culturally neutral as the biological and biochemical bases of animal behavior draw more extensively on research done in other countries than this symposium does [253].

Our points of view in many areas could benefit from greater attention to the work that has been done overseas, particularly that which is published in other languages. Sweden, to take just one example, has provided many interesting, but little-noted, studies which bear on problems we are interested in. Höglund [279] has elaborated and applied Sune Carlson's [97] ideas for describing executive behavior to give a map of the activities of top managers in relation to their external environments. Wirdenius [605a] has studied new ways to describe supervisory behavior. Fältström [185], like Dalton [152] in this country, has done an interesting and sensitive analysis of the ways in which management organizations differ in practice from the formal models we sometimes use to design and describe them. Dahlström [149] has done a detailed field study of communication patterns and problems within industrial organizations.

Four very different Swedish reports cast light on the much-studied questions of employee attitudes and satisfactions: a field experiment with different patterns of supervision in a telephone company (Westerlund [596]), an analysis of the causes behind absence from work in insurance companies (Henriksson [265]), studies of the things that affect feelings of satisfaction among bank employees (Remitz [446]), and a very ambitious comparison of job and free-time behavior of workers in a newly industrialized community and in an established urban center (Segerstedt and Lundquist [468, 469]).

To these we might add studies of goal setting and decision making in marketing organizations (Ramström [445]; Wärneryd [587]), an attempt to develop ways to select top managers from a Parsonian framework of ideas about what is needed (Ramfalk [444]), factor analysis of work group structure (Boalt [77]), and work on intracompany pricing and business planning (Paulsson Frenckner [431, 432]).

Studies like these afford one way to achieve meaningful, if gross, tests of the validity of propositions in organizational behavior. Hope-

---

[2] See also Chapter 11 by Udy in this volume.

fully, we will be able to find ways to attain a greater interchange of hypotheses and data from other groups around the world. Sometime in the tradition of the International Geophysical Year and the Year of the Quiet Sun, it might even be appropriate to plan a year's program to concentrate on the kinds of comparative studies of organizations around the world that would do most to test the theories we now have and to give us a base of new data on which to build better theories.

RESEARCH STRATEGIES

Progress toward effective integration of our knowledge about organizations presumes some positive actions on the part of those engaged in research to broaden the scope and improve the value of the studies we do. One of these actions is to seek, by new empirical work or by review of what has already been done, some accommodation on the assumptions and issues which still divide us. Research in organizations remains an art of advocacy as well as of analysis. On any aspect of organizational behavior that can be named, more facts are needed. On some issues, like the question of how organizations translate information from their environments into definitions of tasks to perform, very little useful data of any kind have been gathered. On other issues, like the effects of different patterns of supervision, we have masses of data—but still not nearly enough to answer very many questions well.

Large-scale systems studies are one promising way of collecting needed data. Even discounting the optimism of some advocates of this approach and acknowledging the difficulties of handling complex networks of variables, there are still signs of progress. The air-defense and logistic policy experiments (Chapman et al., [105]; Enke, [182]) show that, even in large systems, significant sets of relationships among variables can be isolated as manageable subsystems. In Bonini's [79] [3] general simulation of the operations of a firm, in Cyert and March's [143] [4] simulations of specific decision-making subunits within firms, and in many management games, computer programs produce highly realistic matches to the behavior of real organizations. As we develop better languages to characterize the structure of such simulation programs, we have a new language in which to propose hypotheses and theories.

Another important step in research involves replication and elaboration of studies that have already been done. This is perhaps the most efficient way to find out what sorts of concepts and hypotheses

---

[3] See also Chapter 15 in this volume.
[4] See Chapter 16 in this volume.

have long-run survival value. In a few areas we have done replications with highly beneficial results. The early experiments on participative management patterns, for example, draw dramatic attention because of their apparently solid demonstration of the immediate practical benefits of participation. The early research of Lewin, Lippitt, and White [345], Coch and French [129], and the University of Michigan group (Kahn and Katz [100c]) are among the most widely cited studies in the organizational literature. Yet in each case, the original groups have done elaborations of the original experiments (Lippitt and Whyte [358b]; French, Israel, and Ås [207]; Morse and Reimer [407]) and have found that the simple relationships which they first hypothesized between participation, satisfaction, and productivity do not hold up. As a result, at a time when participative notions may be at a peak in terms of popularity with managers, we are reopening many old questions to establish more clearly the conditions under which these methods will and will not work.

The communication network experiments are another example of what replication and elaboration can contribute. The early experiments of Leavitt [333] related job satisfaction to centrality in the communication network. But later studies by Trow [550] and Mulder [409] have recognized the ambiguities in this hypothesis, given the nature of the networks used, and have tested whether satisfaction is most highly related to centrality in the communications system or to other variables that happened in Leavitt's experiment to be coincident with centrality—autonomy in action, and power over the activities of others. Leavitt focused originally on the effects of different network restrictions on task performance. However, Guetzkow and others [241, 242] found that the amount of time given for planning, the communication network that prevailed during the planning period, and the placement of personalities in the network had also to be taken into account in predicting group performance. Work that Shure [497] and McWhinney [386] are now doing is suggesting ways in which the Guetzkow hypotheses should be modified. Some, like Glanzer and Glaser [217], would conclude that we are not able to synthesize much from the kinds of experience we have had with network studies. However, replication and elaboration of the Leavitt experiment have enabled us to ask sharper and more meaningful questions about behavior in communication nets.

The need to study a process by using a variety of subjects in a variety of environments is one important facet of replicative efforts which many recent studies emphasize, e.g., Churchill [121]; Milgram [400]; French, Israel, and Ås [207]. Limited research budgets, timidity about complicated experimental situations, and ready routines for conscripting college students or military personnel produce "knowledge" of limited usefulness. What college sophomores do, alas, may not be much more relevant than the behavior of monkeys for predicting how executives, nurses, or research scientists will perform.

It is also important—as Tannenbaum, Weschler, and Massarik [536] suggest—to increase the span of time over which research groups keep contact with the organizations they are studying. Many of our notions about the effects of leadership style, communication procedures, patterns of participation, new technology, and many other variables are based on experiments or field studies that studied reactions for only a short period of time after a change or a new force was introduced.

Prospects for Real Integration

In the foregoing, I have stressed the diversity of contemporary organizational studies. I have suggested that what is happening—and what we should encourage to happen—is mainly a process of breaking down the loose sets of barriers that now constrain what we notice and accept as appropriate research. I have characterized this as a process of desegregation. What now about the prospects for real integration?

It is unlikely within the foreseeable future that anyone will be able to define the content and scope of organization theory as well as we once thought we could define some areas in physics, biology, or psychology. If we reach an agreement about organization theory, in fact, our experience in these other fields suggests that organization theory will be dead; and the study of the institutions with which it was concerned will proceed with renewed vigor under some other label.

But efforts toward integration are important. It would be useful within the structure of an existing professional society or under the sponsorship of a new society to provide more regular, more highly interdisciplinary forums for the planning and evaluation of research on organizations. It might be useful to have a journal devoted to organizational research which printed a greater variety of kinds of research and attracted a greater variety of readers than the current journals do. Broad efforts like those of March and Simon [367] or Blau and Scott [76] to summarize and structure what we know about organizations also make a major contribution. Although such efforts to integrate are doomed to a short lifetime in such an active field, they play a major role in helping all of us to fill the gaps in our knowledge of what has been done and in provoking at least some of us to question and modify the boundaries and structure which they propose.

PART TWO

Behavioral science perspectives

4

APPLIED ORGANIZATION CHANGE IN
INDUSTRY: STRUCTURAL, TECHNICAL,
AND HUMAN APPROACHES

Harold J. Leavitt [1]

This is a mapping chapter. It is part of a search for perspective on complex organizations, in this instance, through consideration of several classes of efforts to change ongoing organizations. Approaches to change provide a kind of sharp caricature of underlying beliefs and prejudices about the important dimensions of organizations. Thereby, perhaps, they provide some insights into areas of real or apparent difference among perspectives on organization theory.

To classify several major approaches to change, I have found it useful, first, to view organizations as multivariate systems, in which at least four interacting variables loom especially large: the variables of task, structure, technology, and actors (usually people) (Figure 1).

Roughly speaking, task refers to organizational *raisons d'etre*—manufacturing, servicing, etc., including the large numbers of different, but operationally meaningful, subtasks which may exist in complex organizations.

By actors I mean mostly people, but with the qualification that acts usually executed by people need not remain exclusively in the human domain.

By technology, I mean technical tools—problem-solving inventions like work measurement, computers, or drill presses. Note that I in-

---

[1] Many of the ideas in this chapter are expanded and restated in the author's chapter in [366].

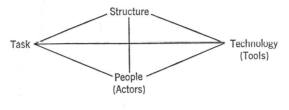

FIGURE 1

clude both machines and programs in this category, but with some uncertainty about the line between structure and technology.

Finally by structure, I mean systems of communication, systems of authority (or other roles), and systems of work flow.

These four are highly interdependent, so that change in any one will most probably result in compensatory (or retaliatory) change in others. In discussing organizational change, therefore, I shall assume that it is one or more of these variables that we seek to change. Sometimes we may aim to change one of these as an end in itself, sometimes as a mechanism for effecting some changes in one or more of the others.

Thus, for example, structural change toward, say, decentralization should change the performance of certain organizational tasks (indeed, even the selection of tasks), the technology that is brought to bear (e.g., changes in accounting procedures), and the nature, numbers, and/or motivation and attitudes of people in the organization. Any of these changes could presumably be consciously intended; or they could occur as unforeseen and often troublesome outcomes of efforts to change only one or two of the variables.

Similarly, the introduction of new technological tools—computers, for example—may effect changes in structure (e.g., in the communication system or decision map of the organization), changes in people (their numbers, skills, attitudes, and activities), and changes in task performance or even task definition, since some tasks may now become feasible of accomplishment for the first time.

Changes in the people and task variables could presumably branch out through the system to cause similar changes in other variables.

We can turn now to the central focus of this chapter, namely, a categorization and evaluation of several approaches to organizational change—approaches that differ markedly in their degree of emphasis and their ordering of these four variables.

Clearly most efforts to effect change, whether they take off from people, technology, structure or task, soon must deal with the others. Human relators must invent technical devices for implementing their ideas, and they must evaluate alternative structures, classing some as consonant and some as dissonant with their views of the world. Structuralists must take stands on the kinds of human interaction that are supportive of their position, and the kinds that threaten to undermine it, etc.

Although I differentiate structural from technical from human approaches to organizational tasks, the differentiation is in points of origin, relative weightings, and underlying conceptions and values, not in the exclusion of all other variables.

This categorization must be further complicated by the fact that the objectives of the several approaches to organizational change are not uniform. All of them do share a considerable interest in improved solutions to tasks. But while some of the technical approaches focus almost exclusively on task solutions, that is, on the *quality* of decisions, some of the people approaches are at least as interested in performance of task subsequent to decisions. Although improved task solution serves as a common goal for all of these approaches, several carry other associated objectives that weigh almost as heavily in the eyes of their proponents. Thus some of the early structural approaches were almost as concerned with maintaining a power status quo as with improving task performance, and some of the current people approaches are at least as interested in providing organizations that fulfill human needs as they are in efficacious performance of tasks.

The several approaches are still further complicated by variations in the causal chains by which they are supposed to bring about their intended changes. Some of the structural approaches, for example, are not aimed directly at task but at people as mediating intervening variables. In these approaches, one changes structure to change people to improve task performance. Similarly, some of the people approaches seek to change people in order to change structure and tools, to change task performance, and also to make life more fulfilling for people. We can turn now to the several varieties of efforts themselves.

The Structural Approaches

Applied efforts to change organizations by changing structure seem to fall into four classes. First, structural change has been the major mechanism of the "classical" organization theorist. Out of the deductive, logical, largely military-based thinking of early nonempirical organization theory, there evolved the whole set of now familiar "principles" for optimizing organizational performance by optimizing structure. These are deductive approaches carrying out their analyses from task backwards to appropriate divisions of labor and appropriate systems of authority. These early structural approaches almost always mediated their activities through people to task. One improves task performance by clarifying and defining the jobs of people and setting up appropriate relationships among these jobs. Operationally one worried about modifying spans of control, defining nonoverlapping areas of responsibility and authority, and logically defining necessary functions.

In retrospect, most of us think of these early approaches as abstractions, formal and legalistic, and poorly anchored in empirical data. They were also almost incredibly naive in their assumptions about human behavior. In fact, almost the only assumptions that were made were legalistic and moralistic ones: that people, having contracted to work, would then carry out the terms of their contract; that people assigned responsibility would necessarily accept that responsibility; that people when informed of the organization's goals would strive wholeheartedly to achieve those goals.

The values underlying these early approaches were thus probably more authoritarian and puritanical than anything else. Order, discipline, system, and acceptance of authority seemed to be dominant values. The objective, of course, was optimal task performance, but within the constraints imposed by the hierarchy of authority.

In one variation or another, such structural approaches are still widely applied. It is still commonplace for consultants or organization planning departments to try to solve organizational problems by redefining areas of responsibility and authority, enforcing the chain of command, and so on.

A second widespread approach to structural change, allied to the first, somewhat more modern and sophisticated and somewhat narrower, too, is the idea of decentralization. The idea of changing organizations by decentralizing their structure was probably more an invention of the accounting profession than anyone else, though it has been widely endorsed by structuralists and by human relators too. Almost nobody is against it. Not too long ago, I heard the senior officer of one of the nation's largest consulting firms remind his large staff of young consultants that their firm was founded on the "bedrock principle of decentralization."

Decentralization affects the performance of tasks partially through its intervening effects on people. By creating profit centers, one presumably increases the motivation and goal-oriented behavior of local managers. One also adds flexibility so that variations in technology appropriate to the different tasks of different decentralized units now become more possible; so do subvariations in structure, and local variations in the use of people. Decentralization can be thought of as a mechanism for changing organizations at a meta level, providing local autonomy for further change. Thus, within limits, decentralized units may further change themselves through the use of any one of the many alternatives available, and perhaps for this reason no group has questioned it, at least until the last couple of years.

Recently, two other structural approaches have shown up, but they have not yet reached a widespread level of application. One of them is best represented by Chapple and Sayles [107]. Theirs is a form of social engineering aimed at task, but via people. They seek to modify the behavior of people in order to improve task performance, but they do it by modifying structure, in this case, the flow of work. Out of the tradition of applied anthropology, they argue that planning of work flows and groupings of specialties will directly affect the morale, behavior, and output of employees. One of the failings of earlier structural models, in their view, is that the design of work was almost entirely determined by task and technical variables, and failed to take account of human social variables. They provide illustrative cases to show that appropriate redesigning of work, in a social engineering sense, affects both human attitudes and output.

I cannot overlook in this discussion of structure the implications of a second approach—the research on communication networks [217]. I know of no *direct* applications of this laboratory research to the real world, though it has had some indirect influence on structural planning. In that research, variations in communication nets affect both routine and novel task performance rather significantly. The results suggest that appropriate communication structures might vary considerably within a complex organization, depending upon the type of task that any subunit of the organization undertakes. Thus for highly programmed repetitive tasks, highly centralized communication structures seem to operate most efficiently, but with some human costs. For more novel, ill-structured tasks, more wide-open communication nets with larger numbers of channels and less differentiation among members seem to work more effectively.

Technological Approaches to Organizational Change

My first entry in this technological category is Taylor's *Scientific Management* [539]. Its birth date was around 1910, its father, Frederick W. Taylor. Its tools were work measurement tools. It bore none of the abstract deductive flavor of the structural approaches. From the classic programming of the labors of Schmidt, the immigrant pig-iron handler at Bethlehem, on to the more sophisticated forms of work measurement and analysis of succeeding decades, Taylorism has constituted a significant force in influencing task performance in American organizations.

Scientific Management, almost from its inception, took a position outside of the task, not of it. Taylor created a new technical skill—industrial engineering—and a new class of specialized practitioners—the industrial engineers. Theirs was a staff skill, a planning skill. They were the organizers and designers of work. The Schmidts were the doers.

Like the early structural approaches, Scientific Management was thus to a great extent ahuman, perhaps even inhuman. For in creating the separate planning specialist, it removed planning from its old location—the head of the doer of work. Many observers, both contemporary and subsequent, saw this phase of scientific management as downright demeaning of mankind. Taylor put his foot deeply into his mouth by saying things like this: "Now one of the very first requirements for a man who is fit to handle pig iron . . . is that he shall be so stupid and so phlegmatic that he more nearly resembles . . . the ox than any other type. . . . He must consequently be trained by a man more intelligent than himself." [2]

But despite the flurry of Congressional investigations and active counterattack by Taylor's contemporaries, Scientific Management grew and prospered, and radically changed structure, people, and the ways jobs got done. Indeed, it spread and flourished until no self-respecting manufacturing firm was without time-study men, methods engineers, work standards, piece rates, and job classification schemes.

The range of Scientific Management, however, was limited by its relatively simple tools largely to the programming of eye-hand and muscle jobs. Though Taylor and his fellows were ready to generalize their methods to almost any organizational problem, the methods themselves fell pretty short when applied to judgment and think-type jobs.

If one asks why Scientific Management flourished, several reasonable answers appear. The environment of the day, despite counterattacks by Upton Sinclair and others, was probably supportive. It was an environment of growth, expansiveness, and muscle flexing. Work in associated disciplines was supportive, too. Psychology, for example, was physiologically oriented, concerned with individual differences

---

[2] Quoted from Taylor [539].

and anxious to be treated as a science. Hence it, too, was measurement happy.[3] Finger dexterity tests meshed neatly with Taylor's motion study.

But most of all, Taylorism, like many other ideas, seemed to be carried by its own operational gimmicks—by its cheap, workable, easily taught techniques and methods.

Scientific Management receded into a relatively stable and un-dramatic background in the late 1930's and 1940's and has never made a real comeback in its original form. But the technological ap-proaches were by no means dead. The development of operations research and the more or less contemporaneous invention and ex-ploitation of computers have more than revived them.

I submit that operational operations research methods for changing organizational problem solving can be reasonably placed in the same category with Scientific Management. They have both developed a body of technical methods for solving work problems. They both are usually *external* in their approach, essentially separating the plan-ning of problem-solving programs from the routine acting out of solutions. Operations research, too, is quickly developing in its op-erational form, a new class of hot-shot staff specialists, in many ways analogous to the earlier staff efficiency man. What is *clearly* different, of course, is the nature of the techniques, although there may be larger differences that are not yet so clear.

The operations research and information processing techniques are turning out to be, if not more general, at least applicable to large classes of tasks that Scientific Management could not touch (Schultz and Whisler [496a]). Now armed with linear programming methods, one can approach a task like media selection in an advertising agency, though it would have been nonsense to time study it.

But note the over-all similarity: Change the setting of the movie from Bethlehem, Pa., to Madison Avenue; the time from 1910 to

---

[3] See for example Bendix's [57] account of the early enthusiasm of industrial psy-chologists. He quotes Hugo Munsterberg appraising the promise of industrial psychology in 1913:

. . . *still more important than the valued commercial profit on both sides is the cultural gain which will come to the total economic life of the nation, as soon as everyone can be brought to the place where his best energies may be unfolded and his greatest personal satisfaction secured. The economic experimental psy-chology offers no more inspiring idea than this adjustment of work and psyche by which mental dissatisfaction with the work, mental depression and discourage-ment, may be replaced in our social community by overflowing joy and perfect inner harmony.*

1962; the costuming from overalls to gray flannel suits; and the tasks from simple muscular labor to complex judgmental decisions. Turn worried laborer Schmidt into worried media executive Jones. Then replace Taylor with Charnes and Cooper and supplant the stopwatch with the computer. It is the same old theme either way— the conflict between technology and humanity.

A distinction needs to be drawn, of course, between operational operations research and other computer-based information-processing approaches, although they are often closely allied. "Management Science" hopefully will mean more than highly operational applications of specific techniques, and organizations are also being changed by simulation techniques and by heuristic problem-solving methods. Their impact has not yet been felt in anything like full force; but tasks, people, and structures are already being rather radically modified by them. In fact, one wonders if these task-directed efforts will not end up having at least as radical an impact on structure and on the role of humans as on task solutions themselves. For out of new information-processing methods we now begin to reconsider the bedrock issue of decentralization and to reconsider the permanency and primacy of human judgments for making certain classes of decisions. All the way round the organization, visible changes are being generated out of technical innovations.

Without delving further into the substance of these more recent technological approaches, it may be worth pointing up one other characteristic that they share with many of their predecessors—a kind of faith in the ultimate victory of *better* problem solutions over less good ones. This faith is often perceived by people-oriented practitioners of change as sheer naïveté about the nature of man. They ascribe it to a pre-Freudian fixation on rationality; to a failure to realize that human acceptance of ideas is the real carrier of change; and that emotional human resistance is the real road block. They can point, in evidence, to a monotonously long list of cases in which technological innovations, methods changes, or operations research techniques have fallen short because they ignored the human side of the enterprise. It is not the logically better solutions that get adopted, this argument runs, but the more humanly acceptable, more feasible ones. Unless the new technologist wises up, he may end up a miserable social isolate, like his predecessor, the unhappy industrial engineer.

Often this argument fits the facts. Operations research people can be incredibly naive in their insensitivity to human feelings. But in another, more gracious sense, one can say that the technological approaches have simply taken a more macroscopic, longer view of the world than the people approaches. Better solutions do get accepted in the long run, because deeper forces in the economy press them upon the individual organization—competitive forces, mainly. Macroscopically these ahuman or people-last approaches may encounter bumps and grinds in the microcosms of the individual firm; but sooner or later, in the aggregate, human resistances will be allayed or displaced or overcome, and the steam drill must inevitably defeat John Henry.

The technological approaches assume some communication among firms, and between firms and the world; and they assume further that the demonstration of more economic solutions will eventually result in their adoption, though the road may be rough.

The technological approaches seem not only to predict the victory of cleaner, more logical, and more parsimonious solutions but also to *value* them. Failure of human beings to search for or use more efficient solutions is a sign, from this perspective, of human weakness and inadequacy. People must be teased or educated into greater logic, greater rationality. Resistance to better solutions is proof only of the poverty of our educational system; certainly it is not in any way an indication that "optimal" solutions are less than optimal.

The People Approaches

The people approaches try to change the organizational world by changing the behavior of actors in the organization. By changing people, it is argued, one can cause the creative invention of new tools, or one can cause modifications in structure (especially power structure). By one or another of these means, changing people will cause changes in solutions to tasks and performance of tasks as well as changes in human growth and fulfillment.

In surveying the people approaches, one is immediately struck by the fact that the literature dealing directly with organizational change is almost all people-oriented. Just in the last four or five years, for example, several volumes specifically concerned with organizational change have been published. All of them are people-type books. They include Lippitt, Watson, and Westley's *The Dynamics of Planned Change* [353]; Lawrence's *The Changing of Organizational Behavior Patterns* [332]; Ginsberg and Reilly's *Effecting Change in Large Organizations* [216]; Bennis, Benne, and Chin's *The Planning of Change* [59]; and Guest's *Organizational Change* [238].

This tendency to focus on the process of change itself constitutes one of the major distinguishing features of the people approaches.

The technological and structural approaches tend to focus on problem-solving, sliding past the microprocesses by which new problem-solving techniques are generated and adopted.

Historically, the people approaches have moved through at least two phases: The first was essentially manipulative, responsive to the primitive and seductive question, "How can we get people to do what we want them to do?"

Although most of us identify such questions with borderline workers like Dale Carnegie, much of the early work (immediately post-World War II) by social scientists on "overcoming resistance to change" dealt with the same issues.

Carnegie's *How to Win Friends and Influence People* [98] was first published in 1936, a few years ahead of most of what we now regard as psychological work in the same area. Like the social scientists that followed, Carnegie's model for change focused on the relationship between changer and changee, pointing out that changes in feelings and attitudes were prerequisites to voluntary changes in overt behavior. Carnegie proposes that one changes others first by developing a valuable (to the other person) relationship, and then using that relationship as a lever for bringing about the change one seeks. One does not attack with logic and criticism and advice. A offers B support, approval, a permissive atmosphere; and having thus established warm, affective bonds (invariably "sincere" bonds, too), A then requests of B that he change in the way A wishes, while A holds the relationship as collateral.

Though social scientists have tended to reject it out of hand, current research on influence processes suggests that the Carnegie model is not technically foolish at all, although we have disavowed it as manipulative, slick, and of questionable honesty.

The Carnegie model, moreover, has some current social scientific parallels. Thus Martin and Sims [371], for example, directly attack the issue of how to be a successful power politician in industrial organizations. They argue that dramatic skill, capacity to withhold certain kinds of information, the appearance of decisiveness, and a variety of other calculatedly strategic behaviors, appear to be effective in influencing behavior in organizational hierarchies.

In fact, Carnegie-like interest in face-to-face influence has finally become a respectable area of social scientific research. Several works of Hovland et al. [284] on influence and persuasion provide experimental support for the efficacy of certain behavioral techniques of influence over others.

But if we move over into the traditionally more "legitimate" spheres of social science, we find that much of the work after World War II on "overcoming resistance to change" was still responsive to the same manipulative question. Consider, for example, the now classic work by Kurt Lewin [531b] and his associates on changing food habits, or the later industrial work by Coch and French [129]. In both cases, A sets out to bring about a predetermined change in the behavior of B. Lewin sets out to cause housewives to purchase and consume more variety meats—a selling problem. Coch and French set out to gain acceptance of a preplanned methods change by hourly workers in a factory. In both cases the methodology included large elements of indirection, with less than full information available to the changees.

But whereas Dale Carnegie built warm personal relationships and then bargained with them, neither Lewin nor Coch and French are centrally concerned about intimate relationships between changer and changee. Their concern is much more with warming up the interrelationships among changees.

Thus 32% of Lewin's test housewives exposed to a group-decision method served new variety meats, as against only 3% of the women exposed to lectures. Lewin accounts for these results by calling upon two concepts: "involvement" and "group pressure." Lectures leave their audiences passive and unpressed by the group, whereas discussions are both active and pressing. Similarly, Coch and French, causing the girls in a pajama factory to accept a methods change, emphasize group methods, seeing resistance to change as partially a function of individual frustration, and partially of strong group-generated forces. Their methodology, therefore, is to provide opportunities for need satisfaction and quietly to corner the group forces and redirect them toward the desired change.

But it is this slight thread of stealth that was the soft spot (both ethically and methodologically) of these early people approaches to change, and this is the reason I classify them as manipulative. For surely no bright student has ever read the Coch and French piece without wondering a little bit about what *would* have happened if the change being urged by management just did not seem like a good idea to the "smaller, more intimate," work groups of Coch and French's "total participation" condition.

One might say that these early studies wrestled rather effectively with questions of affect and involvement, but ducked a key variable—power. Coch and French modified behavior by manipulating participation while trying to hold power constant. In so doing, the artistry of the "discussion leader" remained an important but only vaguely controlled variable, causing difficulties in replicating results and generating widespread discomfort among other social scientists.

Other contemporary and subsequent people approaches also avoided the power problem and encountered similar soft spots. The Western Electric counseling program (Roethlisberger and Dickson [452]) that emerged out of the Hawthorne researches sought for change through catharsis, with a specific prohibition against any follow-up action by counselors—a "power-free" but eminently human approach. Later, users of morale and attitude surveys sought to effect change by feeding back anonymous aggregate data so that the power groups might then modify their own behavior. But the very anonymity of the process represented an acceptance of the power status quo.

It was to be expected, then, that the next moves in the development of people approaches would be toward working out the power variable. It was obvious, too, that the direction would be toward power equalization rather than toward power differentiation. The theoretical underpinnings, the prevalent values, and the initial research results all pointed that way.

But though this is what happened, it happened in a complicated and mostly implicit way. Most of the push has come from work on individuals and small groups, and has then been largely extrapolated to organizations. Client-centered therapy (Rogers [453]) and applied group dynamics (Miles [399]) have been prime movers. In both of those cases, theory and technique explicitly aimed at allocating at least equal power to the changee(s), a fact of considerable importance in later development of dicta for organizational change.

Thus Carl Rogers describes his approach to counseling and therapy:

This newer approach differs from the older one in that it has a genuinely different goal. It aims directly toward the greater independence and integration of the individual rather than hoping that such results will accrue if the counsellor assists in solving the problem. The individual and not the problem is the focus. The aim is not to solve one particular problem, but to assist the individual to grow ([453], pp. 28–29).

At the group level, a comparable development was occurring, namely, the development of the T (for training) group (or sensitivity training or development group). The T-group is the core tool of programs aimed at teaching people how to lead and change groups. It has also become a core tool for effecting organizational change. T-group leaders try to bring about changes in their groups by taking extremely permissive, extremely nonauthoritarian, sometimes utterly nonparticipative roles, thus encouraging group members not only to solve their own problems but also to define them. The T-group leader becomes, in the language of the profession, a "resource person," not consciously trying to cause a substantive set of changes but only changes in group processes, which would then, in turn, generate substantive changes.

Though the T-group is a tool, a piece of technology, an invention, I include it in the people rather than the tool approaches, for it evolved out of those approaches as a mechanism specifically designed for effecting change in people.

In contrast to earlier group discussion tools, the T-group deals with the power variable directly. Thus Bennis and Shepard [59a] comment:

The core of the theory of group development is that the principle obstacles to the development of valid communication are to be found in the orientations toward authority and intimacy that members bring to the group. Rebelliousness, submissiveness or withdrawal as the characteristic responses to authority figures . . . prevent consensual validation of experience. The behaviors determined by these orientations are directed toward enslavement of the other in the service of the self, enslavement of the self in the service of the other, or disintegration of the situation. Hence, they prevent the setting, clarification of, and movement toward, group shared goals.

I offer these quotes to show the extent to which the moral and methodological soft spots of the early manipulative models were being dealt with directly in group training situations. These are not wishy-washy positions. They deal directly with the power variable. Their objective is to transfer more power to the client or the group.

But these are both nonorganizational situations. For the therapist, the relationship with the individual client bounds the world. For the T-group trainer, the group is the world. They can both deal more easily with the power variable than change agents working in a time-constrained and work-flow-constrained organizational setting.

At the organizational level, things therefore are a little more vague. The direction is there, in the form of movement toward power equalization, but roadblocks are many and maps are somewhat sketchy and undetailed. McGregor's [380] development of participative Theory Y to replace authoritarian Theory X is a case in point. McGregor's whole conception of Theory Y very clearly implies a shift from an all powerful superior dealing with impotent subordinates to something much more like a balance of power:

People today are accustomed to being directed and manipulated and controlled in industrial organizations and to finding satisfaction for their social, egoistic and self-fulfillment needs away from the job. This is true of much of management as well as of workers. Genuine "industrial citizenship"—to borrow a term from Drucker—is a remote and unrealistic idea, the meaning of which has not even been considered by most members of industrial organizations.

Another way of saying this is that Theory "X" places exclusive reliance upon external control of human behavior, while Theory "Y" [the theory McGregor exposits] relies heavily on self-control and self-direction. It is worth noting that this difference is the difference between treating people as children and treating them as mature adults [380].

Bennis, Benne, and Chin [59] specifically set out power equalization (PE) as one of the distinguishing features of the deliberate collaborative process they define as planned change: "A power distribution in which the client and change agent have equal, or almost equal, opportunities to influence" is part of their definition.

In any case, power equalization has become a key idea in the prevalent people approaches, a first step in the theoretical causal chain leading toward organizational change. It has served as an initial subgoal, a necessary predecessor to creative change in structure, technology, task solving, and task implementation. Although the distances are not marked, there is no unclarity about direction—a more egalitarian power distribution is better.

It is worth pointing out that the techniques for causing redistribution of power in these models are themselves power-equalization techniques—techniques like counseling and *T*-group training. Thus both Lippitt et al. [353] and Bennis et al. [59] lay great emphasis on the need for collaboration between changer and changee in order for change to take place. But it is understandable that neither those writers nor most other workers in power equalization seriously investigate the possibility that power may be redistributed unilaterally or authoritatively (e.g., by the creation of profit centers in a large business firm or by coercion).

If we examine some of the major variables of organizational behavior, we will see rather quickly that the power-equalization approaches yields outcomes that are very different from those produced by the structural or technological approaches.

Thus in the PE models, *communication* is something to be maximized. The more channels the better, the less filtering the better, the more feedback the better. All these because power will be more equally distributed, validity of information greater, and commitment to organizational goals more intense.

Contrast these views with the earlier structural models which argued for clear but limited communication lines, never to be circumvented; and which disallowed the transmission of affective and therefore task-irrelevant information. They stand in sharp contrast, too, to some current technical views which search for optimal information flows that may be far less than maximum flows.

The PE models also focus much of their attention on issues of *group pressure, cohesiveness,* and *conformity.* The more cohesiveness the better, for cohesiveness causes commitment. The broader the group standards, the better. The more supportive the group, the freer the individual to express his individuality.

These, of course, are issues of much current popular debate. But as factors in effecting change, they are almost entirely ignored by the technical and most of the structural models. In their faith that best solutions will be recognized and in their more macroscopic outlook, until very recently at least, the technical and structural models did not concern themselves with questions of human emotionality and irrationality. If these were treated at all, they were treated as petty sources of interference with the emergence of Truth.

Evidence on this last question—the question of whether or not truth is obscured or enhanced by group pressures—is not yet perfectly clear. On the one hand, Asch [28] has shown in his classic experiments that group pressures may indeed cause individuals to deny their own sense data. On the other hand, Asch [61a] himself has warned against interpreting this denial as an entirely emotional noncognitive process. When ten good men and true announce that line A is longer than line B, and when the eleventh man, still seeking truth, but himself seeing B as longer than A, still goes along with the group, he may do so not because he is overwhelmed by emotional pressure but because "rationally" he decides that ten other good sets of eyes are more likely to be right than his own.

Moreover, some data from some recent experiments being conducted at Carnegie Tech and elsewhere [4] suggest that in-fighting and debate will cease rather rapidly within a group when a solution that is prominently better than other alternatives is put forth. This is to say that people use their heads as well as their guts; though at times in our history we have vociferously denied either one or the other.

Consider next the *decision-making* variable. Decision making, from the perspective of power equalization, is viewed not from a cognitive perspective, nor substantively, but as a problem in achieving committed agreement. The much discussed issues are commitment and

---

[4] As reported in a personal communication from T. C. Schelling, 1961.

consensual validation, and means for lowering and spreading decision-making opportunities.

Contrast this with the technical emphasis on working out optimal decision rules, and with the structuralist's emphasis on locating precise decision points and assigning decision-making responsibility always to individuals.

Summary

If we view organizations as systems of interaction among task, structural, technical, and human variables, several different classes of efforts to change organizational behavior can be grossly mapped.

Such a view provides several entry points for efforts to effect change. One can try to change aspects of task solution, task definition, or task performance by introducing new tools, new structures, or new or modified people or machines. On occasion we have tried to manipulate only one of these variables and discovered that all the others move in unforeseen and often costly directions.

We have more than once been caught short by this failing. The Scientific Management movement, for example, enamored of its measurement techniques, worked out efficient task solutions only to have many of them backfire because the same methods were also evoking human resistance and hostility. The human relations movement, I submit, is only now bumping into some of the unforeseen costs of building a theory of organization exclusively of human bricks, only to find that technological advances may obviate large chunks of human relations problems by obviating large chunks of humans or by reducing the need for "consensual validation" by programming areas formerly reserved to uncheckable human judgment.

Approaches with strong structural foci have also on occasion fallen into the one-track trap, changing structure to facilitate task solution, only then to find that humans do not fit the cubby holes or technology does not adapt to the new structure.

On the positive side, however, one can put up a strong argument that there is progress in the world; that by pushing structural or human or technical buttons to see what lights up, we are beginning gropingly to understand some of the interdependencies among the several variables.

What we still lack is a good yardstick for comparing the relative costs and advantages of one kind of effort or another. We need, as Likert [350] has suggested, an economics of organizational change.

If we had one, we could more effectively evaluate the costs of movement in one direction or another. Likert urges an economics of change because he believes the presently unmeasured costs of human resistance, if measured, would demonstrate the economic utility of organizational designs based on PE models. But such an economics might also pinpoint some of the as yet unmeasured costs of PE-based models. For the present state of unaccountability provides a protective jungle that offers quick cover to the proponents of any current approach to organizational change.

If I may conclude with a speculation, I will bet long odds that, as we develop such an economics, as we learn to weigh costs and advantages, and to predict second and third order changes, we will not move uniformly toward one of these approaches or another, even within the firm. We will move instead toward a mélange, toward differentiated organizations in which the nature of changes becomes largely dependent on the nature of task. We have progressed, I submit; we have not just oscillated. We have learned about people, about structure, about technology; and we will learn to use what we know about all three to change the shape of future organizations.

5

SOME PSYCHOLOGICAL ASPECTS OF ORGANIZATIONAL CONTROL

Victor H. Vroom

Introduction [1]

The ability to control the behavior of its members is a prerequisite of a viable organization. To attain its objectives, each organization must determine the functions that have to be performed, allocate these functions to organization members and establish behavior patterns on the part of its members which lead to the performance of those functions. The necessity of taking individuals with diverse goals, habits, and skills and establishing the patterns of behavior that are consistent with the rational plan of the organization presents an exceedingly difficult and complex problem. Organizations typically develop a multitude of means of dealing with this problem, ranging from the use of a battery of psychological tests for screening prospective organization members to highly elaborate profit sharing plans.

In this chapter we are going to examine certain psychological aspects of the control which organizations exercise over their members. We are assuming that the behavior of individuals as role occupants in formal organizations is not governed by basically different processes than behavior in other situations. Consequently, one source of knowledge concerning the problem of organizational control lies in the data of individual psychology. To this end we will be examining certain basic psychological processes and will try to show their rele-

---

[1] This paper was originally presented at a seminar on the Social Science of Organizations, sponsored by the Ford Foundation and held at the University of Pittsburgh, Pittsburgh, Pa., June 10–23, 1962.

vance for an understanding of the ways in which organizations can and do influence the behavior of their members.

Let us start off by viewing the problem of control in the context of a conception of the nature of a role in a formal organization. Each role may be regarded as consisting of one or more functions (e.g., assembling transistors, teaching students, fixing television sets, etc.) which the role occupant is expected to perform. These functions represent effects which the role occupant is expected to produce on his environment and they represent the basis for inferring the effectiveness of his performance.

In the context of his role, the role occupant is exposed to a variety of situations, $S_1, S_2, \cdots, S_n$, each possessing distinctive stimulus properties. To each stimulus pattern there are one or more *functional* responses that can be made by the role occupant, i.e., responses which produce the required effects on the environment. The specific responses that are functional often vary from one stimulus pattern to another, i.e., S_1 calls for R_1, S_2 calls for R_2, etc. For example, a radar scope operator is exposed to many different signals. Some of these, e.g., those indicating approaching aircraft, call for very different responses on his part than those not indicating approaching aircraft. Similarly, a musician in a symphony orchestra is confronted with different notes, bars, and passages which require that he produce different sounds on his instrument. By definition, the more consistently the role occupant performs responses functionally appropriate to the immediate stimulus, the more effective is his performance.

Some work roles are highly "programmed." The appropriate responses to task-related stimuli are known and codified. It is possible to write down or otherwise communicate the most effective response to each stimulus pattern. Despite the influence of the scientific management movement, which sought to standardize work methods, many work roles remain "unprogrammed." The optimal responses to task-related stimuli are subject to considerable uncertainty and are left to the judgment of the worker.

Let us assume that organizations are interested in controlling the behavior of any organization member only to the extent to which that control is reflected in more effective role performance on the part of that member. Viewed in these terms, the problem of organizational control over members becomes one of creating those conditions under which members reliably and consistently perform appropriate or functional responses to the various patterns of stimulation with which they are confronted, i.e., R_1 to S_1, R_2 to S_2, etc. All of the systems developed by organizations for the purpose of control—from cost accounting procedures to human relations training—are effective only to the extent to which they increase the probability of organization members making functionally appropriate responses to role-related situations. This approach to organizational control is by no means an original one. Baldamus [38], for example, has stressed that industrial production be viewed as "a system of administrative controls which regulate quantity, quality, and distribution of human effort" (p. 1).

With this as our starting point let us examine the relevance of certain aspects of each of the three traditional psychological processes of perception, motivation, and learning.

Perception

The environment of a person at any moment includes a wide range of energy changes. Because of the nature of man's sense organs, only a relatively small number of these energy changes, e.g., sound waves from 16 to about 20,000 cycles per second and electromagnetic waves from 390 millimicrons to 760 millimicrons can be perceived. Such events are potential stimuli which can provide information to the person to guide his behavior.

Even within the range of stimuli, however, there are limitations on how well men can discriminate physically different stimuli. From the time of Ernst Weber, students of behavior have been interested in the conditions affecting the capacity of persons to make these discriminations. In psychophysics, for example, the concept of differential threshold has been introduced to refer to the minimal decrease or increase in some physical dimension of a stimulus needed to produce a just noticeable difference (j.n.d.) in the stimulus.

Whenever an organizational role requires a person to make differential responses to stimuli, e.g., R_1 to S_1, R_2 to S_2, the effectiveness of his performance will vary with his capacity to discriminate these stimuli. One might argue that a major source of ineffectiveness in large-scale organizations is failure of organization members to discriminate stimuli which require different responses. The airline pilot may mistake a mountain for a dark cloud; an employment interviewer may mistake a totally inept applicant for one with executive potential; and a taxi-cab driver may mistake a red for a green traffic light. This is a perceptual problem but it has important organizational implications. An organization can increase the effectiveness of the role performance of its members by creating conditions which increase the probability of the members making appropriate discriminations among role-related stimuli.

One method of doing this is to alter the characteristics of stimuli which require different responses. A significant portion of the work of the engineering psychologist involves determining the discriminability of combinations of task-related stimuli and assisting in the design of displays and equipment which minimize the risk of the role occupant's confusing two or more stimuli to which different responses are required. The objective is to provide displays so that the information needed to do the job is received quickly and accurately.

Another method is to keep the stimulus aspects of roles constant but to select role occupants who have proven capacities to make the relevant discriminations among them. Many psychological tests widely used in personnel selection and placement measure sensory and perceptual abilities. For example, the Minnesota Clerical Test measures a person's ability to make rapid discriminations between identical pairs of names and numbers and those which are slightly different, and it has proved reasonably successful in predicting the performance of workers for whom such discriminations are a necessary part of their jobs.

Insofar as the capacity to discriminate between stimuli can be modified by experience, it is possible for organizations to train individuals to make the discriminations required by their roles. We will take up this third method of organization control over perceptual errors later when we consider the learning process.

Motivation [2]

Most conceptions of the process of motivation are based on the assumption that behavior is purposeful or goal directed. People choose the course of action which they expect will result in the greatest satisfaction, utility, or value. This assumption is probably not applicable to certain classes of responses like reflexes, emotions, and other "involuntary" acts, but seems to be a useful point of departure for accounting for most of the role behavior of individuals in formal organizations.

It follows from this assumption that the effectiveness of a person's performance in a work role will be related to the extent to which performance constitutes a goal or is believed to be a means to the

---

[2] The ideas expressed in this section are developed more fully in Vroom [580].

attainment of a goal. By itself, this proposition is neither testable nor of practical value. Its theoretical and social value is inextricably connected with other assumptions which permit us to make inferences about the goals of individual persons and their expectations concerning how to attain these goals.

It is often asserted (see, for example, Viteles [572] and Likert [350]) that motivation is the core problem in the effective utilization of the human resources of organizations. Reflecting this view, a great deal of research has been carried out on motivational factors in performance, particularly by social psychologists interested in the effect on behavior of the social aspects of the work situation.

Let us consider some of the evidence bearing on the conditions affecting the motivation of workers to perform their jobs effectively.

WAGES

If one assumes that money constitutes a goal and that behavior is goal directed, it follows that persons should perform more effectively in a work role if their wages are directly linked with their performance than if their wages are independent of their performance. The results of a number of different kinds of research investigations are in essential agreement with this proposition.

In laboratory experiments, Atkinson and Reitman [30], Atkinson [29a] and Kaufmann [308] have shown that subjects achieve higher levels of task performance when they are told that they will receive financial rewards for effective performance. A field study in a household appliance factory by Georgopoulos, Mahoney, and Jones [213] indicated a higher proportion of "high producers" among workers who reported that productivity would result in their receiving more money in the long run, than among those who reported that productivity was either irrelevant to or hindered the attainment of money. The relationship between productivity and workers' beliefs about its financial consequences was strongest for those workers who ranked money relatively high in importance. Wyatt [612] carried out a series of field experiments on the effects of different methods of payment in a British candy factory, and found consistent evidence for superior productivity under wage-incentive plans. Finally, Viteles [572] has noted that surveys of companies' experience with wage-incentive plans report substantial increases in productivity following their installation, although he cautions that other changes have frequently accompanied the installation of wage-incentive plans, thus making the effects of the latter difficult to isolate.

PROMOTIONAL OPPORTUNITIES

March and Simon [367] have hypothesized that organizations in which promotion is contingent on performance will be more productive than those "that promote on the basis of family relationships, internal politics, or old school tie" (p. 61). The implicit assumption is that promotions are desired, and that workers will strive to perform more effectively in their jobs if they expect that by doing so they will increase their chances of receiving a promotion.

Although the influence of promotional aspirations on the behavior of individuals in organizations has frequently been the subject of novels, television plays, and even a popular musical comedy, there is little quantitative evidence concerning the effects of promotional systems on performance. The evidence which does exist supports the March and Simon hypothesis.

In a field study of over 600 workers in a household appliance factory, Georgopoulos, Mahoney, and Jones [213] found a higher level of productivity among workers who expect that low productivity will hurt their chances for promotion than among those who believe that it is irrelevant. This difference reaches statistical significance only for those who rank promotion relatively high in attractiveness and who are relatively free to set their pace of work.

SUPERVISION

Insofar as praise or criticism by the supervisor has affective consequences for subordinates, one should expect a relationship between the conditions under which a supervisor extends praise or criticism and the performance of his subordinates. Praise or criticism given unconditionally, or on the basis of unclear or inconsistent criteria, should be less effective in motivating subordinates than that which is contingent on the subordinate's performance.

This point of view is frequently expressed by those writing on the subject of supervision and leadership. For example, McGregor [379, p. 151] has proposed that rewarding subordinates for effective performance and withholding rewards and even punishing subordinates for ineffective performance is a necessary component of effective leadership.

Given a clear knowledge of what is expected of him, the subordinate requires in addition the definite assurance that he will have the unqualified support of his superiors so long as his actions are consistent with those policies and are taken within the limits of his responsibility. Only then can he have the security and confidence that will enable him to do his job well.

At the same time the subordinate must know that failure to live up to his responsibilities, or to observe the rules which are established, will result in punishment.

Existing research on supervision and productivity is largely irrelevant to this proposition. In the main, such research has been aimed at determining personality characteristics or behaviors on the part of supervisors which result in high levels of productivity. Dimensions of supervisory behavior, like consideration (Halpin and Winer [250]) and employee-orientation (Kahn and Katz [100c]), attempt to depict how the supervisor characteristically treats subordinates. Such dimensions do not reflect differential responses by the supervisor to functional and dysfunctional behaviors on the part of subordinates. The available evidence concerning the effects of conditional and unconditional application of rewards and punishments is minimal and cannot be regarded as having satisfactorily answered this question. Kahn [302] reports that employees in high-producing groups in a tractor factory were more likely to report that high productivity is important to their supervisors than employees in low-productivity groups. He suggests that effective supervisors may have succeeded in communicating to their subordinates that at least one of the paths to supervisory approval is to produce at a high rate. Also Fiedler [193] finds that leaders of effective work groups perceive greater difference between most and least preferred co-workers than leaders of ineffective groups, and he proposes that the former are more independent of others and are willing to reject a person with whom they cannot accomplish an assigned task.

THE WORK GROUP

It has long been clear that the performance of individual workers is affected by their relationships with their co-workers. The manner in which a person behaves in the work situation is dependent not only on the formal role requirements and the organizational reward and punishment systems used to implement them but also on norms or standards with respect to behavior which develop out of informal interaction among organization members.

Evidence concerning the effects of the informal work group on productivity dates back to the Hawthorne studies (Roethlisberger and Dickson [452]). In the relay assembly room experiments, the continued increments in productivity seemed to be due, in no small part, to an "esprit de corps" that developed in the group. On the other hand, in the bank wiring room studies in the same organization, there was evidence that the informal work group was instrumental in restricting productivity. Apparently, the effects of the informal organization on performance might be consistent with, or contrary to, the organizations' objectives.

The authors' explanation of these findings is essentially a motivational one. In the relay assembly room, the nature of the relationship between co-workers resulted in a high level of motivation for effective performance, whereas in the bank wiring room, a different pattern of relationship had the opposite effect. If this interpretation is correct, it is necessary to determine the kinds of relationships between workers that serve to increase and decrease their motivation to perform effectively.

It is sometimes suggested that the motivation of workers to perform effectively on their jobs is a direct function of the cohesiveness of their informal work group. There is very little support for such a proposition. French [208] found no relationship between a sociometric index of cohesiveness and a variety of measures of performance among naval recruits; Schachter, Ellertson, McBride, and Gregory [461] and Berkowitz [64] found no over-all differences in productivity between experimentally created groups of high and low cohesiveness, and Seashore [466] found only a slight tendency for groups with high measured cohesiveness to be higher in productivity than those low in cohesiveness.

The experiments of Schachter et al. [461] and Berkowitz [64] indicate that the cohesiveness of a group affects the amount of influence that group members can exert on one another, but that the direction that the influence will take is a function of the norms or standards predominant in the group. Attempts to influence workers to increase or decrease their level of production were less likely to be effective when they were believed to be coming from co-workers in low-cohesiveness groups than from co-workers in highly cohesive groups. The highest productivity was obtained in highly cohesive groups with positive standards regarding productivity while the lowest productivity was obtained in highly cohesive groups with negative standards regarding productivity. These findings are in agreement with the results obtained by Seashore [466] in a large-scale field study in a factory manufacturing heavy machinery.

These findings are interpretable in motivational terms if one assumes that the strength of a person's desire to be accepted by other group members is related to the extent of his attraction to the group. The behavior of persons who are attracted to the group is consequently more likely to be influenced by the demands made by other group members than is the behavior of persons who are unattracted to the group. If one wished to predict not the amount of influence which the group exercised over its members but the direction of this influence, it is necessary to know the behaviors that are likely to be met with approval by other group members and the behaviors that are likely to be met with disapproval. The highest level of performance should occur when the worker strongly desires acceptance by his co-workers, and anticipates that he will receive this acceptance only if he performs effectively. On the other hand, the lowest level of performance should occur where he strongly desires to be accepted by his co-workers, and expects that he will be accepted only if he performs ineffectively.

INTERNALLY MEDIATED INCENTIVES

All of the incentives for effective performance that we have discussed have been externally mediated. We have been assuming that the workers perform effectively in order to receive from other persons desired outcomes or to avoid receiving aversive outcomes. This type of assumption has been characteristic of most treatments of motivation by industrial psychologists. Although the colloquial language of the "carrot and stick" hypothesis has been replaced by more sophisticated concepts, the meaning remains unchanged. For example, Georgopoulos, Mahoney, and Jones [213] and Kahn [302] have described what they call a path-goal approach to productivity. A person's motivation to perform effectively on a task or job is a function of the attractiveness of such externally mediated outcomes as money, promotion, or acceptance by the work group, and his perception of the usefulness of productivity as a path to the attainment of these outcomes.

There is a growing body of evidence suggesting the limitations of this type of model. Successful performances on a task or job may constitute not only a means or a path to the attainment of other goals but also may be a goal in itself. Under certain conditions, successful performance on a task may represent a source of satisfaction and unsuccessful performance a source of dissatisfaction, independent of the externally mediated consequences of this performance.

There have been a number of attempts to specify the conditions under which individuals derive satisfaction from performing successfully on tasks or jobs. McClelland et al. [376] and Atkinson [29] have proposed that persons vary in the strength of their need for achievement, which they define as a predisposition to gain satisfaction from "success in competition with some standard of excellence." The amount of satisfaction derived by a person from success in a task is hypothesized to be directly related to the strength of his need for achievement and to the difficulty of the task. Lending some support to this theory is evidence that persons high in need achievement tend to perform more effectively on tasks than those low in need achievement (Lowell [355]; French [206]; Wendt [595]). Furthermore, this difference is most consistently found where the person is given achievement-orienting instructions (French [206]), when other motives are not aroused (Atkinson and Reitman [30]), or when his subjective probability of success is low (Atkinson [29a]).

Alternative approaches to this problem are suggested by the theoretical work of Adams [5] and of Vroom [579]. Both investigators take as their point of departure the assumption of cognitive dissonance theory (Festinger [190]) that consistency among cognitions is pleasant and inconsistency unpleasant. Consequently, they assume that a person will be motivated to perform effectively when effective performance is more consistent with other beliefs and opinions that he holds than is ineffective performance. Adams and Vroom differ, however, in the kinds of consistency with which they deal. Adams emphasizes the consistency between a person's inputs to his job (such as his level of performance) and his outcomes (such as his wages) and those of other persons. An individual is hypothesized to perform more effectively on a task or job when effective performance serves to reduce feeling of inequity. Supporting this theory is evidence that workers paid on an hourly basis perform more effectively when they are led to believe that they are being overcompensated relative to others than when they are led to believe that they are being equitably compensated (Adams and Rosenbaum [6], Arrowwood, reported in Adams [5]). Presumably, feelings of guilt or inequity resulting from "overcompensation" are reduced by increasing one's level of performance. However, when an "overcompensated" person is being paid on a piece-work basis, inequity should be reduced when his level of performance is decreased. Thus, Adams predicts that "overcompensated" workers, paid by the piece, should perform less effectively than those who are "equitably compensated." This prediction has also received experimental support (Adams and Rosenbaum [6]).

Vroom [579] emphasizes the affective consequences of the degree of consistency between a person's performance and his self-concept. A person is hypothesized to be motivated to perform effectively when effective performance is consistent with his conception of his abilities and with the value he places on these abilities. Supporting this assumption is evidence that persons perform more effectively on tasks when they are led to believe that the task requires highly valued abilities, like intelligence (Kaustler [309], French [206]), and that they perform more effectively when they are led to believe that the task requires abilities which they believe themselves to possess (Kaufmann [308]).

Learning

Many psychological theorists have distinguished two types of consequences of situations and related stimulus events. They may interact with existing properties of the person in determining how the person will respond in the situation, and they may effect changes in the person determining how he will respond to subsequent situations. The term "learning" is typically used to refer to the process by which these longer term effects take place.

The fact that persons are modified by experience greatly simplifies the problem of organizational control. Organizations do not have to work only with the existing behavior patterns of their members, but can change their members in ways that will produce new behavior patterns more conducive to the requirements of their roles. Both formal and informal training procedures are employed by organizations to develop requisite abilities, habits, and knowledge on the part of organization members.

There are, to be sure, many limitations on the ability of an organization to mold its members. These stem both from lack of knowledge of the conditions under which learning occurs and from an inability to create these conditions in organizations. We will now briefly examine some aspects on the learning process which bear on the organizational control of performance.

DISCRIMINATION LEARNING

In our discussion of perception, we have argued that the effectiveness of a role occupant is a function of his capacity to discriminate among patterns of stimulations which require different responses. The physician must be able to tell the difference between an appendicitis and a stomach ache; the automobile mechanic must be able to discriminate a faulty battery from a faulty starter; and a clinical psychologist must be able to tell a mentally retarded patient from a simple schizophrenic. Although organizations can select persons who already have the capacity to make these discriminations, or, in the case of stimulus cues under organizational control, change the cues so that they can be more easily discriminated, training, both formal and informal, can be used to increase the degree to which organization members can make the discriminations required by their roles. Hebb [260] has shown that the discrimination of even elementary stimulus patterns like triangles and circles is not innate but requires a long period of learning with extensive exposure to the stimuli to be discriminated. Similarly, it can be demonstrated that the capacity of a person to discriminate reliably and quickly more complex patterns of stimulation, e.g., a 1965 Ford and a 1965 Chevrolet, can be increased by appropriate training. An understanding of the process by which persons learn to discriminate stimulus objects, although beyond the scope of this chapter, should provide a firm foundation for the design of such training programs.

SKILL LEARNING

A role occupant must not only be able to discriminate situations which call for different responses but he must also know how to respond to each. For example, the physician must know how to treat a stomach ache and an appendicitis as well as how to tell them apart.

Technologically, the problem is to increase the probability that a person will make certain responses to a stimulus situation (e.g., R_1 to S_1) and to decrease the probability that he will make other responses (e.g., R_2 to S_1). The traditional method [3] of changing the probability that a stimulus will result in a response is through the use of rewards and punishments. Thorndike [545] provided a theoretical foundation for this method with his law of effect.

Of several responses made to the same situation, those which are accompanied or closely followed by satisfaction to the animal will, other things being equal, be more firmly connected with the situation, so that, when it reoccurs, they will be more likely to recur; those which are accompanied or closely followed by discomfort to the animal will, other things being equal, have their connections with that situation weakened, so that, when it recurs, they will be less likely to occur (p. 24).

The law of effect and its modern counterpart, Hull's law of reinforcement (Hull [288]), have provided the foundation for most of the experimental and theoretical work on learning. These laws have also led to the identification of a number of variables which affect the relative efficiency of different training methods. Training for a particular job is most effective when it requires the trainee to practice responding to stimuli identical or highly similar to those to which

---

[3] The discussion here is restricted to instrumental rather than classical conditioning. The latter process seems to occur mainly with "involuntary" responses, such as pulse rate and salivation, which are of less significance to the problem under consideration.

he must respond on the job, when the trainee is furnished with immediate and specific knowledge of results, and when he is sufficiently motivated to learn that these "results" constitute rewards and punishments (McGehee and Thayer [377]).

It is by no means clear that positive or negative reinforcement of responses that *have occurred* to a particular stimulus is the only means of affecting the probability that they will be elicited in subsequent occurrences of that stimulus. Among humans who have the use of language, communication eliminates much of the need for direct reality testing. One person can affect the probability of another person making a response to a stimulus not only by rewarding or punishing the response when it occurs but also by communicating that the response will be rewarded or punished. Workers learn what is expected of them in their work roles not only through reinforcement of their behavior but also through communication with others and by observation of the consequences of the behavior of others. Learning of this kind is particularly likely to occur when the responses are, as a result of previous training, already within the repertoire of the person. It is probably of less significance in the learning of skills than in the transfer of existing skills to new situations.

LEARNING OF MOTIVES

Psychologists interested in learning have also attempted to explain the ways in which the motivational properties of events are modified by training or experience. Many outcomes which act as rewards (e.g., money, approval, success, status) or punishments (e.g., disapproval, failure) cannot be attributed to some innate property of the person but are dependent on previous learning.

Most conceptions of the way in which the affective properties of outcomes change as a result of experience involve creating or modifying an association between the outcome and some more basic reward or punishment. The most frequently studied basis for the formation of such associations is contiguity. In experiments with animals, the pairing of neutral stimuli such as lights or clicks, in space and time with the receipt of food, has resulted in the acquisition, by these previously neutral stimuli, of the properties of rewards and positive incentives. Similarly, neutral stimuli, when paired with innately aversive stimuli like shocks or loud noise, act as punishments and negative incentives.

Allport [14] has suggested that the motivational properties of an outcome can be altered by changing its instrumentality for the attainment of other outcomes. His famous principle of functional autonomy asserts that means become ends. Activities that were originally engaged in or outcomes that were sought, in order to satisfy biological needs, are subsequently undertaken "for their own sake." Thus, he asserts that adult motives for achievement, recognition, or affiliation, while growing out of more basic motivational systems, function independently of them.

Although it is customary to think of this learning as occurring relatively early in life, it is at least hypothetically possible for organizations to effect significant changes in the events which are rewarding or punishing to their members. Such changes should be reflected in increased role performance to the extent to which the attainment of rewards or avoidance of the punishments is dependent on the effectiveness of the role occupant.

Existing knowledge regarding the conditions under which learning of motives takes place is far too sketchy to provide much guidance in the control of human behavior. Changes undoubtedly take place in the motives of persons as a result of their experiences in organizations, but too little is known about how, when, and why they occur to be of technological value.

Conclusion

An attempt has been made in this chapter to show the relevance of the psychological processes of perception, motivation, and learning to the technology of organizational control. We have assumed that the objective of organizational control is to increase the effectiveness of the role performance of organization members and have argued that this effectiveness is dependent on (1) the role occupant's capacity to discriminate role-related patterns of stimulation which require different responses and (2) on the extent to which effective performance is a goal or is believed to be a means for the attainment of a goal. The conditions associated with (1) are perceptual in nature, whereas those associated with (2) are motivational.

Organizations can create these perceptual and motivational conditions by changing the properties of role-related stimuli, by selecting role occupants with requisite psychological characteristics, or by training present role occupants. The latter method raises certain basic questions concerning the problem of learning, and some relevant aspects were considered. This chapter has not dealt with all of the determinants of the effectiveness of performance. It is also not proposed that the present state of our knowledge of perception, motivation, and learning is sufficient to provide a basis for a sound technology of organizational control. Existing theory and research does, however, provide a starting point for analysis of the problems and for identifying important variables. It is my hope that attempts, such as this one, to forge a link between the study of organizations and core problems in the field of psychology will increase communication and exchange of ideas between psychologists and organization theorists.

6

THE MOTIVATIONAL EFFECTS OF SOCIAL
DEPENDENCE ON A POWERFUL AGENCY
OF CONTROL

John Thibaut

Introduction [1]

The ideas presented here were stimulated by observations on instances of great courage and heroic striving of assorted great men: religious, military, and revolutionary leaders, explorers, and the like. We have been struck (as have others) by the frequent mention in accounts of these great men of a paradoxical mixture of activism and fatalism in their lives. In many cases there appears to be a strong dependence on a powerful external agency of control, which may sometimes be a form of Deity, an ineluctable historical force, an institution (the Army), etc. It is as though the man belonged to a coalition that gave him a greater strength to strive or to resist than could be commanded by any single individual. This additional source of strength appears not to be "internalized" but is necessarily a separate external thing.[2] These observations, if valid, point to the paradox

[1] This is an amended version of a paper contributed to the Pittsburgh Seminar on the Social Science of Organizations, June 10–23, 1962. The research outlined in this paper is a project of the Organization Research Group which is supported by the Institute for Research in Social Science at the University of North Carolina and by the Group Psychology Branch of The Office of Naval Research, *Nonr-855(04)*.
[2] This is not to deny that a strong achievement orientation resulting in the "internalization" of specific types of activism through "independence training" (as suggested by the line of theory and research summarized in [375]) may not pro-

of the "dependent" person showing behavior ordinarily attributed to the most adventurously independent.

It will be evident that the ideas expressed in the following are not a highly developed theory but represent only the inchoate beginnings of a formulation. It will also be apparent that the ideas are not easy to operationalize and that research on them will be difficult. The two or three studies that we have completed have been aimed at some of the preliminary problems most obviously susceptible to research. Finally, these ideas have not come from the observation of men in organizations. Thus, though an effort will be made to reorient these ideas toward organizational behavior, there is no assurance that they can be justified as applicable to this area.

The Coalition

First, let us introduce one of the main concepts to be used—the coalition. In the triad to be considered here, a coalition is said to exist if two of the parties (A and B) act in concert to affect the outcomes of the third party (C) whose actions, in turn, have common effects on the outcomes of A and B. In the organizational setting, which is the focus of this discussion, our interest centers on the conditions and consequences of the formation of a coalition between a person (P, a member of the organization) and the organization (O, any agency of the organization: the president of the company, the executive committee, a supervisor, or even the vaguely populated "organization in general") vis-à-vis the social and physical environment (E) which is the domain of operation of the organization. According to Thibaut and Kelley [541], the following conditions are promotive of coalition formation between any two parties (in this case P and O): (1) A high correspondence of outcomes across the cells of the outcome matrix describing the consequences of the P-O interaction, i.e., P and O must have some "common interests"; (2) a degree of control over their outcomes by a third party (E), i.e., E must "matter" to them; and (3) the circumstance that, by joint action, P and O can mobilize greater power counter to E's control than by independent action, or simply taking P's point of view, joint action with O must be more effective than acting independently.

---

duce effects that are phenotypically similar to those herein described. The present discussion merely concentrates on an additional mechanism which I believe has been largely overlooked.

If from (3) above, the coalition provides P with distinct advantages, he may be expected to adopt either of two orientations and perhaps over time to oscillate between them:

1. If P's outcomes are not sufficiently correspondent with O's to insure that O's power will be used benevolently, P is likely to adopt an *internal* or *coalition-maintenance* orientation. P's behavior here is aimed at insuring that the coalition remains viable and that it works in his behalf. To do this, he must either improve the correspondence of outcomes between himself and O or increase his power vis-à-vis O without, at the same time, seriously reducing O's contribution to the effectiveness of the coalition.[3] An obvious strategy for P in this case is to ingratiate himself with O; by flattery and related behaviors, P may be able to improve the P-O correspondence of outcomes and insure that O's power (while not reduced) will not be used against him (see [541], Chapter 7). For P to adopt a coalition-maintenance orientation it is necessary, of course, that a communication channel exist from P to O. In many organizational settings such a channel may not exist.

2. If P's outcomes are sufficiently correspondent with O's, P is likely to adopt an *external* or *task* orientation. In this case, P acts in concert with O to induce changes in E or to resist E's control. The support given by the coalition can be expected to contribute to P a confidence and strength that he might not otherwise have. The experiments by Asch [27] on the effects of majority opinion on the judgments of the individual document quite clearly the transforming strength given to the individual when he perceives that a partner is sustaining him. Still, the mere existence of a coalition is not in itself a sufficient basis for activism, no matter how important a precondition. If a coalition with a powerful O is perfect and indestructible, if P believes his outcomes to be in perfect correspondence with those of a powerful agency, he is more than likely to show a very confident but very passive trust in the inevitable.

---

[3] The power of O may be important to P in two different ways. If the outcomes of P and O are noncorrespondent, then a highly powerful O might threaten to take a disproportionate share of any coalition gains made in the joint interaction with E, and hence P's enthusiasm for remaining in the coalition would begin to cool as these reduced gains lose superiority over those outcomes he could achieve independently. However, with high correspondence of P-O outcomes, O's power will be used only in P's behalf, and maintenance problems having to do with the division of coalition gains would be minimal. For a further discussion of these points see [312].

The Concept of Comparison Level

In the following discussion, the heightened intensity or rate of activity referred to may be directed toward either internal or external functions, and, at a later point, we will suggest one of the conditions which may determine which of these orientations is adopted.

First, though, it is necessary to introduce another concept that will be used in the discussion. A concept believed to be useful in this analysis is that of comparison level (*CL*), advanced by Thibaut and Kelley [541], and derived from earlier concepts such as level of aspiration, adaptation level, and reference groups. The general point of view behind all of these ideas is that the evaluations of one's self and circumstances entail relative judgments. The degree of satisfaction experienced by *P* depends partly on the reference persons or groups with whom he compares himself.

The *CL* for a given *P* is defined as the level of outcomes (payoffs, rewards, punishments, etc.) which he experiences to be fairly neutral in value; it is the level of hedonic experience to which he has become adapted and which he expects to receive. Better outcomes are experienced as good and are greeted with a certain amount of elation, the amount depending on how far they exceed the *CL*.[4] Poorer outcomes have negative affective consequences.

The height of the *CL* depends on *P*'s previously experienced outcomes, both those he receives personally and those he knows or believes others to receive (especially others who are perceived to be similar to himself). Particularly important in determining the level of the *CL* are outcomes recently experienced and those that for other reasons have special salience for him. Thibaut and Kelley speculate that those outcomes that *P* views as being under his own control will tend to be highly salient. These include the outcomes he believes to have resulted from his own efforts (that reflect such attributes as his own power, ability, value) and the as yet unattained outcomes which he believes are within his capabilities to achieve. The reasoning here,

---

[4] However, under certain circumstances, abruptly increased rewards may be undervalued by *P*. It would carry us too far afield to go into this in detail, but it may suffice here to suggest merely the following. If *P* comes to develop an adaptation to a certain *proportionality* of rewards to costs, representing his "fair" or "just" outcome, then an abrupt increase in reward unaccompanied by a proportionate increase in cost (say in effort) should create a state of "cognitive dissonance" which can be reduced only by a subsequent increase in (effort) cost or a devaluation of the increased reward.

in brief, is that it is adaptive for P to give prime consideration to outcomes caused by himself.

According to this view, then, the CL depends not simply on P's experienced outcomes but also on the causal interpretations he makes of the source of these outcomes. The less P attributes variations in his outcomes to his own control, or the more he attributes them to an external agency, the lower will be his CL. In other words, if P is under the "fate control" ([541], Chapter 7) of O, his CL will be lower than if his outcomes were under his own control. The matrix in Fig. 1 shows P's outcomes when a powerful O has fate control over him. Note that in Fig. 1, variations in O's behavior are totally responsible for variations in P's outcomes; variations in P's behavior have no efficacy in altering his outcomes.

If the CL of a fate-controlled P is sufficiently low, then outcomes that would be regarded by others (with higher CL's) as quite mediocre will be for him distinctly rewarding. Research in our laboratory by Arthur Miller [401] confirms this expectation. Each subject in Miller's experiment interacted in succession with five different (fictitious) partners in such a way that the subject's outcomes were entirely determined by the behaviors of the partners, who represented, in fact, merely programmed distributions of outcomes determined by the experimenter. CL was varied experimentally by two different procedures: (1) by offering the subject no initial information about the range of outcomes possible in the situation and inducing a CL from the level and variability of outcomes received from his first partner, and (2) by giving the subject (fictitious) pre-experimental information about the levels of outcomes received by a large sample of subjects who had preceded him. On receipt of each outcome, the subject made a utility judgment, the subjective value of the outcome

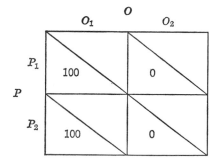

FIGURE 1 O has fate control over P.

to him. For both manipulations of CL, subjects with low CL's showed consistently higher valuations of standard (objectively constant) outcomes than did those with high CL's.[5]

In another recently completed experiment, the results of which have not yet been fully analyzed, we have also found that the judged utility of a suddenly increased reward is related to CL. In this experiment with 10- to 12-year-old boys, subjects with a low CL evaluated the increased reward more positively than did those with a high CL. Here then is a factor that by heightening the reward value of "ordinary" outcomes should contribute in some degree to the motivation of the fate-dependent P. If, as CL declines, the subjective utility of outcomes increases, the incentive to achieving and maintaining such outcomes would be expected to increase, thus providing an impetus to "activism."

Cognitive Dissonance and External Agency Dependence

However, there is more to it than this. For a P who depends on external agencies, the maintenance of his belief that he and a powerful O are in coalition is essential. The steady receipt of exceedingly good outcomes might be expected to confirm and strengthen P's belief in the reality of his coalition with O. Negative outcomes, however, although they should not be affectively so distressing because of his low CL, provide information that disconfirms his belief in the reality of his coalition, in the friendliness of the fates. To the extent that P is strongly committed to this belief and it forms an important part of his view of the world, and to the extent that the negative outcomes experienced are attributed to the fate control of O rather than to the self, then the conditions have been created for the development of cognitive dissonance (Festinger [190]). If it is impossible to deny the negative character of the outcomes, it is likely that P will attempt to reduce the dissonance through strenuous striving to avoid such outcomes and to insure that they do not recur. (Note that the focus of this striving may be either an internal or an external one, that is, P may attempt to reduce dissonance either by heightened effort toward

---

[5] Miller also found that with increasing variance of outcomes (and hence increased power of the source of the outcomes) the partner was increasingly attractive to the subject when the outcome mean was above CL and decreasingly attractive when the outcome mean was below CL. In other words, the subjects preferred benevolent partners to be powerful and malevolent ones to be weak. See [401].

coalition maintenance or by acting directly on E to produce the high outcomes that would symbolize to him a viable coalition.) This may provide an additional motivational base for activism.

Power of the External Agency

In spite of such efforts to reduce dissonance, negative outcomes must recur intermittently if the motivational base is to persist, for two reasons: (1) To prove that the fate-controlling O is powerful. Although there may be many types of evidence of such power, a particularly convincing type of evidence is the range of one's own outcomes. Thibaut and Kelley [541, Chapter 7] define A's dependence on B as the range of outcomes through which B can move A. This range of outcomes is equivalent to B's power over A. Thus for P to be convinced of O's great power (a crucial matter in the effectiveness of the coalition), he must suffer some relatively poor outcomes. (2) To provide a negative end anchor. Independently of the general level of CL and the source of the outcomes, it is probable that the shape of the outcome distribution is influential in determining the subjective utility of the component outcomes. We are suggesting that both extremely positive and extremely negative outcomes may operate as end anchors, with the consequence that remote outcomes on the scale become subjectively even more remote from such anchors. In a symmetrical distribution of outcomes, such effects might be expected to cancel one another out. But in a highly skewed distribution, the few outcomes at the skewed end may be sufficient to establish an end anchor which would displace away from it the numerous modal outcomes. Thus, a negatively skewed distribution (with a few extremely poor outcomes) should produce an overvaluation of the more numerous set of outcomes in the modal region.[6] From the viewpoint of maximum subjective utility, this seems to be the ideal distribution of outcomes. If this reasoning is valid, this would provide another motivational base for energetic striving in the fate-dependent person. The motivational contribution here is like that resulting from a lowered CL: if, *ceteris paribus,* as the distribution of outcomes skews negatively, the subjective utility of modal outcomes increases, then

---

[6] A negative end anchor thus works like a low CL. The argument above is not changed if the reader prefers to view this process either as creating a low CL special to this particular outcome distribution or as lowering the general CL, which for the fate-dependent P would be already relatively low.

the incentive to attaining and maintaining such outcomes would be expected to increase and P's general level of activity should rise.

Experimental Results

Research on this hypothesized end-anchoring effect of extreme outcomes has been recently completed by Carole Brannon Hickey [268]. As in Miller's study, subjects made utility judgments of outcomes received from fictitious partners. In the present experiment, however, each subject interacted with just one partner and the judged outcomes were stimulus materials (developed by Emir Shuford) presented tachistoscopically (to facilitate subjective distortion). Half of the subjects received a negatively skewed distribution of outcomes and the other half a positively skewed distribution, the extreme outcomes being presented at or near the beginning of each series. The two distributions had exactly equal means and ranges. The results of this experiment are quite clear. Objectively identical outcomes in the modal region of both distributions were consistently judged as having significantly greater utility when they were received in the negatively skewed distribution than when received in the positively skewed one. (This difference in judged utility was reported for each of the six common outcome values in the region of the mode.) Subjects receiving the negatively skewed distribution also reported postexperimentally that they were more "satisfied" with their partner (in rating him on a scale of "satisfaction-dissatisfaction") than were those receiving the positively skewed distribution. The former subjects also evaluated their partners more positively on the semantic differential (evaluation dimension) than did the latter subjects; no clear differences appeared on the potency and activity dimensions.

Note an additional fact about this negatively skewed distribution of outcomes. It is precisely the one likely to be attained by a person highly dependent on a very powerful fate that either is predominantly (but not wholly) friendly or is "neutral" but subject to the person's effective (but imperfect) countercontrol. A few negative outcomes occur as a result of the imperfect friendliness of the fate or the imperfect countercontrol of the person, or from the "benign indifference of the universe," as Camus puts it.

The imperfection of either benevolence or countercontrol seems crucial because perfection in this regard would create a total correspondence of outcomes between P and O, and, as we have suggested earlier, this condition is not likely to motivate P to strenuous activity.

For one thing, as we have also commented, it is (perhaps paradoxically) likely to lead to a shrinkage in the power P attributes to O.

Some Generalizations

We are suggesting then that extremely high motivation is most likely to be aroused when P is under the fate control of a powerful O with whom his outcomes are sufficiently correspondent to provide the basis for the formation of a P-O coalition (against E). This generalization has enough latitude in it to permit a further differentiation. Two further possibilities suggest themselves:

1. P's countercontrol over O, though good, is sufficiently imperfect to motivate him to work very hard to maintain and improve his relationship with O. This should produce an *internal* orientation toward coalition maintenance.

2. P's countercontrol over O is both sufficiently effective and stable (though imperfectly so) so that his main focus of activity is directed toward E. This should produce an *external* orientation of acting in concert with O against E.[7]

It may be appropriate at this point to summarize the components conceived to contribute to the general state of strong motivation of the fate-dependent person. First, we have suggested that the very fact of the P-O coalition will increase P's strength and confidence. Second, the relatively low CL of fate-dependent P should lead to relatively high valuation of (modal) outcomes, thus providing an incentive to elevated levels of activity. Third, the negative outcomes that occur through P's imperfect countercontrol of O should tend to disconfirm P's belief in the reality of the P-O coalition and thus produce dissonance-reducing striving to attain superior outcomes and to avoid the recurrence of poor ones. However, negative outcomes function also to provide evidence of the power of O and to serve as negative end anchors. Hence, finally, the occasional occurrence of negative outcomes (serving as end anchors) should produce relatively high valuation of (modal) outcomes, thus providing an additional incentive to activity leading to the attainment of such outcomes.

---

[7] A third possibility exists that O converts his fate control (on this process of conversion, see [541], Chapter 7) thus inducing activity in P. This is likely to lead to a stable P-O coalition only if O dependably converts his fate control in such a way that the outcomes of P and O are highly correspondent; i.e., O causes P to do what he would be motivated to do in the absence of O's exertion of control. Instances of coalitions formed on this basis are likely to be rare.

Some Further Directions of Research

The strategy that is evolving to deal with the questions raised by the foregoing analysis is to work from the simplest forms of the problem back to increasingly complex antecedents. More specifically, we have begun by studying two relatively simple relationships: the effects of CL on utility of new outcomes without regard for the processes that created the differences in CL, and the effects on utility of outcomes in different distributions of outcomes without regard for the processes that created the differences in the distributions.

Assuming that our first experiments continue to turn out favorably, we shall proceed to attempt to take more into account by creating different CL's through manipulating the perceived causality for the outcomes, and by creating different outcome distributions (varying particularly in skewness) by manipulating the perceived friendliness of the sources of such outcomes and the efficacy of the subject's countercontrol over the sources of his outcomes. Similarly, the subject's dependency (or the source's power) will be manipulated by varying the range of outcomes obtained by the subject.

7

PRODUCTION ORGANIZATION EXERCISE:
AN APPLICATION OF EXPERIMENTAL
TECHNIQUES TO BUSINESS GAMES

Bernard M. Bass

Prefatory Remarks [1]

When an executive asks whether his organization should be modified to improve its over-all operations, how can he, how does he, and how might he, find the answer?

When an executive solves a problem in organization design he often searches his own memory for ready-made solutions with which he is already familiar. Most "innovations" in viable organizations are thus borrowed rather than invented [367]. For instance, the line-staff arrangement seems to have been introduced from the military by Taylor around 1911 into manufacturing shopwork; from there it spread into other industries as executives transferred out of manufacturing firms (Fisch [196]).

Besides relying on his own experience and that of his colleagues, he can turn to the wisdom literature, filled with hortatory do's and

[1] Data analysis and evaluation was supported by Contract *N7onr 35609* and carried out by George Dunteman and James A. Vaughan, who also served as staff members in conducting the third exercise reported here. I am also indebted to Drs. Sherman Little, Robert Blake, Charles Furguson, Harold Leavitt, and the many other co-workers in management training laboratories whose ideas were incorporated in these studies.

A more detailed version of selected portions of this report appears in [475a]. Substantial portions also appeared in the April 1964 issue of *Management Science*.

don'ts. Some of the propositions he finds there may indeed be applicable and true, even if untested by scientific standards.

He may also find some help in reviewing past cases and how they were handled, but he can seldom feel comfortable about whether it is possible to generalize from his review.

He may consult laboratory, field, and survey results, but here, too, he will usually find it difficult, if not impossible, to achieve the compound solution required. He will be hard put to synthesize an answer to a real problem from what can be discerned from the individual findings.

He may turn to operations research models to achieve mathematico-deductive solutions, but the assumed men in the model may not accurately simulate, with all their complexities, the real men in the organization—at least at this state in the art.

The executive may test possible ideas about an organizational arrangement of men, money, and materials structured specifically for the purpose. Simulations and games seem particularly appropriate when radical innovations are under consideration. Such innovations are unlikely to have been observed in actual practice, for it is unlikely that real production organizations can tolerate the expense of such experimentation.

WHY HAVE GAMES NOT BEEN USED FOR RESEARCH?

In reviewing the purposes of business games, Stewart [523] commented:

Most intriguing of all is the possibility of using games to pretest business strategies. . . . So far, there seems to have been more talk than action in this field. . . . Some game designers, however, think this is likely to prove by far the most significant application of the technique in the long run.

Can games be used in the same way as pilot plants or wind tunnels for testing designs and strategies? Critics have felt that the games primarily designed for training have not been sufficiently realistic or complicated. But the lack of realism and complication is not a valid argument against the application of games and models for simulating operations.

One must only remember that their function is to portray not a structure, but a process; it is not so much how the models look as how they perform that counts. . . .

The substance of the idea lies in the self-evident statement that two processes are similar if they can be described by the same equations. This becomes possible for the model and nature if the dimensions of the natural process are scaled down in reasonable relationship to one another in the model (Belousov [56], pp. 97–98).

What then has been missing? First, it is probable that most of the cognitive, logical decision making of the exemplary game now in use can be studied by experimentalists with simpler empirical procedures. The typical game is not the tool with which to test specific individual cognitive processes, one by one, any more than a pilot plant is usually necessary to test the tensile strength of a particular alloy. It is when we no longer trust the test-tube findings of several interrelated processes, or the simple stress tests of the alloy, that we build the pilot plant or put the alloy into a specific wing structure to try a "property-rich" simulation. Thus the complex game becomes the recommended experimental procedure when we want to examine questions about the organizational mix, particularly of real men, processes, and materials as they interact. When no simple experiment with all-but-one variable held constant will provide the answers we seek, it will be profitable to simulate the organization.

WHAT KIND OF GAME HAS RESEARCH USED?

In the hundred or more management games designed so far, players are required to allocate men, money, and materials; to invest, to schedule, to arrange; to select and evaluate alternatives; in short, to engage in a wide variety of management decisions primarily associated with the interplay of economic factors. A few of the games such as UCLA's Task Manufacturing Corporation and AMA's General Management force the players to consider *organizational* variables, *per se*. Because of the many decisions required in a short time, participants must organize among themselves the division of labor and responsibility, and the delegation of authority. But these structural questions are secondary to the purposes of these games. System improvement is directly an objective of the University of Pennsylvania's SMART, but here the managerial decisions again are free of the behavior dynamics and emotional aspects of real organizational life. The Case Institute game, requiring the purchase of consonants and vowels and their manufacture into words for sale on a market, illustrates a game that provides a potential research tool for experimenting with the effect of organizational structures on behavior of individuals and groups.

POE: A Game to Test Hypotheses About Organizations

After some trial and error, we believe we have achieved a game, the Production Organization Exercise (POE), which can be used to test hypotheses about *organizations per se*. We present POE, and some preliminary research completed with it, primarily to illustrate a general approach to the study of organizations, not as *the* method. In reviewing the factors we tried to take into account and how we did so, we present certain general ideas about what should be included in organizational simulations intended to have research utility.

COMPETITION

To guarantee a high degree of motivation, we featured, in POE, competition in a common market. Our main purpose in doing so was to incorporate into the game the real-life tendency displayed in intergroup competitions of undervaluing opposing groups and overvaluing one's own organization when making decisions (see [61]). This, of course, is a common feature in most games. It introduces a disadvantage, for control of the course of events is lost by the experimenter compared to a simulation where the subjects play against a standard rather than against each other. The best arrangement would be for organizations to perceive themselves competing, yet all actually be stimulated by the same standard problems.

REDUCING INTERACTION POTENTIAL BY RULE

Interaction potential is the tendency of any two individuals to interact (Bass [47], p. 343). It is low in large groups, causing them to require formal organization to be effective. Problems of the large group can be simulated in the necessarily smaller laboratory group by arbitrarily increasing communication difficulties.

Bavelas' method [51] restricted interaction between subjects to passing notes between designated individuals within a larger communication network. Guetzkow and Simon [242] employed these procedures with success to provide informative analyses of how organization patterns develop under these conditions of low communicativity—low interaction potential—in small groups. As will be seen, interaction potential was reduced in POE by arbitrarily prohibiting any face-to-face communicating at any time by more than one-third of an operating organization.

TANGIBLE PRODUCTS

The "triangular porthole" produced for a profit in POE is a tangible product requiring the literal organizing of men, money, and materials for its production. Inspiration for introducing operational criteria of productivity came from the series of studies of attempted leadership and productivity in quartets by Pepinsky, Pepinsky, and Pavlik [436]; Pepinsky, Hemphill, and Shevitz [435]; and Hemphill, Pepinsky et al. [263], who developed a *manufacturing problem,* in which quartets literally purchased tinker toy material at fixed prices, assembled the toys, and sold them in a fixed market. Economic simplification was maintained in order to focus attention on production.

POE depends greatly on the repertoire of professional, managerial, and technical responses which the laboratory subjects bring into the game. Differing from many decision-making management games, it is probable that much of the significant behavior generated by POE would not appear if the exercise were run by untutored college students. Accounting skills, simplified industrial engineering, and organizational "know-how" are all relevant.

A close approximation of the real thing, without the errors and expense, is afforded by selecting a "diagonal slice" of representatives of management personnel and assigning them to jobs similar to their own in real-life in a highly simplified replica of the real-life organization to which they belong. The critical elements of the real-life organization are maintained in the simulated organization because the operators are representative of the entire personnel who operate the real-life organization.

The Production Exercise

"Companies" of 13 to 15 salaried employees, usually, and preferably, a diagonal slice of the management of a single real company are given up to 24 hours to organize themselves to manufacture products most profitably and efficiently and with most satisfaction to management (6–8 of the men) and the wage earners (6–8). The "going" wages in the community are $3.00 per wage earner per 45-minute work period and $10.00 per manager.

Companies must establish procedures for internal reporting and public financial statements.

In the prototype exercise, companies produce *triangular porthole assemblies* in three models, #8–#10's, #10–#20's, and #8–#10–#20's. For these assembly models, #8's are produced from 8-column sections of IBM mark-sense cards, stapling three sections to form the model. The #10's use 10-column sections and the #20's use 20-column sections as indicated. The assembly of #8–#10's, etc., is as shown in Fig. 1. Samples are provided.

Raw materials (mark-sense cards) are sold freely for five minutes every half-hour once the exercise begins. Once purchased, they are stored, if still on hand the next period, at $0.50 per period raw, and

$1.00 per period if in assembled form. Companies rent staplers and scissors at $50 per unit (simulating capital expenditures).

There is a market at the end of every period the demand of which is known 1½ periods before. Demand at each market can be different, although prices are fixed to build in potential overproduction. If more goods are offered for sale than are demanded by the market, equal amounts will be purchased from competing companies.

Rules prohibit more than one-third of the company meeting face to face at any one time. Violations are fined $100. Factory and office space (4–6 rooms) are provided for each company.

Fifteen-minute rests between 45-minute work periods permit planning, retraining, informational meetings, or vacations.

New products made with the cards and paper cups, like dippers, bowls, teacups, and stars, are demanded in subsequent markets (Fig. 2) to avoid boredom which might develop on the production lines, to provide new types of cost engineering and management decisions, and to introduce problems of retraining, replanning, technological change, and size of product line.

Marketing problems were kept simple and related wherever possible to questions about one's own production and the potential productivity

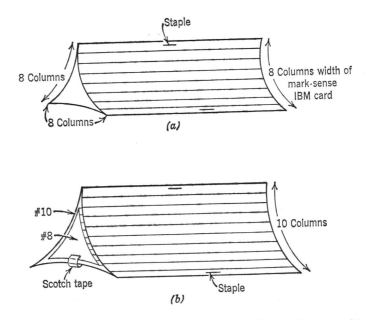

FIGURE 1   (a) #8 triangular porthole. (b) #8-#10 porthole assembly.

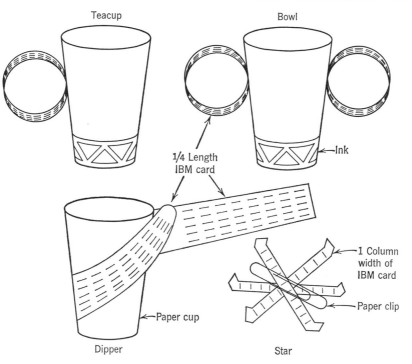

FIGURE 2   New items to be manufactured.

of the competing company. Excess inventories of raw materials and of finished goods had to be avoided because profits could be wiped out by heavy storage costs. Market uncertainties and competitor's decisions and efficiency had to be considered in deciding how much of what to produce. Paramount, however, was the need for each company's management to maintain a productive and satisfied establishment. More than successful intellectual decisions were needed in order to insure this. Real workers and managers were involved in real production—only the monetary exchange was fictitious.

We have completed three trial runs with POE involving a total of 105 salaried personnel from foreman to vice-president. The richness of the results leads us to expect that the method has considerable potential.

SIMPLE VERSUS COMPLEX ORGANIZATION

In a first investigation, near the end of a sensitivity training laboratory held by a single industrial firm, one group formed a relatively simple line-staff arrangement to three echelons (Fig. 3) to meet the needs of the exercise; the other group "searched" its memory and duplicated the more complex line-staff arrangement of its own real home plant (Fig. 4).

In the competition that ensued, the simpler organization showed a considerably greater profit after four production periods than the more complex organization. The simpler manufacturing concern was able to market 60% more product in dollar value, yet did so with lower operating costs than the complex organization. The complex organization had a less adequate inventory control system and failed to maintain as healthy a posture in the market as did the simpler company.

According to attitude surveys of the participants in both companies, taken during rest periods, there was a steady increase in satisfaction with company operations in the simpler organization, while there was a correspondingly steady decrease in satisfaction in the complex organization. Both companies declined in feelings of responsibility for company operations, although members felt more responsible in the complex organization and were more attracted to their own company. Goals became much clearer in the simpler organization towards the end of the exercise, while the reverse took place in the more complex

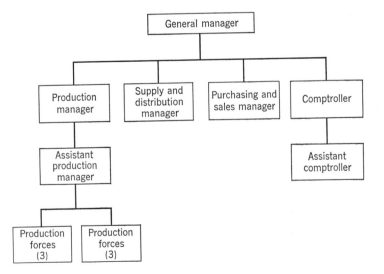

FIGURE 3   An example of a chart for a line-staff organization to produce port-holes.

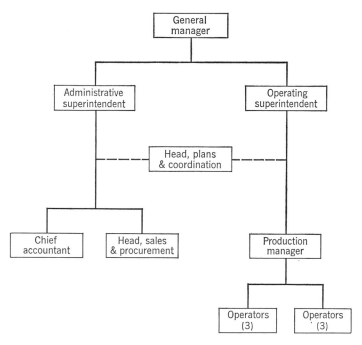

FIGURE 4   An example of a chart for a complex organization to produce portholes.

arrangement. Satisfaction with fellow employees increased more in the simpler organization.

Evidence for the validity of the simulation was found in the positive association between over-all satisfaction and status (importance of position) in the simulated organization, duplicating the usual correlation found in real life. Also, as in real life, lay-offs and strike threats began to appear; engineering modifications were introduced without concern for their human impact but only on the basis of engineering economics; and important trade secrets were lost because their value as secrets were not realized.

LINE-STAFF VERSUS OVERLAPPING COMMITTEES

With minor modifications, a second study was conducted again in a sensitivity training laboratory of the same industrial firm but with new subjects. This time we introduced an independent variable beforehand, differentiating the two competing companies. One of the competitors was given explicit directives to operate by means of individual decision making and responsibility, while the other was forced to adopt committee decision making as the basis of its organizational life. Since all decisions in the latter company were to be made by committees of three men or more, and since each manager could be a member of more than one committee, an arrangement of overlapping committees was constructed. Likert [349] has proposed superimposing overlapping committees on a line-staff organization, and we went one step further and eliminated the line-staff, in accord with suggestions by Fisch [196] that the line-staff arrangement may be obsolete.

Relative efficiency. Despite its novelty and awkwardness, this *formal* arrangement of overlapping committees (Fig. 5) outproduced and outperformed its traditional line-staff competitor. Profits were almost five times greater; sales volume was 157% greater; yet operating and inventory costs were considerably lower in the company managed by overlapping committees. In almost every respect, the overlapping committee organization was cited both by its own participants

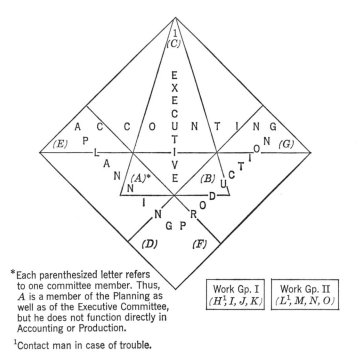

*Each parenthesized letter refers to one committee member. Thus, *A* is a member of the Planning as well as of the Executive Committee, but he does not function directly in Accounting or Production.

[1]Contact man in case of trouble.

Work Gp. I	Work Gp. II
(H^1, I, J, K)	(L^1, M, N, O)

FIGURE 5

as well as by outside consultants as the more effective of the two organizations.

Labor-management problems. The competing line-staff organization had a good deal of labor difficulty. Following directives, line-staff management told the wage earners to "take off," and that they would be told what and how to do things just before production began. Since all production decisions were to be made by individual superiors, workers were left free to create, and what they created was a strong union movement. During the ensuing collective bargaining, negotiations were conducted poorly and the labor force began work highly dissatisfied.

Decision making and operation. Planning was relatively inadequate among the overlapping committees since they failed to take into account their own much more satisfactory worker relationships and productivity, and failed to capture the much larger portion of the market that they could have gained had planning been adequate.

The flexibility of the overlapping committee organization was illustrated by the much greater number of promotions and rotations effected among its management than was possible in the line-staff organization. The usual difficulties in upward communication seemed much less significant in the overlapping committee organization, according to a postexercise questionnaire. Managers actually were rated more influential in the overlapping committees, despite the abolition of the authority-obedience chain of command.

In this postexercise questionnaire of 162 items answered by managers and wage earners of the two competing organizations, 109 statistically significant differences emerged. Analysis of variance was used to ascertain whether these differences were caused by differences between the structures of the two organizations, by differences between management and labor in general, or by the interaction between structural differences and differences in job status.

Management in *both* companies saw more task and interaction effectiveness, more maturity and stability, smoother and more adaptive operations, and greater flexibility and ease of communications than did the workers within the same companies. On the other hand, wage earners in *both* organizations saw more conflict, disorganization, indecision, splintering, insecurity, unpredictability, and rigidity coupled with poor communications and access to information in their respective companies. Yet, in comparison, to *all* members of the line-staff company, *all* members of the overlapping committee organization felt more satisfied with effectiveness, productivity, and management, and were more inclined to agree that there was equal participation, cooperation, and goal clarity. In comparison to all members in the overlapping committee company, all members of the line-staff organization, regardless of their status, found their company to be relatively more unbalanced, overstaffed, bureaucratic, disorderly, indecisive, and resistant to change. They saw more confusion, splintering, involvement, and carelessness and rejection of their own leadership.

Analysis of the interaction between structure and status suggested that the union success achieved by the wage earners of the line-staff organization compensated for their company's failure in the market place. They completed the exercise with a sense of victory not shared by their own management, and so they were almost as happy with the over-all outcomes as were the management and wage earners of the overlapping committee organization who won the actual manufacturing competition in sales, productivity, and profits.

A THREE-WAY COMPETITION

Thirty-nine participants in a more traditional management training program concerned with economics, cases, and business issues, and drawn from many different large and small enterprises, were asked to operate in groups of 13, the simple, the complex, and the overlapping committee organizations. To minimize preproduction effects, each player was assigned to his specific job as well as to his organization.

Although, again, the simple line-staff was found slightly superior in productivity to the complex line-staff, both were clearly operated more profitably than the overlapping committee. In the same way, players in the simple organization were most satisfied with how their organization worked, its communications, its labor relations, and its management, and the overlapping committee organization was least satisfied. Figure 6 profiles the statistically significant mean responses of players (according to appropriate analyses of variance) in describing their own organizations at the end of the game. It is interesting to see that the simple organization, despite instructions not to do so, actually made considerable use, much more so than the complex company, of decisions by committee.

The productive inadequacy of the overlapping committee centered in its failure to produce its allowable market quota of more complex porthole assemblies, which, in turn, seemed due to excessive concern with efforts to minimize waste and storage costs. In the critique after

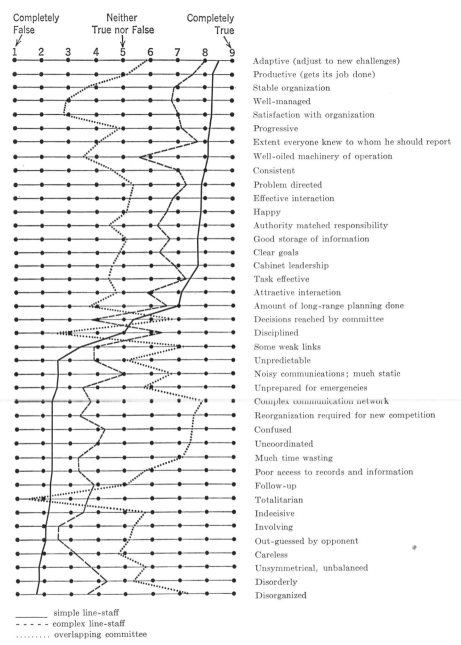

Completely False — Neither True nor False — Completely True

1 2 3 4 5 6 7 8 9

Adaptive (adjust to new challenges)
Productive (gets its job done)
Stable organization
Well-managed
Satisfaction with organization
Progressive
Extent everyone knew to whom he should report
Well-oiled machinery of operation
Consistent
Problem directed
Effective interaction
Happy
Authority matched responsibility
Good storage of information
Clear goals
Cabinet leadership
Task effective
Attractive interaction
Amount of long-range planning done
Decisions reached by committee
Disciplined
Some weak links
Unpredictable
Noisy communications; much static
Unprepared for emergencies
Complex communication network
Reorganization required for new competition
Confused
Uncoordinated
Much time wasting
Poor access to records and information
Follow-up
Totalitarian
Indecisive
Involving
Out-guessed by opponent
Careless
Unsymmetrical, unbalanced
Disorderly
Disorganized

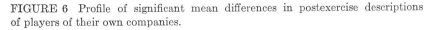

———— simple line-staff
- - - - - complex line-staff
.... overlapping committee

FIGURE 6 Profile of significant mean differences in postexercise descriptions of players of their own companies.

the exercise, it became clear that particularly damaging to the chances of success of the overlapping committee organization was its operators' initial negative reaction to being "stuck" with an unfamiliar and, they believed, unworkable organization. Actually, considerable effort was exerted, particularly by a key member of the executive committee to convert the organization into a traditional line-staff arrangement, while, counter to instructions, much committee action took place in the companies organized to simulate individual decision-making hierarchies.

In future studies where radical innovations are tried, we will need to pay attention to resistance by the players to the unfamiliar. Thus, operation of an overlapping committee organization may require considerable training in the kinds of personnel and group factors usually covered in sensitivity training programs, none of which was given to these players before they were forced into using a system so heavily dependent on consensual decisions. Turning the matter around, how well managers can successfully operate a committee-type organization might be the basis for evaluating the utility of a sensitivity training program.

Conclusions

THE ISSUE OF RELIABILITY

In some respects, we have described only three cases needing considerable replication before any reliance can be placed on our inferences. On the other hand, our inferences are drawn on samples in identical fashion, as in any investigation of two or three different divisions of a company, or two or three small companies, using different managerial approaches. However, our chances for replication are obviously much greater than for those collecting data from real-life organizations. One example of a recurring phenomenon seen in all three trials of POE is the effort to unionize. Unions actually developed in only two out of the seven companies studied (both eventually signing contracts). One of these created considerable difficulty for its management. But in all three trials, considerable agitation for unions occurred. Management strategy was the same in the first and third trials—they promoted the agitators to middle management. In the second trial, unions developed with one company suffering protracted negotiations, stoppages, picketing (during rest periods), and the like. All union drives were local except in the third exercise where an effort to form an international union of all wage earners in the three companies was foiled by a timely promotion.

THE ISSUE OF UNREALITY

Many of the phenomena expected in real-life industry occurred during the exercises; phenomena such as the correlation of status and satisfaction, the union-management polarization in collective bargaining, and the acceptance of satisfactory rather than optimum levels of productivity. Nevertheless, the simulation was different in many respects from real-life operations. The powerful motivations of real job security and real monetary reward could only be substituted for by competitive desires and the normal concerns about winning rather than losing a game, loyalty to one's team, and short but intensive visibility among peers.

But the difference, in some senses even additional to the possibilities of controlled replication, favors simulation over real-life observation for research purposes; for more may happen in simulation in less time than ever might occur under similar circumstances in real life. For example, when partial lay-offs of workers were considered by management in the first study, they were not executed because it seemed highly possible that the entire work force would have gone on strike if any workers had been laid off. Many so stated afterwards. What we see here in miniature is a collapsing of time coupled with potential overexcitation of behavior illustrative of what might occur in much less dramatic form or actually only be felt, but not acted out in real-life industry. Many of the same feelings and tendencies are generated in a much shorter, quicker, and sharper way than in real life.

FURTHER RESEARCH APPLICATIONS

Many other independent variables, which could not heretofore be subjected to experimental attack, can be systematically examined with POE or similar games. Thus national differences in style of organization could be simulated and contrasted. For example, the technical-commercial dual management practiced in Germany can be contrasted with the line-staff system common to the United States.

Radically different modes for arranging productive organizations might be developed and tested by taking advantage of the revolution in computer technology and automation now in progress. For example, extending an idea recently advanced by Leavitt and Whisler [337],

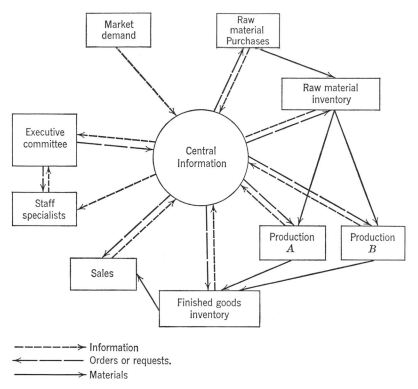

FIGURE 7 Functional chart of an information-matter-energy processing system for manufacturing.

one can envisage, as in Fig. 7, a productive organization as a logical *information-matter-energy* processing system instead of the traditional *man-materials-money* system. This novel arrangement would have stores of information and materials. Decisions as to what to produce, how much to produce, and who should produce it would all be optimized mathematically in advance when market demands for finished goods were ascertained. Raw materials and finished goods inventories would likewise be optimized. The executive committee assisted by its staff of specialists would need only to decide on broad program changes rather than on any particular operating decisions since the latter would all be mathematically optimum for prevailing conditions. But how would those men servicing central information, central materials, and production accept machine decisions? What new human factors would be introduced? Would labor and management negotiations improve with the "errorless" computer information available? POE might help to answer these questions.

The utility of many other organizational propositions could be subject to experimental test: selected personnel practices, management by objectives, performance appraisal interviews, open horizontal channels of communications, mergers, decentralization, and operational goals.

FURTHER STUDIES

During 1963–1964, the Production Organization Exercise was refined considerably with the collaboration of James A. Vaughan and run with success permitting five or six companies of 15 business executives each to compete. Four such runs now provide data for analysis for the comparative performance of 26 "companies" under standardized conditions.

In this University of Pittsburgh version (UPPOE), marketing has been made more complex. A company's sales quota for a given period depends on how much more it advertises each of its products than its competitors and how much it underprices them. Ceiling prices prevent an explosive inflation. Management has to choose whether to continue to produce items a and b, to add item c to its line, to discontinue a and b, etc. Issues of retraining and replanning arise. Technological discoveries can be capitalized for exploitation or they can be ignored.

Firms that fail to gain a sufficient market for what they can produce can make agreements to sell excess production to competitors who have more of a market than they can meet. They can "pirate" each other's labor force and management, form active labor unions, consider mergers, perform special services (at agreed upon prices) for each other and try to "rig" each other's markets.

In the most recent experiment, three "bottoms-up" companies have competed with three "top-down" organizations. The "bottoms-up" organization was designed by Paul R. Lawrence of Harvard and Murray Horwitz of New York University. The organization contains planners, representatives and operators. Everyone has a job with problems to solve. There is no traditional hierarchy. The design aims to maximize the satisfaction of all members with the organization. The "top-down" organization was designed by Ralph Stogdill of Ohio State University and Harold J. Leavitt of Carnegie Tech to maximize the adequacy of the organization's response to the external environment. To ensure that the 100 graduate business students who operated in "bottoms-up" and "top-down" companies were not overly resistant to these radically different plans, Drs. Lawrence and Stogdill lectured on the rationale of their respective arrangements, then served as management advisors during the organization process.

Generally, the "bottoms-up" firms showed greater gains in net worth and more satisfied operators and managers than the "top-down" organizations with which they competed.

8

THE ABSORPTION OF PROTEST:
A WORKING PAPER

Ruth Leeds

Introduction—The Nonconformist and the Enclave [1]

The usual fate of the nonconformist who occupies a position of some responsibility in a complex organization has been established: the cleric who waivers from the true path goes on retreat; the maverick army officer is appointed to an innocuous position; the recalcitrant political party deputy is temporarily suspended.[2] If temporary suspension or relegation to an insignificant position does not suffice to curb the nonconformist, he is gradually eased out of the organization. But what happens when an organization is faced with not just a single nonconformist but with several who form a cohesive enclave in its midst? The organization—specifically incumbents of positions superordinate to the nonconformists—must now check not just one individual but many who could potentially divert organization resources from their current commitments, undermine organizational effectiveness, or form a front capable of capturing control of the organization.

To control a nonconforming enclave, the organization has to employ techniques other than those typically used to check a single noncon-

---

[1] This paper is the theoretic part of a project initiated and directed by Amitai Etzioni. I very much appreciate the ideas, comments and time he gave to it. I am indebted to John C. Pock for reading critically several drafts of this paper. His many suggestions and willingness to argue with me over questionable points have been invaluable in adding clarity to it.
[2] Amitai Etzioni [184], pp. 241–244. This paper represents an expansion of an idea briefly discussed by Etzioni, pp. 245–248.

formist. An individual's nonconformity often as not stems primarily from personality factors although structural determinants do contribute to it. The nonconformity of an enclave, which is shared by all its members, stems primarily from structural determinants rather than personality factors. Hence, different techniques are called for to check nonconforming enclaves.

There is one organizational technique—the subject of this chapter—that is particularly suited for controlling wayward groups. It consists of integrating the protest of the nonconforming enclave into the organization by converting it into a new legitimate subunit. Through conversion, the nonconforming enclave obtains a legitimate outlet for its nonconformity, and thereby contributes to the attainment of legitimate goals of the organization. The conversion from nonconforming enclave to legitimate subunit will be called the protest-absorbing process. Protest absorption might take as little as a year or as long as a generation. Regardless, by the end of the process, the nonconforming enclave and the top authorities of the organization reach an accommodation such that the enclave is given some autonomy to pursue a specific activity (usually the activity which was the focus of the nonconformity), but, at the same time, it is expected to abide by the regulations and restrictions to which all legitimate subunits adhere.

Protest absorption is a structural "weapon" available to the organization. It is a weapon insofar as it is used to control nonconforming groups. It is a structural weapon insofar as its effectiveness rests on formal changes in the organizational structure, that is, on the formal positions of subunits vis-à-vis each other. As will be seen, the weapon is unleashed through the exercise of *authority*, although *power* is a variable in the protest-absorption process. Protest absorption should not be confused with co-optation which comes about through power differentials between the co-opters and the co-opted regardless of the authority structure.[3] Although reductionist concepts like power and charisma are variables in the protest-absorption process, they are not the major explanatory concepts. Structure and authority are the key concepts to an understanding of protest absorption, although these terms will be used only rarely to avoid awkward phrasing.

Organizational analyses which generate theories about the organization as if all structures were cut from the same cloth must be qualified when applied to specific organizations, e.g., a prison, an army, or a factory. The development of a comparative approach permits the enrichment of organizational theories by adding statements of regularities

---

[3] Philip Selznick [476].

within one type of organization to statements of universal uniformities. Given this consideration, the first step is to delineate the type of organization in which protest absorption is expected to be an effective weapon. Then we can characterize the nonconforming enclave and the process by which it is converted into a legitimate and quiescent unit. The appendix presents an outline of cases which *illustrate* the protest-absorption model. Since this paper represents both an exploratory study and a preliminary report, we are not concerned here with the frequency with which the model is approximated.

Normative Organizations and the Distribution of Charisma [4]

Organizations can be characterized by the nature of the primary power that is used to control its lowest ranking participants. *Coercive* organizations, e.g., prisons, keep order through the use of physical force (or the threat of it); *utilitarian* organizations, e.g., factories, keep order primarily through monetary rewards; *normative* organizations, e.g., churches, elicit compliance through the allocation and manipulation of symbolic rewards. For reasons to be evident shortly, protest absorption is expected to occur most frequently in normative organizations.

Two other major characteristics distinguish the normative from the coercive and utilitarian organizations. First, a normative organization tends to demand a high degree of commitment and loyalty from its members, often to the point that members are expected to give their primary allegiance to the organization. The priest is symbolically wedded to the Church; in those organizations where secular marriage is permitted, the wife is drawn into the structure and is known by its name, e.g., a navy wife.[5] Voluntary exiting from the organization is perceived as a sign of insufficient loyalty; for example, resignation from academic departments tends to precipitate feelings of resentment and rejection among the professors who remain.[6] Criticism of the organization's institutionalized norms and methods is also taken as a sign of insufficient loyalty.

Second, most offices in normative organizations have charisma ascribed to them. The performances associated with the position of priest or military officer are charismatic and are symbolized by such devices as special dress, badges of office, and ritual courtesies. The

---

[4] Based on Etzioni [184].

[5] Arthur K. Davis [393a].

[6] Theodore Caplow and R. J. McGee [95], p. 66.

charismatic elements of a particular office enrich the organization's symbols and rituals with additional meaning, and increase their reward value for the loyalty and discipline which lowest ranking members exhibit. Moreover, personal contact with an incumbent of a charismatic office is itself perceived as a reward by members. Thus charismatic power in its routinized form re-enforces the normative power of the organization.

At the same time that charisma helps to generate loyalty and discipline among the personnel, it also is a potential disrupter of discipline and loyalty to the organization itself. The problem is present in latent form when the lower participants of the organization attribute the functionally specific charisma of office to a *particular* incumbent, and, in so doing, generalize the charisma so that it takes on diffuse characteristics. Where this occurs, the participants make personal commitments to the particular individual who occupies a charismatic office rather than to the office itself. If the charismatic officer uses these particularistic commitments for purposes that are functional to the organization as a whole (or for purposes that do not generate dysfunctions), then the problem remains latent. The case might be, however, that the charismatic employs these commitments to challenge organizational hegemony and integration, and to compete against regular subunits (sometimes laterally related) for resources, thereby undermining the organization's allocation and reward system. (That such a situation might occur indicates both the desirability and the apparent impossibility of routinizing charisma.)

The potential strain between charisma and discipline is greatest in those organizations where the gift of grace parallels the formal organizational chart, being characteristic of many offices as well as the top ones, and yet where formal authority is centralized. The Catholic Church and wartime military organizations are the major examples of organizations that have charisma distributed throughout their lines combined with a strong, centralized authority structure. Protest absorption is more likely to be used in these organizations to control nonconforming enclaves than in normative structures which have the potential for strain between charisma and discipline but lack a strong central authority (e.g., Protestant denominations and the early Catholic Church).

The Process of Protest Absorption

The potential strain between charisma and discipline erupts into a tempest in a tepid teapot with the formation of a nonconforming enclave. More often than not, the enclave is led by a charismatic who is concerned with devising new ways for carrying out his responsibilities more effectively. The leadership of the enclave is strengthened by able lieutenants. The enclave itself is endowed with a militant spirit; its members are eager to undertake large-scale tasks and to execute them with novel strategies. The organization, grown weak internally in one or several respects, either cannot or prefers not to initiate change (although from some objective perspective change might be functionally required if the organization is to continue being effective). Protest absorption has two major consequences for the organization: it checks the nonconforming enclave by turning it into a legitimate subunit which remains loyal to the organization and it permits the introduction of change. The descriptive model of protest absorption contains three parts: (1) The characteristics of the nonconforming enclave; (2) the state of the organization; and (3) the process of absorbing protest.

THE NONCONFORMING ENCLAVE

Two conditions are basic to the emergence of a nonconforming enclave. First, some members of a normative organization must attribute personal charisma to an official. This provides the official with an opportunity to lead a loyal following over which diffuse influence and control can be exercised. Second, the official must have tendencies toward nonconformity and unorthodoxy, and must disregard at least some traditional norms and strategies. Once the official has proved his capacity to acquire a personal following, he may be referred to as the enclave leader; once he leads in unorthodox directions, the enclave becomes a nonconforming group.

The leader's nonconformity stems in large measure from his position in the organization. Assume that the leader is in unit C_4 (Fig. 1). Assume further that C_4 is not functioning effectively with regard to

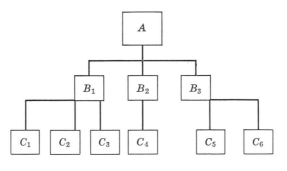

FIGURE 1   Boxes denote units in organization.

its subunit goals. Lack of effectiveness could stem from one or several factors. For example, the unit is functionally peripheral and so does not receive the optimum quantity and quality of inputs, or the unit is a long established one which has become more concerned with self-maintenance than with attainment of goals; or changes in the unit's environment have occurred which make present methods and procedures obsolete; or contingencies have emerged for which there is no formal provision. In short, the unit's responsibility for goals far exceeds its capacity for attainment of goals, thereby making it relatively ineffective.[7] One response to lack of effectiveness is to exercise trained incapacity, that is, to continue conforming to rules and procedures which have become inappropriate.[8] A second response is to search for new rules and procedures which would permit increased unit effectiveness. The first response is symptomatic of functional rationality and the second of substantive rationality.[9] The leader, either in his capacity as head of C_4 or as a member of it, exercises some degree of substantive rationality and assumes responsibility for devising methods which will make the unit more effective. Increased unit effectiveness would permit him to fulfill his own particular position more adequately.

In large measure, one's position determines whether one perceives the discrepancy between responsibility and control, and whether one chooses to respond functionally or substantively to it. The greater the responsibility for goal attainment or the greater the environmental contact associated with a given position, the more likely is the incumbent to respond substantively rather than functionally. In our simplified organization chart, the A level has over-all responsibility for organization goals; the C level is responsible for subunit goals. Moreover, both A and C levels have some contact with the environment. The B level serves internal coordination and communication functions. On a probability basis, then, the enclave leader is more likely to occupy a position in A or C rather than in B. To simplify presentation of our model, we assume that the enclave leader is located in C.

The leader's nonconformity is not to be confused with deviancy. Unlike a deviant, a nonconformist does not hide his dissent from the prevailing norms. He publicly challenges the efficacy of the existing norms and their applicability to specific situations in the hope of

---

[7] See Etzioni [184], pp. 77–79 for a discussion of effectiveness.
[8] R. K. Merton [391], p. 198.
[9] Karl Mannheim [364], pp. 112–117.

changing them without destroying the organization. The nonconformist justifies his challenge of the status quo by appealing to what the organization recognizes as its highest morality or its ultimate set of values.[10] The official who emerges as a leader of a nonconforming enclave is justified in saying, in the area of his specific responsibility, "It is written . . . but I say unto you . . ." on two counts. First, because he has charisma attributed to him, and second, because as a nonconformist he is oriented to existing rules only in a negative sense—to challenge them.[11]

Concomitant with his personal charisma and tendency toward nonconformity, the leader also has a flair for originality which permits him to create new strategies, ideologies, and symbols to counter those of the organization.[12] The development and implementation of new strategies come to represent the goal of the enclave. The new ideology and symbols serve as extensions to the leader's charisma in welding the enclave into a cohesive, dynamic group.

The charismatic rarely leads the enclave by himself.[13] He is usually assisted by lieutenants who support his unorthodox tactics and innovations, and spearhead the enclave with their own missionary fire and ability to influence others. The leader, by granting his lieutenants some autonomy in a specialized area like procuring supplies, insures that they will remain subservient to him. Since the lieutenants are likely to promulgate their own ideas, a limited amount of autonomy

---

[10] If the leader appeals to a morality or values not recognized by the organization, the likelihood of protest absorption is reduced and the organization will resort to other means to check him. Orde Wingate was able to organize and arm Jews to quell Arab raids on the British pipelines in Palestine in the late 1930's, despite British policy not to give arms to Jews. Wingate also hoped that his Special Night Squad would form the basis for a Jewish army which would help to pave the way for Palestine's independence. Wingate's advocacy of a cause which extended beyond military purlieus led to his recall from Palestine, and probably helps to account for the rapid deJudification of the Special Night Squad. See Christopher Sykes [532].

[11] R. K. Merton [392], pp. 725–726, and Max Weber [590], p. 361.

[12] Dorothy Emmet [181], p. 258. The problem of what an administrator should do with the single nonconformist, the "creative genius," the person with a flair who is "beyond good and evil," receives excellent treatment by Professor Emmet. She feels that a solution might develop if the administrator has the capacity to comprehend different roles; with such understanding the administrator might create a special role in the organization for the nonconformist. In the present context, protest absorption would require the administrator to have some understanding of structure. Emmet does not deal with the problems presented by a group of nonconformists.

[13] See Weber [590], p. 360.

may prevent rival ideas and methods from disrupting the unity of the enclave.

The energy and zeal of the nonconforming enclave are focused on innovations, which often assume the form of techniques intended to facilitate attainment of organizational goals. New techniques might be more effective in attaining existing goals by permitting higher output or they might revitalize goals which have grown fallow. (Later we shall have more to say about the enclave's objectives and their bearing on the protest absorption process.) In essence, the enclave maintains a high commitment to the basic goals of the organization, and desires to display this commitment through recognition of its innovations. The commitment inspiring the nonconformists is frequently viewed as higher than that possessed by others in the organization. The perceived or alleged discrepancy between the extremely high degree of loyalty to basic organizational values exhibited by the nonconforming enclave and the moderate degree of loyalty exhibited by other organization participants is likely to provoke conflict. Other participants have little tolerance for the enthusiasm of the enclave, for, by comparison, they appear less diligent and less loyal to the organization.

The nonconforming enclave is further distinguished by an unorthodox atmosphere which permeates many aspects of its life. This atmosphere varies from extreme austerity and asceticism to romance, adventure, and heroic sacrifice. The unorthodox behavior of the enclave, whether reflected in the wearing of special clothing or in reckless courage, not only sets the enclave apart from the rest of the organization but also contributes to its cohesiveness and strength. A member can readily identify with a group symbolized by noticeable objects or mannerisms. If the group merits esteem from outsiders, it can be bestowed on easily recognized members. The symbols of unorthodoxy also facilitate recruitment in that they help publicize the group to potential members who share similar values and similar tendencies toward nonconformity.

In summary, the nonconforming enclave is characterized by a leader whose charisma of office has become personal. He pursues a course of action or cause which is perceived as unorthodox, and for which he creates symbols and an ideology. His immediate lieutenants are nonconformers in their own right, although less influential and original than the leader. The cause served is usually a means to revive allegedly neglected organizational goals or to achieve present organizational goals more effectively. Lastly, a peculiar aura, either of asceticism or of romance, envelops the enclave, contributing to its integration and highlighting its dedication to its cause.

THE STATE OF THE ORGANIZATION

Although nonconformity can erupt at all times, a cohesive nonconforming enclave is likely to emerge in a context in which one or a combination of the following variations of organizational weakness is prevalent. If, over time, the legitimacy of the organization procedures decreases generally or within any subunit, charisma tends to shift from office to person among those dedicated to the ultimate purposes of the organization. If an organization is insensitive to potential nonconformity (due to such factors as inadequacies of communication networks), control mechanisms might not be activated in time to forestall a nonconforming official before he gains a personal following.[14] If an organization's internal authority is weak, owing to the corruption of officers responsible for enforcing conformity or owing to the lack of (or limited) control over enforcement facilities, then whatever control mechanisms the organization might employ are ineffectual. Finally, resources diverted outside the organization to meet an external challenge, or stoppage of inputs, limit the availability of the means needed to combat nonconformity.

Once the enclave emerges, mild checks to contain the nonconformity are no longer adequate. If the organizational elite ousts the leader, his immediate lieutenants could assume control of the enclave, or members of the enclave might follow their leader and form the beginnings of a competing structure. Such a possibility is particularly threatening when the organization enjoys a monopoly or duopoly position. If the organization is one of several of its kind, then one more similar structure in the environment makes little difference. Finally, if both the leader and the members of the enclave are dispersed throughout the organization, in an effort to disband the group, nonconformity might be spread rather than eliminated.

Given the inadequacy of control techniques which are typically applied to single nonconformists, the organizational elite must choose between several alternatives: condemnation, avoidance, expulsion, or

---

[14] In some instances the "following" emerges first and then casts about for a leader. According to Erle Wilson's less romantic account of the Bounty mutiny, the potential mutineers were ship's sailors, who, on becoming cognizant of each other's discontents, recruited Fletcher Christian to be their leader. Subsequent events indicated that the choice was not entirely fortunate, for Christian lacked the capacity to live up to the charisma which his followers attributed to him. See Erle Wilson [605].

protest absorption. The first three alternatives are not effective in containing the nonconformity unless the enclave itself is quite weak to begin with. Condemnation contains the danger of widening the rift between the enclave and the rest of the organization by forcing a polarization of issues.[15] Avoidance, which means consciously taking little account of the existence of the enclave, sidesteps the danger of polarization.[16] During the period that the organization elite ostensibly ignores the enclave, however, the enclave might grow in size and strength instead of dying out. Expulsion of the enclave represents a costly loss of resources which might yet be channeled to serve organizational goals.[17] Also, expulsion could lead to the emergence of a rival structure (albeit it does permit tightening of organizational ranks). The negative consequences which might result from attempting to control the enclave through condemnation, avoidance, or expulsion are particularly dysfunctional to the organization when it displays one or more signs of weakness. Although protest absorption also entails some dangers, it is a more promising way of checking nonconformity on several counts.

If protest absorption is successful, it not only eliminates the pocket of nonconformity but also strengthens the organization by providing it with the services of an energetic, devoted group. Moreover, the process permits the legitimation of innovation which better equips the organization to face external challenges or to attain its own goals more effectively. Protest absorption can also lead to the elimination of nonconformity without the emergence of a devoted group or the introduction of innovation. This form results when the organization provides the enclave with an "opportunity to fail." When the enclave protests about matters beyond its ken or original bailiwick, and it is accorded legitimacy in the area of protest, it is likely to fail because it lacks the skills and knowledge to carry out the now legitimate activity. Any nonconformity which survives outright failure is expected to be sufficiently weakened so as to be eliminated easily. Should the enclave succeed despite its opportunity to fail, then the organization can reap the benefits. The risk accompanying protest absorption is that the nonconforming enclave may, during the time that the organization attempts

---

[15] Z. Brzezinski [89], pp. 9–10.

[16] *Op. cit.*, pp. 11–12.

[17] A recent report of the AFL-CIO council stated:

It is obvious that expulsion as such does not cure the offending practices. And, what is more important, once outside the federation the membership of such an organization is no longer accessible to corrective influences from the parent body through education and persuasion. (Quoted in the *Reporter*, October 26, 1961, p. 18.)

to check it, gain access to the key power positions and, subsequently, assume control of the total structure.

THE PROCESS OF PROTEST ABSORPTION

Once the nonconforming enclave has been converted into a new legitimate subunit, the organization is strengthened. During the protest-absorption process, however, the organization, especially that sector of it in which the enclave has erupted, faces a series of internal battles involving several levels of its hierarchy. The charismatic leader and his followers oppose those persons who formally are their immediate superiors. These shall be called the middle hierarchy and represent the enemy in the battles. Insofar as the organization has a centralized top hierarchy which can exercise authority over the middle hierarchy, these battles tend not to be fought to the death of one or the other set of combatants. Instead, the top hierarchy intercedes and more or less arbitrarily terminates the conflict. Protest absorption essentially is a process whereby the top hierarchy attempts to balance the two opposing forces—members of the nonconforming enclave against members of the middle hierarchy who are the immediate superiors of the former.

In some instances, units which are laterally related to the nonconforming enclave will also be aligned with the middle hierarchy in opposing the enclave. In other cases, the opposition will be made up only of heads of laterally related units and an opposing middle hierarchy will be absent. The varying composition of the "enemy" depends upon the location of the enclave in the organizational structure. The general pattern, however, might be diagrammed as shown in Fig. 2.

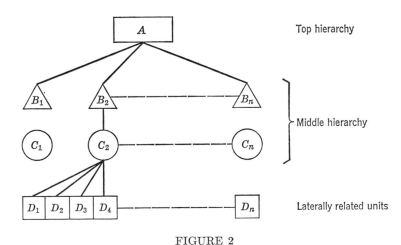

FIGURE 2

Assume that the enclave erupts in D_4. If the leader is the head of D_4, the enclave will encompass the entire unit. If the leader is only a member, the enclave will set itself up as $D_{4'}$. In either case, the enclave will have to contend with C_2 who is responsible for D_1–D_4. Directly, or indirectly, the enclave will also have to contend with the other D units. The emergence of the nonconforming enclave creates increased competition for resources among the D units. In addition, they perceive themselves as being cast in an unfavorable light by the enthusiasm and heightened activity of the enclave. Hence, the D units will pressure C_2 to suppress the enclave. The D units do not always form part of the opposition to the enclave; another variation is that C_2 might also be directly in charge of one D unit as well as having general responsibility for the entire D section. Such structural variations in the formation of the opposition to the nonconforming enclave do not affect the general pattern of protest absorption, although they help to explain slight variations from case to case. Hence, for simplicity's sake, in describing the process we shall limit the opposition to the middle hierarchy, although the reader should bear in mind that the opposition can vary in its composition.

Incumbents of positions constituting the middle hierarchy are more likely to exhibit "trained incapacity" than incumbents of other levels. Hence, they are usually incapable of comprehending the significance of the enclave's protest. Furthermore, their positions are threatened by the enclave, both because it reveals that their loyalty to basic values of the organization is not as strong as it could be and because it indicates that they cannot make use of the authority vested in them to maintain order in their own bailiwicks. Their response to the enclave is to attempt to suppress it through such means as closing the communication links between the charismatic leader and the top hierarchy, restricting the enclave members' freedom of movement, and reducing the resources available to them. From the perspective of the middle hierarchy, the use of such techniques represent the full exercise of their rights of office.[18] From the perspective of the nonconforming enclave, such techniques are obstructions which indicate that the organization is against it, and hence, to carry out its cause, the enclave must try to be even more dynamic and more cohesive.

If the charismatic leader is to demonstrate his basic loyalty to organizational values and if he is to gain recognition and legitimation

---

[18] When legitimate techniques fail to quell the enclave, the middle hierarchy might resort to illegitimate or nonlegitimate ones. Paradoxically, it is at such times that the middle hierarchy overcomes its "trained incapacity."

for his cause, he must have access to the top hierarchy. When such access via regular channels is barred, the leader develops his own routes to the top. Frequently this is done through an intermediary who is outside the organization but has legitimate access to the top echelon. Insofar as the charismatic leader is able to establish a particularistic relationship with such an intermediary which is beyond organizational control, he has relatively easy access to the top.

The particularistic communication line gives the nonconforming enclave some leverage in an attempt to have its cause recognized and legitimized. That the intermediary is willing to use his power over the top hierarchy in behalf of the enclave is regarded by its members as a significant step forward and as a sign of incipient legitimation.

At the same time that a particularistic communication line gives the enclave hope that its cause will be successful, it also produces potential instability and unreliability. First, the communication line is maintained at the will—or the whim—of the intermediary, which means that it can be opened and closed arbitrarily. Second, a particularistic request to the top hierarchy in behalf of the nonconforming enclave might elicit informal instructions to the middle hierarchy which it can easily overlook in its continued attempts to obstruct the enclave.

In some instances the charismatic leader need not resort to particularistic communication channels for he might be able to go to the top directly; [19] or the attention of the top hierarchy might be drawn to the nonconforming enclave as a result of the conflict between it and the middle hierarchy, especially if the conflict has affected task performance adversely.

Regardless of the means by which the attention of the top hierarchy is directed to the enclave, the leader who has gained this attention can demonstrate his basic loyalty to organizational values and communicate his ideas for their more effective realization in the hope of gaining official approval. Concerned with blocking such approval, the middle hierarchy urges the top to suppress the enclave. The top hierarchy is interested in enhancing general organizational effectiveness, and, by extension, is concerned with maintaining internal order. With its broader, more substantive, perspective, the top is more amenable to innovation than the middle hierarchy, especially when faced with internal weakness or external challenge. Hence, the top is more likely

---

[19] The leader's ability to communicate with the top hierarchy directly is determined in large part by other capacities, roles, and statuses which he might have within or outside of the organization.

to accede to some demands of the nonconforming enclave, especially if its leader is backed by a powerful intermediary, than to the insistence of the middle hierarchy that the enclave be thoroughly curbed or eliminated.

The first round in the protest-absorption process is completed when the top hierarchy recognizes the nonconforming enclave and gives it a modicum of autonomy to pursue its advocated innovation. This is followed by several more rounds of obstruction by the middle hierarchy, unorthodox communication to the top by the nonconforming enclave, and a gradually increasing grant of resources, autonomy, and legitimacy to the enclave by the top hierarchy. With each round the enclave comes closer to approximating a new legitimate subunit.

In exchange for autonomy and legitimacy from the top hierarchy, the enclave must agree to accept certain stabilizers. The stabilizers are mechanisms to insure the loyalty of the new unit to the organization and its conformity to organization regulations. First, the protest-absorbing unit is expected to develop rules, subject to approval by the top echelon, to guide its conduct; any changes in these rules are also subject to approval by the top. Second, the unit must accept a regular source of finance through which it will acquire all or most of its inputs. In this way, unauthorized appropriations of resources and competition with existing units for available resources are minimized, and the frustrations of an irregular source of income, typical of a group during its nonconformist period, are avoided. Third, and most important, the unit's activity is limited to a particular sphere of operation, usually that for which the leader and his followers advocated their innovation.[20]

With the introduction of stabilizers, the leader's personal charisma becomes attenuated. The personal charisma is reconverted to charisma of office as the leader (or his successor) assumes legitimate control of the protest-absorber unit. Furthermore, the most radical members of the former enclave perceive the leader as bowing to the dictates of the top hierarchy, thereby betraying the cause; they cease to accept the leader as a charismatic figure, leave the unit, and, where possible, even the organization. The more visible to his followers are the leader's

---

[20] The nature of the task limitation imposed on the protest-absorber unit is in part determined by the form of the organization's division of labor, i.e., whether it is structured along geographic lines such that each unit engages in the same task but in a different locality, or around functionally specific lines where each unit engages in its own speciality, or is a combination of geography and functional specificity. See C. I. Barnard [44], p. 129 ff.

negotiations with the top hierarchy, the more likely is this to be the case. In fact, the top hierarchy could reduce the leader's personal charisma considerably by sending a representative directly to the members of the enclave to grant it legitimacy. By circumvonting the leader, the top hierarchy gives the impression that it has been wise enough to recognize the value of the enclave's cause of its own accord and so no credit need be given to the leader who has spearheaded the cause. Circumvention of the leader does present certain dangers, however. Such a procedure is most likely to be successful only if the representative has instructions to grant all or the most important of the enclave's demands. Otherwise, enclave members are likely to perceive the visitation of the representative as an attempt by the top hierarchy to sabotage the cause. Since, in most cases, the top is unlikely to grant major concessions in one fell swoop, this danger is almost always present and serves to strengthen the enclave. A second danger is that the representative himself might be affected by the leader's charisma and join the enclave rather than fulfill his orders.

Occasionally other stabilizers are also introduced, e.g., limiting the size of the protest-absorber unit, appointing a special supervisor to watch for and check any excessive enthusiasm which the unit might display, and restricting the use it may make of its particularistic communication channel. Generally, these particular stabilizers are instituted if the newly legitimized unit still remains somewhat recalcitrant in its adherence to organization rules.

The conformity of the unit is further enhanced through pressures arising within it to replace the instability of its charismatic nature with the stabilizing characteristics which accompany routinization. The nonconforming enclave, like the large-scale charismatic movement, faces "everyday" problems of economic and administrative organization. For example, the unit at some point must provide for the selection of a successor to replace its charismatic leader. (The criteria for selection may be established either by the enclave or by the organization.)

The external pressures toward protest absorption and the internal pressures toward routinization eventually tame the nonconforming enclave and convert it into a quiescent unit concerned with maintaining order in its own bailiwick.[21] The unit may show signs of quiescence simultaneously with its legitimation through protest absorption, or after a period of dynamism during which it expands and gives devoted service to the organization. Its concern with expansion and innovation

---

[21] Robert Michels [398], pp. 174–175.

is replaced by one of self-maintenance. The zeal and energy of the unit are dissipated in legitimized action without being replenished. Once the original members of the unit are gone, or have become concerned with preserving their newly legitimized positions within the organization, the verve that sparked the unit when it was a nonconforming enclave cannot be sustained. Successors to key positions in the unit most likely have been socialized by the organization, and tend to resemble the middle hierarchy more than the original members of the enclave.

The unit's agreement to restrict itself to a specialized sphere of operation is itself another contributing factor to the emerging quiescent period. The agreement helps to preclude the possibility that the unit will attempt innovation beyond its allotted sphere; and whatever success the unit has in its speciality also drains it of further nonconformity. Success is its own detriment when the question of new risks arises: members of the unit prefer to maintain rather than gamble their resources and status on a new venture.

Another factor in the elimination of nonconformity from the unit is time itself. Norms which the enclave had revitalized once again become eroded through increasing lack of strict adherence to them. Members of the unit remain committed to their once-new methods even though they have become outmoded and ineffectual. The unit as a whole is no longer dedicated to the ultimate values of the organization but rests content with the sinecure provided it through protest absorption.

The factors that contribute to quiescence—cessation of innovation, dissipation of zeal and energy, emergent conservative tendencies, modification of norms, and the obsolescence of methods—also set the stage for new protest and new forms of nonconformity, which are likely to erupt because the unit legitimized through protest absorption is more vulnerable to the strains between charisma and discipline than are other units. Its history of nonconformity remains unforgotten and lends it an aura of prestige, thereby distinguishing the former enclave from ordinary units. It is further distinguished by having institutionalized a more arduous socialization period for its recruits. Finally, its standards tend to be more strict and demanding than those of the organization as a whole, even with the corroding effects of time. These factors not only militate against the complete integration of the unit into the organization but also make it extremely attractive to recruits, particularly to those who tend to be strongly or rigidly committed to its original values. In short, the unit, limited to its own sphere of action, tamed by stabilizers, concerned with its own well-being, and yet, endowed with the aura of its unorthodox past which facilitates recruitment of potential nonconformers, nurtures a fertile field for the regeneration of a nonconforming enclave and another cycle of protest absorption.

In summary, the process of protest absorption follows several steps. A nonconforming enclave is able to gain some power within the organization because the latter is internally weak or faced with an external crisis. To check the internal threat without further weakening itself, the organization forms a new administrative unit to absorb the enclave, based on the institutionalization of new norms. The emergence of the unit represents a *Sturm und Drang* period: the enclave demands more autonomy and resources so that it can pursue its course of action while the organization reluctantly grants some autonomy and resources, and permits some innovation, in order to maintain peace and overcome the crisis confronting it. The *Sturm und Drang* begins to subside when the enclave achieves the status of a more or less legitimate unit within the organization, and is virtually quelled as the unit loses its initial *élan*, no longer taking on new ventures and becoming concerned with its own maintenance. From the perspective of the top hierarchy of the organization, protest absorption is a process of encapsulation. The nonconforming enclave becomes encased in a network of stabilizers which limits its freedom of action.

Implications of Protest Absorption for the Organization

In large measure, the significance of protest absorption for the organization as a whole depends upon the bearing which the enclave's cause has on the core policies and practices of the organization. From the standpoint of its proponents, the cause usually has a greater degree of significance for core policies than the top hierarchy is willing to acknowledge.

It is convenient to formalize what is generally involved here by means of a continuum in which the cause advocated by an enclave is scaled relative to the degree with which it is likely to affect core policies and practices. Then, as in Fig. 3, the enclave can be characterized as to where it *aspires to be* on the continuum, and where it is *willing to be placed*. The organization can be characterized as to where it would *like* to locate the enclave, and where it is *willing to place it*. The shaded area indicates the range of acceptability for an enclave and its organization; in this instance there is an overlap, although this is not necessarily always the case. Moreover, the ranges

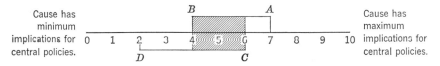

FIGURE 3   *A*. Enclave desires cause to have value of 7. *B*. Enclave willing to accept value of 4. *C*. Organization willing to permit value of 6. *D*. Organization prefers value of 2.

of acceptability can shift in the course of the protest-absorption process.

Once these ranges are known, further statements can be made about protest absorption. Where there is an overlap in ranges, protest absorption should prove more successful in controlling the enclave's nonconformity than where such an overlap does not exist. In the case where an overlap is absent (or in the case where the organization makes strong attempts to place the enclave below its minimum acceptable position—in Fig. 3 this would be below 4), the enclave will retain its zeal and unorthodoxy in order to attempt to achieve its cause in the face of control measures. For as the enclave is forced toward the lower end of the continuum, its cause becomes more attenuated, and its chances are lessened for realizing the goals which sparked it in the first place.

Furthermore, by locating the ranges of acceptability, we can predict approximately the number of rounds the protest-absorption process is likely to undergo. More rounds can be anticipated as the overlap between the two ranges is lessened. For the organization will usually try to check the enclave by locating it as low on the continuum as it can, while the enclave will continue its nonconformist activity until it is located as high on the continuum as it can be.

The more that protest absorption takes place at the higher end of the continuum, the more likely it is that an organization's central policies and practices will undergo a change. This is likely, if only for the reason that the more central the protest-absorber unit is to the organization, the more probable it is that its members will be promoted upward in the hierarchy until they reach the top.[22] The variables which determine where, on the continuum, the enclave will ultimately be absorbed, are those involved in the protest-absorption process it-

---

[22] The most cogent illustration of this process can probably be found in the history of the United States Air Force and of the submarine and aircraft carrier units in the United States Navy.

self: the degree of weakness of the organization, the strength of the nonconforming enclave, the power of the intermediary, the nature of the stabilizers, etc. Thus the protest-absorption process can lead to a long-term chain reaction of major changes in the organization, as well as check nonconformity and introduce a particular innovation.

Finally, protest absorption can have implications for organizational policy for dealing with nonconformity. An organization which has had long experience with nonconformity, e.g., the Catholic Church, might institutionalize the rounds of protest absorption. This means that, as a nonconforming enclave emerges, it "automatically" will be converted into a new subunit over several stages, as it is able to meet criteria specified by the top hierarchy. If the adoption of protest absorption as a conscious organization policy is carried out effectively, an organization will strengthen its ability to cope with nonconformity and to implement changes flowing upward from the bottom.

APPENDIX

Some Historical Examples

Following a presentation of a middle-range theory model, ideally, one should develop indicators for the variables that make up the model, and then collect a sample of cases to test the model. Traditional limitations of time and space prevent the realization of the ideal. To facilitate comprehension of the protest-absorption model, however, the history of two nonconforming enclaves are presented in Table 1. One enclave emerged within the Carmel Order in sixteenth-century Spain under the leadership of St. Teresa. The second enclave began when Claire Chennault was faced with the problem of developing a Chinese Air Force in the late 1930's.

Space does not permit even a skeleton consideration of other enclaves. Examples abound however. To name a few: Orde Wingate's Special Night Squad, his Gideon Force which fought in Ethiopia, and his long-range penetration unit known as the Chindits; the Cistercian Order which began as an enclave within the Benedictine Order, and the Trappist Order which emerged from the Cistercian Order, etc. Our examples have been limited to military groups and to the cenobitic structures of the Catholic Church, not only because these are normative organizations with strong centralized authorities but also because of availability of data. The reader should bear in mind, however, that nonconforming enclaves and their containment through protest ab-

Table 1   History of Two Nonconforming Enclaves

	Discalced Carmelites, 1562–1593	Flying Tigers, 1941–1960
Organization	Catholic Church	United States Army
Leader	St. Teresa	General C. L. Chennault
Lieutenants	St. John of the Cross	Colonel C. V. Haynes Colonel R. L. Scott
Cause	Greater concern with salvation. Revive asceticism of early Carmelites. Concern with action as well as contemplation, e.g., praying for the souls of others. This was to lead to emphasis on missionary work.	Develop and put into action fighter pilot tactics. Train American pilots in the use of fighter planes. Furnish air support for Chinese land forces and fight delaying action against Japanese.
Symbols	Alpargatas (hemp and rope sandals). Rough material for clothing.	Flying Tiger sharks painted on planes. Cowboy boots instead of regulation military boots.
State of Organization	Carmel Order had its strict Rule modified in 1432. By the sixteenth century, adherence to the modified rule had become lax. Nuns spent time in gossip rather than in prayer. Spanish Church beginning to seethe with reform to meet challenge of Reformation.	Tactics for use of planes not developed at pace commensurate with technological progress. Tendency by military to view planes as auxiliary to infantry and artillery. Lack of preparation to deal with onset of World War II.
Middle hierarchy	Officials of Carmel Order in Spain and Italy.	Generals Bissell and Stilwell.
Top hierarchy	The Pope	President Roosevelt
Intermediary	Philip II of Spain	Madame Chiang Kai-shek
Obstruction techniques	Teresa assigned for three-year period to head of a Carmel convent to halt her activities. Excommunication of nuns who voted for Teresa when her three-year term was concluded. Assigning Calced confessors to Discalced houses. Kidnapping and imprisoning friars loyal to Teresa.	Limiting allocation of supplies and personnel. Detaining Flying Tiger recruits in India, enroute to China, to indoctrinate them against Chennault. Attempting to select Chennault's chief of staff for him.
Stabilizers	Constitution for Discalced providing for a centralized government.	Induction of Flying Tigers into U. S. Army which meant that group would have to adhere to military regulations.
Origin of enclave and rounds of protest absorption	Within convent at Avila, Teresa gained small following. Permission granted to start her own house.	Chennault invited to China by Madame Chiang Kai-shek to develop Chinese Air Force. From 1936–1940, Chennault fought Japanese with whatever pilots and equipment drifted to China. From 1940–1941, American Volunteer Group organized; group commanded by Chennault and paid by Chinese government.
	1. Discalced established as separate province, 1579. Free to establish religious houses. Subject to General of Order of Spain. 2. Established as separate congregation, 1587. Subject to General of entire Carmel order but elected its own Vicar-General. 3. Established by papal bull as separate order, 1593, subject only to Pope. 4. In succeeding centuries Discalced Order engaged in missionary work and spread beyond the boundaries of Spain.	1. AVG transformed into China Air Task Force and inducted into USAAF, July 1942, subject to Bissell as head of parent 10th Air Force. 2. CATF converted into 14th Air Force, March 1943, subject to Stilwell's command as head of China-Burma-India theatre. 3. No further rounds of protest absorption occurred, for General Marshall felt that Chennault should continue under Stilwell's command, but Stilwell was instructed to give Chennault all that he asked for. 4. 14th Air Force deactivated in 1960.

NOTE: For references pertaining to Table 1, see the following:

Discalced Carmelites:
Nigg, Walter, *Warriors of God*, New York: Alfred A. Knopf, 1959.
Peers, E. A., *Handbook to the Life and Times of St. Teresa and St. John of the Cross*, Westminster, Maryland: Newman Press, 1954.
———, *Spirit of Flame*, New York: Morehouse-Gorham, 1945.
St. Teresa, *Life of St. Teresa* (trans. by Rev. John Dalton), New York: P. J. Kennedy & Sons, N.D.
Zimmerman, B., *Carmel in England*, London: Burns & Oates, 1899.

Flying Tigers:
Romanus, C. F. and Sunderland, R., *Stilwell's Mission to China*, Washington, D. C.: Office of the Chief of Military History, Dept. of the Army, 1953.
Scott, R. L., *God is my Co-Pilot*, New York: Ballantine, 1959.
———, *Flying Tiger: Chennault of China*, New York: Doubleday, 1959.
Wedemeyer, A. C., *Wedemeyer Reports*, New York: Henry Holt, 1958.

sorption can occur in other normative organizations. An example is the Fund for the Republic which has been described as "Paul Hoffman's severance pay." In his unofficial biography of the Ford Foundation, Dwight MacDonald writes: [23]

. . . the Foundation's trustees decided that (the program) should be implemented by a new agency, which finally emerged in December, 1952 as the Fund for the Republic. . . . Hoffman originally supported Hutchins in proposing it, and its establishment coincided with Hoffman's extrusion from the Foundation. . . . The Fund's elephantine gestation is perhaps explained by the dilemma of the Ford trustees . . . who found themselves being chivied by Hoffman and Hutchins into doing something that was as "controversial" as it was logical on the basis of the program they themselves had adopted.

---

[23] Dwight MacDonald [359], p. 71.

9

SOURCES OF POWER OF LOWER PARTICIPANTS IN COMPLEX ORGANIZATIONS

David Mechanic

Introduction [1]

It is not unusual for lower participants [2] in complex organizations to assume and wield considerable power and influence not associated with their formally defined positions within these organizations. In sociological terms they have considerable personal power but no authority. Such personal power is often attained, for example, by executive secretaries and accountants in business firms, by attendants in mental hospitals, and even by inmates in prisons. The personal power achieved by these lower participants does not necessarily result from unique personal characteristics, although these may be relevant, but results rather from particular aspects of their location within their organizations.

Informal Versus Formal Power

Within organizations the distribution of authority (institutionalized power) is closely if not perfectly correlated with the prestige of positions. Those who have argued for the independence of these variables [3]

[1] Paper presented at the Ford Foundation Seminar in the Social Science of Organizations, University of Pittsburgh, June 10–22, 1962.

[2] The term "lower participants" comes from Amitai Etzioni [184], and is used by him to designate persons in positions of lower rank: employees, rank-and-file, members, clients, customers, and inmates. We shall use the term in this paper in a relative sense denoting position vis-à-vis a higher-ranking participant.

[3] Robert Bierstedt [71].

have taken their examples from diverse organizations and do not deal with situations where power is clearly comparable.[4] Thus when Bierstedt argues that Einstein had prestige but no power, and the policeman power but no prestige, it is apparent that he is comparing categories that are not comparable. Generally, persons occupying high-ranking positions within organizations have more authority than those holding low-ranking positions.

One might ask what characterizes high-ranking positions within organizations. What is most evident, perhaps, is that lower participants recognize the right of higher-ranking participants to exercise power, and yield without difficulty to demands they regard as legitimate. Moreover, persons in high-ranking positions tend to have considerable access and control over information and persons both within and outside the organization, and to instrumentalities or resources. Although higher supervisory personnel may be isolated from the task activities of lower participants, they maintain access to them through formally established intermediary positions and exercise control through intermediary participants. There appears, therefore, to be a clear correlation between the prestige of positions within organizations and the extent to which they offer access to information, persons, and instrumentalities.

Since formal organizations tend to structure lines of access and communication, access should be a clue to institutional prestige. Yet access depends on variables other than those controlled by the formal structure of an organization, and this often makes the informal power structure that develops within organizations somewhat incongruent with the formally intended plan. It is these variables that allow work groups to limit production through norms that contravene the goals of the larger organization, that allow hospital attendants to thwart changes in the structure of a hospital, and that allow prison inmates to exercise some control over prison guards. Organizations, in a sense, are continuously at the mercy of their lower participants, and it is this fact that makes organizational power structure especially interesting to the sociologist and social psychologist.

CLARIFICATION OF DEFINITIONS

The purpose of this paper is to present some hypotheses explaining why lower participants in organizations can often assume and wield considerable power which is not associated with their positions as

---

[4] Robert A. Dahl [147].

formally defined within these organizations. For the purposes of this analysis the concepts "influence," "power," and "control" will be used synonymously. Moreover, we shall not be concerned with type of power, that is, whether the power is based on reward, punishment, identification, power to veto, or whatever.[5] Power will be defined as *any force that results in behavior that would not have occurred if the force had not been present.* We have defined power as a force rather than a relationship because it appears that much of what we mean by power is encompassed by the normative framework of an organization, and thus any analysis of power must take into consideration the power of norms as well as persons.

I shall also argue, following Thibaut and Kelley,[6] that power is closely related to dependence. To the extent that a person is dependent on another, he is potentially subject to the other person's power. Within organizations one makes others dependent upon him by controlling access to information, persons, and instrumentalities, which I shall define as follows:

1. *Information* includes knowledge of the organization, knowledge about persons, knowledge of the norms, procedures, techniques, and so forth.

2. *Persons* include anyone within the organization or anyone outside the organization upon whom the organization is in some way dependent.

3. *Instrumentalities* include any aspect of the physical plant of the organization or its resources (equipment, machines, money, and so on).

Power is a function not only of the extent to which a person controls information, persons, and instrumentalities but also of the importance of the various attributes he controls.[7]

Finally, following Dahl,[8] we shall agree that comparisons of power among persons should, as far as possible, utilize comparable units. Thus we shall strive for clarification by attempting to oversimplify organizational processes; the goal is to set up a number of hypothet-

---

[5] One might observe, for example, that the power of lower participants is based primarily on the ability to "veto" or punish. For a discussion of bases of power, see John R. P. French, Jr., and Bertram Raven [100b].

[6] John Thibaut and Harold H. Kelley [541]. For a similar emphasis on dependence, see Richard M. Emerson [180].

[7] Although this chapter will not attempt to explain how access may be measured, I feel confident that the hypotheses concerned with access are clearly testable.

[8] [147].

ical statements of the relationship between variables taken two at a time, "all other factors being assumed to remain constant."

A CLASSIC EXAMPLE

Like many other aspects of organizational theory, one can find a classic statement of our problem in Weber's discussion of the political bureaucracy. Weber indicated the extent to which bureaucrats may have considerable power over political incumbents, as a result, in part, of their permanence within the political bureaucracy, as contrasted to public officials, who are replaced rather frequently.[9] Weber noted how the low-ranking bureaucrat becomes familiar with the organization—its rules and operations, the work flow, and so on, which gives him considerable power over the new political incumbent, who might have higher rank but is not as familiar with the organization. While Weber does not directly state the point, his analysis suggests that bureaucratic permanence has some relationship to increased access to persons, information, and instrumentalities. To state the hypothesis suggested somewhat more formally:

H1: Other factors remaining constant, organizational power is related to access to persons, information, and instrumentalities.

H2: Other factors remaining constant, as a participant's length of time in an organization increases, he has increased access to persons, information, and instrumentalities.

While these hypotheses are obvious, they do suggest that a careful scrutiny of the organizational literature, especially that dealing with the power or counterpower of lower participants, might lead to further formalized statements, some considerably less obvious than the ones stated. This kind of hypothesis formation is treated later in the paper, but at this point I would like to place the discussion of power within a larger theoretical context and discuss the relevance of role theory to the study of power processes.

Implications of Role Theory for the Study of Power

There are many points of departure for the study of power processes within organizations. An investigator might view influence in terms of its sources and strategies; he might undertake a study of the flow of influence; he might concentrate on the structure of organizations, seeing to what extent regularities in behavior might be explained through

---

[9] See [393b].

the study of norms, roles, and traditions; and, finally, more psychologically oriented investigators might concentrate on the recipients of influence and the factors affecting susceptibility to influence attempts. Each of these points of departure leads to different theoretical emphases. For our purposes the most important emphasis is that presented by role theorists.

Role theorists approach the question of influence and power in terms of the behavioral regularities which result from established identities within specific social contexts like families, hospitals, and business firms. The underlying premise of most role theorists is that a large proportion of all behavior is brought about through socialization within specific organizations, and much behavior is routine and established through learning the traditional modes of adaptation in dealing with specific tasks. Thus the positions persons occupy in an organization account for much of their behavior. Norms and roles serve as mediating forces in influence processes.

While role theorists have argued much about vocabulary, the basic premises underlying their thought have been rather consistent. The argument is essentially that knowledge of one's identity or social position is a powerful index of the expectations such a person is likely to face in various social situations. Since behavior tends to be highly correlated with expectations, prediction of behavior is therefore possible. The approach of role theorists to the study of behavior within organizations is of particular merit in that it provides a consistent set of concepts which is useful analytically in describing recruitment, socialization, interaction, and personality, as well as the formal structure of organizations. Thus the concept of role is one of the few concepts clearly linking social structure, social process, and social character.

Many problems pertaining to role theory have been raised. At times it is not clear whether role is regarded as a real entity, a theoretical construct, or both. Moreover, Gross has raised the issue of role consensus, that is, the extent to which the expectations impinging upon a position are held in common by persons occupying reciprocal positions to the one in question.[10] Merton has attempted to deal with inevitable inconsistencies in expectations of role occupants by introducing the concept of role-set which treats differences in expectations as resulting, in part, from the fact that any position is differently related to a number of reciprocal positions.[11] Furthermore, Goffman has criticized role

---

[10] Neal Gross, Ward S. Mason, and Alexander W. McEachern [236].
[11] [390].

theory for its failure to deal adequately with commitment to roles [12]—
a factor which Etzioni has found to be related intimately to the kind
of power exercised in organizations.[13] Perhaps these various criticisms
directed at role theory reflect its importance as well as its deficiencies,
and despite the difficulties involved in role analysis, the concept of role
may prove useful in various ways.

Role theory is useful in emphasizing the extent to which influence
and power can be exercised without conflict. This occurs when power
is integrated with a legitimate order, when sentiments are held in
common, and when there are adequate mechanisms for introducing persons into the system and training them to recognize, accept,
and value the legitimacy of control within the organization. By providing the conditions whereby participants within an organization
may internalize the norms, these generalized rules, values, and sentiments serve as substitutes for interpersonal influence and make the
workings of the organization more agreeable and pleasant for all.

It should be clear that lower participants will be more likely to
circumvent higher authority, other factors remaining constant, when
the mandates of those in power, if not the authority itself, are regarded as illegitimate. Thus as Etzioni points out, when lower participants become alienated from the organization, coercive power is likely
to be required if its formal mandates are to be fulfilled.[14]

Moreover, all organizations must maintain control over lower participants. To the extent that lower participants fail to recognize the
legitimacy of power, or believe that sanctions cannot or will not be
exercised when violations occur, the organization loses, to some extent, its ability to control their behavior. Moreover, insofar as higher
participants can create the impression that they can or will exert sanctions above their actual willingness to use such sanctions, control over
lower participants will increase. It is usually to the advantage of an
organization to externalize and impersonalize controls, however, and
if possible to develop positive sentiments toward its rules.

In other words, an effective organization can control its participants
in such a way as to make it hardly perceivable that it exercises the
control that it does. It seeks commitment from lower participants, and
when commitment is obtained, surveillance can be relaxed. On the
other hand, when the power of lower participants in organizations is
considered, it often appears to be clearly divorced from the traditions,
norms, and goals and sentiments of the organization as a whole. Lower

---

[12] [219].   [14] *Ibid.*
[13] Etzioni [184].

participants do not usually achieve control by using the role structure of the organization, but rather by circumventing, sabotaging, and manipulating it.

Sources of Power of Lower Participants

The most effective way for lower participants to achieve power is to obtain, maintain, and control access to persons, information, and instrumentalities. To the extent that this can be accomplished, lower participants make higher-ranking participants dependent upon them. Thus dependence together with the manipulation of the dependency relationship is the key to the power of lower participants.

A number of examples can be cited which illustrate the preceding point. Scheff, for example, reports on the failure of a state mental hospital to bring about intended reform because of the opposition of hospital attendants.[15] He noted that the power of hospital attendants was largely a result of the dependence of ward physicians on attendants. This dependence resulted from the physician's short tenure, his lack of interest in administration, and the large amount of administrative responsibility he had to assume. An implicit trading agreement developed between physicians and attendants, whereby attendants would take on some of the responsibilities and obligations of the ward physician in return for increased power in decision-making processes concerning patients. Failure of the ward physician to honor his part of the agreement resulted in information being withheld, disobedience, lack of cooperation, and unwillingness of the attendants to serve as a barrier between the physician and a ward full of patients demanding attention and recognition. When the attendant withheld cooperation, the physician had difficulty in making a graceful entrance and departure from the ward, in handling necessary paper work (officially his responsibility), and in obtaining information needed to deal adequately with daily treatment and behavior problems. When attendants opposed change, they could wield influence by refusing to assume responsibilities officially assigned to the physician.

Similarly, Sykes describes the dependence of prison guards on inmates and the power obtained by inmates over guards.[16] He suggests that although guards could report inmates for disobedience, frequent reports would give prison officials the impression that the guard was unable to command obedience. The guard, therefore, had some stake

---

[15] Thomas J. Scheff [463].
[16] [533].

in ensuring the good behavior of prisoners without use of formal sanctions against them. The result was a trading agreement whereby the guard allowed violations of certain rules in return for cooperative behavior. A similar situation is found in respect to officers in the Armed Services or foremen in industry. To the extent that they require formal sanctions to bring about cooperation, they are usually perceived by their superiors as less valuable to the organization. For a good leader is expected to command obedience, at least, if not commitment.

Factors Affecting Power

EXPERTISE

Increasing specialization and organizational growth have made the expert or staff person important. The expert maintains power because high-ranking persons in the organization are dependent upon him for his special skills and access to certain kinds of information. One possible reason for lawyers obtaining many high governmental offices is that they are likely to have access to rather specialized but highly important means to organizational goals.[17]

We can state these ideas in hypotheses, as follows:

H3: Other factors remaining constant, to the extent that a low-ranking participant has important expert knowledge not available to high-ranking participants, he is likely to have power over them.

Power stemming from expertise, however, is likely to be limited unless it is difficult to replace the expert. This leads to two further hypotheses:

H4: Other factors remaining constant, a person difficult to replace will have greater power than a person easily replaceable.

H5: Other factors remaining constant, experts will be more difficult to replace than nonexperts.

While persons having expertise are likely to be fairly high-ranking participants in an organization, the same hypotheses that explain the power of lower participants are relevant in explaining the comparative power positions of intermediate- and high-ranking persons.

The application of our hypothesis about expertise is clearly rele-

---

[17] As an example, it appears that 6 members of the cabinet, 30 important sub-cabinet officials, 63 senators, and 230 congressmen are lawyers (*New Yorker*, April 14, 1962, p. 62). Although one can cite many reasons for lawyers holding political posts, an important one appears to be their legal expertise.

vant if we look at certain organizational issues. For example, the merits of medical versus lay hospital administrators are often debated. It should be clear, however, that all other factors remaining unchanged, the medical administrator has clear advantage over the lay administrator. Where lay administrators receive preference, there is an implicit assumption that the lay person is better at administrative duties. This may be empirically valid but is not necessarily so. The special expert knowledge of the medical administrator stems from his ability legitimately to oppose a physician who contests an administrative decision on the basis of medical necessity. Usually hospitals are viewed primarily as universalistic in orientation both by the general public and most of their participants. Thus medical necessity usually takes precedence over management policies, a factor contributing to the poor financial position of most hospitals. The lay administrator is not in a position to contest such claims independently, since he usually lacks the basis for evaluation of the medical problems involved and also lacks official recognition of his competence to make such decisions. If the lay administrator is to evaluate these claims adequately on the basis of professional necessity, he must have a group of medical consultants or a committee of medical men to serve as a buffer between medical staff and the lay administration.

As a result of growing specialization, expertise is increasingly important in organizations. As the complexity of organizational tasks increases, and as organizations grow in size, there is a limit to responsibility that can be efficiently exercised by one person. Delegation of responsibility occurs, experts and specialists are brought in to provide information and research, and the higher participants become dependent upon them. Experts have tremendous potentialities for power by withholding information, providing incorrect information, and so on, and to the extent that experts are dissatisfied, the probability of organizational sabotage increases.

EFFORT AND INTEREST

The extent to which lower participants may exercise power depends in part on their willingness to exert effort in areas where higher-ranking participants are often reluctant to participate. Effort exerted is directly related to the degree of interest one has in an area.

H6: Other factors remaining constant, there is a direct relationship between the amount of effort a person is willing to exert in an area and the power he can command.

For example, secretarial staffs in universities often have power to make decisions about the purchase and allocation of supplies, the allocation of their services, the scheduling of classes, and, at times, the disposition of student complaints. Such control may in some instances lead to sanctions against a professor by polite reluctance to furnish supplies, ignoring his preferences for the scheduling of classes, and giving others preference in the allocation of services. While the power to make such decisions may easily be removed from the jurisdiction of the lower participant, it can only be accomplished at a cost—the willingness to allocate time and effort to the decisions dealing with these matters. To the extent that responsibilities are delegated to lower participants, a certain degree of power is likely to accompany the responsibility. Also, should the lower participant see his perceived rights in jeopardy, he may sabotage the system in various ways.

Let us visualize a hypothetical situation where a department concludes that secretarial services are being allocated on a prejudicial basis as a result of complaints to the chairman of the department by several of the younger faculty. Let us also assume that when the complaint is investigated, it is found to be substantially correct; that is, some of the younger faculty have difficulty obtaining secretarial services because of preferences among the secretarial staff. If in attempting to eliminate discretion by the secretarial staff, the chairman establishes a rule ordering the allocation of services on the basis of the order in which work appears, the rule can easily be made ineffective by complete conformity to it. Deadlines for papers, examinations, and the like will occur, and flexibility in the allocation of services is required if these deadlines are to be met. Thus the need for flexibility can be made to conflict with the rule by a staff usually not untalented in such operations.

When an organization gives discretion to lower participants, it is usually trading the power of discretion for needed flexibility. The cost of constant surveillance is too high, and the effort required too great; it is very often much easier for all concerned to allow the secretary discretion in return for cooperation and not too great an abuse of power.

H7: Other factors remaining constant, the less effort and interest higher-ranking participants are willing to devote to a task, the more likely are lower participants to obtain power relevant to this task.

ATTRACTIVENESS

Another personal attribute associated with the power of low-ranking persons in an organization is attractiveness or what some call "personality." People who are viewed as attractive are more likely to obtain access to persons, and, once such access is gained, they may be more likely to succeed in promoting a cause. But once again dependence is the key to the power of attractiveness, for whether a person is dependent upon another for a service he provides, or for approval or affection, what is most relevant is the relational bond which is highly valued.

H8: Other factors remaining constant, the more attractive a person, the more likely he is to obtain access to persons and control over these persons.

LOCATION AND POSITION

In any organization the person's location in physical space and position in social space are important factors influencing access to persons, information, and instrumentalities.[18] Propinquity affects the opportunities for interaction, as well as one's position within a communication network. Although these are somewhat separate factors, we shall refer to their combined effect as centrality [19] within the organization.

H9: Other factors remaining constant, the more central a person is in an organization, the greater is his access to persons, information, and instrumentalities.

Some low participants may have great centrality within an organization. An executive's or university president's secretary not only has access, but often controls access in making appointments and scheduling events. Although she may have no great formal authority, she may have considerable power.

COALITIONS

It should be clear that the variables we are considering are at different levels of analysis; some of them define attributes of persons, while others define attributes of communication and organization. Power processes within organizations are particularly interesting in that there are many channels of power and ways of achieving it.

[18] There is considerable data showing the powerful effect of propinquity on communication. For summary, see Thibaut and Kelley [541], pp. 39–42.

[19] The concept of centrality is generally used in a more technical sense in the work of Bavelas, Shaw, Gilchrist, and others. For example, Bavelas defines the central region of a structure as the class of all cells with the smallest distance between one cell and any other cell in the structure, with distance measured in link units. Thus the most central position in a pattern is the position closest to all others. See Harold Leavitt [358a].

In complex organizations different occupational groups attend to different functions, each group often maintaining its own power structure within the organization. Thus hospitals have administrators, medical personnel, nursing personnel, attendants, maintenance personnel, laboratory personnel, and so on. Universities, similarly, have teaching personnel, research personnel, administrative personnel, maintenance personnel, and so on. Each of these functional tasks within organizations often becomes the sphere of a particular group that controls activities relating to the task. While these tasks usually are coordinated at the highest levels of the organization, they often are not coordinated at intermediate and lower levels. It is not unusual, however, for coalitions to form among lower participants in these multiple structures. A secretary may know the man who manages the supply of stores, or the person assigning parking stickers. Such acquaintances may give her the ability to handle informally certain needs that would be more time-consuming and difficult to handle formally. Her ability to provide services informally makes higher-ranking participants in some degree dependent upon her, thereby giving her power, which increases her ability to bargain on issues important to her.

RULES

In organizations with complex power structures lower participants can use their knowledge of the norms of the organization to thwart attempted change. In discussing the various functions of bureaucratic rules, Gouldner maintains that such rules serve as excellent substitutes for surveillance, since surveillance in addition to being expensive in time and effort arouses considerable hostility and antagonism.[20] Moreover, he argues, rules are a functional equivalent for direct, personally given orders, since they specify the obligations of workers to do things in specific ways. Standardized rules, in addition, allow simple screening of violations, facilitate remote control, and to some extent legitimize punishment when the rule is violated. The worker who violates a bureaucratic rule has little recourse to the excuse that he did not know what was expected, as he might claim for a direct order. Finally, Gouldner argues that rules are "the 'chips' to which the company staked the supervisors and which they could use to play the game";[21] that is, rules established a punishment which could be withheld, and this facilitated the supervisors' bargaining power with lower participants.

---

[20] [232].
[21] [232], p. 173.

While Gouldner emphasizes the functional characteristics of rules within an organization, it should be clear that full compliance with the rules at all times will probably be dysfunctional for the organization. Complete and apathetic compliance may do everything but facilitate achievement of organizational goals. Lower participants who are familiar with an organization and its rules can often find rules to support their contention that they not do what they have been asked to do, and rules are also often a rationalization for inaction on their part. The following of rules becomes especially complex when associations and unions become involved, for there are then two sets of rules to which the participant can appeal.

What is suggested is that rules may be chips for everyone concerned in the game. Rules become the "chips" through which the bargaining process is maintained. Scheff, as noted earlier, observed that attendants in mental hospitals often took on responsibilities assigned legally to the ward physician, and when attendants refused to share these responsibilities the physician's position became extremely difficult.[22]

"The ward physician is legally responsible for the care and treatment of each ward patient. This responsibility requires attention to a host of details. Medicine, seclusion, sedation and transfer orders, for example, require the doctor's signature. Tranquilizers are particularly troublesome in this regard since they require frequent adjustment of dosage in order to get the desired effects. The physician's order is required to each change in dosage. With 150 patients under his care on tranquilizers, and several changes of dosages a week desirable, the physician could spend a major portion of his ward time in dealing with this single detail.

"Given the time-consuming formal chores of the physician, and his many other duties, he usually worked out an arrangement with the ward personnel, particularly the charge (supervisory attendant), to handle these duties. On several wards, the charge called specific problems to the doctor's attention, and the two of them, in effect, would have a consultation. The charge actually made most of the decisions concerning dosage change in the back wards. Since the doctor delegated portions of his formal responsibilities to the charge, he was dependent on her good will toward him. If she withheld her cooperation, the physician had absolutely no recourse but to do all the work himself." [23]

In a sense such delegation of responsibility involves a consideration of reward and cost, whereby the decision to be made involves a question of what is more valuable—to retain control over an area, or to delegate one's work to lower participants.

---

[22] Quoted with permission from Scheff [463].
[23] *Ibid.*, p. 97.

There are occasions, of course, when rules are regarded as illegitimate by lower participants, and they may disregard them. Gouldner observed that in the mine men felt they could resist authority in a situation involving danger to themselves.[24] They did not feel that they could legitimately be ordered to do anything that would endanger their lives. It is probably significant that in extremely dangerous situations organizations are more likely to rely on commitment to work than on authority. Even within nonvoluntary groups dangerous tasks are regarded usually as requiring task commitment, and it is likely that commitment is a much more powerful organizational force than coercive authority.

Summary

The preceding remarks are general ones, and they are assumed to be in part true of all types of organizations. But power relationships in organizations are likely to be molded by the type of organization being considered, the nature of organizational goals, the ideology of organizational decision making, the kind of commitment participants have to the organization, the formal structure of the organization, and so on. In short, we have attempted to discuss power processes within organizations in a manner somewhat divorced from other major organizational processes. We have emphasized variables affecting control of access to persons, information, and facilities within organizations. Normative definitions, perception of legitimacy, exchange, and coalitions have all been viewed in relation to power processes. Moreover, we have dealt with some attributes of persons related to power: commitment, effort, interest, willingness to use power, skills, attractiveness, and so on. And we have discussed some other variables: time, centrality, complexity of power structure, and replaceability of persons. It appears that these variables help to account in part for power exercised by lower participants in organizations.

---

[24] Gouldner [232].

10

ROLES, GOALS, AND VALUE STRUCTURES IN ORGANIZATIONS

Bruce J. Biddle

Introduction [1]

Many terms now used in social psychology may be said to suffer from connotative bloating. Words are used in vague and amorphous ways, sometimes in "thoughtful" articles where they are discussed in isolation from related concepts, sometimes in empirical research where the operations used are unrelated or opposed to those used elsewhere. As a result, such potentially useful terms as *function, action, attitude, group,* and *culture* have lost nearly all denotative significance and connote merely a range of interest areas or general set of concerns. But for proliferation of meanings, logical circularity, outright disparate usage, and sheer muddle, *role* and *goal* lead all the rest!

It is not that these terms should be obliterated. On the contrary, they suggest interest areas necessary for the study of organizations. Indeed, we cannot do without them. It is necessary, however, that we achieve a common usage for these terms. If role refers to behavior, for instance, it should not simultaneously be used for cognitive structure or official prescription. If goal is an element of the life space, it should not also be used for a description of institutional purpose or group intention.

[1] This paper was prepared in connection with a contract from the Group Psychology Branch, Office of Naval Research. In part the conceptual structure was developed while the author was conducting research supported by the Cooperative Research Program of the Office of Education, Department of Health, Education, and Welfare.

It shall be my thesis that these terms have been used as elements in three distinct systems of concepts for analyzing behavior, and that confusion is generated in contemporary research through refusal to recognize the unique characteristics of each system. I will defend my viewpoint with a general discussion of the three systems, with parallel definitions of several terms in the three systems, and with application of the distinctions made to familiar examples of organizations.

Many of the distinctions made in this chapter were developed originally for role theory.[2] In fact, I shall refer to the broad context of this chapter as "role theory," although recognizing that I am attempting to summarize materials from several disciplines with this title.

Three Conceptual Systems

A major assumption of this chapter is that three separate conceptual systems are needed when dealing with behavior in the organization. It shall be shown that such terms as "role" or "goal" may be defined within each of these three alternate conceptual systems, but that implications of the definitions differ markedly between the systems.

THE OVERT SYSTEM

It may be assumed that human beings emit a number of characteristics or qualities which constitute the raw data of the social sciences. These include behaviors and unchanging features such as sex or age. For simplicity, I shall consider only behaviors. Let us agree on what constitutes a behavior, however.

As used here, *behaviors* are overt events which are emitted by acting human beings and which tend to change rapidly over time. Behaviors are transitory, patterned, voluntary, directed, purposeful, molar, and meaningful. Behaviors may be viewed in many ways. One way splits the socially meaningful unit—behavior—into smaller units—actones —which describe the individual movements of muscles and organs. Another way splits behavior into its socially meaningful components; for instance, action, manner, social target (if any), implied end state of action, and so on.

Regardless of how we choose to look at them, behaviors differ from one another in terms of content, and we must make use of content to describe behavior. The term "aggression," for instance, is an abstrac-

---

[2] See Biddle [67].

tion which maps only one quality of multifaceted behaviors and should not be confused with the raw behavioral events which are mapped.

At the lowest level of abstraction, it is convenient to classify human behaviors in terms of content dimensions or *frameworks*.[3] In general, each framework is conceptually independent of other frameworks. Thus a "vocal" behavior can be described in terms of "loudness," "timbre," "pitch," and so on. Each framework consists of two or more mapping points (which may or may not be ordered) which are exclusive alternates for displaying behavior.[4] Any given behavioral event is mappable into only a small number of frameworks. For instance, a "vocal" behavior cannot be rated for "albedo" or "saltiness." Finally, it is possible to consider more than one type of mapping for a set of behaviors. As will be seen, a single behavior can be mapped only simply, but a set of behaviors can be mapped in several fashions.

However complex may be the mapping process, the meaning of any human behavior at the overt level is given by its mappings into a finite number of frameworks, and the frameworks chosen represent a shared system of concepts common in the culture of the mappers. In general, overt concepts involve no assumptions about what is going on "inside" the actor, nor are they dependent upon characteristics of the organization as a supra-individual entity. Overt mappings are direct, objective, at a low level of abstraction, and require a minimum of observation time.

To summarize: Concepts of the overt system consist of direct mappings of behavioral events into a finite set of frameworks. The type of overt concept is specified by the choice of framework and mapping rule. In general, overt concepts imply nothing other than immediately evident qualities emitted by an actor.

THE COGNITIVE SYSTEM

In contrast with concepts of the overt system, some concepts describing behaviors apply to phenomena which we presume are taking place in the minds of actors and which serve to mediate between stimulus events and output behavior for the individual. A social observer might conclude, for instance, that behaviors which were overtly "aggressive" were covertly "motivated by hostility." Such terms as *motive, norm, value, goal, expectation, cognitive dissonance, force,* and the like, refer to hypothetical processes which may be reflected in a number of differing behavior types depending upon the situation.

---

[3] The choice of the term "framework" is made to connote frame of reference.
[4] The mapping of behaviors into framework points is always one-to-one.

Cognitive concepts are designed to account for patterns of similar behavior emitted by a single person and involve a variety of mentalistic connotations.

Operations for cognitive concepts are more complex than those for overt concepts. As a rule, cognitive concepts are operationalized in three different ways: (1) *By assumption*—the individual is assumed to experience a cognitive phenomenon because of some stimulus condition impinging upon him. (2) *By report*—respondents are often asked to report their cognitive experiences by answering interview questions and the like. (3) *By result*—actors who choose certain behavioral alternatives are presumed to behave as a result of cognitive factors. It is suggested that a fourth method of operationalization— the finding of neuronic analogues for cognitive concepts—is not yet possible. Until it is, cognitive concepts are judged to be most adequate when they predict both behavioral outcomes and phenomenal experiences.

THE OFFICIAL SYSTEM

Finally, some concepts apply to the description of a codified consensus about the organization. Such terms as *foreman, job description, the law, table of organization,* and the like, have reference to a set of specifications and rules for governing human conduct in the organization. The official system is codified, that is, written down (in literate societies), and exists apart from and independent of the behaviors or cognitions of the individual actor. Modal behavior in the organization or modal cognitions of actors may or may not be at variance with the official system.

The complexity of organizations in Western society is facilitated by a written official system. But an official system can also exist in the ritualized regulations of a preliterate society. In fact, one of the major reasons for ritual is the re-establishment of an official system analogue in the consensual cognitive structure of ritual participants in a society where written regulations are unknown.

Concepts Which Cut Across Systems

Although there are many concepts which are unique to the three systems discussed in this chapter, several concepts including role and goal tend to cut across the systems. These latter are discussed in the following.

IDENTIFICATION OF THE PERSON

Organizations are characterized by a division of labor. That is, sets of persons may be identified who perform differently from others and who are treated in a unique fashion by others. Moreover, such sets of persons tend to be designated, to be the target of expectations or norms, and to be codified as a "slot" in the official system. To a certain extent, persons who are members of such a set may be replaced by other persons of similar training and aptitude. Such functionally differentiated sets are commonly termed "positions," [5] and the positional concept will now be defined in terms of each system.

(*Overt*) *Position.* This is a set of persons who exhibit similar behaviors or who are treated similarly by others. The sociologically sophisticated reader may be surprised to discover that a position is basically a "set of persons" and not a "location in a social system." The definition given above follows from the low level of abstraction to which the overt system is confined. It should be pointed out, however, that in proto-organizations positions may be observed in just the sense implied by the foregoing definition without either recognition of positions by the actors or codification of the relationship. This suggests that the overt system may occasionally exist without either its cognitive or official counterparts.

(*Cognitive*) *Position.* This is a cognitively identified set of persons for whom a cluster of unique cognitions are maintained either by themselves or others.

It should be noted that cognitive positions are restricted in comparison with their overt counterparts. First of all, cognitive positions are identified in the life space of the person. Usually this identification takes the form of a *designation* or name given to position members; for instance, foreman, president, policeman, or teacher. In a few instances a position may be identified in terms of some shared characteristic; for instance, "all persons having batlike ears," although designations are a more popular method of identification. Secondly, cognitive positions are associated with a cluster of unique cognitions held for the position. We shall return to cognitions which may be held for a position in the next section.

(*Official*) *Position.* This is a designation (for persons) associated with defined tasks relating to other designations. In the official system the persons who may constitute a position are ignored in favor of the designation and tasks with which they are associated.

---

[5] Anthropologists have commonly used the term "status" to refer to a position. Hammond [531a] has suggested that status "has two additional connotations— statistically that of magnitude on a single dimension and socially that of respect." For instance, Jaques [293] used the term "status" to mean "the value attaching to a role or stratum of roles." Because of these needless connotations, the more neutral term, position, is to be preferred.

It should be clear that official, overt, and cognitive positions may not coincide. Indeed, in the average organization only a skeletal framework of official positions is laid out. Informal, overt, positional relationships appear; although the autistic individual may deal with persons in terms of a unique set of positional designations he, alone, maintains. Yet, throughout role theory, the distinction between these three concepts is ignored in favor of a single term, "position." Why is such a sloppy usage common?

There are two reasons—convenience and ignorance. In many cases one is either interested solely in positions of the official system or it may be assumed that official positions are represented in overt and cognitive systems. It is also true, however, that we know little about positional relationships among the three systems. To what extent, for instance, are nonofficial, overt positions represented in the cognitive systems of actors? To my knowledge this problem has not been studied. For the rest of this chapter, however, it is assumed that the term "position" refers to a designated set of persons represented equally in the official, overt, and cognitive systems.[6]

CONCEPTS OF STANDARD

The simple mapping of an individual human behavior into an overt framework may be called a *trace*. If we choose to map a number of behaviors into a single, overt framework, a trace distribution is generated. If the behaviors chosen are restricted to a single acting population and context, such a trace distribution is referred to as a *behavioral standard*.

Behavioral standard. This describes a distribution of behavior traces for a given overt framework, actor, and context. As defined here, the behavioral standard is a component of the overt system; or, in other terms, the standard is an objective assessment of behavioral events. It is, of course, true that selection of a framework for rating behavior is arbitrary, but each framework selected is an instrument with which one can assemble slices (standards) which are objective representations of behavioral events. It should also be observed that a behavioral standard may be applied to a single actor or to the behaviors emitted by an acting position. Finally, as used here, the concept of context implies physical location, social situation, time, and/or other specifications of the situation.

---

[6] Additional discussions of the concept of position may be found in Hughes [287], Benoit-Smullyan [60], Neiman and Hughes [415], Argyle [20], Gross, Mason, and McEachern [236], and Biddle [67].

Let us turn now to the cognitive analogue of a behavioral standard. It has been pointed out by many authors that human beings can hold a variety of orientations to the social events about them.[7] Role theory has dealt mainly with cognitions of two types of orientation applying to behavior: beliefs and values. Since both types of orientation are germane to the study of the organization, I shall give a much abbreviated discussion of two cognitive analogues to the behavioral standard—the *expectation* and the *norm*.

Expectation. This is a cognition consisting of a belief (or subjective probability distribution) held by a person which maps behavior traces for a cognitively held framework, actor, and context.

Norm. This is a cognition consisting of a value (or approval distribution) held by a person which maps behavior traces for a cognitively held framework, actor, and context.

The definitions of norm and expectation are deceptively simple.[8] It should be noted that both have the forms of distributions, since belief or value may be defined for each point of a behavioral framework. We may conveniently represent a typical expectation as in Fig. 1. In this figure, the abcissa represents a framework (in this case, "loudness"), whereas the left-hand ordinate measures subjective probability. The expectation given is for loudness of a certain class of behaviors exhibited by an acting position ("mothers") in a context and directed towards another target position ("preschool children") The dotted line in Fig. 1 represents the objective behavioral standard after which the expectation is modeled and should be read against the right-hand ordinate.

Figure 2 presents a comparable norm dealing with the same subject material. In contrast with subjective probability represented in Fig. 1, it may be seen that approval is conceived as a two-signed orientation running from negative to positive values. The distinction in sign of approval has given rise to the popular terminologies, *positive norm* and *negative norm*, referring to the regions on the framework corresponding to maximum approval and disapproval. It will be noted that there are two regions of disapproval suggested in Fig. 2.

---

[7] The concept of orientation is laid out in Parsons and Shils [430].

[8] Note that in neither definition is the concept of mapping adequately spelled out, since mapping rules for cognitive concepts should be based upon perceptual theory. There is reason to believe, for instance, that expectations are not "assembled" from "cognitive traces" but are wholistic units which are defended against contradicting information (Festinger [190]).

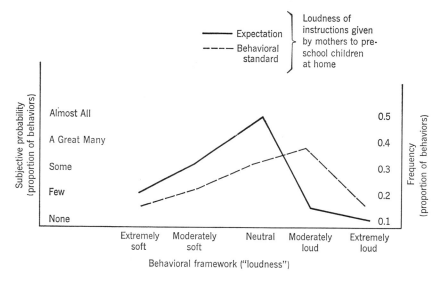

FIGURE 1   A typical expectation.

Implicit in the definitions of norm and expectation is the notion that both may be held by a single subject person. Expectations or norms may be said to be shared among subjects if and only if the cognitions held by all are minimally similar. It should also be noted that expectations and norms are conceptually independent. Both types of cognitions have been studied for many years, but only recently have they been studied jointly. It seems reasonable to postulate for approved positions that there would be a tendency for positive norms and expectations to coincide. A much more complex relationship would

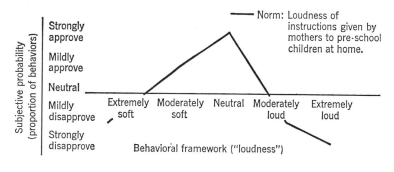

FIGURE 2   A comparable norm.

be predicted for such a disapproved position as, let us say, Nazi prison guards.

It is not assumed here that value and belief orientations are the only ones that might be treated fruitfully in role theory. Indeed, affective response, power, legitimacy, and numerous other orientations could be dealt with similarly and might account for some types of social behavior. However:

1. Value and belief are the only two orientations that have received extensive coverage in role literature to date.

2. The dominance of these two orientations probably reflects the "grand theories" of sociology which stress that consensus of value and belief are necessary for social stability.

3. The more esoteric the orientation, the less predictive utility will it have.

4. Unfortunately, many authors writing in the role field do not even recognize the distinction between expectations and norms. As we shall see, this distinction is crucial for understanding certain processes in the organization.

As has been pointed out by many theorists, human beings also form cognitions about the cognitions of others. That is, persons hold ideas about what others are thinking; moreover, these ideas are often as determinative of their behavior as are their own preferences or needs.

It is convenient to make a distinction in role theory between *own* and *attributed* cognitions. Up to this point I have treated own cognitions exclusively; norms and expectations held by the person which map behaviors of others. The own norm or expectation involves only the *subject person* who holds a cognition and the *object actor* for whose behavior the cognition is held. The attributed cognition, in contrast, involves three persons. There is first of all the *subject person* who holds the cognition. Then there is the other, or *sentient object,* to whom the norm or expectation is attributed. Finally, there is the *object actor* whose behavior is (once again) under discussion.

Examples are in order. We are interviewing a parent about the role of a public school teacher. The parent says, "I don't like teachers to smoke [own norm], but I realize that many teachers do smoke today [own expectation]. On the other hand, I feel that school officials neither want teachers to smoke [attributed norm] nor do they think teachers actually do smoke [attributed expectation]." In this example the person holding cognitions was the parent, the sentient object to whom cognitions were attributed was a position, "school officials," and the actor whose behaviors were under discussion was the position, "teachers."

It should be clear from the above examples that no assumption is made here about correspondence between own and attributed cognitions. Nor is it assumed that cognitions attributed to others are necessarily an accurate representation of what those others are thinking. Nor, finally, is it assumed that either own or attributed cognitions are necessarily a veridical mapping of the comparable behavioral standard. As will be seen in the following, each of these conditions suggests a distinct type of organization model with differential behavioral effects.[9]

Turning, finally, to the official system, it may be observed that most statements made in the official system about behavior are prescriptive in their orientation, which contrasts with the existential orientation of the overt system or the value and belief orientations of the cognitive system. For example, it may be specified that "minimum production will exceed 20 widgets per day," and so forth. We shall refer to such prescriptive statements as *tasks*.

Task. This is an official prescription which maps behavior traces for an officially held framework, actor, and context. It is instructive to compare the distributional form of a typical task with those of behavioral standard, expectation, and norm. Simple tasks may be single-valued as when a single behavioral alternative is specified. A more complex form of prescription specifies minimum or maximum standards, and a still more complex form lays out a range of acceptable behaviors or even a mean and variance. As a general rule, however, tasks have a simpler form than the other concepts of standard.

To review briefly: A behavioral standard is a distribution of behavior traces, an expectation is a subjective probability distribution, a norm is a value distribution, and a task is a prescriptive distribution. Each concept is limited in application to a single framework, actor, and context. It is not assumed that any of these concepts necessarily correspond with any of the others in a functioning organization; indeed, cases where they do not correspond will be taken up presently. Each concept is a unit, but not the only unit, of a conceptually distinct system of analysis.

---

[9] The most sophisticated discussion of norms available in the literature is presented by Jackson [292], while Gross, Mason, and McEachern [236] present an approach to role theory based upon norms. Sarbin [459] presents an approach based upon expectations. Biddle, Rosencranz, and Rankin [69] have studied norms and expectations in interaction.

CONCEPTS OF ROLE

The term "role" has been used in each of the three systems of analysis discussed herein.[10] Wherever used, it has appeared as a summing term—role as a collection of behaviors, or expectations, or tasks, or something. As the units and methods of summation are distinct in the three systems, three separate summing terms will be used in this paper.

A collection of behaviors for a single actor is termed a *performance*. As used here, a performance is roughly equivalent to the more common term, "role behavior," except that it includes both shared and idiosyncratic types of behavior. However, the concept of a collection of behaviors is not operational in itself. We may use the earlier definition of behavioral standard to provide a usable and formal definition of performance.

Performance. This is the set of behavioral standards applying to a given actor and context over the set of useful frameworks. As defined, a performance is limited to involve only "useful" content frameworks and thus excludes the measurement of performance aspects in which the observer does not happen to be interested. This suggests that while behavioral standards may be objective, the content of a performance depends upon the subjective judgment of an observer. For instance, it is possible to conceptualize a performance in terms of an *a priori* theory only to discover at a later date that performances measured using frameworks of that theory are useless for making certain kinds of predictions.[11] Under ideal conditions a performance would be measured with a maximum number of frameworks, and those frameworks which represented unfruitful dimensions of behavior would be discarded at a later date.

The concept of *role*, in the cognitive system, represents a different form of summation.

Role. This is a set of cognitions maintained for an actor in a context by a subject person. It should be pointed out that: (1) Involved

---

[10] "Role" has been used as an overt system term by Newcomb [416] and Jaques [293], as a cognitive system term by Coutu [139], Videbeck and Bates [571], and as an official component by Getzels and Guba [214]. It has also been used in numerous other ways (see Biddle [67]).

[11] Something like this is happening to psychoanalytic theory today. Ideally the way to approach a performance would be with the prescriptions of participant observation—an unbiased mind containing a large number of frameworks using one that might assemble a very broad picture of behavior. In actual practice, many participant observers are restricted to frameworks suggested by their training. The best objective technique yet available for studying a performance seems to be that of Barker and Wright [43].

in a role are both norms and expectations and both own and attributed cognitions. (2) A role can be held by a single person. It can also be shared, but only if both the cognitively held frameworks and cognitive distributions are shared. (3) Role, like performance, is limited to an actor and a context. It is possible, however, for persons to maintain roles for an acting person or position which are pan-contextual. For instance, Negroes may be mapped as "always" dirty, stupid, musical, etc. This gives rise to a secondary concept, the *total role,* which is not useful in the overt system.

A role is not strictly comparable to a performance in terms of content coverage. A role is limited to frameworks which are salient for the subject person, whereas a performance is measured by frameworks which are useful for displaying the varieties of behavior exhibited by an actor. This suggests that many useful frameworks for any given performance must not be represented in roles held by even a trained observer. In terms of content, a role is simpler than a performance.

The equivalent concept in the official system, *job,* is simpler than either role or performance. This is caused by the limited and codified nature of the official system. Usually an official system presents only a small number of tasks which are applicable to a given actor and context.

Job. This is the set of tasks maintained for an actor in a context. One may also, without creating confusion, speak of *total jobs* which summarize tasks for an actor across all contexts dealt with in the overt system.

Summarizing briefly: A performance consists of a set of behavioral standards, a role of a set of cognitions maintained by a subject person, and a job of a set of tasks maintained in an official system. All three terms are limited to an actor (who may be either a person or a position). All three terms are normally limited to a context, although role and job may be expanded so as to include all contexts. Ordinarily, a role will involve fewer content frameworks than a performance, and a job involves still fewer frameworks. A role, however, involves several different types of cognitive elements. Once again, no implication is suggested regarding performance-role-job equivalence.

CONCEPTS OF GOAL

Goal concepts are not closely related to the focus of role theory. In fact, with one exception [12] role concepts can be discussed without

---

[12] Goals are occasionally (and sloppily) used to define the context of a norm or role. For example, one might encounter the following definition: "The role

recourse to goals. However, much of organizational behavior may be said to be goal oriented, and once again the goal concept has been used as an element of all three systems of analysis.[13]

To the extent one assumes that behaviors are goal directed, behaviors may be seen as tending towards *end states*. Confining our discussion, once again, to behavioral conditions, end states may be mapped as single or contiguous points of overt frameworks. This suggests that a second, nonsimple mapping of behavior into overt frameworks is possible.[14]

End trace. This is the point (or contiguous region) of an overt framework towards which the behavior of an actor in context appears to tend. As used here an end trace does not (necessarily) involve motivation or even recognition by the actor that he is moving towards the specified state-of-affairs. Involved only is the assumption that behaviors change as a function of time. Often, for instance, behaviors appear to be cyclical in form. The individual eats on a regular and periodic basis, and the observer may conclude that "satiety" is an end trace towards which the periodic process of "eating" tends. It is also possible to use the concept of end trace hypothetically, as when one observes that meetings are never "completely organized." End traces may be applied, of course, to the behaviors of a single person actor or to an acting position. An end trace may or may not be mappable into a framework where the behaviors of an actor generate a behavioral standard. However, it should be emphasized that an end trace is usually thought of as a single-point map, and the behaviors of an actor (usually) receive only a single end trace mapping for any single context.

The concept of *goal*, as a cognitive element, involves connotations beyond those of end trace. We may assume that persons are capable of cognitively mapping end traces either for their own or for other behavior. But to declare that an end trace is a goal implies that there exists an energy system leading the person to behave in ways which

---

of the teacher is to instill knowledge in the mind of the pupil." Such a statement emphasizes context but does not give behavioral information.

[13] Tolman [549], Allport [15], Bindra [72], and Young [614] have emphasized the overt characteristics of goals. Lewin and his students have used goal for a variety of purposes including both cognitive and official (see, for instance, Zander [617]). March and Simon [367] use goals in both the cognitive and official systems.

[14] Once again, a careful spelling out of end trace mapping is avoided in this paper. As a rule, trace mapping is immediate, while end trace mapping involves the detection of behavioral change. End trace mappings are many-to-one between behaviors and end traces.

will move towards end trace attainment. Several sources for goal energy have been suggested, focusing upon both value and affect. For purposes of this chapter, it shall be assumed that goals are valued, which leads to a definition.

Goal. This is a cognition consisting of a value held by a person which maps an end trace for the behavior of an actor in a context. Goals are, in this sense, directly analogous to norms. Goals may be held, for instance, either for oneself or for another actor (person or position). They may be idiosyncratic to the individual or they may be shared among several persons. The end trace which is mapped may or may not correspond to the overt end trace exhibited by the actor. In fact, if an actor does not conform to a norm held by a subject person, under the definition that norm becomes a type of goal. It should be emphasized, however, that goals are usually treated as single points or compact regions within a framework, whereas norms are usually assumed to exhibit a range of approved points. It is also worthwhile noting that an expectational analogue (or subjective probability mapping of an end trace) exists as a cognitive component and has received a somewhat confused treatment in the level of aspiration literature. Finally, persons are also capable of attributing goals to others.

The official equivalent of an end trace—the purpose—is, like task, prescriptive in orientation. But prescriptions do not provide for any distinction between behavioral end states and behaviors now emitted. A task may be applied equally to work in progress or to production aspired to. Of what utility is an additional term?

It is characteristic of official systems that a logical ordering of tasks is given. That is, little tasks are set up in order to facilitate bigger tasks which, in turn, are justified in terms of supertasks. This logical ordering of tasks may or may not characterize a given person's cognitive system and is not often studied in the overt system (except by functional integrationists). However, ordering is an obvious characteristic of the official system, and it is useful to specify those tasks, or purposes, which specify the ultimate aims of the organization.

Purpose. This is a task for the organization which serves to justify other tasks and which is itself unjustified within the official system. It is useful to review the relationships between end trace, goal, and purpose. An end trace maps a behavioral condition towards which an actor appears to tend, a goal is a valued end trace, a purpose is a task for the organization in terms of which other tasks are justified. End traces have as their referent the existent behavioral system. Goals are justified in terms of the idiosyncratic value structure of the person holding them. Purposes are logically primitive tasks serving to justify

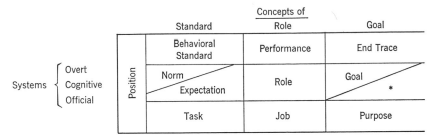

*There is no clear, expectational analogue of the goal concept. See page 163.

FIGURE 3   Relationships among concepts.

other tasks in the organization. All three concepts may be applied to single person actors or to acting positions. There is, once again, no assumption of correspondence between end traces, goals, and purposes; and various models for the organization stem from their interaction.

A CONCEPTUAL MODEL

Relationships among the several concepts defined in this paper are symbolized in Fig. 3. It will be observed that the concept of position cuts across all three systems of analysis. Behavioral standard, performance, and end trace belong to the overt system; norm and expectation, role, and goal are of the cognitive system; task, job, and purpose are found in the official system.

In the last part of this chapter I shall apply these concepts in a discussion of organizational functioning. The reader may want to refer to Fig. 3 during this discussion.

Organizational Models

It is beyond the scope of this chapter to review the many propositions which have been advanced for organizations and which can be conceptualized by using the concepts discussed here. Rather than attempt such a review, I shall give example propositions while discussing familiar organizations.

THE MISSING PURPOSE

It is tempting to assume, as many organization theorists have done,[15] that purposes are always present and serve to justify the or-

---

[15] See, for instance, Oeser and Harary [424].

ganization. It would follow from such an assumption that the purpose precedes the organization in time, and that any organization which loses its purpose will soon dissolve. Yet organizations exist—and prosper—with no clearly defined purpose. The best example of this in contemporary society is the educational organization.

We are all familiar with the public school. Public education in America is ubiquitous to all communities, and most of us have contact with the schools in one form or another some time during our lives. Involved in the schools are persons occupying defined positions and exhibiting recognizable behavior standards leading toward known end states. Moreover, roles are held by educational participants for one another, and there is marked similarity in roles held by persons representing various positions. Finally, the typical school exhibits a hierarchy of status relationships which is enforced by an—occasionally repressive—official system. In short, the school, the school system, or the state or national education association is a viable, growing, active organization.

Yet, the school does not have a purpose. Documentation for this claim may be gained either through conversation with educators or by reading the newspapers. Individual schools may have stated purposes thrust upon them by pressure groups operating in the local school board. School systems may even state such broad purposes as support of country, God, or mother. But one looks in vain for clearly stated tasks for public education in terms of which individual tasks in the school are justified.

What are the effects of such a missing purpose? Several propositions may be suggested.

PROPOSITION 1. Lack of purpose leads to proliferation and conflict in goals.

A pungent demonstration of this proposition is given to us by Stringfellow Barr [46, pp. 34–35] in discussing the small college:

There's no common purpose. The trustees want to prevent subversion and stay solvent. . . . [The president] wants to get publicity and, eventually, if it isn't too late, a bigger job somewhere else. The department heads want to raid each other for students, especially for majors, and thereby enlarge their departments. The professors want to publish, get promoted, get famous, and meanwhile stave off their creditors. . . . The wives of the professors . . . are socially ambitious and go in for cutthroat competition. The men students try to make fraternities, make athletic teams, avoid study, and then graduate somehow or other. The girls try to make sororities and find a husband. The parents of the students hope their offspring won't "get ideas." The dean of women hopes the girls won't conceive anything more dangerous than a concept before they find husbands. And the alumni hope the teams will win, and hunt promising high-school athletes to send us.

But if we talk with educators, we are also given to understand that the reason why no common purposes are statable for education is because of the very disagreement in goals which is engendered by lack of purpose. This suggests that Proposition 1 may also be reversed.

PROPOSITION 2. Conflicting goals lead to a lack of purpose.

Another effect of the missing purpose seems to be that of increasing the amount of goal-setting activity in the organization.

PROPOSITION 3. Lack of a purpose leads to behaviors which have as their end traces the stating of a purpose.

Dewey [165] has pointed out that to have an educational system which serves disparate goals makes for a vigor which some other institutions (and societies) do not have. This observation suggests a corollary to Proposition 3.

PROPOSITION 4. Lack of a purpose leads to wider and more flexible behavioral standards in the organization.

Two other useful effects of lack of purpose in the organization have been suggested by Frank [202].

PROPOSITION 5. Lack of a purpose leads to an increase in the amount of control superiors can exert over subordinates in the organization.

PROPOSITION 6. Lack of a purpose leads to increased dependence of the organization on reality factors.

It should not be implied that all effects of the missing purpose are salubrious. The absence of agreed-upon purposes in education also makes it difficult to evaluate performance. Let us assume that we know what kinds of teaching produce given effects in terms of pupil learning (which we do not). How are we to establish standards of teacher excellence unless we can agree on what effects we wish to produce? Such speculations lead to two propositions.

PROPOSITION 7. Lack of a purpose leads to competing task systems which conflict with one another.

PROPOSITION 8. Lack of a purpose leads to evaluating performance in arbitrary terms (such as by years of tenure) rather than in terms of task conformity.

Finally, it seems reasonable that the public cannot remain oblivious to the organization which functions without clearly stated directions.

PROPOSITION 9. Lack of a purpose leads to low public esteem for the organization.

This last proposition should not be taken to mean that it is unpleasant to work in the purposeless organization. Far from it; I take it that most academicians have chosen to work for just such an organization, and take a cut in salary, precisely because of the many advantages resulting from unclarity of purpose. One is, frankly, far freer to pursue one's idiosyncratic interests in general education than one would be in General Motors.

CHANGE OF PURPOSE

A quite different challenge is posed by the phenomenon of change in purpose. An organization with clearly stated purposes decides to change directions; perhaps to meet new competition, perhaps to avoid technological obsolescence, perhaps because the management is bored! What are the effects of change in purpose?

A dramatic example of change in purpose recently occurred in the March-of-Dimes. Here was a thriving organization, eminently successful in collecting money, enjoying status relationships with two of the most successful positions in our society (scientists and physicians), with a staff of hundreds and offices in all major cities, suddenly faced with success! Imagine, if you will, the thoughts of the March-of-Dimes executive who hears sudden rumors of the impending polio vaccine. The entire justification of the organization will soon vanish; should not one flee before the catastrophe strikes? It is tempting to suggest that loss of purpose increases the probability of organizational collapse, and yet the March-of-Dimes survived. Buckled about with positions, jobs, and low-level tasks—and armed with a shared goal to preserve the organization—the personnel has succeeded in making a changeover from the polio purpose to the birth defect purpose. This suggests a number of propositions.

PROPOSITION 10. Loss of purpose leads to disorientation of the overt and cognitive systems and to the goal of creating another purpose.

PROPOSITION 11. Loss of purpose decreases the valence of organizational membership.

PROPOSITION 12. Loss of purpose leads to a restriction of behavioral standards in favor of extant tasks and a tightening of behavioral norms.

PROPOSITION 13. Radical change in purpose leads to lowering of public esteem for the organization.

PLURALISTIC IGNORANCE IN THE ORGANIZATION

There is a common tendency in normative integrationist theories of social structure to assume that organizations function smoothly only when cognitive systems are accurate, veridical, and shared.[16] Thus, persons are presumed to both share and be aware of each others' norms for the behavior of all position members. At the very least, if people should disagree about behavioral norms, they must each be aware of the others' thinking in order to plan intelligent activity with the others.

In contrast with this broad assumption, Schanck [462] has shown that under certain conditions the members of a community might share a wholly mistaken view of the norms of the group. Thus, there might exist an agreed-upon view of "public opinion" which corresponded neither with the norms of community members nor with the behavioral standards of position members. Schanck observed that for such a *pluralistic ignorance* to occur it was necessary to restrict either communication or behavioral observation, or both.

In a recent study, I and others have shown that pluralistic ignorance exists in the school system.[17] It was discovered that, for such teacher behavioral frameworks as "discipline," "watching for cheaters," "supervision," and the like, respondents attributed to "People in General" and to "School Officials" much more conservative norms than were actually held by these positions. That is, members of the public were felt to want more disciplining, supervision, watching, and so on than was reflected in the own norms revealed by respondents sampled from these positions. This distorted view of public opinion was held by teachers, parents, and pupils alike. Only school officials were able to assess the truly liberal norms held by other school officials, and they shared in the general ignorance of public opinion on these issues.

We have speculated that such a phenomenon as pluralistic ignorance in the organization might stem from rapid social change paired with the legitimizing of reactionary public outcry. Many persons may assume that the public continues to think of teachers in terms of the values of small-town America, particularly when they listen to the

---

[16] The distinction between normative and functional integration stems from Durkheim [176] and is discussed in Freedman et al. [205].

[17] See Biddle, Rosencranz, and Rankin [69], Volumes 2 and 3, and Biddle, Rosencranz, Tomich, and Twyman [70].

criticisms of the superpatriots, those interested in a "classical" education, or the know-nothings who delight in attacking the public school. If this explanation is correct, conservative stereotypes should be observable for many public positions. It may be speculated, for instance, that public opinion in the South regarding desegregation is actually more liberal than one is led to believe by reading the newspapers— for surely here is a field where public outcry is on "one side of the fence."

It may also be true that teachers are peculiarly vulnerable to conservative stereotypes due to their ambiguous position of giving personal service in a public organization and their inability to form professional groups which would set and enforce standards for their profession. This latter interpretation suggests that conservative pluralistic ignorance might be a regular feature of public organizations and would apply to such positions as nurses, social workers, or civil service employees.

Whatever its etiology, conservative pluralistic ignorance for the teacher is probably maintained through restrictions of both communication and behavioral observation. School officials and teachers must rely upon the reports of others for a description of teacher behavior, while parents depend on the dubious reporting of their own children. The school system is also notorious for lack of communication between positions due to inadequate administration, lack of time, poor facilities, and, above all, poor motivation.

These observations suggest two propositions relating to the genesis of pluralistic ignorance:

PROPOSITION 14. Pluralistic ignorance results when behavioral observation is curtailed, discussion of norms or expectations is restricted, clearly stated tasks are at a minimum, and/or discussion of norms is slanted.

PROPOSITION 15. Pluralistic ignorance is more likely to occur for positions in the public domain than for positions defined privately in the organization, more likely for public organizations and for organizations or professional societies having poorly stated purposes.

It is probable that the conservative stereotype of the school official is also facilitated by duplicity. It should be noted that school officials share in the general ignorance of public opinion concerning the teacher. The average school official, then, is faced with "representing" a public whose standards run counter to his own (he thinks). This suggests that school officials exhibit a double standard of performance; conservative values for teacher behavior supported and enforced in public, liberal standards held in private. Thus, the school official is not only forced into upholding standards which he does not share but we presume he adds to his burdens by appearing as an authoritarian "fuddy-duddy" in the eyes of others.

Other positions must also suffer from conservative pluralistic ignorance for the teacher. Parents and teachers are probably constrained from expressing opinions which they believe run counter to public opinion and to the norms of school officials. Teachers, particularly, appear unaware of the liberal norms they share with school officials, and must be burdened when attempting to satisfy a set of values which they do not believe in and which are not shared by school officials or the general public. This suggests three propositions dealing with the effects of pluralistic ignorance.

PROPOSITION 16. Pluralistic ignorance leads to the restriction of communication and the slanting of normative discussions.[18]

PROPOSITION 17. For members of the position to which pluralistic ignorance is applied (teachers), pluralistic ignorance leads to the establishment of behavioral standards at odds with own norms, to the restriction of behavioral standards, and to dissatisfaction.

PROPOSITION 18. For members of positions holding pluralistic ignorance (school officials, parents), pluralistic ignorance leads to the establishment of inappropriate behavioral standards, to reduction of the status of their own position, and to dissatisfaction.

These outcomes are strictly negative ones. In contrast, a number of authors have suggested that systematic deceptions are useful, or even necessary, in the smooth operation of organizations.[19] It has been suggested that deceptions allow for certain kinds of control and enable individuals to avoid direct threats to status or reward. Thus, the negative effects of pluralistic ignorance may sometimes be preferable to other alternatives. We need a comprehensive theory of the organization which will deal with pluralistic ignorance and other forms of deception.

ROLE CONFLICT AND COGNITIVE DISSONANCE

Two closely related terms have recently appeared in the literature of role which are useful for understanding the organization. In common with other terms in role theory, *role conflict* has been used for a

---

[18] Taken together, Propositions 14 and 16 suggest that pluralistic ignorance tends to be self-perpetuating, once established.

[19] These include Machiavelli [360], Lenin [339], Selznick [477], Sorel [511], and Goffman [218].

variety of purposes.[20] I shall assume here that any two disparate cognitions which are held for a common actor constitute a conflict. For instance, should the foreman and shop manager hold disparate norms for work production, it may be said that a role conflict exists for the worker to whom the norms apply. It should be pointed out, however, that there are only two ways in which the worker can be affected by such a conflict. He may (correctly) attribute conflicting norms to the sentient others involved, or he may receive the behavioral effects of the others' norms with or without understanding the reasons for their behavior.

In contrast with role conflict, *cognitive dissonance* has as its focus the existence of cognitive disparities within the life space of a single person.[21] For instance, the subject person who attributes conflicting norms to sentient others experiences cognitive dissonance, but cognitive dissonance would also be experienced if the norms were held for another position of which the subject was not a member. The basis of cognitive dissonance is logical inconsistency (which may appear among any cognitions held by the subject person, for instance, between a norm and an expectation), while the basis of role conflict is that of inconsistent cognitions held for an actor. It is postulated that the existence of cognitive dissonance is, in and of itself, motivating to the individual, whereas role conflict affects the individual only when he experiences its effects. Role conflict may, however, be reflected in overt disorganization without anyone being aware that it exists.

A number of theorists [22] have begun to treat small groups as if they had systemic properties which were similar to those of the life space. Applied to the organization, such theories would suggest that behavioral standard conflict is resolved in the overt system by mechanisms which are analogous to those whereby cognitive dissonance was resolved in the cognitive system. My position would be that tendencies of the organization to clarify the overt system by promoting and enforcing tasks was not a "basic property" but rather a peculiar condition of certain organizations.

For example, certain kinds of organizations may encourage disorganized or random behavior in order to promote purposes of the organization. A summer camp, for instance, may have periods of "free time" when only a bare minimum of social control is exercised and

---

[20] Biddle and Twyman [68] have provided a review and bibliography for role conflict.

[21] The term "cognitive dissonance" was coined by Festinger [190].

[22] See, for instance, Sherif [488], Festinger et al. [191], Newcomb [417], Heider [261], and Scott [465].

individual campers are encouraged to do anything they feel like, including "running, hollering, and carrying on." Other organizations may tolerate or encourage a professional "gad fly" whose job it is to question basic assumptions and generally stir things up. Such exceptions are rare, however, and behavioral standard conflict seems to be an anathema to many organizations. Several propositions are suggested:

PROPOSITION 19. Role conflict produces disruption in the overt system and (with communication) cognitive dissonance and dissatisfaction for the position member to which it applies.

PROPOSITION 20. Role conflict is more likely in organizations with poorly defined task structures and organizations where purposes are being changed.

PROPOSITION 21. Behavioral conflict is occasionally promoted by organizations for specific purposes, but only when carefully regulated by tasks.

PROPOSITION 22. Organizations will take steps to reduce behavioral disruption which is not governed by tasks whenever disruption exceeds a minimum level of toleration.

Summary and Conclusion

It has been the thesis of this chapter that three conceptual systems are necessary for understanding the organization. *The overt system* presents concepts dealing with behavioral and overt events at a low level of abstraction. *The cognitive system* is concerned with the "thoughts" that individuals have about social events and which serve to organize their behavioral responses. *The official system* is built out of codified consenses which are public domain and which serve as the skeleton around which the organization is constructed.

A number of terms have been defined for the three systems including position, concepts of standard (behavioral standard, expectation, norm, task), concepts of role (performance, role, job), and concepts of goal (end trace, goal, purpose) ; and it has been shown that these concepts have different implications within the three systems.

Finally, the concepts outlined were used in a discussion of several problems related to the functioning of the organization. In the process, a number of propositions were suggested for empirical study.

Careful separation of elements of the organization will lead towards the assemblage of a tested, logico-deductive structure of propositions that predicts. Without such careful usage it is difficult to see how we are to build a social science.

11

ADMINISTRATIVE RATIONALITY, SOCIAL SETTING, AND ORGANIZATIONAL DEVELOPMENT

Stanley H. Udy, Jr.

Introduction [1]

The fact that modern organization theory has been developed from data drawn almost exclusively from contemporary western industrial society has had both advantageous and disadvantageous consequences. On the positive side of the ledger, this situation has unquestionably—if sometimes unwittingly—aided theoretical development by materially simplifying the data to be studied. For modern industrial culture is, in many respects, quite invariant relative to the variety exhibited among nonindustrial social forms and the differences manifested between industrial and nonindustrial societies. The researcher who restricts himself to the study of organizations in modern western culture is thus essentially holding a great many cultural contextual variables constant, and, consequently, is better able to investigate other sources of variation under specified cultural conditions. It is therefore no accident that organization theory has probably reached its highest level of sophistication in the areas of economics, psychology, and in the sociology of internal administrative operations.[2]

---

[1] This is an expanded version of [561]. We are indebted to Professor W. W. Cooper of the Carnegie Institute of Technology for helpful comments and suggestions.

[2] See, for example, the summary treatments of March and Simon [367] and Blau and Scott [76].

From another viewpoint, however, this rather restricted empirical scope of organizational analysis has had serious drawbacks. Sociological organization theory of institutional scope has not been highly developed, precisely because contextual elements cannot appropriately be held constant in such theory but must explicitly be introduced as variables. Furthermore, the relative lack of such variables in organization theory is, we think, more serious than is often suspected. Quite apart from purely intellectual academic interest, there is considerable practical applied value in constructing models which describe a "general case." The reason for this is that many "constant" contextual elements of industrialism are really only relatively constant, in that the range of variation which they exhibit under industrial conditions is only a small portion of their total possible range. Some of the more important examples involve variation in mode of recruitment, and patterns of incentives and rewards. Despite the relatively small range of variation exhibited by such elements in industrial culture, the variation present can have such important implications as to suggest that even the most narrowly conceived theoretical approaches should take account of such variables. If this is to be done, systematic knowledge must exist of their total possible range of variation and its implications. A "general case" must be developed. Pressures toward such development have increasingly been felt. For example, in the areas of "human relations" and "informal organization" in industry, failure to recognize that certain "constants" are, in fact, variables has sometimes led to situations in which commonplace organizational phenomena, notably in the case of "informal organizations," have had to be treated as "exceptions" merely because available theoretical models lacked sufficient generality to encompass them.

Another source of need for more attention to the "general case" in sociological organization theory results more directly from the extension of industrialism to newly developing areas and consequent organizational problems entailed by a change from a nonindustrial to an industrial economy. The need is rather obvious in this area, where it is especially important to be able to project patterns of social and organizational change against a "general case." [3]

Such considerations led us to undertake over the course of the past five years a series of comparative studies of formal organizations engaged in the production of material goods in nonindustrial societies.[4]

---

[3] See [252] and [404].

[4] Other principal studies by the author in this series include [557], [558], [559]. Also see "Comment" by A. L. Stinchcombe and "Rejoinder."

The aim was to introduce broad variations in contextual elements; the present analysis forms one of this series. One may define a *formal organization* as any social group engaged in pursuing explicitly announced objectives through manifestly coordinated efforts, and, at the same time, describe an entity that appears to be culturally universal. It is thus possible to utilize ethnographic data compiled by anthropologists to study such organizations comparatively in different societies, and thereby systematically introduce wide variations in the socio-cultural settings of the organizations. Similarly, a focus on production *per se* can render technological variations highly visible, and thus make their variation relatively easy to explore. Our objective throughout has been to seek broad generalizations about variations in organization structure relative to its social setting and the technology involved, and thus contribute to filling some of the "gaps" in organization theory which we have discussed.

For the most part our work has been based on a "master sample" of 426 organizations in 150 societies. The societies were drawn in accord with the criteria set forth by George P. Murdock.[5] The organizations represent the sum total of those described in the ethnographic sources consulted for the societies concerned. On this score, data were drawn essentially from the Human Relations Area Files and supplemented by additional ethnographic materials. The 426 organizations involve widely varying types of technological problems, as encountered in various forms of agricultural work, hunting, fishing, collection, construction, manufacturing, and stock-raising. The societies are distributed over all of the world's culture areas and range from the most "primitive" to some of the more socially complex "traditional" and "peasant" types. A variety of "experimental" treatments was thus possible relative to the influence of social setting and technology on organization structure; such was the subject of our first and most extensive analysis.[6] Typical of the results obtained is the finding that technological complexity sets rather definite and measurable lower limits on the number of levels of authority in an organization, and that the existence of levels beyond this lower limit can be accounted for by a multilevel status structure in the social setting combined with ascriptive recruitment. This situation sets the stage for a number of other considerations. It appears, for example, that social conditions which make it easy to establish a multilevel authority system in response to a high degree of technical complexity are somewhat at odds

---

[5] [412].
[6] See [557], Chapters 3–4.

with social conditions making for rational planning, specific jobs, and explicit decision rules. Thus highly complex organizations under severe pressures to operate efficiently would appear to suffer from a great many more basic problems than mere internal structural confusion.[7]

The Present Study

The present study deals with the problem of "rationality" in administration—what it involves organizationally, and what social conditions are associated with it. Few, if any, concepts employed in social science are fraught with so many difficulties. In the first place, the term is understood in both a "formal" as well as a "substantive" sense, to use Max Weber's terminology. *Formal* rationality is present in any social situation to the extent that the means employed to reach specified objectives are planned in accord with the best available scientific knowledge. *Substantive* rationality, on the other hand, is present to the extent that all objectives pursued in the situation are logically compatible with a given system of values.[8] One can, in principle, apply either of these usages to the actions of an individual or a collectivity acting as a unit without encountering serious problems, provided one is willing to grant the "givens" specified. It is rather in the analysis of the composition of collectivities that the most severe sociological problems arise. To a very limited degree, the idea of formal rationality can be extended to the composition of social units through the theory of games.[9] A more fundamental problem to organization theory, however, is the question of combining formal and substantive rationality in the same system. Historically the classic instance is perhaps the "problem of order" in utilitarian social philosophy; namely, the problem of accounting for the existence of society assuming it to be composed of discrete individuals striving rationally for the same ends in a context of scarce resources. The solution to this problem, of course, as has been widely pointed out, is that cultural values distribute ends among categories of persons differentiated in the social structure and, at the same time, motivate "nonrational" behavior in given circumstances. In other words, the problem of substantive rationality resolves itself into the question of how cultural values distribute objectives in such a way as to allow for formally rational behavior in certain segments of society, with a minimum of conflict.[10]

---

[7] [559].

[8] See [590], pp. 115–118; also [428], pp. 640–649.

[9] See, for example, [576] and [24].   [10] [428], pp. 87–94 and 697–719.

In the analysis of formal organization, the problem is somewhat similar, except that the behavior of the collectivity as a whole is expected to be formally rational, as well as the behavior of the individual participants *qua* members. The problem of "administrative rationality," then, emerges on an intervening, substantive level. It is a question of determining what social structures are appropriate to an organization which is not only expected to behave in a formally rational manner as a collectivity, but whose members are also expected to behave in formally rational ways in their several capacities.

We may thus presume rationality to be present in a formal organization to the extent that role expectations are based on planning for explicit organizational objectives. In a more sophisticated statement, Cyert and March characterize a rational system as being oriented to produce choices through standardized search procedures in such a way as to "maximize the expected return to the system" in terms of "a well-defined preference ordering over possible future states." [11] Two major determinants of the degree of administrative rationality in an organization thus suggest themselves: The first is the extent to which the structure of the organization defines and motivates planned collective behavior; the second is the degree to which behavior in the social setting is independent of behavior in the organization, from the standpoint of the individual member. This paper will thus first attempt to isolate organizational-structural requisites of rationality and to analyze their interrelations. It will be found that the requisites herein isolated form a Guttman scale in terms of which the organizations studied can be compared as to degree of rationality. Second, we shall explore relationships between the rationality scale and the institutional and social settings of the organizations studied, in an attempt to assess the independence from societal ascription of organizations lying at different points on the scale. Finally, we shall propose some hypotheses about the development of rationality in organization.

Data and Methods

Data are drawn from 34 formal organizations engaged in the production of material goods in 34 nonindustrial societies; information is based on anthropological monographs and the Human Relations Area Files. The analysis was limited to organizations having three or more levels of authority, inasmuch as previous work suggested that only such organizations would be of sufficient complexity to be of interest

---

[11] [143].

for present purposes.[12] The 34 organizations studied are part of the sample of 426 organizations in 150 societies, described earlier. Fifty-six of the original 426 cases proved to have three or more levels of authority and offered sufficient data for purposes of the present analysis. Twelve of them, however, had already been employed in an *ex post facto* extrapolation of a scale containing four of the seven items used in the scale developed in the present study.[13] Since one of our desires was to test the previous result, these 12 cases were dropped, leaving 44 organizations representing 34 societies. Under the not entirely realistic assumption that organizations in different societies represent independent events while those in the same society do not, only one organization per society was finally used, it being drawn at random when the society offered more than one potentially usable case on the basis of a survey of pertinent ethnographic material. Of the resulting 34 organizations representing 34 societies, 11 are African, 12 North American, and the remaining 11 are distributed over the Circum-Mediterranean, Insular Pacific, East Eurasian, and South American regions.[14] The geographical distribution of the sample is therefore unfortunately somewhat unbalanced. The extent to which this imbalance reflects the actual distribution of complex production organization as opposed to complete data is not known, except that it may be noted that materials on South American societies are quite sparse.

Administrative Rationality and Its Structural Requisites

We shall assume that rationality as herein conceived minimally involves orientation to *limited objectives,* defined for present purposes as objectives explicitly restricted only to the production of certain products. This simple criterion of rationality is, of course, far from ideal but represents the closest operational approach possible of our data to "explicit objectives" or "a well-defined preference ordering of future states." We shall thus assert that "highly rational" organizations possess limited objectives in this sense, by definition. The problem now becomes one of exploring the structural requisites of an organizational orientation to limited objectives. In an earlier study it had been found that all organizations with limited objectives also involved *segmental participation,* that is, explicit definition of the terms of participation by some mutual contractual agreement, but that

---

12 [557], pp. 36–41.   14 [412].
13 [556].

not all organizations with segmental participation had limited objectives.[15] Since a reasonable common-sense interpretation of this relationship is at hand (unrestricted terms of participation seem likely to invite goal displacement), it was decided to hypothesize that segmental participation precedes limited objectives at the upper end of the rationality scale. Reference was then made to another previous study [16] that found (in a sample different from the present one) the following characteristics to be related to segmental participation on a scale in the following descending order: *Performance emphasis* (expected dependence of the quantity of the reward on the amount and/or quality of work done); *specialization* [17] (the concurrent performance of three or more qualitatively different operations by different members); and *compensatory rewards* (allocation of money or goods in kind by members of higher authority to members of lower authority in return for participation).[18] Reasonable theoretical interpretations seemed possible for these findings as well. Segmental participation would seem to be difficult without some explicit attention being drawn to performance. Similarly, unless roles are specialized relative to one another such that the particular content of each is stable and discretely identifiable, any emphasis on performance would seem tenuous. Specialization, in turn, is always potentially difficult to institutionalize, since it is always at least partially determined by technical considerations. Functionally, compensatory rewards constitute a mechanism whereby specialization can be "artificially" institutionalized by management through its control over the reward system. Furthermore, there is some reason to believe that compensatory rewards constitute the *only* mechanism that can reliably do this. Empirically, there appear to be only two possible

---

[15] See footnote 4.

[16] [556].

[17] We have elsewhere defined "specialization" as a continuous variable (i.e., the number of different operations performed simultaneously by different members; see [557], pp. 22–23). In a social context of the type discussed here, however, it seems proper to regard specialization as discontinuous; the number "three" was chosen as the cutoff point because three is the smallest number of roles in one system wherein ego is faced with the problem of defining relationships between two alters in a way independent of ego's relationship with either of them.

[18] See [76], pp. 205–206, 224–225. Blau and Scott regard this characteristic as indicative of "hierarchical dependence." We find that compensatory rewards indeed do represent hierarchical dependence but only one possible form which it may take. Other possible forms would be the use or threat of force, manipulation of approval needs, etc. We would argue that if organization is to be rational it is important that hierarchical dependence be restricted to compensatory rewards.

alternatives: (1) manipulation of already existing social obligations and (2) the use of force.[19] The first of these alternatives presupposes a fortuitous and highly improbable identity of technical activities and social roles; the second is subject to serious limitations as a continuous mode of control, particularly in organizations that are at all complex. If this line of reasoning is correct, compensatory rewards are requisite to specialization, except under extremely improbable social conditions.

A review of pertinent literature on administration revealed that the items so far mentioned are often assumed to be structural correlates of administrative rationality and suggested two further items on which data were available: *specific job assignment* (continuous assignment by management of particular people to particular roles), and *centralized management* (the existence of a single internal source of ultimate authority).[20] The former was placed on the scale between specialization and performance emphasis on the grounds that roles had to be specialized to be assigned and that particular people had to be associated with particular roles to be rewarded for performance in a consistent fashion. Centralized management was placed at the beginning of the scale on the grounds that management could not consistently allocate compensatory rewards without being centralized.

In sum, our argument suggests that organizations, which, from an administrative standpoint are "completely rational" in that they involve limited objectives, also tend to involve segmental participation, a performance emphasis, specific job assignments, specialization, compensatory rewards, and centralized management. In turn, organizations with segmental participation may or may not involve limited objectives, but tend to possess the other five characteristics, and so forth. Thus our argument theoretically suggests a scale which would order organizations according to degree of administrative rationality, ranging from those possessing no rational characteristics or possessing only a centralized management to those possessing all seven characteristics up to and including limited objectives. It is in this sense that some organizations studied may be said to be "more rational" than others.

Our next step was to determine whether or not the data actually scaled in this manner. The organizations studied had previously been coded in another connection, according to the presence or absence of

---

[19] See [557], Chapter vii.
[20] See, e.g. [590], pp. 225–226; [589], pp. 196 ff.; [591], p. 95; [367], pp. 12–33 and [23], pp. 12–13.

the items in the scale. The coding was done on the basis of ethnographic descriptions; a few examples are perhaps in order.

One of the most rational organizations in our terms occurs among the Navaho, and is set up explicitly for the purpose of hunting antelope by locating and driving the game through a V-shaped stockade into a corral. The organization is reported as set up explicitly for the purpose of hunting and as such does not appear to do anything else; it does carry on rituals, but only those felt to be instrumental to hunting. We thus report "limited objectives." Twenty to 50 men simply agree to go hunting, elect one of their number to superintend distribution of the game to those who agree to join, and ask a man reputed to be a good hunter to agree to lead them on an explicit basis. We thus report "segmental participation" and a "performance emphasis," the latter because "good hunters" received more game than others. The leader is further reported as making specific job assignments on the basis of ability: the fastest runners are assigned to drive, others are stationed at the open end of the V, and older men detailed at the corral. Thus "specific job assignment" and "specialization" are reported. Since the game is distributed to participants by an elected official, we report "compensatory rewards." The presence of a leader indicates "centralized management." [21]

House building among the Kabyles provides an example of a somewhat less rational organization, and also illustrates certain coding problems notably absent in the preceding case. Typically, houses are constructed by the members of the household concerned, with the aid of a cooperative organization known as the *touiza*. The resulting unit, however, serves a variety of purposes other than house building, notably various community ritual and political functions. It does not, therefore, possess "limited objectives" by our definition. By the same token, participation in the organization is not "segmental." There is no agreement that an effort will be made to limit the content of interactions only to what is relevant to house building; on the contrary, there is every expectation that fraternal and ceremonial activities will be freely mixed with work. An exception to this situation, however, is a relatively recent tendency to hire a stonemason and a carpenter, temporarily at appropriate stages of construction, on contractual bases. Only two people are involved on a temporary basis, and evidently not invariably. Thus we decided to code "segmental participation" as "absent."

---

[21] [271].

The coding of "performance emphasis" also presented some problems. It is clear from the account that rewards are allocated differentially by office (those in charge of work groups, as well as the mason and carpenter, receive more than others). It is less clear that amount and/or quality of work done is relevant. The degree of zeal put forth by a worker at least partially depends on his kinship ties with the owner, and to that extent is independent of rewards. But it is also evident that performance makes some difference. Those who work hard can legitimately expect more help from the owner in the future. There is also some indication that people who do work of particularly good quality are rewarded with "choice pieces" of food. We thus report a "performance emphasis" to be present.

The presence of specific job assignments as well as specialization, compensatory rewards, and centralized management is clear. People are assigned to particular jobs either by the owner or the stonemason. A rather high degree of specialization is often reached. In the course of wall construction, for example, approximately twelve workers perform at least four explicitly differentiated activities: carrying stones; carrying water; mixing mortar and passing it to the mason; laying stones. The owner is expected to reward workers liberally with feasts, and is himself ultimately in charge of all work.[22]

In the case of Betsileo wet rice field cultivation, operations are under the central management of the owner who compensates workers with a feast. At various points in the process, as many as five different activities occur at once. For example, in preparing the rice field and transplanting shoots from the nursery into the field, the young men drive cattle around in the mud to reduce the soil to an even consistency; the middle-aged men level the field with hoes; the young women plant the rice shoots; the old women transport the shoots from the nursery and pass them to the young women; and the old men regulate the water level in the field. Specific job assignments appeared not to be made but rather to occur "automatically" on the basis of age and sex differentiation, as the above example illustrates. The evidence, though, is not entirely clear on this point. On the other hand, the account explicitly states that performance is not a factor in rewards—one need simply be present and working. Also, the organization performs religious, familial, and community functions in addition to work, and some of these activities extend to the work situation.[23]

The other 31 cases were similarly coded, with the results shown in

---

[22] [373].

[23] [172], especially pp. 434–440.

Table 1: × denotes the presence of a characteristic, 0 its absence. In general, the results are consistent with the hypotheses proposed.

Since much of the theoretical basis of this scale is probabilistic, one would expect some exceptions. Deviant cases were thus examined in detail and proved to be of two general types. The first involved the

Table 1   Administrative Rationality in 34 Nonindustrial Production Organizations *

Society from which Organization was Drawn	Limited Objectives	Segmental Participation	Performance-Emphasis	Specific Job Assignment	Specialization	Compensatory Rewards	Central Management
Iroquois	×	×	×	×	×	×	×
Navaho	×	×	×	×	×	×	×
Paiute	×	×	×	×	×	×	×
Sanpoil	×	×	×	×	×	×	×
Sinkaietk	×	×	0	×	×	×	×
Nambicuara	×	×	0	×	×	×	×
Otoro	0	×	0	×	×	×	×
Hopi	0	×	0	×	×	×	×
Tikopia	0	0	×	×	×	×	×
Kabyles	0	0	×	×	×	×	×
Jukun	0	0	×	0	×	×	×
Tallensi	0	0	×	×	0	×	×
Haida	0	0	0	×	×	×	×
Haitians	0	0	0	×	×	×	×
Dahomeans	0	0	0	×	0	×	×
Tarahumara	0	0	0	×	0	×	×
Turkana	0	0	0	×	0	×	×
Camayura	0	0	0	×	0	×	×
Betsileo	0	0	0	0	×	×	×
Trobrianders	0	0	0	0	×	×	×
Pukapukans	0	0	0	0	×	0	×
Malay	0	0	0	0	×	0	×
Bemba	0	0	0	0	0	×	×
Crow	0	0	0	0	0	×	×
Ifaluk	0	0	0	0	0	×	×
Ila	0	0	0	0	0	×	×
Kikuyu	0	0	0	0	0	×	×
Lobi	0	0	0	0	0	×	×
Papago	0	0	0	0	0	×	×
Sotho	0	0	0	0	0	×	×
Winnebago	0	0	0	0	0	×	×
Dogon	0	0	0	0	0	0	×
Tarasco	0	0	0	0	0	0	0
Tibetans	0	0	0	0	0	0	0

* Coefficient of reproducibility = 0.95.
For references see Udy [557], pp. 139–158 ff.

absence of expected specialization or performance emphasis—the apparent loci of most of the deviance. The reason why so much deviation centers on these characteristics seems to be that the presence or absence of each of them, in contrast to the other items, is in part a function of purely technical considerations. Certain kinds of tasks, as for example many involving agriculture or construction, are by nature cumulative and do not lend themselves particularly to specialization, although there is no reason why they cannot be otherwise rationally organized. The Tallensi, Tarahumara, and Camayura cases appear probably to be of this variety. They suggest that rationality involves specialization only where the latter is clearly relevant technologically. Similarly, whether or not rationality involves a performance emphasis appears to be technologically relative. Where activities are highly routinized with a minimum of uncertainty involved, performance seems less likely to be emphasized, despite the presence of other rational characteristics. The Nambicuara, Otoro, and Hopi cases may well be of this variety. In sum, it appears that specialization and a performance emphasis tend in effect not to be a part of rational administration unless their presence clearly contributes to technical efficiency in the physical sense.

The other class of exceptions may be purely a function of the research methodology and is thus possibly more apparent than real. A characteristic was coded as "absent" not only when its existence was explicitly denied but also in instances where it was simply not reported, provided the context was such that it seemed reasonable to assume that the ethnographer would have reported it had it been present. This procedure, of course, tended to result in "overreporting" absences. On this score the single deviant omissions for the Sinkaietk, Dahomeans, Pukapukans, and possibly the Turkana are dubious; the "absent" characteristics may actually be present. By the same token, the Betsileo case may involve specific job assignments; the description is not entirely clear on this point. General explanations for other exceptions are not apparent.

The results were adjudged to be consistent with the hypothesis, although our interpretation of some of the exceptions suggests the desirability of complicating the model with some contextual variables deriving from technology. We suggest that the scale items indicate a cumulative emphasis on specificity of organizational roles and decision rules such that (1) explicit limits for individual rationality are established and motivated, and (2) interrelated procedures relative to collective rationality are established.

The Institutionalization of Rationality

We now wish to explore and explicate the hypothesis that administrative rationality involves relative independence of the organization from its social setting. Central to this hypothesis is the idea of social involvement, developed in a previous paper. *Social involvement* is defined as the institutionalization of participation and motivation in the organization through expectations and obligations existing independently of the organization in the social setting.[24] One would expect socially involved organizations to be less rational on the grounds that they are less independent of the social setting. The presence in the organization of opportunities to express general social values would inhibit the development of highly specific roles and procedures. In addition, one would expect organizations that are not socially involved to be highly rational under an assumption of structural substitution; that is, if functions are not performed in the setting, they would presumably have to be built into the organization.

Two indicators of social involvement are proposed. The first describes the basis on which people are socially expected to participate in the organization. Participation is least socially involved when it is purely voluntary, and expected on the basis of self-defined self-interest. The Navaho hunting party described earlier provides an example of such a low degree of social involvement. Men simply decide they want to go on a hunt. Beyond a minimal expectation that men in general hunt from time to time, and the knowledge that hunting produces necessary food, there exists no special social mechanism which compels particular men to hunt at particular times. A somewhat more socially involved situation occurs when participation, though still voluntary for specific occasions, is nonetheless expected to be proferred most of the time because of a general community obligation over and above self-interest. Participation in the Kabyle *touiza* is a case in point; one is expected to come most of the time whether one wants to or not (particularly if one wishes any future cooperation from others), yet at the same time one is free to refuse on specific occasions. The most socially involved situations occur when participation is compulsory on the basis of an ironclad community reciprocity rule, or kinship, or political ascription. Refusal is met with severe sanctions, extending even to ostracism or death. In the Betsileo case, for example, relatives are obliged to assist in rice cultivation largely

---

[24] [559].

because they are relatives, with considerable pressure exerted, owing to the short time period during which transplanting is possible. In the Tibetan case, a variety of officials may requisition forced labor for a variety of purposes. All 34 cases were thus coded according to whether participation was voluntary on the basis of self-defined self-interest, voluntary but a community obligation, or compulsory, with this order of categories presumed to reflect increasing social involvement. Exploration of the relationship between these categories and the rationality scale as set forth in Table 1 shows that rationality and social involvement do indeed vary inversely. Results are summarized in Table 2 in which scale types 0–3, 4–5, 6–7 are combined respectively for ease of presentation, in as much as their separation adds no information.

A second indicator of social involvement is the separation of ownership from management; such separation may be considered an indication of independence of the organization from its setting, other things being equal. The form which such separation generally assumes is either one in which the leader of a work party is simply not the same person as, say, the owner of the field worked on, or a situation wherein land or raw materials are cooperatively or communally owned. Table 3 compares organizations having *independent proprietorship* (control of the ultimate disposition of the means of production not vested in management) with all other organizations with respect to rationality. Explorations revealed that "highly rational" organizations (defined as scale types 6–7, comprising the eight most rational organizations in the sample) exhibit only independent proprietorship.

Table 2   Rationality and Basis of Participation

	Rationality Scale Type		
Basis of Participation	6–7 (Iroquois-Hopi)	4–5 (Tikopia-Camayura)	0–3 (Betsileo-Tibetans)
Voluntary, self-interest	8	0	0
Voluntary, community obligation	0	9	0
Compulsory	0	1	16

$\chi^2 = 62.79$ $P < 0.001$ d.f. $= 4$

Table 3   Rationality and Proprietorship *

	Highly Rational Organizations	Other
Independent proprietorship	8	7
Other	0	18

$$Q = +1.00$$
$$\chi^2 = 9.93$$
$$P < 0.01$$

* One case was omitted owing to lack of data.

We thus conclude that the mechanisms by which rational administration is institutionalized are such as to produce a certain independence of the organization from its social setting. As is the case with
individual members relative to the organization, so is the case of the
organization relative to its social setting; rational administration requires that an "area of discretion" be defined within which manipulative planning is free to occur.

The Social Setting of Rational Administration

The preceding discussion suggests that it is more difficult for rational administration to develop in social settings that emphasize
traditional ascriptive relationships. Previous research suggests that
this may be especially likely where differences of power and status
are ascribed, since such differences seem particularly likely to be
part of social involvement patterns.[25] Accordingly, the settings of
"highly rational" organizations were compared with the settings of
all other organizations with respect to three presumed indexes of the
general presence of ascription in the society concerned: (1) the presence of a hereditary stratification system with at least three classes
or castes; (2) the presence of hereditary political succession; (3) the
presence of slavery in any form.[26] Combined results appear in Table 4.
The hypothesis is rather weakly confirmed; none of the relationships
is statistically significant at the 0.05 level, but all are in the expected

---

[25] [559].
[26] Data are drawn from Murdock [412].

*Table 4   Rationality and Ascriptive Elements in Social Settings ***

	Complex Hereditary Stratification		Hereditary Political Succession		Slavery	
	Present	Absent	Present	Absent	Present	Absent
Highly rational organizations	0	7	4	3	2	6
Other organizations	10	15	16	7	11	14
	$Q = -1.00$		$Q = -0.26$		$Q = -0.40$	
	$\chi^2 = 2.42$		$\chi^2 = 0.02$		$\chi^2 = 0.29$	
	$P > 0.10$		$P > 0.98$		$P > 0.50$	

* Cases lacking data omitted.

direction, and the stratification relationship approaches significance. No highly rational organization in the sample existed in a setting with a complex stratification system. Furthermore, Table 5 indicates what at first glance seems to be a surprising finding—rational organization is negatively associated with the existence of a centralized government transcending the local community. The relationship, however, is not statistically significant. We report it because, in the type of

*Table 5   Rationality and General Centralized Government ***

	General Centralized Government	
	Present	Absent
Most rational organizations	1	7
Other organizations	12	13
	$Q = -0.73$	
	$\chi^2 = 2.33$	
	$P > 0.10$	

* One case omitted owing to lack of data.

society dealt with here, strong central government indicates a hierarchical feudal order wherein political power permeates the entire social order, and is hence probably simply another index of ascription. If so, this result is consistent with our hypothesis.

Development of Rational Administration

It is very hazardous to attempt to extrapolate hypotheses concerning organizational evolution or development from cross-sectional data of the type on which this study is based. As our earlier theoretical argument indicates, a scale does suggest a structure of requisite elements. It does not, however, indicate prerequisites. One cannot conclude from our scale, for example, that centralized management must precede compensatory rewards in a temporal sequence of development. Similarly, a scale *per se* implies nothing about causal relationships among the items in it. It simply describes a modal static state of affairs.

One can, however, use such a scale to predict types of problems that different developmental sequences will probably entail. For example, if specialization should be the first rational characteristic to develop in an organization, the scale implies that such an organization, if it is to be stable, must immediately develop a centralized management and compensatory rewards. Unless it proves to be the case that rational administrative characteristics are likely to develop simultaneously—and we shall presently see that at least in many cases this is highly unlikely—one may hypothesize that a developmental sequence that follows the scale pattern will probably entail fewer problems and tensions than one which does not.[27]

It is further possible to infer certain constraints and problems that seem likely to arise at specific points in organizational development. First, the institutional system appears to be markedly discontinuous relative to administrative rationality. An increase in rationality beyond specialization evidently involves a radical change in institutional arrangements; ascriptive social involvement is abandoned in favor of self-commitment. Similarly, an increase beyond a performance emphasis involves another such change—the introduction of the norm of self-defined self-interest in commitment, as well as the separation of proprietorship from management. But between points of discon-

---

[27] On the other hand, it may be impossible to develop administrative rationality without generating problems and tensions.

tinuity, it appears possible for rationality to fluctuate independently of the institutional system, provided the requisite pattern suggested by the scale is maintained. Thus, for example, given an institutional adjustment to specific job assignments, performance can either be emphasized or not, with no institutional implications one way or the other. By the same token an organization with no rational characteristics at all can develop a centralized management, compensatory rewards, and specialization without encountering institutional difficulties. But if either of these organizations were to proceed further in rational development, its mode of institutionalization would have to change considerably.

The fact that Table 2 is symmetrical suggests that the converse of the preceding argument may also be valid, insofar as obligation to participate is concerned. It appears that, if participation is institutionalized as voluntary commitment based on self-defined self-interest, the organization must at least involve segmental participation plus, in principle, the five other characteristics lower on the scale. Also, participation based on self-commitment in a context of kinship or community obligations implies an organization at least sufficiently rational to possess specific job assignments, together with specialization, compensatory rewards, and a centralized management. On the other hand, where participation is purely ascriptive or based on compulsory reciprocity, no rational elements need necessarily be present.

One may next ask: In what kinds of societal settings is administrative rationality, together with its requisite institutional arrangements, most likely to be found? Owing to gaps in the data, our analysis at this point is necessarily quite fragmentary. If complex hereditary aristocracy, the existence of slavery, hereditary succession to political office, and complex government are viewed as rough indexes of an ascriptive emphasis in the culture concerned, Tables 4 and 5 suggest, as one might suppose, that organizations in settings where ascription is stressed are themselves likely to be highly socially involved, and hence possess nonrational administrative systems. It is particularly noteworthy that complex hereditary stratification is absent from the setting of all the most rational administrative systems. But this relationship is not symmetrical, and the situation with respect to the other social setting variables is not nearly so marked. One infers, therefore, that, to some extent at least, fairly rational organizations can be institutionalized in quite "hostile" settings. Also, it would appear that a propitious setting does not in itself guarantee rational administration. Why might this be so?

We have already seen that certain elements of rationality—notably specialization and performance emphasis—are at least partially functions of technical, as opposed to institutional, influences. If in a more general sense it is the case that administration tends to be no more rational than is technically necessary, one would indeed expect to find instances of relatively nonrational administrative systems in settings where rationality would in principle be possible, merely because in the instances concerned rationality would be technically unnecessary.

A second reason may stem from the type of ascription present in the social setting. Stinchcombe has suggested that where rationality is a general cultural value, ascription may not markedly inhibit rationality in administration, on the grounds that the major effect of ascription is to infuse the organization with general cultural values.[28] It is possible that the Iroquois case in our sample partially illustrates this type of situation. It is known that Iroquois culture placed a high valuation on efficiency and achievement, with socialization measures taken to assure the differential competence of hereditary political officials. The Iroquois organization in our sample is highly rational, yet exists in a society with a complex government involving hereditary political officials. Complex hereditary stratification is absent, however. Furthermore, participation is based on self-defined self-interest. It may be that a general valuation of rationality simply tends to make possible nonascriptive recruitment in otherwise ascriptive settings. Modern industrial society may largely fit in this category. But even in the presence of a high cultural valuation on efficiency and rationality, ascriptive recruitment can still be disruptive to organizational operations by introducing competing goals and loyalties, however "rationally" they are individually viewed. It would seem that there are limits to the extent to which the effects of ascription on administration can be offset by institutional arrangements.

Conclusions

In a sample of 34 nonindustrial production organizations, 7 organizational characteristics associated with administrative rationality were found to scale in a cross-sectional comparative analysis in such a way as to suggest that rationality involves a cumulative emphasis on specificity of organizational roles and decision rules. The rationality scale was further found to be highly negatively associated with

---

[28] See [525].

the degree to which the organization is socially involved with its setting; administrative rationality appears to require some modicum of organizational independence. Rationality was somewhat less closely negatively associated to settings having traditional ascriptive elements. From these findings it was possible to infer certain differentials in problems of organizational development under varying conditions.

PART THREE

Interdisciplinary perspectives

12

THE CUMULATION OF ROLES INTO HOMOGENEOUS STRUCTURES

Harrison White

Introduction [1]

Sponsor to protegé, sender to receiver, subordinate to superior are but a few of the asymmetric relations ubiquitous in organizations. Normally one thinks of formal organizations as composed of offices assigned fixed duties whose empirical interrelations define the structure of relations among offices. There is a converse view: asymmetric relations define relative roles which can be cumulated indefinitely until closure is reached at the boundaries of the organization. In this view, organizational structure is defined as the articulation of chains of cumulated roles which define the indirect role relations between each pair of men.

---

[1] A detailed account of the analysis sketched here, including application to four tribes, can be found in [599]. A. Weil and R. R. Bush were the first to apply modern algebra to the study of classificatory kinship, and their papers are reproduced as appendices in the above reference. J. Kemeny, J. Snell and G. Thompson developed this early work further, and the reader will find their book [314] a helpful reference in other respects as well. Major aspects of the general topic of trees and networks are ably summarized in [63] and [451]. Unfortunately none of this work is helpful, as far as I have been able to discover, for the problems raised here about kinship systems. It should be possible eventually to find parallels between kinship structures as treated in this chapter and modern accounts of the atomic structure of magnetic crystals and of electric switching circuitry. The best single reference on the mathematical approach described in this chapter is [354]. A general account of Australian kinship systems can be found in [179].

The word "relative" has another meaning, "kinsman." It is in the kinship systems of tribes in Australia and nearby areas that the idea of a formal organization as a structure of cumulated roles has been worked out most completely. From examples of these kinship systems and the generalizations derived later, we can get ideas for new ways to analyze existing formal organizations as well as for new types of organization. Native intelligence is no monopoly of civilization, and it should not be surprising that men at a stone-age level in some respects outdistance us in some aspects of social organization.

To understand the underlying logic, we will trace out how and why our type of kinship relations might evolve into an Australian one. The core principle of this evolution turns out to be consistency in the structure of role relations, which leads to homogeneity. Hierarchy is the antithesis of Australian kinship systems. Even very complex ones are, in principle, homogeneous; the structure looks the same from every position.

Family trees are a familiar example of the branching diagrams, called simply trees, which are the natural tool to begin with. Marriage is with prescribed types of kin in Australian systems; thus branches of the tree we start with are joined in regular patterns, forming the networks and lattices in two and more dimensions illustrated later. The structure of such networks can be described economically in algebraic terms, and we indicate how the detailed work of deriving a catalogue of possible systems is carried out mathematically. A given network can be rolled up into any of a very large number of closed structures of groups of kinsmen by a variety of social events, and without mathematical guidance we would be lost in the welter of an astronomically large number of possible systems. Anthropologists seem unaware of the variety of kinship systems logically possible and may too often force the data for a tribe into a simpler mold than is appropriate.

Trees of Kin Roles

Brother and other relatives are social inventions—roles. A biological rationale is usually provided in a culture, but the criteria for assignment of one person to the role of brother to another vary from culture to culture in ways having nothing to do with biology. It is position in a structure of roles which perhaps most clearly distinguishes a kin role like brother from other roles with similar role behavior like friend. The brother (B) role at once implies sister (Z), father (F), mother (M), son (S), daughter (D), wife (W), and husband (H) roles, to begin with. Some tribes do not use the roles of brother and sister, but rather think only in terms of roles for what we would call elder brother, elder sister, and younger sibling. Nonetheless the familiar list of eight primary kin roles will serve as a convenient starting point.

Like other types of roles relevant to the structure of formal organizations, kin roles can be cumulated. Ego recognizes that each of his seven close relatives is his own ego with a field of seven kin roles, some of whose occupants are not occupants of any of the seven roles closest to ego. In a given culture, the cumulation of kinship roles can be represented as a tree with fixed rules as to the types of branches that emerge from a given type of branch. Brother's father will not define a new role in a society without polyandry, for example, nor will mother's husband be a role distinct from father.

Two of the primary roles can be replaced by cumulated roles to simplify notation; it is convenient to replace mother by father's wife (*FW*), and daughter by son's sister (*SZ*). Figure 1 demonstrates the branching rules for a tree in which all kin roles familiar to us are specified. One can see how dense and complex the tree will become in even the third and fourth steps; within 30 steps of ego, there will be more branches in the tree than people in the world.

Kin relations could be extremely confusing for ego in the small inbred tribe where he is trained to view everyone in a kin role, for there could be a bewilderingly large variety of roles vis-à-vis ego combined in a given person. But compound kin roles are not imposed

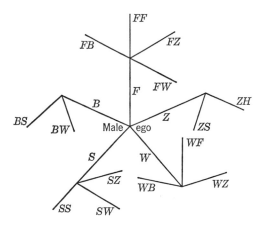

FIGURE 1 The first two steps in a tree which specifies efficiently all kinship roles we recognize. *B* stands for brother, *Z* for sister, *F* for father, *S* for son, and *W* for wife, while, for example, *WZ* stands for wife's sister.

on society by biological constraints; in some sense they have been institutionalized *by* a tribe as the primary means of defining and regularizing social relations among members. One would expect that in such a tribe kin roles are defined and compounded according to laws which have evolved so as to minimize ambiguity in role relations among concrete persons. The tree in Fig. 1 will not do.

In principle, or as an ideal type, the Australian kinship system is one in which a consistent structure of social relations among members can be built solely on the basis of kinship roles as extended by a process of cumulation as in a tree. Consistent is the key word. Social relations mean norms, and the assertion is that social relations are consistent only if all members of the society agree when a norm is violated in a given instance. Whenever two persons considered identical in role by a third are differentiated by a fourth, there exists potential disagreement between the latter on the application of norms, the incest taboo case below being an example.

Consider a tribe through the eyes of one man taken as ego in the role tree. He wishes to place the other members at the nodes of his tree. He perceives not only role relations they have to him but also role relations between them implied by their relations to him. A new role relation, say, *alter*, describes the identity relation that ego perceives between two persons in the same role with respect to ego; e.g., Mac and Sam, both brothers of his father, are alters in ego's view.

If kin roles are to place the members of a tribe in a clear and mutually consistent structure of relations, the following properties are essential.

AXIOM 1A. In the kin role tree of a given person as ego, if two persons are alters in one node of the tree, then in any other node in which one appears the other must also appear as an alter to the first.

AXIOM 1B. The tree of kinship roles must be such that all persons who are alters (have equivalent roles) with respect to one person as ego must be alters with respect to any other person as ego.

Important consequences result from Axiom 1, the two parts taken together. No male kinship role may be differentiated from a kinship role which would be related to the former as brother to male ego, nor may a female kinship role lead to a distinct branch for the role of sister to it. Anthropologists call this the principle of brother equivalence and term kinship systems which obey it as "classificatory." Why from a formal abstract view is brother so different from son that the former role must be reduced to alter but not the latter?

Some minimal roles, F, H, W, of the idealized tree specified in Fig. 2 can hold but one person with respect to an ego, whereas the other roles, B, Z, S, in the minimal set can hold an indefinite number of people. Axiom 1 requires that all initial plus compound branches hold at most one person or, else, all branches can hold an indefinite number of persons with respect to ego.

Two examples will show how our kinship tree violates Axiom 1 and leads to an inconsistent structure of role relations. Consider three brothers, John, Joe, and Jim, each of whom has a wife and a son. In terms of our kin role tree, John's son views Joe's and Jim's wives as alters, behavior toward whom is guided by identical norms. To Joe's son, Joe's wife is, of course, mother (or father's wife, to be consistent in our terminology), whereas Jim's wife would be in the role of father's brother's wife. Obviously Axiom 1 is violated. The role "father" must apply to all three men in the eyes of each son, and, of course, all three wives must be alters to satisfy Axiom 1.

A man may not marry his sister, nor equivalently may a woman marry her brother. This word formula for an incest taboo is applicable in all societies, though the operational meaning varies. Obvious as it seems, the taboo has a curiously powerful impact in a society in which perceptions and acts are governed solely by kinship roles. Let the same three men's wives each have a brother and a sister recognized as such as in our terminology. In John's eyes Jim's wife's brother is alter to Joe's wife's brother, as are the two wives' sisters. Necessarily in John's role tree, the brother of Jim's wife is in the relation of brother to the sister of Joe's wife. Therefore to John marriage between them violates the incest taboo, but in either Joe's or Jim's eyes no such thing occurs.

A consistent kinship structure looks the same to every ego, not only the abstract role tree but also the structure of role relations among concrete individuals. Another way to put it is that the application of norms governing role behavior is homogeneous. Norms that a person recognizes as governing a specific role relation of his with another person he can invoke as equally applicable to the mutual behavior of two other people whom he perceives as in that same role relation.

Since brother is alter to ego, father's brother is alter to father, etc., in a classificatory kinship system, at most four branches lead out from each node in the kinship tree. Suppose we associate one's sister's son with her husband; so from the branch for sister only the single branch to her husband is split off. Then we can omit all branches for female roles, it being understood that to each node representing a male role is attached the sister as well. To each node are connected

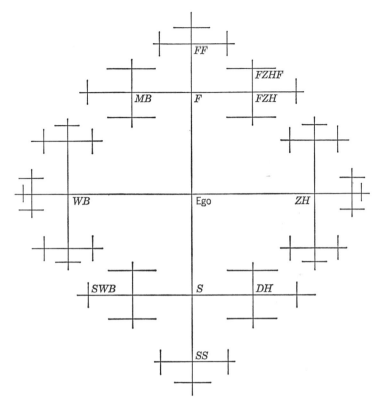

FIGURE 2   Tree of kin roles for a classificatory system. Only male roles are shown explicitly.

the same four branches, to father, son, wife's brother, and sister's husband. Figure 2 shows the first four steps from ego in the resulting tree. It is much simpler and more regular than the tree in Fig. 1, but even so there are 1,456 nodes no more than six steps from ego.

A stipulation is in order. Consider two compound roles in the kin tree which are given the same name in that tribe, just as *FF* and *MF* are both called grandfather by us. They may nonetheless be recognized as distinct roles. In other words, an occupant of one is not the alter of the occupant of the other, if the respondent who uses the joint role name for those two men is questioned as to the positions of the latter in the compound role tree recognized in that society. A near relative of the two men would certainly use different role names for them. Axiom 1 is not violated by such terminological inconsistency. It is unreasonable to expect kinship terminology in itself to reveal the full distinctions among roles that a native draws where appropriate.

His behavior toward distant relatives is not ordinarily governed by norms stringent and variable enough to require distinctive names in everyday usage for each distant compound role he recognizes.

There remains a basic ambiguity. Some role for brother or sibling of the same sex is institutionalized even in societies with classificatory systems; certainly such kin terms and role prescriptions are reported. This conflict is resolved when kinship roles are differentiated into public and private aspects. Kin roles as cumulated into trees for classificatory systems are not the total content of kinship relations perceived by individual members of tribes. These roles are only the public aspect of kinship relations, the aspect relevant in the eyes of tribe members to the place of individuals in the tribe as a whole. Exactly what concrete behavior patterns the tree roles regulate is an empirical question, but choice of marriage partners, through which new parts of the tree are identified, should clearly be one.

Marriage Rules and Networks

In a small tribe a man can hardly avoid marrying a girl who is kin to him. If different men married girls related to them in different ways, either the skein of kinship relations would become very involved and inconsistent or else the tree itself would collapse partially. It is not surprising that a variety of rules have evolved in different societies prescribing what type of kin a man must marry.

One common rule prescribes mother's brother's daughter as the category of kin from which a man's wife should be chosen. In effect, the classificatory role "wife" becomes indistinguishable from the classificatory role MBD, and the same native kinship term will apply to both; so the nodes for WB and MBS in Fig. 2 should be coalesced. Every man is to marry his MBD; so at each successive step in the tree, each node should be welded to the node which stands to it in the relation of $ZHMBS$. The general tree in Fig. 2 collapses into the two-dimensional net shown in Fig. 3.

One's mother's brother's daughter is one's first cousin in our terms. Two other kinds of first cousin, FBD and MZD, are in classificatory logic just siblings, since all FB are classificatory fathers and all MZ are classificatory mothers. All girls in a given relation to a man must be treated the same way; so marriage to these two "parallel" cousins is prohibited by the incest taboo against marrying one's sister.

It is important to realize how wide a variety of actual genealogical kin are included in a classificatory category. Not only the two first cousins above but also second cousins like $FFBSD$ or $MFBDD$ are ego's classificatory sisters, whatever the marriage rule. When marriage is prescribed with MBD, the field of eligible spouses is much wider than actual mother's actual brother's actual daughter; for example, not only $MMZSD$ but also $MMBDD$ are equivalent to MBD.

Figure 3 can easily be described in algebraic terms. Let W be the operator which transforms each node representing a role to the next node to the left representing its WB, and let C shift the network down a rung, the transformation of father into son. In this operator notation, the "product" WC defines an operator which first transforms to WB and then to S, while CW combines the same two operators in inverse order. In Fig. 3, W and C clearly are isomorphic to unit vectors pointing left and down respectively, and operator multiplication corresponds to vector addition. Hence $WC = CW$, or in algebraic terms W and C, commute with each other. The tree in Fig. 2 can also be described in terms of these operators, but as long as there are no marriage rules to define closed loops in the tree, algebraic manipulations are sterile.

Father's sister's daughter is the fourth type of first cousin. If marriage is prescribed with FZD, the kinship tree condenses into a more complicated network, as shown in Fig. 4. Here an arrow is drawn from each node to the node which stands in the relation of WB; i.e., the arrow runs from husband to wife. Moving left in the diagram means going toward the WB node only in alternate generations. This alternation in direction is reflected in the algebraic condition for FZD marriage, $WC = CW^{-1}$. Here W^{-1} means the inverse operation to W, $WW^{-1} = I$, where I is the identity or "do-nothing" operator corresponding to 0 in ordinary addition and 1 in ordinary multiplication. No longer do W and C commute.

If by the marriage rule the ego can marry both his MBD and his FZD, then by classificatory logic the two roles are equivalent and the

MBMB				
	MB	F	FZH	
	WB	Ego	ZH	
		S		

FIGURE 3   Network into which the tree of classificatory kinship roles is folded when marriage is prescribed with MBD.

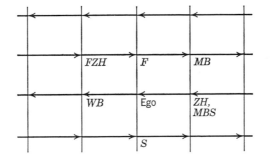

FIGURE 4 Network of kin roles for marriage prescribed with *FZD*. Each arrow runs from husband to wife's brother.

corresponding nodes should be coalesced. It is easy to see from Figs. 3 and 4 that the result must be the ladder in Fig. 5. In algebraic terms since both

$$WC = CW$$

and

$$WC = CW^{-1}$$

then

$$CW = CW^{-1}$$

and $W = W^{-1}$; i.e., W is equivalent to its inverse so that the marriage transformation must be represented by a reciprocal arrow.

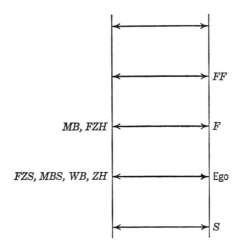

FIGURE 5 Network of kin roles when the wife role is equivalent both to *MBD* and to *FZD* roles.

Any relative can be specified by the sequence of operators which transforms ego into that relative. It is clear from Fig. 2 that in any classificatory kinship system the product of some sequence of the operators W, W^{-1}, C and C^{-1} will take one from ego to any classificatory relative of his. The operator transforming ego to mother and mother's brother is $C^{-1}W$. The condition for MBD marriage is thus $C^{-1}WC = W$, or after premultiplying both sides by C, $WC = CW$, as stated before.

In many tribes marriage is forbidden with first cousins and instead prescribed with some types of second cousins (who are by definition the grandchildren of siblings). Of the 16 types of second cousins logically possible (given one is male and one female), 4 are siblings in classificatory terms and 4 are first cousins. Hereafter only the remaining eight types are called second cousins. As one might expect, a rule prescribing marriage to any one type of second cousin alone does not reduce the tree to a two-dimensional network as in Figs. 3 and 4. The eight types fall into four pairs,

(a)	$FMBSD$	and	$FFZSD$
(b)	$MMBDD$	and	$MFZDD$
(c)	$MMBSD$	and	$FFZDD$
(d)	$FMBDD$	and	$MFZSD$

in which one second cousin becomes equivalent to the other if men exchange their classificatory sisters in marriage. That is, if $W^2 = I$, each of the pairs reduces to a single distinct classificatory relationship, just as FZD and MBD become equivalent if $W^2 = I$. (Such "sister exchange" in itself does not reduce the tree of Fig. 2 into any network, but rather into a tree in which each horizontal trunk is condensed as in Fig. 5 into a single link of reciprocal arrows.)

Only in one case, $FFZDD$, does prescribed marriage with a single type of second cousin reduce the tree even to a three-dimensional network. This structure is shown in Fig. 6, where the trunks representing lines of descent from father to child are drawn as dotted lines to improve clarity. The reader should check for himself that from *each* node in this complex grid an arrow goes to the node representing its $FFZDD$, the node of which does not contain any other first or second cousins. Contrary to appearances, the network is completely homogeneous. In algebraic terms, the operator transforming ego to his $FFZDD$ is the product $(C^{-1})(C^{-1})(W^{-1}C)(W^{-1}C)$. Thus the marriage rule for Fig. 6 is

$$C^{-2}W^{-1}CW^{-1}C = W$$

which is the same as

$$(W^{-1}C)^2 = C^2W$$

Note that

$$(W^{-1}C)^2 \neq W^{-2}C^2$$

since then

$$WC = CW$$

and marriage with MBD would be prescribed.

If marriage is prescribed with both second cousins in a pair, only for pair (a) i.e., $FMBSD$ and $FFZSD$, is the result a two-dimensional network. This network, in which marriage is prescribed with both $FMBSD$ and $FFZSD$ so that they are equivalent and $W^{-1} = W$, is drawn in Fig. 7. The algebraic condition is

$$WC^2 = C^2W$$

since the operator for $FMBSD$ is $(C^{-1})\,(C^{-1}W)\,(C)\,(C)$.

Pairs (a) and (b) have a special affinity. If marriage is prescribed with $FMBSD$ from pair (a) and $MMBDD$ from pair (b), but not with the other two so that $W^2 \neq I$, the tree is reduced to the three-

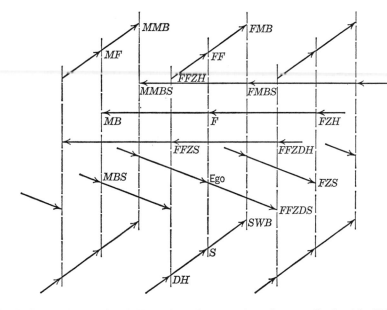

FIGURE 6   Network of kin roles when marriage is prescribed with $FFZDD$ alone among all first and second cousins, drawn in three-dimensional perspective. Each solid arrow runs from the node for a husband (H) to the node for his wife's brother (WB). Lines of descent through successive generations of males are dotted to insure visual clarity.

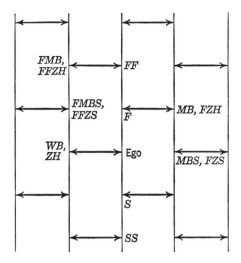

FIGURE 7 Network of kin roles when marriage is prescribed with $FMBSD$ and $FFZSD$ alone among all first and second cousins. Sisters are exchanged in marriage ($W^2 = I$).

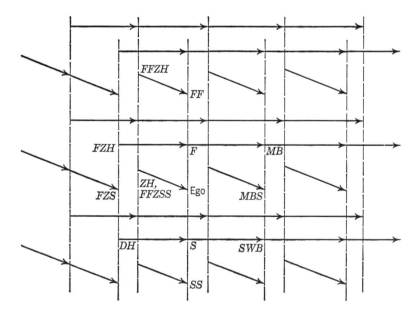

FIGURE 8 Network of kin roles when marriage is prescribed with $FMBSD$ and $MMBDD$ alone among all first and second cousins.

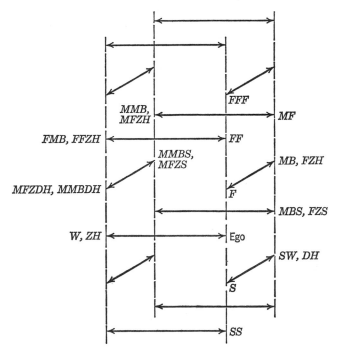

FIGURE 9 Scaffolding into which the tree of classificatory kin roles is folded when marriage is prescribed with *FMBSD, FFZSD, MMBDD,* and *MFZDD* but no other second or first cousins.

dimensional network in Fig. 8. If still $W^2 \neq I$, but marriage is prescribed with the other two second cousins in the pairs, *FFZSD* and *MFZDD*, the tree is reduced to a more complex three-dimensional network. This network has the same framework as in Fig. 8, but the direction of arrows is reversed in every second plane. The marriage condition for *MMBDD* in algebraic terms is

$$(C^{-1}W)^2 = (WC^{-1})^2$$

which like the rule for *FMBSD* is suggestive of the simple commutative rule for *MBD* marriage,

$$CW = WC$$

If, finally, marriage is prescribed with all four types of second cousins in pairs (a) and (b), so that all are equivalent to the wife role and to each other, the tree is folded into the four-sided scaffolding shown in Fig. 9. The algebraic conditions which define this scaffolding are

$$W^2 = I \quad CW \neq WC$$

$$C^2W = WC^2 \qquad (CW)^2 = (WC)^2$$

Pairs (c) and (d) also have a special affinity, and marriage for them clashes with marriage for the four types in (a) and (b). If just the four second cousins in pairs (c) and (d) are eligible spouses and hence equivalent, the algebraic conditions are

$$W^2 = I \quad WC \neq CW \quad (WC)^2 = C^2W \qquad (CW)^2 = WC^2$$

The four-sided scaffolding to which the general tree is reduced is shown in Fig. 10.

Marriages and Closed Structures

Australian tribes are so small, it is impossible to assign a different group of people to each node in the tree of kin roles (whoever is taken as ego), even after the tree is condensed into a simple network such

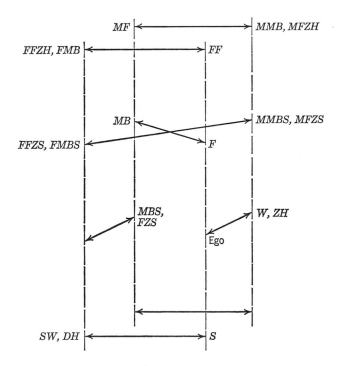

FIGURE 10 Scaffolding of kin roles when marriage is prescribed with *FFZDD*, *MMBSD*, *FMBDD*, and *MFZSD* only, of second and first cousins.

as the one for *MBD* marriage in Fig. 3. Many nodes will contain a lot of people; e.g., if ego's mother had a lot of brothers, there could be dozens of men assigned to the *MBS* role. Because of the cumulative effects of age differences between siblings, people of the same age may be assigned to nodes several generations apart, while to the same node may be assigned young boys and men long dead. Yet by Axiom 1, if two people are alters in one role, each must appear in all the nodes in which the other appears, whoever the person taken as ego; otherwise the kinship system is not consistent. It follows that the same group of persons must appear repeatedly at various nodes in the tree.

Some nodes may be bare of living representatives. Men assigned the node to the right of a bare node in Fig. 3 are in a pickle: their prescriptive right to marry *MBD* does them little good. In any case, there will often be too large a group of classificatory brothers for the available numbers of girls of the right age who are *MBD* to them. The surplus men will marry available girls assigned to some other node in the tree, preferably a node far away so that the deviation from marriage norms is not too obvious. The same surplus may continue long enough to build up a tradition of marriage to the other node. Then men in the original node are publicly viewed as also being assigned to the node for husbands of the girls they married. Close relatives of the men must then also be assigned to additional nodes, by Axiom 1.

The final result of such marriages of convenience, in a tribe where classificatory logic is applied relentlessly, can be to "roll up" a network of kin roles as in Fig. 3 into a closed figure, such as in Fig. 11. Of course, Fig. 11 could also result from the imposition of additional prescriptive rules of marriage and descent. There are but four generations in each descent line in Fig. 11, and in many tribes there is an explicit rule that *FF* and *SS* are equivalent roles—they are given the same name.

Figure 11 represents the payoff of our analysis. It shows how a society can be divided into a relatively small number of distinct kin groups through an evolution guided by classificatory logic. Let us call each kin group a *clan:* all men in a clan are classificatory brothers, interchangeable in the kinship structure. No longer does the effect of kinship relations in grouping people have to be relative to whose viewpoint one assigns to be ego's. Clans are very much like fixed offices in a formal organization; in the structure in Fig. 11 each person is objectively allocated to a fixed clan which can be given a permanent name, not dependent on who is ego. Kin relations can be derived from clan membership as well as vice versa.

It is by no means easy to find how many consistent ways there are

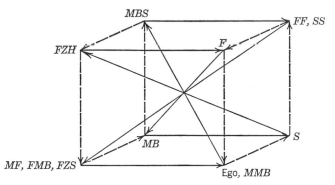

FIGURE 11   Closed structure of eight clans into which network of kin roles for *MBD* marriage (Fig. 3) can be folded, as a result of traditions of marriage. All men in a clan are classificatory brothers. Each solid arrow runs to the clan of *WB*; each dotted arrow runs to the clan of *S*.

to roll up a network of kin roles into a closed structure of clans. The simplest approach is to start from the other end by deriving from Axiom 1 a set of axioms which must be satisfied in any consistent and homogeneous structure of clans. The operators introduced before can be regarded as permuting the clans, and, in fact, the set of operators generated by W and C will constitute a finite group of permutations. It can be shown that all structures of clans can be deduced from the regular representation of the elements of such finite groups by matrices. There are remarkably few such structures. For example, among 16 clans, one can construct 4 consistent structures in which marriage is with *FZD* but not *MBD*, 26 structures where marriage is with *MBD* but not *FZD*, and 2 additional structures in which marriage is with both *FZD* and *MBD*. Consistent structures of clans in which marriage with first cousins is prohibited are even less common. For example, only when the number of clans is a multiple of eight can one construct structures in which just the four types of second cousins in pairs (*a*) and (*b*) are eligible spouses (see Fig. 9), and there are only two such structures for each multiple of eight.

Conclusion

Aborigines do not use algebra or construct three-dimensional models of the structures of their kinship systems, but they understand the cumulation of kin roles into trees and networks very well indeed, and for many an anthropologist they have drawn in the sand diagrams as complex as Fig. 11. Several times in analyzing field reports, I have been forced to the conclusion that the observer oversimplified the ideal structure to which the natives oriented their concrete behavior. Anthropologists are not addicted to the systematic reporting of hard data, but it is often possible to deduce a kinship system from the structure of kinship terminology supplemented by a few genealogies.

Certainly, a model like Fig. 11 is an ideal type: not all choices of spouses and kinship appellations conform to it. Repairs and adjustments are often called for; many of these tribes number but a few hundred and the demographic variability is great. Under the pressure of mixing with other tribes, a conscious change of ideal structure may be adopted by a tribe. If constrained within the framework of a completely consistent system, evolution of kinship relations can only proceed in the direction of fewer clans and a simpler structure, but elders have been known to reassign roles arbitrarily.

Neither in its evolution nor functioning need a kinship system be dependent on conscious understanding of it in its totality by participants, who need only follow the rules as directly applied to themselves. Therefore we can hope to find analogues functioning in more familiar organizations. It is unlikely that we will uncover systems of relational terms as well organized as a set of classificatory kin terms. Given data in the form of sociograms, a first step would be to develop a self-consistent search procedure to identify a set of "clans" as groups of men equivalent with respect to the bases of choice. One of the main results of this as of the kinship analysis would be to discover what indirect role relations can consistently be combined between a pair of men, e.g., in one of the diagrams which types of relatives appear in the same node.

The manifest authority structure and Table of Organization of a bureaucracy need not match a latent structure deduced from the cumulation of the role relations between pairs of actors. For that matter, role relations need not be the content of the "arrows" or transformations for the mathematical machinery we have developed to work. For example, "marriage" could be taking over another man's job. Or the "clans" could be tasks and a "descent" arrow could be the assignment of precedence between tasks. Nor need one be limited to a basis of two types of transformation, although there must be at least two for a homogeneous structure based on them to have a structure which is not trivial. With such novel interpretations of the permutations which are the formal core of our analysis, one would, however, have to reexamine the applicability of Axiom 1 and the meaning of homogeneity.

13

EXPLORATORY MODELS IN THE THEORY OF BUDGET CONTROL

A. Charnes and A. Stedry

Introduction [1]

The problems and processes of budgetary control tend to be sufficiently complex and subtle so that a variety of attacks appear to be in order. There is, of course, a literature in accounting, administration (public and private), etc., which has attempted a distillation of experience in order to discover "principles" or to reach for certain "normative" or "prescriptive" rules for budgeting which are deemed to be (a) valid under certain circumstances and (b) sufficiently precise as guides to practice. See, e.g., Stedry [516] for relevant citations. More recently the area has begun to be studied by means of methods and concepts common to the various sciences. Argyris [21], for example, reports a field study approach to some of the "human" problems of budgeting and Simon, Kozmetsky, Guetzkow, and Tyndall also dealt

[1] We would like to express our appreciation for suggestions and helpful comments by W. W. Cooper in preparation of this paper. We also acknowledge the contribution of Selwyn W. Becker in pointing out recent work in aspiration level theory relevant to our models, and to Trevor Sainsbury for his thorough review of the manuscript.

The research underlying this paper was undertaken for the project *Temporal Planning and Management Decisions under Risk and Uncertainty* at Northwestern University, under contract with the U. S. Office of Naval Research. Reproduction of this paper in whole or in part is permitted for any purpose of the United States Government. Contract Nonr-1228(10), Project NR 047-021. This paper is a revised version of an earlier paper which appeared as Northwestern University O.N.R. Research Memorandum No. 43.

with aspects of this problem as one part of a total field study [503] of the "controllership function." Subsequently, Stedry [516] applied the techniques of classical (psychological) laboratory experimentation as one part of an inquiry which included analytical models of a deterministic (differential equation) variety. Finally, C. P. Bonini [79] has utilized the techniques of computer simulation, and subjected them to statistical verification, as yet another way to study aspects of budgetary procedures in terms of their bearing on information-action processes for a firm in a "behavioral-economics-accounting" setting. See also Bonini, Chapter 15, this volume.

These and other approaches should, and will, be continued, of course, and still other approaches will probably also be investigated. Here we propose to use, or extend, parts of modern mathematics—notably Markov processes, decision theory, and search theory—in order to study what might be accomplished by purely mathematical formulations directed toward models of budgetary control which are probabilistic in nature.

It is proposed, so far as possible, to develop models which are consistent with, or pertinent to, previous findings in psychology and economics, and to known parts of the problems of "rational" budgetary management. Particular emphasis is placed on literature dealing with "levels of aspiration" in psychology and the ideas of profit maximization or cost minimization [2] in economics.

It is neither possible nor desirable, at present, to rest research in model development on the existing states of knowledge in psychology, economics, or other disciplines, or even to confine the developments so that a precise correspondence is always achieved. For one thing, a universal consensus has not yet been achieved on the underlying categories and, furthermore, these ideas have not generally been developed in a way that always makes them immediately pertinent and applicable to the problems and processes of management budgeting or goal-setting.[3] Furthermore, there are certain very significant problems in budgeting where neither evidence nor theorizing appears to be

---

[2] More generally the reference is to "benefits" and "penalties" as interpreted via, say, utility functions, e.g., of von Neumann-Morgenstern type, where risk or uncertainty is involved.

[3] See the discussion and references—e.g., to the so-called marginalist controversy in economics—as given on p. 11 ff. in [248]. It is also of interest to observe here that psychologists at the conference (where this paper was presented) were not in unanimous agreement even on the pertinence of aspiration level theory in general or even in universal agreement on the "facts" resulting from experiments in this area.

available. The so-called principle-of-exceptions approach, which is widely used in budgeting and cost accounting, is a case in point. Although, from the standpoint of attempting to minimize the amount of executive time spent on items which are not of critical importance, it is desirable to focus on exceptions—i.e., those items which are not proceeding according to some predetermined plan—this focus appears to have resulted in communication between supervisor and subordinate only when something has "gone wrong." This would appear to have the undesirable side effect (from a psychological standpoint) of making supervisor-subordinate communication one of criticism and distribution of (possibly implicit) punishment. Thus the supervisor-subordinate relationship may be viewed with hostility, and the quantitative information or control devices associated with such communication marked for particular attack. However many the protestations against the use of budgets as devices for distribution of rewards and penalties (as, for example, the treatment by Hill and Gordon [270], Chapter 17), it is not clear that most, if not all, of the systems commonly in use which have an evaluative as well as informational function can escape reward-penalty distribution entirely. The question might be restated in terms of the relative desirabilities of two systems: (1) where the feedback from the systems largely carries negative reward implications (i.e., where an individual's information from the system is "where he went wrong" combined with a request for explanation of the unfavorable item); or (2) a system where explicit rewards and penalties are incorporated, and the attainment of the goals set is associated with specific positive reward rather than merely the absence of implicit punishment. Such questions are, however, beyond the scope of this chapter, where the focus is on the levels of goals rather than on the environment in which they are received.

Although the budgeting literature has been characterized by "assuming away" complications in human behavior, psychological treatments of aspiration level have been focused on the manner of formation of aspiration levels rather than the behavioral implications of the levels formed.[4] Furthermore, the literature on level of aspiration seems to have been preoccupied almost entirely with "single task" situations, whereas the principle-of-exceptions approach, as it appears in the management literature, is only operative in multiple-task situations.[5] Furthermore, under risk-probability conditions, which are of

---

[4] See, e.g., the discussion in Stedry [516], Chapter 3, for elaboration.

[5] See, e.g., Cooper and Savvas [135], where this point is made more vigorously.

interest here, the formal literature of economics has not been able to reach any consensus even on the meaning of "rationality." [6]

This chapter is concerned with three models of supervisory behavior in response to a budget control system: (1) a supervisor who has only one goal; (2) a supervisor in a multiple goal setting operating via the principle of management by exception; and (3) a "search oriented" model for a supervisor operating under a more general reward structure and with diminishing returns to scale of effort.[7] All of the models are probabilistic in character. For instance, (1) is examined via a so-called finite Markov chain model, whereas the model for (2) utilizes more general (classical) statistical notions which are then adapted to the ideas of decision theory in order to indicate how rational choices of effort allocation might be made under risk conditions. The latter ideas, in turn, are related to certain ideas such as increasing and decreasing returns to effort, by analogy with classical economics, and undoubtedly other analogies could also be found to ideas like returns to scale in information theory, psychophysics, etc., when alternative possibilities are under consideration and only probability estimates are available.

Whereas the models under (1) and (2) conform to the classical *a priori* notions of probability, statistics, etc., this is not necessarily true for the models in (3). Here the "search density functions" recently propounded in the operations research literature are utilized. The densities are only *relative* rather than absolute frequencies, since a "probability of one may not be achieved even when the density is integrated over its entire range.[8] Thus, a sought-for object may not be detected or a wanted goal may not be achieved with certainty even with "infinite" amounts of search or effort.

Although the latter ideas have a certain appeal in connection with aspiration level or level-of-achievement phenomena, we have not attempted to document or exploit directly these aspects of search theory and probability distributions. It seemed better, all things considered, to alter model constructions to achieve some connection with known

---

[6] That is, no consensus has been reached apart from the pure formalisms of "utility maximization." See, e.g., Charnes and Cooper [115] for ways of characterizing differing objectives that might well be considered under operational conditions.

[7] This may also be interpreted as diminishing returns to "scale of information." See, e.g., Marschak [369] and Shubik [491].

[8] See, e.g., Koopman [322]. To convert these functions to "true" densities, we must divide by the *a priori* probability of detection with up to infinite amounts of search or effort.

patterns of human behavior than to attempt to force the latter into classical definitions of probability. Here, then, as in the other cases, we have attempted to stay as close as possible to the received ideas of science and known problems of budgetary management. It is perhaps desirable to note, now, however, that these are only initial explorations. We have not attempted to exhaust all possibilities or even to survey and evaluate them, and, in fact, only certain aspects of the models (1) through (3) are covered in this chapter.

A Dynamic One-Variable Model

Relevant comments on the nature and shortcomings of our exploratory models will be introduced at suitable points herein. We shall also attempt to relate these developments to research by others that have been reported in the literature of psychology, economics, sociology and accounting. For instance, findings, and possible further research, in level of aspiration theory (or experimentation) will be examined after first introducing our one-goal one-variable model as follows.

We assume the existence of a set of performance values $Q = \{q^j\}$, $j = 1, \cdots, n$, which are ordered such that, if $j > k$, the performance q^j is preferred to the performance q^k. We wish to leave the nature of this preference relation as general as possible. The set Q might be interpreted (1) as a collection of production levels attainable at the same cost and quality but with possibly different supervisory effort (in which case $j > k$ implies $q^j > q^k$), or (2) as a collection of cost figures under unvarying quality and output (where higher costs would represent lower performance), or (3) a less well-structured set of "states of being" in which the relation $j > k$ implies that the performance q^j by this segment of the organization contributes more to organizational goals than performance q^k. We require, however, that these states of being can be recognized, both by the supervisor whose performance is being evaluated and by the person or persons who prepare budgets and evaluate performance.[9] Our use of the term "supervisor" here

---

[9] This does not imply complete understanding on the part of the supervisor of "how his budget is set," an impossibility if any but the least sophisticated techniques of forecasting and resource allocation are utilized in translating organizational goals into subentity plans. It should be emphasized that insistence upon *complete* understanding must, implicitly or explicitly, deny the existence or usefulness of, for example, linear programming planning tools. We merely hypothesize the existence of a description of the performance of the subentity such that the attainment or nonattainment of a particular "state" can be jointly recognized by the supervisor of the subentity and the evaluator of his performance.

should be understood as descriptive of the *budgeted* employee, not the preparer of the budget.

We do not require that a cardinal measurement of value exist for the different states. Instead, we assume that the transition from state q^j to state q^{j+l} (a more preferred state where l is positive) in one period with a given probability of occurrence requires an amount of effort which is a monotone increasing function of l and independent of j. The preference field is assumed, for convenience, to be strongly ordered, although it is possible that an extension to the case in which a member of a set of equally preferred states [10] can be attained with equal effort from another state.[11]

The level of effort which the supervisor will expend is assumed to be related to the performance value which he strives to attain, i.e., his aspiration level, relative to its current value. If he aspires to a future performance level equal to or less than his present performance, the effort he will expend toward improvement [12] will be small and, hence, the likelihood of improvement will likewise be small. If, on the other hand, his goals are so much higher than his previous performance that the effort he would need to expend to attain them is beyond his capabilities, a state of discouragement (with attendant sharp diminishing of effort, or at least effective effort) is likely to ensue, again decreasing the likelihood of improvement but, in addition, increasing the likelihood of a sharp decrease in performance, a phenomenon not usually associated with modest aspiration levels.[13] Between these values

---

[10] Analogous to an optimum in the linear programming formulation where alternate optima exist.

[11] Clearly, a transition to a performance of a lesser value to the organization than the most advantageous value that can be obtained with a given amount of effort is desirable from the standpoint of neither the supervisor nor the organization. We visualize a situation somewhat analogous to the game of chess in which, when a player has a number of equally good moves available to him (i.e., one period transitions to positions of equivalent value), we mean that the subsequent moves from these positions (as far as he can determine) will place him in positions of equivalent value although the actual positions may depend upon the choice of the immediate move.

[12] Improvement may be defined as a transition from the present level, say q^j, to level q^{j+k} with $k > 0$ in accordance with the ordering scheme defined above.

[13] A discussion of the effect of aspiration levels on performance with some empirical evidence can be found in Stedry [516]. It should be stated, however, that psychologists have been largely concerned with the determination of aspiration levels rather than their effect on performance. A notable exception is the study of Siegel and Fouraker [499] which produces strong evidence for an (externally induced) aspiration level substantially affecting performance. Much evidence exists for the substitution of stereotypes for intuitive behavior resulting in sub-

of "too low" and "too high" aspiration levels lie values which, by their stress-producing characteristics promote effort, the effect of which is to reduce the discrepancy between aspired and actual performance, i.e., to reduce stress.[14]

Under certain assumptions, the discrepancy between aspired and current performance levels should be, for optimal performance, just short of the point at which discouragement is produced.[15] The deterministic model, although possibly adequate for some situations in which a definitive relationship can be found for the effect of increased effort on performance, does not represent the situation more often encountered in practice. Increased effort [16] increases the likelihood of improvement but does not ensure it. Decreased effort or stereotyped response patterns [17] increase the likelihood of maintenance of the current or lower performance level but do not preclude accidental, i.e., "windfall," improvement.

Aspiration Level Assumptions

We can make our assumptions about aspirations somewhat clearer as follows. Let q^j represent the level of performance which a certain supervisor achieves in a period where $j = 1, \cdots, n$. We then assume that this supervisor has a set of aspiration levels which can be represented as $A \equiv \{a^{j+k}\}, k = -l, \cdots, -1, 0, 1, \cdots, m$. Thus the representative term in this set, which is a^{j+k}, is to be interpreted as the supervisor's aspiration in terms of the number of levels of improvement in excess of his current performance he will strive for in the next period. In other words, an individual who is now performing at level q^j and is trying to attain a performance of q^{j+k} will be said to have an aspiration level defined by a^{j+k}. Note that $k < 0$, which means that aspirations will be lowered, is possible while $k \geq 0$ means that

---

stantially diminished performance under "too much" stress (e.g., too large a discrepancy between aspired and actual performance) although the determination of the saturation point is difficult.

[14] Stress-reducing activity has been hypothesized and observed in many contexts. Cf. the treatment here with that of March and Simon [367], Chapter 3, and dissonance reduction observed by Festinger [190].

[15] As described by Stedry [516], Chapter 2.

[16] Throughout this paper we consider effort to be entrepreneurial effort—that which manifests itself in the search for new alternatives—as discussed by Simon [501], March and Simon [367], Charnes and Cooper [110], and others. A study which relates innovation in an organization to aspiration levels has been reported by Haberstroh [246].

[17] Which, since they do not constitute search or innovatory behavior, do not represent "effort" although they may be accompanied by a good deal of frenzy.

aspirations will either be raised or left unchanged. Note also that the range of j is n whereas the aspiration level set contains $n + l + m$ elements. Thus we permit the existence of aspiration level states which are not technologically feasible. Then we partition the set as follows. For the aspirations a^{j+k} which are technologically feasible, we let $j + k$ run from 1 to n. For aspiration levels which are not technologically feasible, we arrange the a^{j+k} so that $j + k = -l + 1, \cdots, -1,$ 0, and $j + k = n + 1, \cdots, n + m$ so that the indices 1 to n are excluded from this set. We thus admit the possibility that technologically infeasible aspirations may be required to achieve certain performance states q^j which are technologically feasible.[18] We recognize that we both trespass on current budgeting theory and on that psychological theory which presumes that such aspirations, since they cannot be fulfilled, are personally damaging to their holders. However, since we possess evidence [19] that such aspirations can produce superior performance without adversely affecting satisfaction with performance on the task,[20] we deem it prudent to include them for consideration as available aspirations in our models.

Although the process of aspiration level formation has been extensively investigated, the existing evidence does not allow us to propose a model which can rest upon much more than "reasonable assumptions." We shall consider an individual's aspiration level to be that level of performance which, if he achieves it, will be associated by him with a feeling of "success," and if not, "failure." [21] Whereas the now classic article of Lewin, Dembo, Festinger, and Sears [346] hypothesizes a choice of aspiration level at something close to a 50% (subjective) probability of success, a study reported by Becker and Siegel [54] and, in particular, recent investigations of Becker and

---

[18] Technological feasibility here refers to the ability of an organism as well as the existing state of knowledge (managerial, scientific) which it has available along with plant and machinery, worker ability, etc.

[19] See Stedry [516].

[20] See Stedry [517].

[21] This definition proposed by Becker and Siegel [54] is used rather than the widely accepted one proposed by J. D. Frank [203]: "The level of future performance which an individual, knowing his level of past performance in that task, explicitly undertakes to reach." The latter does not allow for formation of aspirations in a task which has not been previously performed, a phenomenon well known to exist. Furthermore, the mention only of "past performance" implies at least lack of emphasis on other factors influencing aspiration level determination, such as group norms, performance in similar tasks, externally suggested goals, etc., all of which have been shown to have some effect.

Parsons [53] indicate subjective probability of success for individual aspirations almost evenly distributed over the range from 0 to 100%.

What is of interest, however, is that some individuals will aspire to levels the accomplishment of which will be extremely easy, while others will aspire to the "impossible," even in the absence of externally suggested explicit goals, and so we cite some of the partial evidence that bears on this point. Siegel and Fouraker [499] report an experiment in which externally suggested (by the experimenter) goals appear to be accepted as aspiration levels almost with probability 1. Stedry [516] reports a high probability of acceptance of external goals as aspiration levels which tends to diminish (but not disappear) as the external goals approach levels which have a very low likelihood of attainment. Although the effect of varying reward attached to the attainment of an externally suggested goal on its internalization, i.e., the probability that it will be accepted as the aspiration level, has not been explicitly investigated, the use of more or less explicit rewards in the experiments cited above, which tend to indicate an acceptance of external goals, contrasts markedly with experiments of Chapman and Volkmann [104] which show little effect of external suggestions on aspiration in an experimental situation where (even intangible) reward attached to performing up to the suggested level seems to have been minimized. Simon, however, hypothesizes [501] that, if a goal is externally or internally suggested to an individual and it is satisfactory, he will accept it and seek no further for goals since searching for alternatives requires effort. If, on the other hand, it is unsatisfactory, he will search until he finds a satisfactory one, but no further.

While each of these studies has focused primarily on a single determinant of aspiration level—e.g., previous performance, or social norms, or an externally presented goal—aspiration levels set in a budgetary systems environment have at least two determinants. Specifically, an individual generally has some feedback from his past performance on which to formulate some estimate (or expectation) of his future performance. In addition, he has a goal which is presented to him by his superordinate [22] in the form of a budgeted performance for the period. Presumably, the aspiration level actually formed will result from the forces exerted by these two quantities—the expectation for future performance and the superordinate's aspiration for his per-

---

[22] It is generally considered that budgets are applicable and applied to people in supervisory positions, and hence the subject of our study is a budgeted supervisor. Rather than refer to this supervisor's "supervisor," we will refer to the former's supervisor as a "superordinate."

formance—in a manner as yet unspecified. The superordinate's goal (or budget) is then perceived as a mechanism for *influencing* the aspiration level of the subordinate.

In the light of available evidence, we propose a model having the following properties (which at least do not conflict with the extant evidence). For a given level of reward attached to attaining an external goal, the probability of acceptance of a goal initiated (or suggested) by a supervisor will be high if it is at or close to an individual's own *a priori* expectation of his probable performance. The probability of acceptance will be high if the goal represents a level of difficulty which has been attained previously; the probability of acceptance will diminish rapidly as the goal rises above the previously attained level. However, should the individual's expectation exceed previously attained levels, the probability of acceptance will be high for an external goal, as long as it is at or below, but not too far below, the expectation, but will diminish rapidly as the goal rises above the expectation; if the external goal is above or is substantially below the individual's expectations, the individual will, with a high probability, accept the expectation in lieu of the external goal. Increasing reward will increase the probability of acceptance of the goal since this will reduce, relatively, the factors which act as attractive forces for competing levels.

If we further assume that the current acceptance probabilities are independent of the absolute level of performance j, but depend only upon k, the number of levels of aspired improvement,[23] a table of acceptance probabilities for aspiration levels under several different budget "policies" might be constructed, as shown in Table 1, where b^{j+i} is defined as a budget set at i levels above current performance.

Model Details

In Table 1 it is assumed that the individual's performance expectation is one level above his current performance. Clearly these figures are shown merely for explanatory purposes, and there is no empirical justification for the use of the numerical values chosen or for confining the probabilities for each budget to only three possible levels.

Bearing these points in mind, we can now explain the entries of Table 1 as follows. Suppose the budget is set at b^{j+1}, i.e., the budget is

---

[23] It will be recalled that the effort expended in improving performance from q^j to q^{j+k} was constructed (by appropriate choice of the "distance" between various performance levels) independent of j.

Table 1   *Probability of Acceptance of an Aspiration Level k Levels Above Current Performance Given a Budget i Levels Above Current Performance and Expected Improvement of One Level*

		Aspiration Levels				
	$k =$ $i =$	−1	0	1	2	3
Budgets	−1	0.4	0.2	0.4		
	0	0.1	0.6	0.3		
	1		0.1	0.8	0.1	
	2		0.1	0.6	0.3	
	3			0.8	0.1	0.1

directed to raising this supervisor's aspiration level by one unit above current performance. By assumption the supervisor had formed an expectation of improvement by one unit and might, on the basis of this expectation, have already previously decided to raise his own aspiration by this amount. We must allow, however, for the influence of other (unspecified) environmental factors, so we have not assumed that this will produce agreement with probability one. We have, instead, assigned a probability of 0.8 to the "acceptance" of this change on the supervisor in the form of incorporating it in his own level of aspiration. See the entry at the intersection of row $i = 1$ and the column $k = 1$. We have also indicated in this same row $(i = 1)$ that the supervisor will change his previously decided aspirations, so that, with a probability of 0.1 in both cases, he will either (1) aspire only to his current level of performance (row $i = 1$ and column $k = 0$) or (2) raise his own aspirations two units above his current performance (row $i = 1$, column $k = 2$). He will in no case, under this "budget policy," move to $k = -1$ or $k = 3$. That is, the blanks under these columns for row $i = 1$ represent a zero probability of having the supervisor change his aspirations either by $k = -1$ (a change to one unit below his current performance) or by $k = 3$ (three units above it).

It will be noted that, in general, the column $k = 1$ contains the highest probabilities. But this is not universally true. For instance, if no budget change is made $(i = 0)$, then the supervisor has a high probability ($=0.6$) of not changing his aspirations in the direction he had

Table 2   Probability of Attaining Performance q^{j+h} in the Next Period Given Aspiration Level a^{j+k} in the Current Period

		Performance Levels		
$k =$	$h =$	-1	0	1
Aspiration Levels	0	0.3	0.6	0.1
	1	0.2	0.2	0.6
	2	0.6	0.3	0.1

previously decided upon. Also, if the budget is revised downward, below current performance, then the probability distribution (see row $i = -1$) is bimodal and, in fact, a so-called U-shaped distribution.

From a management standpoint, the main interest in aspiration levels lies in their effect on performance (rather than vice versa), and so we now single this out, via Table 2, preparatory to combining these into an aspiration level-performance interdependency model. The cells of Table 2 are to be interpreted as transition probabilities. In particular, they represent the probability that an individual who has attained performance q^j in period t will attain a performance level q^{j+h} in period $t + 1$ when his aspiration level in the latter period is a^{j+h}. It is assumed again that these probabilities are independent of j.

Although the data of Table 2 are again purely hypothetical, we may briefly indicate some aspects of its construction. As indicated in the foregoing section, it is likely that there will be a high probability of attainment for q^{j+h} with aspiration level a^{j+k} when $h = k$, provided that k is not too large.[24] Also, values in the vicinity of k will then tend to have a relatively high probability of attainment. On the other hand, high values of k (e.g., those which exceed a tolerable amount of stress) may cause discouragement or a tendency to stereotyped behavior which is represented in Table 2 as a high probability of recurrence of current performance, or, possibly, as a level below current performance.

---

[24] For example, the transition to k may be technologically infeasible.

A possible array of transition probabilities relating aspirations to performance levels in period $t + h$ is shown in Table 2. To see how some of the preceding assumptions are incorporated in these probabilities, refer to the row opposite $k = 2$. It has here been assumed that $k = 2$ constitutes a level of stress which is too great. This is reflected in a very high probability of performance deterioration, as witness the 0.6 entry under the column $h = -1$ in this row, followed by the next highest probability $(=0.3)$ of only achieving the current level of performance in period $t + h$. Finally, the entry under $h = 1$ is 0.1 while, for a^{j+2}, as well as all other cases, there is zero probability of attaining q^{j+2}.

Now we wish to combine the budget-aspiration effects of Table 1 with the aspiration-performance effects of Table 2. This will yield the transition matrix of Table 3. To construct a complete transition matrix for this system, it is necessary to specify the transition probability from the state q_t^{jk}, i.e., the joint occurrence of a performance of q^j in period t and aspiration level a^{j+k} for period $t + 1$ to state $q_{t+1}^{j'k'}$, where j' and k' are the new values of performance and aspiration levels respectively.

Table 3   Probability of Transition from State q_t^{jk} to State $q_{t+1}^{j'k'}$ with Budget Policy $i = 1$

| | | | Period $t + 1$ | | | | | | | | | | | |
| | | $j' \rightarrow$ | 1 | | | 2 | | | 3 | | | 4 | | |
$j \downarrow$	$k \downarrow$	$k' \rightarrow$	0	1	2	0	1	2	0	1	2	0	1	2
	0		0.09	0.72	0.09	0.01	0.08	0.01						
1	1		0.04	0.32	0.04	0.06	0.48	0.06						
	2		0.09	0.72	0.09	0.01	0.08	0.01						
	0		0.03	0.24	0.03	0.06	0.48	0.06	0.01	0.08	0.01			
2	1		0.02	0.16	0.02	0.02	0.16	0.02	0.06	0.48	0.06			
	2		0.06	0.48	0.06	0.03	0.24	0.03	0.01	0.08	0.01			
	0					0.03	0.24	0.03	0.06	0.48	0.06	0.01	0.08	0.01
3	1					0.02	0.16	0.02	0.02	0.16	0.02	0.06	0.48	0.06
	2					0.06	0.48	0.06	0.03	0.24	0.03	0.01	0.08	0.01
	0								0.03	0.24	0.03	0.07	0.56	0.07
4	1								0.02	0.16	0.02	0.08	0.64	0.08
	2								0.06	0.48	0.06	0.04	0.32	0.04

(Period t labels the left rows)

* *Note:* j = performance level.

k = aspiration level expressed as the number of levels above current performance.

i = budget level expressed as the number of levels above current performance.

This is merely the product of the appropriate probabilities shown in Tables 1 and 2. The probability, for example, that an individual in state $q_t^{j,1}$ will attain a performance of q^{j+1} in the period $t + 1$ is (from Table 2) 0.6. Given a budget for period $t + 2$ of $i = 1$, i.e., a budget of $j + 2$ which is one level above period $t + 1$ performance, he will be in state $q_{t+1}^{j+1,0}$ with probability 0.06, state $q_{t+1}^{j+1,1}$ with probability 0.48, etc., using the budget acceptance probabilities in the appropriate row $(i = 1)$ of Table 1.

To continue our investigation, let us assume $n = 4$ and a consistent budget policy of setting the budget for the next period at one level greater than that attained in the current period $(i = 1)$. The matrix of transition probabilities for budget policy i we shall denote by $[P_{jk,j'k'}^i]$, where $P_{jk,j'k'}^i$ is the probability, with budget policy i, that an individual at performance level j and aspiration level $j + k$ in period t will in period $t + 1$ have attained performance level j' and aspiration level $j' + k'$. $[P_{jk,j'k'}^i]$ for all states—performances and aspiration levels—is shown in Table 3. It will be noted that some compression is necessary for the large and small values of j. Arbitrarily it has been assumed that, if the transition (as indicated in Table 2) would be to a performance level which was less than 1 or greater than 4, the transition probabilities for these "impossible" values are added to the smallest or largest possible value as applicable. Although this will cause some distortion in this small exploratory problem, the effect of this "compression" should become negligible [25] as the number of possible levels reaches a realistic order of magnitude. In Table 3, the only "uncompressed" rows of the transition matrix are those of transition from performance levels 2 and 3. Performance level 1 transition probabilities are "compressed" on the left, the probabilities of transition to performance level 1 in period $t + 1$ consisting of the combination of probabilities of "maintaining the status quo" $(h = 0)$ and of dropping in performance $(h = -1)$. Similarly the transition probabilities from performance level 4 are compressed on the right.

Asymptotic Behavior of the Model

Let π_t^{jk} be the probability that, in period t, the supervisor will be at performance level j with aspiration level for the next period k levels above j. Then let

---

[25] Provided that the compression does not produce any absorbing states, i.e., states which, once arrived at, will not be left. An absorbing state will occur if compression produces some $[P_{jk,j'k'}^i] = 1$ for $j = j'$ and $k = k'$, provided that some means of arriving at that state exists.

$$\pi_t = (\pi_t^{1,-l}, \cdots, \pi_t^{j,k}, \cdots, \pi_t^{n,m}) \tag{1}$$

so that π_t is a vector of $n(m + l + 1)$ components. The vector π_t then represents the vector of probabilities for the states of performance and aspiration of the supervisor in period t, with the additional condition

$$\sum_{k=-l}^{m} \sum_{j=1}^{n} \pi_t^{jk} = 1 \tag{2}$$

Given any initial set of probabilities π_0, if the transition matrix A represents a Markov process which is completely ergodic,[26] there exists a limiting vector (which we shall denote by α) such that

$$\lim_{t \to \infty} \pi_t = \lim_{t \to \infty} \pi_0 A^t = \alpha \tag{3}$$

This limiting steady-state vector also has the property [27]

$$\alpha A = \alpha \tag{4}$$

as well as the property of any probability vectors, viz.,

$$\sum_{k=-l}^{m} \sum_{j=1}^{n} \alpha^{jk} = 1 \tag{5}$$

Analysis of the matrix of Table 3 readily yields:

$$\alpha = [\alpha^{10}, \alpha^{11}, \alpha^{12}, \alpha^{20}, \alpha^{21}, \alpha^{22}, \alpha^{30}, \alpha^{31}, \alpha^{32}, \alpha^{40}, \alpha^{41}, \alpha^{42}]$$

$$= \tfrac{1}{150} [1, 8, 1, 2, 16, 2, 4, 32, 4, 8, 64, 8] \tag{6}$$

At steady state, then, the supervisor will be twice as likely to be at performance level 2 than performance level 1, twice as likely at level 3 than at 2, and similarly, twice as likely at 4 than at 3. Also, as would be expected, his aspiration levels for the next period will be at 0, 1, or 2 levels above his current performance in probability ratios corresponding to the probabilities of budget acceptance shown in Table 1. Namely, a budget, $i = 1$, will be accepted as the aspiration level with probability 0.8, and aspiration equal to current performance or one level higher than the budget will be equally likely with probability 0.1.

It would be of interest to continue our investigation with an analysis of the steady-state probabilities should the budget $i = 1$ be accepted with probability 1. The transition matrix in this instance is shown in Table 4. This matrix is readily seen to represent an ergodic set

---

[26] As defined by Kemeny and Snell [313].
[27] *Ibid.*

Table 4   Probability of Transition from State q_t^{jk} to State $q_{t+1}^{j'k'}$ with Budget Policy $i = 1$ and Budget Acceptance as Aspiration Level with Probability 1

			Period $t + 1$											
	j ↓	k ↓	$j'\to$ 1			2			3			4		
Period t			$k'\to$ 0	1	2	0	1	2	0	1	2	0	1	2
	1	0		0.9			0.1							
		1		0.4			0.6							
		2		0.9			0.1							
	2	0		0.3			0.6			0.1				
		1		0.2			0.2			0.6				
		2		0.6			0.3			0.1				
	3	0					0.3			0.6			0.1	
		1					0.2			0.2			0.6	
		2					0.6			0.3			0.1	
	4	0								0.3			0.7	
		1								0.2			0.8	
		2								0.6			0.4	

(consisting of those states for which $k = 1$) and a transient set.[28] We may thus deal with a reduced matrix, D, consisting of the transition probabilities for the ergodic set, or

$$D = \begin{bmatrix} 0.4 & 0.6 & & \\ 0.2 & 0.2 & 0.6 & \\ & 0.2 & 0.2 & 0.6 \\ & & 0.2 & 0.8 \end{bmatrix} \tag{7}$$

---

[28] It may be observed that the probability of transition to any state for which $k \neq 1$ is $=0$. Thus, whatever aspiration level an individual initially has, he will be in a state with $k = 0$ after the first transition.

The limiting vector, α, for the transition matrix of Table 4, becomes

$$\alpha = \tfrac{1}{40} [0, 1, 0, 0, 3, 0, 0, 9, 0, 0, 27, 0] \qquad (8)$$

the supervisor being three times as likely to be in performance level 2 as in 1, etc.

Absolute budget acceptance (i.e., acceptance with probability 1) does not, however, produce more favorable results in all circumstances. If a budget $i = 0$ is specified and accepted with probability 1, then

$$\alpha = \tfrac{1}{40} [27, 0, 0, 9, 0, 0, 3, 0, 0, 1, 0, 0] \qquad (9)$$

produces a mirror image of the performance level probabilities of the vector with a budget $i = 1$. Furthermore, if a budget $i = 2$, which is accepted with probability 1 as an aspiration level, then too much stress is produced for the individual to behave in a manner which improves his performance and the effect is even more unfavorable. In this situation, the steady-state vector becomes

$$\alpha = \tfrac{1}{259} [0, 0, 216, 0, 0, 36, 0, 0, 6, 0, 0, 1] \qquad (10)$$

which represents a very high likelihood of residing in the lowest performance level and, incidentally, forever at an "intolerable" level of stress.

The results of the various steady-state analyses are summarized in Table 5. Although it is unwise to draw firm conclusions from analysis of a single example, one hypothesis is suggested. The hypothesis suggested is that budget acceptance *per se* does not guarantee best performance. Although it is possible, at least in theory, to produce budget acceptance with probability arbitrarily close to 1 by introducing a reward attached to budget attainment so large that neither realistic expectations nor random influences will be effective in counteracting its force, it is useful to note the relatively small improvement in performance produced by raising the budget acceptance probability to 1. An improvement also may be observed when, for a budget $i = 0$ or $i = 2$, instead of acceptance of the budget as the aspiration level with certainty, a probability of acceptance of 0.8 is specified, and a more favorable aspiration level (from the standpoint of probable effect on performance) is accepted with probability 0.2.

We are thus faced with many questions which might be asked vis-à-vis "rational" budgeting. Strict adherence to budgeted goals may, in fact, be detrimental. Whether the rewards for such adherence be tangible or otherwise, the danger inherent in adherence to motivationally unsound (albeit "technically" sound) budgeted goals might suggest some care in the selection of appropriate rewards. We do not infer, however, that reward should be absent since, at least in the

Table 5   Steady-State Limiting Probabilities of Performance at Level j for Various Budgets and Probabilities of Acceptance as Aspiration Level

	Budget Accepted with Probability = 1			Budget Accepted with Probability < 1		
Budget	$i = 0$	$i = 1$	$i = 2$	$i = 0$	$i = 1$	$i = 2$
Probability that:						
$\quad\quad\quad$ 0	1	0	0	0.8	0.1	0
$k =\quad$ 1	0	1	0	0.2	0.8	0.2
$\quad\quad\quad$ 2	0	0	1	0	0.1	0.8
Steady State 1	0.675	0.025	0.834	0.386	0.067	0.629
Performance 2	0.225	0.075	0.139	0.276	0.133	0.242
Level $j =$ 3	0.075	0.225	0.023	0.197	0.267	0.093
Probabilities 4	0.025	0.675	0.004	0.141	0.533	0.036

present model, expected behavior under "no reward" would fall far short of possible performance.

Multiple-Variable Budgeting

Although the investigation of one-variable (i.e., one supervisory goal) models for budgets, aspiration levels, and performance levels is far from complete, we here initiate an investigation of models in which a supervisor simultaneously supervises several tasks which are budgeted. This will help us to develop more quickly the advantages or deficiencies of the present approach in achieving a realistic and rational theory. We undertake the simultaneous development of "one-variable" and "multivariable" budget models because we feel there is some uncertainty about the applicability of an unconstrained single-variable model (with profit as the single variable or goal most commonly assumed) even in the case of an independently operating business, to say nothing of quasi-independent or completely interdependent subentities within a large corporation.[29]

---

[29] In describing General Motors, one of the most vivid examples of decentralized management and divisional independence, Drucker [169] states, ". . . central management does not hesitate to interfere directly and even ruthlessly when

Although the single-variable model may be useful for providing insights into behavior in more complex situations, the introduction of competing goals at this juncture would seem to be of interest should our investigations show that these additional considerations necessitate a revision [30] in what might be considered "basic principles" of budget setting policy.

As in the single-variable case, we assume that the over-all level of effort is determined by the amount of stress, as measured by the difference between aspired and actual performance levels.[31] In this instance, however, we assume that this over-all effort is determined by the combination of several such disparities, and allocation of effort is determined both by the size of the disparity and the relative rewards attached to the attainment of the budgeted goals pertaining to each of the performance levels involved. Moreover, we assume that the likelihood of acceptance of a budget for a particular performance variable is dependent on the relative reward attached to attainment *and* the remaining requirements of effort due to the other budgets within the supervisor's purview. We might consider a short-run expected reward function of the following form:

$$R_t = R_t^0 + \sum_{i=1}^{n} \rho_i E(z_i^+) - \sum_{i=1}^{n} \pi_i E(z_i^-) \tag{11}$$

where z_i^+ is 1 when [32] $s_{it} \geq b_{it}$ and 0 otherwise, and, conversely, z_i^- is 1 when $s_{it} < b_{it}$ and 0 otherwise. s_{it} and b_{it} are, respectively, the actual

---

ever the interests or policies of the business are at stake" (p. 62). This interference and perhaps the desire to avoid it provide competition for the divisional profit maximization goal. Later (p. 65), Drucker describes two distinct performance measurements: efficiency, a profitability measure determined with the aid of a form of variable budgeting scheme known as "base pricing," and share of market. It is indicative that even in what might be considered an attempt at the ultimate in decentralized management, more than one goal is seen to prevail. Further evidence of such incompatibility has been provided by Whinston [597], Chapters V and VI, in certain automobile manufacturing companies.

[30] See [516].

[31] A variant of this concept has been presented by March and Simon [367] vis-à-vis the difference between aspired and actual reward levels. Stedry [516], Chapter 2, has presented a budget related model of this process. Cooper and Savvas [135] have built on this concept of budget-produced stress, which they term "Stedry pressure," in investigating the effects of pressure on aspiration and performance with various response parameters.

[32] That is, z_i^+ and z_i^- are defined relative to

$$R_t = R_t^0 + \sum_{i=1}^{n} \rho_i P(s_{it} \geq b_{it}) - \sum_{i=1}^{n} \pi_i P(s_{it} < b_{it}).$$

performance and budgeted performance for the ith item in the tth period. R_t is the supervisor's expected reward in the tth period while ρ_i and π_i are the amounts by which the base reward $R_t{}^0$ is increased or decreased, respectively, in the event of attainment or nonattainment of budgeted performance for the ith variable, and $P(x)$ is the probability of the event x.[33] $R_t{}^0$ may be interpreted as the amount which the supervisor is paid for his presence on the job. This would be expected to increase over time while in the same position, and may be large in practice.[34] The difference between changes in $R_t{}^0$ and changes in the other components of R_t are sometimes referred to as the difference between "seniority raises" and "merit raises." Although we are assuming equation 11 as a short-run function and thus assume ρ_i and π_i constant, it is likely that they will change over time for the same individual in the same position in practice. The direction of these changes would not appear to be consistent—the neophyte may be forgiven his errors more readily than one experienced in the position —although, in general, increases in relative rewards and decreases in relative punishments (i.e., increasing latitude or "freedom of action") may be expected with time.

Under "management by exception," it is often the case that only negative or unfavorable budget variances—i.e., nonattainments—are examined. Most of the psychological literature would inveigh against this practice which is at least implicitly punitive and nowhere rewarding. In these instances, it would appear that since "punishment" is not intended but rather merely an investigation into the cause of the nonattainment, the punitive result of nonattainment [35] of a budget in an unimportant area may be rendered indistinguishable from a shortcoming in an important one. In this situation, or one in which no rewards are given for attainment and equal punishments are im-

---

[33] We continue the practice of the single-variable model of considering increases in performance to be improvements although here we use continuous variables rather than discrete intervals.

[34] Although, to return to the General Motors example, Drucker [169] points out that, "For . . . executives, particularly for the senior men, the bonus is in normal years a very important part of their income" (p. 58).

[35] The logical inconsistency in the assumption that a budget can exercise meaningful control unless some reward, stated or otherwise, is associated with attainment or punishment with nonattainment has been dealt with at length by one of the authors in [516]. Argyris [21] documents the perceived punitive effect of the "higher up's" phone call, whether or not intended for its punitive value. Psychological studies which show absence of action in the presence of insufficient motivation are numerous.

posed for each nonattainment, $\rho_i = \rho_j = 0$ and $\pi_i = \pi_j = \pi$ so that equation 11 becomes

$$R_t = R_t^0 - \pi \sum_{i=1}^{n} P(s_{it} < b_{it}) \tag{12}$$

The functions representing rewards in equations 11 and 12, of course, are simplifications. In practice, rarely will an individual's rewards change as frequently as short-run budgets, although for an annual budget this might appear reasonable. If one assumes a reward function without positive incentives, a further assumption that R_t^0 increases rapidly enough with t so that R_t does not decrease might be made. Thus equation 12 need not imply an actual decrease in total reward, but only that the rate of change of reward is affected adversely by unfavorable variances.

Paradoxically, a short-run reward function may be noted in many firms at both ends of the management hierarchy but more rarely in the center (i.e., middle management). At the lowest level of supervision, rewards are frequently tied in with production of a supervisor's department. At the highest level, executives holding large amounts of stock in their companies may experience large financial gains or losses as a result of a decision which becomes public (or even semipublic) knowledge, the publication of a quarterly earnings report, or other relatively short-run phenomena. Values observed in practice might be taken to be a smoothed form (e.g., moving average) of the predicted values of R_t in our equations if such a correspondence is desired. Questions of how quickly reward and punishment should follow performance, or whether the reward function should be recast in terms of probability of promotion (instead of reward at the present level), are beyond the scope of this chapter.

Returning to equation 12, let us assume that the expected value of performance in the ith variable in the tth period, μ_{it}, is a linear function of the effort allocated to this variable, viz:

$$\mu_{it} = s_{i,t-1} + \frac{E_i - \bar{E}_i}{\alpha_i} \tag{13}$$

$$i = 1, \cdots, n \qquad \mu_{it}, s_{i,t-1}, E_i\bar{E}_i \geq 0, \qquad \alpha_i > 0$$

where $s_{i,t-1}$ is the performance level in the period $t - 1$ of the ith variable,[36] E_i is the level of effort allocated in the tth period to performance in

---

[36] Although s_{it} will be assumed a random variable, $s_{i,t-1}$ is viewed as a parameter in the distribution of s_{it} and not a random variable.

the ith variable, $\bar{E}_i$ is the level of effort necessary to sustain the previous period's performance, and α_i is an arbitrary constant converting effort into units of improvement, hence representing the relative level of difficulty of improvement for the ith product.

A Neo-Classical Model

For the purpose of illustration, we investigate behavior embodied in a model which assumes that a supervisor will act rationally, i.e., will maximize his expected reward, under the conditions as presented in equations 12 and 13, and an assumed specific distribution for the performance variable. In the absence of information about distribution of performance of supervisors, we assume normality.

More specifically, let us further assume that the actual performance s_{it} is normally distributed about μ_{it} with variance σ_i^2, which is independent of t and E_i, or: [37]

$$f(s_{it}) = (2\pi)^{-\frac{1}{2}}\sigma_i^{-1} \exp\left[-\frac{1}{2}\frac{(s_{it} - \mu_{it})^2}{\sigma_i^2}\right] \tag{14}$$

From equation 12, if the supervisor wishes to maximize one period reward, he will minimize the sum of the probabilities of failure of attainment subject to an over-all effort constraint or:

Minimize

$$\sum_{i=1}^{n} \int_{-\infty}^{b_{it}} f(s_{it})\, ds_{it} \tag{15}$$

subject to

$$\sum_{i=1}^{n} E_i \leq M$$

where M is the maximum effort he is willing to exert. It can be shown that, with the chosen functional, the inequality is equivalent to the assumption that:

$$\sum_{i=1}^{n} E_i = M \tag{16}$$

Thus we obtain a classical minimization problem in which the Lagrangian function may be written:

$$L = \sum_{i=1}^{n} \frac{1}{\sqrt{2\pi}\,\sigma_i} \int_{-\infty}^{b_{it}} \exp\left[-\frac{1}{2}\frac{(s_{it} - \mu_{it})^2}{\sigma_i^2}\right] ds_{it} + \lambda\left(\sum_{i=1}^{n} E_i - M\right) \tag{17}$$

---

[37] It is also assumed that the rewards of this supervisor are independent of the rewards of any other, and conversely.

Now, let

$$y_i = \frac{s_{it} - \mu_{it}}{\sigma_i} = \frac{s_{it}}{\sigma_i} - \frac{s_{i,t-1} + (E_i - \bar{E}_i)/\alpha_i}{\sigma_i} \qquad i = 1, \cdots, n \quad (18)$$

Then, performing the indicated changes of variable,

$$L = \sum_{i=1}^{n} \frac{1}{\sqrt{2\pi}} \int_{-\infty}^{\frac{b_{it} - s_{i,t-1} - (E_i - \bar{E}_i)/\alpha_i}{\sigma_i}} \exp\left(-\tfrac{1}{2}y_i^2\right) dy_i + \lambda \left(\sum_{i=1}^{n} E_i - M\right)$$

$$(19)$$

Differentiating with respect to E_i and λ,

$$\frac{\partial L}{\partial E_i} = -\frac{1}{\alpha_i \sigma_i \sqrt{2\pi}} \exp -\frac{1}{2} \left[\frac{b_{it} - s_{i,t-1} - (1/\alpha_i)(E_i - \bar{E}_i)}{\sigma_i}\right]^2 +$$

$$+ \lambda = 0, \qquad i = 1, \cdots, n \quad (20)$$

$$\frac{\partial L}{\partial \lambda} = \sum_{i=1}^{n} E_i - M = 0 \tag{21}$$

for optimality.

The second derivatives are, however, of interest, in as much as it is not obvious in this case that an optimal (as opposed to a pessimal) solution will result from the solutions of equations 20 and 21. Specifically,

$$\frac{\partial^2 L}{\partial E_i^2} = \frac{1}{\sqrt{2\pi}} \left[-\frac{b_{it} - s_{i,t-1} - (1/\alpha_i)(E_i - \bar{E}_i)}{\sigma_i}\right]$$

$$\times \left(\frac{1}{\sigma_i \alpha_i}\right)^2 \exp -\frac{1}{2} \left[\frac{b_{it} - s_{i,t-1} - (1/\alpha_1)(E_i - \bar{E}_i)}{\sigma_i}\right]^2 \tag{22}$$

which are ≥ 0 if, and only if,

$$b_{it} \leq s_{i,t-1} + \frac{E_i - \bar{E}_i}{\alpha_i} = \mu_{it} \qquad \text{for all } i = 1, \cdots, n \tag{23}$$

It would appear that, for the classical solution to hold, required, or budgeted, performance b_{it} must, for all performance areas, be at or below the expected value, μ_{it}; alternatively, for normal distributions such as equation 17, all budgets must be set at a level sufficiently low to provide a probability of attainment of one half or more.

Equation 23 may better be perceived as:

$$E_i \geq \bar{E}_i + \alpha_i(b_{it} - s_{i,t-1}) \tag{24}$$

and it will be shown (by way of example) that, although effort E_i will eventually be allocated so as to satisfy equation 24 for nonzero

E_i, it is rather the result of the ex-post allocation which sets $E_i = 0$ for some i. Proceeding in this way, it is possible to achieve a probability at least one half of attaining whatever budgets may be set; i.e., even when the classical solution does not hold, procedures are available for eliminating some activity areas from the set and allocating effort over the remaining ones.

This process is analogous to the device used in classical economics of eliminating products such that, if production is to be undertaken at all, it will be increased to at least the point of rising marginal cost where effort, here, is viewed as a cost.[38]

For an optimum to exist (in the sense of classical economic techniques) it is necessary but not sufficient that

$$\sum_{i=1}^{n} E_i = M \geq \sum_{i=1}^{n} \alpha_i(b_{it} - s_{i,t-1}) + \sum_{i=1}^{n} \bar{E}_i \qquad (25)$$

a weaker result which follows immediately from equations 23 and 24.

This model would seem to indicate the value of investigation, beyond the scope of this chapter, of decision-theoretic methods for providing an optimum under less restrictive conditions. A systematic method of elimination of "too difficult" variables on which to obtain rewards, leaving a subset for which the classical conditions hold, appears possible.

Manipulation of equation 20 yields, as a decision rule for allocation,

$$E_i = \bar{E}_i + \alpha_i(b_{it} - s_{i,t-1}) \pm \alpha_i\sigma_i \sqrt{2 \ln \frac{1}{\lambda\alpha_i\sigma_i\sqrt{2\pi}}} \qquad (26)$$

To satisfy the inequality shown in equation (25), the positive square root must be chosen. Let

$$\bar{M} = \sum_{i=1}^{n} \bar{E}_i + \sum_{i=1}^{n} \alpha_i(b_{it} - s_{i,t-1}) \qquad (27)$$

We then obtain:

$$M - \bar{M} = \sum_i \alpha_i\sigma_i \sqrt{2 \ln \frac{1}{\lambda\alpha_i\sqrt{2\pi}\,\sigma_i}} \qquad (28)$$

---

[38] It should be noted that, in "classical economics," the efforts of individuals within the firm have not been perceived as accompanied by "cost." The concept of "motivational cost," introduced by Cooper and Savvas [135] in this connection, is suggested as a possible vehicle for translating the findings (and techniques) of economics into viable contemporary organization theory.

For real solutions to exist,

$$\ln \frac{1}{\lambda \alpha_i \sqrt{2\pi} \, \sigma_i} \geq 0 \qquad \text{or} \qquad \lambda \alpha_i \sqrt{2\pi} \, \sigma_i \leq 1 \tag{29}$$

With these equations one can solve, by numerical methods, an illustrative problem. We present a two-variable example, with the following parameters assumed:

$$b_1 = 26 \qquad\qquad b_2 = 16$$
$$s_{1,t-1} = 25 \qquad\qquad s_{2,t-1} = 15$$
$$\bar{E}_1 = 10 \qquad\qquad \bar{E}_2 = 20$$
$$\alpha_1 = 1 \qquad\qquad \alpha_2 = 2$$
$$\sigma_1 = 4 \qquad\qquad \sigma_2 = 3$$

where b_i is the budgeted performance for the period and $s_{i,t-1}$ is the previous period's performance attainment with $i = 1, 2$. Similarly, for these same i, $\bar{E}_i$ is the effort required for zero expected improvement, α_i is the effort required per unit expected improvement, and σ_i is the standard deviation of the distribution of the s_{it} about the expected improvement.

For a classical optimum to exist with these parameters, substitution in equation 23 yields $E_1 \geq 11$ and $E_2 \geq 22$; i.e., the effort allocated to each variable must be sufficient to provide for $\mu_1 \geq 26$ and $\mu_2 \geq 16$, permitting a probability of an improvement of one unit in each variable or of budget attainment of 0.5 or greater. By an heuristic method, it is possible to find values of total effort less than that amount for which the classical optimum conditions are fulfilled.

The largest value of λ for which the condition of equation 29 obtains is, with the chosen parameters [39]

$$\lambda = \inf \left\{ \frac{1}{\alpha_1 \sigma_1 \sqrt{2\pi}} \, ; \, \frac{1}{\alpha_2 \sigma_2 \sqrt{2\pi}} \right\}$$

$$= \inf \left\{ \frac{1}{4\sqrt{2\pi}} \, ; \, \frac{1}{6\sqrt{2\pi}} \right\} \tag{30}$$

$$= \frac{1}{6\sqrt{2\pi}}$$

Substituting this value for λ in equation 26 we obtain $E_2 = 22$ (the minimum value) and $E_1 = 14.6$. Thus, for total levels of effort in

---

[39] inf $\{x; y\}$ may be read "the lesser of x or y." The condition is so stated as to render both solutions for ($i = 1$ and $i = 2$) real.

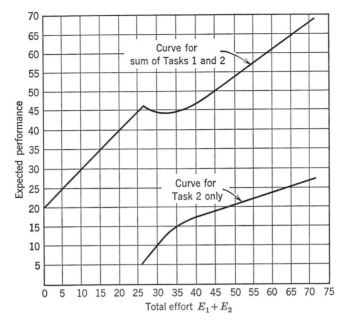

FIGURE 1   Expected performance vs. total effort.

excess of 36.6 units, the classical conditions prevail. By numerical methods, it is found that below a total effort of 26 units, all of the effort, for maximum reward, is allocated to the first task, i.e., the task indexed by subscript 1. The percentage of total effort allocated to variable 1 decreases from 100% to a low of 36.6% at a total effort level (M) of 50 units, then increasing as the effort level increases.

The expected value of performance in variable 2 and the combined expected values are shown in Fig. 1.[40] If we assume that management desires to maximize the sum of the expected values, it will be noted that in a portion of the upper curve, additional effort actually decreases this sum. Hence, as even this simple example shows, it can be dangerous for management to proceed by the often recommended routes of unaided trial and error, using only experience as a guide. For instance, as the upper curve of Fig. 1 shows, a management might be led to move backwards if it happened to be experimenting in the region $25 \leq E_1 + E_2 \leq 33$, whereas if the whole chart were avail-

[40] It will be noted that performance, albeit at a very low level, continues to be observed in task 2 even though no supervisory effort is allocated to it.

able, it could see that much better results could be achieved at very high levels of $E_1 + E_2$.

This example indicates some of the possibilities for an analysis of the way in which the goals of management may be quite different from those produced by a supervisor attempting to maximize his reward. As shown in Fig. 1, the ratios of expected performance in the two products approach the ratio of the budgets only as the amount of effort expended grows large.

The parameter α_i may be interpreted as a difficulty coefficient since it represents the amount of effort required to effect a unit improvement in expected performance. If the amount of effort is small, all effort will go to that variable for which the product of the standard deviation and difficulty coefficient is smaller, i.e., that variable for which the combined effects of the difficulty of improvement and uncertainty are smaller. Furthermore, no increase in the budget of the neglected variable can change this situation until the supervisor has passed the minimum level of effort required. In fact, raising the budget can only increase the total level of effort that will be required for the change to a two-variable allocation.

Because of the computational effort required for calculation of similar multivariable models, we shall not consider here more than two variables. The two-variable case is presented to show the possible effects of the combination of a "rational" supervisor and a budget control scheme. In the current example, "irrational" behavior of a supervisor might be more satisfactory in terms of management goals, i.e., a supervisor who will allocate his effort in such a way as to attain the budgeted amounts rather than to maximize his reward. Without being logically conclusive, the example does suggest that if rationality is to be assumed, some budgets other than the desired amounts must be used in order to produce the desired effort allocation. On the other hand, if the budgets are to be set equal to the desired amounts, means of convincing the supervisor to act "irrationally" must be discovered.

In practice, budgets and goals quite different from desired attainments are sometimes proposed to assure arrival at the desired attainments.[41] Such goals, particularly goals perceived as impossible, one expects, from psychological experiments, to have deleterious effects in one-variable situations, such as, for example, we have considered in

---

[41] See, for example, Charnes and Cooper [111] and [113] for a discussion of the role of "unattainable" goals in management practice and references to such uses in central management of the U.S.S.R.

the section starting on p. 216. A multivariable (task) situation is more immediately germane to the problems of budgetary practice—as witness, for instance, the widely cited and used principle of management by exception. In contrast to the single-variable case, it is not possible to specify the results without more experimental evidence than is now available. Furthermore, it is not possible even to specify whether a withdrawal of effort on some variables is undesirable, managerially speaking, until adequate descriptions of the related tasks are available along with economic measures of their costs and benefits.

A Model Based on the Theory of Search

In the previous section, a model was presented in which a normal distribution of performance about an expected value of one variable, the latter a linear function of effort allocated to a particular variable, was assumed. In proceeding further, it would seem that, if possible, a distribution should be found which allows for diminishing returns to scale with increasing effort. The normal distribution is not a convenient one to employ toward this end. Instead, using a discrete distribution of a particular kind, one can introduce diminishing returns and reduce the complexity of the analysis as well. Another advantage of recourse to such distributions is that the reward function becomes a convex function of the effort allocated to each variable.

The model presented here draws upon the theory of search introduced by Koopman [322]. The specific distribution used here is a modification of that presented by Charnes and Cooper in [110].[42] The departure of the distribution used here from their model will be discussed more fully below.

Assume that there exist n performance areas and that, for each, a performance level exists to be designated s_j. This performance level is further assumed to be capable of attaining the discrete values a_{ij}, to be interpreted as the ith performance value which the jth variable can attain. The probability that s_j will attain a value at or above a_{ij} will be designated $P(s_j \geq a_{ij})$, i.e., the probability that, in the jth area, performance will achieve a level at or above an "ith rung" on a ladder (scale) of values.

We assume the relevant probability distribution is adequately described by a function of the form

$$P(s_j \geq a_{ij}) = k_{ij}(1 - e^{-\alpha_j \rho_j}) \tag{31}$$

---

[42] The terminology in this section differs from that of previous sections to be consistent with that of [110].

where

$$i = 1, \cdots, \infty$$

$$j = 1, \cdots, n$$

$$k_{ij} \geq k_{lj} \text{ implies } i \leq l \qquad \text{for all } i, l \geq 1$$

Further we specifically hypothesize [43] an "easy" level, a_{0j}, which can be attained with certainty regardless of the effort expended, *viz.*,

$$P(s_j \geq a_{0j}) = 1 \tag{32}$$

where

$$a_{ij} > a_{0j} \qquad \text{for } i > 0$$

In equation 31, ρ_j is the amount of effort allocated to the jth performance variable, $\alpha_j > 0$ is an arbitrary constant, $0 \leq k_{ij} < 1$. It can be shown that it is necessary for $k_{\infty j} = 0$ in order that the probabilities of attainment of discrete levels sum to 1.

The last inequation of equation 31 represents a lexicographic ordering relating the magnitude of the k_{ij} to the values attained by the a_{ij}. It is seen that

$$k_{ij} \equiv \lim_{\rho_j \to \infty} P(s_j \geq a_{ij}) \tag{33}$$

That is, k_{ij} is the limiting probability of attainment of the ith performance level as effort is increased without bound. Thus the ordering on the k_{ij} merely provides that no more difficult level of performance can be attained, at the effort limit, with greater probability than an easier one, and conversely. It is assumed that k_{ij} is a function of past performance and technology and, hence, independent of any decision in the current period. In the analysis by Charnes and Cooper [110], this parameter is the limiting probability for discovery of a target as effort devoted to search in the jth region grows large. In their model, however, only one level of performance is admitted, i.e., finding the target. Thus, the limiting probability which they use (h_j) for the probability that the target will be in the jth area requires no second subscript as does the k_{ij} here, which depends upon the performance value to be attained. Also it will be noted—see equation 31 —that as $\rho_j \to 0$, the probability of attaining any level above some minimum level a_{0j} (which can be attained with no managerial effort allocated to the jth variable) approaches zero. The positive constant α_j represents the relative "sensitivity" of the jth variable to increased effort, i.e., the rate at which the limiting probability is approached as ρ_j is increased.

As a short-run model, this formulation would appear to have correct qualitative qualities. It includes both a technological con-

---

[43] Thus we alter the earlier search theory work of Koopman [322], p. 507.

straint on possible performance independent of the manager's activity and a variable portion over which he does have control. Product interdependence is introduced to a limited extent through a constraint on over-all managerial effort.

Let us then assume that management can set a budget at the bth level of performance for the jth budgeted variable, i.e., management can choose a particular value of performance a_{bj} from the set $\{a_{ij}\}$ where it is assumed throughout that b may take on a different value for each j but the additional subscripting is omitted for simplicity. The probability of budget attainment may then be expressed as

$$P(s_j \geq a_{bj}) = \begin{cases} k_{bj}(1 - e^{-\alpha_j p_i}) & b = 1, \cdots, \infty \\ 1 & b = 0 \end{cases} \tag{34}$$

Thus $b = 0$ is seen to be an attainable budget in the strict sense. All other budgets are attainable with some probability less than 1, depending upon the amount of effort allocated to their attainment.

Let us then assume that the supervisor's expected reward is the sum of a fixed amount and a portion which depends upon performance in the period, and the latter is determined by the attainment and nonattainment of his various budgets. Clearly if a supervisor is to be judged against a standard, some result must be expected from the judgment. That these rewards and punishments are not usually meted out period by period, as discussed above, is not a serious criticism of this approach in as much as these cumulative effects should be in some sense significant, although perhaps subject to an unusual form of discounting where later attainments are seen as more significant than early ones.[44]

We shall adhere to the usual practice which judges black variances as "good" and red variances as "bad" without specifying the degree of redness or blackness formally.[45] It is assumed that a reward R_j is administered for attainment and a punishment L_j for nonattainment of the jth product budget. The expected reward may be expressed, then, as

$$E(R) = R_0 + \sum_{j=1}^{n} R_j P(s_j \geq a_{bj}) - \sum_{j=1}^{n} L_j P(s_j < a_{bj}) \tag{35}$$

---

[44] This might be termed "informational" discounting, similar to the weighting factors used for decision making by Holt, Modigliani, Muth, and Simon [281].

[45] Because we are using a discrete distribution, a_{bj} may be considered to represent, in fact, a range about the stated budget which is considered to be just attaining the budget. The usual application of the "principle of exceptions" in fact allows such a range (or threshold) before an "exception" is recognized.

We shall number the products so that:

$$a_{hj} > a_{0j} \qquad j = 1, \cdots, m \tag{36}$$

$$a_{bj} = a_{0j} \qquad j = m + 1, \cdots, n \tag{37}$$

Clearly those products for which $a_{bj} = a_{0j}$ simply contribute to the fixed reward, and the rational manager will not allocate effort to them provided there is at least one product for which $a_{bj} > a_{0j}$. We shall assume that such possibilities are always present, i.e., the set $\{a_{bj} \mid b > 0\}$ is not empty.[46] Eliminating fixed rewards, the manager, if he acts rationally, will attempt to:

Minimize

$$C = \sum_{j=1}^{m} (R_j + L_j)k_{bj}e^{-\alpha_j \rho_i}$$

subject to

$$\sum_{j=1}^{m} \rho_j = \rho \tag{38}$$

Thus he attempts to obtain the maximum reward for the effort he ex-pends. For simplicity, let

$$h_j = (R_j + L_j)k_{bj} \qquad j = 1, \cdots, m \tag{39}$$

Then the problem can be stated: [47]

Minimize

$$C = \sum_{j=1}^{m} h_j e^{-\alpha_j \rho_i}$$

subject to

$$\sum_{j=1}^{m} \rho_j = \rho \qquad \rho_j \geq 0 \tag{40}$$

For an optimum in the large, the necessary and sufficient conditions established by Kuhn and Tucker [326] require that the normal to

---

[46] Otherwise, at least in the short run, the manager cannot improve his reward by expending effort, so the allocation problem would be trivial.

[47] This problem is almost identical to that presented by Charnes and Cooper except that, although the (known) h_j's are nonnegative here, there is no additive constraint on the h_j's and also the α_j's are permitted to be different whereas in the cited paper, $\alpha_j = \alpha_k = \alpha$. The h_j's could, of course, be normalized by a suitable choice of units for $(R_j + L_j)$. This would have no effect on the algorithm, since it amounts to merely multiplying the functional C by a positive constant. For this reason, $\Sigma_j \rho_j = \rho$ is substituted in this formulation for the constraint $\Sigma_j \rho_j = 1$, which they use since their α can be conveniently chosen to normalize ρ_j, whereas here, each of the α_j's would need to be changed to reflect a difference in over-all effort ρ.

the functional in equation 40 be expressed as a nonnegative linear combination of the normals to the constraints that are critical, that is, the constraints that are satisfied as equalities. By an interpretation analogous to that used in [110] and earlier in [119], these conditions become

$$\frac{\partial C}{\partial \rho} = (-\alpha_1 e^{-\alpha_1 \rho_1} h_1; \; -\alpha_2 e^{-\alpha_2 \rho_2} h_2; \; \cdots; \; -\alpha_j e^{-\alpha_j \rho_j} h_j; \; \cdots; \; -\alpha_m e^{-\alpha_m \rho_m} h_m)$$

$$= -\mu(1, 1, \cdots, 1_j, \cdots, 1) + \sum_{j=1}^{m} v_j(0, 0, \cdots, 1_j, \cdots, 0) \tag{41}$$

where $v_j \geq 0$ and $v_j = 0$ if $\rho_j > 0$ so that

$$\alpha_j e^{-\alpha_j \rho_j} h_j = \mu \qquad j \in J$$
$$\alpha_j h_j = \mu - v_j \qquad j \notin J \tag{42}$$

where $J = \{j \mid \rho_j > 0\}$. J is therefore the set of all indices for which ρ_j is positive whereas $j \notin J$ means that the associated ρ_j are not members of this set. In other words, for $j \notin J$ we have $\rho_j = 0$ in all cases.

Now let

$$\hat{f}_j = \ln(\alpha_j h_j) \tag{43}$$

Then these expressions may be written as:

$$\hat{f}_j - \alpha_j \rho_j = \ln \mu \qquad j \in J \tag{44}$$
$$\hat{f}_j \leq \ln \mu \qquad j \notin J \tag{45}$$

Rewriting equation 44 as

$$\frac{\hat{f}_j}{\alpha_j} - \rho_j = \frac{\ln \mu}{\alpha_j} \tag{46}$$

and recalling, by conditions imposed in equation 40, that

$$\sum_{j=1}^{m} \rho_j = \sum_{j \in J} \rho_j = \rho \tag{47}$$

we can sum equation 46 to obtain

$$\sum_{j \in J} \frac{\hat{f}_j}{\alpha_j} - \rho = \ln \mu \sum_{j \in J} \frac{1}{\alpha_j} \tag{48}$$

or

$$\ln \mu = \frac{1}{\sum_{j \in J} 1/\alpha_j} \left(\sum_{j \in J} \frac{\hat{f}_j}{\alpha_j} - \rho \right) \tag{49}$$

Recalling that $\alpha_j \rho_j > 0, j \in J$, we can now rewrite equation 45 as

$$f_s \le \frac{1}{\sum\limits_{j \in J} 1/\alpha_j} \left(\sum\limits_{j \in J} \frac{\hat{f}_j}{\alpha_j} - \rho \right) < \hat{f}_r \tag{50}$$

for all $r \in J$ and $s \notin J$.

The necessary and sufficient condition for the selection of indices $r \in J$ becomes

$$\min\limits_{r \in J} \hat{f}_r > \frac{1}{\sum\limits_{j \in J} 1/\alpha_j} \left(\sum\limits_{j \in J} \frac{\hat{f}_j}{\alpha_j} - \rho \right) \ge \max\limits_{s \notin J} \hat{f}_s \tag{51}$$

and the optimal $\rho_r{}^*$, $r \in J$, and $\nu_s{}^*$, $s \notin J$, becomes

$$\rho_r{}^* = \frac{1}{\alpha_r} \left[\hat{f}_r - \frac{1}{\sum\limits_{j \in J} 1/\alpha_j} \left(\sum\limits_{j \in J} \frac{\hat{f}_j}{\alpha_j} - \rho \right) \right] \tag{52}$$

and

$$\nu_s{}^* = \mu - \alpha_j h_j \tag{53}$$

Since the ideas incorporated herein may well prove immediately useful in both search and effort allocation, we should consider how an algorithm might be synthesized for practical applications. The lemma proved by Charnes and Cooper [110] for the case of a single α can, in fact, be extended for this purpose as follows:

LEMMA: If

$$\hat{f}_{l+1} > \frac{1}{\sum\limits_{h=1}^{l} 1/\alpha_j} \left(\sum\limits_{j=1}^{\rho} \frac{\hat{f}_j}{\alpha_j} - \rho \right)$$

then

$$\hat{f}_{l+1} > \frac{1}{\sum\limits_{j=1}^{l+1} 1/\alpha_j} \left(\sum\limits_{j=1}^{l+1} \frac{\hat{f}_j}{\alpha_j} - \rho \right)$$

PROOF:

By hypothesis

$$\hat{f}_{l+1} \left(\sum\limits_{j=1}^{l} \frac{1}{\alpha_j} \right) > \sum\limits_{j=1}^{l} \frac{\hat{f}_j}{\alpha_j} - \rho$$

so that

$$\hat{f}_{l+1} \left(\sum\limits_{j=1}^{l} \frac{1}{\alpha_j} \right) + \frac{\hat{f}_{l+1}}{\alpha_{l+1}} > \sum\limits_{j=1}^{l} \frac{\hat{f}_j}{\alpha_j} + \frac{\hat{f}_{l+1}}{\alpha_{l+1}} - \rho$$

and therefore

$$\hat{f}_{l+1} \left(\sum\limits_{j=1}^{l+1} \frac{1}{\alpha_j} \right) > \sum\limits_{j=1}^{l+1} \frac{\hat{f}_j}{\alpha_j} - \rho$$

Hence, as was to be proved,

$$\hat{f}_{l+1} > \frac{1}{\sum\limits_{j=1}^{l+1} \alpha_j} \left(\sum_{j=1}^{l+1} \frac{\hat{f}_j}{\alpha_j} - \rho \right)$$

Now, without loss of generality, we may renumber the $\hat{f}_j$'s so that $\hat{f}_1$ is the largest. If

$$\alpha_1[(\hat{f}_1/\alpha_1) - \rho] \geq \hat{f}_2$$

then the entire effort allocation will be to the first variable. If

$$\hat{f}_2 > \alpha_1 \left(\frac{\hat{f}_1}{\alpha_1} - \rho \right)$$

by the lemma

$$\hat{f}_2 > \frac{1}{1/\alpha_1 + 1/\alpha_2} \left(\frac{\hat{f}_1}{\alpha_1} + \frac{\hat{f}_2}{\alpha_2} - \rho \right)$$

and effort is allocated to variable 2. The process is continued until some $\hat{f}_{m_{J+1}}$ is found such that

$$\frac{1}{\sum\limits_{i=1}^{m_J} 1/\alpha_1} \left(\sum_{i=1}^{m_J} \frac{\hat{f}_i}{\alpha_i} - \rho \right) \geq \hat{f}_{m_{J+1}}$$

The set J is then determined, and the optimal values and shadow prices (the $\nu_s{}^*$ which represent the cost of allocating a unit of effort to an area s, $s \not\subset J$) may be found by substitution in equations 52 and 53.

We note here, as in the foregoing section, that, barring weighting functions for the rewards, the supervisor will allocate his effort to the least difficult tasks first. Since $\hat{f}_j = \ln(\alpha_j h_j) = \ln \alpha_j (R_j + P_j) k_{bj}$, and by raising the budget one lowers k_{bj}, management drives the supervisor away from this variable. Also, the lower the sensitivity of changes in performance to changes in effort α_j, the less likely the jth variable is to be chosen for allocation of effort. However, once ρ is sufficiently large to allocate any effort, the amount of effort allocated to the jth variable will increase with decreasing α_j for α_j sufficiently large. In the absence of specific rewards and weights to differentiate among budgets, this becomes a very rational mode of behavior for the manager.

Optimal Management Policy

When a supervisor behaves in the fashion predicted by the above multigoal model, a question arises as to whether this behavior may be channeled in such a way as to provide an optimal effort allocation by another criterion. Specifically, is it possible, by a suitable choice of goals and weights (rewards), to transform a superordinate's desire to maximize profit into an identical effort allocation where the supervisor is maximizing his reward with respect to goals?

Let us suppose that management (superordinate) seeks to maximize a weighted sum of the expected values of performance,[48] subject to a constraint on the over-all effort that will be put forth by the supervisor, which may be expressed as:

Maximize

$$\sum_{j=1}^{n} \beta_j E(s_j)$$

subject to

$$\Sigma \rho_j = \rho \tag{54}$$

From equation 31 it will be noted that

$$P(s_j = a_{ij}) = \begin{cases} (k_{ij} - k_{i+1,j})(1 - e^{-\alpha_i \rho_i}) & i \geq 1 \\ 1 - k_{1j}(1 - e^{-\alpha_i \rho_i}) & i = 0 \end{cases} \tag{55}$$

$$E(s_j) = (1 - e^{-\alpha_i \rho_i}) \left[\sum_{i=1}^{\infty} (k_{ij} - k_{i+1})a_{ij} - k_{1j}a_{0j} \right] + a_{0j} \tag{56}$$

Let

$$\lambda_j = \beta_j \left[\sum_{i=1}^{\infty} (k_{ij} - k_{i+1})a_{ij} - k_{1j}a_{0j} \right]^{49} \tag{57}$$

For optimization, the fixed elements can be ignored, and a maximization of the negative is equivalent to minimizing the positive of a function. Hence we can replace the functional and objective in equation 54 by:

Minimize

$$\sum_{j=1}^{n} \lambda_j e^{-\alpha_i \rho_i} \tag{58}$$

This function will be identical to the one in equation 38 if the rewards and budget are chosen such that

$$(R_j + L_j)k_{bj} = \lambda_j \tag{59}$$

We have thus provided a sufficient (although not necessary) condition for management (or superordinate) goals to be satisfied by rational behavior on the part of the supervisor. It is not required, however,

---

[48] Which could, of course, be profit contribution from each of n activities.

[49] By definition, $a_{ij} > a_{0j}$, $k_{ij} \geq k_{i+1,j}$, $i \geq 1$. Hence,

$$\sum_{i=1}^{\infty} (k_{ij} - k_{i+1,j})a_{ij} - k_j a_{0j} > a_{0j} \left[\sum_{i=1}^{\infty} (k_{ij} - k_{1i+1,j}) - k_j \right] = 0$$

that the supervisor maximize profit. He may, instead, maximize with respect to the attainment of a set of discrete performance levels or goals.

Summary

We have presented three stochastic models of budgetary response—the response to one or several goals—made by a supervisor. In the absence of empirical evidence for the validity of the assumptions made it is, of course, impossible to draw conclusions on the basis of such hypothetical models. Nevertheless they provide some guidance as to kinds of situations which are relevant, at least qualitatively, in management budgetary practices. They also supply guidance on the types of information which would be valuable as well as providing a tool for analysis when (and if) such validation becomes available.

The first of these models dealt with a single goal set for a supervisor by his superordinate—e.g., a profit goal in a responsibility accounting system. It was assumed that his probability of acceptance of the presented goal was in part a function of the improvement in performance subsumed under the goal vis-à-vis his own expectations for performance and in part a function of other variables not explicitly examined, e.g., personal goals in nonwork-related activities. Should a supervisor reject the presented goal, he may accept other goals (probabilistically) as his own aspiration for the task. His performance attainment is an assumed stochastic function of his aspired performance for this period and his previous performance. Through the power of methods of analysis that are available for Markov processes, it was possible to examine the possible dynamic effects of consistent budget policies, taking the supervisor's goal-response pattern as a given.

We note, in this first model, that a high probability of high performance is not achieved by budgets which cause aspirations to be raised to that level *per se*. This is achieved rather by budget changes which, when accepted, affect performance in a way that is likely to result in an increase rather than a decrease or lack of change from a previous period. This, it may be noted, carries some further implications with reference to current budgetary practice, which focus on levels rather than changes of levels in budgeting. The models here suggest the desirability of budgeting on the basis of trends and "budgeted improvement" rather than from the standpoint of a fixed level only determined on such grounds as accuracy or attainability.

We also note that the value to management of a budgetary scheme, in terms of long-run performance probabilities, is not a monotone function of probability of budget acceptance. Thus, a budget which is badly chosen can, under certain conditions, produce poorer performance if it is accepted as an individual's aspiration level than if it is not. It may be similarly inferred that a participative budgeting scheme, although increasing the likelihood of budget acceptance, might produce aspiration levels which would be far from those that could be used to effect optimum performance. Such participative budgeting could thus produce poorer performance than a budget which is only partially accepted but modeled on relevant economic as well as psychological grounds. Likewise, the dangers of increasing acceptance (e.g., through large rewards and penalties upon budget attainment or failure) become obvious if the aspiration level produced will not contribute to improved performance. Hence a preoccupation with budget acceptance, especially when the resulting contributions to supervisory performance are not well understood, can frustrate one of the main purposes of business budgeting.

In the second and third models we have sacrificed the dynamic character of the first in order to investigate the possible consequences when more than one goal is introduced. It is, of course, difficult to envision managerial situations which are pertinent to budgeting and in which only one goal is present. Even in responsibility accounting systems, where a department's profit is pointed to as a sole measure,[50] company policy constraints serve as goals as in chance-constrained programming.[51] Furthermore, a supervisor may also have internal goals and informal organization goals as well, e.g., high morale level of his subordinates, which may constrain him and require effort expenditure on his part.

As our analysis of the first of these two multiple-goal models showed, an optimal effort allocation by the supervisor could produce expected attainment quite different from that embedded in the goals of his superordinate. If, in this instance, the superordinate desired expected performance at the goal (provided sufficient effort would be expended by the supervisor) he could use: (1) a different reward structure;[52] (2) different stated goals from his "true" desires; or (3) training of the supervisor to behave in a nonself-optimizing manner.

---

[50] This may be more frequently advocated than practiced, however. See, for instance, the cases discussed by Whinston, Chapter 21, in this volume.

[51] See Charnes and Cooper [115].

[52] As, for example, used in the goal-programming model of Charnes, Cooper, and Ijiri [116] and Ijiri [291], where the objective is minimizing the distance between the goals and the (in this case, expected) performance. Their models are particularly applicable to the case where there is insufficient effort available in as much as they provide the solution which is closest to the presented goals.

The second of the multiple goal models sheds light on the problem of how to increase effort allocated to a particular area. It will be noted from the form of the expressions for the optimal solution that the criterion for selection of an area for *any* effort allocation, i.e., that $\alpha_j \eta_j$ be sufficiently large, increases linearly with α_j (sensitivity to effort), k_j (limiting probability of attainment) and $(R_j + L_j)$ the relative reward for attainment. An increase in the difficulty of a goal in an area where no effort is now being allocated, with a resulting diminishing of α_j or k_j, or both, cannot produce an increase in the effort allocated to it. Only lowering the difficulty of the goal or raising the relative reward can move this area into that set where effort is allocated. Where an area is already in the set to which effort is allocated, increasing goal difficulty, given certain conditions,[53] will increase effort allocated to the area until $\alpha_j \eta_j$ is too small for any further allocation. Thus we find that it is possible that increasing goal difficulty up to a point can improve performance but after a critical difficulty level is reached performance drops off sharply. Thus we find the behavior of a single area in the context of a multiple-goal model to be similar to the effects postulated with the single activity dynamic model.[54] The multiple-goal case is, of course, more complex but it is interesting to note that this "critical level" of difficulty, at which effort allocation to an area ceases, need not be stated *a priori* but rather follows from the economic characteristics of the goal-attainment model.

The power of these models to predict behavior depends, of course, on the validity of the underlying behavioral assumptions. It may, however, prove to be much easier to provide operational tests for the predicted behavior (performance and effort allocation) than to undertake a direct validation of the underlying assumptions. In this event, it may be possible only to state that behavior is "as if" the assumptions were correct. This can be tested, of course, by reference to a particular situation. It can be further tested by generalization to behavior in situations other than ones for which the model was formulated.

The evidence for or against the validity of these models is not now available. Indeed, empirical testing of the response to goals and rewards in an organizational setting is a critical area for further research in organizational behavior.

---

[53] It is impossible to state these precisely unless one specifies the relationship between k_j and α_j as difficulty is increased. Specifically, the optimal allocation is a decreasing function of α_j but an increasing function of k_j, while increasing goal difficulty may diminish either or both.

[54] And the earlier single-goal model postulated by Stedry [516].

14

EFFECTS OF AUDITING RECORDS:
INDIVIDUAL TASK ACCOMPLISHMENT
AND ORGANIZATION OBJECTIVES

N. C. Churchill and W. W. Cooper

Introduction [1]

This chapter reports on a study which was designed to examine certain managerial concepts related to auditing and some of the effects that may be expected when people are subjected to the experience of an audit. Managerial (supervisory) and accounting types of audit were both included in order to investigate properties of the corresponding basic audit processes when used jointly or separately as instruments for managerial control relative to (1) specific task performance and (2) over-all organizational requirements.

The term auditing is rather broad and has a variety of connotations in management and accounting practice. Hence it was deemed necessary, at the start, to distinguish and isolate specific aspects of these processes that might be amenable to examination in the current state of knowledge and also to consider ways for conducting studies that could provide a basis for establishing suitable generalizations amenable to scientific inquiry and validation. The area of accounting audits was

---

[1] This chapter was written as part of the contract "Planning and Control of Industrial Operations," with the Office of Naval Research and the Bureau of Ships, at the Graduate School of Industrial Administration, Carnegie Institute of Technology. Reproduction of this chapter in whole or in part is permitted for any purpose of the United States Government. Contract Nonr-760(01), Project NR-047011.

chosen for an initial study emphasis. This area was also circumscribed further in a variety of ways. For example, aspects such as the types of recommendations that might result from an actual audit were not included in this study. Attention was focused rather on the basic audit itself—referred to as the audit *per se*.

The study reported on here is to be viewed as only the first of a series of investigations into the audit process and the use of auditing as an instrument of managerial control.

Organizations, Auditing, and Control

Auditing is a pervasive managerial activity the origins of which go back to antiquity.[2] The audit process is utilized by managers at virtually every level of an organization hierarchy as some part (virtually daily) of their managerial-supervisory duties. Specialists—internal auditors—perform audits which cut across departmental lines and operate up and down the chain of command; and still other specialists from outside the organization perform audits on the organization as a whole. Yet, despite its widespread, almost ubiquitous, use in practice, there appears to be a persistent tendency to associate the word "audit" and even the audit function with its practice by accountants. There is a further tendency to narrow it to the task of examining certain specialized records and supporting documents. This is, of course, an inadequate characterization of auditing even as it is currently practiced by accountants; it is even more inadequate as a characterization of audits as a part of the total managerial function; and finally, this view of auditing tends to obscure the potential value that auditing might have either as a supplement or an alternative to current modes of managing that are now characterized (possibly loosely) as "direct supervision."

One reason, perhaps, for this limited view of the audit process is that the modes of executing the managerial audit are very numerous, and little, if any, effort has been made either to study or codify these aspects of the supervisory function. Indeed, it may even be the case that individual managers may themselves fail to perceive the occasions for performing an audit and hence fail to notice the effects produced by their examination, or even the effects that are produced when an audit is *anticipated* in terms of pending "external" examinations of ongoing operations.

---

[2] See, for example, the references to the use of audit practices by the Fuggers, Welsers, and the Medici in R. de Roover [162].

Choice of Study Area and Topics

Some explanation is probably now in order concerning the choice of an accounting emphasis for this first study. There were various reasons for electing this particular emphasis and some of these may be summarized as follows. First, we observe that there is not a great deal of guidance in this area that can be secured by reference to results of preceding scientific studies of the audit function.[3] Second, we observe that auditing—and especially the accounting audit—is indirect in its effects and involves a variety of complex and subtle processes. Under the circumstances it seemed best to attempt to secure the maximum amount of explicit guidance, and the best source appeared to be the literature of accounting theory and practice.[4]

We should probably now also observe that the experiment was designed so that certain aspects of a supervisory (as distinguished from an accounting) audit could also be studied. This was done because we wish ultimately (*a*) to utilize these results as, possibly, a better starting point for analysis of supervisory audits, and (*b*) to study the possible advantages of various supervisory-accounting audit combinations. The best way to secure the wanted isolations, at least initially, seemed to involve study of the accounting audit process, *per se*, and, in particular, to study it as a process of record examination only—as distinguished from (*a*) formulating and submitting explicit recommendations, and (*b*) actual observation of task performance.

As will subsequently be indicated, we sought to study and distinguish between the effects of an actually executed audit and the effects that might ensue when an audit was only anticipated. We further subdivided the study by selecting subjects for the experiments from (1) industrial personnel who had experienced previous exposures to actual commercial audits, and (2) college students who had not had any such previous experience. Finally, we distinguished between immediate performance of a certain prescribed task and certain "over-all" organization goals which were associated with the records that were to be maintained by the subjects. The association between records maintenance and over-all organization objectives was designed into the experiment because it is often viewed this way in actual management practice, and because this design permitted accounting audit variables

---

[3] There is, of course, a considerable literature on psychological (and other) studies of the supervisory function which includes, undoubtedly, the audit aspects of supervision as one part of a total conglomerate.

[4] The literature of administrative and organization theory (and practice) does not appear to have given very much explicit attention to the audit function.

to come into play in a way that could be relatively easily manipulated and distinguished from the supervisory audit variables that were also studied.

The audit variables are here viewed as one of a variety of managerial control instruments. Generally speaking, managerial control is concerned with bringing about conformance between plans and their execution, and *vice versa*.[5] More specifically, we are here concerned with the potential effects (or value) of such control instruments as a way of bringing about desired—or desirable—modes of behavior in a way that might be used to reduce (or otherwise alter) the actual, direct, supervision which might otherwise be necessary in order to achieve a balance in conformance between the plans and their execution at various levels of an administrative-supervisory hierarchy. We might, for instance, consider certain elements of supervision that presuppose a certain degree of expertise with respect to the tasks that are to be planned or executed. Then we might distinguish these from an expertise directed towards an examination of the records which, for one reason or another, are supposed to be maintained with reference to task plans and their execution. Finally, we might further separate the supervisory authority (and responsibility) that is normally associated with the preparation and direction of workers on a specific task and then distinguish these from the record examination process where no such responsibility, or authority, is delegated to or assumed by the persons who perform this function.

Note that, from this standpoint, the "accounting type" of audit, at least as here conceived, proceeds on the assumption that the preliminary training, instructions, etc., have all been handled by the supervisor. That is, the record examination presumes that a certain level of subject competence has already been attained not only on the tasks to be performed but also on the record-keeping activities which are then subjected to an independent audit examination. Proceeding on this assumption, then, we want to examine, if possible, the effects that such an independent audit inspection (or its anticipation) might have on the conduct of a set of tasks [6] where the primary responsibility and authority have previously been fixed on the supervisor.[7]

---

[5] See, for example, A. Charnes and W. W. Cooper [113], Vol. I, pp. 39–40, and A. Stedry [516].

[6] Note, we do not here concern ourselves with the problem of coordinating the activities of numerous individuals in the sense, say, that this is discussed by A. Whinston in Chapter 22 of this volume.

[7] We are here concerned with control of individual activities where two different objectives are involved rather than the dynamics of multiple activity controls and aspirations that A. Stedry and A. Charnes [518] deal with.

Accounting Audits

Having now indicated our choice of subject area—accounting audit —we next need to distinguish the aspects studied, so that there will not be a confusion of the results of this study as they might bear on other facets of an accounting audit encountered in actual practice. A review of contemporary American literature on auditing reveals that there is no general agreement on the definition of the term "audit" or "auditing," and, in fact, very little has been written concerning audit theory.[8] There is sufficient consensus, however, relative to certain audit characteristics so that it is not too difficult to define at least some of the essential characteristics of an audit as it would be performed by a professional accountant in the United States (or elsewhere) today, or as they have been in evidence over a considerable period of years. Briefly, the process is concerned with procedures for examining actions or, more precisely, the *evidence* of actions and an ascertainment of whether these findings correspond to certain more or less defined criteria as to the directions and modes of implementation that were assumed to be governing. In addition, both the design of the investigation and the evaluations effected are supposed to be executed by persons possessed of certain minimum levels of competence, expertise, and experience,[9] and these persons are also supposed to be able to implement their investigations and appraisals in a wholly objective manner.

The activities of a professional public practitioner of auditing are probably most easily understood when he is regarded as an expert on contemporary managerial control systems. Indeed, especially when auditing large organizations, the chief emphasis is likely to turn toward study and appraisal of the over-all managerial controls. In the formal literature of accounting, this is usually described relative to certain types of mechanics for checking—so-called people-to-people checks, people-to-documents checks, documents-to-documents checks, etc., and, finally, even procedure-to-procedure or company-to-company checks.[10] Often this study or appraisal is accompanied by a report of findings and recommendations for altering the system of internal control in a variety of ways after first test checking (or sam-

---

[8] R. K. Mautz and H. A. Sharaf [374], pp. 1–3.

[9] For example, as evidenced by a written examination, certain criteria of training, background, and experience.

[10] For example, in the validation of the so-called *bona fides* of accounts payable records, subsidiary-parent controls, etc. See, e.g., R. M. Trueblood [551].

pling) the actual functioning of the instant system in a variety of ways.

We will not be concerned here with studying these somewhat complicated systems approaches and, in fact, as has already been said, we shall not be concerned with the effects even of recommendations that might flow from an audit.[11] In contrast to the more usual approaches, however, we shall not confine ourselves to performance and appraisal in terms of the issues related to expertise in current applications. We shall, instead, focus on the audit process itself and call it *audit per se* in order thereby to indicate that it is an essential ingredient of every kind of audit. We shall then focus on the possible behavioral consequences of *audit per se* in highly simplified laboratory situations, so that we may be able to draw inferences or gain insights into managerial as well as accounting aspects of audit.

Audit Anticipation

To appraise the choice that was actually made for this experiment, it is first necessary to understand some of the kinds of audit variables that were to be examined. Consider, for instance, the problem of "audit anticipation." A person who is informed—or otherwise led to believe— that an audit will occur may be expected to modify his behavior in anticipation of this event. In particular, the modification that is evoked may be determined, to some extent, by the criteria that this individual supposes that an auditor might employ when conducting his examination. Evidently it will also depend on the kinds of further acts or consequences that might be expected to flow if an audit uncovers some evidence of nonconforming or deviant behavior.

We leave aside, for the moment, whether or not the evoked responses are based on correct anticipations in order to emphasize that we are here dealing with something which has the nature of a sociological influence function.[12] We also want to point up the possible relevance of these influence function ideas for their bearing on audits and managerial-supervisory practices in general and, conversely, to utilize the audit process as a way of gaining further insight and knowledge of the way influence functions might operate in other sociological contexts.

---

[11] We are also not essentially concerned with such issues as objectivity, accounting competence, etc. For further discussion of these topics and their possible relevance to further scientific research, see either N. C. Churchill and L. N. Teitelbaum [123] or N. C. Churchill and W. W. Cooper [122].

[12] J. G. March [365].

Note that these anticipations may screen or conceal the effects of an audit when it is actually conducted. This is true with respect to actions that are subject to supervisory audit as well as with respect to the records of these actions that are subject to accounting audit. The problem tends to be further compounded in the latter case since deviant behavior may be continued, or accentuated, in concert with efforts to amend or alter the records that otherwise might serve as a source of revelation leading to possible punishments or rewards.

An experiment designed to test such audit anticipation effects necessarily confronts certain difficulties at the present stage of knowledge. The situation is something less than clear, for example, as to the nature and variety of the responses that might be studied.[13] Also, these responses might themselves be subject to change as a consequence of previous exposures to audit examinations. The latter, in turn, might be dependent upon the kinds of audits that were utilized as well as the various supervisory-accounting audit combinations that could be employed, and so on.

For the present study, it was therefore decided to confine the experiment to certain modest objectives concerning audit anticipation. It was decided, for example, to utilize two sets of subjects distinguished according to whether they might reasonably be supposed to have either some or no experience with actual commercial audits—i.e., the way such audits might be conducted and their possible consequences. The "no experience" subjects were drawn from the body of college students at Carnegie Institute of Technology. The "some experience" subjects consisted of a selected panel of persons who, by previous interview, were known to have had some exposure to actual commercial audits.

Of course, the selection of a group with "some experience" does not exhaust the numerous dimensions in which an audit experience might be encountered. The aspects of an audit, as it might actually be observed in practice, are likely to differ from layer to layer in the usual company hierarchy. For instance, at some of the higher echelons, the auditor is likely to be concerned, in the main, with over-all systems appraisals. At other echelons he is likely to be observed when he

---

[13] There was, for example, no available literature with which to contrast the perceptions of auditees and auditors concerning the nature and proper functionings of an audit examination even in the sense of an accounting audit. Hence it was necessary to initiate field studies in order to obtain at least a general feel for the kinds of characterizations that ought to be admitted for consideration in the experiments. (These field studies, which are still under way, will be reported separately when the full results have been finally assembled and analyzed.)

is "test checking" by examining particular records or documentary evidence, verifying inventory details, and so on.

To avoid becoming enmeshed in the multidimensional complexity of a systems evaluation study, it was decided to select an industrial group at the lowest possible hierarchy where an audit exposure could have been experienced. It was further decided to proceed, if possible, to a layer that was sufficiently removed from actual audit contacts so that the contamination that might be due to some familiarity with sophisticated professional audit concepts could be avoided (or at least minimized).[14] Finally, in order to keep the desired industrial subject group sufficiently homogeneous—e.g., with respect to supervisor-accounting audit exposure mixes—it was decided that all persons should be drawn from the staff of one industrial enterprise and that these persons should have operated under the same supervisor on very similar kinds of tasks.

Accounting and Supervisory Audit Combinations

For the purposes of our study, we distinguished between accounting or, perhaps, more exactly,[15] independent audits [16] and supervisory audits in several ways. First, we restricted the independent audit so that it was confined to the records the subjects were supposed to maintain. This involved recording entries which would (a) facilitate task performance and (b) provide a basis for subsequent analysis. By way of contrast, we oriented the supervisory audit so that it would tend to be associated very closely in the subjects' minds with final accomplishments on the immediate task. To emphasize further this aspect of a supervisory audit, we disassociated it almost entirely from any examination of the records that were being maintained by the subjects and from the methods followed by the subjects in obtaining their task results.

---

[14] Further subsequent experiments are planned which will tap this aspect of auditing by reference to staff members of practicing professional CPA firms.

[15] As we previously explained, we do not wish to give an impression that we actually tested the effects of an audit as it might be conducted by a full-time professional accountant.

[16] The term "independent" is to be interpreted here as meaning that the auditor was not to be regarded as either (a) an expert who was knowledgeable about the actual task or (b) a person whose motivation or reward structure was tied to task performance. Furthermore, he was not to be tied to the chain of supervisor authority and responsibility but rather (a) was to be an expert in examining records for any task and (b) was to represent an "over-all" organization of which the experiment was a part.

We further distinguished between independent and supervisory audits by reference to the motivation that was likely to be imputed to the performance of each of these functions. In particular, the experiment was designed so that the supervisory audit was closely associated with the amount, quality, and speed of accomplishing output on the immediate task—what we call the "output check" as distinguished from "record inspection." By way of contrast, the independent audit examination was designed to be closely associated with over-all organization goals (or requirements) via the records to be maintained by the subjects and by the task solution methods as reflected in the records. Some care was utilized in order to communicate this facet of the experiments to the subjects and, in particular, some degree of conflict between task accomplishment and record maintenance was included in the experiment that was finally designed so that we could thereby re-enforce the distinction between over-all organization and task considerations.

Of course, two different persons were utilized to represent the independent audit and supervisory functions. An attempt was made to create an atmosphere which would cause the experimental subjects to believe that the supervisor was closely associated with the actual outcome of the task, whereas the independent auditor was primarily concerned with records and, in particular, the methods of task solution that had been followed according to the records.

The nature of the task and the experimental design utilized are discussed more fully in subsequent sections and in the appendix to this chapter. Here we should note that the supervisory role also caused us some concern, especially in its bearing on the supervisory (output check) and the independent (record examination) audit. We finally decided that it was probably best to avoid any attempt to separate the audit (output check) aspect of supervision from any of the other ordinary supervisory functions. Since the experimenter would be required, in any event, to inform or generally instruct the subjects and perform other supervisory functions as well, it seemed best to design the experiment so that he (i.e., the experimenter) would rather naturally be accorded the role of a supervisor by the experimental subjects. In particular, the experiment was designed so that the person who was in charge of its actual execution would also conduct the output checks according to a prearranged schedule. The questionnaires completed by the experimental subjects indicate that this aspect of the experimental design was successful.

Somewhat less success was experienced in conveying the role of the independent auditor to the experimental subjects. The problems here involved several kinds of considerations. Note, for example, that here we were taking a somewhat different tack from that employed in most experimentation in that we were attempting to design into the experiment an "observer effect," which we could control and measure. We were also trying to do this in an indirect manner. In particular, our effort here was directed toward an observer effect via the records rather than via the actual tasks with which the subjects were concerned. In addition, we wanted to convey an impression of an observer who possessed considerable expertness at record examination but had virtually no expertness (or concern) with the results of the task itself. Judging from the responses to questionnaires completed by the subjects (at the end of their experimental trials), we were not very successful in conveying this image of an expert examiner.[17] We apparently did succeed, however, in creating a setting in which the subjects tended to associate the independent audits with over-all organization objectives and to distinguish, at least to some extent, between these objectives and the immediate task accomplishments. In particular, the subjects tended to respond both in the audit anticipation and in the actual audit situations as though the auditor were conducting his examinations and applying criteria that differed from those that would be applied if he were motivated only by task accomplishments. We were, therefore, apparently able to communicate aspects of the kind of *set* sometimes associated with the differences in the supervisor and audit viewpoints in actual management. In this view, a supervisor is often more concerned with results on the actual task than with the methods of achieving these results; he is notably more concerned with task results than in the propriety with which other associated procedures (e.g., record maintenance) are executed. In this same view, an almost opposite concern is ascribed to the auditor. His concern is less with the actual task accomplishments and more with the propriety of the procedures utilized, their conformance to previously prescribed norms or policies, and so forth.[18]

We call attention to this particular facet of the experiment because it was exactly this supposed "means-ends" difference which was uti-

---

[17] We were motivated here by reference to ordinary conceptions of the public accounting (and other) audit functions as performed across a variety of organizations and industries.

[18] This is sometimes paraphrased by asserting that accountants are motivated by a "third party interest." That is, in evaluating transactions the accountant is less concerned with advantages or disadvantages to the immediate parties and more concerned with the possibly affected interests of "third persons," e.g., the general public, governmental units, stockholders, or more remote tiers of managers.

lized to bring into the experiment a conflict between over-all organization goals and immediate task accomplishments. This was further amplified, of course, and the experiment was, in fact, designed so that an emphasis on propriety would necessarily be achieved at some cost in immediate task accomplishments.

The Experimental Task

There were, of course, many other considerations, including deliberate (or inadvertent) omissions,[19] that entered into the selection of a task that would lend itself to this kind of study. The main criteria of selection, however, were conceived in the following terms:

1. The task must be capable of performance by the experimental subjects without any need for observation or participation by anyone else.

2. The task must involve only easily explained procedural steps leading to its completion.

3. The task must permit not only the accomplishment of a definite, easily determined output but also the method used in producing the output should produce a trail of evidence in sufficient and systematic detail, so that it would always be possible to ascertain the actual procedures used in a way that admitted of ready comparison with the subjects' own records.

4. The task must be rich enough in possible methods of attack and methods of solution so that a method could be initially given to the subjects in an easily comprehended manner, and variations from this method could be utilized by the subjects either to improve or worsen their performance.[20]

5. The output and method of performance should be susceptible of influence by a penalty-reward system.

6. The task should have some of the same content—at least in very basic or elementary senses—as some of the tasks that may be audited in society.

The task that was finally selected consisted of an adaptation of a "trouble-shooting" experiment used by Marx, Goldbeck, Bernstein, and Hillex at the University of Missouri,[21] modified for use in a study

---

[19] N. C. Churchill [121].

[20] In addition, the task finally selected admitted of mathematical characterizations which could be used to establish optimum performance and optimum methods of achieving this performance.

[21] Marx, Goldbeck, and Bernstein [372] and Goldbeck et al. [220].

of problem-solving strategies and information-processing behavior by J. D. Folley at Carnegie Institute of Technology.[22] The task involved searching through and locating one possible block in an array of 100 displayed on a problem board.[23] The problem was presented so that the subjects would perceive it in terms of searching for a source of contamination (the particular block) in a large water supply system. The structure of the problem allowed various methods to be used in its solution. These methods were represented by the sequence of tests that the subjects made in trying to solve the problem. A test of the output of any block could be made by pressing a pushbutton in the desired block. This produced a binary response on the problem board. Every time such a button was pressed, an apparatus in another room recorded the number of the button pressed. The sequence of the buttons pressed then produced a search pattern which represented the method that the subject used in solving the problem.

One particular method of solution was reported to the subjects as an organizational objective and was also made a part of the auditor's criteria. Although this procedure had desirable characteristics in that it led the subjects to solve the problem more rapidly and quite efficiently, it was not optimal in the sense that it required the pressing of buttons which logical deduction could eliminate. The subjects were rewarded by 25 points for solving the problem correctly, and penalized 2 points for each button pressed; hence a criterion of score maximization would be in conflict with procedural adherence and, in fact, this conflict was presented to the subjects. The subjects were also instructed to record the number of each button pressed in the proper sequence in a data log (books of account) provided for the purpose. The experimental setting is depicted in Fig. 1.

The subject was thus given four objectives: (1) Solve the problem correctly; (2) press as few buttons as possible; (3) follow the procedures given; and (4) maintain proper records in the data log. Their performance with respect to each one of these objectives was a separate, measurable, experimental variable.

Experimental Results

In general, the experiment indicated that the actual occurrence of an *audit per se* exerts an effect on the behavior of those audited, even where there is no direct connection between the auditor's findings and

---

[22] [199].

[23] The task and apparatus are presented in further detail in Appendix B.

the penalty-reward structure. The main direction of this effect appeared to be toward conformance patterns in which the behavior of those who were audited tended to move toward the auditor's criteria. The results of the experiment indicate that the subjects who were audited consider the auditor as being concerned with comparing their

FIGURE 1 Experimental setting. (See Fig. 2, Appendix B for overlay being removed.) 1. Scoreboard on left; data log at bottom; specimen problem on panel. 2. Light at top is initial source; lights at bottom are final sinks. 3. Red light on if contaminated; green light on if not contaminated. 4. Red or green light in each block is activated while button is pressed. 5. If red is activated, water output from block is contaminated. 6. Problem: find *initial* red, the *source* of contamination. 7. Black lines are permanent. Others on plastic overlay to show water flow connections for specimen problem.

actions against some "organizationally desirable" standard. Even without exact knowledge of the over-all organization or the desiderata, the subjects tended to respond as though the criteria that the auditor was employing were in conformance with certain "organizational goals."

We should note that the subjects were not given any explicit information on how the audit would be performed or the kinds of criteria that the auditor would use. Moreover, his actions were not directly connected with any penalty-reward structure on record-keeping aspects of the experiment. In short, we relied on the audit—or its anticipation —to provide its own "informational effects."

It cannot be assumed, of course, that even an actual auditor's true criteria are accurately perceived by those audited or even that the auditor can always articulate these criteria when asked. In fact, the perception of his criteria is the cause for action regardless of the correspondence of this perception to the true basis of evaluation.[24] Notice, then, that the experiment suggests that audits may conceivably be employed as managerial control instruments when certain kinds of actions are desired, even in the absence of an expert, well-trained auditor.[25] This is brought into view most prominently by the audit anticipation variable when its effects are exhibited even in the absence of a subsequent actual audit so that, then, the quality or expertise cannot be known in any concrete sense.[26]

Some qualifications should be entered here. Although all aspects of the evidence concerning the effect of the anticipation of the audit were not definitive, two conclusions emerged. The first is obvious: to be effective, an audit of historical actions should have, or at least be perceived as having, the power to go beneath the apparent evidence to determine what, in fact, did happen. The second is that the anticipation of an audit as studied in this experiment did produce behavioral effects, but the direction of these effects was unexpectedly sensitive to

---

[24] Since audits cross organizational structures and move up and down the chain of command—examining some actions in one group and supposedly related actions or events in another—the perception of the people in any one part of the organization may easily be based on partial evidence and an auditor's actions may consequently be misperceived.

[25] We are, of course, not referring to the actions of an auditor as an expert in evaluating or designing business control systems.

[26] Of course, allowance must be made for halo effects carried over by the industrial subjects who were previously exposed to commercial audits. However, this tends to re-enforce the point especially since the auditor used in their experiments was not a trained accountant but rather a behavioral scientist—with the added qualification of a mustache and a general auditor's "mien."

the characterization of the impending audit and to the type of organizational personnel involved.

The difference between the types of subjects—industrial and academic—in their reactions to audit anticipation was, perhaps, somewhat surprising. The industrial subjects significantly decreased the errors they made in the record while the student subjects reacted significantly in the opposite direction and increased the number of record errors. Although this may be attributable to anxiety and confusion resulting from knowledge of an impending examination, it may also be indicative of a class of people or of backgrounds that would behave perversely to the knowledge of an audit. In either case, additional study is certainly needed before we can seriously entertain the hypothesis that knowledge of an audit causes certain individuals to behave to the detriment of themselves or of the organization. The point to be made here, however, is that, conceivably, various kinds of audits may have perverse effects if applied uniformly without respect to persons and organization structure.

The supervisor's output evaluation had no noticeable effect on the student subjects, but caused the industrial subjects not only to significantly increase the number of problems solved correctly but also to increase the errors made in the record. These results suggest the pervasiveness of the supervisor's influence not only on the output but also on the method of task performance and on the information produced by his subordinates.[27]

Finally, the interactions should be noted. For the student subjects, the audit occurrence and the supervisory output check each tended to increase (but not significantly) the care with which the problems were solved and the records maintained. Moreover, no significant additions were achieved when the two were applied jointly on these subjects. For the industrial subjects, the combination of audit anticipation and supervisory check increased significantly the number of problems solved correctly. However, the combination of audit anticipation, supervisory check, and audit occurrence significantly decreased the number of problems solved correctly.

These results suggest that various kinds of audit mixes may have

---

[27] Where a manager of, say, a decentralized branch is evaluated unidirectionally, e.g., on profits made or on units produced, the influence of his concern with this "output" may permeate the organization, and result in unconscious or even well-intentioned bias in the actions or reports of his subordinates. This may be true even when their rewards or penalties are less involved than his in the performance attained.

countervailing tendencies so that nothing is really added and, further-more, that an "excessive" amount (or combination) of examinations may even be detrimental. Of course, the results of this experiment are only indicative. But they do bear on possible managerial strategies which are worthy of further examination in terms of possible mix com-binations of audits and supervision, especially as these are reflected in a structure of organization relations, spans of control, and related con-siderations. The possibility must be at least entertained that an inju-dicious use of control devices may, of itself, give rise to a need for further controls, and so on.

Conclusions and a Program for Further Research

Recent research [28] into the problems and practices of decentralized managements has suggested that there is some need for further under-standing and improvement of the existing methods for securing co-ordination and control. We refer, of course, to the human agents of management and leave aside the improvements that are possible via the development of new mechanical and mathematical devices.[29]

In this connection we can point out that there is some justification for examining the practices of management itself—particularly ad-vanced managements—to ascertain how these have been evolving in order to grapple with problems that theoretical research has already suggested is present, and which may become pressing, as organizations continue to increase in size and complexity. Audit, and especially ac-counting audit, is a case of possible interest in that "third party" con-trol now plays a very prominent role in the performance of these du-ties, although in ways that are not always completely documented and well understood.

Some of the main gaps in our understanding have already been sug-gested in considering, for example, how accounting and managerial (supervisory) audits may relate and conflict with one another, how they may affect different classes of persons in different kinds of or-ganization frameworks, and so on. We have also taken some pains to distinguish between "audit anticipation" and "audit occurrence," not only to clarify the preceding issues but also the kinds of expertise that would be needed for adequately using these two different aspects of

---

[28] See, e.g., Chapter 22 of this volume by A. Whinston dealing with price-cost guides for managerial decision making in decentralized entities. See also Chapter IX and Appendix D in A. Charnes and W. W. Cooper [113].

[29] See Chapter 4 of this volume by H. J. Leavitt.

audit per se. Of course, the results reported in our experiments might take a different cast when extensions are attempted to other aspects of accounting audit such as: (1) potential disclosure [30] of recorded results (and methods) as usually envisioned in the so-called "attest function"; or (2) possible recommendations, of different kinds, to persons under audit, in terms of possible transmittal to their superiors or others; and (3) examining and evaluating total control systems as distinguished from the simple kinds of records test checking that were studied in this case.

We have already indicated that we did not examine accounting in its so-called advisory or "management service function" capacities where, again, a certain kind of expertise relative to the tasks and its associated methodologies must, apparently, be presumed. We also did not plan any systematic study of the utilization of accounting audits that were directed to the information needs for obtaining coordination in a multiple-person multiple-task situation in an organization hierarchy. On the other hand, the experiment does suggest the possible use of accounting-type audits as one link in a possible chain of informational devices. Note that we are here conceiving of a task-oriented supervisor who might possibly achieve superb performance in his immediate task environment only at a much greater resulting cost, to the total organization, by driving his activity to a point where the attainment of other organization goals is thwarted.

A common view of the accounting audit process directs attention to its use as a device for explicitly transmitting information up the chain of command in order to enable higher management echelons to evaluate and direct the activities that are being undertaken at lower tiers of the organization. The experimental evidence suggests, however, that an *audit per se*—or even its anticipation—may be utilized to transmit "information" downward in accordance with certain perceived "audit criteria," even when the latter are not explicitly stated and even (under audit anticipation) when no auditor is present to serve as a transmitting vehicle.

Evidently more is needed, however, before any really firm conclusions can be reached. One part of the studies now planned will undertake a more precise characterization of the nature of the audits that are, or might be, employed, and the kinds of information or audit

---

[30] Especially disclosures of the kind associated with the certification of statements for third-party examination or use, e.g., the so-called short form reports and supporting statements that are usually released under an opinion audit by an independent CPA.

images that they are likely to transmit.[31] Such a study would probably best be conducted, at least in part, in a field context of the kind suggested by, say, the Simon, Kozmetsky, Tyndall, and Guetzkow inquiries into the controllership function.[32] Because of the considerable professionalization that has accompanied the development of the audit process, however, it will probably be best to plan this kind of study so that it will include various tests and characterizations of audit procedures as these are conceived and executed by full-time professional auditors. If these are to yield something more than a series of verbal characterizations, however, something more than the usual field interview techniques will be required. In particular, it is hoped that the initial field inquiries can be made to yield protocols that will lend themselves to computer simulations. These could then be elaborated and, possibly, validated by synthesizing a variety of auditlike situations to predict how actual professional auditors would perform under the indicated circumstances, and to evaluate this performance against the known aspects of the simulation. The simulation, including recording and systems defects, should, of course, be designed with the standards and criteria of actual audit practice in mind if it is to supply the kinds of insights that are wanted. Presumably then the simulation can also be used either to predict the performance of actual auditors under similar "real-world" conditions or else to ascertain how real-world auditors will actually perform under conditions that the simulations may generate.

Of course, further laboratory testing is also in order. Since many obviously important audit variables were not included in the present inquiry, one evident course of extension is thereby immediately indicated. Some other kinds of preparatory work are in order, however, before the full gamut of these extensions to all aspects of an ordinary audit can even be begun with any real hope of success. As a case in point, a focus on the systems control aspects of an audit will almost certainly require the use of explicit mathematical models, and, possibly, new mathematical and statistical techniques,[33] especially when

---

[31] In the taxonomy suggested by Dr. George Briggs, the intended meaning here would perhaps be better rendered by "transformation"—as distinguished, according to Dr. Briggs, from information "transmission" or "translation." See Briggs [84], from whom we also borrow the following very apt statement: "Information processing within the human components of a system is a private affair which can be specified only by influence or analogy, the latter being a form of influence. . . ."

[32] [503].

[33] See, e.g., R. M. Trueblood and R. M. Cyert [552], p. 69.

auditors are being simultaneously deployed at various points in an organization hierarchy. Then, at last, we might obtain a vantage point from which we could proceed from task performance and organization analysis—by bits—to the even grander problem of multiple-variable organization designs.

These remarks are intended to form an appropriate closing note by suggesting that such inquiries might offer a fruitful meeting ground for behavioral science-management science developments in understanding or improving management practices. Further details concerning the experiment and some of the results secured are set forth in the appendices.

APPENDIX A

The Experimental Setting

THE SUBJECTS IN THE EXPERIMENT

The experiment was performed on two types of experimental subjects—industrial personnel who had been subject to professional audits and college students who had had no such experience.

These two groups were selected for several reasons. First, it was desirable to work with people who had actually been audited as well as with those that had not. Second, since the variables being tested had real-world counterparts, the desire was to include real-world subjects rather than base the conclusions strictly upon the performance of the traditional "college sophomore." Finally, it was of interest to ascertain, for future work, whether the choice of subjects was a critical factor in the experimental results.

In analyzing the performance of these two groups, two methods were used. In the first, all seven groups of eight subjects were treated as separate replications (or trials) of the three experimental variables. In the second, a contrast was made between the college students—engineers and industrial management majors—and the industrial personnel. In effect, the differing populations from which the subjects were drawn was considered as an explicit experimental variable.

The use of industrial subjects made it infeasible to test the individuals in the experiment for personal qualities or characteristics such as aptitudes or intelligence. Such comparisons of peer group capabilities not connected with job performance were, it was discovered, looked upon with some suspicion as providing an opportunity for rationalizing or implementing discriminatory practices that might otherwise not be available to the company supervisors. Consequently, the experiment was arranged so that performance on the first set of five problems could serve not only as a learning experience and a means of generating a record for the audit variable but also as a measure of task performance which would be of value in analyzing the experimental results.

THE EXPERIMENTAL DESIGN

A factorial design was used in the experiment. The subjects performed 13 task problems, 3 during a training session, a set of 5 under identical conditions, prior to the application of the experimental variables, and a set of 5 after the treatments were applied. The division of the 10 experimental problems into two groups of 5 each was necessary to provide an audit trail prior to the application of an audit. It further allowed the use of covariance analysis on the assumption that performance in the first group of problems could be taken as representative of the individual characteristics of the subjects.

As mentioned above, the analysis was first made by using as experimental variables the audit occurrence, the audit anticipation, and the supervisory output check. Another analysis was made which specifically included the difference in personnel as between the industrial and the student subjects as a fourth variable. Although this violates the condition of covariance analysis, at least in principle, the result of the four-factor analysis was compared to that of the three factor analysis, and the interpretation of the results was made with this condition in mind.

A questionnaire was also administered to the subjects at the completion of each experimental session. Although the questions were not intended to be tabulated statistically, they were useful both in checking the conduct of the experiment and providing some insight into the results.

THE EXPERIMENTAL MEASURES

The three behavioral patterns measured in the experiment were task accomplishment, procedural adherence, and record maintenance.

Task accomplishment. The number of problems solved correctly was taken as the primary measure of task accomplishment.

Record maintenance. Since each subject was told to record the number of each interrogation (tests) he made of the problem board as well as the result, the measure of record maintenance was the number of discrepancies between the tests actually made and those that were recorded.

Procedural adherence. Each subject was given a set of procedures to follow in solving the problems. These procedures called for a set but different pattern of tests to be made on each problem. Any tests that should have been made according to the procedures but were in fact not made by the subject are referred to as procedural omissions while those made that were not called for by the procedures during the portion of the experiment covered by the procedures are called additions to procedure. Since each test was made under a two-point penalty arrangement, it was hypothesized that there would be some tendency to omit rather than add to the tests specified by the procedures. Consequently it was anticipated that the omissions would provide a significant, easily handled, measure of procedural adherence.

APPENDIX B

The Task and the Experimental Apparatus

DESCRIPTION OF THE TASK

The problem-solving task used in the audit experiment was presented to the subjects on a problem board (shown in Fig. 2). Each task consisted of 100 blocks—representing 100 water-processing stations—arrayed on a problem board (see Fig. 2) in 10 columns of 10 blocks each. Each block was connected vertically to the block in the same column directly below it, and the bottom block in each column was connected to a pair of column-indicator lights—one red and one green. These vertical connections represented water flows from a single source at the top of the board down through the columns to the indicator lights at the bottom. There were ten connections between blocks in different columns, called cross connections. Both the vertical and cross connections were one-way connections only, and the direction of the connection was indicated by arrow heads on the problem board. These cross connections represented the only flows possible *between* blocks in different columns. Each block was numbered and contained a red light, a green light, and a pushbutton the purpose of which was to activate one of the lights in the block—the light remaining on only while the button is being pressed [34]—the color of the light (red or green) (bad or good) being used to signify the condition of the water flowing out of that block.

---

[34] This procedure was followed, as permitted by the experimental apparatus, in order to make part of the record-keeping process useful to the subject.

FIGURE 2 Problem board and plastic overlay.

The problem board was connected to a recording apparatus concealed from subject's (S) view in another room which was used to record each block tested, and the order in which the tests were made, as the S's proceeded with their tasks. An exact record was thereby made available both on "task" and "method" which could be compared, as desired, with the records maintained by any S.

THE CONDUCT OF THE EXPERIMENT

Each S was presented the problem board upon which a particular pattern of cross connections was displayed and with one column-indicator light glowing in each column. No lights within the blocks were on, however. The subject was instructed to solve the problem by finding the *one* water-processing station (block) that was the source of all the contamination (red lights) in an otherwise pure water system (pure water represented by green lights).

The problem is solved by analyzing the pattern of red or green indicator lights at the bottom of the columns and the cross connections (cross flows) that were present. Information about the flow out of any water-processing station is obtained by pressing the button in the block representing that station. This button activates either the red or the green light within the block and, accordingly, indicates the state of the water flow leaving that block. A solution is achieved whenever a subject finds the block that has only pure flows (green lights) going into it and a red light indicating contaminated output going out. (Blocks with red inputs were not candidates as the contamination source since red flows propagated themselves through the system.) The problems were set up so that they were solvable and had the specified unique source—one and only one block serving as the source of all contamination in the entire system.[35]

Although it is possible to isolate a *group* of blocks which contain the solution to the problem by analyzing both the pattern of lights at the bottom of the columns and the cross connections present, in all but one of the 13 problems given the subjects, it was necessary to press at least one button to gain further knowledge of purity of the flows in order to solve the problem.

The problems given the S's were sufficiently complex so that both the time taken to solve and the number of buttons pressed could not simultaneously be minimized. Although either could be made an objective of the experiment, it was felt that the number and pattern of buttons pressed lent itself more easily to examination of the solution method.

The pressing of a button in a block was represented to S's as a test of the output of that particular water-processing station. They were told that such a test would require the expenditure of considerable time and money and, hence, they were to minimize the number of tests made—to solve the problems by pressing as few buttons as possible.

To provide suitable variety in the task problems given to subjects, as well as to facilitate problem change, the cross connections were

---

[35] The problem board is designed, however, to admit either more complex arrangements or simpler ones (by reducing the number of rows and columns) as desired for subsequent experimental studies.

mounted on plastic overlays which were placed over the face of the problem board. Figure 2 shows the specimen overlay of Fig. 1 as it is being removed.

It was desired to have an experimental apparatus that would admit of easy transport, e.g., to company offices for studying industrial S's, and it was also desired to arrange matters so that only a small amount of time would be needed to change the wiring for the experiment and the problems for any S. The first problem was handled by keeping the experimental apparatus fairly small and light. The second was handled by appropriately designed switches which changed the circuitry in accordance with predesigned plastic overlays for each problem in a series. Finally, relay arrangements were designed so that a recording machine (an old desk calculator) could be concealed in another room to follow exactly the sequence of trials used by each S.

In the experiment, 13 different problems were given the subjects

FIGURE 3   Wiring from back of panel to switches used by experimenter to effect changes in problems.

using 7 different patterns of cross connections. The responses to the pressing of a pushbutton in any block and the color of the column indicator lights were controlled by a switch panel on the back of the problem board (see Fig. 3). In this way, both the pattern of cross flows and/or the sources of contamination could be changed in less than a minute.

APPENDIX C

The Experimental Results

The complete experimental results are not reproduced here.[36] Neither the raw experimental data nor the responses to the questions are included. Only an indication of the pattern of the F test results, using the four treatment analyses, are shown for the three main measures—the number of problems solved correctly, the number of errors made in the record and the number of omissions.[37]

In this presentation (Table 1), the following notation is used for the experimental variables:

$$A = \text{audit occurrence}$$
$$E(A) = \text{anticipation of an audit}$$
$$S = \text{supervisory output check}$$
$$P = \text{personnel variable}$$

---

[36] They are described in their entirety in N. C. Churchill [121].

[37] The latter was used as a measure of the lack of procedure adherence.

*Table 1   Experimental Results—F Ratios with the Sign of
the Corresponding Treatment Effect. Covariance Analysis of
Untransformed Data. (The P Variable is Possessed by the
First-Named Subject Group.)*

Treatment Effect	Student Group I and Industry	Student Groups I and II	Student Group II and Industry
	Errors Made in the Record		
$E(A)$	−4.48	+5.53 *	−5.86 *
S	+11.24 ‡	+0.83	+9.44 †
$P, E(A)$	+9.18 †	+0.10	+4.07
P, S	−13.90 ‡	−0.15	−8.35 *
$A, E(A), S$	−5.14 *	−1.00	−3.42
	Problems Solved Correctly		
P	+16.25 ‡	−4.32	+23.47 ‡
$E(A)$	+3.80	+0.37	+1.82
S	+5.82 *	−0.30	+3.21
P, S	−3.12	+1.40	−6.33 *
$E(A), S$	+7.11 *	+0.37	+9.19 †
$P, E(A), S$	−4.07	+0.00	−4.86 *
$A, E(A), S$	−5.93 *	−1.40	−11.18 ‡
$P, A, E(A), S$	+5.82 *	+0.83	+3.23
	Number of Tests Omitted from Those Required by the Procedures		
A	0.15	−4.11	−8.05 *
P, A	0.13	5.00 *	−6.66 *

* Significant at 5% level.
† Significant at 1% level.
‡ Significant at 0.5% level.

15

SIMULATING ORGANIZATIONAL BEHAVIOR

Charles P. Bonini

Introduction [1]

Simulation has long been a tool of research in the physical sciences. More recently, simulation has been used to reproduce and study business and military systems. Here, in general, the major emphasis has been upon physical flows of goods, materials, orders, and funds. The purpose of this chapter is to discuss an extension of simulation techniques into organization theory research.

In general, a simulation model must specify the rules of procedure in each part of the system under study, and it must also specify the connections between the various parts. Thus, if we are to simulate an organization, we must note the behavior patterns for the various parts of the organization and the ways that these parts interact. As with simulations of physical systems, it is not possible to include all the factors, i.e., all the organizational variables, but only those deemed most important. This simplified model serves as a tool for research on organizations.

Uses of a Simulation Model

We shall here concern ourselves only with a specific type of organization—the business firm—which has been of interest to persons

[1] This research was sponsored in part by the U. S. Office of Naval Research through Carnegie Institute of Technology and in part by the Western Management Science Institute. The computations were performed at the Western Data Processing Center, University of California, Los Angeles. I am deeply indebted to W. W. Cooper and R. M. Cyert for guidance during the course of this research.

in various disciplines. In addition to behavioral scientists and organization theorists, this kind of organization has been studied, rather naturally, by students of general management, marketing, manufacturing, and finance. Accountants, who have had major responsibility for the quantitative data used, have studied firms with the intent of siphoning off appropriate information.

Economists, too, have been concerned with the business firm and its influence on the economic market place. Psychologists and sociologists are curious about the behavior of groups and individuals in the firms, and management scientists have been interested in optimizing certain management functions.

Each of these groups has tended, of necessity, to look at the firm from its own particular perspective, concentrating on certain aspects while ignoring others. Yet, each discipline has accumulated some wisdom and insight about business firms and their organizational processes. A model of the firm which would synthesize these various views and make use of this accumulated information is the aim of our simulation study.

In contrast to these other approaches, however, our study is directed toward a comprehensive model of the firm. By this we refer to a model arranged so that propositions can be measured not only against the assumptions and experience of any one discipline but also against a complete business system with its characteristic interconnections and feedbacks. Thus, to choose an example from management science, we might evaluate the effects of various inventory rules not only upon inventory holding costs, depletion costs, and manufacturing costs but also upon the whole business system via the organizational and communication constraints imposed by these various inventory re-order procedures.

By this means we might obtain new insight into any of several disciplines and, possibly, advance the developments of models for complete business systems. Let us now consider how the model could be useful in organization research.

The first use of such a study is to *formulate* hypotheses about the behavior of real-world firms—hypotheses that indicate relationships among organizational, environmental, or communication variables, and the reactions of the over-all organization. A great many of these propositions will not be gross generalizations but will be valid in certain kinds of organizations or under certain conditions. Again, these propositions may be of a negative variety, specifying that particular variables do not affect organizational behavior.

Propositions formulated by simulation models can then be verified by other forms of organizational research. That is, they can be tested in the laboratory or subjected to extensive field research.[2] Thus, simulation can provide a valuable method for "question asking" about business behavior.

Simulation may also be used to *verify* propositions or hypotheses that have been or can be advanced on more theoretical grounds. This can be done by considering organizational effects upon a broader or more comprehensive set of variables than was the case when theoretical formulations were originally undertaken in a particular discipline. Again, to emphasize a point, such a simulation approach permits us to study the effects of an organization variable on the complete business system rather than on a specific part. In the process we may, perhaps, expect to cast new light on old issues. We shall be interested, for example, in whether known, already accepted, propositions about the proper kinds of costs for individual decision making remain valid when extrapolated to a complex system involving interacting decisions related to each other by various kinds of organization ties, information flows, etc. It is often supposed, for instance, that better decisions will occur when the costs used for these purposes are as current and up-to-date as possible. This may be the case at the level of individual decisions for specific business functions and activities. On the other hand, it does not follow that this is necessarily true when cost information is used to evaluate individuals acting in an organization hierarchy.[3]

A Specific Simulation Model

We have discussed the utility of simulation models in research on organizations. We now turn to a discussion of a specific model and the research accomplished using this model.

We have indicated that such a model should be comprehensive in two ways: (*a*) It should embody theory and experience from the various disciplines that have studied organizations, in particular, business firms, since our model is of this kind; and (*b*) it should be a systems model designed so that effects can be traced throughout the whole organization. This can be done as follows: We view the firm as composed of a series of decision centers—places in the firm where a decision is made. Associated with each decision center is a

---

[2] A discussion of the relationship between simulation, laboratory experimentation and field study research is incorporated in Chapter 28 of this volume by J. E. McGrath.

[3] See [79], pp. 123 ff.

set of *decision rules*. Each decision rule is a program specifying completely how a decision is made. Since information is necessary for decision making, the complete flow of information within the firm must also be specified. This flow of information is called the *information system* of the firm. Of course, there are organization arrangements, personality factors, etc., to be considered, too, for their possible effects on behavior.

Table 1 shows the general organization of the firm and the decisions made by the various decision centers in the firm. It is impossible in this summary to list all aspects of the organization design arrangements or even the various decision rules employed in the model. But we shall discuss the general nature of the decision rules and then illustrate the rules by a few specific examples.

The first point of note about the decision rules is that many of them are behavioral rules; that is, they involve psychological variables such as pressure, organizational slack, bias, aspiration levels, and so on. Thus, the model portrays the behavior of individuals in the firm in addition to the flows of cash, production, and information. Other decision rules are based directly upon economic theory. Finally, a large class of decision rules are what might be labeled "rule-of-thumb" decision rules. These rules represent how businessmen operate, or might operate, and are derived largely from the received body of business literature. These rule-of-thumb procedures are neither optimal nor do they necessarily represent the most common business practice. They are intended to be only reasonably good reflections of how businessmen do, or could, behave, as determined from relevant texts, business cases, etc.

To illustrate the kinds of decision rules employed in the model, we have chosen an example for more detailed discussion: For each individual in the firm an *Index of Felt Pressure* was constructed. This index is intended to represent the sum total of the various pressures exerted upon the individual. Specifically, the factors making up the index for a salesman are listed in Table 2, together with the weights attached to each factor.

These represent, more or less, the formal factors affecting a particular salesman. Of course, a large number of informal factors could be added, such as personality conflicts with his superior, etc. These cannot be dealt with here. Instead, we note that the foregoing index was designed to provide connections between information flows in the firm and one kind of behavioral variable, namely, pressure.

In this model, a main factor influencing an individual in the performance of his job is the amount of his felt pressure. Not all indi-

Table 1   Decisions Made at Various Levels in the Firm

Executive Committee

1. Formulate sales cost and expectations.
2. Determine the projected profit level.
3. Set price.
4. Set administrative budgets.
5. Exercise control over the manufacturing vice-president and the general sales manager.

General Sales Managers

1. Determine preliminary sales and budget estimates.
2. Set sales quotas for sales districts.
3. Influence sales administrative expense.
4. Exercise control over the district sales managers.

District Sales Managers

1. Determine district sales forecasts.
2. Set quotas for salesmen.
3. Influence sales administrative expense.
4. Exercise control over the salesmen.

Salesmen

1. Make a territory sales forecast.
2. Expend sales effort.
3. Bargain with the district sales manager about sales quota.

Industrial Engineering Department

1. Revise production cost standards.

Manufacturing Vice-President

1. Determine preliminary cost and budget estimates.
2. Set the "target" level of operations.
3. Influence manufacturing administrative expense.
4. Exercise control over the plant supervisor and the industrial engineering department.

Plant Supervisor

1. Set the immediate level of operations for the plant.
2. Request revisions in production cost standards.
3. Exercise control over the foremen.

Foremen

1. Influence variable manufacturing costs.
2. Request revisions in production standards.

Table 2   Index of Pressure for a Salesman

Factor	Weight
1. Index of pressure of his superior (the district sales manager)	25
2. His quota relative to his sales in the past month	40
3. Sales of the "average" salesman in his district relative to his sales	10
4. 0.75 + (percentage of his product less than 75% of quota)	10
5. His total quota for the past quarter relative to his total sales for the last quarter	15
	100

viduals react in the same manner to pressure. Some salesmen meet increased pressure by increasing effort and selling more (on the average); others react adversely to pressure and slightly decrease sales effort; others react to pressure by borrowing sales from the future (convincing customers to overstock); and still others react by reducing the variability of sales (calling only on relatively "sure" customers). As pressure diminishes, a phenomenon called "organizational slack" gradually develops and results in inefficiency within the firm.[4]

The rule used for planning provides a second example of a behavioral decision rule in the firm. A profit goal is set by the firm as a function of past profits. If projected estimates do not produce an expected profit up to the goal level, then cost estimates, sales forecasts, and prices are examined and revised in that order. If these revisions all fail to produce a satisfactory result, then the goal itself is reduced. This process is repeated until a "satisfactory" level of projected profits is obtained.[5] The necessity of re-examination and revision of estimates increases pressure in the firm.

These two examples illustrate the type of rules used in the model of the firm. In addition to psychological concepts, a variety of business rules are inculcated into the model. There are, for instance, decision rules by which budgets are set, production is scheduled, and cost standards are determined. These parts of the model were designed

---

[4] R. M. Cyert and J. G. March [142]. See also [143].
[5] See [144].

by reference to more or less documented aspects of current business practice. Market behavior aspects of the model, on the other hand, are represented in accordance with standard economic demand theory.

Experimentation with the Model

The general method of experimentation with the model is as follows: We make changes in information flows within the firm, changes in decision rules, or changes in the firm's environment. We then note the effects of these changes upon the behavior of the firm. Eight specific changes were selected for study in this experiment. Although space limitations prohibit our explaining the eight hypotheses in detail, we can at least enumerate them as follows:

CHANGES IN THE EXTERNAL ENVIRONMENT OF THE FIRM

1. *External world variability.* (Stable costs and sales versus fluctuating costs and sales.)
2. *Market growth trend.* (Slow cyclical pattern of market growth versus fast irregular growth.)

CHANGES IN THE DECISION SYSTEM

3. *Loose vs. tight industrial engineering department.* ("Loose" or "tight" standard costs.)
4. *Amount of contagion of pressure in the firm.* (Degree to which an individual transmits his "felt pressure" to his subordinate.)
5. *Sensitivity of individuals to pressure.*
6. LIFO *vs. average cost method of inventory valuation.*

CHANGES IN THE INFORMATION SYSTEM

7. *Knowledge by the general sales manager of the company inventory position.*
8. *Emphasis upon current period information vs. past information for control purposes.*

Experimental Design

In each of the eight aforementioned changes there were two alternatives for environmental conditions, for decision systems, or for information systems in our firm. We consider now the experimental design used to measure the effects of these changes.

First, we are interested in the effect of each change by itself. Moreover, we want this effect to be as general as possible, so we want it measured over many organizational arrangements (i.e., over all possible combinations of other changes). We have instituted a 2^8 factorial design to do this. The measurement of the main effects in the design will correspond to the effects mentioned above.[6]

In addition, we wish to measure the degree to which main effects are dependent upon each other. For example, a fast market growth may have an effect only when there is an organization sensitive to pressure, and not otherwise. These are interaction effects and can be measured in a factorial experimental design. Only the first-order or two-factor interactions were considered important in this analysis. Accordingly, a one-fourth replicate (a complete replicate would involve $2^8 = 256$ cases) of 64 cases was used. This was sufficient to estimate the main effects, the two factor interactions, the block effects (below), and to perform an analysis of variance.

Because it is possible for initial conditions to influence the results, and because we want to measure the possible effects of different starting conditions, we divided the 64 observations into 4 blocks. In one set of conditions the firm was initially profitable, in a second set quite unprofitable; the other 2 blocks represented middle conditions.

Each of the 64 observations mentioned represented a run of our simulation model under different conditions (i.e., different combinations of the alternatives). In each run the firm was simulated for 108 periods (months). The following measures were used to describe the behavior of the firm over time: indexes of price, cost, and inventory; dollars of profits; dollars of sales adjusted for market trend; and a summary index representing a compilation of the "felt pressure" within the firm.

Results

The results of the experiment are presented in detail elsewhere.[7] We shall now describe some of the important results.

EFFECT OF HIGH VARIABILITY IN THE EXTERNAL ENVIRONMENT

The firm, in a highly variable environment, had lower costs, higher sales, and greater profits than when the environment was relatively stable. High variability also increased pressure within the firm. This effect was quite significant and was largely independent of the other alterations in the model.

---

[6] For a discussion of the experimental design terminology and the specific design used, see [155], Chapters 7 and 10.

[7] Charles P. Bonini [79], Chapters 9 and 10.

Before explaining the reasons for this effect, we should discuss the meaning of "high variability." When the firm is in a highly variable environment, the foremen and salesmen are faced with greater monthly fluctuations in manufacturing costs and sales (i.e., the standard deviations of the probability distributions determining costs and sales are much larger in the highly variable environment). In a relatively stable environment, the fluctuations in costs and sales are more moderate.

The reason for the effects of high variability can best be understood by tracing its impact upon the profits of the firm. If costs and sales fluctuate widely from period to period, then profits would also be volatile. This, occasionally, causes the firm to do quite poorly and a crisis situation develops. Pressure is increased, costs are cut, sales are increased, and, in general, the slack is cut out of the organization. A crisis of this nature is probably less likely to develop when the external world is more stable.

Increased variability had a favorable effect upon the profit of the company and caused a significant increase in pressure within the firm. Variability kept the firm more "on its toes" and more likely to take advantage of cost and market opportunities when the occasion arose.

This opens up some interesting questions with respect to variability, uncertainty, etc., and its possible effects on business practice viewed from the standpoint of the complex organization. One might have argued that, in a more stable environment, the firm would be able to predict more accurately and, hence, to plan more efficiently. This has been suggested, in fact, in some parts of economic theory and, indeed, firms spend considerable sums of money on forecasting presumably for the purpose of reducing uncertainty and variability. Also on the empirical side, accounting systems are sometimes designed or operated in ways that explain away variability and smooth fluctuations in profits.

Yet the result obtained from our analysis is in direct opposition to these prescriptions and practices. The conclusion need not be reached, however, that these are incorrect. It may be the case that these students have overlooked important psychological-organizational factors; e.g., variability may increase pressure and keep a firm more "on its toes." Thus for complex organizations, the elimination of variability and the reduction of uncertainty may not always be wholly desirable from a profit standpoint. This study has merely raised a hypothesis, of course, and further research is needed. There are also other factors which could be included in the model and which may have a bearing upon the result. In particular, we could include the possibility of an individual's resignation from the firm under extreme pressure. Also, we might expect that learning or some other adjustment mechanisms might tend to dull the effect of variability.

EFFECT OF "TIGHT" VERSUS "LOOSE"
INDUSTRIAL ENGINEERING DEPARTMENT

Strong effects appeared when the industrial engineering department changed its method of revising production cost standards. *A "tight" industrial engineering department reduced cost in the firm, but it also caused a large decrease in sales. Thus, the profits of the firm did not change significantly.* Hence, we have a counterbalancing effect. When costs are reduced, pressure upon profits and sales is alleviated, and the level of total sales is allowed to fall. On the other hand, when cost standards were "loose" and costs high, the sales department increased its efforts to keep up profits. In general terms, the effect of loose standards in one sector of the organization tended to be counterbalanced by better performance in another sector.

This result may be rather surprising although it is not completely unknown in business practice. Major cost-cutting campaigns are not uncommon. Neither are major sales and promotional efforts. It is oftentimes implicitly assumed that these activities are independent of behavior in other parts of the firm but, as our results suggest, this may not be wholly valid. For, even when the firm is organized so that technologically the parts are independent, there may be important interconnections through the goal-setting procedures in the organization. That is, if one part of an organization is concerned largely with an over-all goal (and does not place primary emphasis upon some *independent* subgoal), then its performance could easily be negatively correlated with performance in other parts of the organization. This is simply because, to repeat, better performance by the other departments can make achievement of the over-all goal easier and hence relax pressure on the given department.

This result also poses an interesting question about information in organizations. On the surface, it would seem desirable to give individual groups information about the progress of the whole organization so that they can see their contribution to the over-all effort and be motivated to perform better. But the result here is exactly the opposite. Knowledge of the over-all profit level caused poorer performance rather than better.

Again, this result merely suggests or hypothesizes an organizational variable that perhaps has been unduly neglected in small group experimentation or individual psychology studies. In these studies it has not been possible to consider remote or secondary effects of actions, the complex interconnections of tasks, and the heavy burdens of information processing required. But, of course, our model studies here are not designed to validate such generalizations. They are meant only to raise questions about existing propositions in psychology, say, as they might be extrapolated into a complex organization, and further studies are indicated.

EFFECT OF LIFO

The effects of a LIFO approach to inventory valuation have been widely discussed in the accounting literature along with the topic of changing from one basis of inventory valuation to some other basis.[8] A change in the method of inventory valuation did have certain effects upon the behavior of the firm. *The LIFO method of inventory valuation greatly increased profit when the firm operated in a highly variable environment, but had little effect in a relatively stable environment.* Thus, LIFO exaggerated the effects of a highly variable environment noted earlier, since it charges current costs against profits[9] (rather than using a smoothed average inventory value). In a relatively stable environment, the fluctuations in cost were minor and the effect of LIFO was negligible.

Note that the whole organization is affected by what appears to be a change in a simple accounting procedure. Here is an example of an information procedure which had some surprising results when measured against the total business system. LIFO is commonly justified either on grounds of savings in tax dollars or on grounds of providing a better approximation to replacement costs. We are suggesting that there may be some very important second-order organizational effects that have been largely ignored.

EFFECTS OF CONTAGION OF PRESSURE

Contagion of pressure refers to the degree to which an individual in the organization can transmit his own "felt pressure" to his subordinate. *An increase in the amount of contagion of pressure directly*

---

[8] LIFO (Last In, First Out) is an accounting technique that attempts to charge approximately current costs against current profits and to value inventory at some base-year price. See Thomas M. Hill and Myron J. Gordon [270], pp. 227–235. LIFO is most often used only for annual external reporting, whereas we have used it here for monthly internal reporting. In addition, it is likely that the same result could have been obtained by FIFO (First In, First Out).

[9] This is only approximately true, since some past costs are also included if unit sales exceed production in a given period.

reduced cost. Sales were also affected (increased) when the firm operated in a highly variable environment. This leads to the hypothesis that the effect of contagion is dependent upon the number of levels in the hierarchy through which contagious pressure must pass. In our model, for instance, manufacturing, having fewer levels, was affected directly by a change in the amount of contagion; sales, with more hierarchical levels, was affected only when variability was also present.

Let us use this last result to illustrate the use of the simulation model in formulating hypotheses. Note that we are suggesting a new organizational variable—contagion of pressure—and hypothesizing its effects upon the organization. Note also the relationship between this variable and another organizational variable—the number of hierarchical levels and the dependence of the effect upon external conditions. Thus, we have formulated some well-defined propositions which could be studied further in the laboratory or in the field. These studies may confirm our simulation results, or they may disprove them in a way that will also increase or deepen our understanding of organizations.

Conclusion

Let us summarize briefly what we have done. We constructed a simulation model of a hypothetical business firm. The model relates to real organizations in four ways: First, the decision rules are patterned upon received knowledge from the disciplines of economics, psychology, sociology, and business practice. Secondly, the complete model should and does behave in ways that are pertinent to at least some aspects of real-world business operations. Thirdly, we can pose questions and formulate hypotheses based upon experimentation with the model. These hypotheses have potential relevance for real-firm behavior. They are also formulated so they can be verified by field and laboratory tests. Fourthly, the model can be used to test hypotheses that have been advanced by others, perhaps in different contexts or with simpler models.

We might compare experiments with the model to controlled laboratory experiments with organizations. The difference is that we have behavioral decision rules instead of behaving individuals. The advantage is that experimentation is feasible and statistical control is possible. The results reported above indicate the possible value of such an approach. Of course, none of these results are claimed to be decisive; they merely suggest where future research is indicated. This research will include more simulation with refined and expanded models.

Field studies and possibly laboratory studies are also indicated. Finally, the results suggest fresh attempts at study and theorizing about behavior in complex organizations.

In summary, we have a fine hypothesis generating mechanism. Thus far, however, its main virtue lies in its ability to raise many questions that are pertinent not only for management but also for related disciplines.

16

THE BEHAVIORAL THEORY OF THE FIRM:
A BEHAVIORAL SCIENCE—ECONOMICS
AMALGAM

R. M. Cyert and J. G. March

The Organization as a System for Making Decisions [1]

Consider an organization as a system for making decisions. In the case of a business firm, we imagine an organization that makes decisions on price, output, investment, marketing strategy, and so on. Let us view such decisions as the primary output of the organizations, in the sense that we wish to develop a theory that will explain the choices organizations make on such decisions. We wish to develop such a theory by examining the mechanisms used by human organizations to resolve conflict and make choices. To emphasize the conviction that a theory of organizational decision making must depend on propositions about human behavior, we have called the theory "a behavioral theory of organizational decision making." It might as easily be called the "psychology or sociology or politics of choice in complex human organizations."

It is reasonable to describe an organization as making decisions. As a result, it is reasonable to describe an organization as having goals and as having expectations about future states of the world.

[1] The research described here is part of a long run study of organizational decision making at the Graduate School of Industrial Administration, Carnegie Institute of Technology. It is supported by grants from the Ford Foundation and from the school's own research funds. The research is reported in detail in R. M. Cyert and J. G. March [143].

Partly to avoid the anthropomorphic argument, some of our colleagues prefer to describe organizations as "information processing systems." Such a description has a number of advantages; but it should neither unnecessarily obscure the utility of concepts like organization goals and organization expectations nor conceal the general utility of considering an organization as a decision system exhibiting choice behavior. In this chapter we wish to describe a number of models of choice behavior by organizations and to suggest several basic phenomena that seem to be important to the psychology of organizational choice.

Organizational Choice and Rationality

We have found it convenient to study organizational decision making against a background of a model of rational choice. Substantial elements of rationality are exhibited by most systems we would call "purposive." Thus, although many of the more interesting features of a model of individual or organizational choice are in some sense "irrational," the major thread is one of rationality. The rational model to which we refer is a simple one:

1. We assume the system has a well-defined preference ordering over possible future states of the world.

2. We assume the system has some procedures (called "search") for gathering information about alternatives available to it and the probable consequences of pursuing those alternatives.

3. We assume the system makes choices (including the choice of how much to search) so as to maximize the expected return to the system in terms of the preference ordering.

Such a model has been used extensively in the economic study of organizational choice. It has been used extensively (although less explicitly) in the study of human choice. There are technical problems associated with using the model. There are many economists and psychologists who think it is of use only in normative models; but it provides a basic framework for the examination of decision-making systems. In effect, we propose to use it as a norm, as a set of axioms subject to a modest list of qualifications and constraints.

Since the axioms of rationality perform essentially this same function in a wide variety of psychological and economic theories of choice, the heart of a behavioral theory of organizational decision making for all purposes of communication lies not in the widely shared axioms but in the less widely shared qualifications and constraints. We assume that organizations are in a general way attempting to be rational. They are attempting to achieve those states of the world they prefer rather than those states of the world they consider less attractive. However, we also assume that this effort is constrained by some relatively severe limits on the cognitive capacity, the computational speed, and the internal goal consistency of large complex organizations. As a result, we can perhaps best characterize this behavioral theory of organizational decision making as a theory of an *adaptively rational* rather than an *omnisciently rational* system.

Key Concepts in a Behavioral Theory of Organizational Choice

We can identify four critical concepts that we would use to modify the classical axioms of rationality. First, the quasi-resolution of conflict; organizations do not have a simple preference ordering over possible future states of the world. Second, uncertainty avoidance; organizations tend to avoid uncertainty rather than deal with it by calculations of expected return. Third, problemistic search; search decisions are dictated by specific problems rather than calculations of expected return. Fourth, organizational learning; organizations learn from their experiences and modify procedures (at several levels) over time. We consider each of these briefly below.

QUASI-RESOLUTION OF CONFLICT

Any decision-making system of interest is a system for resolving conflict over scarce resources. An organization is such a system. Essentially, it is a coalition of participants. For purposes of the theory, we assume that the participants of the organization have well-defined preference orders. The preferences of the various participants are mutually inconsistent in the sense that not every participant's most preferred alternative can be achieved. Thus, if the organization is to make decisions, some procedure for resolving conflict must be discovered. It is convenient in many theories of economic organizations to assume the conflict is resolved by the bargaining associated with purchasing various factors of production (e.g., labor, capital, etc.), and that once the bargaining is completed the organization has a single, consistent set of goals—the organizational objective.

Our observations on organizations lead us to a different view. Organizations, as we observe them, do not have a single, internally consistent goal at a particular point in time. Instead, they exist with considerable conflict and potential conflict. What they decide at one point in time is often apparently inconsistent with what they decide at another time. What is decided in one part of the system is often apparently inconsistent with what is decided in another part. Instead of a single overriding goal, organizations have a series of more or less independent goals. Instead of a single decision center, organizations have a number of decision centers, each dealing with some subset of the organizational goals.

Specialization and delegation are used to reduce the complex conflict situation facing the systems as a whole into a series of simpler, less conflicting situations. The organization divides its decision problems into subproblems, but it does so under circumstances in which there is no guarantee that the conflict will be thereby resolved. There is no guarantee that local decisions satisfying local demands will necessarily provide a joint decision satisfying all demands on the system. Thus, an organization requires mechanisms for facilitating over-all consistency.

We can cite here two such mechanisms. First, the use of aspiration-level goals. The criteria for choice actually used by the systems take an aspiration level form rather than a "maximize" or "minimize" form. For simplicity, we assume in the theory that the demands of the organization participants (and, therefore, the goals of the organization) are stated in terms of acceptable levels of reward, performance, etc. Thus, we assume a profit goal of the form, "Profits must exceed $X" rather than of the form, "Maximize profits." Aspiration level goals impose relatively weak consistency demands on the system. Ordinarily, we will expect a "solution" to such a system to be nonunique in the sense that more than one allocation of resources will meet the joint demands. At the same time, aspiration level goals tend to under-exploit the environment and thereby leave excess potential resources to absorb potential inconsistencies in local decisions.

Second, the sequential attention to goals. Ordinarily when we talk of "consistency" of goals or decisions we refer to some way of assessing their internal logic at a point of time. As a result, in many theories of organizational choice, we are inclined to insist on consistency within a cross section of goals. Such an insistence seems to us inaccurate as a representation of organizational behavior. Organizations resolve conflict among goals, in part, by attending to different goals at different times. The business firm is likely to resolve pressures for two conflicting behaviors by first doing one and then doing the other. The resulting time buffer between goals permits the organization to solve one problem at a time, attending to one goal at a time.

UNCERTAINTY AVOIDANCE

To all appearances, at least, uncertainty is a feature of organizational decision making with which organizations must live. In the case of the business firm, there are uncertainties with respect to the behavior of the market, the deliveries of suppliers, the attitudes of shareholders, the behavior of competitors, the future actions of governmental agencies, and so on. As a result, much of modern decision theory has been concerned with the problems of decision making under risk and under uncertainty. The solutions involved have been largely procedures for finding certainty equivalents (e.g., expected value) or introducing rules for "living" with the uncertainties (e.g., game theory).

Our studies indicate quite a different strategy on the part of organizations. Organizations avoid uncertainty. They avoid uncertainty in two major ways. First, they avoid the requirement that they correctly anticipate events in the distant future by using decision rules emphasizing short-run reaction to short-run feedback rather than anticipation of long-run uncertain events. They solve pressing problems rather than develop long-run strategies. Second, they avoid the requirement that they anticipate future reactions of other parts of their environment by arranging a negotiated environment. They impose plans, standard operating procedures, industry tradition, and uncertainty-absorbing contracts on that environment. In short, they achieve a reasonably manageable decision situation by avoiding planning where plans depend on predictions of uncertain future events and by emphasizing planning where the plans can be made self-confirming through some control device.

We assume that organizations make decisions by solving a series of problems. Each problem is solved as it arises. Then the organization waits for another problem to appear. Where decisions within the firm do not naturally fall into such a sequence, they are modified so that they will do so.

This assumption of a fire department organization is one of the most conspicuous features of our models. Under a rather broad class of situations, such behavior is rational for an organization having the goal structure we have postulated. Under an even broader set of situations, it is likely to be the pattern of behavior that is learned by an organization dealing with an uncertain world and quasi-resolved goals. It will be learned because, by and large, it will permit the organization to meet the demands of the members of the coalition.

Classic models of oligopoly ordinarily assume that firms make some predictions about the behavior of their environment, particularly those parts of the environment represented by competitors, suppliers, customers, and other parts of the organization. Certainly such considerations are important to any decisions made by the firm. Our studies lead us, however, to the proposition that firms will devise and negotiate an environment so as to eliminate the uncertainty. Rather than treat the environment as exogenous and to be predicted, they seek ways to make it controllable.

In the case of competitors, one of the conspicuous ways in which this is accomplished is through the establishment of industry-wide conventional practices. If "good business practice" is standardized (through trade associations, journals, word-of-mouth, external consultants, etc.), we can be reasonably confident that all competitors will follow it. We do not mean to imply that firms necessarily enter into collusive agreements in the legal sense. Our impression is that frequently they do not. But they need not do so to achieve the same objective of stability in competitive practices.

In a similar fashion, the internal planning process (e.g., the budget) provides a negotiated internal environment. A plan within the firm is a series of contracts among the subunits in the firm. As in the case of industry conventions, internal conventions are hyperstable during the contract period and tend to be relatively stable from one period to the next (e.g., in resource allocation). As a result, they permit each unit to avoid uncertainty about other units in making decisions.

PROBLEMISTIC SEARCH

The theory of choice and the theory of search are closely intertwined. Necessarily if we argue that organizations use acceptable level goals and select the first alternative they see that meets these goals, we must provide a theory of organizational search to supplement the concepts of decision making. In our models we assume that search, like decision making, is problem-directed. By problemistic search we mean search that is stimulated by a problem (usually a rather specific one) and is directed toward finding a solution to that problem. In a general way, problemistic search can be distinguished from both random curiosity and the search for understanding. It is distinguished from the former because it has a goal; from the latter because it is interested in understanding only insofar as such understanding contributes to control. Problemistic search is engineering rather than pure science.

With respect to organizational search, we assume two major things: (1) Search is motivated. Whether the motivation exists on the buyer or the seller side of the alternative market, problemistic search is stimulated by a problem, depressed by a problem solution. (2) Search is simple-minded. It proceeds on the basis of a simple model of causality until driven to a more complex one.

Search within the firm is motivated by problems. A problem is recognized when the organization either fails to satisfy one or more of its goals or when such a failure can be anticipated in the immediate future. So long as the problem is not solved, search will continue. The problem is solved by either discovering an alternative that satisfies the goals or by revising the goals to levels that make an available alternative acceptable. Solutions are also motivated to search for problems. Pet projects (e.g., cost savings in someone else's department, expansion in our own department) look for crises (e.g., failure to achieve the profit goal, innovation by a competitor). In the theory we assume that variations in search activity (and search productivity) reflect primarily the extent to which motivation for search exists.

In addition, we assume that rules for search are simple-minded. They are simple-minded in the sense that they reflect simple concepts of causality. Subject to learning, search is based initially on two simple rules: (1) Search in the neighborhood of the problem symptom. (2) Search in the neighborhood of the current alternative. These two rules reflect different dimensions of the basic causal notions that a cause will be found "near" its effect and that a new solution will be found "near" an old one.

The neighborhood of symptom rule (rule 1) can be related to the subunits of the organization and their association with particular goals and with each other. A problem symptom will normally be failure on some goal indicator. Initial reaction, we assume, will be in the department identified with the goal. Thus, if the problem is the failure to attain the sales goal, the search begins in the sales department and with the sales program. Failing there, it might reasonably proceed to the problem of price and product quality and then to production costs.

The neighborhood of existing policy rule (rule 2) inhibits the movement of the organization to radically new alternatives (except under circumstances of considerable search pressure). Such an inhibition may be explained either in terms of some underlying organizational assumptions of continuity in performance functions or in terms of the problems of conceiving the adjustments required by radical shifts.

When search, using the simple causal rules, is not immediately successful, we assume two developments. First, the organization uses increasingly complex ("distant") search. Second, the organization introduces a third search rule: (3) Search in organizationally vulnerable areas.

The motivation to search in vulnerable areas stems from two things. On the one hand, the existence of organizational slack will tend to lead search activity in the direction of slack parts of the organization. On the other hand, certain activities in the organization are more easily attacked than others, simply because of their power position in the system. One general phenomenon is the vulnerability of those activities in the organization for which the connection with major goals is difficult to calculate concretely (e.g., research and development in many firms). In either case, a solution consists either in absorbing slack or in renegotiating the basic coalition agreement to the disadvantage of the weaker members of the coalition.

ORGANIZATIONAL LEARNING

Organizations learn. To assume that organizations go through the same processes of learning as do individual human beings seems unnecessarily naive. But organizations exhibit (as do other social institutions) adaptive behavior over time. Just as adaptations at the individual level depend upon phenomena of the human physiology, organizational adaptation uses individual members of the organization as instruments. But we believe it is possible to deal with adaptation at the aggregate level of the organization, in the same sense and for the same reasons that it is possible to deal with the concept of organizational decision making.

We focus on adaptation with respect to three different phases of the decision process: adaptation of goals, adaptation in attention rules, and adaptation in search rules. We assume that organizations change their goals, shift their attention, and revise their procedures for search as a function of their experience.

The goals with which we deal are in the form of aspiration levels, or—in the more general case—search equivalence classes. In simple terms, this means that on each dimension of organizational goals there are a number of critical values, critical that is from the point of view of shifts in search strategy. These values change over time in reaction to experience, either actual or vicarious.

We assume, therefore, that organizational goals in a particular time period are a function of (1) organizational goals of the previous time period, (2) organizational experience with respect to that goal in the previous period, and (3) experience of comparable organizations with respect to the goal dimension in the previous time period. Initially at least, we are inclined to assume a simple linear function,

$$G_t = a_1 G_{t-1} + a_2 E_{t-1} + a_3 C_{t-1},$$

where G is the organizational goal, E the experience of the organization, C a summary of the experience of comparable organizations and $a_1 + a_2 + a_3 = 1$. The parameters in this goal adaptation function are important attributes of the organization. a_3 reflects the organization's sensitivity to the performance of competitors or other comparable organizations. a_1 and a_2 reflect the speed at which the organization revises goals in the face of experience. In some cases, we will want to define two values for a_3, one for when comparative experience exceeds the organization's goal and a different one for when it is below the goal. Similarly, we may want to allow the effect of the organization's experience to depend on whether it exceeds or is below the goal.

Just as organizations learn what to aspire for in their environment, they also learn to attend to some parts of that environment and not to others. One part of such adaptation is in learning search behavior. We will consider such phenomena in a moment. Here we wish to note two related, but different, adaptations. First, in evaluating performance by explicit measurable criteria, organizations learn to attend to some criteria and ignore others. For example, suppose an organization subunit has responsibility for a particular organizational goal. Since this goal is ordinarily stated in relatively nonoperational terms, the subunit must develop some observable indices of performance on the goal. Among the indices objectively available to the subunit, which will be used? Observation suggests this is a typical case of learning. Subunits in the short run do not change indices significantly. But there are long-run shifts toward indices that produce generally satisfactory results (i.e., in this case, usually show the subunit to be performing well).

Second, organizations learn to pay attention to parts of their environment and experience and ignore other parts. We have assumed parameters in the goal-adaptation function reflecting the sensitivity of the organization to past goals, past performance, and external comparisons. These parameters are not fixed. We would expect them to change over time so as to produce results (in the form of goals) that are satisfactory to the important groups in the coalition. At the same time, we have represented by C in the goal-adaptation function a summary description of comparable organizations. Concealed in such an abstract form is organizational learning with respect to what is properly comparable. With which attributes of which organizations should we compare ourselves? Although in a relatively short-run model we might reasonably consider this fixed, we would expect that in the long run we would require a model in which such attention factors changed.

Finally, if we assume that search is problem-oriented, we must also assume that search rules change. Most simply, what we require in the models are considerations of the following type. When an organization discovers a solution to a problem by searching in a particular way it will be more likely to search in that way in future problems of the same type. When an organization fails to find a solution by searching in a particular way, it will be less likely to search in that way in future problems of the same type. Thus, the order in which various alternative solutions to a problem are considered will change as the organization experiences success or failure with alternatives.

The Basic Structure of the Organizational Decision-Making Process

We have described four basic concepts that seem to us fundamental to an understanding of the decision-making process in a modern, large-scale business organization. The quasi-resolution of conflict, uncertainty avoidance, problemistic search, and organizational learning are central phenomena with which our models must deal. In our judgment, the natural theoretical language for describing a process involving these phenomena is the language of a computer program. It is clear that some parts of the theory are susceptible to representation and solution in other forms. But the general structure of the process can be conveniently represented as a flow chart. Such a flow chart is outlined in its most general form in Fig. 1.

Figure 1 is intended to illustrate two things. On the one hand, it shows abstractly the step-by-step decision process. For convenience, we have started the process at the point of receiving feedback from past decisions. Since the decision process is a continuous one, this start is arbitrary. Starting from the feedback, the figure shows the sequence of steps taken by a particular subunit in the firm with respect to a specific decision and a specific goal. Other decisions by other subunits using other goals would occur in parallel with this one. Loose connections among the subunits and decisions are secured by the environmental feedback and (when indicated) by expanded search.

At the same time, the figure shows (by the vertical columns) the relation between the basic concepts of the theory and the decision process flow chart. At a general level, each of the concepts is represented in a decision process having this structure. Obviously, when a specific decision in a specific context is considered, this abstract description of the process must be substantially elaborated with specific content.

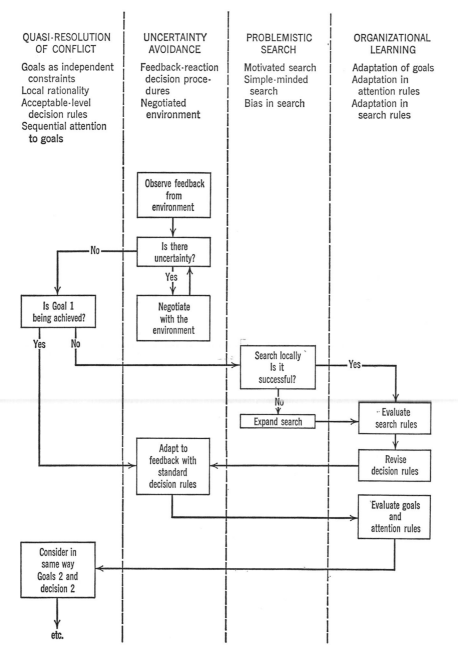

FIGURE 1   Organizational decision process in abstract form.

Three Models of Organizational Choice

To illustrate the application of such general concepts to the development of models of organizational decision making, let us describe briefly three different models built upon the theory. Each of the models has a different purpose. Taken together, they suggest both the range of relevance of the concepts and some of the limitations on their use.

Each of the models is in the form of a computer program, although in some cases it would be possible to present them in the form of difference equations. The analyses have been made by simulation rather than by explicit solution of the equations. The first model is a model of price and output determination in one department of a large metropolitan department store. It is based on close empirical observation of the organization involved and a comparison is made between the predictions of the model and the actual behavior of the organization. The second model is a model of output determination in a major American duopoly, the can industry. It is based on theoretical assumptions about the organizations involved and a comparison is made between the time series predictions made by the model and the actual observed time series. The third model is a general model of price and output determination. It is an abstract representation of organizational decision making in an American oligopoly.

MODEL 1: PRICE AND OUTPUT DETERMINATION IN A DEPARTMENT STORE

The model was developed by Cyert, March, and Moore.[2] The organization studied is one department in a large retail department store. The firm involved is part of an oligopolistic market consisting (for most purposes) of three large downtown stores. The firm is organized into several merchandising groups. Each of these groups has several departments. The firm, in total, has more than 100 departments. We have studied, with varying degrees of intensity, the price and output decisions in about a dozen of the departments. From these dozen we have chosen one department for investigation and developed a detailed model of its decisions. In our judgment, the decision processes described for the one department could be generalized with rather trivial changes to other departments in the same merchandising group, with somewhat more substantial changes to other departments outside the immediate

---

[2] See [143], Chapter 7, pp. 128–148.

group, and without major alteration to many departments in a modern retail department store.

The model predicts the department's decisions with respect to the following:

1. Sales forecasts (total amount by season and by month).
2. Advance orders (total amount).
3. Reorders (timing and amount).
4. Regular pricing (for each item).
5. Sales pricing (for each item).
6. Markdown pricing (for each item).

To test the model the behavior of the department was observed in a period subsequent to the period over which the model was generated. The following results were obtained:

1. Ninety-five percent of the monthly sales estimates were predicted to within 5%.
2. For the four seasons in which tests were feasible, one advance order prediction was within 1%, two were within 10%, and one was within 20%.
3. No data available to test the reorder predictions.
4. In an unrestricted random sample of 197 items, the regular price was predicted correct to the penny 95% of the time.
5. In an unrestricted random sample of 58 items, the sale price was predicted correct to the penny, 96% of the time.
6. In an unrestricted random sample of 159 items, the markdown price was predicted correct to the penny, 88% of the time.

In general, we conclude that it was possible to develop a model of organizational decision making that substantially simulated some (though by no means all) of the major discretionary decisions of this organization.

MODEL 2: OUTPUT DETERMINATION IN A DUOPOLY

The model was developed by Cyert, Feigenbaum, and March.[3] The duopoly considered was the American can industry. The industry is substantially dominated by two firms (American Can Company and Continental Can Company). Originally (early in the century) it was essentially a monopoly of American. Continental represented an offshoot. On the basis of these facts, we formed a series of hypotheses

---

[3] See [143], Chapter 5, pp. 86–99, and [144].

about differences between the organizational decision making in the two firms. We then simulated their decisions in a market having the apparent demand characteristics of the period from 1913 to 1956, and observed the share of market gained by the two firms and their profit ratio over that period.

The resulting time series are compared with the actual time series obtained from Moody's Industrials. In general, the time series show a rather surprising fit to the actual data. See [144], pp. 81–95.

MODEL 3: A GENERAL MODEL OF PRICE AND OUTPUT DETERMINATION

The first two models described represent attempts to predict specific decisions by specific organizations. They are two of a number of such efforts.[4] Suppose, however, that we wished to construct a more general model of organizational decision making. Such a model should be susceptible to two kinds of uses. It should be useful as a framework within which to construct specific models. Optimally, it should provide a structure that is invariant over a wide variety of organizations and depends on changes in the parameters to reflect variations among the organizations. Secondly, it should permit general propositions about families of organizations and their reaction to certain environmental conditions.

We have developed such a general model of price and output determination in a large, modern corporation. The model was developed by Cohen, Cyert, March, and Soelberg.[5] We will not attempt to describe the model in detail. It has been programmed in GATE for analysis on any computer system having a GATE compiler. However, the decision process postulated in the model can be described in gross terms.

The organization makes three basic decisions each time period. (1) The price to be charged for the firm's product is determined. As in most models of oligopoly, price is viewed here as a decision variable, not simply the direct result of market mechanisms. (2) The output to be produced during the next time period is set. The organization decides how much of the product will be produced over a relatively brief future time period. (3) A general sales and marketing strategy is chosen. The organization makes a decision on the amount of sales

---

[4] For example, G. P. E. Clarkson ([143], Chapter 10, pp. 253–267, and [127]) has developed a model for the trust investment decisions of a bank. Given some simple attributes of the account, the model predicts which stocks will be purchased for each account and in what amounts. G. Haines has developed a model to predict the decision making behavior of a laboratory organization, a team playing a complex business game.

[5] See [143], Chapter 8, pp. 149–236.

effort to be expended and the amount of investment to be made in sales promotion.

Associated with each of these decisions is a set of relevant goals. The organization relates each decision (at least in the first instance) with its own set of goals. Insofar as possible, decisions within one decision area are made only with respect to the immediately relevant set of goals. The primary interconnections among goals come through feedback and expanded search where local goals cannot be achieved.

Thus, we have three sets of goals. (1) A profit goal. The profit goal is an aspiration level with respect to profits. It is connected most directly with the pricing decision. (2) A set of inventory and production goals. The inventory goal is in the form of minimum and maximum limits on inventory size relative to sales. The production goal is a production smoothing objective in the form of constraints on variation in output level. The inventory and production goals are related immediately to the output decision. (3) A set of sales goals. We consider three kinds of sales goals. The organization has aspiration levels for market share and for sales. It also has a preference for maintaining or improving (i.e., having a relatively lower price) its relative price position.

Because the decision process is segmented into three sets of decisions each having its own set of goals, it is convenient to think of the organization as being departmentalized into three subdivisions. These subdivisions—pricing, sales, production—operate relatively independent of each other. Each makes decisions independently, subject to a few cross departmental pressures.

Each decision is made on the basis of feedback from past results. The organization adjusts goals and procedures on the basis of such feedback. The organization uses search to solve problems when problems exist, avoids search when problems do not exist. In fact, at the most general level, the decision process in each department of each firm can be described as shown in Fig. 2.

The model has not been analyzed in detail as yet. Since it involves many parameters, the first major task of analysis has been to devise a procedure for determining the properties of the model and its sensitivity to variations in certain parameter values. The first stages of that analysis have been completed. It indicates that such output as profits, market shares, prices, and inventories are particularly sensitive to a few key parameters; but it is not clear whether that information can be used to simplify the model. The second major task is the comparison of the output of the model with real-world data. The model generates time series of decisions (and consequences of decisions) that can be compared with actual series for directions of movement,

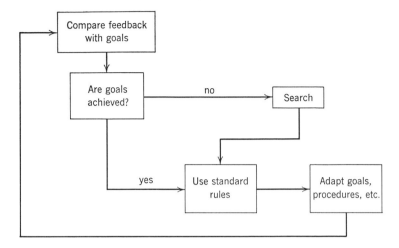

FIGURE 2 Decision process in each department.

characteristics of cycles, reaction patterns, differentiation of organizational strategies, etc. The output generated thus far does not appear to be "unreasonable" in some crude sense (for example, different organizations learn different decision strategies, the organizations seem to be able to adapt relatively successfully to their environment), but no direct attempt has yet been made to link the model to specific firms or industries.

Implications for the Study of Choice in Complex Organizations

In general, we think the development of these models and the theory underlying them indicate three things:

1. They indicate that it is reasonable and fruitful to consider the organization as a basic unit for the study of choice.

2. They suggest that computer simulation models are a convenient form for models of organizational choice.

3. They provide support for the view that a useful theory of organizational choice will be an adaptive rather than a purely rational theory, and that it will have psychological as well as economic components.

17

ORGANIZED DECISION-MAKING: A PROPOSAL FOR STUDYING THE INFLUENCE OF ENTREPRENEURIAL AVERSIVENESS TO RISK-TAKING ON BUREAUCRATIC STRUCTURE

James E. McNulty

Introduction [1]

The character of recent empirical research on organizational questions has taken two paths. On the one hand, we have more or less global approaches. Here one might cite in the recent literature the study of Guetzkow and Bowes [240] or, perhaps, as a more vivid example, the organizational simulations carried on at the RAND Corporation (Geisler [212]).

On the other hand, we have had some highly focused studies of questions on specific organizational questions. The experimental reports of

[1] The theoretical economics work underlying this paper was done in the main during the Summer of 1961 under a grant from the Ford Foundation funds administered by the Wharton School of Finance and Commerce. Research design ideas were developed while the author held a Ford Foundation Faculty Fellowship which he spent in the Department of Psychology of the University of Pennsylvania. The previous empirical work alluded to in the text was done under a grant from the Bureau of Business and Economic Research, Southern Section, of the University of California. The first draft of the paper itself was prepared under the auspices of and for the first Seminar in the Social Science of Organization, sponsored by the Ford Foundation and held at the University of Pittsburgh in June of 1962. Special acknowledgment is due to Dr. Murray A. Geisler of the RAND Corporation for making a number of helpful criticisms and comments.

Cyert, March, and Starbuck [145] on bias and conflict in organizational estimation are examples of this kind of work. The work started by Bavelas [52] on the effects of communication patterns in task situations and carried on by others (Leavitt [333]) is another example.

It is probably a fair statement to say that global research procedures have tended to go hand in hand with problems of organization structure and the more finely focused research with questions in the area of participant behavior. Increasingly, however, exceptions must be taken to this statement, especially with the development and use of man-machine simulative procedures for research.

This chapter is likely to turn out to be a case in point. We are concerned with the effects on key organizational contours of entrepreneurial, or "top management," attitudes towards risk-taking. This concern, by the argument set forth above, should put us in the global-approach camp.

However, the grosser forms of global approaches have turned out, for us at least, to be of questionable value in testing hypotheses about the effects of aversion to risk. What we shall suggest for our essentially structural organizational question is a procedure which is somewhat encompassing. Nevertheless it amounts to a controlled experiment in which risk aversiveness is manipulated in various ways. Moreover, the recommended procedure involves a study of human behavior in an environment specified with respect to certain organizational contours as well as externally.

The first of the four following sections describes our initial hypothesis development and the results of a rough global test to which the hypothesis was put. Then we shall discuss a more advanced and, as it turns out, diametrically opposed hypothesis. Our third and main task will be to outline the elements of a more decisive test of the newer hypothesis. The concluding section discusses some of the implications, for certain other areas of business research, of a validated and extensively used testing procedure of the type proposed.

Decentralization and Risk Avoidance

The idea of centralizing bureaucratic structures for purposes of risk avoidance has been a pervasive one, arising in such diverse places as discussions of efficient socialist economies and treatises on the efficient financial management of large business enterprises. To the author's knowledge, however, the first statement of the idea as a descriptive assertion relating to behavior on the part of the decision maker is implied in the early work of the economist Frank Knight ([318], 1946 reprint).

Knight was concerned especially with the likelihood of response errors made by the managerial subordinates of his entrepreneur ([318], p. 311). He also seemed to feel that, even if the entrepreneur himself were not concerned, his financial backers would be and would effectively prohibit any real delegation of authority with respect to resource allocation to financially nonresponsible managerial subordinates of the entrepreneur ([318], pp. 297 ff.). Thus on two counts—risk aversiveness on the part of the entrepreneur, and/or a similar aversiveness on the part of the financial backers of an enterprise—he looked forward to problems connected with the delegation of authority to subordinate (Knight called them "hired") managers and, hence, by diminishing returns reasoning, finite limits on the size of business enterprise.

All of this has a certain ring of reasonableness from a number of points of view. From modern psychophysics we know that individual responses to signal stimuli are widely distributed for a variety of reasons, including purely perceptual characteristics of the individual, the frequency of presentation of the signals against "noise" backgrounds, and the character of the payoff matrices confronting individual subjects. The latter force, moreover, was long ago noted qualitatively in the business literature by Gordon [230].

Similarly Dean [158] and others have made us aware of the pressures which frequently bear on top managements to meet a normative profit standard dictated by the performance of similar firms and industries, if not by larger classes of firms. Moreover, since the norms usually represent averages, a management may try to make the average rather than entail the risks frequently associated with going above the average.

Finally, the annals of business literature and the experience of the author are replete with examples of interference by investors in an enterprise, particularly by institutional investors in fixed income obligations, to insure that capital will be preserved and obligations met. Generally speaking, the result of such interference is tighter control of the operating affairs of the enterprise. This, of course, is roughly what we mean by the term "centralization."

The author had on hand some data on organization changes in a group of Southern California growth companies (McNulty [384]). Some financial data on the publicly held firms in the group were obtained. It was then possible to make some comparisons between changes in over-all financial structure and changes in global organization structure. The working hypothesis was that those enterprises which became more debt-ridden during the period covered by the study of organization change would also show obvious signs of increasingly centralized management, and vice versa.

Admittedly, not all holders of fixed income obligations undertake to interfere in the affairs of an enterprise and not all equity investors are passive. It must be conceded, moreover, that subjective estimates of risk and degree of aversiveness to risk are likely to vary among investors. Finally, the gross organizational measures which were used in the comparison, e.g., those designed to get at changes in centralization and decentralization of management, were equivocal to say the least.

Despite these problems of experimental design, we entertained hopes for evidence confirmatory to the hypothesis. However, what confirmatory indications appeared were beset by contradictions. We found that if the changes in organization structure were taken as a whole, then the debt and organization changes appeared somewhat more related, at least as regards the companies showing increases in debt as a percentage of total assets. All of the companies which added management echelons in the face of a rising debt ratio also added presumably centralizing staff units and/or committees and/or reported more attention by top management to the details of running the business.

On the other hand, it was found that the relationship between debt change and changes in the number of management echelons indicated a relatively strong *positive* association. Such an association, of course, points to an hypothesis which is diametrically opposite to the working hypothesis which engendered the comparison. That is to say, there is the suggestion at least that decentralization of management is useful as a mechanism for risk avoidance.

At this point one is always faced with the choice of gathering more data, presumably *via* a better experimental procedure or, on the other hand, reconsidering his original thinking before trying further empirical investigation. The latter course was chosen, giving the hypothesis now to be developed, and suggesting the investigative procedure to be discussed below.

Response to Internal and External Sources of Risk

In their summary of the work of the sociologists on the subject of bureaucracy, March and Simon [2] note the likelihood of "unanticipated

---

[2] [367], pp. 34–37.

responses" of organizational participants to bureaucratic rules. The implication is that tight control of an organization from the top is not likely to reduce the risks which arise from peculiar responses and actions of organizational participants. On the contrary there may well be a compounding of errors with severe effects on the goals of the enterprise.

This latter notion is indeed borne out by recent investigations of stochastic programming problems in operations research. Here risk and uncertainty arising both from the characteristics of the external world and from within the enterprise have been considered at some length. The basic observation that has been made is that programming matrices whose coefficients and/or parameters are in fact random variables lead to distributed payoffs, the extent depending upon the dispersion characteristics of the random variables and also upon the number of them.

A first corollary is that we expect a decline in expected payoff with a symmetrical increase in the dispersion of a random variable contained in a programming matrix (Quandt [443]). Of perhaps greater importance is a second corollary observation that the addition of an independent random variable to a programming matrix (such as is the *de facto* effect of greater centralization) results in the decline in the probability of some planned payoff obtaining. This will be the case when resources and outputs are not perfect substitutes for each other (Jensen [297]).

Hence risk aversion should lead an informed top management, operating under the usual pressures for a respectable relative profit performance, to arrange things such that planning matrices are appropriate (1) to the management's aversiveness to risk, (2) to the subjective probabilities associated with profit expectations chosen for planning matrices of different sizes, and (3) in view of a not unlikely requirement for trading income for risk, the economic consequences of smaller planning matrices. One expects penalties with smaller operations of course because of various kinds of "indivisibilities" in technique and equipment.

Such action will lead to product and/or geographic diversification as a means for dealing with uncertainty. Or it may lead simply to what March and Simon have called "self-containment" of organizational units. But the outcome is, in the present context, not very important, except for reasons of experimental convenience, since in either case the effect on organization structure and organized decision-making is easily demonstrated to be a more decentralized bureaucratic structure [383]. Thus we arrive at our revised hypothesis concerning the relationship between entrepreneurial risk aversiveness and bureaucratic structure, namely, that risk aversiveness should lead to decentralization.

Three remarks should be made at this point, since they will have a bearing on any reasonable test of the revised hypothesis. First we must point out that there are likely to be differences in risk aversiveness, either natural or induced, among managements and, therefore, differences in the respective characters of bureaucratic structures developed in enterprises. The point at issue here is, in the jargon of economics, the shape of the entrepreneurial marginal utility function for money. Although we expect certain broad similarities among entrepreneurs, out of environmental and cultural considerations, we have every reason to expect important differences in detail [154].

A second point is that we may find differences in aversiveness to risk for given managements at different levels of resource base, that is to say, in different economic circumstances. Our particular hypothesis here would be that managements operating from larger resource bases would be less risk-averse to larger programming matrices than would be the case if the resource base were smaller (Friedman-Savage [209]). This hypothesis does not necessarily mean that bureaucracy would be centralized to the highest management echelon. It seems more likely, out of "span of control" considerations, that the manifestation would be larger, more highly centralized major operating units.

Thirdly in practice we may well find differentially decentralized bureaucracies among enterprises whose managements are equally risk aversive and whose resource bases are approximately the same. The reason for these expected differences is that a number of other considerations of the external environments in which given enterprises operate are likely to have an influence on bureaucratic structure and also the characteristics of the participants of enterprises.[3] Hence the influence of one or two factors, such as aversiveness of top management to risk and size of resource base, may be obscured in observations of real-life phenomena.

A Model to Test for Entrepreneurial Risk Aversion

How then do we put our notion of entrepreneurial risk aversiveness to the test? Clearly one must first have an unambiguous measure of the state of risk aversiveness. These measurements must be taken from the behavior of subjects existing in a world characterized by

---

[3] See [383].

risks and also by the usual reward structures which we have come to associate with top management action in an uncertain world.

In addition, it would be desirable for purposes of control to offer subjects the same set of choices: presumably a set of organizational choices differentiated by the dimensions of the programming matrices associated with each choice. The implication of planning-matrix decomposition obviously needs careful investigation. Although one might not want to treat the subjects like Professor Skinner's rats, there is a clear need for uniform treatment of the subjects and for appropriate orientation.

What we are suggesting here is a set of experimental games to be played by a group of subjects operating under specified conditions. Although the main object is to note organization choices, as defined above, it would seem desirable first to present the experimental problem simply as one of choosing among monetary gambles, with the size of payoffs and the associated probabilities corresponding roughly to those in the subsequent "organizational game." Each player would be offered a percentage of his winnings. This problem could be run several times with initial "kitties" of varying amounts being presented to the several subjects. The objects of such a preliminary procedure would be two: First, to gain pristine information about the reactions of subjects to monetary risk situations in changing economic circumstances; and, second, to gain information which would reveal any utility or disutility associated with a "real life" as compared with an obviously simple gambling situation.

With the completion of these preliminary investigations, the organizational game series would be presented to the subjects. The precise problem would involve the choice of a single, large planning matrix with a large, but low, probability payoff, or groups of smaller sized matrices with smaller, but higher, probability payoffs. One would want to run the organizational game series initially along the lines of the preliminary monetary gambling problem, with strictly symmetrical monetary payoffs, each subject in isolation from any other subject, and one play per specified "kitty."

If the main experiment is to be meaningful, however, it would seem necessary to introduce certain complexities into the rules of procedure. The first of these would be a nonsymmetrical reward structure, as seems to be true of the environment in which contemporary business managements operate. Second, the reward and penalty base ought to be expanded to include, especially (1) exclusion from the game if losses exceed certain amounts, (2) special bonuses or status symbols for continued "winning of planned profits" and retention of earnings, and (3) information on the performance of other subjects.

There are several criticisms to be made of the investigative procedure which we outline here. For one thing, our subjects are likely to be college students rather than business executives. There may be real personality differences between college students and business executives as far as incidence of risk aversiveness is concerned.

A second and related point is also not new. Our simulation of real-life pressures during the organizational gaming series is assailable on the grounds that exclusion from the game, etc., will not have the same impact on a subject as the possibility of loss of job on an operating top executive.

Finally, there is a third criticism which also involves personality. This criticism arises from the likelihood that the population of top executives is probably more preselected for responsiveness to the demands of task situations than college students. Such preselection is certainly contemplated in most of the executive recruitment and advancement schemes with which the writer is familiar. Although one could attempt to identify subjects on this basis and split them for purposes of analysis, the general effect should be to weaken any observable association between aversion to risk and behavior in terms of bureaucratic structure choices. We should expect a greater amount of dysfunctional behavior from students. Problems of the sorts just discussed should be the subject of auxiliary studies so that their impact on the validity of the main experimental results can be assessed.

Possible Experimental Results

The experiments outlined in the foregoing have not yet been run. In the happy thought that our experiments were run successfully what at most would we have?

There would appear to be two important benefits, one directly relevant to organization matters, the other relevant to broader questions of business behavior. First, we should have a reasonably direct answer to the question of whether or not aversiveness to risk, either pristine or induced by circumstances roughly analogous to those prevailing on the contemporary business scene, has any important bearing on the character of bureaucratic structures as chosen by our subjects. Such a direct answer would, in turn, throw light on the existence or absence of what the author elsewhere [383] has called the "dominant utility function" of an enterprise. It would thereby speak to the important methodological question raised by Cyert and

March [247*b*] as to whether the organization should be treated as the usual economic monolith, or, as they suggest, as a sociological example of an *n*-person game.

As far as still broader questions of business behavior are concerned, strong confirmatory findings would be most significant from the standpoint of predicting market, financial and other policies of an enterprise, once its bureaucratic structure has been ascertained. This possibility was advanced, then apparently partially rejected by Cyert and March.[4] Nevertheless it is something which, as March and Simon have implied, under certain conditions "ought to be."[5] For this reason the prospect seems worth pursuing.

The realization of either benefit would, in the writer's opinion, make the proposed experimentation worth while. Realization of both would indeed be a "breakthrough" for a science of management.

---

[4] [141] and [145].

[5] [367], pp. 142 ff.

18

MEASURING CENTRALIZATION OF CONTROL IN BUSINESS ORGANIZATIONS

Thomas L. Whisler

Introduction

In social science research the distribution of control within an organization has frequently been treated as an independent variable, with various aspects of group performance and individual welfare as dependent variables. However, clear definition of the concept of centralization and an empirically useful measure of it (the relation of the two is close) have been rare.[1] Consequently, empirical research in which the control structure is a variable has lacked rigor.

This chapter proposes a measure of the structure of control within business organizations based upon the distribution of financial compensation in them. The proposal could theoretically apply to any organization that rewards its members primarily with money or money equivalents. However, the argument is most compelling when applied to profit-seeking organizations. Furthermore, the data used in this chapter come entirely from business organizations.

It will be argued that the distribution of compensation within an organization mirrors the distribution of control over the activities and output (goal achievement) of that organization. The degree of concentration in the distribution of compensation reflects the concentration of control (centralization) in the organization. Measures of concentration or inequality in the distribution of compensation thus become measures of centralization.

---

[1] In the final section of this chapter, the measure proposed here will be compared with possible alternatives.

Control and Compensation

Roles in a task-oriented group have been analyzed in a variety of ways. Here it is proposed that the role structure be described in terms of the proportionate control found in each role. In this context control means effective influence upon everything affecting goal achievement of the group. Thus, in a true peer group (for example, an equal partnership) roles would have equivalent control assigned to them. Hierarchies would exhibit a variety of patterns of assymetrical control, approaching, as a limit, vesting of all control in one role, and none in the rest. The peer group represents the extreme in decentralization of control, the limiting case of hierarchy the extreme in centralization.

The concept of control used here may seem novel, especially to sociologists and social psychologists, referring as it does to control over organizational goal setting and goal achievement through allocation of human and nonhuman resources, choice of production techniques, selection and analysis of information, choice of level of personal energy expenditure, and all the other thousands of ways in which the pattern of individual decision, and subsequent behavior, modifies the direction and level of group activity. The concept differs from the more traditional one (usually associated with the word "authority") only by removing the assumption that an individual's influence on group welfare must always be mediated by his influencing (controlling) another individual. The kind of control referred to here is exercised in some degree by *every individual* in an organization.

The concept actually is a familiar, common-sense one. Social scientists and administrators alike, when discussing the act of delegating additional control to a member of a hierarchy (by another member), customarily define it as giving the second member more "decision-making authority," more freedom of choice. ("Choice" relates to goals, aspiration levels, and methods and techniques of goal achievement.) The problem in past analyses has been that although pair relationships were analyzed in terms of delegation, no viable concept or method existed for so analyzing the organization as a whole, despite the common tendency to characterize organizations in terms of their degree of centralization. The measure proposed in this paper is aimed at dealing with this problem directly.

In the bureaucratic organization, roles are formally structured and control explicitly assigned by those in top leadership positions (their own roles included). It is usually recognized that this can be done only imprecisely and that often the particular persons assigned to these roles will help determine the exact limits of control exerted.

However, the distinguishing characteristic of the bureaucracy (and, presumably, its great advantage) is the rational structuring of roles and the careful selection of individuals to fill them.

It seems reasonable to assume that control can be assigned in a variety of alternative patterns in these bureaucracies. We need not assume that all patterns of assigned control will be equally efficient, nor that an organization at any moment of time will have the most efficient distribution, nor that every variation in pattern produces a sensible difference in group performance. We assume only that different distributions of control can be made and are made.

The pattern of control that is established determines an homologous pattern of role demands made upon the individuals who fill these roles (or, in the language of business organizations, a grant of authority carries a corresponding measure of responsibility). These role demands can be expressed in terms of individual attributes: innate intelligence, acquired special or general knowledge, energy, sensitivity and insight, daring—any attribute associated with individual contribution and commitment to organization goals based upon *his present activity and upon past investment in himself.*

It is assumed that these attributes are unevenly distributed in a population, with individuals who possess them in high degree, singly or in combination, being relatively scarce. Given a general preference in organizations for those who possess more, rather than less, of these attributes, we have the necessary and familiar conditions for a structure of labor prices in a society in which individuals sell their services to organizations.

Furthermore, if we assume the existence of broad, reasonably competitive labor markets, we can assume that the organization which pays monetary compensation to those who participate in its activities will not be able to influence prices significantly, but must regard them as constraints on its choice of control structure. In other words, the leadership of the organization will establish what it conceives to be a satisfactory pattern of control in the role structure, given the prices it must then pay to staff these roles adequately. Given the same set of prices in the market, alternative control patterns would produce different compensation patterns.

Business firms commonly act just about this way, devising job analysis and job evaluation schemes which make an assessment of role demands and then deriving from this a compensation structure.[2] The official structure of compensation in the firm is periodically ex-

---

[2] William B. Wolf [608], Chapter 15.

amined in light of market changes, and discrepancies—as evidenced through difficulties in finding people to fill jobs, or through evidence of maneuvering and bargaining to obtain overvalued jobs—are rectified. Every organization also has some scheme for assessing individuals, which is a counterpart to the one used in assessing jobs. Discrepancies between the control structure and the compensation structure can occur not only because of market changes but also because of changes in individuals, and because of initial imperfections in analysis of the control or compensation structures. Those discrepancies may be rectified by adjusting *any* of the variables—the role, the actor, or the compensation. This process tends to be continuous, consisting of marginal adjustments throughout the organization.

It thus becomes possible to infer the control structure of the organization from its compensation structure, and to compare organizations with one another at the same or different points in time. The compensation structure is a datum commonly preserved in economic organizations and is thus available at little cost (at least, to the organization itself).

Complications do exist, of course, in calculation of monetary compensation. Deferred income, bonuses, fringe benefits, all pose measurement problems.

More serious is the matter of nonpecuniary income. The problem is important in the present discussion since it is often assumed that the less uniformly control is distributed in a group, the less enjoyable is work for those with little control (and the more enjoyable for those with greater control). Hence, it might be argued that the elite would sacrifice some money income in order to wield great power in a hierarchy, while those with little power would demand compensatory wages. If this effect were powerful enough, the relationship between control and compensation posited earlier would be offset or even reversed.

In fact, however, the distribution of the "taste for controlling others" in a labor market is unknown. At least one psychologist has argued that it is reasonable to assume a taste for being controlled (he does not phrase it this way) in a substantial part of the population.[3]

Under such circumstances it seems that we may either assume (as economists often do) that nonpecuniary returns introduce no systematic error into the analysis, or that their effect is simply to make the observed differences in money income distributions less pronounced than they would be in the absence of such returns.

---

[3] See, for example, Robert N. McMurry [382].

Finally, the possibility exists that an organization might persist in paying some of its members above the market rate (for the quality and quantity of labor rendered). This implies existence of error in the job-and-man-assessment procedures. If the error is persistent and is not uniform throughout the job structure, the pattern of control would be obscured. Conceivably, an error of this type could be tested by comparing turnover rates for different jobs in the organization. Those with near zero turnover might be assumed to be overpaid. However, turnover is correlated with age. In the absence of empirical age/turnover norms, error in compensation would not be detected in this way. Further, turnover measurement involves observation over some (past) period of time. It is possible that at the moment of observation (of the distribution of control) previously observable errors in compensation no longer exist or that new ones have just developed.

It is assumed herein that errors of the kind just discussed are not large, that they arise from changing market conditions and from shifting task content, as well as from administrative lags and lapses in assignment and reassignment of individuals within the job structure. Hence, these overpayments will appear here and there in varying patterns in the compensation structure and will have the effect of reducing to some degree the precision and reliability of the measure discussed in this article. Errors of this kind should be less serious in profit-seeking organizations than in those not subject directly to market pressures.

The Measurement Problem

It would be immensely convenient to have a numerical index of control, so that one could test statements of the kind: "A Company is more highly centralized than B Company"; "K Company's announced policy of decentralizing authority has had no practical effects"; "The larger the firm in any given industry, the more decentralized its authority structure"; "Computers tend to centralize authority"; "The rate of return varies inversely as the degree of centralization in the company"; etc. Thus, attention was focused initially on the possibility of devising an index of inequality of compensation.

The experience of economists who have studied income distribution is illuminating. They, too, have sought ways of measuring or describing inequality in these distributions. However, as one student points out, summary indexes of inequality inevitably give rise to ambiguities and inconsistencies.[4] "Meaningful study of inequalities requires that

---

[4] Mary Jean Bowman [83], p. 2.

their patterning and not merely over-all summary measures on degree of inequality be given careful attention." [5] The various indexes that have been devised are of extremely limited value.[6]

Various graphical techniques—Lorenz diagrams, Gini charts, lognormal plots, etc., are useful for quickly showing the profiles of distributions. They permit qualitative comparison of two or more distributions throughout their ranges. For quantitative comparisons, a simple comparison of ratios of cumulative values at specific points is as effective a method as can be devised. For example, we might compare, in several organizations, the percentage of the total compensation paid to the highest paid quartile of members of each of those organizations, to the upper half, to the lowest paid 2%, etc.

In the remainder of this chapter we shall use such of the display techniques as seem most appropriate to the purpose at hand. Unfortunately, the prospect of deriving a convenient *index* of centralization must yield to the reality of the properties of the frequency distribution, since the basic concept in this paper does involve such a distribution.

Three empirical illustrations of application of this control concept and measure make up the remainder of this chapter:

1. An examination of the behavior of compensation patterns during a corporate reorganization emphasizing decentralization at the management level.

2. A comparison of the proposed compensation measure in several organizations with a survey of perceived influence patterns in these same organizations at the same point in time.

3. Examination of compensation distributions in a number of firms in different industries to see if an anticipated size effect is visible.

The point of the first two illustrations is to make some common-sense tests of the proposed measure: Does it behave the way it "should?" Since no generally accepted measure of organization control now exists, in the strict sense the proposed measure cannot be validated. It is, in fact, both measure and definition and must stand on its own feet in terms of its theoretical defensibility and logical appeal. It is offered as a criterion; its appeal must develop, in part, from such "concurrent validity" checks.

The third illustration—the size-effect test—ties the measure in with the economic theory of the firm. Such a test should simultaneously check the sensitivity of the measure, buttress this particular concept

---

[5] *Ibid.,* p. 16.
[6] Mary Jean Bowman [82].

of control, and provide evidence of the constraints imposed by organization size.

A Case: The Behavior of Compensation Distributions During a Corporate Decentralization Campaign

The *K* Company, about 100 years old, shifted from a functional
form of organization to a product-division form in 1955. This change
actually began three years earlier with the installation of a new
president. This president, and his vice-president for organization, conceived the structural change as a major first step in a long-term
campaign to decentralize control within the company. The second
part of the program involved overt persuasion, starting with a clear
policy statement on the part of the president, and a follow-up evaluation on the part of the vice-president.

The president's memorandum to executives (in late 1957) said, in
part:

*The time has come to make a large scale, concentrated effort toward true de-
centralization in all areas of our company. . . .*
*By decentralizing we place decision-making power closer to the place where
problems are occurring from day to day in many areas in our business. This
gives us faster, more accurate decisions. . . . Each decision-making manager
in [the Company] should:*

1. *review personally with the people under him, their individual authority
   and accountability;*
2. *insure that delegated decision-making power is in balance with delegated accountability;*
3. *begin a planned program of additional delegation under the philosophy
   of decentralization outlined in this statement.*

A follow-up memorandum by the vice-president (in 1958) established the company's "organization philosophy":

*To establish a working climate throughout all levels and all areas of [the
Company] which both encourage and allow all employees to contribute to the
maximum of their ability, experience and willingness to apply their ability. In
establishing this working environment we believe in creating a oneness of purpose by furthering the "small business concept"—a concept of putting together a number of homogeneous groups that have a common final interest.
Our program for the fulfillment of this organization philosophy is an aggressive policy of divisionalization and decentralization.*

DIVISIONALIZATION *is the recognition and establishment of the different busi-
nesses in which [the Company] is engaged, and placing together men with
common objectives and goals so as to achieve complete integration of such*

*important functions as production, procurement, accounting, sales and mar-
keting—all integrated with some broad corporate philosophies and goals.*

DECENTRALIZATION *is the placement of action, authority and accountability
closest to the place where the greatest number of important, timely facts exist.*

If this organization restructuring and hoped-for attitude change
achieved the intended goals of top management, the compensation
structure should reflect it. It was possible to get the distribution of
monthly salaries (managerial and nonmanagerial) paid in 1955, 1958,
and 1960. Also available were total wage and salary payments. No
breakdown of hourly rated workers is available.

Table 1 shows the redistribution effects in the salaried group. Decentralization effects began to appear in 1958 at top levels. Lower-salaried
levels lost some control (according to our measure) in 1958 but regained
it by 1960.

*Table 1   Percent of Total Salaries Paid to Stipulated Fractions
of Salaried Employees in K Corporation: 1955, 1958, and 1960*

Salary Levels	1955 ($n = 3,594$)	1958 ($n = 3,450$)	1960 ($n = 4,020$)
Top 1 percent	5.09	4.92	4.51
Top 2 percent	8.07	7.90	7.00
Top quartile	42.34	42.36	41.32
Median and above	67.33	67.37	66.30
Bottom quartile	13.45	13.20	14.67
Bottom 5 percent	2.29	2.19	2.34
Bottom 2 percent	0.84	0.75	0.86

Table 2 shows some ratios where total wage and salary payments
are used as a base. We see the interesting fact that decentralization
in the corporation as a whole is focused in the very top levels, while
the upper quarter of those on the payroll appear to have actually
acquired increasing control. These countertrends undoubtedly reflect
several things: product divisionalization with growth of division staff,
automation at the blue collar level, and effective results from the
decentralization drive at the very top.

The conclusions from the data must be tentative, until it is possible
to examine earlier periods (to separate effects of different trends). It
should be noted that unavailability of bonus and fringe compensation
probably causes an understatement of the concentration of control

Table 2   Percent of Total Wages and Salaries Paid
to Stipulated Fractions of Those on the Payroll in
K Corporation: 1955, 1958, and 1960

	1955 ($n = 8,800$)	1958 ($n = 7,300$)	1960 ($n = 7,150$)
Top 1 percent	4.11	4.02	3.93
Top 2 percent	6.38	6.35	6.22
Top 25 percent	34.23	34.83	36.77

in all three years, since these kinds of compensation bulk large at the extreme upper end (due to bonuses).

The Compensation Measure Compared with a Measure of Perceived Influence

A measure of perceived influence in an organization, the *control graph*, has been developed at the Survey Research Center of the University of Michigan.[7] It is based upon a questionnaire administered to members of an organization, the respondents being asked to indicate the degree of influence which other individuals at various specified organizational levels have on the respondents' jobs. The means of these responses (by level of respondent) are plotted as shown in Fig. 1. The two control graphs shown pertain to two small units of a nationwide corporation. These units are hundreds of miles apart, but perform identical functions. The compensation distributions (wages and salaries for all personnel) for the same two units are shown in Figs. 2 and 3. The compensation data are from the payroll period in which the questionnaire was administered.[8]

If the concept of control or influence implicit in the control graph were the same as that set forth early in this chapter, the compensation measure and this sociometric measure should rank order a group of organizations in the same way in terms of the degree of centralization of control within these organizations.

---

[7] Arnold S. Tannenbaum [534] and [535].

[8] Dr. Arnold Tannenbaum of the University of Michigan generously provided summary questionnaire data. Company management, anonymous at their request, went to substantial trouble to construct summary compensation information.

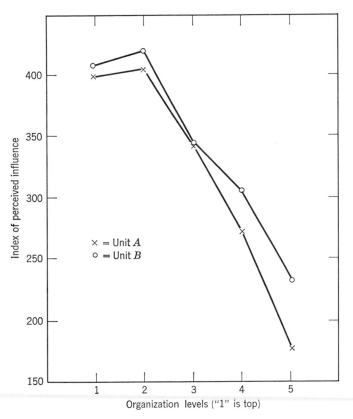

FIGURE 1   Control graph, units A and B, X Corporation.

The evidence from these two nearly identical (in size and function) units is mixed. The very top level is perceived by those in the organization to have less influence on their own jobs than does the second level. (See Fig. 1.) On the other hand, one can see that the curve for A has a slightly steeper slope than does B, indicating, as does the compensation measure, a greater concentration of control in A.

Another comparison of this sort is shown in Figs. 4 and 5. The control graph data (Fig. 4) were respondents' perceptions of influence exercised over their jobs by corporate management (level 1) and the top three levels of divisional management. The respondents included those who made up these latter three levels. Again, the highest level is perceived to have only moderate influence. The compensation data shown in Fig. 5 cover levels 2, 3, and 4, as shown on the control graph.

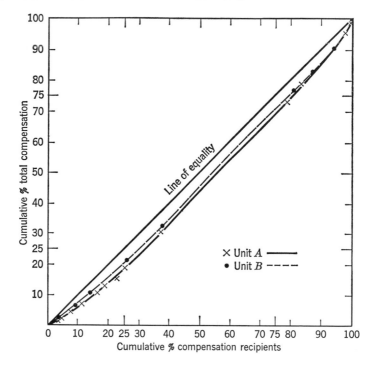

FIGURE 2   Lorenz diagram—compensation distributions, units A and B, X Corporation.

The slopes of the control graph curves order the divisions A, I, C, in concentration of control, while the compensation curves (at the upper end only) order them I, A, C. These results must be considered inconclusive.[9]

We deduce from the shape of the control graphs that respondents (as they have been instructed to do) relate the influence of others to their own jobs and not to the general accomplishments of the firm. The relatively low influence of the topmost level is probably a measure of the proportion of his time which the top executive or top executive group devotes directly to problems of the firm rather than dealing with them through the mediation of others in the firm.

Since the compensation measure deals essentially with individual

---

[9] The survey data have an additional degree of unreliability introduced by ambiguous terminology used in the questionnaire, in describing organization levels to respondents. This questionnaire was similar to the Survey Research Center instrument, but was not designed by the Center.

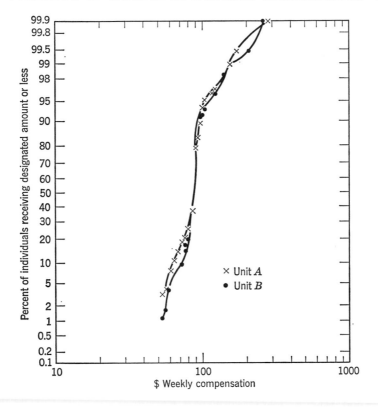

FIGURE 3   Compensations diagram, units A and B, X Corporation, on log-normal paper.

marginal contributions to goal achievement without inquiry as to whether or how others are manipulated in this process, there is reason to doubt that the two measures deal with the same phenomenon. We might expect that in traditional, simple line organizations with tightly integrated effort, the perception of influence would parallel the control structure as it is revealed by compensation distributions. On the other hand, in organizations where large numbers of "professionals" are used—people who spend a large fraction of their time dealing directly with problems of the organization—the perception of influence would be less closely related to the actual pattern of control. A pharmaceutical firm or an advertising agency would perhaps furnish examples of the latter situation, a distributing firm of the former.[9a]

[9a] Other data are being analyzed to test further the possible relationship of these two measures.

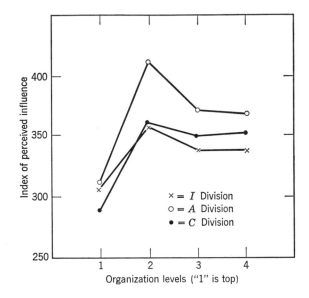

FIGURE 4   Control graph, *I*, *A*, and *C* divisions, *K* Corporation.

Size and Industry Differences

A search for multicompany compensation data resulted in getting partial distributions on a number of companies. These data were compiled from a survey conducted by a professional association in the field of business management for its own purposes.

Consequently, the data have deficiencies. In the survey, all data were grouped, reducing the amount of information. Illegible data reduced the size of an already small sample ($N = 48$). Comparisons among companies had to be restricted to the proportion of total compensation paid to the top 2% and 5% of the payroll.

Figures 6 and 7 show these percentages. Income ratios are plotted against size of firm. Where data are considered without industry identification, we get suggestive visual evidence of correlation because of the general downward sweep of the observations. In several industries as many as three firms were represented. Distinctive symbols were used on the charts for such firms and straight lines fitted freehand to the three industry observations. These lines were deliberately positioned to see if the data were consistent with the hypothesis that decentralization of control at the top of a firm is correlated with firm size (measured by number of employees). With just three points, a

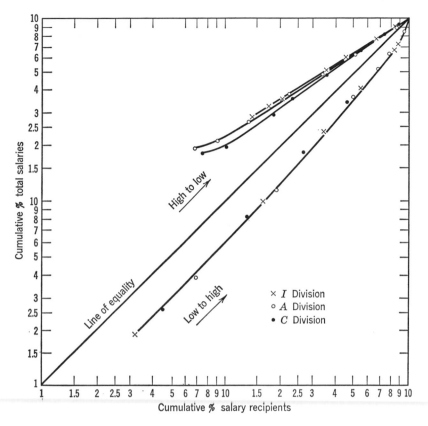

FIGURE 5   Gini chart, I, A, and C divisions, K Corporation.

number of straight lines could be so fitted, of course. So that the fact that lines with the expected negative slope can be fitted merely permits one to say that the hypothesis is not disproven by the data.

The hypothesis is really a combination of hypotheses. One comes from the economic theory of the firm. In seeking to explain why firms encounter "diseconomies" as they grow in size (a necessary condition for there to be more than one firm in an industry), the hypothesis is advanced that as increasing numbers of people engage in a joint activity, an increasing *proportion* of them must be used to coordinate the efforts of others.[10] Although economists do not specify the level

[10] See George J. Stigler [524], pp. 128–138.

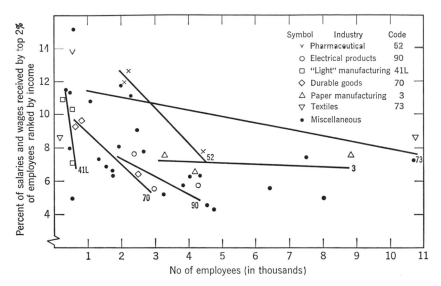

FIGURE 6 Percentage of compensation paid to the top 2% of payroll in 48 companies.

in the hierarchy at which these "coordinators" exist, it is clear that they must exist at a high enough level so that they can, in fact, direct others, while coordination itself implies the existence of still higher-level policy—and policy makers. The coordinators would thus make up a large part of the familiar middle management group. The output of the coordinators is a part of the total output of the group as defined in the early part of this paper. As their proportions grow, the control in the upper levels is distributed more evenly, even if one regards the coordinators' output as being in part "uneconomic."

A joint hypothesis, also from economics, is that increasing size permits increasing specialization.[11] Control and planning functions can be given to specialists—a "task dilution" of managerial positions. This is one of the sources of "economies" of size. The effect again, however, is decentralization of control.

The effect-of-size hypotheses appear tenable especially if one considers the lower limit where organizations become very small. The ability of one or two men to oversee all operations at first hand, to make most of the necessary computations and choices, and to com-

---

[11] Frank H. Knight [319], pp. 15–23.

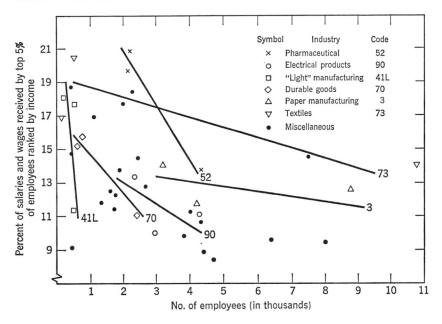

FIGURE 7 Percentage of compensation paid to the top 5% of payroll in 48 companies.

municate them to the remainder of the organization, frequently results in highly centralized control.

These hypotheses do not invalidate the earlier assumptions of optional control structures being available to the organization. Size may impose constraints, but only in one direction. To return to the case of decentralization of control in the *K* Corporation (p. 320), *the control structure became steadily more decentralized despite the fact that organization size decreased during the five-year period studied.* The size hypotheses are assymmetrical. They say that decentralization must increase as size increases, but not that centralization must increase as size decreases.

No hypothesis exists to explain the apparent differences in slope among industries. These differences could well arise from having only three observations per industry. Industry-associated factors may well exist, perhaps associated with differences in production technology.[12]

Again, the data are meager. Two things are needed to test further

---

[12] Joan Woodward [610].

the relationship between size and control structure—a much greater range and volume of data, and some theory or theories of organizational growth against which to analyze it. The theory will probably lag rather than lead further display of data. Acquiring the data is in itself a challenge since organizations, private and public alike, treat compensation data as privileged information.

The Compensation Measure and Alternatives

The concept of centralization is important in the theories of social scientists and biological scientists.[13] It has even been presented as an important variable in all systems.[14] Rarely, however, has anyone attempted rigorous definition of centralization. Even less often has quantitative measurement been attempted.

Economists have examined various empirical measures of the degree of deviation of a given market organization from the free competitive model (the model of maximum decentralization of economic power): [15] These measures, using cost, price, output, and employment data in various ways, whatever their merits in the market context, are not adaptable to measuring centralization of control in an administrative bureaucracy. Several attempts have been made to describe centralized and decentralized models of administrative price-fixing systems.[16] These models have much in common with those set up in the communications networks experiments of social psychologists.[17]

Sociologists directly concerned with processes and structures of influence and control in groups have used two techniques to infer patterns of control and influence in groups, interaction analysis [18] and questionnaire. In the first technique, influence patterns are inferred from interaction patterns but so far as the author is aware, no attempt has been made to scale these patterns in order to permit direct com-

---

[13] For example, Frank H. Knight [319], pp. 23–31; Henry C. Simons [504], pp. 1–39; Leonard D. White [600], p. 15; Robert F. Bales [100a]; Dorwin Cartwright [99]; S. N. Eisenstadt [178]; C. L. Prosser and F. A. Brown [442], pp. 619–628; Karl Pribam [439]; V. G. Dethier and E. Stellar [164], Chapters 3, 4, and 5; W. C. Allee et al. [11], pp. 413 ff.

[14] Ludwig von Bertalanffy [573], p. 150.

[15] E.g., John E. Maher [363]; Arthur M. Ross [455] and [456], especially pp. 57–140; A. C. Harberger [251].

[16] See Jacob Marschak [247c]; Thomas Marschak [370].

[17] H. J. Leavitt [333].

[18] E. C. Chapple and C. Arensberg [106]; R. F. Bales [40].

parisons of control structures in different groups.[19] In the questionnaire technique, a variety of methods of capturing and scaling members' perceptions of control or authority relationships in groups have been tried. (One of these, the control graph,[20] was discussed earlier in this chapter.) However, as Tannenbaum points out,[21] these methods almost always focus upon the interpersonal relationship between supervisor and subordinate (the control graph is an exception). Hence, definition and measurement of the pattern of authority in the total organization is not attempted, even if it were possible to do so.[22]

Research will surely continue on the interaction and questionnaire techniques, but as empirical measures of control, both techniques suffer from the limitation that they call for on-the-spot generation of data not ordinarily collected by the organization itself. Historical comparisons become possible only when it happens that comparable data had been previously collected. The compensation measure proposed in this paper overcomes this limitation to a great extent.

Some writers have discussed centralization of control in terms of the level (in the leadership hierarchy) at which decisions are "made." [23] Attempts have also been made to give some empirical content to such a definition.[24] A major difficulty has been that of giving meaning to "decision-making" in the organizational context. In many cases it is possible to find the person who makes the formal choice of action for the organization, but not identified in this way are those who have formally or informally influenced this choice by searching for and selectively presenting information, and assigning probabilities to various outcomes contingent upon the choices made. For example, in modern organizations, it is common to use staff for research and advice

---

[19] Paul R. Lawrence [332] distinguishes degrees of *delegation* among three supervisory situations in terms of interaction patterns. However, his analysis is confined to two-man events; it is not clear how generalizations about entire organizations could be made in these terms.

[20] Arnold S. Tannenbaum [534] and [535].

[21] Arnold S. Tannenbaum [534], pp. 50 ff.

[22] For example, Ralph M. Stodgill [526]. Those who analyze dyadic relationships in behavioral rather than perceptual terms, further relax the assumption of transitivity implicit in the perceptual approach. See Robert L. Davis [157]. True hierarchy thus becomes a special case, the one we take as given in our present analysis.

[23] To cite just a few examples: H. J. Kruisinga [324]; Helen Baker and Robert R. France [37]; David Bicknell Truman [553]; Ernest Dale [150].

[24] Ernest Dale [150], pp. 107 ff.; Bernard H. Baum [50], Chapter 7; Wilfred Brown [87], p. 81.

and to use committees as decision bodies. Who, then, "makes" the decision?

Not only is the location of decision making important to this definition of centralization, so also is the "size" or importance of the decision. One measure that has been proposed for this is the dollar value of the resources which the individual may commit without permission from others.[25] The profile of the distribution of control would thus be drawn in terms of the relative dollar value of autonomous decisions at various levels in the managerial hierarchy.[26]

This measure carries an additional difficulty. For only a fraction of all organizational decisions can a present value be established even approximately. Large commitments of capital are so valued, but the endless stream of day to day decisions which influence and modify the outcome of investments made earlier, but which do not involve further commitments of capital, cannot be (practically) valued in this fashion. This is especially true in what are usually called "staff" functions.

Other concepts relevant to the structure of control in bureaucratic organizations can be found in the literature. They invariably appear to suffer from one or more of the weaknesses mentioned previously. Brown's policy-setting measure, for example, focuses exclusively upon dyadic relationships—the superior's behavior toward his subordinate.[27] Such a concept is not useful in describing the pattern of control in the organization as a whole. Jaques' concept of maximum time span of discretion as a measure of responsibility also focuses upon dyadic relationships.[28] Although he has proposed a measure which is a role correlate and could, thus, conceivably be expanded into a measure of the group control structure, his interests lie elsewhere, and he has not so expanded it.[29]

Considering alternative concepts and measures, the compensation measure of the distribution of control proposed in this paper seems to offer the only currently viable empirical measure of this important dimension of organizations, except for the control graph. The relation of the control graph and the distribution of compensation needs further exploration. A promising way to make such exploration would

---

[25] E.g., Dale [150], p. 107; Louis A. Allen [13], pp. 162 ff.
[26] Allen [13], p. 164, suggests such a measure as a "ready index" of decentralization without explaining how these data on decision values would be converted to an index.
[27] Wilfred Brown [87], pp. 81–93.
[28] Elliott Jaques [294].
[29] See Jaques [294], especially Chapters 8 and 9.

be through a longitudinal study using *both* measures in such a situation as the K Corporation, where a strenuous decentralization program is in process. Another good test would be a similar study in a firm undergoing intensive computer application, where centralization of control is to be expected.[30]

Above and beyond the interesting possibilities from cross-comparison of compensation distributions and control graph data, the compensation measure proposed has some distinctive advantages:

1. It makes possible an historical study of organizations, since pay data are retained for some years in most organizations.

2. It has objectivity. One is freed from complete dependence upon assertions of a research observer concerning the control structure of a firm.

3. It is inexpensive.

4. It can be related directly to theory in sociology, economics, and social psychology (especially role theory and the theory of the firm).

5. It permits interfirm, intermarket, and cross-cultural comparisons, avoiding problems of scaling and semantics. For example, one is aware that inequality of distribution of skills and knowledge is much sharper in some countries (e.g., Egypt) than in others (e.g., the United States). One would thus expect most organization control structures in the U. S. to be less centralized than in Egypt. Most important, the compensation measure makes this a testable hypothesis.

The major disadvantage of the measure is that it applies only to organizations using money compensation. Lesser difficulties have already been discussed.

---

[30] Harold J. Leavitt and Thomas L. Whisler [337].

19

DECISION-MAKING, THE FIRM,
AND THE MARKET

James D. Thompson [1]

Decision-Making as a Unitary Concept

Decision-making as a unitary concept is crumbling under a variety of attacks.

Simon distinguishes *programmed* and *nonprogrammed* techniques for making decisions.[2] Economists and statistical decision theorists consider the activity under varying degrees of *risk* and *uncertainty*. March and Simon distinguish between *analytic* and *bargaining* processes.[3]

From a different starting point, Thompson and Tuden suggest four *strategies* for organizational decision-making, of which the analytic (or *computational*) and *bargaining* are two, the others being *judgmental* and *inspirational*.[4] They suggest that each strategy is appropriate for a different kind of issue, and that for each kind of issue and its associated strategy, there is an appropriate type of organizational structure.

Thompson and McEwen have approached decision-making as it is influenced by the environment, suggesting that the decision process

---

[1] This is a revised version of a paper originally presented to the Seminar on Social Science of Organizations, University of Pittsburgh, July, 1962. I am also grateful to C. Edward Weber and W. W. Cooper for helpful reactions to an earlier version.

[2] Herbert A. Simon [502].

[3] James G. March and Herbert A. Simon [367].

[4] James D. Thompson and Arthur Tuden [542a].

(as it operates on goal-formulation problems) shows variations under different conditions of competition and cooperation.[5]

It is a step forward to learn that one of our central concepts contains significant variations, but still we do not know very much about the association between decision-making variants and variations in organizational structures and processes. This chapter will attempt:

1. To find relationships between the Thompson-Tuden typology of decision strategies and the Thompson-McEwen analysis of competition and cooperation,

2. To relate ideas from (1) with certain phenomena considered by the theory of the firm, and finally,

3. Via an hypothetical example, to develop and clarify some of the preceding material for its possible bearing on the processes of uncertainty handling in organizations and on linkages that might be made between the social science of organization and the theory of the firm.

Decision Issues and Decision Strategies [6]

A decision *issue* arises whenever a choice is to be made between or among alternatives. Different types of decision issues can be characterized or defined by differences in the *uncertainties involved*.[7]

Frequently the uncertainty in a decision issue lies in our understanding of the relevant *cause-and-effect relationships*. Perhaps we are not sure whether A, B, or C will yield more of what it is we are seeking. Sometimes we are confident about this question but uncertain about the costs or undesired effects which might accompany the desired payoffs.

Perhaps just as frequently the uncertainty of an issue lies in our *preferences* regarding alternative possible outcomes. Even when we are sure that A produces X, while B produces Y, we are uncertain as to whether we prefer X to Y.

On either question, of course, uncertainty may be a matter of de-

---

[5] James D. Thompson and William J. McEwen [543].

[6] This section is a somewhat new interpretation of one portion of the earlier paper.

[7] I am ignoring the important distinction between risk and uncertainty. For present purposes, risk—where probabilities are known—is treated as a special case of uncertainty. The distinction is important in selecting among tools for decision making but does not appear to make a difference in the selection of a *strategy* as that term is used in this paper.

gree, but if we dichotomize these continua and work only with the extremes, four types of decision issues are defined and we can suggest a strategy for each:

Preferences About Possible Outcomes

		Certain	Uncertain
Beliefs	Certain	Computation	Compromise
About			
Causation	Uncertain	Judgment	Inspiration

Where there is certainty regarding both preferences and causation, i.e., where a preference hierarchy is understood and where knowledge is believed to be available, decision-making is a technical or mechanical matter. In its extreme form, this situation requires no genuine choice, since the problem-solution appears as common sense. But in many instances the appropriate techniques for equating cause-effect knowledge with known preferences are complicated. The data may be so voluminous, for example, that only an electronic computer can make sense of them; or the particular activities involved may be so intricate that only the highly trained specialist can arrive at the appropriate choice. In either event, the strategy for decision is straightforward analysis, and we term this "decision by computation."

When causation is uncertain—or disputed—but preferences are clear, decision-making takes on new difficulties. This situation may arise from the complexity of an issue which defies objective analysis. For example, which of two human beings would most effectively (on any criterion) meet the myriad anticipated and unexpected demands and opportunities which will arise in four years in the Presidency of the United States? In such cases we may resort to judgments of likelihood, whereas on issues of a more repetitive nature, we may resort to probability estimates. Perhaps just as often this situation occurs because of contradictory or competing explanations or theories. In an organizational context this situation frequently involves differential perception and interpretation of reality. In all such cases, where preferences are clear but causation uncertain, we will refer to the strategy for decision as one of *judgment*.[8]

On occasion there is certainty about the expected consequences or outcomes of available alternatives but ambiguity in the ordering of preferences regarding such "facts." This is not an infrequent situation

---

[8] For some game theory counterparts see Martin Shubik [493].

in organizations with multiple goals that are not commensurable and, hence, where attainment of one goal does not substitute for failure to attain another. If resources are scarce, as they usually are, alternative courses offer attainment in one direction at the expense of another. The appropriate strategy where causation is clear but preferences are uncertain thus appears to be one which will accommodate competing preferences. We will refer to this strategy as *decision by compromise*.

The final type of issue is one in which there is uncertainty both as to causation and as to preferences. It is difficult to conceive of a group whose members share neither goals nor understanding, and a group in this plight on vital issues probably is nearing disintegration. Although this situation seems far removed from usual discussions of organized decision-making, it may have empirical as well as theoretical relevance. The most likely action, perhaps, is decision not to face the issue, and organizations which are paralyzed on certain issues may, in fact, be preserving their integrity. On occasion, however, someone in the organization attains and articulates enough imagination to create a new vision or image or belief, and thereby pull together a disintegrating or paralyzed organization. Whatever the particular form of leadership exercised, it seems that decisions where there has been uncertainty about both causation and preferences are *decisions by inspiration*.

Role of the Environment in Defining Issues [9]

Thompson and McEwen conceive of a continuum of organizational power in environmental relations, ranging from the organization which dominates its environment to one completely dominated. If we conceive of organizations as embedded in some sort of exchange network, each needing supports or benefits from others, it appears that most organizations must adopt strategies for coming to terms with their environments.[10] These strategies may be broadly classified as *competitive* or *cooperative*.

Competition here refers to that form of rivalry between two or more organizations which is mediated by a third party. It includes scrambling for resources as well as for customers or clients, and in a com-

---

[9] This section is a somewhat new interpretation of one portion of the earlier paper.

[10] See Sol Levine and Paul E. White [341].

plex society it includes rivalry for potential members and their loyalties. In each case a *third party* makes a choice among alternatives, two or more organizations attempt to influence that choice through some type of appeal or offering, and choice by the third party is a vote of support for one of the rivals and denial of support to the others involved.

Bargaining or compromise—treated here as one form of cooperation —refers to the negotiation of an agreement for the exchange of goods or services between two or more organizations. Unlike competition, bargaining involves direct interaction with other organizations in the environment rather than with a third party. Bargaining, therefore, appears to invade the actual decision process. To the extent that the second party's support is necessary, he is in a position to exercise veto over final choice of alternatives, and hence takes part in the decision.

A second form of cooperation, *cooptation*, has been defined as the absorption of new elements into the organization as a means of averting threats to its stability or existence.[11] To the extent that it is effective, it places representatives of an "outside" organization in a position to participate in the decision process from its beginning. By the same token, it further limits the opportunity for one organization to choose arbitrarily from among alternatives.

The third form of cooperation, *coalition*, refers to a combination of two or more organizations for a common purpose. To the extent that it is operative, two or more organizations act as one with respect to certain goals. It requires a commitment for joint decision of future activities and thus places additional limits on unilateral or arbitrary decisions.

Some Connections Between the Two Schemes

The computational strategy seems most appropriate for strictly internal matters, for it requires clarity of goals and relative certainty of causal relations, and these usually occur only in those situations over which the organization has *unilateral control*. The computational strategy, therefore, does not appear to be appropriate where interaction with other organizations is imperative; it does not appear to correspond to any of the situations of competition or cooperation, although we will shortly modify this statement.

---

[11] Philip Selznick [476].

Under competitive conditions, the organization keeps unilateral control of its preference hierarchy. But because it must behave toward prospective customers, suppliers, and other third parties in the light of its *expectations* about the behavior both of rivals and of prospects, cause-and-effect relations are uncertain. Competition, therefore, defines a situation calling for the judgmental strategy.

The situation calling for bargaining seems to be directly translatable into the cell defined as an issue for compromise and, hence, for the bargaining strategy. In both schemes, the issue is defined by competing or incommensurate preference hierarchies. Presumably, however, two parties do not come together for bargaining purposes unless each has some fairly clear beliefs about cause-and-effect relationships involved.[12] Essentially, then, bargaining seems to occur when causation is certain but preferences uncertain.

Hence, to compete, the organization retains certainty about its outcome preferences but faces uncertainty regarding causation. To bargain, the organization retains certainty about causation but faces uncertainty regarding outcome preferences. Can an organization reduce or remove either type of uncertainty when it must relate to its environment?

Cooptation and coalition appear now to be devices operating specifically to reduce environmental uncertainty.

By coopting relevant environmental units, the organization gains knowledge of their actions and plans, i.e., it reduces or removes uncertainty regarding causation. It does this by yielding freedom on the question of preferences, for cooptation means a commitment to those preferences which are jointly held by the coopting and coopted organization. But while certain preference alternatives are foregone, the remaining range of preferences is clear. Thus cooptation is a means of replacing uncertainty with certainty, and provides a basis for computational decision strategies.

Coalition now appears as a higher degree of cooptation, i.e., it places even greater limitations on freedom to establish preferences, but results in certainty both of preferences and causation. Hence coalition, like cooptation, defines a situation for which computation is an appropriate decision strategy. In summary:

---

[12] It is also possible to conceive of the early phase of bargaining to be devoted to clarification of causation questions before tangling directly with preferences.

Preferences About Possible Outcomes

		Certainty	Uncertainty
Beliefs About Causation	Certainty	Unilateral action based on dominance or shared control —Computation	Bilateral action based on compromise —Bargaining
	Uncertainty	Multilateral action based on action and reaction —Judgment	

Functional Differentiation Within Organizations

Suppose our entrepreneurial talents lead us a conclusion that there is a wide-open field for the production and marketing of aardvark kennels. Since it became fashionable to have an aardvark as a pet, aardvark owners have been using dog kennels. But it is obvious that dogs and aardvarks are different. Hence there is an unmet need.

Once we have the idea, we can design and plan an aardvark kennel, set up a pilot operation in the lab, and experiment with production processes to standardize them. As soon as we take this man-machine process out of the lab, however, we must add to our *technical* organization some new organizational elements to handle the problems which our laboratory had handled during the experimental stage. We need to surround our technical *core* organization with organizational components to provide the necessary inputs and to distribute the outputs.

The technical core of our firm operates optimally only when it is supplied with a constant flow of ingredients which conform to desired standards and only if the man- and machine-components are adequate, in place, and operable at the desired times. In short, the technical core conforms to our efficiency designs only if there is uniformity, regularity, predictability, and reliability—the absence of uncertainty. Since nothing must interfere with or surprise the technical core, we should isolate it from the environment of the organization, leaving entirely to other components of the firm to fend off intrusions, iron out irregularities, maintain resource stocks at levels which insure that shortages never occur, and sell aardvark kennels quickly enough that the technical core never clogs up. Ideally (from this point of view), we would divorce the at-work sector of the lives of our employees from other sectors, and we would ensure that their interactions at work were solely governed by work flow requirements. The achievement of this state of affairs will be the responsibility of our personnel input component.

By insisting that the input components and output components smooth out all irregularities and remove all uncertainty, we have created a technical core with a clear-cut outcome preference or criterion and with a known set of cause-effect relations or means-ends links. If occasional problems do arise (obviously because "they" goofed), they can be settled by experts via the computational strategy. Hence we can appoint engineers to supervise and control this technical core, and they can apply scientific management, operations research, and similar techniques to the production of aardvark kennels.

The stability and efficiency we have achieved with our technical core was gained by isolating it from the organization's environment. If we assume that the environment is dynamic, we have automatically assigned to the input component and/or output component the task of off-setting or overcoming the uncertainties in that environment. These components must procure supplies, recruit employees, and obtain financing from an uncertain environment; they must also sell kennels to the people who own aardvarks.

This leads to the scheme depicted in Fig. 1, with an isolated, highly protected technical core employing the computational decision strategy, but with input components and output components spanning the boundaries of the organization, therefore acting with reference to the environment, and therefore forced to rely on the judgmental (competitive) decision strategy or the bargaining (compromise) decision strategy.

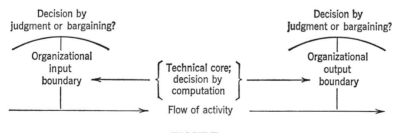

FIGURE 1

We are now ready to advance four general propositions:

PROPOSITION 1. Variations in environmental conditions will bring about changes in decision strategies for input and output components of the firm.

PROPOSITION 2. Variations in environmental conditions can penetrate the input and output "buffers" and cause changes in the technical core of the organization.

PROPOSITION 3. Variations in environmental conditions will alter the dependence of input, technical core, and output components relative to one another.

PROPOSITION 4. When input or output components transfer uncertainty rather than absorb it, there will be conflict among input, technical core, and output components.

These propositions taken together focus on "internal" uncertainties stemming from "external" uncertainties. This is a topic avoided by economists' models of the firm, which do not allow for internal uncertainty because their interest has been on the action of environments —markets—rather than on the behavior of firms themselves.

Environmental Concepts Relevant to the Firm

To explain and illustrate these propositions we need variables which can be used to characterize environments. The most sophisticated concepts of organizational environments available undoubtedly lie in economics. Unfortunately for present purposes, however, the precision of economic theory with respect to the firm has been achieved by unduly heavy emphasis on price.

For present purposes therefore we will rely on the earlier definitions of competition and cooperation which, though cruder than those of economists, seem more pertinent. Neither will we make the further distinctions between pure competition, imperfect competition, and monopoly that are usual in economic analysis. Instead, we will conceive of a firm selling in a market where it is, first, the only producer; then we will allow for consumer reaction and subsequent entrance of other producers. We will also assume an initial situation in which there is more customer demand than can be supplied at the prevailing price, and we will then let this situation become reversed; in the vernacular we will consider first a "sellers' market," then a "buyers' market."

Although this approach sacrifices precision for convenience, it will underscore the possibilities of attempting to link organizational and economic considerations.

History of the Aardvark Firm: Phase I

When we take our firm out of the pilot trials and set up actual production facilities, we are reasonably certain about a number of things. Millions of aardvarks are housed in dog houses and none have aardvark kennels. We know we can mass produce kennels designed specifically for aardvarks. We have the design and we know the appropriate production techniques and sequences. We know the kinds of man-skills and machine-skills needed, and the kinds of raw materials required.

Important uncertainties exist, however, about the market. If aardvark owners become convinced that aardvark kennels are significantly more appropriate for their pets than are dog houses, we are bordering on monopoly in a sellers' market. Otherwise, we are simply a late entrant into an already established and competitive market in which productive capacity is at least equal to demand and perhaps exceeds it, thereby creating a buyers' market.

The crucial question in Phase I, therefore, is whether our output component can establish in the market the notion that our aardvark kennels are uniquely superior. Since aardvarks appeal to all ages and sexes, and are practical pets for all except the destitute and those living in high-rise apartments, it is difficult to predict in the abstract the preference scales of aardvark owners, or of aardvarks, or of those who may soon acquire aardvarks.

Success in Phase I, therefore, depends on success of decision-making in the *output component, using a judgmental strategy.*

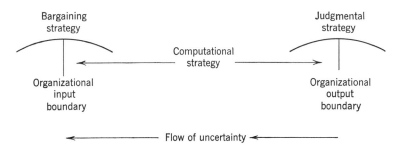

FIGURE 2

The uncertainty about the market cannot be entirely absorbed by the output component. Some is passed back to the technical core, which must have several sets of computations, each based on a different set of assumptions about the outcome of the promotion effort. The uncertainty as to which set of computations will be chosen provides an unstable base for the input component, which must, therefore, bargain with various suppliers rather than recruit or purchase competitively; i.e., it must convince suppliers to deal on a contingency basis, providing small lots initially but standing ready to deliver larger lots on short notice and on favorable terms. In Phase I, then, our scheme looks as shown in Fig. 2.

The input component is dependent on the technical core, which, in turn, is dependent on the output component. Each absorbs some of the uncertainty contained in the market, but each passes some back, with the input component transferring some of the uncertainty to suppliers.

History of the Aardvark Firm: Phase II

Because our promotion campaign was successful, we now enjoy a sellers' market in which we are the only significant supplier. New purchasers of aardvarks automatically demand one of our kennels, and millions of owners realize how inadequate their dog houses really are.

The output problem is essentially one of maintaining good will by establishing a priority system and efficient shipping schedules. These are matters to be handled via the computational strategy. By removing uncertainty, environmental changes have produced a change in decision strategy at the output boundary (Proposition 1). The technical core is operating on a three-shift schedule, having discarded alternative computations (Proposition 2) and employing a computational strategy which maximizes quantity. The input components are busy competing for raw materials, personnel, and services; the shift from negotiation to competition entailed a shift from the bargaining to the judgmental decision strategy (Proposition 1). The scheme in Phase II, therefore, is as shown in Fig. 3.

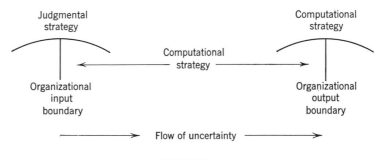

FIGURE 3

The output component is dependent on the technical core, which in turn is dependent on the input component; the flow of uncertainty is from the input side, spilling over into the technical core, and eventually affecting the output component.

History of the Aardvark Firm: Phase III

The boom is now over. Several dog house producers have added aardvark kennels to their lines, and together we can produce kennels faster than people buy them. Our problem is to capture a share of the market which equals our production capacity, and let our rivals cut their production back. How do we achieve this situation, now that we face a buyers' market?

We need somehow to make our kennel appear to consumers to be significantly different from others, through one or some combination of four variables: price, design, quality, or propaganda. Since propaganda is the easier, we already have tried it, without success. We also tried a combination of propaganda and modest changes in design (i.e., adjustments at the *end* of the production sequence), by introducing eight colors of paint. This production modification merely called for substitution of one variable for another in the technical equation in a way which did not alter other variables or relationships in the production process. That gave us only a temporary advantage, however, for our rivals could quickly and easily make the same shift.

It has now become clear that we can remain fat and saucy only by pricing below our competitors or by major design modifications. Since we prefer not to sell at low prices, we have opted for new designs, and our engineers have come up with the following innovations: (1) Air conditioning for aardvark kennels; (2) an ultra-violet delouser; (3) a hi-fi installation; and (4) a device which sprays the aardvark with deodorant each time he comes out the kennel door. Since some customers will want kennels plain, some will want kennels with everything, and some will want various combinations, we now offer 16 different models.

The problem for our output component involves logistical questions, such as how many of each model to warehouse in each territory, and various operations research techniques are available to handle this. They can be used, however, only after certain judgment questions have been answered, such as when and where and how to promote the various models. Despite logistical decision tools, then, the judgmental strategy is the essential one for the output component. This involves a change corresponding to environmental change (Proposition 1).

The technical core still uses the computational strategy, but its problems have been magnified by the variety of production runs it must employ to produce 16 different models. Each calls for rearrangement of parts of the production sequence, adjustment of machinery, etc. Each change, therefore, reduces the quantity that can be produced in a given time, and increases costs of production. Although we have avoided cost as our prime consideration, we still must be realistic. The result is that the technical core no longer has a clear-cut criterion to be optimized, and the predictability, regularity, etc., which it faced in Phases I and II has been sharply reduced (Proposition 2). For the technical core, there is pressure to clarify its goals, which can be done only by extracting favorable quotas from the output component.

Thus *between* the technical core and the output component, the situation calls for compromise via the bargaining strategy, with the technical core wanting guaranteed quotas which call for long production runs of a single model, and the output component wanting flexibility in production (Proposition 4). The output component faces uncertainty in consumer reaction to the various models and to their promotion, and would prefer that the technical core absorb a large measure of that uncertainty.

Uncertainty is also passed back to the input component, for it does not know how many hi-fis, air-conditioners, deodorizers, or delousers to buy. It wants to purchase small lots of each, but to be certain that additional orders will be filled promptly if they become necessary. These conditions cannot be met by competition, so the input component is forced to bargain with suppliers. (This change in response to environmental changes is consistent with Proposition 1.) This situation of monopolistic competition in a buyers' market can be depicted as in Fig. 4.

Uncertainty enters from the output component, is relayed to the technical core, and then to the input component. (This switch from Phase II is consistent with Proposition 2.)

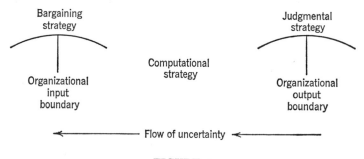

FIGURE 4

History of the Aardvark Firm: Phase IV

The aardvark craze is over. Like chihuahuas, aardvarks are here to stay, but the avant garde has turned to white mink. Propaganda has little effect in differentiating our product from those of rivals. Owners have decided that pampering is damaging to the personalities of aardvarks, hence most of our models can be discontinued.

If we want to stay in business, we face stiff competition unprotected by monopoly, unless:

1. We enter into mutual *cooptation* with our rivals, to form a cartel, i.e., we allow them to participate in our decisions about where to sell, and which models to offer, in exchange for our participation in their decisions on similar questions.

2. We enter into a *coalition* with Sears, Roebuck, in which they become our marketing agency and we become their producing agency.

Because the cartel arrangement is illegal, we have decided on the second alternative as a way of reducing the uncertainties of cut throat competition. The only way we could obtain a contract with Sears was to accept a low price ceiling. We have, of course, transferred our output costs to Sears, but still we face a reduction in profits.

We have become a satellite, with the output component (now in the form of a powerful outsider) wielding the power, but with regularity, routinization, and predictability restored for our technical core. This allows the technical core to concentrate on cost as the variable to be minimized, thus increasing the difference between what Sears pays and what we spend.

Once our production process has been adjusted to minimize cost, however, the only flexibility we have in our profit picture lies in reducing the cost of inputs. Now it is our ability in bargaining—both with labor and suppliers—which can make or break us. If our inputs component is on the ball, it will from time to time find special buys on inputs which do not quite meet the specifications established by our technical core, and which, therefore, would require adjustments by the technical core which *its* computational strategy does not allow. Now the stage is set for conflict between the input component and the technical core (Proposition 4). The situation can be depicted in Fig. 5.

The technical core now is dependent both on Sears (at the output "boundary") and on the input component, and the input component is dependent on the contract with Sears. Uncertainty enters from the input side and is partly transferred to the technical core, but must stop there. (This change is consistent with Proposition 3.)

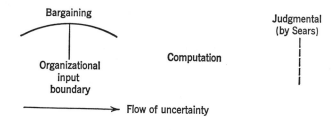

FIGURE 5

Conclusion

March and Simon have drawn attention to the important process of *uncertainty absorption* in complex organizations.[13] I hope I have presented a case for the hot-potato aspect of uncertainty absorption, i.e., which parts of the organization are to absorb the uncertainties stemming from the environment? Perhaps in this area lie important sources of "informal organization" and of "human relations conflict" in dynamic organizations.[14]

In any event, I vote to dissolve this firm which is now caught in a cost-price squeeze. Besides, there's something more appealing about mink.

---

[13] [367].

[14] For a revealing empirical study on this topic, see George Strauss [528].

PART FOUR

Management science perspectives

20

THE MATHEMATICAL REPRESENTATION
OF THE INDIVIDUAL IN MODELS OF
ORGANIZATION PROBLEMS

Maynard W. Shelly, II

Introduction [1]

To Percy, a ballbearing-eyed experimental psychologist who specialized in making sense out of responses to nonsense syllables and confidently examining the guessing habits of others, man was an object to be treated with rigor; he saw little hope for incorporating the characteristics of man into models of organization problems because any initial attempt in this direction could not be regarded as testable or usable by his fellow experimentalists.

To Priscilla, a dark cashmere-eyed social psychologist, who refused to define things sharply for fear that her points would be misunderstood, man was a mass of unintelligible motives and aspirations; she saw little need for incorporating the characteristics of individuals into models of organization problems because the position of men in organizations could be understood without an analysis of the organization problems they faced. When this was not possible, the problems were too immense to be analyzed anyway.

[1] The approach to problems of the organization included in this chapter has profited from many comments and suggestions. The author would, in particular, like to acknowledge the helpful suggestions and assistance given by W. W. Cooper. The author would also like to acknowledge the helpful assistance given by Yvonne Holmes in the preparation, correction, and proofreading of the final manuscript.

To Melvin, a mathematician inoculated against being too abstract, life was a series of inequalities which could only be repressed by adopting a system's viewpoint; he saw little need for incorporating the characteristics of individuals into models of organization problems because there would always be a systematic way to avoid the ephemeral problems humankind created.

To Oratio, an organization theorist, an organization analyst, and an organization man, the organization as a social structure was a source of consultation capable of supporting a bewildering array of intellectual interests when these interests were firmly rooted in the realities of twentieth-century life; he saw little need for incorporating the characteristics of individuals into models of organization problems, because, managementwise, it was easier to find another individual who would fit the old groove.

To Grover, who was a graduate student of Percy, Priscilla, Melvin, and Oratio, and who sincerely wanted to mature into a first-rate manager, administration was a matter of learning to deal with facts that got your hands dirty; he was not interested in learning how to develop models of organization problems which incorporated the characteristics of individuals because this might make the things he had already learned less useful.

Thus, Percy, Priscilla, Melvin, and Oratio made no attempts to include explicitly individual differences into their models of organization problems. It is unlikely that Grover will either. But is there really, behind these varied reasons, a good reason why models of organizational problems cannot include explicitly and formally some of the characteristics of individuals, characteristics which may belong to only very small sets of individuals? This chapter attempts to show in a preliminary way that the answer is "no."

The preceding question really has several parts. The first involves an explication of what is meant by "incorporate." The second part, involving the preceding explication of "incorporate," consists of showing, for a variety of organization problems how, if possible, this incorporation might be begun. The final part of the question concerns the usefulness of such an incorporation of individual characteristics into models of organizational problems.

We shall consider the characteristics of individuals to have been successfully incorporated into models of organizational problems if the inclusion of these characteristics leads to interesting problems. We shall not demand that the products of the incorporation be useful; as we have indicated, this is a separate question. (There is a tendency in management science to combine the attributes of interesting and useful, because management science arose from dealing with "real people making real decisions"; if something is not seen as potentially useful, it may be regarded as inherently uninteresting to management scientists.)

The remainder of this chapter is almost exclusively concerned with the second part of the question—to show, in, as yet, a fragmentary and incomplete way—that the explicit and tentatively formal incorporation of individual characteristics into a range of observed organization problems leads to the germs of interesting problems. (Since interest is a quite personal type of thing, as are all scientific innovations, the same verdict may not be rendered by every reader.)

Since the only real criterion of usefulness is use, this chapter will ignore for the most part the third and final part of the question.

Perhaps because individual characteristics have not been explicitly incorporated into models of organization problems, very often a bipolarization has developed for treating the individual in the organization. Leavitt (Chapter 4) has termed these the "people approaches" versus the "structural" and, more recently, the "technological approaches" to organizations. In the former, emphasis is placed on the aspirations and needs of people and the structure of organization problems is pretty much ignored, whereas in the latter, individuals are regarded as replaceable units subservient to a particular structure.

This dichotomization may also reflect a schism in values. Indeed, such a conclusion will be reached at the termination of this chapter. The persistent and unavoidable conflict between those needs finding an expression in the organization structure (those consistent with organizational goals) and those not finding such an expression is very difficult to adjudicate, and it is often easier simply to take one side or the other. It is then quite a short step to develop representations of organization problems which proselyte for the side chosen. Thus to deal with the problems posed in this chapter may represent an unwanted compromise for either those firmly committed to the "people position" or to those firmly committed to the "structural position."

The Need for a Single Model for
Describing Organizational Problems

The tendency to bipolarize organization problems has often yielded irrelevant abstractions. The abstractions have often been confined within a preconceived framework prescribing what the problems should be rather than being based, as well, upon perceptions of the problems by organizational members. There is always this set of dual problems.

To consider the individual without considering the structure in which he is embedded is to ignore the effects of structure upon individual behavior.[2] To consider the individual without considering the structure is also to ignore the "fact that changes at one point in the system may bring about related changes in many variables throughout the system." [3] We need a framework which *simultaneously* considers both viewpoints. But the effects of an organization's structure upon the individual are being ignored by many psychologists (Katzell [307], Leavitt [335]). The possible effects that individuals can have upon communication patterns (e.g., in small groups, see [277] and [520]) is being ignored by the structurally oriented for although organizations are among the most "rationally" contrived units of human association, it cannot be expected that their goal-oriented structure will determine their behavior (Simon [457e]). Indeed, Cooper [134] has contended that, ultimately, organization design and analysis are intimately connected with the whole fabric of society.

THE INDIVIDUAL AND ORGANIZATIONAL BEHAVIOR

Organizations' existence depends upon the individuals in them being able to share parts of the environment. This permits their behavior to show the interdependence required for organizational behavior to exist, for, as Simon [457e], p. 158, has noted, the individuals in an organization must indeed "exhibit a high degree of internal cohesion" relative to the dependence of organizations on each other.

In studying any organization we are concerned with its parts and their interrelations. The assimilation of the organizational environment by the individual determines in part his relations to others. It is this assimilation of the environment by the individual which accounts for much of the regularity as well as initiates many of the changes in an organization. A major source of organizational change in the government agencies studied by Blau [75], for example, was the (perceived and assimilated) unanticipated consequence of new procedures or the (perceived and assimilated) accumulated effects of established procedures. The question is then not whether the individual is important, but how to represent the assimilation of the organization en-

---

[2] For example, as shown in studies of behavior in communication nets: Leavitt [333], Shaw [479], Shelly and Gilchrist [487].

[3] [578], p. 415.

vironment by the individual in the mathematical analysis of organizational problems.

Representation of the Individual in Analyzing Organizational Problems

The individual in the organization has been portrayed as both a stimulus-bound, role-dominated creature and as a free, need-motivated, goal-seeking human being. The representation chosen is partly a product of the orientation and experiences of the scientist representing the individual. The complexities of an organization makes the adoption of some viewpoint unavoidable, but different views need not be incompatible. For example, consider the (exaggerated) views of the individuals in the organization of a "hard-headed" experimental psychologist and a "clinically oriented" social psychologist, both of a decade ago.

The experimentalist was used to varying the stimuli when changing from one experimental condition to the next, and then finding ways to substantiate the *differences* he found in behavior between experimental conditions. He had done many experiments in which the control of the stimuli was very important. He thought of a stimulus rather than a situation. His experimental rooms were blandly and monotonously colored. The theories he had worked with and helped to extend were theories based upon experimental manipulations of stimulus conditions. They were theories of how stimuli led to responses. He had few techniques and often no desire to study the relationships between responses in a single subject. It was simpler, and perhaps just more aesthetically pleasing, to assign subjects randomly to experimental conditions among which there were stimulus differences. If the subjects showed wide variability, this psychologist simply increased the size of the experimental groups. When he approached the problems of an organization, he continued to view the individual as dominated by those stimuli present, which, in an organization, could be largely those determined by a person's position within the organization.

The clinically oriented social psychologist felt that laboratories were too confining, and that it was not possible really to understand the subjects when they came in, sat in a black booth, and pushed telegraph keys or, in more affluent laboratories, pulled computer connected switches. This psychologist preferred interviews, the use of projective techniques, or the observation of interactions viewed through a one-way mirror, all of which involved the same individuals day after day. He got to know his subjects; he watched them make different responses to the same situations time after time. He saw relationships between responses which were different for different subjects. After an angry outburst some always turned inward into themselves, while others kept up a rapid, agitated conversation. The theories that this psychologist worked on and helped to extend were theories which related responses and judgments to basic personality traits. It always seemed as though differences in behavior were related to differences in basic personality traits if one looked *deep enough*. One could observe that the environmental stimuli were simply hurdles to be leaped over by insights. Thus, this psychologist wanted the subjects to be as free as possible of distracting influences, and so he usually *removed any source of stimulus change*. When he approached the analysis of organizational problems, he looked at the characteristics of the individuals involved in the problems. Each problem became unique.

Both of these viewpoints are important and are not necessarily in conflict with each other. The "hard-headed" experimentalist was impressed by the observation that when you instructed the individual person that certain stimulus differences were important, he learned to *respond differently* to the different stimuli. The social psychologist was impressed by the observation that when a quiet, restful room was used, subjects showed *behavior which was consistent* and even repetitive. Thus, the apparent conflict between the views of the two psychologists is perhaps more an accommodation to those things they believe they understand than a fundamental and irreconcilable difference.

This is probably also true of the resulting descriptions of man in organization problems. The person in the organization shows *consistency* in his behavior partly because certain responses are relatively isolable from stimulus changes, and partly because the stimulus conditions are relatively constant from day to day—a condition which can be perpetuated by a relatively rigid organizational structure. The person shows *inconsistency* or change partly because stimulus conditions change, and partly because his behavior is not completely controlled by his immediate environment. Behind both these stimulus-conditioned and these relatively constant responses are the "perceptions" of the individual in the organization.

This chapter is concerned with the analysis of some organization problems in terms of what will be called "personal structures." Although "Proponents of structure, as opposed to mere quantity, have seldom been popular in America . . . and their arguments usually set aside," [4] when problem solving in a complex situation is studied, the importance of such imposed "perceptual" structures becomes quickly evident. "Learning to characterize in an effective way the task environment is an important and prevalent type of human learning." [5] In response to a talk on blind variation in problem solving (Campbell [616a]), Newell said ([616b], p. 229): "You start with a problem and the first thing you try to do is to put structure on the problem." He admitted that blind variation takes over at some point, but the interesting thing, he said, was how you got from the large space of possible solutions to the small space of probable solutions. Indeed, it is this possibility of momentary changes in "perceptual" structures that helps to make learning in complex situations as efficient as it is (Simon [233d]).

The "perceptual" structure of an individual clearly affects his behavior in the organization—in ways which may be quite subtle and intricate.

Administrative man is limited . . . by constraints that are part of his own psychological makeup. . . . The fact that these limits are not physiological and fixed, but are instead largely determined by social and even organizational forces, creates problems of theory construction of great subtlety. . . .[6]

In the remainder of this chapter, we shall be concerned with how this "perceptual" structure or, as we shall choose to call it, this *personal structure*, can be represented so that its implications and usefulness in models about and for the organization can be explored.

THE PERSONAL STRUCTURE OF THE INDIVIDUAL
MEMBER OF AN ORGANIZATION

The approach to the "individual-in-the-organization" herein considers the individual to be characterized by the correspondence between his judgments and sets of environmental states within the organization. Two executives, for example, might be distinguished in part by the differences in the set of organizational states to which they apply a judgment such as "This organization is adequately staffed." The collection of the judgments together with the collection of the sets of environment states to which the judgments may be applied by the individual will be called the individual's *personal structure*. We will be concerned with the use to which personal structures can be put in analyzing certain organizational problems.

Before proceeding further, two things should be said. First, the

---

[4] [210], p. 285.   [5] [616c], p. 161.   [6] [457e], p. 162.

mathematical development of the concept of "personal structure" is still in its youth if not its infancy. Consequently, it is only possible to use the concepts associated with personal structures in quite restricted situations; thus the illustrative situations employed herein will be quite simple. It is hoped that the extension of the ideas to more complex situations will be intuitively acceptable, although very likely technically difficult to accomplish.

Second, only the most central of ideas will be presented to avoid lengthening this chapter.[7] This restriction will permit using diagrammatic analogues in place of mathematical developments and concepts. Although the analogues will not be exact models of the mathematical development, they will probably give a better idea of how the concepts can be extended than could the inclusion of the mathematical developments themselves. Often it will be possible to give only verbal sketches of the relation of personal structures to organizational problems.

We shall let an individual be denoted by P (or by Q or R). We shall permit this person P the ability to make a finite set of judgments. This set of judgments will be denoted by Φ. An individual judgment, in particular the ith judgment, will be denoted by ϕ_i. The complete set of environmental states will be denoted by X. The organization will be denoted by O, and the set of organizational states (the different states the organization can be in) will be denoted by X_O.

We shall assume that the individual in an organization does not change spontaneously with regard to those environmental states for which a particular judgment *may be true*.[8] Therefore, there is constantly a fixed set of environmental states for which a particular judgment may be true for a particular individual in the organization. We shall call these sets of states A-sets.[9] Thus, for example, if we

---

[7] For the mathematical representation of personal structures, see [482] and [483]. Related but prior developments, using a topological rather than an algebraic approach, are contained in Shelly [481]; an exploratory application of the concepts of personal structures to the psychotherapeutic situation is contained in Shelly [486f]. Two further papers are nearing completion and should be published in the near future: Shelly [484] and [485].

[8] As is obvious upon a moment's reflection, those judgments which are true for a particular environmental state depend upon the state the individual P is in. Personal structures depending upon the state of the individual have been called realized personal structures and are discussed in Shelly [485]. They will not be discussed in this chapter because of complications they introduce.

[9] A-sets can be viewed as upper bounds for the set of environmental states for which a judgment can be true. The corresponding A-set in a realized personal structure will always be contained in the A-set of the personal structure.

consider a particular judgment, say ϕ_i, the set of environmental states for which that judgment may be true will be denoted by A_i. The set of all A-sets corresponding to the judgments Φ will be denoted by **A**. The personal structure of **P** depends upon the set of judgments Φ and the associated set of A-sets, **A**, in the environment X. The personal structure of **P** will be altered if Φ is changed, if the correspondence between ϕ_i and the states of the environment is changed, or if the states of the environment are restricted, e.g., to the organization.

Judgments can have at least two types of relationship to each other with reference to states of the environment. The first relation is that of *combination*—two or more judgments may be true for a single environmental state. The second relation is that of *uncertainty* —it may not be clear as to whether one or more judgments can be true of an environmental state. If we identify the combination of judgments with "conjunction" and the uncertainty between judgments with "disjunction," then the set of judgments under the operations of combination and uncertainty become a set of propositional functions (or a Boolean algebra). The A-sets are a representation of the judgments when the following is true. The intersection of two A-sets corresponds to the A-set for the combination of two judgments, and the union of two A-sets corresponds to the A-set of the uncertainty of the two judgments. We shall consider all combined and uncertain judgments to be included in Φ. Those judgments in Φ which are neither the combination of judgments nor a judgment expressing the uncertainty between judgments will be called *primary judgments*.

The judgments or the set of A-sets of a personal structure can also be treated as a Boolean ring. One of the advantages of considering these structures to be rings is that it tends to place more direct emphasis upon the two operations—that of combination and uncertainty. It also facilitates the algebraic identification of certain logical concepts—an area of activity currently known as algebraic logic.[10]

The basic form of the diagrammatic analogue of the mathematical structure to be used is presented in Fig. 1. We shall let A-sets be represented by the areas enclosed by a single continuous line. States of the environment to which a judgment may be applicable are thus represented by points within a closed boundary line. The number labeling the A-set will be the index of the corresponding judgment. The possible states of the environment (or organization environment) may be represented by an encompassing rectangle, as in Fig. 1, or simply as the union

---

[10] For review of the area of algebraic logic, see [329] and [249].

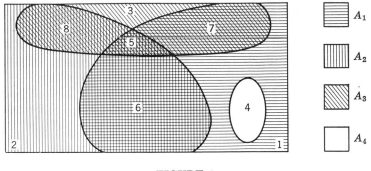

FIGURE 1

of all represented A-sets. In Fig. 1, $\mathbf{P}$ is assumed to have a total of four primary judgments, ϕ_1, ϕ_2, ϕ_3, ϕ_4, and hence four basic A-sets. Note that A_4 is *not* included in A_1. When we include both combinations of judgments which are true for at least one environmental state, then $\mathbf{P}$ has a total of eight primary and composite judgments: ϕ_1, ϕ_2, ϕ_3, ϕ_4, $\phi_1 \wedge \phi_2 \wedge \phi_3 = \phi_5$, $\phi_1 \wedge \phi_2 = \phi_6$, $\phi_1 \wedge \phi_3 = \phi_7$, $\phi_2 \wedge \phi_3 = \phi_8$, and all the uncertain judgments which can be obtained from combinations of these primary and composite judgments.

In the following we shall be concerned with the judgments and the corresponding A-sets for more than one person. By identifying a judgment that an individual *does not use* with the null set, we can consider that Φ represents the set of judgments for every individual. If the judgment for two different individuals has the same subscript, then it will be the same for both individuals. Hence, we need only identify the A-sets of different persons. We shall do this through the use of superscripts. Consider, for example, the judgment ϕ_i for both individual $\mathbf{P}$ and $\mathbf{R}$. The A-set corresponding to ϕ_i for $\mathbf{P}$ will be denoted by $A_i{}^{\mathbf{P}}$ and the A-set corresponding to ϕ_i for $\mathbf{R}$ will be denoted by $A_i{}^{\mathbf{R}}$.

THE EMPLOYMENT OF THE CONCEPT OF PERSONAL STRUCTURE IN THE REMAINDER OF THIS CHAPTER

We have discussed the need for a model of the individual-in-the-organization which can reflect the interpersonal aspects of organizational problems. Since the organization is in part composed of the individual members, we need a model of the individual-in-the-organization which can depict significant differences between individuals. Since the complexity of the organization often forces us to partition it into smaller subparts, the contribution of significant individual differences in these smaller subparts is emphasized and we need models of organizations which can be partitioned into parts which are dominated by the perceptions of individuals in such parts.

In the remainder of this chapter we shall try to show how personal structures can be used to fill these types of needs. We shall try to indicate that it is possible to represent the individual mathematically in such a way that some organization problems can be *explicitly* related to differences (or similarities) among individuals in the organization. Some of the problems approached will be "translations" of recognized organizational problems, while others will be problems either suggested by the particular approach or suggested by the emphasis of this chapter. In the analysis of these problems, some conjectures will be made, but these will be more for the purpose of illustration than for the purpose of stating or suggesting conclusions.

Some General Comments about Personal Structures and Organizations

In this section we shall make some general remarks about possible relationships between personal structures and organizational behavior. In the remainder of the paper we may abbreviate "personal structure" by PS. The set of organizational states for which a particular judgment may be true will be called an *organizational A-set* to distinguish it from an ordinary *A*-set. Usually, however, when an organizational *A*-set is referred to, the fact that it is an organizational *A*-set will be implicit rather than explicit. Two *A*-sets or organizational *A*-sets of different persons which are equal or "nearly" equal will be called *congruent*. When two *A*-sets of different persons for the same judgment are quite different they will be called *incongruent*.

Let us first consider some possible effects of characteristics of personal structures upon organizational functioning. Suppose there are a set of judgments, Φ', upon which hinge the major decisions in an organization. For example, in a military organization such a set of judgments might be those concerned with threat evaluation. If the *A*-sets associated with these judgments are congruent for all major administrative personnel in an organization, then the organization will probably (depending upon influences external to the organization) display a stability of behavior even under a succession of managers from within the organization. If a primitive society can be considered to be an organization, then with the environment limited and unchanging and with the set of judgments Φ itself quite limited and unchanging, we can expect the "organizational" *A*-sets of different members to be congruent. Hence, the *A*-sets corresponding to a core of important judgments Φ' would also be congruent. Consequently, successive leaders might produce relatively few changes in comparison with modern organizations, where successive leaders may have vastly different backgrounds, and even view the set of core judgments Φ' differently.

We have ruled out spontaneous changes in an individual's personal structure; this means that we shall not consider in any detail the problems associated with the "stability" of an A-set. If, however, the A-sets associated with the judgments of Φ' are "unstable" and constantly changing, then this is somewhat the same as having a rapid succession of leaders with different backgrounds where we identify differences in background with incongruence in A-sets. In this case we could expect some instability in the behavior of the organization.

Certain general organizational policies may also influence the congruence of organizational A-sets. For example a policy of restricted interaction of organizational personnel may have several possible effects. It may decrease the congruence between A-sets and lead to something resembling anarchy. It may, on the other hand, increase the congruence of A-sets within a particular section of the organization, but decrease the possibilities of communication between sections.

A policy of extensive interaction, like that advocated by proselyters for the "new management," may have the desirable effect of increasing the congruence of A-sets associated with judgments in Φ' and, hence, increase agreement on principle decisions. Increased interaction may, however, also increase the number of judgments applicable to organizational states and this might affect the stability of the set of judgments Φ' itself.

Some More Specific Relations between Personal Structures and Organizational Problems

In this section we shall be concerned with some of the more specific problems an organization encounters in its attempts to reach certain goals. More specifically, we shall employ the concept of personal structures in: (1) A general discussion of organizational decision making; (2) an analysis of a simplified interpretation of organizational control; (3) an analysis of some major problems in selections between alternative actions; and (4) brief analyses of some still more specialized organizational problems.

THE DECISION PROBLEM IN THE ORGANIZATION

One of the advantages of an approach which takes into consideration the decision maker's view of the world in analyzing organizational decision making is that it is possible (although perhaps difficult) to consider the organization from the viewpoint of the decision maker. When the personal structure is formally described, it becomes possible to assess some of the effects of differences in the personal structures of the major decision makers upon organizational behavior. As an example it becomes meaningful to assess formally some of the effects of subgoals, e.g., personal subgoals, upon the behavior of the organization. It focuses attention upon, among other factors, the neglected role of interpersonal understanding in problem solution. Even within individual problem solving there is the problem of the dichotomy between the languages of perceiving and acting; "How hard a problem will be depends on the simplicity or complexity of the rules that define the correspondence between the two languages (those of perceiving and acting)." [11] When, as in organizations, we have a person making decisions who must depend upon others' perceptions as well as his own the problem of translation becomes connected with interpersonal understanding. The process of influence (and hence agreement on solutions) depends "not only upon interpersonal relations between influencer and influencee but also upon the structure and accepted rules of transformation of language employed by them." [12] The use of the PS is well suited for an analysis of this type of organization decision problem.

The organizational decision problem thus has aspects which, while perhaps present in broad interpretations of individual decision making, at least assume a position of increased importance in the context of the organization. Cyert and March [247b], among others, have pointed out that the organizational decision problem is a legitimate focus for research and organizational decisions may be mediated by quite different processes than individual choices.

Little is yet known about how business decisions are actually made (Cyert and March [247b]; Holt [233b]). It may turn out that some general policies have over-all effects upon the organizational decision problem. Restricting the type of communication to those which had been transmitted in the past, for example, may minimize the difficulties resulting from differences in PSs. The quality of the decisions made may not be improved, however. Policies which minimize the

[11] [233d], p. 113.
[12] [457e], p. 160.

difficulties which could result from differences in PSs by letting people get together and indirectly familiarize each other with some of the bounds to their more important A-sets may facilitate the making of some decisions but again this does not assure a minimum quality to the decisions made.

THE PROBLEM OF ORGANIZATIONAL CONTROL

We shall interpret the problem of organizational control to be one of deciding whether or not the organization is in a specified set of organizational states. For example a personnel executive may consider the organization, from his point of view, to be under control when the personnel turnover and absences due to sickness are below a certain level; i.e., the organization is in the A-set associated with the judgment that there is less than a critical amount of absenteeism and turnover. We shall use ϕ_c as the generic notation for the judgment that the organization is under control.

An organization may be too large, however, for all major decision makers to be in positions where they can make all the necessary judgments themselves. Therefore the problem of organizational control may involve reliance of principle decision makers upon information they obtain from others, i.e., it becomes in part a problem of interpersonal understanding. This is true *even* if we do not consider the fact that words are imperfect transmitters about the state of the organization, and *even* if we do not consider the fact that the decision maker may completely lack certain information. For even under such circumstances, problems of control and interpersonal understanding may arise from the lack of congruence of the A-sets of corresponding judgments.

To explore the type of problem we can consider when we can directly and formally represent the personal characteristics of decision makers, we shall consider an organization in which **P** and **Q** are both major decision makers. Let **P** be the one who makes the decisions and let **Q** be a "deputy" who makes decisions in **P**'s absence.[13] If we assume that the PS of **P** does not correspond exactly to the PS of **Q**, what can we say about **Q**'s decisions in **P**'s absence? To compare **P**'s and **Q**'s decision making, we need a reference point. If this reference point is **P**, the senior executive, then the question becomes the following: How can the decisions **Q** makes be related to

---

[13] There are, of course, problems, even within the framework of this chapter, concerning control of the organization by **P** alone, but we are more interested in those which are more uniquely the control problems of an organization.

those **P** would make? To analyze this question, we must consider the relation of **Q**'s PS to **P**'s PS. If the corresponding A-sets of **Q** are finer than those of **P** for judgments about control of the organization (i.e., if **Q**'s A-sets are contained in **P**'s A-sets—**Q** has a more *differentiated* PS), then **Q** will not take actions to change the organizational state when **P** would have taken such actions. If, on the other hand, the corresponding A-sets of **Q** are less fine than those of **P**, then **Q** will take some actions when **P** would not.

To give some further insights into the problem of organizational control from an interpersonal point of view, we consider **P**'s and **Q**'s ability to discriminate between organizational states.[14]

Let x_1 and x_2 be two of the states of the organization. There are several ways in which **Q** can distinguish or partially distinguish between these two states. If we consider a particular judgment, say ϕ_1, this may be true for state x_1, but not true for state x_2, or conversely. Two states will be said to be *partially distinguishable* by the judgment ϕ_i if the judgment can be true for one state but cannot be true for the other. More formally, using $\mathfrak{D}$ to denote "partially distinguishable" and adding a subscript to denote the judgment involved, we have for the definition of partial distinguishability

$$x_1 \mathfrak{D}_i x_2 \iff \phi_i(x_1) = \phi_i \quad \text{and} \quad \phi_i(x_2) = 0$$

or

$$\phi_i(x_1) = 0 \quad \text{and} \quad \phi_i(x_2) = \phi_i$$

where "$\iff$" stands for "if and only if," and where ϕ_i is the judgment i as a function (much as *"yes"-and-"no"* is a judgment function in a psychophysical experiment—either "yes" or "no" may be made in response to any presented stimulus) and $\phi_i(x_1) = \phi_i$ means that the judgment ϕ_i is actually made in response to the state x_1 while $\phi_i(x_1) = 0$ means that ϕ_i is not applicable to state x_1.

Q may also distinguish between two environmental states when (*a*) one judgment is true of one state, (*b*) another is true of the other state, but (*c*) neither is true of both states. When all three conditions hold, we shall say that the two states are *distinguishable* by the two judgments. More formally, two organizational states x_1 and x_2 are distinguishable by the judgments ϕ_i and ϕ_j (where distinguishability is represented by $\overline{\mathfrak{D}}$ and the subscripts are the indices of the two judgments) when the following holds:

---

[14] The following discussion of types of discrimination is largely based on Shelly [481] and upon a paper by Shelly presented at the September 1961 meetings of the American Psychological Association entitled "Judgments and Organizational Control."

$$x_1 \overline{\mathfrak{D}}_{ij} x_2 \iff [\boldsymbol{\phi}_i(x_1) = \phi_i \quad \text{and} \quad \boldsymbol{\phi}_j(x_2) = \phi_j$$

$$\text{and} \quad \boldsymbol{\phi}_i(x_2) = 0 \quad \text{and} \quad \boldsymbol{\phi}_j(x_1) = 0]$$

or

$$[\boldsymbol{\phi}_i(x_1) = 0 \quad \text{and} \quad \boldsymbol{\phi}_j(x_2) = 0 \quad \text{and} \quad \boldsymbol{\phi}_i(x_2) = \phi_i \quad \text{and} \quad \boldsymbol{\phi}_j(x_1) = \phi_j]$$

On the basis of the preceding two definitions, we obviously have the following relationships:

$$x_1 \mathfrak{D}_i x_2 \iff x_2 \mathfrak{D}_i x_1$$

$$x_1 \overline{\mathfrak{D}}_i x_2 \iff x_2 \overline{\mathfrak{D}}_i x_1$$

$$x_1 \overline{\mathfrak{D}}_{ij} x_2 \implies x_1 \mathfrak{D}_i x_2 \quad \text{and} \quad x_1 \mathfrak{D}_j x_2$$

We shall now reconsider some of the relations between the decisions of **P** and of **Q**. Thus, let x_{t_1} be a state of the organization at time t_1 which is recognized as being clearly under control, i.e., a state for which $\boldsymbol{\phi}_c(x_{t_1}) = \phi_c$. Then suppose that the decision to take action to "restore the organization to control" at time t_2 requires that $x_{t_1} \overline{\mathfrak{D}}_{ic} x_{t_2}$ for some i, i.e., the new state at time t_2 is distinguishable from x_{t_1} under our preceding definitions. Under what circumstances will **P** and **Q** make the same decision? They will make the same decision if $A_c{}^P$ and $A_c{}^Q$ are the same and the union of all of those A-sets disjoint from A_c is the same for both **P** and **Q**. Note that it is not necessary that all the A-sets disjoint from A_c be the same, but that simply their union be the same.

Suppose now we make the same assumption about the state x_{t_1} but require that for action to be taken to restore O to a "state of control" at time t_2 we need only $x_{t_1} \mathfrak{D}_c x_{t_2}$. In this case, however, **P** and **Q** will make the same decision if and only if $A_c{}^P = A_c{}^Q$. Thus, when partial distinguishability is required, then complete congruence of $A_c{}^P$ and $A_c{}^Q$ can guarantee that the decisions of **Q** will be the same as **P** would also make.

Although the preceding is only a very simplified analysis, it is hoped that it has at least shown how personal structures can be made an integral part of the analysis of organizational control from the viewpoint of individual differences.

THE CHOICE BETWEEN ALTERNATIVE ACTIONS

In the preceding section we have concentrated upon those judgments which underlie a decision to act. We now go beyond this "predecision" behavior and examine executive action from the viewpoint of personal structures and individual differences. (The analysis will be restricted by the difficulties in approaching the relation of action to personal structures—for an initial attack on this problem see [484].)

There are two principal problems in incorporating actions into a model involving personal structures. First, the same actions may not appear the same to different persons in the organizations. Second, not only may the actions themselves be viewed as being different but also the same action may be viewed as having different results. We shall consider each of these in turn.

The fact that the same act might be perceived differently by different individuals is probably not surprising. This follows from the approach already adopted, for any act can be looked upon as a "continuous" *sequence of environmental states* when viewed from initiation to termination. Since we have already permitted different persons to associate different judgments to the same environmental states it follows that they may see an act as "passing through different states." Thus, under this development, we see that individuals may have different perceptions of the same act. Conversely, of course, different acts—consisting of different sequences of states and consequences—may be viewed as the same act.

Instead of considering an act to be a "sequence" of states, we will now assume that an act will be perceived as a "whole" and that different individuals may see the same "whole" act differently; i.e., individuals may attach different judgments to the "same act" or the same judgment to "different acts." Thus, we shall treat responses somewhat the same way we have treated states of the environment (see [484] for a more detailed development).

An act, symbolized by **a**, will be defined to change an environment from one state x to another $a(x)$. This new state of the environment, $a(x)$, falls in some A-sets of an individual but not in others. The result of the act will be viewed differently by two individuals if the A-sets containing the changed environmental state differ for the two individuals.

We can now consider the relation of acts to organization decisions when the analysis considers individual differences. We will proceed as follows. Let us consider again the PSs of **P** and **Q**. The PSs of **P** and **Q** may be the same, but **P** and **Q** may perceive the *acts* as being different, or **P** and **Q** may perceive the acts as being the same but may, through their individual PSs, view the *results* of the act differently. This gives rise to two principal cases that we shall consider.

First let **P** and **Q** have the same PS but view the acts differently. In this situation they cannot agree on the choice of an alternative, even though they agree upon the characterization of the current state of the organization, and even though they agree on the characterization of the state they want the organization to go to. In this situation (without considering the possibility of changing the PS of either **P**

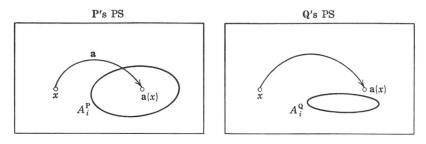

FIGURE 2

or **Q**), **P** must either completely delegate the choice of action to **Q** and hold him responsible for achieving the organization state that they agree upon, or he must make the choice himself. It may not be feasible to change the judgments of **P** or **Q**, for the critical judgments may be very difficult to change or success in changing such critical judgments might have undesirable "side effects."

Suppose, secondly, that **P** and **Q** agree upon their labeling of the act but have different PSs. In this case, they may see the same act as being required in different situations, or they may see the same act as producing different results. This latter possibility is presented in Fig. 2, where the action **a** is perceived as the same by both **P** and **Q**, but the results of the act are perceived as being different.

In Fig. 2, the A-set for **P** corresponding to the judgment ϕ_i is larger for **P** than for **Q**, and hence **P** sees the action producing a result that **Q** does not see.[15]

THE PS IN MORE SPECIALIZED ORGANIZATIONAL PROBLEMS

The importance of the PS in analyzing organizational problems arises from the fact that, even in highly computerized operations,[16] it is still man who, upon the basis of his perceptions of the world and the organization in particular, makes many of the decisions. This may

---

[15] We are again speaking here as though all the states of the set A_i were something accessible to the memory of both **P** and **Q**. This is obviously not the case. A part of this unrealism—that concerned with fixed A-sets being available in memory—is taken care of through the introduction of A-sets dependent upon the state of the individual (Shelly [485]).

[16] Computerization does not always lessen the dependence upon PSs. Automation, for example, may eliminate the jobs of 50 persons not requiring an IQ above 100 but require the more highly refined PSs of 15–20 persons with much higher IQs. Such persons may be much more difficult to obtain.

be especially true of "terminal" decisions. When men make the decisions, two questions of organization and information design immediately arise: (1) Given a particular PS, what kind of information should be funneled to a particular man so that he can make the "best" decision possible? (2) Given certain unalterable characteristics of the type of information, what PS characteristics permit the best use of this information in making decisions? Aspects of both of these questions will appear repeatedly in the following.

We have previously discussed the problem of organization control in very broad terms. There we saw one way how judgments of individuals within the organization could become one of the factors influencing the future states of an organization. The judgments of the individuals, through their effects upon the selection of an act, also place constraints on future states of the organization. In a very large organization especially, these judgments can become difficult to "control," since the larger the number of persons compounds the difficulty of controlling how they see or structure the possible states of the organization. Larger numbers of persons also permit greater opportunities for variation in the people joining an organization. This provides further opportunity for variation in the circumstances which can arise within the organization, and consequently, for variation in the interaction between persons within the organization. In the following we shall examine some aspects of this "generalized problem of organizational control" from the viewpoint of individual differences.

In an organization certain judgments are more critical than others. The control of persons within an organization then centers around establishing the congruence of those A-sets associated with the more critical judgments Φ'.

Consider now the quite common situation in which an action by one person must be followed by a suitable action by another person. Let the first person be $\mathbf{Q}$ and the second person be $\mathbf{P}$. Suppose that action $\mathbf{a}_i$ follows whenever $\mathbf{Q}$ makes judgment ϕ_i, and when this occurs, it should be followed by $\mathbf{P}$ taking action $\mathbf{a}_j$. In order for $\mathbf{P}$ to take action $\mathbf{a}_j$ (which we are assuming will be dependent upon his making judgment ϕ_j), the state to which the organization is changed to by $\mathbf{a}_i$ must be included in A_j; i.e., we must have $\mathbf{a}_i(A_i) \subset A_j$. If the inclusion is strict, then occasionally $\mathbf{P}$ may take action $\mathbf{a}_j$ without $\mathbf{Q}$'s having taken action $\mathbf{a}_i$. Depending on circumstances, this may or may not be undesirable.

If we have a whole sequence of such required actions $(\mathbf{a}_i)$, $i = 1, \cdots, k$ and their associated judgments, such that $\mathbf{a}_i$ must immediately precede $\mathbf{a}_{i+1}$; then by a simple extension of the preceding development, we must have $\mathbf{a}_i(A_i) \subset A_{i+1}$ for $i = 1, \cdots, k$. Such a nesting property may not be difficult to achieve. If, however, there are certain difficulties associated with action $\mathbf{a}_i$ being taken when action $\mathbf{a}_{i-1}$ has not preceded it, then the problem of organizational control could become very difficult. In this situation the fundamental problem may be *to design an organization* so that action $\mathbf{a}_i$ being taken without $\mathbf{a}_{i-1}$ has at most the cost of wasted effort associated with it.

The problem of coordination between parts of an organization is, like the problem of control, dependent in part on the relations between the PSs of individuals within the organization. Coordination depends upon the communication of information. But here the term "information" is meant to include concepts used in one part of the organization, which may not be really understood by other parts of the organization. Thus, while organizational control is largely concerned with the congruence of A-sets corresponding to common judgments coordination is more concerned with judgments which may have no A-set in the PS of some organization members. (We can, of course, also have the problem of coordination if the judgments are held in common and only the A-sets themselves differ.)

We shall consider the problem of coordination to be one of communicating information concerning the state of one part of an organization to another part of the organization when the judgments employed (i.e., method of description used) differ for the communicating parts. We shall label the two parts of the organization O_o (for the part of the organization originating the communication) and O_r (for the part of the organization receiving the information). There are several ways of defining more formally what is to be meant by "a part" of an organization. We shall, however, take what appears to be the simplest formalization; we shall, within the set of states of the organization, consider two disjoint subsets, and each of these subsets of states will be considered to be "a part" of the organization.[17]

Accepting the preceding definition of "a part" of the organization, we can apply the approach of this chapter to a further analysis of coordination. Consider first the situation in Fig. 3, where $\mathbf{Q}$ is the senior executive of O_o and $\mathbf{P}$ is the senior executive of O_r. Let both $\mathbf{P}$ and $\mathbf{Q}$ have the same judgments ϕ_1, ϕ_2, and ϕ_3, each applying the judgments to *only their part of the organization*. Now, even though both have the same judgments, coordination is not possible, for the sets $A_1{}^Q$ and $A_1{}^P$, for

---

[17] Perhaps a preferable, but more complex, way of representing parts of an organization would be to consider the states of a part of the organization to be "marginal images" of a product space which represents the states of the organization as a whole.

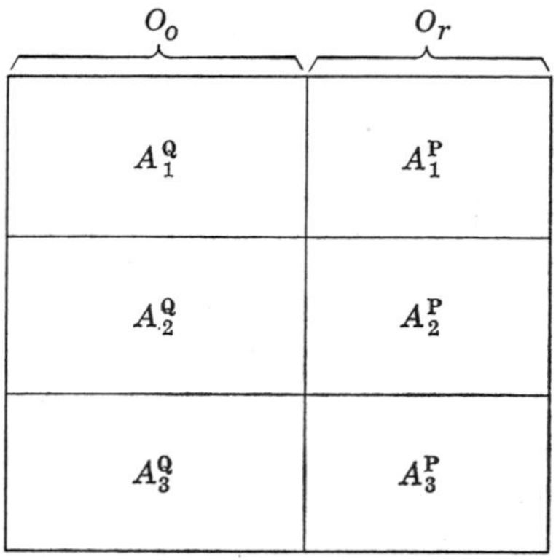

O_o O_r

A_1^Q	A_1^P
A_2^Q	A_2^P
A_3^Q	A_3^P

FIGURE 3

example, are completely disjoint. If **P** must base his choice of action partly upon the basis of the state of O_o, then he has no real basis for making a decision. Hence, there must be some way of relating the A-sets A_i^Q and A_i^P for coordination to take place.

Consider now a third individual in the organization whom we shall designate by **R**. Let this person have as the domain of his A-sets the entire organization as in Fig. 4 (where the dotted lines represent the A-sets for **P** and **Q**). If **R** says that O_o is in a state for which the judgment ϕ_1 is true, **P** may feel that he can choose an act dependent upon ϕ_1^P for he knows that, within the range of his experience, both he and **R** make the same judgment in response to the same state in O_r.

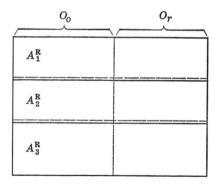

FIGURE 4

We can also consider the situation in which **Q** and **P** have completely disjoint sets of judgments. This situation is represented in Fig. 5. Obviously, here again coordination is impossible for there is no basis for **P** making use of any of **Q**'s judgments about the state of O_o in selecting any action.

Previously, the problem of coordination consisted of finding ways for **P** to estimate the domains of the judgments applicable to states in O_o. It is possible, however, that **Q**'s principal interest in the states of O_o is in what might follow from these states with regard to the future states of O_r. In such a case **Q** does not need to know the domain of the judgment ϕ_i (the A-set A_i) in O_o. In the situation depicted in Fig. 5, **P** does not necessarily have to know the A-sets of the judgments ϕ_1, ϕ_3, and ϕ_5 in the perception of **Q** if he knows, for example, that $\phi_1 \rightarrow \mathbf{a}_1(x) = x_1^P$, where "$\rightarrow$" means "leads to" and x_1^P is a state in A_1^P; this latter information will be sufficient. There are, of course, other phases to intra-organization coordination which could be discussed, but in the following we shall restrict ourselves as indicated.

Consider now the situation depicted in Fig. 6. The judgments of **Q** are ϕ_1^Q and ϕ_2^Q which are applicable to states in O_o. The judgments of **P** are ϕ_3^P, ϕ_4^P, ϕ_5^P, and ϕ_6^P, of which ϕ_3^P and ϕ_4^P are applicable to O_o, and ϕ_5^P and ϕ_6^P are applicable to O_r. (The A-sets of **Q** are outlined with dashed lines and those of **P** by solid lines.) If we assume that the action **Q** selects depends upon the judgments he applies to the states of O_o, then the judgments **P** applies to states in O_o are useless because these judgments give him no information as to what action **Q** will select. Consequently, **P**'s judgments about O_o do not give him any information about the future states of O_r.

We can also have a need for coordination when, as in Fig. 7, **P**'s judgments about O_o correspond to **Q**'s and their A-sets are congruent,

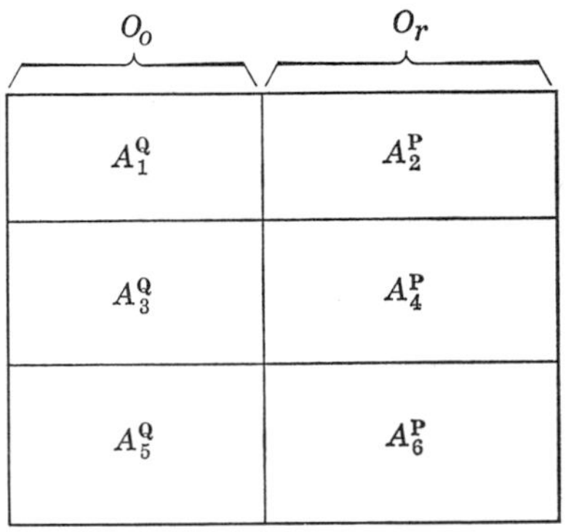

FIGURE 5

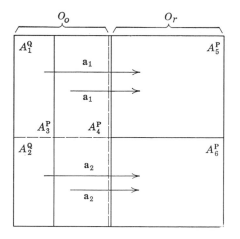

FIGURE 6

but his judgments about O_r are inappropriate for determining the *results* of **Q**'s actions. In this case, his judgments are not sensitive to the results of the actions **Q** selects. (Again **Q**'s A-sets are outlined by dashed lines.)

We can now describe at least two possible roles for a coordinator. A coordinator **R** who can make all the judgments which both **P** and **Q** can make could understand what was going to happen and report

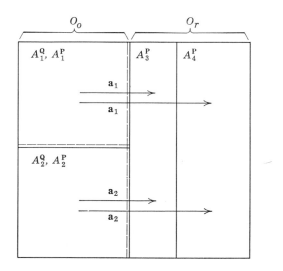

FIGURE 7

this in a "meaningful" way to **P** (for he would have **P**'s judgments as well as **Q**'s). A second role can develop when **P** is already able to make all of the judgments **Q** can make. Therefore, in order to make a contribution (*a*) **R**'s *A*-sets would have to be more congruent to the *A*-sets of **Q** than **P**'s, or (*b*) **R** would have to have judgments whose *A*-sets corresponded satisfactorily to the *ranges* of the alternative actions selected by **Q**. In these cases it would then be necessary to delegate to **R** (as "coordinator") the authority to respond to the state of O_o or to the results of the actions **Q** selects. In the preceding case, **R**, as a coordinator, acts largely as an interpreter (*interpretive coordination*) and in the last situations, **R**, as a coordinator, acts as a specialist (*specialized coordination*). We might offer the hypothesis that, any time specialized coordination is necessary, the coordinator will have more organizational power than when interpretive coordination is possible. The rise of the scientifically educated manager may be regarded as evidence for the greater influence of a specialized coordinator.

In addition to problems of control and coordination there are, of course, other types of organizational problems in which the PS of the individual members becomes clearly important. We briefly mention a few below. The problems of planning and adjusting to change are discussed separately in the next section.

The "age-old" problem of the individual *versus* the organization may be viewed as an extension of the problem of coordination. Let us assume for the purposes of speculation, that identity for the individual is closely associated with the existence of relatively unique judgments. Then the desire (or need, as some would have it) to achieve an identity within the organization can be viewed as a force which creates problems of coordination. The solution of the problems of coordination takes organizational time, effort, and possibly funds, and so will be objected to in varying amounts by the organization.

Very closely related to the problem of creating or maintaining an individual's identity is the problem of the newly arrived individual in the organization. Having not learned the organizational culture (those judgments and their associated *A*-sets which are congruent for almost all organizational members), he may, in spite of selection techniques, have a PS quite different from the remaining members of the organization. He will have to make discriminations which he cannot make, and there will be discriminations he does make which are irrelevant. He may, for example, only partially distinguish between two organizational states when he needs to distinguish more fully between two organizational states, and so on. The newly arrived individual's PS needs to be changed with reference to the decisions he is to make. We know little about what changes need to be made, especially if it is desired to minimize effort.

Another phenomenon clearly associated with organizational culture and the PSs of individual members are the successive waves of new judgments, or "okay" words. Certain judgments have a value associated with them long before their A-sets become stabilized. Because of the unstable nature of the A-sets associated with these fad words, the problem of communication becomes more difficult although their frequency of usage may give the opposite illusion. The A-sets may mean different things to different persons in different parts of the organization and, hence, they may lead to "uncoordinated changes" in different parts of the organization.

Organizational Change and Planning

Change, and the achievement of stability in the face of change, are of fundamental importance in modern organizations. In particular, the changing environment of the organization produces "compensating" intraorganizational changes which may become the central concern of some of those analyzing organizational behavior (e.g., Forrester [233a]; Haberstroh [457b]).

Change within or external to the organization requires the initiation of many new organizational activities. March and Simon [367] have in this regard pointed to the importance of the search activities in solving the organizational problems produced by some type of change. The organization of search activities, however, leads to many of the same problems met in the managing of research—one of the major ones being that the activity can only be evaluated through its use by others, and these others may not have the time to understand fully the information presented (Rubenstein [457d]). Thus, change may not be adjusted to successfully and the organization may, in some intuitive sense, become "unstable." To delay a decision may risk a buildup of instabilities until a major crisis is reached, but, alternatively, to make a decision quickly can involve risks of unforeseen consequences and magnitudes (e.g., described in Blau [75]).

The personal structures of individuals in the organization play a central role in both prevention or "correction" for change (discussed earlier under "Organizational Control") and in the adjustment to change (the problem of "stability"). "The area of control is intimately connected with organization design and analysis. These are, in turn, intimately connected with individual character formation and behavior and ultimately with the whole fabric of society" (Cooper [134]). Because of the role that personal structures play in organizational adjustment to change, we have the following fundamental problem: An organizational environment in which the possibility of change is not viewed as threatening is one in which, simultaneously, controls over unstabilizing change have been weakened. Personal structures conducive to perceiving alternative solutions are not the type most amenable to the receipt of specific instructions. Thus, recursive adjustment, and the techniques of recursive adjustment (e.g., those employed in chance constrained programming) [18] begin to play prominent roles for organizations reacting to a changed environment where maintenance of stability is a continuing problem. We shall, nonetheless, ignore most of the sequential aspects in order to continue to keep things simple.

EFFECTS OF CHANGE

We have already alluded to the effects of one specific type of change—those effects resulting from introducing a new person into an organization. With the introduction of a new person into a major decision-making post, new judgments, or new A-sets for old judgments, affect organizational behavior. The result is that other persons within the organization must learn new judgments and/or alter their A-sets for established judgments. Thus, the PS of a major decision maker can be very important as a specific source of change. In the remainder of this section, however, we shall be concerned with change and its effects on a more general level.

Change, whether internal or external to the organization, places stresses upon communication. Change leads to the introduction of new concepts and changes the domain (the A-sets) of old concepts. The concepts (or judgments) used in the organization may often change in *clusters*, as occurs, for example, when a new technology contains so many new concepts that new parts of an organization must be formed by collecting persons who are experienced in employing these new or changed judgments. Once such sections are established there arise the problems of communicating between those already established parts of the organization and the new parts of the organization. This, of course, creates problems of coordination such as those which were previously discussed.

Even if an organization does not establish a new section (in response to environmental changes), there may arise many communication

---

[18] See Charnes and Cooper [112].

difficulties. The organization must communicate with the external world and, to do this, it must adopt at least some of the concepts of the external world. A further difficulty here is that the A-sets of members external to the organization and those internal to it may not be congruent because judgments used extensively within an organization may derive their *primary significance from an organizational context*. This may be particularly true for newly introduced judgments. Then certain members of the organization must essentially function as "coordinators" with the external world. But by their very functioning as coordinators, they may lose part of their "organizational culture" and thus find it difficult to communicate with other individuals within the organization.

The difficulties of a single person or a part of the organization communicating with other parts of the organization may be further increased through the way the organization has been structured. The structure of the organization—the division of the organization into "boxes"—may lead the parts of the organization to adopt certain judgments and their associated A-sets internally, and thus limit diversification of PSs for members of that part of the organization. Thus, a "solution" to problems of interpersonal communication within one part of an organization may increase the problems of communication of that part with other parts of the organization. *Too good* a solution to the problem of interpersonal communication within a part of the organization *may even make changes external to that part "unperceptible"* in that new states of the organization will be neither completely nor partially distinguishable from old states of the organization.

Probably one of the most important effects of intra- or extraorganizational change is that actions no longer accomplish certain ends. The old routines are destroyed. This may simply be because the new judgments produce changes in the A-sets for old judgments which (a) lead to the conclusion that the old results of acts are not good enough or (b) alter the domain of acts so that what appear to be "old" actions, because they are tied to the same judgments, no longer accomplish the same ends. These two situations are portrayed in Fig. 8.

In Fig. 8a, the A-set for ϕ_j, the states of which are desired results for action a_i, is shifted; the old action a_i no longer leads to a desired state, the desired state now being in A_j' rather than in A_j. In Fig. 8b, the domain of the action a_i is "shifted" so that the action a_i (labeled a_i') now produces different results. A similar analysis holds if we consider ϕ_i and ϕ_j to be new "more organizationally acceptable" judgments.

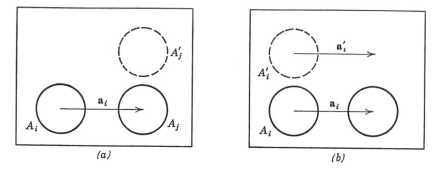

(a)   (b)

FIGURE 8

Destruction of all or part of a routine implies that the previous organizational culture is also destroyed to some extent. Individuals are then forced back upon judgments (and their corresponding A-sets) which are now held in common with fewer organization members so that, once again, the difficulties of interpersonal understanding are increased.

It often seems desirable to effect adjustments to intra- or extra-organizational change in a way that will cause minimal alterations in the structure or personnel of the organization. This often means, however, that decision-making authority is shifted, at least indirectly, through making substitutions among those who occupy the roles of advisor. If there are persons who are already in the organization with PSs adequate to understand the changed situation, then the change may be adjusted to within a minimum of disruption in the total organization. Such persons are able to make the significant discriminations. An organization may be designed to achieve such an adjustment to change. For example, a military organization may continue to maintain a number of specialists, even though some of these specialists may never be needed. Thus, when the organization already has individuals whose PSs permit them to understand the changed situation, then the organization is able to use individuals who perhaps already share a large part of the organizational culture with other members. When, on the other hand, the organization does not contain such members, then they may have to "import" individuals who do not share much of the organizational culture. This may itself produce further changes.

The ability to adapt to change, of course, also depends upon the adaptability of individuals within the organization. If the PSs of the individual members can be easily altered, then the organization may adapt to changes quite easily although, of course, this is not always necessarily the case. On the other hand, if the individuals cannot easily be taught to make new discriminations and drop old ones, then the adjustment to change will almost certainly be a difficult process.

PLANNING CHANGE

In planning and executing plans (programming), we begin to deal with a somewhat different problem. The planning of change might be viewed as a "rational" adjustment to changes which are occurring. It would seem, however, to go beyond this. Adjustment to changes which have occurred is pretty much the problem of organizational control. It is recognized that the organization is in a state to which some or several judgments indicating dissatisfaction are attached. In planning for change, however, it is expected that *unless something is done*, judgments of dissatisfaction *will be made* at some future time. The role of PSs is apparently different for the two types of processes.

Unless things are really falling apart at the seams in the adjustment to change, there are usually spots of crisis and this localization of crisis reduces the information processing problems for the major decision makers. The contingencies which must be considered in planning change are much greater and the details can become too numerous and complex to be absorbed by a single individual. Even though a computer program may be able to handle thousands of variables, the individual planners, *prior to the development of the program*, have placed a considerable amount of structure on the situation.[19] Thus, those estimates of crisis points in the future of an organization may become very dependent upon the personal structures of the major planners.

When we begin to approach plans for points of time quite distant in the future, the contingencies increase even more. The need to place some type of order regarding these contingencies increases still more, and the plans will probably depend more and more upon the characteristics of the personal structures of the major planners. The mass of contingencies can make the more distant situation so ambiguous

---

[19] This statement is based upon the proposition that decision makers wish to understand the decision they are making. It may eventually become necessary (in order to achieve certain goals) that this restraint be given up. In such a case, although we may plan segments of history, we shall watch it unfold much as when we did before we could meticulously plan such segments of history.

that demanding decisions from a planner is somewhat like forcing him to respond with descriptive phrases to an ink blot.

To analyze these problems, let us assume that those A-sets which are organizationally large (e.g., those A-sets which include large numbers of organizational states) will be the most influential for the planner. Under this assumption, let us make a somewhat finer analysis of the problems of planning to illustrate how personal structures can be used in the analysis of planning. If future plans do indeed depend quite heavily upon the personal perceptions of the major planners, those attempting to control the organization must do one of two things. They must either (a) make the plans themselves or control the perceptions of those who do make the plans, or (b) they must be certain that the plans are sufficiently modifiable through execution so that most "undesirable" influences can be eliminated. We shall discuss these alternatives below.

If it is desirable to control the effect of the personal structures of those making long-range plans then, under the preceding assumption, it is desirable to ensure that the PS's of these planners contain large organizational A-sets which are congruent to those of the major executives or policy makers. This is apparently one of the purposes of defining "organizational objectives." If these objectives (as judgments) cover large ranges of desirable organizational states, then they may have a large influence on the plans made by the planners. If, furthermore, these objectives are relatively impersonal (e.g., are common to many organizational members with congruent A-sets), then it is easier to replace planners should the need arise.

Continuing with the assumption that large A-sets have a significant influence on plans, there may be further ways of refining the control of plans. One possible way is through confining plans to intersections of A-sets. For example, let **P** be a major executive of an organization and let **Q** be a planner. Now if **P** selects judgment ϕ_i *and* makes certain that A_i^Q is congruent to A_i^P, he may confine planning activities to states for which this judgment holds. The planner is to select organizational states *contained within* A_i^P. Thus, instead of defining an over-all goal the major decision maker may only define subgoals (goals within a category). Through the forcing of plans into such categories the major decision maker may be more easily able to control the nature of plans.

In Fig. 9 we give an example of how the device of using only subgoals might work to the advantage of the major executive, **P**. Figure 9a presents the part of the PS of **P** containing the A-set A_i^P and the organizational "goal" A-set, A_g^P; Fig. 9b presents the part of the PS of **Q** containing the A-set A_i^Q, and the organizational "goal" A-set A_g^Q. It can

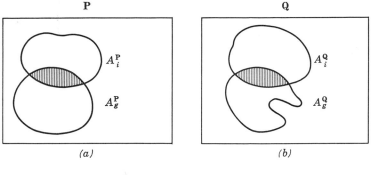

P

Q

A_i^P

A_g^P

A_i^Q

A_g^Q

(a)

(b)

FIGURE 9

be seen that whereas the sets A_i^P and A_i^Q are congruent, the A-sets A_g^P and A_g^Q, the organizational "goal" A-sets, are quite different. By restricting the goal A-set to A_i^Q, **P** can obtain a subgoal set, $A_i^Q \cap A_g^Q$, which is approximately equal to his own subgoal set $A_i^P \cap A_g^P$. It should also be clear that if **P** pushes the categorization too far he is again in difficulty. Policy makers need methods based on other than intuition for executing this procedure.

We have said that a second way a major organizational executive or policy maker could control the planning process is through the programming phase. By programming we shall mean what would generally come under the execution of plans. We shall consider a plan to consist of a set of contingent statements of the form, "If ϕ_i is true, then take action a_j." We shall assume an execution of a plan to be the plan *plus* any additions to the plan made by the person in control of the execution. Only a single example will be presented.

Figure 10*a* presents a part of the PS of **P**, a major decision maker who is in control of executing a plan. The set A_i^P is a set which is congruent for all organization members of the organization. The set A_d^P is a set of organizational states considered by **P** to be desirable.

In Fig. 10*b* the plan is represented. It says that, if judgment ϕ_j is true, then take action a_k. $a_k(A_j)$ is the image of the set A_j under the action a_k, i.e., it is the set of organization states which result from taking the action a_k for every state in the set A_j. As can be seen, it does not overlap very much with the set A_d^P outlined by a dashed line.

Figure 10*c* shows the execution of the plan by **P**. He restricts the plan to a subset of A_i^P (indicated by the shaded part of A_i^P) and in this way restricts the results of the plan so that most of the resulting organizational states are regarded as desirable by **P**. (The result of the executed plan is also shown by a shaded area.)

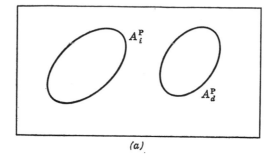

(a)

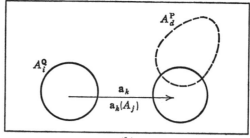

(b)

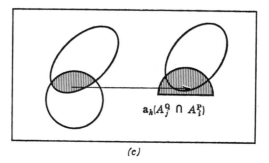

(c)

FIGURE 10

Although the examples in this section are based upon actual observations (which have been highly distilled however) it is still clear that if this kind of analysis is to be of other than intuitive help to decision makers a great deal more detailed development, including many estimation procedures, needs to be provided. Yet it is hoped that the preceding shows that even in complex areas, e.g., in the area of planning and the execution of plans, it is feasible to formally consider certain *individual* characteristics in the analysis of organizational problems. This is, after all, the point of the entire chapter.

Personal Structures and Personal Satisfactions

THE SOCIAL GOALS OF AN ORGANIZATION

In the preceding we have spoken as though organizations, or at least sections of organizations, had single goals. This is not the case, even for parts of an organization, for there is no clear agreement on what is to be meant by "best." As decision making technology evolves, indeed, the meaning of "best" becomes less clear [486]. Organizations do have multiple goals; ". . . it seems reasonable enough to say that few if any firms maximize opportunity profit." [20] Indeed, "all social units, including organizations, are multifunctional units" [21] and as such have multiple goals.

This is altogether natural. The organization can offer the individual in it many satisfactions, many of which are highly personal. It can create an atmosphere which the individual finds appealing or unappealing, friendly or unfriendly, and so on. Its structure, as well as its functions, creates parts of the content of the jobs it provides. If for the moment we are permitted to draw a speculative conclusion we might say that, on the basis of available information, the atmosphere an organization emits may detract from personal satisfactions, but its structure, through adding content to jobs, is the primary source of personal satisfaction from an organization. Herzber, Mausner, and Synderman [267] studied the satisfactions of accountants and engineers and found the job context to be the factor which detracted from job satisfactions. Gurin, Veroff, and Feld [245] also found that factors extrinsic to the job could detract from the satisfactions of the job. Both studies, as well as a study by Morse [406] found, however, that the primary satisfactions were obtained from the content of the job itself. With increased automation we shall consequently have to modify the structure of the organization to put new content into jobs. It will probably be necessary to restore some of the depleted satisfactions an organization can offer by imaginatively contrived organizational structures which both create new values and new jobs. But this is getting beyond ourselves and, indeed, beyond the somewhat modest aims of this chapter—to show that the role of individual differences can be explicitly included in the formulation of a variety of organizational problems.

---

[20] [125], p. 47.
[21] [183], p. 259.

PERSONAL STRUCTURES AND SOCIAL GOALS

In the preceding sections we have discussed possible ways of using the concept of personal structures to analyze simplifications of observed organizational problems. Most of the organizational situations discussed contained problems because there were circumstances in these situations which could impede progress toward some over-all organizational goal. However, in the immediately preceding subsection we have argued that organizations have multiple goals and that among these multiple goals are the personal and social needs of its members.

A question now arises with respect to how easily personal structures can be employed in analyzing the problems of achieving personal satisfactions for members of an organization. Although the major aim of this chapter has been to relate personal structures to an analysis of some of the more widely observed organizational problems it is believed that the concept of personal structure will prove to be particularly important for the analysis of organizational problems which restrict the attainment of the personal and social satisfactions of the organizational members.

It is well documented that social satisfactions need not conflict with the goals of efficiency and profit. In one study by the Institute for Social Research,[22] "The units achieving the best performance [were] much more likely than the poor performance units to have [had] managers who [dealt] with their subordinates in a supportive manner and [built] high group loyalty and teamwork." In one plant, production estimates failed to be met for three years until a reorganization occurred which created more horizontal relationships as well as extended incentive pay; following this reorganization production estimates were exceeded. Other studies have confirmed these findings (e.g. [301], [305], and [306]). In the remainder of this section, however, we shall be only peripherally interested in the contributions of personal satisfactions to other goals, such as increased efficiency. Instead, we shall be concerned with the problems of organization design which *directly* promote personal and social satisfactions as goals in themselves.

THE DESIGN OF INTERPERSONAL OPTIMIZATION

The emerging social problems of organizations are already becoming apparent, and several writers and speakers have already made proposals for their solution or amelioration. Increased decentralization and delegation (McGregor [457c]; Cordiner [137]; and Likert

---

[22] Likert [348], p. 458.

[348]) and more horizontal relationships (Jasinski [295]) have been proposed to mitigate the impersonalizing effects of the new technology. As a counter measure, personnel men have been urged to take broader roles in organizational planning (Henneman [264]; Kyle [328]; and Odiorne [423]), and there have been charges made that social scientists have been too conservative in their treatment of the organization's emerging social problems—charges that social science representatives in organizations have become "servants of power" instead of the creators of new values (Baritz [42]).

But will the social climate of America, with its puritanical origins, sanction the large expenditures of effort which would be required in designing organizations which will have personal satisfaction as a principal goal? The answer would seem to be "yes," with increasing frequency. Ever since the pioneering study at Western Electric Company's Hawthorne Works in the late 1920's and early 1930's,[23] increased importance has been attached to the position of individual satisfactions in an organization. It is true that the implicit restraint here, and in many subsequent studies, was that the improved social climate also result in increased efficiency, but there are growing indications that even this restraint is being relaxed.

Unhappiness, chronic disappointment, loneliness, and any number of other "mental" complaints are no longer being viewed only as inevitabilities of human existence. National programs for improved mental health are one evidence of this. Nor are we without experience in organizations devoted to such ends. The design of organizations like country clubs—if "design" is a proper word—are cases where, in some loose way, the optimization of member happiness is an objective. We can probably expect the tendency to accommodate organizations to the relevant individuals to increase, and especially so as we develop suitable ways of effecting designs. "This, in turn would probably lead to different social fabrics and it might also produce a different 'Social Ethic.'"[24] Nor is this possibility confined only to the work of management scientists, administrative theorists, and others whose interest is in organization design. The growing stress in psychotherapy on environmental circumstances will, for instance, also contribute to designing organizations to accommodate the personal needs of their members.

From the *point of view of personal structures*, an analysis of some of the fundamental problems which might be encountered in the de-

---

[23] [452].
[24] [134], p. 59.

sign of an organization for optimizing interpersonal relations is discussed in Shelly [486f]. Generalizing directly the ideas of that paper to organizations, however, leads to new problems.

The major theme of the above mentioned paper on intentional optimization was that it was desirable to eliminate those judgments which were unpleasant, but that the psychotherapist's own personal structure limited him to actions which were *intended* to optimize the patient's adjustment but might not achieve this goal because of "misperceptions." In the organization there is the additional restriction that one act *necessarily* affects a large number of persons, *each of whom has a different personal structure*. Therefore, within the organizational context, there needs to be additional criteria as to what is best or at least "desirable."

Therefore, since in an organization there are at least two persons and these persons will differ in their personal structures, the problem of interpersonal optimization involves the employment of two criteria. The first, the one discussed in Shelly [486f], is the one used in determining those organizational states unpleasant for each member of the organization; more expansively, the first criterion is something like a utility function for the individual members of the organization defined over the possible states of the organization. The second criterion must reflect the negative values attached to various types of dissatisfaction for different members of the organization; again, the second type of criterion can be viewed as a variety of social utility functions defined over the set of possible organizational states. One thing seems clear, however, as Churchman and Eisenberg [486c] have pointed out, within organizations (or groups in their case) the "best" will have to be based as much upon differences between persons as upon their similarities.

If we focus on differences in PSs, then the problem of optimizing interpersonal relations in an organization can be viewed in part as an extension of the problem of organizational control discussed earlier in this chapter. In the problem of organizational control, we considered two persons in the organization, P and Q, and made some comparisons of the decisions they would make based upon their PSs. Then the specific decision considered was whether or not the organization was in a state which required some action to be taken to try to restore the organization to a state of "control." If we call those judgments where the organization was not in a state of control "unpleasant judgments," and simultaneously consider these unpleasant judgments for both P and Q, then we have established an organizational analogue of the "therapeutic" situation described in Shelly [486f]. We have thus presented a method for analyzing, in a highly simplified way, some of the problems of interpersonal satisfactions in an organization.

In the following we will very briefly expand upon this approach. The aim will be to present in slightly more detail the type of problems raised. Let the A-set of unpleasant states for **P** be denoted by $\tilde{A}^\mathbf{P}$ and the corresponding A-set for **Q** by $\tilde{A}^\mathbf{Q}$. If $\tilde{A}^\mathbf{Q} \subset \tilde{A}^\mathbf{P}$ and we keep the organization from going into any of those possible organizational states unpleasant to **Q**, but *only* to **Q**, then **Q** will presumably be "happy" but there will remain possible organizational states which are unpleasant to **P**. If, on the other hand, we "eliminate" all of those organizational states unpleasant to **P**, then we will have reduced the "richness" of the organizational environment for **Q** because we shall have "eliminated" possible organizational states which were pleasant for **Q**. If neither of the A-sets $A^\mathbf{P}$ and $A^\mathbf{Q}$ are contained in the other but they intersect then we can consider eliminating, for example, $A^\mathbf{P} \cap A^\mathbf{Q}$ or $A^\mathbf{P} \cup A^\mathbf{Q}$ with the same attendant problems. The problems are increased greatly when we consider larger numbers of persons.

Preventing certain organizational states from being realized may affect organizational behavior in general, and in particular the achievement of other goals. For example, the requirement that the organization not realize certain states, effectively eliminates certain actions because the results of these acts may fall largely, though perhaps not wholly, in the set of undesirable organizational states. Certain other actions may be reduced in frequency because some of the "eliminated" organizational states may be the primary "precursors" to these other actions. Both of the preceding effects may, of course, have secondary effects that eliminate certain organizational states which are quite desirable.

The preceding and really *very* elementary analysis of some of the problems of optimizing interpersonal relationships in the organization may appear to be a long way from that which is truly "interpersonal." If this perception of distance exists, it may be because the reader, to use Fingarette's phrase,[25] has became a "victim of metaphor." We have far too long felt that the only way to discuss problems of emotional adjustment was to use words having emotional significance themselves.

Conclusion

In the preceding we have considered abstractions based on a variety of problems faced by organizations, some of which were abstractions

---

[25] [195].

of actual observed problems. We have been concerned with showing how these abstract problems could be formally translated into problems of interpersonal relationships through the concept of "personal structure." The goal was to demonstrate feasibility rather than to present solutions. In concluding with a brief discussion of the problems of achieving personal satisfaction in an interpersonal situation, it was hoped to make it apparent that *the conflict between the individual and the organization was one of values and not one of difficulties in constructing models*—that the difficulty of representing both the organizational structure and the individual structure simultaneously in the analysis of the same problem is a problem of ethics and not of science.

The importance attached to the individual in the organization as opposed to the structure of the organization is an evaluative decision made prior to constructing a model of the organization or its problems. It is not necessary to choose between the two extremes. Any degree of balance desired can be obtained. That the issues have not always been clear should not be surprising. "Our science is developed; our ethics is not. This is very sad, but not very odd." [26]

Of course, it is not wholly adequate to show only that models which formally mix the structure of individual and the organization are feasible. It is necessary to show that the result is also useful. This could not be done in this present chapter, but it can be hoped that the approach has at least conveyed an impression of potential usefulness. The existing analogue models in this chapter have been obviously too simple to accommodate the complexities of the organizational world. Judgments are concatenated. Judgments change. Judgments may have different meanings in different sequences. Judgments may sometimes be imbedded in selected sequences of judgments at one time while at other times they may be relatively free. If A-sets are to have any meaning, there must be ways of estimating their boundaries. This is not an easy task, and the task is even less easy when we consider that A-sets may vary with the state of the individual decision maker.

Beginning with selected, organizational problems, the approach of this chapter can be adapted to the contingencies of "existence" in several ways. One approach, stressed in Shelly [482], is to concentrate on certain "critical" judgments and their A-sets and attempt to construct the remainder of the personal structure from the personal structure corresponding to the critical judgments. Another is to describe in terms of PSs the actions available to different members and in this way set bounds on planned organizational changes.

---

[26] [124], p. 1.

Turning now to analytical tools, we can observe that the preceding approach was essentially algebraic. A topological approach in which the A-sets can become either open or closed sets is also a very natural one. In particular, through the use of separation spaces,[27] discriminability can be directly used to establish a topology on the space of organizational states.[28] We can also use very few properties of personal structures and then examine the relations between these simplified personal structures when they are placed in different networks. For example, we can consider the organization as a graph and then consider the relations between the personal structures of persons in a minimal covering subgraph [29] of the organizational graph. Via this route, the effects of some of the characteristics of personal structures of persons forming a minimal path in the organization could also be investigated.

Many other extensions which would improve potential applicability are also possible. The preceding examples were intended only to show that the ideas of this chapter can be extended so as to meet directly the methodological problems that were covered over by the oversimplifications employed in this chapter.

Now we turn to criteria of "acceptability." The ultimate acceptability of any model of organizational problems will have to depend upon what is considered to be "desirable" as well as "best." Within the decision making framework, it is becoming increasingly unclear as to what is meant by "best." It would seem that the meaning of "best" and the limits on achieving it can be most easily understood when "best" is measurable by some criterion which can be applied independently of individual variability. In this way the acceptability of the model of a problem may be clear even when a "best" cannot be delineated. On the other hand, when it is *subjectively clear* as to what "best" means, then we may also be able to decide upon the acceptability of models for organizational problems. For example, judgments may be used for assigning quantitative values to organizational problems, to providing the criteria for linear programming problems, etc.[30] But it is not always easy to specify, in a formal way, even the more standard goals of an organization [486d], and sometimes we must be content with, at best, a collection of ill-defined problems [486e]. Man has an ability to reduce information, but he appears to be more limited in his ability to make comparisons [486g], and this will always affect the problems he can formulate which are personally significant to him. What man can achieve in the

---

[27] [583].
[28] [481].

[29] [425].
[30] [32] and [486b].

way of conceptualizing "best" is dependent upon a ladder of "higher order" concepts, constrained in some vague way by whatever limits might exist on the evolution of his brain. Even when an explicit criterion of "best" is available, sequential adjustment is the rule rather than the exception. When "best" is itself evolving as a concept, sequential adjustment will become even more essential.

The concept of acceptable models of organizational problems is itself subject to change and sequential adjustment. The analysis in the chapter suggests, however, that the direction of this change will be towards improved ways for incorporating the structure of the individual into organization models. Organization for achievement of the "best," it is predicted, will depend more and more upon the inclusion of particular combinations of structural and individual characteristics into a single model, and even an initially limited success may be enough to accelerate progress in this direction.

21

MEASUREMENTS OF DECISIONS

I. J. Good

Introduction [1]

In this chapter I shall try to analyze, in a quantitative manner, a part of the process of making a decision.

I do not know to what extent the work is a contribution to statistics, to the theory of rationality, to psychology, or to the "mathematics of philosophy." To some extent the work is metaphysical, but I think no more than Jungian or Freudian psychology. It is well known that in the philosophy of the law no one has succeeded in completely eliminating metaphysical ideas, especially in connection with right and wrong, and blame and credit. The decision process is closely related to these matters, so that one can expect great difficulties in avoiding metaphysics entirely in its analysis.

One of the functions of philosophy is to define words that are too difficult for the makers of dictionaries. Of special interest to current statistics and management science is the decision process. Tukey [555], for example, complained that no adequate definition of a decision had been given in the literature of decision theory. This chapter begins with a suggested definition.

It is more difficult and mathematically more interesting, but perhaps less important, to consider quantitatively the process of deciding. I am going to argue that two aspects of a decision are the *change* of mind and the *variation* of mind with respect to a class **E** of acts, and that both can be expressed in terms of the "credibilities" of **E**, these credibilities being functions of time. The fact that it is possible to carry

---

[1] This is a completely revised version of a previously published paper [228].

out the analysis quantitatively lends extra credence to the qualitative description of a decision.

Decisions and Conclusions

We begin by suggesting a definition of a "decision."

Let **E** denote a set of mutually exclusive and exhaustive acts, $E_1, E_2, \cdots, E_n$, which a man might perform with a view to achieving some assigned purpose. It is convenient here to regard the time at which an act is performed as part of its definition. If the man is rational, he will act as if he had estimated the expected utility—for him —of each act, and he will perform the one of largest expected utility. Under this formulation, the man will automatically take into account the loss of utility due to postponement of his decision, and also the rate at which new information can be made available. It will, for example, often be sensible to make a decision when the rate is low (Good [222a]). If the man is a manager, the acts will often be commands which will trigger off other activity in his organization. (Strictly speaking, *each* act, E_i, is a class of practically equivalent acts.)

Some definitions of rationality imply that the man must be capable of thinking with infinite rapidity, but in the real world such an assumption is unrealistic, and therefore a good decision depends as much or more on good judgment as on good reasoning. This fact leads one to consider the notion of degrees of rationality, but this matter will not be pursued further here. The interested reader will find a discussion of this notion in Good [229]. There is another aspect of the decision process which should be discussed.

From time to time, during the decision process, we have assumed that the man is conscious of the subjective probability P_i, that he will perform the act E_i $(i = 1, 2, \cdots, n; P_1 + P_2 + \cdots + P_n = 1)$. This probability will usually be at least approximately equal to his subjective probability that E_i is in some sense the "best" act. When P_i becomes close to 1, for some i, we say that the man *thinks* he has decided to perform act E_i, or thinks he has reached a decision.

Apart from the subjective probabilities P_i, it is convenient to suppose that there are also *credibilities* p_i, i.e., unique rational degrees of belief or intensities of conviction, otherwise known as *logical probabilities*, based on all the information available to the man, and that there are also physical probabilities $\mathfrak{p}_i$, which by definition are based on the entire state of the world and all true laws of nature, known or unknown. (For an account of kinds of probability, we strongly recommend Good [223].)

A man's subjective probabilities are also his assessments of the credibilities, unless he is trying to fool himself, which we shall suppose he is not doing. But we are assuming that there are true credibilities, and that the man's assessment of them might be very inaccurate. We also assume that the credibilities exist at each moment t, whereas the man might make his assessments only occasionally.

If one of the credibilities p_i becomes close to 1, and if the man's estimate P_i is also close to 1, then the man has actually made a decision which, on the evidence available to the man, is unlikely to be reversed. Since no credibility of a future empirical event can be equal to 1 ("nothing is certain"), a decision can be reversed at any time before the corresponding act is performed, even if no new evidence comes in. If the man thinks that the credibility is exactly 1 he would be wrong. (More generally he can think he has made a decision when he has not done so.)

We are suggesting that to decide to perform an act E_i is a mental event which occurs if and only if p_i and P_i are *both* close to 1, provided that they remain close to 1 until the act is performed. If the subjective probability P_i is close to 1 but the credibility p_i is not, then, as said before, the man only thinks he has made a decision. If, on the other hand, the credibility is high, but the subjective probability is not, then the man does not know his own mind. If in such a state of mind a man actually performs the act E_i, then either the act is a habitual one that does not require a decision or else he has acted while the balance of his mind was disturbed.

The subjective probabilities and credibilities in the above definitions must be in the light of information available to the man: we would not say that a man had decided to leave a Public House if only *we* knew that he was shortly to be ejected, although some people might claim that he had unconsciously decided to leave! This explains why the definition is not framed in terms of the physical probabilities, p_i.

A peculiarity of the process of deciding is that the subject simultaneously *estimates* the credibilities (his estimates being his subjective probabilities), *generates* the credibilities, and affects the physical probabilities of the acts. A reluctance to accept the idea that there are several kinds of probability must, I think, lead to difficulties in analyzing the process of making a decision. Note that the "given" evidence must include the state of mind, both conscious and unconscious, of the subject; in fact, quite often in the process of reaching a decision, the only relevant evidence that varies is this state of mind.

When a decision is reached and not reversed, we can retrospectively say that the decision was made at the earliest time at which the sub-

jective probability and the credibility both reached some convention-
ally high value, such as 0.99, and did not thereafter sink below this
value. It is seldom easy to estimate this moment; for example, when
a man signs a contract, we can be sure only that he made the decision
at some moment preceding the signing, provided that he was in his
right mind. In the game of chess, on the other hand, the decision to
make a move can hardly precede the action by a long period of time,
otherwise the player would simply be wasting time on his own clock.
In both these examples, the moment at which the decision becomes
overtly clear is when it becomes costly to reverse it.

A conclusion is a decision in which the act E_i is itself a mental event,
usually the provisional acceptance of a hypothesis. By convention, we
may assume that the hypothesis does not simply state that one act is
better than another!

Tukey [555] said that there ought to be a conclusion theory as well
as a decision theory. I would agree with him in resisting the conquest
of the whole of statistics by "decision theory" if by this expression is
meant a theory in which all possible actions have to be listed in advance of experimentation or observation. But this is not what I personally mean by a theory of rational decisions or behavior. (See, for
example, Good [221], [222], [224], [229] and Smith [508].) In fact,
to emphasize that such a theory should cover conclusions just as much
as any other decisions, I now prefer the name *theory of rationality*.

It could be argued that the conclusion of accepting a hypothesis
is liable to have unknown effects in the future. But this is also true
of any other decision. To say that we need a theory of conclusions
as well as a theory of rationality would be like saying that we need
geometry as well as mathematics. We need a theory of rationality,
with special reference to a theory of conclusions and to a theory of
values.

The Zero-Order Approximation to the Change
of Mind with Respect to a Class of Acts

One aspect of the process of coming to a decision, as described
above, is a variation of the "vector" $\mathbf{p} = (p_i)$ with time. If the credibilities are $\mathbf{p}(t) = (p_i(t))$ at time t, then, in some sense, the "length"
of the path traced out by the point $\mathbf{p}(t)$ in n dimensions in a duration
$t_0 \leqq t \leqq T$ should represent the total "variation of mind," with respect to the class of acts, and the shortest possible such length, when
only $\mathbf{p}(t_0)$ and $\mathbf{p}(T)$ are assigned, should represent the "change of

mind." We shall suggest that there is a natural definition for the length of the path, even if the point $\mathbf{p}(t)$ moves discontinuously.

The vector function $\mathbf{p}(t)$ may be regarded as corresponding to a sequence, F, of mental events. We denote the total variation of mind in F, with respect to the acts $\mathbf{E}$, by $D(\mathbf{E}: F)$, a numerical function of the events $\mathbf{E}$ and F. In Good [228] this was called the "decisionary effort," but this name was misleading since the "variation of mind" ignores the efforts of imagination and judgment in assessing the utilities and probabilities.[2]

Let $\mathbf{p}(t_0) = \mathbf{p}$, $\mathbf{p}(T) = \mathbf{q}$. In order to arrive at a quantitative definition for $D(\mathbf{E}: F)$, we shall first introduce an approximation, $D_0(\mathbf{E}: F)$, in which only $\mathbf{p}$ and $\mathbf{q}$ are taken into account and the *history* of the distribution throughout the duration of F is ignored. We call $D_0(\mathbf{E}: F)$ the "zero-order approximation to the variation of mind in F with respect to $\mathbf{E}$." It may also be regarded as the zero-order approximation to the change of mind.

We wish then first to assign a definition to

$$D_0(E_1, \cdots, E_n: F) = D_0(\mathbf{E}: F)$$
$$= D_0(p_1, \cdots, p_n; q_1, \cdots, q_n) = D_0(\mathbf{p}; \mathbf{q})$$

where $\mathbf{p} = (p_1, p_2, \cdots, p_n)$ is an ordered set of nonnegative numbers whose sum is 1, and likewise for $\mathbf{q}$. It should be noticed that the functional symbol D_0 is used in two related senses. In the second sense, D_0 is a function of $2n$ real variables.

I shall adopt what philosophers of science call the desideratum-explicatum approach.

Let us assume the following desiderata, of which all but the fourth seem to me to be convincing, whereas the fourth one seems to me to be reasonable if we wish to obtain a simple explicatum. (The fifth and last desideratum is given in the next section.)

(i) $D_0(\mathbf{p}; \mathbf{p}) = 0$, $D_0(\mathbf{p}; \mathbf{q}) > 0(\mathbf{p} \neq \mathbf{q})$, *and* D_0 *is a continuous function in the open domain of definition.* (If there is no change in the credibilities when time varies, we naturally take the variation of mind to be zero, and if there is some change we take the variation of mind to be positive.)

(ii) *If* $G_1, G_2, \cdots, G_s$ *are exhaustive and mutually exclusive, and have "nothing to do" with* E_1 *nor with* F, *then*

---

[2] The colon in $D(\mathbf{E}: F)$ may also be read as "provided by" as in the analogous notations for "amount of information," "weight of evidence," "degree of corroboration," and "causal support." See Good [225], [226], [227].

$$D_0(E_1 \cdot G_1, \cdots, E_1 \cdot G_s, E_2, \cdots, E_n \colon F) = D_0(\mathbf{E} \colon F) \qquad (1)$$

(Here E_1 is simply one of the events $E_1, E_2, \cdots, E_n$. Any one of them would have served just as well.)

(iii) *The zero-order approximation to the variation of mind involved in two separate decisions having nothing to do with each other is some continuous function of the two separate zero-order approximations, increasing in each when the other is held constant. Symbolically, for some Ψ,*

$$D_0(p_1 p_1', \; p_1 p_2', \; \cdots, \; p_n p_m'; q_1 q_1', \; \cdots, q_n q_m') = \Psi(D_0(\mathbf{p}; \mathbf{q}), D_0(\mathbf{p}'; \mathbf{q}'))$$
$$(2)$$

where $\mathbf{p}'$ and $\mathbf{q}'$ are m-dimensional vectors of real nonnegative components, adding up to 1 in each case, and where m need not be equal to n. *Moreover Ψ is "commutative" (symmetric),*

$$\Psi(D_0(\mathbf{p}; \mathbf{q}), D_0(\mathbf{p}'; \mathbf{q}')) = \Psi(D_0(\mathbf{p}'; \mathbf{q}'), D_0(\mathbf{p}; \mathbf{q}))$$

and "associative,"

$$\Psi(D_0(\mathbf{p}; \mathbf{q}), \; \Psi(D_0(\mathbf{p}'; \mathbf{q}'), D_0(\mathbf{p}''; \mathbf{q}'')))$$
$$= \Psi(\Psi(D_0(\mathbf{p}; \mathbf{q}), D_0(\mathbf{p}'; \mathbf{q}')), D_0(\mathbf{p}''; \mathbf{q}''))$$

where $\mathbf{p}''$ and $\mathbf{q}''$ are equidimensional vectors of real nonnegative components adding up to 1 in each case.

It follows from Abel's first theorem (Abel [3]; Aczél [4], p. 176) that there exists an increasing continuous function Φ, such that $\Phi(0) = 0$ and

$$\Phi D_0(p_1 p_1', \; \cdots, \; p_n p_m'; q_1 q_1', \; \cdots, q_n q_m') = \Phi D_0(\mathbf{p}; \mathbf{q}) + \Phi D_0(\mathbf{p}'; \mathbf{q}') \quad (3)$$

so that $\Phi D_0(\mathbf{p}; \mathbf{q})$ has an additive property. (In spite of the omission of brackets, the reader will presumably not forget that Φ is a functional symbol.) In Good [228] it was assumed that D_0 itself had this additive property, but I now think that this assumption was unwarranted since it too much resembles the assumption that the length of the hypotenuse of a right-angled triangle is equal to the sum of the lengths of the other two sides! For the same reason, I now find equation 6 of Good [228] unconvincing and have therefore omitted the content of Sections III and IV of that paper.

It would be convincing now to assume that

$$D_0(p_1, \; \cdots, \; p_n; q_1, \; \cdots, \; q_n) = D_0(p_{i_1}, \; \cdots, \; p_{i_n}; q_{i_1}, \; \cdots, \; q_{i_n})$$

wh ere $(i_1, i_2, \; \cdots, \; i_n)$ is any permutation of $(1, 2, \; \cdots, n)$; and also that

$$D_0(p_1, p_2, \; \cdots, \; p_r, p_{r+1}, \; \cdots, \; p_n; q_1, \; \cdots, \; q_r, p_{r+1}, \; \cdots, \; p_n)$$

depends only on $p_1, p_2, \cdots, p_r, q_1, q_2, \cdots, q_r$, i.e., that

$$D_0(p_1, \cdots, p_r, p_{r+1}, \cdots, p_n; q_1, \cdots, q_r, p_{r+1}, \cdots, p_n)$$

$$= D_0(p_1, \cdots, p_r, 1 - p_1 - \cdots - p_r; q_1, \cdots, q_r, 1 - q_1 - \cdots - q_r)$$

if

$$p_1 + \cdots + p_r = q_1 + \cdots + q_r$$

But in place of these two assumptions we shall make the following much stronger assumption:

(iv) There exists a continuous function ϕ of two variables such that

$$\Phi D_0(\mathbf{p}; \mathbf{q}) = \phi(p_1, q_1) + \cdots + \phi(p_n, q_n) \tag{4}$$

In view of the additive property of equation 3, this assumption seems reasonable. It might be possible to replace the function Φ in equation 4 by an arbitrary function, and later to prove that it must be proportional to Φ, but I have not succeeded in doing this.

For any x and y, we have from (ii) and (iv):

$$\phi(x\lambda_1, y\lambda_1) + \cdots + \phi(x\lambda_s, y\lambda_s) = \phi(x, y) \tag{5}$$

whenever

$$\lambda_1 + \cdots + \lambda_s = 1 \qquad \lambda_1 \geq 0, \cdots, \lambda_s \geq 0$$

This can be shown (Appendix I) to imply that the function ϕ is of the form

$$\phi(x, y) = (y - x) \psi\left(\frac{y}{x}\right) \tag{6}$$

If we take $\psi(x) = A + B \log x$, where A and B are constants, then equation 3 is easily seen to be satisfied, and, in fact, this form is necessary as well as sufficient (Appendix II). The fact of sufficiency is, mathematically, already known (Kullback [327], p. 23). The constant A does not affect the explicatum, and B can be absorbed into the logarithmic base. If this is done, the base must exceed unity, in virtue of the desideratum (i).

Thus

$$\Phi D_0(\mathbf{E}: F) = \sum_i (q_i - p_i) \log \frac{q_i}{p_i} \tag{7}$$

and only the function Φ remains unselected. It will be selected in the next section.

For a continuous distribution, having a density function that is changed from $u(x)$ to $v(x)$ by the event F, we should naturally write

$$\Phi D_0(u, v) = \int (v(x) - u(x)) \log \left[\frac{v(x)}{u(x)}\right] dx \qquad (8)$$

Generally $\Phi D_0(u, v)$ is the sum of the expected "weights of evidence" per observation (Good [221]) when discriminating between two hypotheses, when one is true and when the other is true. It is called the "divergence" between the two distributions u and v (or $\mathbf{p}$ and $\mathbf{q}$) by Kullback [327], and we shall adopt this name here.

The Change of Mind with
Respect to a Class of Acts

As t increases from t_0 to T, the distribution $\mathbf{p}(t)$ might sometimes change discontinuously. Let us suppose that there are at most an enumerable number of discontinuities, $\tau_1, \tau_2, \tau_3, \cdots$.

Now dissect the closed interval $[t_0, T]$ into an enumerable number of nonoverlapping and abutting intervals $[t_j, t_j']$ $(j = 1, 2, \cdots)$, such that the points $\tau_1, \tau_2, \cdots$ never fall at points of dissection. (t_{j+1} need not be equal to t_j'; in fact the ordering of the subintervals is immaterial.) We then naturally define the variation of mind with respect to $\mathbf{E}$, contained in F, as

$$D(\mathbf{E}:F) = \lim \sum_{j=1}^{\infty} D_0(\mathbf{p}(t_j); \mathbf{p}(t_j')) \qquad (9)$$

the limit being taken as the "fineness" (maximum length of any subinterval) of the dissection tends to zero.

What this definition expresses is that the variation of mind with respect to $\mathbf{E}$ is equal to the "length" in some sense of the path traced out by the point $\mathbf{p}(t)$. When using this form of words, it is necessary to remember that the path may be discontinuous.

Among all continuous paths with assigned end points there will be one path, or perhaps more than one, along which the variation of mind is as small as possible. This minimum will be called the *separation* between the two distributions $\mathbf{p}(t_0)$ and $\mathbf{p}(T)$. It turns out to be the least variation of mind, for all paths from $\mathbf{p}(t_0)$ to $\mathbf{p}(T)$, *continuous or otherwise*, as a consequence of our selection of the function Φ, so that it can also be described as the change of mind between instants t_o and T. As our fifth and final desideratum we assume:

(v) *If the distributions* $\mathbf{p}(t_0)$ *and* $\mathbf{p}(T)$ *are distinct, their separation is positive (not zero); and if none of the probabilities* $p_i(t_0)$ *and* $p_i(T)$ *is zero or 1, the separation is not infinite.*

Consider a path for which $\mathbf{p}(t)$ is continuous and differentiable. Write $p_i(t) = x_i{}^2(t)$ so that the point representing $\mathbf{p}(t)$ is now a point on the sphere $\Sigma x_i{}^2(t) = 1$. (Bhattacharyya [66]). Corresponding to the instants t and $t + \delta t$, the divergence is approximated by

$$4 \sum_i [\delta x_i(t)]^2 \tag{10}$$

We can satisfy condition (v) by taking the function $\Phi(u)$ proportional to u^2, and not to any other power of u. Hence, for the sake of simplicity, let us select $\Phi(u)$ proportional to u^2. The constant of proportionality is not important, but we take $\Phi(u) = 4u^2$ for reasons that will appear. Hence

$$D_0(\mathbf{E}: F) = \frac{1}{2} \left[\sum_i (q_i - p_i) \log \frac{q_i}{p_i} \right]^{\frac{1}{2}} \tag{11}$$

one half of the square root of the divergence.

Among continuous differentiable paths, the least variation of mind is obtained by traveling along a great circle of the sphere, and its magnitude is equal to the geodetic distance. This *separation* between two probability distributions was discussed in detail by Bhattacharyya [66], who described it as a measure of divergence, but we have here adopted the name "divergence" for $4(D_0(\mathbf{E}: F))^2$.

In view of Appendix III, we see that the smallest variation of mind does, in fact, require a continuous path. In so far as variation of mind is a measure of effort, we see that it wastes effort to move discontinuously in the space of credibility distributions. Also, among discontinuous paths, the best ones consist of short steps (see equation 14 below).

It seems reasonable to assume that all thinking is discontinuous in that it seems to consist of a sequence of distinct concepts, each of duration say one third of a second. But if the steps are short, we can refer to continuous variation of mind without being very misleading. (See also the remark at the end of Appendix III.)

In Good [228] I claimed that a smooth decision was effortless, but this was a mistake based on the assumption that $\Phi(u)$ was the function u. Even on that assumption it was *possible* for a continuous path to have positive length, provided that it was nondifferentiable. For example, the typical path of a Brownian motion would have positive length. But the present analysis seems to me to be decidedly more reasonable and less metaphysical.

In accordance with our present definition, equation 9, $D(\mathbf{E}: F)$ can be expressed as the sum of the D_0's at all the discontinuities, plus the lengths of the paths on the sphere $\sum_i x_i^2(t) = 1$ corresponding to all continuous rectifiable parts of the whole path.

The *vacillation* of F with respect to $\mathbf{E}$ can be measured by the percentage by which the variation of mind exceeds the change of mind. This vacillation arises from two sources: (1) discontinuous jumps (jerky thinking) and (2) unnecessarily circuitous paths. Vacillation is justifiable when the "given" information is very variable.

Although F is a mental event, it will often reveal itself in overt behavior, as for example when a chessplayer's hand moves indecisively, and perhaps jerkily, from one piece to another. Although this might be done illegally in an attempt to put the opponent off, it more often indicates mental vacillation. Thus the notion of vacillation has some meaning to the behavioral psychologist.

Allocation of Responsibility

The measurement of variation of mind, including degrees of vacillation or of its opposite, decisiveness, has some bearing on questions of allocation of responsibility between different people in an organization.

Suppose we consider mental events, F_A and F_B, occurring in two people, A and B. Superficially, these mental events might be very similar and yet the first man might be the one who is making the decision, in relation to a class of acts $\mathbf{E} = (E_i)$, because he happens to be the man in charge. Here (E_i) are supposed to be acts performable by an organization to which both men belong. F_A might have much more effect than F_B on the credibility distribution $\mathbf{p}$.

Next suppose that A and B are two advisers to the chief of an organization, and suppose that the chief calls them in to his office alternately in order to discuss some decision problem. We might have a picture such as Fig. 1, where the black line represents the path taken by the credibility distribution when A is interviewed, and the dotted line is the path when B is interviewed. Strictly, the diagram should be on a sphere, but it is drawn on a plane for convenience.

Here A appears to cooperate much more effectively with the chief than does B. Three times A has helped the chief to arrive smoothly at much the same opinion, whereas, when the chief and B discuss the problem, they dither all over the place, and sometimes even shift their ground discontinuously. It is possible however that B sometimes comes up with a startling and original idea.

But now let us replace B by C, as in Fig. 2. It is well known that

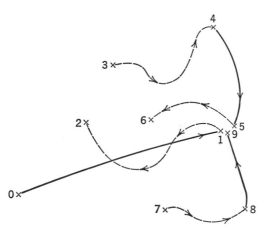

FIGURE 1 *A* versus *B*. *A*'s effects are illustrated by the continuous lines from 0 to 1, 4 to 5, and 8 to 9, whereas *B*'s correspond to the broken lines and also to the jumps from 2 to 3 and from 6 to 7.

the economist Stephen Leacock [332a] pointed out that *C* always loses.

It will be seen that *C* is almost totally ineffective in helping the chief. Whereas *B* vacillates, he at least might be stimulating and educational; but *C* does not vacillate since he hardly thinks at all.

This method of thinking about the decision process seems to me to be at least picturesque, and it is interesting that underlying it there is a quite natural and almost unique analytic model.

But when one is concerned with the science of *kudology*, that is, the allocation of credit and blame, it seems to me that there are some other very different relevant arguments. If some event *E** occurs which is either highly desirable or highly undesirable, it is often important, especially for legal purposes, to know to what extent it was caused by some earlier event, *F**. By means of arguments en-

FIGURE 2 *A* versus *C*. *C*'s effects are illustrated by the broken lines and are always small.

tirely different from those used in this chapter, it seems to be possible to analyze this problem, and to supply explications for the *tendency* of F^* to cause E^* and also for the degree to which F^* actually caused E^* (Good [226], [227]). When trying to decide whether to promote a man, it seems that, in principle, his *tendency* to cause desirable results and not to cause undesirable ones is more important than whether he *actually* caused them; but owing to the difficulties in collecting information, it might often be excusable to judge by results. When we wish to judge a driver's carelessness in an accident, we regard it as very relevant whether any one was killed; but if we knew enough about the circumstances, we might see that the accident was one that could easily have happened with any other average driver at the wheel.

For reasons that would take too long to give here, the measure suggested for the tendency of F^* to cause E^* is

$$\log \frac{P(\overline{E^*}|\overline{F^*} \cdot U)}{P(\overline{E^*}|F^* \cdot U)} \tag{12}$$

which can also be described as the "weight of evidence" against F^* if E^* does not occur. Here U represents the state of the world just before F^* occurred, together with all laws of nature known or unknown. In the particular case in which only one man's thoughts are relevant, and he is aware of *all* the relevant circumstances, the tendency of the mental event F to cause E_i is, in the previous notation,

$$\log \frac{1 - p_i}{1 - q_i} = \log \frac{1 - \mathfrak{p}_i}{1 - \mathfrak{q}_i} \tag{13}$$

since in this case the credibilities equal the physical probabilities. Thus when a decision to perform the act E_i is made in the light of *all* relevant circumstances, it has, as we might expect, a strong tendency to cause the act E_i. (For $\mathfrak{q}_i$ is close to 1.) This result is mentioned not because it will surprise anyone but because its self-evidence lends some support to the reasonableness of the explications given of a decision, and of tendency to cause.

APPENDIX I

From equation 5, we see successively that

$$s\phi\left(\frac{p}{s}, \frac{q}{s}\right) = \phi(p, q)$$

when s is a positive integer; and

$$s\phi\left(\frac{s'x}{s}, \frac{s'y}{s}\right) = \phi(s'x, s'y)$$

$$= s'\phi(x, y)$$

when s' is a positive integer. Therefore

$$\phi(\lambda x, \lambda y) = \lambda\phi(x, y)$$

when λ is a positive rational, and so for all real positive λ, since ϕ is continuous. (In the argument, x and y must be small enough to bring all the arguments into the range $0, 1$.) It follows that $\partial\phi/\partial x$ is a function of x/y, so that ϕ is y times a function of x/y, and this is equivalent to equation 6. (Compare Good [225], p. 325.)

APPENDIX II

In equation 3, take $m = n = 2$, and $p_j' = p_j$, $q_j' = q_j$ $(j = 1, 2)$. Then let $x = q_1/p_1$, $y = q_2/p_2$. We find that

$$(1 + x)(1 - y) \psi(x^2) + 2(xy - 1) \psi(xy) + (1 - x)(1 + y) \psi(y^2)$$

$$= 2(x - y)[\psi(x) - \psi(y)]$$

On this identity, perform the operation $\partial^2/\partial x \, \partial y$ (successive partial differentiation with respect to x and y) and, in the result, put $x - y$. We got

$$(x^2 - 2x - 1) \psi'(x) + x^2(x^2 - 1) \psi''(x^2) + 2\psi'(x) = 0$$

where the prime denotes differentiation. Put $x = e^u$, and $\psi'(x) = f(u)e^{-u}$, and we get

$$f(u) - f(2u) + f'(2u) \sinh u = 0$$

Differentiate ν times (where ν is any positive integer) by making use of Leibnitz's formula for the νth derivative of a product, and put $u = 0$. We find, by induction on ν that the νth derivative of f at the origin vanishes for all ν. Hence f is a constant, and so $\psi'(x) = A/x$, $\psi(x) = B + A \log x$, as required.

APPENDIX III

Let $\mathbf{p} = (p_i)$, $\mathbf{r} = (r_i)$, $p_i \geq 0$, $r_i \geq 0$, $i = 1, 2, \cdots, n$, $\Sigma p_i = \Sigma r_i = 1$, $\mathbf{p} \neq \mathbf{r}$. We shall show that the *separation* between the two distributions is smaller than $D_0(\mathbf{p}; \mathbf{r})$. We already know that the separation is at least as small as the length, on the unit sphere (see p. 399) of any continuous path. To complete the proof, all we need to show is that there is some continuous path joining $\mathbf{p}$ to $\mathbf{r}$ and having length less than $D_0(\mathbf{p};\mathbf{r})$. We first state a fact of some interest in itself, namely, that if $q_i = \alpha p_i + \beta r_i$ $(i = 1, 2, \cdots, n)$, where $\alpha + \beta = 1$, then

$$D_0(\mathbf{p};\mathbf{q}) + D_0(\mathbf{q};\mathbf{r}) < D_0(\mathbf{p};\mathbf{r}) \tag{14}$$

an "antimetric" property (Kullback [327], p. 35). The proof of this is left to the reader. By repeated application of this fact (the case $\alpha = \beta = \frac{1}{2}$ being enough), we see that we can obtain a path consisting of short pieces for which the total of the D_0's is less than $D_0(\mathbf{p};\mathbf{r})$. It is also easy to see that the total of the D_0's, when all the segments are short, is approximately equal to the length of a continuous path from $\mathbf{p}$ to $\mathbf{r}$, and this completes the proof. (It was in order to make this true that we selected $\Phi(u)$ as $4u^2$ rather than as some other multiple of u^2.) Note that we have proved, by a literally circuitous method, that

$$\cos^{-1}(x_1y_1 + x_2y_2 + \cdots + x_ny_n) < \sqrt{\frac{1}{2} \Sigma (y_i^2 - x_i^2) \log \frac{y_i}{x_i}} \tag{15}$$

where

$$\Sigma x_i^2 = \Sigma y_i^2 = 1 \qquad x_i > 0 \qquad y_i > 0 \qquad (i = 1, 2, \cdots, n)$$

For example, if $n = 2$, $x_1 = \frac{3}{5}$, $y_1 = \frac{4}{5}$, $x_2 = \frac{5}{13}$, $y_2 = \frac{12}{13}$, then the two sides of equation 15 are 0.5826 and 0.5903. The closeness of these numerical values indicates that "variation of mind" over a continuous path is well approximated by the value for a discontinuous path having only moderately short steps. Thus the notion of a continuous path is not overly idealized.

22

PRICE GUIDES IN DECENTRALIZED ORGANIZATIONS

Andrew Whinston

Introduction [1]

This chapter deals, primarily, with the use of prices as a means for achieving efficient allocation of resources within a decentralized system such as a business firm. We shall be mainly concerned with two general classes of problems: efficiency of resource allocation and coordination of the results of operations. These problems are examined with special reference to cases when external effects are present.

By a decentralized decision-making system we refer to the following: Given m decisions or actions to be made and n decision makers $(1 < n \leqq m)$, each decision maker is assigned a subset of the m decisions. For the over-all system, there is given a criterion function and a space of possible choices involving the m decisions. Each decision maker is assigned a space of possible choices and a criterion function involving at least the decision variables which he can par-

[1] This paper is based on Chapters 5 and 6 of my doctoral dissertation [597], written under the supervision of Professor W. W. Cooper. I am especially indebted to Professor Cooper in both the development and presentation of these ideas. I am also indebted to O. A. Davis, W. R. Reitman of Carnegie Institute of Technology, Mr. R. M. Trueblood of Touche, Ross, Bailey & Smart, and Mr. W. W. Sick of the Ford Motor Company.

The research was supported by the Office of Naval Research and the Bureau of Ships, at the Graduate School of Industrial Administration, Carnegie Institute of Technology, Contract Nonr-760(01), Project NR-047011, and Cowles Commission for Research in Economics under Task NR-047-006 with the Office of Naval Research.

tially or totally control. In this chapter we shall be studying decentralized decision systems which use prices as a guide for the decisions to be made in choosing between alternate courses of action. Here, however, we view prices primarily in terms of their information content and explore their uses and limitations from this point of view along with other possible devices, e.g., administrative-organization arrangements, that can be used for reenforcement and extensions of the indicated price guides.

We can perhaps distinguish this information theoretic approach to prices by calling them, say, the "transfer prices" of industrial practice, as these have emerged from the cost-accounting transfers that double-entry bookkeeping had previously developed around the cost-collection centers for decentralized decisions. Thus, in the context of controlling transfer prices, these cost-collection centers become profit centers with some degree of freedom allowed for managerial negotiations and price setting between the centers. The objective is to secure a best or efficient set of operations (a) in each profit center and (b) in the total company. By an efficient decentralized system, we refer to a comparison with the achievement of the over-all goal by the actions of each decision maker and the highest possible level of the criterion function achievable in terms of the allowable decision space.

By an external effect—or, more briefly, an "externality"—we refer to events that flow from the decisions of particular managers and affect the criteria or space of possible decisions that are used by others to guide their actions. In particular, externalities are said to be present when the relevant decision variables are not entirely under the control of the manager whose decision is being considered. We need to know, then, how such a person might, or should, behave in such circumstances. In particular, where prices are used to guide such decisions, we need to know the consequences of sole reliance upon, say, a mechanism that might be used to form such prices and also when such mechanisms might yield prices that do not achieve full efficiency (or coordination) in the decisions that affect the allocation of resources. In cases where the mechanisms fall short, it is natural to inquire in what ways they might be altered or supplemented to provide an attainable bettering of these decisions.

Some Observations on Practices and Problems in Company Decentralization

INTRODUCTION

The first part of this chapter will report on certain findings that were obtained from field interviews and discussions with officials of certain companies which utilize mechanisms of decentralization and coordination which, in part, depend on transfer prices and like devices. Such discussions were carried out in depth with only a limited number of officials from two particular companies. Hence, though this is supplemented by some further discussions with others, the results can hardly be regarded as providing a representative picture of the current state of such corporate practices or problems. These discussions, however, did prove fruitful, at least to the author, in providing insights into the nature of specific kinds of problems likely to be encountered when such devices of decentralization are used. This aspect of the interpretations gained from these field inquiries will be emphasized in the following.

Furthermore, such descriptive material will provide the reader with an introduction and background to problems of a more theoretical and normative nature, as will be discussed in the second part of this chapter.

An official statement from one of the visited companies reads:

The direct responsibility for managing company line operations rests with the general manager of the division. Under our form of organization, each division represents a separate profit center for the purpose of management control, and the general manager is accountable for earning a satisfactory rate of return on the assets employed in his operation.

The intent of this statement is clear, of course, but it is also susceptible to various interpretations. Partly this is caused by a natural ambiguity which arises from the fact that there is, in general, no precisely defined collection of words which meets the needs of managerial usage. Indeed, even the terms "decentralization" and "centralization" are usually characterized only as a matter of contrast or emphasis—i.e., degree of centralization or decentralization—from one organization situation to another and by reference to the particular aspects of the organization which are under immediate consideration.[2]

For purposes of theoretical economics, we may assume, of course,

---

[2] See, e.g., H. Simon et al. [503].

that decentralization occurs at the entrepreneurial (or customer) level when each individual is subject only to the limits imposed by market mechanisms [3] and the resources that are available for his disposition. That is, the decentralization which is implicit in a freely functioning price mechanism is relatively complete in the sense that each entrepreneur, say, has whatever autonomy he desires in making decisions to commit such resources as he may have available. In the absence of externalities, the decisions are his own in the sense that operational mechanisms are available, at least in principle, so that each entrepreneur can analyze the variations he encounters and isolate the parts due to his own decisions from the parts which are due to actions by others. Moreover, when decisions are successful, then still further resources are placed at his command, and so on.

The manager of a company division encounters a somewhat different situation. "Externalities" are likely to be present so that either (a) some further direction is necessary to provide him with supplementary information as required for him to guide even his own decisions or (b) further coordinating mechanisms may be imposed to insure the range of benefit-penalty relations arising from externalities is taken into account. The imputation mechanism is further clouded by hierarchical layers along with tiers of line-staff relations, so that it may not be possible to determine precisely his own role in effectuating any particular decision. It is true, of course, that promotion mechanisms and other devices may be used to reward "successful" managers or to punish "unsuccessful" ones in ways that are analogous to the penalty-reward systems provided in theoretical economics for transferring the responsibility for administrating larger or smaller amounts of the social assets between "better" and "worse" entrepreneurs. But the possibility of different situations must also be considered for internal management. Thus, one division manager may have his profit center "earnings" transferred to another part of the company, even when he is "successful" and, in any event, the resulting profit accumulations are rarely left to his own autonomous discretion for further disposition.

Similar remarks apply, of course, to possible access to further sources of funds from "outside" the company and an individual division manager is rarely, if ever, given complete autonomy to acquire or dispose of significant amounts of capital facilities. This suggests that, perhaps, a treatment of the topic of autonomy for a completely decentralized system might best be focused on the decisions involving

---

[3] Other social institutions like the law and mores are, of course, also operative.

current operations such as acquiring and disposing of the materials needed in production. To some extent this is true, but even here some qualification is needed where, for instance, the possibility of procurement or sale via "outside" sources is encountered in the various divisions of a firm.

DECENTRALIZATION ON CURRENT ACCOUNT IN TWO COMPANIES

We shall return to this topic for further general treatment after first considering the issues in more concrete form. For this purpose, we now summarize the general policies of two companies where outside purchases are permitted as part of the autonomy granted to managers under certain conditions. In this case, the division managers *must,* as a general rule,[4] buy from inside sources in all cases where the company has facilities available for "efficient" use in producing the indicated items. The following statements, which are actually patterned after a policy memorandum of one company but which accurately describes the procedures of both, provide a guide in such cases:

1. The company should produce internally items which are important because of "design, performance, or other characteristics, or because of the company's investment in unique facilities."

2. If the company has a large investment in facilities, and they can be operated profitably and efficiently, then the company's facilities should be used.

On the other hand, outside sources *may* be used when the following is true:

1. If investments in facilities are small and qualified suppliers exist and they charge a smaller price than the present internal supplier.

The following points were also made:

1. Outside "distress" prices should not be used in sourcing decisions. (This instruction evidently raises some question as to what is a valid outside price.)

2. An attempt should be made to "split" certain items where valuable technical data may be obtained. A split item is one which is supplied partly internally and partly from an outside company. (This characterization of split term procurements indicates that, in fact,

---

[4] I.e., proposed deviations must first be appealed and receive justification for authorization before the action is completed.

divisional managers may have very little say about whether purchases are to be made within the company or outside it.)

We shall next describe the procedure used as to the "sourcing" [5] of a part within the company. Here certain questions naturally arise such as (1) the discretion that should be allowed a division manager in determining which of various divisions to order from, especially if the part in question had not previously been fabricated in the company; or (2) the discretion that should be given to a potential supplying division for deciding whether it would be worthwhile to invest capital in order to supply the part. Company officials indicated that the following procedures were utilized to resolve such questions: Ordering divisions are supposed to take the initiative and have primary responsibility for sourcing all items, but old sourcing patterns are to continue. When a question arises as to how a new part is to be sourced, it is up to the manufacturing staff (a central staff unit) to indicate what division should be the supplying division. All questions of sourcing which involve capital expenditure or new investment are subject to central staff review and approval.

Even after the sourcing problem is decided, however, there remains a further question as to the price at which such goods are transferred. In a "centralized" firm, the price would be either a standard cost [6]— if a standard cost system [7] obtained—or some version of an actual accounting cost. In a "decentralized" firm, a possibly different price may be used to effect such transfers in order to allow for some profit-or-loss margin, in addition to the accounting costs, inclusive or exclusive of overhead.

Since a transfer price may sometimes differ considerably from the related standard or actual cost figures, a question naturally arises as to how such prices should be set. Some have suggested the use of competitive outside prices, and in a rough general way this practice is often followed.[8] There are, however, certain qualifications and refinements which need attention. For instance, in one of the firms that was visited, three different classes of goods with associated criteria were distinguished as follows:

Group I. Items for which prices of competitive producers are not available and cannot be reliably approximated by comparative analysis.

---

[5] This term is borrowed from the company's usage where it has the following meaning: The determination at the origin of production of some specified item.
[6] Plus, possibly, imputed variances from other departments.
[7] See E. L. Kohler [320].
[8] See, e.g., Joel Dean [159].

Group II. Items purchased from both outside suppliers and company sources (split items).

Group III. Items, other than split items, for which prices of competitive producers are available or can be reliably approximated by comparative analysis.

We shall discuss the pricing of items in Groups II and III first. These present the least difficulty to the organization. The policy for Group II (split items) is for the transfer price of a split item to be the same as the price paid to the outside supplier with various possible adjustments for differences in specification, volume, engineering, services, royalties, inbound freight, etc. Thus Group-II prices may be estimated in a fairly unambiguous manner. However, at the firms interviewed, split items tended to be a minor consideration in practice. To be sure, various qualifications to the use of outside prices may need to be made to allow for other considerations. This may lead to some difficulty, but, at least in the firms that were interviewed, little use was made of any possible deviation from the outside price in Group-II cases.

Group-III items present the same problem as Group-II items and, with suitable qualifications, the usual point of reference is an outside market price. A supplying division may, of course, refer to one or more qualifications in order to justify a higher-than-market price, but such appeals are usually ignored by the central staff unit concerned with arbitrating disputes. Below, further elaborations will be made, and certain tentative hypotheses suggested, in order to provide a possible rationale for this presumably "biased" procedure.

As far as the companies are concerned, Group-I prices cause considerable difficulty because their determination seems arbitrary to affected officials. In terms of dollar value, they are heavily predominant over Groups II and III. A company statement reads:

Group I prices are to be established on the basis of the estimated costs of an efficient producer plus a markup on the assets utilized.

Material costs, direct labor, and overhead are computed to reflect what an efficient producer would charge. Current assets are estimated, and a return is thereby determined and applied to total costs to reflect the utilization of such assets by an independent producer in the current conduct of their business. Longer-range factors are also considered. Fixed assets are included at their undepreciated book value. A further profit markup is then computed from this source and added to the costs to obtain the transfer price.

Such practices are, of course, open to dispute and disagreement because they lack an objective verified basis in fact of the kind that is

supplied, say, by voucher and invoice support for ordinary accounting cost entries. Therefore certain further machinery is supplied in accordance with the following statement, which is an excerpt from a
policy memorandum, of the procedures to be followed:

*If the buying or selling division believes that the profit markup being applied
to a particular part [in Group I] is inappropriate, the issue should be referred
to the Vice-President Finance for discussion.*

The above case does not exhaust the possible variations for com-
puting transfer prices, of course, and for further perspective we now
refer to the specific practices of one of the companies that was visited.
These are somewhat similar to, although not identical with, those practices which have already been discussed. Here, listed in the order of
preference accorded to them by company policy, are the criteria to be
used in determining transfer prices in this case:

a. Lowest current bona fide *price or quotation of an outside vendor, consistent with sound purchasing practice.*

*b. Estimated cost of the design differences between the part to be priced
and a similar part for which a current* bona fide *price or quotation is available.*

*c. Estimated cost differences due to design, volume, engineering, service,
royalties and other relevant factors between the part to be priced and a
similar part for which an acceptable price exists.*

*d. Estimated cost of an efficient producer plus the amount of profit that
an efficient producer can expect to receive.*

*e. Estimated cost of producing the part or assembly with efficient utiliza-
tion of major equipment and facilities which exist at the source plant plus
a normal profit for that type of operation.*

Further administrative arrangements are also utilized which allow
for possible challenges and other adjustments in accordance with the
following procedures: (*a*) Supplying division submits to an ordering
division its price quotation, which includes cost of operation, engineering specifications, and prints as determined from estimates based on its
accounting records. On this basis the ordering division will quote a
price. (*b*) The ordering division has a responsibility to check on the
cost quotation furnished by the supplying division. (*c*) Each division
has a staff of cost analysts who check the data for possible challenges.
A challenge is generally made on the basis of information about competitors' costs, but challenges can also be based on the cost figures or
the rules under which they have been synthesized.[9]

---

[9] For example, by referring to company manuals or other authoritative documents on accepted accounting practices.

A distinction formulated along the line of the preceding distinction between Group I and other group categories may also be used here for clarification. A Group-I product price, as already observed, lacks the kind of objective justification that is normally available for items in Groups II and III. A Group-I price can also give rise to trouble because this kind of product (for which no competitive suppliers are available) also suggests the lack of any real alternative for the ordering department. On the other hand, careful analysis by reference to the company's costing conventions does permit a challenge and adjustment possibility that may prove extremely profitable for the ordering division.

Presumably under a centralized management system, such challenge and increased profit possibilities would not exist. Under the indicated decentralization and transfer price system, haggling could continue indefinitely, possibly even as a game strategy, with resulting injury, perhaps, to other company operations. To foreclose this possibility, however, the following rules are utilized: Price settlements are to be completed within 30 days.[10] Furthermore, once a price is established, it holds for an entire production run of the product. (Hence gains or diseconomies from small "nuisance" orders thereby tend to be eliminated.)

Exceptions to the latter rules, of course, are allowed, but these must be justified by reference to alterations of the following kind: (a) Design of the product; (b) general level of wages or material costs; (c) competitive price components used in establishing the costs that underlie the derived price. On the other hand, cost variations resulting from efficiency variations in the supplying department are not generally regarded as justifying a further adjustment in an already established price for a given production run.

A distinction must be made, of course, between managerial and other sources of efficiency variations. For instance, technological changes may cause a shift in the relevant cost functions, or the dynamics of a learning-curve situation may also have to be allowed for in new item production. Dynamic factors like these are subject to negotiation and adjustment. But, except in unusual circumstances, once the dynamic path of the cost curve is agreed on, it cannot be altered on the basis of actual results—which are thus seen to be implicitly imputed to managerial efficiency only.

---

[10] In the event that a price is not settled on within the time allocated for negotiations, the matter is referred to the staff of the Vice President for Finance. The latter is empowered to make a final determination, subject only to the qualifications noted above for further *post facto* adjustments.

In one company the Product Analysis Department handled price disputes. For that company a price dispute over a Group-II or III item has usually revolved around a price quotation for a similar part obtainable from an outside vendor. Detailed data on the vendor are then supplied, including such items as reputation, tool capacity, and details of any deviation in the vendor's product. A challenge involving a Group-I product generally involves a listing of specific disagreements on certain cost items. In such cases, the Product Analysis Department generally reviews the data and issues a recommended price. This may be appealed to an Arbitration Board which makes a final binding decision.

COMPOSITION OF DISPUTES OVER TRANSFER PRICES

The use of certain types of administrative mechanisms for arbitrating or otherwise resolving disputes over transfer prices has just been noted. But the disputes are also of interest *per se* for supplying insight into the use of such decentralization devices and some discussion of them is warranted. Consider, therefore, the following case which was examined and discussed with relevant company officials: A supplying division claimed that it rightly should be able to charge a price higher than the market price on one of its Group-III items. The market price was based on the selling price of a vendor who possessed a modern, efficient plant. The manager of the supplying division, however, was required to operate with an old outdated plant. Since the division manager had no authority to make the capital expenditures needed to modernize this plant, he claimed that he was penalized for something beyond his control. He claimed that such an organizational situation created bad "managerial psychology."

In this case, the office of the Vice President for Finance made the following decision:

Since the primary objective of the intra company pricing system is to provide a means of measuring performance against known competitive levels, competitive practice with regard to costs and piece price must be followed. In the case of this part, there is an adequate knowledge concerning competitive practice to make this possible.

This case was discussed with company officials who had assisted the Vice President in the analysis leading up to this conclusion. They did not deny that the supplying manager's plant was outdated. Their justification may be paraphrased somewhat as follows. If this manager were forced to accept a transfer price which would cause him to lose money under his current operating procedures, the division would be able to find sufficient ways to save on expenses in order to show a profit again.

In a sense the "conflict" that was thus created might be viewed as a "test" of the managerial (innovating) ability of the affected official and his staff. Other "conflicts" were also observed, e.g., use of different criteria for judging performance even when these were not wholly consistent. From one standpoint, these "price guides" thus represented part of a "control" system rather than serving only as a guide to coordinated rational action in the sense that usually obtains in formal economics. It may be observed, in particular, that the policies and procedures utilized, as per the preceding discussion, did not assume, as in economic theory, that the supplying division was in fact utilizing an optimum production function. Rather it appears that the transfer price mechanism was being used to bring about a closer approach to the technologically feasible optimum. Also this company did not make explicit and systematic use of the mechanism of transfer prices as a way of providing incentives that might bring about additional plant investments. The latter were handled, rather, by other parts of the budgeting-administration machinery.

Another aspect of the kinds of situations which may be operative can be illustrated by a dispute that arose in another company. One division supplied a certain part to several other divisions within the company. Other companies in the industry purchased this same part from one independent producer. Thus the independent supplier had a much higher volume than the internal supplier. The internal supplier claimed that his division was entitled to a higher transfer price than the outside price, because his smaller volume arose from company-wide considerations that were outside his division's control. The Product Analysis Department decided against this division's claim for much the same reason as in the dispute which was discussed above. Established competitive prices were said to provide a desirable norm and the fact that the supplying division could not increase its volume (e.g., by outside sale) to obtain the supposed economies of scale was ignored.

Before proceeding to further cases, we wish to make certain remarks here. In the traditional approach to budgetary accounting, a commonly accepted opinion is that managers should only be held responsible for costs which they at least partially control. The above disputes suggest that this is not always true. Volume considerations, the condition of the plant that must be used, etc., may well lie entirely beyond an individual manager's control, but the resulting costs are nevertheless charged against his budget. On the other hand, the question of optimum practice even of a nonoptimal plant or volume must also be considered, as it apparently was in the preceding cases. Thus the transfer price issues discussed here have also helped to highlight certain aspects of budgetary practice. From a budgetary point of view, the transfer pricing mechanism may be used, as in the above cases, as a way of setting an upper bound on an "acceptable" cost level. If a division manager, when faced with a lowered acceptable cost level (as in the above disputes), is able, in fact, to lower costs, then this procedure may be considered justifiable unless, or until, still better alternatives for managing can be supplied in such situations.[11]

We now return to other cases. Another basis for dispute in one company arose over the method of scheduling production. When transfer prices were negotiated, a tentative schedule of deliveries was agreed upon. However, the ordering division, because of varying demand for its product, sometimes found it necessary to alter the delivery schedule. This alteration, which affected the supplying division's costs, was not permitted to affect the price at which the goods were transferred. Supplying divisions continually point out that the fluctuations are not their responsibility and, therefore, they should not be penalized. On the other hand, the indicated fluctuations were also beyond the control of the ordering division. Evidently, then, no beneficial incentive effect could be expected from merely raising the transfer price and, in any event, the supplying division's appeal was denied. No change in the transfer price was permitted.

Other disputes can arise because of interactions in the productive processes. A particularly striking case of this occurred in one of the companies examined where two different divisions alternatively shared the same production line. One division claimed that the other was not providing proper maintenance and, by saving on its own maintenance, was causing excess maintenance costs to be shouldered by the other division. That is, the complaining division argued that its maintenance costs could be reduced if only the alternate user of this production line were somehow made to conduct its own maintenance "efficiently." Because of frequent occurrences of these cases, this company established a policy under which only units with "separate" assets could be formed into decentralized divisions. In this particular case, other solutions are conceivable. For example, each unit could be directed to budget for a minimum level of maintenance, or a special maintenance unit could be formed to service the production process. But note

---

[11] A similar argument has been made by A. Stedry [516] on the general problem of what are good budgets.

that these proposals would be organizational or "mixed system" rather than pure price solutions.

In the next section, we shall study in a more formal manner some problems raised here. We shall be concerned, in particular, with the question of how a large decentralized organization can effectively generate suitable transfer prices both when externalities are absent and present.

Price Guides Within a Decentralized Organization—a Normative Approach

In contrast to the last section, where we were mainly interested in a descriptive approach of decentralized behavior, we will focus here on how a decentralized organization might best be coordinated from a price (information-theoretic) standpoint. For our purposes, we shall introduce several models representing organizational decision making. The aim of these models will be to allow us to focus on the role of price guides, on questions of the implications of externalities and other features, and to do so in terms of easily manipulated mathematical expressions where complexes of interacting variables and constraining conditions are involved.

FIRM AS A DECENTRALIZED DECISION MAKER

We begin with the consideration of the case for a degree of decentralization in the firm. Two main points are to be made here. The first has to do with problems of motivation and the second with the consequence of human cognitive limitations for the managerial span of control.

Although we emphasize the formulation of a desirable over-all plan of behavior for the organization via decentralization, e.g., the planning problem, in fact, discussions of decentralization in the business literature very often emphasize the control or motivational aspects. Writers have claimed that, with the introduction of profit centers, top management may be better informed as to weakness and strengths of the organization in specific areas.[12] Writers such as Argyris and Likert,[13] for example, have emphasized factors that motivate middle and lower management by means of certain characteristics of a decentralized organization. Setting management goals and rewards, both

---

[12] The control aspect is emphasized by J. Dean [159].
[13] See C. Argyris [22] and R. Likert [348].

salary and promotional, as some functions of the profit of the decentralized unit may be effective forms of budgeting.[14]

On the other hand, many of these writers have failed to relate these aspects of subunit behavior and motivation to the problem of *over-all* optimization in either its coordination or efficiency senses. In particular, they have tended to ignore any consideration of information theoretic devices, e.g., prices, which can be used to guide each subunit into a coordinated scheme of over-all efficiency by reference only to the motivational devices that they suggest for consideration.

A fundamental argument for decentralization which underlies our interest in the subject, but is not reflected in our formal discussion, is the concept of "bounded rationality" as presented by Hayek and Von Mises.[15] We may do no better than quote Hayek:

As decentralization has become necessary because nobody can consciously balance all the considerations bearing on the decisions of so many individuals, the coordination can clearly not be effected by "conscious control," but only by arrangements which convey to each agent the information he must possess in order effectively to adjust his decisions to those of others. And because all the details of the changes constantly affecting the conditions of demand and supply of the different commodities can never be fully known, or quickly enough be collected and disseminated, by any one centre, what is required is some apparatus of registration which automatically records all the relevant effects of individual actions, and whose indications are at the same time the resultant of, and the guide for, all the individual decisions.

This is precisely what the price system does under competition, and which no other system even promises to accomplish. It enables entrepreneurs, by watching the movement of comparatively few prices, as an engineer watches the hands of a few dials, to adjust their activities to those of their fellows. The more complicated the whole, the more dependent we become on that division of knowledge between individuals whose separate efforts are coordinated by the impersonal mechanism for transmitting the relevant information known by us as the price system.

Then we may note, in particular, that Hayek assumes it is always possible to arrange a price mechanism so that each individual can, in fact, effect the necessary cost-price calculations needed for his own best interests. Of course, when this is true, then under certain very

---

[14] For a discussion of experimental approaches to motivation and budgeting, see A. Stedry [516]. See also A. Charnes and A. Stedry in Chapter 14 of the present volume.

[15] See F. Hayek [255] and L. von Mises [575]. A discussion of the Hayek viewpoint is also to be found in March and Simon [367], p. 203.

general circumstances, an efficient over-all decision will emerge when each unit pursues its own goals efficiently. There are certain questions which require further attention, however, before this kind of assumption and this kind of generalization are extended from a free, market-oriented economy into the actual operation of decentralized (but managed) business firms.

MODELS OF RESOURCE ALLOCATION WITHIN THE FIRM

The general purpose of this section is to study decentralized resource allocation within the firm. For this we need a model of resource allocation and decision making.

Let $x_1, \cdots, x_n$ be certain decision variables such as level of an output, level of a service, etc. In general, x_i ($x_i \geq 0$, $i = 1, \cdots, n$), represents a quantifiable operation within the firm. Of course, certain organizational and physical constraints are imposed on these decision variables. Let $g_{ij}(x_i)$ be the amount (in appropriate units) of the jth constraint utilized by the ith decision variable when some value of x_i is specified. Then we can write $\sum_i g_{ij}(x_i) \leq K_j$ for each of the $j = 1, \cdots, m$ constraints that we shall consider.

We define a function $\Phi(x_1, \cdots, x_n)$ to be "separable" if it can be written in the form $\sum_i \Phi_i(x_i)$, where each Φ_i is a function of only one variable. The functions involved in the following model are all separable. In a subsequent section of this chapter, we discuss the implications of relaxing this condition but, for the present, we assume that the $g_{ij}(x_i)$ are separable and write $\sum_i g_{ij}(x_i) \equiv g_{1j}(x_1) + \cdots + g_{nj}(x_n) \leq K_j$ for each of the $j = 1, \cdots, m$ constraints.

We should next observe that these constraints need not be restricted to problems in economic resource limitations only. An example of such a constraint originating from a different quarter might be given as follows: Assume some organization, while wishing to maximize profit, is also concerned that it does not "overly penetrate" the market. (This constraint may be derived from a fear that an over-all domination of several markets may result in antitrust suits.) Let K_j be measured in percentage of market penetration so that K_j itself measures the maximum amount of total increase in market penetration that this organization will allow. Evidently then each $g_{ij}(x_i)$ in $\sum_i g_{ij}(x_i)$ measures, as a function of its own x_i, the increase in market penetration which results from assigning any specified values to the relevant variables.

We shall assume that within the specified structural constraints the firm is attempting to maximize an over-all profit function [16] of the form $f(x_1, \cdots, x_n) \equiv \Sigma f_i(x_i)$. Then our immediately relevant model is

I.
$$\max \sum_{i=1}^{n} f_i(x_i) \tag{1}$$

subject to

$$\sum_{i=1}^{n} g_{ij}(x_i) \leq K_j \qquad j = 1, \cdots, m \tag{2}$$

$$x_i \geq 0 \qquad i = 1, \cdots, n \tag{3}$$

We further assume that every g_{ij} is convex, which in classical economics terminology means that we are essentially making an assumption of decreasing marginal productivity. We also assume that each f_i is strictly concave, which implies decreasing marginal profitability in each $f_i(x_i)$.

With these assumptions, we proceed to obtain the following as sufficient conditions [17] for a choice of $x^0 \equiv (x_1{}^0, \cdots, x_n{}^0)$ and $\lambda^0 \equiv (\lambda_1{}^0, \cdots, \lambda_m{}^0)$ that will maximize Σf_i:

$$\frac{\partial f_i}{\partial x_i} - \sum_{j} \lambda_j{}^0 \frac{\partial g_{ij}}{\partial x_i} \leq 0 \qquad i = 1, \cdots, n \tag{4}$$

$$x_i{}^0 \left(\frac{\partial f_i}{\partial x_i} - \sum_{j} \lambda_j{}^0 \frac{\partial g_{ij}}{\partial x_i} \right) = 0 \qquad i = 1, \cdots, n \tag{5}$$

II.

$$\sum_{i=1}^{n} g_{ij}(x_i{}^0) \leq K_j \qquad j = 1, \cdots, m \tag{6}$$

$$\lambda_j{}^0 \left(\sum_{i=1}^{n} g_{ij}(x_i{}^0) - K_j \right) = 0 \qquad j = 1, \cdots, m \tag{7}$$

$$x_i{}^0, \lambda_j{}^0 \geq 0 \qquad \text{(all } i, j) \tag{8}$$

Certain interpretations are now in order. First the values of the $\lambda_j{}^0$ which satisfy these conditions may be interpreted as "prices." In fact, each $\lambda_j{}^0$ is a so-called efficiency price associated with the jth constraint. Thus if the jth constraint is applied to a transfer of goods between various organization units, then λ_j would be referred to as a "transfer price"—i.e., the price per unit at which a purchasing or selling unit

---

[16] As measured by the difference between revenue and variable plus fixed costs.
[17] These are known as the Kuhn Tucker conditions. See H. Kuhn and A. Tucker [326].

trades the good—and at an optimum, as above, the λ_j would be associated with efficiency in achieving the over-all objective.

The term "efficiency" has a special significance in that it is associated with an optimal solution to a problem involving multiple objectives [18]—e.g., the differing objectives of numerous managers each responsible for one phase of a decentralized set of operations. These differing objectives and especially their quantitative implications need not be known to everyone in the organization, except via the "prices" that result from their activities. An "optimum" is attained whenever the prices can be arranged so that all activities in the decentralized subdivisions will be carried on in an efficient and coordinated manner. Such prices are called "efficiency prices" [19] in order to distinguish them from all other kinds of price-cost mechanisms that might also be employed. See, e.g., the transfer prices discussed earlier in this chapter.

Suppose, for instance, that the jth constraint refers to a physical limitation imposed, say, by a machine capacity. The amount, quality, etc., of this capacity is known only to the manager who has it under his charge. Given the fact that this capacity is fixed, the problem is to determine a price that will ration the available capacity so that a "best" use level is attained for this facility relative to all opportunities and all constraints everywhere in the system.

The λ of II have this "efficiency property" but, of course, a problem is still present in that it is still necessary to specify some kind of machinery that will (a) ensure attainment of these values and (b) interfere as little as possible with the intended degree of decentralization. Here we shall have recourse to a certain "iterative" [20] procedure which will help to illuminate these sorts of issues even though it is not now possible, in general, to supply (always) an effective solution procedure.

To obtain our immediate objective we proceed "organizationally" as follows: We refer to the variable x_i as an activity of the organization. To each activity we assign a manager who is responsible for choosing an optimal level of the activity. The manager is instructed to make his decision on the basis of the various efficiency prices of the "inputs" of fixed resources needed, the direct revenues and costs of the unit, and the technology relevant to the unit—e.g., the input re-

---

[18] See, e.g., T. C. Koopmans [323]. See also Chapter IX and Appendix D in Vol. I of A. Charnes and W. W. Cooper [113].

[19] See, e.g., Koopmans, *loc. cit.* or Charnes and Cooper, *loc. cit.*

[20] The procedure has been discussed extensively by K. Arrow and L. Hurwicz in [26].

quirements of fixed resources needed for different levels of the activity. Each manager is, in fact, instructed to choose, on the basis of the information just enumerated, an activity level which will maximize the profits of his unit and, when efficiency prices prevail, this should (at least under certain circumstances) produce an over-all efficient state for the entire firm as well.

The iterative procedure can then be accorded the following interpretative development. For any given $\lambda_j(t)$, each manager chooses $x_i^*(t)$ so that it is the maximizer of

$$f_i(x_i) - \sum_{j=1}^{m} \lambda_j(t) \, g_{ij}(x_i)$$

This defines, then, a function $\Phi_i(\lambda_1(t), \cdots, \lambda_n(t))$ for each manager. Prices are adjusted by the following rule

$$\frac{d\lambda_j}{dt} = \begin{cases} 0 \text{ if } \lambda_j = 0 \text{ and } K_j - \sum_{i=1}^{n} g_{ij}[x_i(t)] > 0 \\ \ell \left\{ \sum_{i=1}^{n} g_{ij}[x_i(t)] - K_j \right\} \qquad \text{otherwise} \end{cases} \tag{9}$$

$$j = 1, \cdots, m$$

where ℓ = a dimensionality factor
$x_i(t) = \Phi_i[\lambda_i(t), \cdots, \lambda_n(t)]$.

Systems of this sort [21] were first discussed by Koopmans in his original paper on decentralized resource allocation,[22] in which he introduced the terminology of helmsmen, custodians, and managers. His development was, of course, only static and dealt with the maintenance only of already achieved efficient production possibilities.[23]

We may, in fact, follow Koopmans, at least in part, and view each "custodian" as an official who is in charge of allocating a specific fixed resource and who proceeds according to equation 9 or its difference equation equivalent. Roughly, the custodian raises the price if the resource is in excess demand and lowers the price if it is in excess

---

[21] As we have formulated the model of a decentralized solution to the organizational decision problem, there may be in principle an infinite number of calculations to perform by each manager. Thus, in any practical application of the ideas suggested, modification would be required. One writer in discussing this aspect of the problem has suggested that a truncation of the process be made after a given interval of time. See T. Marschak [370].

[22] *Op. cit.*, Koopmans [323].

[23] *Loc. cit.*, pp. 93 ff. See also A. Charnes and W. W. Cooper [113], Chapter IX.

supply. Helmsmen, on the other hand, are officials who do not know the fixed resources or how they are being utilized. Their job is to supply suitable criteria via the $f_i(x_i)$ to "managers." The latter (i.e., managers) are also assigned a role in the resource allocation and this role is played in accordance with the following rules: [24]

Do not engage in activities that have negative profitability. Maintain activities of zero profitability at a constant level. Expand activities of positive profitability by increasing orders for the necessary inputs with, and offers of the outputs in question to, the custodian of those commodities.

Convergence and stability properties of systems like this can be verified by reference to Uzawa,[25] and so we shall not find it necessary to supply a detailed mathematical development for this.

Assuming that the required convergence and stability properties are at hand, we can provide an interpretation as follows: The manager for each activity refers to any of the indicated internal prices and then reaches an optimal decision for himself on the basis of his own technology. Custodians or a central staff group proceed on the basis of information supplied by managers about their decision to allocate correctly the jointly used resources of the company by varying the internal prices. To operate effectively, each manager need concern himself only with his internal operations and the information received from a central staff group.

We have now provisionally achieved one of our objectives—on the indicated assumptions—in that the equilibrium solution to the above iterative decentralized scheme is (a) an optimal solution for the over-all system that is compatible with (b) efficiency in each subunit. By optimal we mean that no better solution exists in terms of the given organizational goal.[26]

COST ACCOUNTING

In the previous section we considered several problems associated with the management of decentralized organizations. However, our discussion proceeded at a theoretical level and we made no reference to problems associated with the specification of the kinds of data which are required for the decentralized decision making system to proceed effectively.

---

[24] Koopmans [323], *ibid.*, p. 94.

[25] H. Uzawa [565].

[26] We refer to a profit goal only for convenience and definiteness. Any quantifiable goal is admitted.

In this section we first interpret the ideas already introduced in terms of certain basic concepts in cost accounting. After noting similarities and divergencies, we shall stress some important uses that certain cost concepts may have for problems of planning and managerial decision making, even though these concepts are not used in current accounting practice. Mainly the discussion will be limited to aspects of cost accounting developed to deal with managerial planning problems as distinct from accounting for financial reporting.

A fundamental distinction is made in cost accounting between period costs and direct costs. This distinction has been stated in the following terms: [27]

Period costs are those costs incurred for keeping manufacturing and marketing capacity in readiness regardless of the extent to which such capacity is utilized. Included are not only costs associated with plant and equipment, but also costs of maintaining a basic organization and expenditures for advertising and research which management has committed itself to make. In the absence of change in capacity or other existing commitments, the amount of period cost incurred runs with time but is independent of variations in activity within the range for which provision has been made. Direct costs are the additional costs incurred only if specific goods are produced and sold. In total, direct costs tend to vary directly with volume of production or other cost incurring activity. Within limited ranges of volume, this variation also tends to be proportional to volume and hence unit cost tends to be constant in amount.

This distinction between the two types of costs is also related to two divergent cost-accounting methods. In one type of cost accounting system, only the direct product or activity costs are recorded in the accounts of the particular product or activity. This is a so-called "direct costing system," which is to be contrasted with a "fully allocated costing system." In a "fully allocated cost system," period costs are assigned to various products in some arbitrary fashion. Thus product costs at various stages of fabrication would be different for the two methods of recording costs.

Advocates of direct costing have stressed its use as a tool in managerial decision making: [28]

By knowing the rate at which profit varies with volume (i.e., the marginal income ratio), management can determine the expected addition to profit from a proposed increment in volume when the capacity provided by period costs is not fully utilized. The same data also provides a guide to selecting the most profitable products, customers, or other segments when the available volume of business exceeds capacity of existing facilities.

---

[27] [414].   [28] *Ibid.*, p. 31.

Note that the use of a fully allocated cost system does not necessarily imply that information finally used for decision making would diverge between the two types of cost systems. Major emphasis is on the desirability of having direct cost figures immediately available from the account books instead of having to adjust the cost figures to eliminate the period cost elements. In a large organization with several levels of fabrication, the processing of cost figures may become a large task and, in practice, the time and costs involved in translating the cost figure may actually result in decisions based on fully allocated costs. The following comments by one company as reported in the National Association of Accountant's Research Report No. 37 [414] are indicative of this:

Under whole (fully allocated) costs, we would not know the profit contribution of this product except by recalculating our costs and breaking out the fixed expenses. Frequently, there is not time to do this before we quote. We would decide under whole (fully allocated) costs that we do not want this business, not knowing it would contribute $14,000.

In the criterion function we have used $f_i(x_i)$ as the profitability of the ith unit. This can be evidently represented in terms of $r_i(x_i) - c_i(x_i)$, where $r_i(x_i)$ is the revenue factor and $c_i(x_i)$ represents the direct costs, e.g., labor or material cost for various outputs x_i. A realistic situation could be represented by a piecewise continuous function indicating that different ranges of production would cause different costs to be operative.[29] Costs which caused the discontinuities would typically be referred to in the literature of cost accounting as either semivariable or semifixed costs. Fixed costs were not explicitly introduced in the model, although they would be represented in the criterion function as any costs independent of the decision variables.

The correctness of using direct costs as the basis for short-run decisions on price and output when the organization is operating below capacity is generally acknowledged, at least in theoretical discussions of cost accounting. However, for the case where the firm operates near capacity, there is no systematic way for synthesizing cost data that will enable the managers to decide on a most efficient use of the scarce fixed facilities. Thus consider the following statement: [30]

---

[29] The problem of maximizing with discontinuities could in principle be handled by integer programming techniques, at least in cases where the functions are piecewise linear and separable. See Charnes and Cooper [113], Chapter XVIII, for example. See also Ijiri [291], Chapters 1 and 2.

[30] [414], p. 32.

When the volume of goods that can be sold exceeds the production capacity of available machines, the highest net profit results from using machine capacity to produce those products which return the largest marginal income per machine hour.

For the case where only one facility is used to capacity, and costs, revenues, and utilization of the particular facility are constant per unit over the entire range of output of the various goods, this is a correct procedure. With variability in costs, etc., the procedure can give only rough approximation depending on the level of outputs for which the measurements are made. For the case when several fixed resources are used to capacity, there would seem to be no guide available to decide on the correct output combination.

In principle, a correct solution to the problem of determining the optimal output combination for an organization could be solved by formulating and solving a large programming problem. This would entail a large problem of gathering and processing the data on the technology of the firm and also pose a serious computational problem. For the moment, however, we wish to consider decentralized schemes for generating correct decisions and the required data.

We have seen that the imputed prices play a fundamental role in allocating these fixed resources. For correctly chosen [31] λ_j, the fixed resource will be properly allocated. The per unit opportunity cost λ_j for the resource is considered, from the point of view of the divisional unit, on the same basis as direct money cost. However, it does not represent a money cost to the over-all firm.[32] Thus a cost-accounting system for its managerial decision-making uses should include, with the money direct costs, the opportunity costs if the information which

---

[31] For a discussion of computational schemes for determining values of λ_j, see the last section of this chapter.

[32] The charging of divisions for the use of fixed resources should not be confused with a fully allocated cost system since, as we are concerned to emphasize, λ_j is an opportunity cost determined by reference to outside as well as inside opportunities. The usual fixed-charge (fully allocated cost) approach is more difficult to rationalize, however, except possibly as a rule-of-thumb long-run average approach or else as a device for cash conservation for eventual repurchase of new equipment, uncertainty allowance, etc. Of course, the assumptions underlying such approaches may not be valid at all, e.g., for optimization, and other approaches now available could be used instead. For instance, actual constraints could be formulated and charges made for the use of cash on a strict opportunity cost basis. Similar remarks could be made with respect to "user cost" in view of the utilization of historical depreciation expenses, etc.

For further discussion of such approaches, see A. Charnes, W. W. Cooper and M. H. Miller [118]. See also H. M. Weingartner [592].

the "cost-prices" designate are to impound in themselves the benefits and penalties that will be incurred over all of the alternatives that are available to every one of the decentralized departments. We may thus regard this result as one mode of improving the costing and transfer-pricing devices that are now being used by industrial firms.

DIFFICULTIES IN GUIDING DECENTRALIZED DECISION MAKING DUE TO THE EXTERNALITY PROBLEM

We have discussed one of a variety of models that might be used to represent decisions for efficiency within a decentralized firm. Decentralized resource allocation supplemented with price guides was seen to be useful, at least under the assumptions that were made. However, it was indicated that further study and experimentation were needed before definite conclusions could be drawn concerning the practicality of such an approach.

In this section we consider some further difficulties with the use of price guides when we weaken the assumptions concerning a decomposable technology, i.e., separability of the functions. These difficulties raise serious problems of how to organize a meaningful decentralized price system. We shall also see that traditional problems discussed in the organization theory literature such as conflict, communication, misbehavior among subsidiary units, etc., can also be interpreted in these terms as one way to cast further light on them by our more general model.

We shall proceed by successively generalizing the static model of an organization that was introduced earlier. Suppose we have

$$\max f_1(x_1,x_2) + f_2(x_2) + \cdots f_n(x_n) \tag{10}$$

subject to

$$\sum_{i=1}^{n} g_{ij}(x_i) \leq K_j \qquad j = 1, \cdots, m \tag{11}$$

$$x_i \geq 0 \tag{12}$$

This model is identical with the earlier one except that the profit for unit one depends on the activity level of unit two. That is, $f_1(x_1, x_2)$ is not separable since it involves two variables in its arguments.[33] This could arise in the case where decisions of a management associated with x_2 affected, say, the demand curve for the output of activity x_1. A case in point may be one in which increases in x_2 values shift the demand

---

[33] It is also assumed that $f_1(x_1, x_2)$ cannot be transformed into functions that are separable (The latter property is sometimes referred to as "weak separability.") See, e.g., Charnes and Cooper [113], Chapter X.

curve for x_1 to the right. This would thereby increase the demand for x_1 while causing a loss—or reduced profit—on x_2. The latter would then become a "loss leader" and the pricing problem would then involve a way of determining how to optimize the total profit on these two items.

The original stipulation to manager two was to choose $x_2{}^*$ for given prices as the maximizer of

$$f_2(x_2) - \sum_{j=1}^{m} \lambda_j g_{2j}(x_2)$$

$$x_2 \geqq 0$$

In the present case, from the point of view of over-all welfare of the firm, manager two should choose rather $\hat{x}_2$ as the maximizer of

$$f_1(x_1, x_2) + f_2(x_2) - \sum_{j=1}^{m} \lambda_j g_{2j}(x_2)$$

$$x_2 \geqq 0$$

In general $x_2{}^*$ will differ from $\hat{x}_2$.

Note that the immediate result of this is that manager two is required to act in a way which is inconsistent with the presumed goal of maximal profit for his own particular unit. A further difficulty for manager two even if (possibly altruistically) he decided to act solely in the best interest of the company, he still would not have the information—from prices only—that would enable him to do this to everyone's best advantage. This is true because, for given prices, his optimal choice depends, via $f_1(x_1, x_2)$, on the choice of x_1 by the manager of activity one. The difficulty is even further compounded in that the latter chooses $x_1{}^*$ as the maximizer of

$$f_1(x_1, x_2) - \sum_{j=1}^{m} \lambda_j g_{1j}(x_1)$$

$$x_1 \geq 0$$

for given prices. The optimal choice for manager one will, assuming $f_1(x_1, x_2)$ cannot be written as $f_{11}(x_1) + f_{12}(x_2)$ (i.e., separable in the variables), depend on the choice of manager two. Even if manager two were correctly motivated and the form of the function $f_1(x_1, x_2)$ were communicated to him, there still remains a difficulty in each manager's choice of an optimal value because of the simultaneity of the decision.

On this kind of point Professor H. Simon has written the following: [34]

. . . *each individual, in order to determine uniquely the consequences of his actions, must know what will be the actions of the others. This is a factor of fundamental importance for the whole process of administrative decision-making.*
. . . *Instability may result even if activity is cooperative, provided the participants are insufficiently informed.*

These examples indicate the class of problems which develop when separability of the functions is no longer assumed. When this assumption is relaxed we have the problem of "externalities" whose presence —at least in certain forms—means that the price guides no longer give sufficient information to guide the individual decision makers in making correct decisions even on their own accounts much less in terms of over-all organizational goals and constraints.[35]

There are two problems which arise: The first is that a manager is not motivated to take into account the consequences of his actions on the welfare of other divisions since these consequences do not affect his own reward structure. The second arises from the fact that a lack of separability is closely associated with the appearance of uncertainty. This uncertainty results in a loss of efficiency for the decentralized system unless some way can be found to reduce or eliminate the ambiguity which ensues because one manager's decision variables are dependent, at least in part, on decisions by others in such a way that he cannot ascertain, from prices alone, as to how his own conduct should be guided.

The above case provides a simple illustration which can be handled in a variety of ways, but in more complex cases a reorganization of the entire hierarchical structure of a firm may be needed. For instance, such a reorganization might be effected by combining two divisions into one single decision-making unit to eliminate the externality problem. This may be desirable—or even necessary—under certain circumstances, but some caution is needed in that the purpose of decentralization thereby tends to be frustrated and certain advantages may thereby be lost.

Consolidation of units affected by externalities is, of course, only one approach. Another involves the use of organizational constraints. This may be illustrated as follows. Assume that two divisions affected

---

[34] H. Simon [500].
[35] See O. A. Davis and A. Whinston [156].

by each other's externalities sell in a competitive market. We can then represent, for given outside and internal price guides, the profits of each unit in the following form.

$$p_i x_i - C_i(x_1, x_2) \qquad \text{for } i = 1, 2$$

where p_i represents "price" and C_i represents cost.

Now suppose that the manager of one of these units—call this "unit one"—is faced with the problem of choosing x_1 without being informed concerning the choice x_2 of division two. Also unit one fails to take into consideration his effect on unit two. As an extreme case, we assume that the manager of division one has no information concerning the intentions of division two.

A reasonable course of action for the manager of unit one to follow in this circumstance is to select an output level which provides a certain security level,[36] i.e.,

$$\max_{x_1 \geq 0} \min_{x_2 \geq 0} [p_1 x_1 - C_1(x_1, x_2)]$$

so that, by analogy with the theory of games, it is assumed that the manager of unit one makes his own best (maximizing) choice of x_1 under a guarantee that he will get at least the amount that the worst possible corresponding x_2 choice admits.

We obtain as necessary conditions for the achievement of these objectives:

$$p_1 - \frac{\partial C_1}{\partial x_1} \leq 0 \qquad x_1 \left(p_1 - \frac{\partial C_1}{\partial x_1} \right) = 0 \qquad x_1 \geq 0 \qquad (13)$$

$$- \frac{\partial C_1}{\partial x_2} \geq 0 \qquad x_2 \left(- \frac{\partial C_1}{\partial x_2} \right) = 0 \qquad x_2 \geq 0 \qquad (14)$$

From equations 13 and 14 a solution $(\hat{x}_1, \hat{x}_2)$ is obtained. By a similar argument a max min solution for division two is obtained $(\tilde{x}_1, \tilde{x}_2)$. In general $(\hat{x}_1, \hat{x}_2) \neq (\tilde{x}_1, \tilde{x}_2)$ which means, in turn, that each unit will act on the basis of information which, ex-post, may turn out to be incorrect.

In order to illustrate the role of constraints, assume that division one

---

[36] The question of a reasonable course of action in these circumstances is a debated point. See Chapter 13 of Luce and Raiffa [356] on this point. However, Charnes and Cooper in an interesting reformulation of the problem have demonstrated that criteria suggested other than the max min rule have implicit, in their formulation, certain information about the opponent's behavior. For the moment, however, we wish to impose a strict assumption of no information. See Charnes and Cooper [113], Chapter XI.

causes large diseconomies to division two at low outputs—e.g., $C_2(x_1, x_2)$ is a monotonically decreasing function of x_1 for each x_2—but that the price for division one's output rarely falls so low that it will produce at such low output levels. Consider the effect of a central unit announcing that unit one is now subject to a constraint of the form

$$x_1 \geq K > 0$$

This constraint is arranged so that it will be redundant for division one and thus does not alter its max min level. However, from the viewpoint of division two, this is an important piece of information. Division two selects x_2 in accordance with

$$\max_{x_2} \min_{x_1} [p_2 x_2 - C_2(x_1, x_2)]$$

subject to

$$x_1 \geq K > 0$$

Now the necessary conditions become

$$p_2 - \frac{\partial C_2}{\partial x_2} \leq 0 \qquad x_2\left(p_2 - \frac{\partial C_2}{\partial x_2}\right) = 0 \qquad (15)$$

$$-\frac{\partial C_2}{\partial x_1} - \lambda \geq 0 \quad \text{or} \quad \frac{\partial C_2}{\partial x_1} \leq -\lambda \qquad x_1\left(\frac{\partial C_2}{\partial x_1} + \lambda\right) = 0 \quad (16)$$

$$\lambda(x_1 - K) = 0 \qquad x_1 \geq K \qquad (17)$$

By our assumptions $\tilde{x}_1 = K$ and $\tilde{x}_2$ is the solution of equation 15 when $x_1 = K$. Note

$$C_2(K, x_2) < C_2(0, x_2) \qquad (18)$$

for every x_2, by the monotonicity assumption.

We now wish to show that the security level has increased. Assuming that the original max min solution for division two without constraints is $(0, x_2^*)$, where zero is chosen because of the monotonicity condition. Note that the solution (K, x_2^*) could be chosen by manager two. By equation 18, this would give him a greater security level than the original solution $(0, x_2^*)$. He may yet choose an even better solution from the point of view of his security level, but in any event the new solution will have a larger security level than $(0, x_2^*)$, his original solution.[37]

---

[37] This suggests that a possible area for research is the design of optimal constraints. Note that, although a constraint may increase the security levels of the individual units, this is not necessarily an actual improvement in over-all return to the organization. This question must also be investigated further.

PROBLEMS OF PRICE GENERATION

In this chapter we have focused on some possible uses of prices as more or less suitable guides for decentralized resource allocation within a firm. In earlier sections we indicated the particular form in which price guides would enter into the delegated preference ordering of a decentralized manager. We also discussed difficulties which may arise in pure reliance on individual managers in such a system. In this section we now turn to the question of how price guides may be generated within the firm and we do this in a general context where externalities may be either present or absent.

Assume that the technology of an organization is such that it lends itself to some degree of decentralization, or that suitable administrative devices can be imposed so as to make decentralized resource allocation feasible at a particular level. There remains now a question of how suitable price guides may be generated. In dealing with the economic system as a whole, conceived of as a collection of independent economic units, it is reasonable to think of price guides being automatically generated through a market mechanism. However, most discussions of business organizations in the literature of administration treat the firm not as a collection of *independent* economic units but as an entity with a structure characterized by a high degree of hierarchical interdependence. Therefore, to complete our treatment of the uses of price guides in business organizations, it will be necessary for us to show how these prices may also be generated in an interdependent hierarchical system. Specifically, we will develop an iterative model with the following characteristics: At each stage of the iterative process, divisional managers make decisions with respect to price guides provided by the central staff. The central staff, which need not have knowledge of divisional technologies, receives these decisions from the divisions and determines price guides based on these decisions, the over-all organizational constraints, and the criterion function of the over-all organization.

Earlier in the chapter a gradient adjustment mechanism was presented as a type of decentralized scheme for determining price guides. This was partly suggested by means of an analogy to the devices presumed to be used in the clearing of economic markets. A drawback in this method, as proposed, however, arises in connection with the problem of how to deal with a truncated form of the process. In general, the process only converges to an optimum with infinite time. Hence only a truncated version appears to have any promise of practical use.

A major difficulty then arises because at any time before the achievement of an optimum the constraints are not satisfied, so that it becomes immediately necessary to decide how the demands and supplies of the various units should be finally determined. It is also acknowledged that the gradient adjustment method is generally inefficient for solving nonlinear programming problems, which is the form in which we have presented the organizational decision problem. For these two reasons we present an alternative scheme.

Price generation in the absence of externalities. We begin by developing a model for a hierarchically structured organization, with each division considered initially as a single decision unit. Let X denote the set of all possible activities in the organization. We partition the set X into m blocks or collections of activities, each block representing the activities carried out by a particular division. Thus let $x_i^j = i$th activity in jth division, so that x_i^j is an activity variable whose level is to be determined within the relevant division $j = 1, \cdots, m$.

Corresponding to this partition we have the following organization model:

$$\max \sum_j \sum_i c_i^j x_i^j$$

subject to

I.
$$\sum_j \sum_i a_{zi}^j x_i^j \leq b_z \qquad z = 1, \cdots, \ell$$

II.
$$g_q^j(x_1^j, \cdots, x_{i_j}^j) \leq R_q^j \qquad q = 1, \cdots, m_j \qquad (A)$$

$$x_i^j \geq 0 \qquad j = 1, \cdots, m$$

Type-I constraints are interdivisional while type II are intradivisional, i.e., they are constraints on variables in a particular division. We assume that g_q^j are convex differentiable functions and $g_q^j(0) = 0$. c_i^j is the net profit per unit of activity i in division j.

The administrative process may be described in the following manner: Each division supplies tentative proposed activity levels [38] $X^{j0} = (x_1^{j0} \cdots x_{i_j}^{j0})$ to a central staff group assigned to coordinate the interdivisional constraints. These initial proposals are made with each division having exact knowledge of the part of the criterion function affecting its activities and the relevant type-II constraints. Verbally, the task of the central staff group is to scale down or re-evaluate the proposals of the various divisions in some optimal fashion. Based on the scaled-down proposals, the central staff issues tentative price guides for use by the divisions in making their next proposals. The process continues for a

---

[38] The second superscript refers to the number of the iteration.

fixed number of iterations after which the central staff, based on the proposals of the divisions, issues a set of activity levels that each division should produce. The final set of activities satisfies all constraints since alterations generally will have been made in the divisional proposals.

In order to amplify the above remarks, let $X^{j0} = (x_1{}^{j0} \cdots x_{i_j}{}^{j0})$ for $j = 1 \cdots m$ be the initial proposals of the various divisions. Then the central staff problem is the following: [39]

$$\max \sum_{j=1}^{m} \sum_{i=1}^{i_j} \lambda_0{}^{j0} c_i{}^j x_i{}^{j0}$$

subject to

$$\sum_{j=1}^{m} \sum_{i=1}^{i_j} \lambda_0{}^{j0} a_{zi}{}^j x_i{}^{j0} \leq b_z \qquad z = 1, \cdots, \ell \tag{B}$$

$$0 \leq \lambda_0{}^{j0} \leq 1 \qquad j = 1, \cdots, m$$

This is a linear programming problem for the unknown variables $\lambda_0{}^{j0}$.[40] Solving this problem by the simplex method, we obtain a set of dual variables for the constraints which are interpretable as imputed prices. These can be interpreted as the tentative price guides.

Using the tentative price guides each division j solves the following nonlinear programming problem:

$$\max \sum_i c_i{}^j x_i{}^j - \sum_z \sum_i \pi_z{}^1 a_{zi}{}^j x_i{}^j$$

subject to

$$g_q{}^j(x_1{}^j, \cdots, x_{i_j}{}^j) \leq R_q{}^j \qquad q = 1, \cdots, m_j \tag{C}$$

$$x_i{}^j \geq 0$$

where $(\pi_1{}^1 \cdots \pi_\ell{}^1)$ are given prices.

For the moment we simply assume that each division can solve the divisional problem to obtain a solution $(x_1{}^{j1} \cdots x_{i_j}{}^{j1})$.

Each division communicates the new tentative proposals to the central staff group. The procedure already described could be repeated, solving

---

[39] The reader will note that we are drawing on a computational scheme suggested for linear programming problems made by Dantzig and Wolfe [153]. They give a brief interpretation of their method for decentralized decision making within the firm. See p. 102, paragraph 1, in their article.

[40] By assuming linearity we obtain direct access to the simplex method as a way to determine the tentative price guides. Since the constraints will very often refer to transfer of goods, a linearity assumption is not unreasonable. However, the basic ideas developed do not depend on linearity of the organizational constraints or the criterion function.

for λ^{j1} in model B with values $\{x^{j1}\}$ instead of $\{x^{j0}\}$. However, we proceed in a different fashion by finding the optimal convex combination of the initial proposal with the present proposal in each division. This procedure guarantees monotonicity for the value of the criterion function.[41] Thus we have the following central staff problem

$$\max \sum_{j=1}^{m} \sum_{i=1}^{i_j} \lambda_0{}^{j1} c_i{}^j x_i{}^{j0} + \sum_{j=1}^{m} \sum_{i=1}^{i_j} \lambda_1{}^{j1} c_i{}^j x_i{}^{j1}$$

subject to

$$\sum_{j=1}^{m} \sum_{i=1}^{i_j} \lambda_0{}^{j1} a_{zi}{}^j x_i{}^{j0} + \sum_{j=1}^{m} \sum_{i=1}^{i_j} \lambda_1{}^{j1} a_{zi}{}^j x_i{}^{j1} \le b_z \qquad z = 1, \cdots, \ell$$

$$\lambda_0{}^{j1} + \lambda_1{}^{j1} = 1$$

$$\lambda_0,{}^{j1} \lambda_1{}^{j1} \ge 0 \qquad \text{for each } j$$

$$(D)$$

New price guides are obtained and in turn new divisional proposals are generated.

Each division then is instructed to produce

$$(\tilde{X}^{jT}) = \lambda_0{}^{jT}(X^{j0}) + \lambda_1{}^{jT}(X^{j1}) + \cdots \lambda_T{}^{jT}(X^{jT}) \qquad (E)$$

where, of course,

$$\sum_{\tau=1}^{T} \lambda_\tau{}^{jT} = 1 \qquad \text{for each } j$$

It is possible to prove that this solution procedure always satisfies every constraint at all stages and, hence, that the constraints are all satisfied whenever the process terminates. Instead of supplying such a proof, however, we here concentrate on a simple illustrative example.

Suppose we have two divisions so that $j = 1, 2$ and let

$$g_1{}^1(x_1{}^1, x_2{}^1) \le R_1{}^1$$

$$g_2{}^1(x_1{}^1, x_2{}^1, x_3{}^1) \le R_2{}^1$$

represent type-II constraints for the first division. Then let

$$g_1{}^2(x_1{}^2, x_2{}^2, x_3{}^2, x_4{}^2) \le R_1{}^2$$

be the only interdivisional constraint for division $j = 2$.

Given the functional for the entire organization as

$$(c_1{}^1 x_1{}^1 + c_2{}^1 x_2{}^1 + c_3{}^1 x_3{}^1) + (c_1{}^2 x_1{}^2 + c_2{}^2 x_2{}^2 + c_3{}^2 x_3{}^2 + c_4{}^2 x_4{}^2)$$

---

[41] This is easily seen since the space of possible solutions for the second iteration contains the space of possible solution to the first iteration.

the division $j = 1$ solves the problem

$$\max (c_1{}^1 x_1{}^1 + c_2{}^1 x_2{}^1 + c_3{}^1 x_3{}^1)$$

subject to

$$g_1{}^1(x_1{}^1, x_2{}^1) \leq R_1{}^1$$

$$g_2{}^1(x_1{}^1, x_2{}^1, x_3{}^1) \leq R_2{}^1$$

$$x_i{}^1 \geq 0 \qquad \text{for } i = 1, 2, 3$$

while the division $j = 2$ solves

$$\max (c_1{}^2 x_1{}^2 + c_2{}^2 x_2{}^2 + c_3{}^2 x_3{}^2 + c_4{}^2 x_4{}^2)$$

subject to

$$g_1{}^2(x_1{}^2, x_2{}^2, x_3{}^2, x_4{}^2) \leq R_1{}^2$$

$$x_i{}^2 \geq 0 \qquad \text{for } i = 1, 2, 3, 4$$

Assuming that these problems can be solved—e.g., assuming that the indicated constraining subsets are consistent—we obtain

$$X^{10} = (x_1{}^{10}, x_2{}^{10}, x_3{}^{10})$$

$$X^{20} = (x_1{}^{20}, x_2{}^{20}, x_3{}^{20}, x_4{}^{20})$$

as the activity levels proposed by each of these divisions for central staff consideration. Assuming only one interdivisional constraint, then the central staff proceeds to solve for the values of λ^{j0} in

$$\max \lambda_0{}^{10}(c_1{}^1 x_1{}^{10} + c_2{}^1 x_2{}^{10} + c_3{}^1 x_3{}^{10})$$

$$+ \lambda_0{}^{20}(c_1{}^2 x_1{}^{20} + c_2{}^2 x_2{}^{20} + c_3{}^2 x_3{}^{20} + c_4{}^2 x_4{}^{20})$$

subject to

$$\lambda_0{}^{10}(a_{11}{}^1 x_1{}^{10} + a_{12}{}^1 x_2{}^{10} + a_{13}{}^1 x_3{}^{10})$$

$$+ \lambda_0{}^{20}(a_{11}{}^2 x_1{}^{20} + a_{12}{}^2 x_2{}^{20} + a_{13}{}^2 x_3{}^{20} + a_4{}^2 x_4{}^{20}) \leq b_1$$

where the terms in the parentheses are now all known constants and the variables $\lambda_0{}^{j0}$ are further constrained by [42]

$$0 \leq \lambda_0{}^{10} \leq 1$$

$$0 \leq \lambda_0{}^{20} \leq 1$$

The latter is an ordinary linear programming problem and, hence, has dual constraints that may be written [43]

---

[42] It is evident that this problem always has a solution, at least for the cases $b_1 \geq 0$, if only because the choices $\lambda^{11} = \lambda^{21} = 0$ are admitted.

[43] The symbol "$\gtrless$" means "less than, equal to, or greater than."

$$\pi_1(a_{11}{}^1x_1{}^{10} + a_{12}{}^1x_2{}^{10} + a_{13}{}^1x_2{}^{10} + a_{13}{}^1x_3{}^{10})$$

$$\gtreqless (c_1{}^1x_1{}^{10} + c_2{}^1x_2{}^{10} + c_3{}^1x_3{}^{10})$$

depending on whether $\lambda_0{}^{10} = 1$, $0 < \lambda_0{}^{10} < 1$ or $\lambda_0{}^{10} = 0$, respectively, and

$$\pi_1(a_{11}{}^2x_1{}^{20} + a_{12}{}^2x_2{}^{20} + a_{13}{}^2x_3{}^{20} + a_{14}{}^2x_4{}^{20})$$

$$\gtreqless (c_1{}^2x_1{}^{20} + c_2{}^2x_2{}^{20} + c_3{}^2x_3{}^{20} + c_4{}^2x_4{}^{20})$$

depending on whether $\lambda_0{}^{20} = 1$, $0 < \lambda_2{}^{20} < 1$ or $\lambda_0{}^{20} = 0$ respectively. Finally, the condition

$$\pi_1 \geq 0$$

also applies.

The solution to the latter problem results in new prices which are designated as $\pi_1{}^1$. The latter are then used, as in model C, to form new divisional problems. For $j = 1$, the new problem is

$$\max (c_1{}^1x_1{}^1 + c_2{}^1x_2{}^1 + c_3{}^1x_3{}^1) - \pi_1{}^1(a_{11}{}^1x_1{}^1 + a_{12}{}^1x_2{}^1 + a_{13}{}^1x_3{}^1)$$

subject to

$$g_1{}^1(x_1{}^1, x_2{}^1) \leq R_1{}^1$$

$$g_2{}^1(x_1{}^1, x_2{}^1, x_3{}^1) \leq R_2{}^1$$

$$x_i{}^1 \geq 0 \qquad \text{for } i = 1, 2, 3$$

For $j = 2$, the problem to be solved now becomes

$$\max (c_1{}^2x_1{}^2 + c_2{}^2x_2{}^2 + c_3{}^2x_3{}^2 + c_4{}^2x_4{}^2)$$

$$- \pi_1{}^1(a_{11}{}^2x_1{}^2 + a_{12}{}^2x_2{}^2 + a_{13}{}^2x_3{}^2 + a_{14}{}^2x_4{}^2)$$

subject to

$$g_1{}^2(x_1{}^2, x_2{}^2, x_3{}^2, x_4{}^2) \leq R_1{}^2$$

$$x_i{}^2 \geq 0 \qquad \text{for } i = 1, 2, 3, 4$$

Thus each of the divisions now reaches a new solution

$$X^{11} = (x_1{}^{11}, x_2{}^{11}, x_3{}^{11})$$

$$X^{21} = (x_1{}^{21}, x_2{}^{21}, x_3{}^{21}, x_4{}^{21})$$

which, in general, will differ from the X^{j0} values by virtue of the "opportunity cost" information that is now impounded in the previously determined $\pi_1{}^1$ values.

With the two solutions, X^{j0} and X^{j1}, in hand, the central staff now alters its procedure. Instead of continuing as before, a new direct problem is determined in which the objective is to form an optimal convex combination of the preceding solutions relative to the data of the interdivisional constraint. That is, the following problem is now stated by the central office staff:

$$\max \left(\lambda_0^{11} \sum_{i=1}^{3} c_i^{1} x_i^{10} + \lambda_1^{11} \sum_{i=1}^{3} c_i^{1} x_i^{11} \right) + \left(\lambda_0^{21} \sum_{i=1}^{4} c_i^{2} x_i^{20} + \lambda_1^{21} \sum_{i=1}^{4} c_i^{2} x_i^{21} \right)$$

subject to

$$b_1 \geq \left(\lambda_0^{11} \sum_{i=1}^{3} a_{1i}^{1} x_i^{10} + \lambda_1^{11} \sum_{i=1}^{3} a_{1i}^{1} x_i^{11} \right) + \left(\lambda_0^{21} \sum_{i=1}^{4} a_{1i}^{2} x_i^{20} + \lambda_1^{21} \sum_{i=1}^{4} a_{1i}^{2} x_i^{21} \right)$$

$$1 = \lambda_0^{11} \qquad\qquad + \lambda_1^{11}$$

$$1 = \qquad\qquad\qquad\qquad \lambda_0^{21} \qquad\qquad + \lambda_1^{21}$$

$$0 \leq \lambda_0^{11}, \lambda_1^{11}, \lambda_0^{21}, \lambda_1^{21}$$

This is, again, a linear programming problem in the variables λ_0^{j1}, λ_1^{j1} since the expressions appearing inside the summation signs are all known constants. Moreover, the preceding solutions can all be obtained by choosing the values of λ_0^{j1} and λ_1^{j1} equal to zero or one, as required, and so the new functional value must be at least as great as the preceding ones. Any solution of this problem will satisfy the interdivisional constraint. By hypothesis, also, each division is choosing only x_i^{j} values that satisfy its own intradivisional constraints. Hence all constraints are satisfied.

Because the new central office problem that was just exhibited is an ordinary linear programming problem, it will have an associated dual problem from which new price guides may be determined, e.g., via the simplex method. On the other hand, it may also terminate the process at this stage, in which event division $j = 1$ is instructed to produce

$$\tilde{X}^{11} = \lambda_0^{11} X_0^{10} + \lambda_1^{11} X_1^{11}$$

or

$$(\tilde{x}_1^{11}, \tilde{x}_2^{11}, \tilde{x}_3^{11})$$

$$= (\lambda_0^{11} x_1^{10} + \lambda_1^{11} x_1^{11}, \lambda_0^{11} x_2^{10} + \lambda_1^{11} x_2^{11}, \lambda_0^{11} x_3^{10} + \lambda_1^{11} x_3^{11})$$

where the $\lambda_0^{11}, \lambda_1^{11} \geq 0$, $\lambda_0^{11} + \lambda_1^{11} = 1$ are optimal values obtained by solving the above linear programming problem. The values for $\tilde{X}^{21}$ are obtained in a similar fashion from the optimal values of λ^{21} and the preceding x_i^{20}, x_i^{21} which were already available.

Enough has probably been said to indicate, now, how the procedure may be applied in more general situations. It is probably also evident that numerous problems still remain to be confronted. Nothing has been said, for instance, about methods for controlling the point of termination. The problem of externalities remains to be considered when these phenomena occur in the intradivisional constraints and, finally, certain game theoretic problems may also be encountered; for instance, an announced termination point (or even an unannounced one) may cause the division managers to adopt strategies that are more or less optimal for themselves at the expense of over-all objectives, and it is even possible that they may enter into coalitions with other division managers for still better opportunities at strategic exploitation. On the other hand, the indicated approach is related, at least formally, to currently employed procedures in budgeting by means of which physical quotas, transfer prices, etc., are established and it does offer certain further advantages in that suitable solution (or bounding) procedures may be devised, at least in principle, for rapidly studying the consequences that might ensue from the kinds of production-costing-marketing that are being considered.

Generalization to case where externalities are present. The foregoing discussion assumed the absence of externalities. The question naturally arises as to whether pricing schemes can be utilized within a divisionalized organization when externalities are present. In this section we shall consider an extension of the scheme just presented to account for such externalities. To maintain the continuity of the argument, we view the decision problem on the divisional level. Thus externalities exist when the technology and criterion function of at least one division is affected by the activities contained in another division.

Suppose that division η affects the technology of a subset of the rest of the divisions which we refer to as Y. For simplicity of the description, each division in Y is affected by the same activity in division η. Call this activity $x_i^{*\eta}$. We proceed by asking each division in Y to propose in addition to its own tentative activity levels a tentative level of $x_i^{*\eta}$ which would be optimal for that division. In the game theory analogy, each player specifies not only his own strategies but also the strategy he would like his opponents to play. In general, each player's specification of the strategies will differ. The central staff group, with only a knowledge of the over-all criterion function and the tentative proposals, solves a programming problem (linear if the criterion function is linear) to determine a preliminary set of "consistent" strategies. It uses these to determine preliminary price guides. Each player in this N person nonzero sum game now faces a new payoff matrix, and again specifies the strategies for the players involved. This process continues for a predetermined number of iterations after which the central staff group issues a set of consistent strategies for each division to follow. As in the previous discussion, the central staff need not have any knowledge of the technology.

To formalize and clarify this verbal discussion, let us consider the following model. This assumed organization is of the same form as presented in model A except that externalities are introduced as indicated below. Thus our model is of the form:

$$\max \sum_j \sum_i c_i{}^j x_i{}^j$$

subject to

I.

$$\sum_j \sum_i a_{zi}{}^j x_i{}^j \le b_z \qquad z = 1, \cdots, \ell$$

II.

$$g_q{}^j(x_1{}^j, \cdots, x_{i_j}{}^j) \le R_q{}^j \qquad j \notin Y$$

$$g_q{}^j(x_1{}^j, \cdots, x_{i_j}{}^j; x_{i*}{}^\eta) \le R_q{}^j \qquad j \in Y$$

$$q = 1, \cdots, m_j$$

$$x_i{}^j \ge 0 \qquad j = 1, \cdots, m$$

For each division $j \in Y$ we define a new variable $x_{i_{j+1}}^j$ to replace $x_{i*}{}^\eta$. Thus we have for $j \in Y$,

$$g_q{}^j(x_1{}^j, \cdots, x_{i_j}{}^j; x_{i_{j+1}}^j) \le R_q{}^j$$

and

$$x_{i_{j+1}}^j = x_{i*}{}^\eta$$

for each $j \in Y$. The new model obtained by this transformation of variables is obviously equivalent to the original problem in the sense that the optimal solutions to both models are the same. We shall proceed using the modified model. We write the model in the form:

$$\max \sum_j \sum_i c_i{}^j x_i{}^j$$

subject to

I.

$$\sum_j \sum_i a_{zi}{}^j x_i{}^j \le b_z \qquad z = 1, \cdots, \ell$$

$$x_{i_{j+1}}^j - x_{i*}{}^\eta = 0 \qquad j \in Y$$

II.

$$g_q{}^j(x_1{}^j, \cdots, x_{i_j}{}^j) \le R_q{}^j \qquad j \notin Y$$

$$q_q{}^j(x_1{}^j, \cdots, x_{i_{j+1}}^j) \le R_q{}^j \qquad j \in Y$$

$$x_i{}^j \ge 0$$

Note that the consistency condition on the selection of strategies is now part of the type-I constraints.

We can now bring the present discussion to a close by observing that the solution and pricing procedures are analogous here to the previous case of no externalities. Thus we can then say we have at least illustrated an approach to generating price guides in a decentralized or quasi-decentralized firm. The partitioning of the information is still achieved since the central staff only need be informed of the projected plans of the various units but, in contrast, to earlier schemes these are models only of "quasi-decentralization" in that the central staff makes the final decision on plans.

Conclusion

The examples presented in this chapter are illustrative rather than exhaustive even for the two companies that were examined in any detail. Nevertheless, they have served to help us point up certain issues in a concrete fashion. Decentralization as understood and practiced in these companies bears, at best, only a partial relation to the economist's conception of a Smithian "invisible hand" which leads each unit to act to the best interests of an over-all society by striving only to promote its own best interests by reference to a suitably arranged system of prices.[44]

Additional points have also emerged from our discussion of the practices utilized by the companies that were discussed earlier in the chapter. From the point of view of planning, i.e., deciding on output, type of product, etc., little authority was decentralized. However, from the point of view of cost control, we found that much responsibility was delegated to divisional managers. Each division was highly motivated through a "profit" incentive[45] to improve its own cost structure and to challenge and thus improve the cost basis of the other divisions from which it purchased products.

Note, now, how this differs from the traditional preoccupation of economic theorists with decentralization in planning decisions only. Partly this arises because of the different kinds of institutional structures that are assumed. (For instance, in "market economics" there is no "higher authority" to which an entrepreneur can appeal for a higher price merely because he has been assigned a less than adequate plant or volume.) Differences also arise because of other simplifying as-

---

[44] For a recent discussion of decentralization in the firm from the point of view of classical economics, see K. J. Arrow [25].

[45] The term "incentive" seems appropriate in that the division managers knew, or believed, that the "profit" records generated by their activities would affect their prospects for promotion within the company.

sumptions which are made for various reasons in formal economics but which cannot be made in practical company operations. For instance, the assumption of equality of access to available technology, at a price, cannot be made in the latter cases. Neither can the primitive organization assumptions of economic analysis be carried over into this context. Control of cost incurrence by delegated subordinates does not exist as a problem in economic theory and therefore the organization and information forms needed to secure such cost control are also nonexistent.[46]

In the later parts of this chapter we discussed in a more formal manner questions of decentralization of decision making. We were concerned with the organization of a decentralized system and the specific role of price guides once a formal model is presented. We saw that price guides were used to coordinate independent decision makers when certain resource or other types of constraint limited the possible choices open to each decision maker.

By adding certain complications into the model in the form of nonseparable functions, we found that difficulties arose in pure reliance on price guides. This suggested a possible study of more general decentralized systems, e.g., systems which employ other devices besides prices for coordination.

In the final section of the chapter we studied an operational scheme for determining price guides. We introduced a hierarchy in terms of a central staff coordinating unit and various divisional subunits. The central staff relied on activity proposals of divisional managers in order to determine price guides. Divisional managers, in turn, relied on price guides supplied by central staff to determine their tentative proposals.

This chapter has explored decentralized decision making within the firm. We have presented a discussion of present practices to suggest topics for theoretical research. We have also developed several theoretical models which should suggest areas for improvement in present practices.

We can perhaps best now refer once more to some of the assumptions that are usually made in formal economic analysis. For this purpose we may find it useful to employ the usual terminology of economics and distinguish between the following three types of cases:

---

[46] Even in the activity analysis models of T. C. Koopmans [323], the technological matrix is assumed to be given and not subject to further variation.

1. Each entrepreneur can determine the total profit he will obtain from each of his possible decisions, irrespective of the actions of his competitors.[47]

2. Each entrepreneur can determine an optimal strategy—i.e., a "best profit strategy"—without reference to competitor reactions, but the total profit he will obtain from an optimizing decision depends on actions taken by his competitors.

3. Some entrepreneurs cannot even determine an optimal course of action—much less their total profits—unless they first know the decisions that will be made by competitors.

Case 1 is probably sufficiently clear, and case 2 may be thought of in terms of a game theoretic analogy wherein an entrepreneur knows that his best choice is row i of a payoff matrix, but he cannot know his a_{ij} payoff until another player has designated the jth column as his choice. It can be shown that the properties of dominance and separability are closely associated.[48] Case 3, on the other hand, involves (in general) problems of nonseparability and, as a consequence, uncertainty in the decision-making processes.

Much of the behavioral science literature on organizations appears to assume that the main problem is to ensure that each person is doing his best. Yet, as is easily shown, the optimization in each separate part of a firm will not generally produce an over-all optimum, and it is also possible, of course, that the individual optima are not even compatible with each other or a constraint system of the firm. Perhaps the extreme form of decentralization entailed in a market economy has rather naturally caused economists to avoid a like course of analysis. Thus, even in case 1, it is not assumed that an over-all (Pareto) optimum is achieved except under special conditions like those in the theory of perfect markets.

By assuming that market prices will generally lead to decision-making units that "internalize" any "externalities" which may be present, much of the literature in economics has tended to ignore case 3. When this is done, it is possible to conceive that the desired optima (e.g., via specified over-all "welfare functions") will be obtained either directly via market prices or via "pricelike" devices

---

[47] Terms like "entrepreneur," "competitors," "profit," etc., are here to be accorded only generic significance in that they are assumed to include terms like "managers," "collaborators," "benefits," or "penalties," etc.

[48] These and other aspects of the present discussion are treated extensively in my doctoral dissertation [597].

such as taxes and subsidies. Then, without too much strain on the information processing capabilities for the relevant "entrepreneurs," it is possible to conceive that they will be led by an "invisible hand" to an over-all optimum while merely pursuing their own best interests, e.g., by reference to the immediate "facts" only of their own situations.

The growth of large corporate enterprises has been associated with various experiments in "decentralization" and related managerial devices. One such device is represented by the so-called transfer pricing arrangements discussed earlier in this chapter. Some of the literature in accounting, business practice, etc., has here drawn on available theory in economic analysis. But some caution is then needed. In particular, it cannot be safely assumed that the problem of externalities is not present within the firm or that, when present, the externality problem will be solved in the way that a market economy is assumed to solve it. Yet, as we have already seen, the externality problem requires various forms of organization intervention, quota setting, etc., which are very different from the "prices" or "pricelike" devices of economic theory. Thus, the mechanisms discussed in the final sections of this chapter generally produced only "mixed systems" in which prices could form at best only part of the total arrangements for achieving an over-all optimum.

This chapter does not, of course, exhaust all of the problems and possible routes of solution, model making, etc. Only some of the problems requiring further attention were briefly mentioned. There is, for instance, the problem of internal incentives since, unlike the arrangements of market economics, the division managers of a firm are not usually given full authority to dispose of the book profits which accrue from their activities. As we also observed, the problems of "controlling" behavior of division managers is apparently a factor to be considered.

Economic theory has very little to offer on problems like these. It thus seems fair to conclude that a mixed behavioral science-economic approach [49] is probably the best course to follow in any study of the kinds of organization-information arrangements that could be effected for practical managerial use. But then it might be assumed that such "mixed" approaches might also yield results of further value such as (1) the limits of prices when serving as a general guide to economic development or (2) the kinds of motivation-aspiration phenomena that may appear when various kinds of pricing artifacts are used. This is by way of saying, of course, that progress in these kinds of studies

---

[49] And other approaches, too, of course.

need not stop at the boundary set by managerial applications. They may well prove fruitful in providing insight or knowledge for other parts of economics and the behavioral sciences generally.

APPENDIX

In this appendix we shall take the opportunity to amplify certain mathematical questions which were raised in this chapter. Consider the set of convex constraints for the jth division

$$g_q{}^j(x_1{}^j, \cdots, x_{i_j}{}^j) \leq R_q{}^j \qquad q = 1, \cdots, m_j$$

and the set

$$X^j = \{x^j = (x_1{}^j, \cdots, x_{i_j}{}^j) \mid g_1{}^j(x_1{}^j, \cdots, x_{i_j}{}^j) \leq R_1{}^j, \cdots,$$

$$g_{m_j}{}^j(x_1{}^j, \cdots, x_{i_j}{}^j) \leq R_{m_j}{}^j, x_1{}^j \geq 0, \cdots, x_{i_j}{}^j \geq 0\}$$

Assuming the consistency of the constraints, the set X^j is convex. Boundedness may be assured by introducing a "regularizing" constraint of the form [50]

$$\sum_{i=1}^{i_j} x_i{}^j \leq K^j$$

Thus each X^j may be considered as a closed, bounded convex set.

THEOREM I. A closed, bounded convex set is the convex hull of its extreme points.

Proof. The proof is based on an induction argument using the dimensionality of the space. However, we omit the proof.

From Theorem I, any point $x^j \in X^j$ can be represented as

$$x^j = \sum_{\eta \in I_j} \lambda_\eta{}^j e_\eta{}^j$$

$$\Sigma \lambda_\eta{}^j = 1 \qquad e_\eta{}^j \in E^j$$

$$\lambda_\eta{}^j \geq 0$$

where I_j represents an index set, and E^j is the set of extreme points of the set X^j. Using the above expression, the nonlinear programming problem studied may be written, employing matrix notation, as:

$$\max \sum_{j=1}^m \sum_{\eta \in I_j} \lambda_\eta{}^j C_j e_\eta{}^j$$

---

[50] See Charnes and Cooper [113].

subject to

$$\sum_{j=1}^{m} \sum_{\eta \in I_j} \lambda_\eta{}^j A_j e_\eta{}^j = b$$

$$\sum_{\eta \in I_j} \lambda_\eta{}^j = 1 \qquad j = 1, \cdots, m$$

$$\lambda_\eta{}^j \geq 0 \qquad \text{all } j, \eta$$

where C_j are row vectors and A_j are matrices of appropriate order. Define

$$A_j e_\eta{}^j = d_{\eta j}$$

$$C_j e_\eta{}^j = C_{\eta j}$$

Then we may write the above in the form

$$\max \sum_{j=1}^{m} \sum_{\eta \in I_j} \lambda_\eta{}^j C_{\eta j}$$

subject to

$$\sum_{j=1}^{m} \sum_{\eta \in I_j} d_{\eta j} \lambda_\eta{}^j = b$$

$$\sum_{\eta \in I_j} \lambda_\eta{}^j = 1 \qquad j = 1, \cdots, m$$

$$\lambda_\eta{}^j \geq 0 \qquad \text{all } j, \eta$$

We may further define $q_{\eta j} = \begin{bmatrix} d_{\eta j} \\ u_j \end{bmatrix}$, where u_j is the jth unit vector having m components. Therefore we have

$$\max \sum_{j=1}^{m} \sum_{\eta \in I_j} \lambda_\eta{}^j C_{\eta j}$$

subject to

$$\sum_{j=1}^{m} \sum_{\eta \in I_j} q_{\eta j} \lambda_\eta{}^j = b_0 \qquad b_0 = \begin{pmatrix} b \\ 1 \\ \vdots \\ 1 \end{pmatrix}$$

$$\lambda_\eta{}^j \geq 0 \qquad \text{all } j, \eta$$

Dantzig and Wolfe [51] have pointed out that for the case where the sets $\{E_j\}$ are all finite, we need not know all extreme points to

---

[51] [153].

initiate the algorithm. It is only necessary to know those extreme points which are associated with basic columns. These extreme points are generated as part of the process of deciding which column should next enter the basis. These observations are also valid for the case of an infinite number of extreme points.

To amplify these remarks, consider that at a certain stage of the iteration we have a basis matrix B which is nonsingular. It follows that we can write any basic feasible solution as $\Lambda_B = B^{-1}b_0$. Let $\Pi = (\Pi_1, \Pi_2) = C_B B^{-1}$ be the vector of simplex multipliers for the current basis, where C_B is a row vector of elements $C_{\eta j}$ which correspond to the columns of B. Then let

$$Z_{\eta j} - C_{\eta j} = C_B B^{-1} q_{\eta j} - C_{\eta j} = (\Pi_1 A_j - C_j) e_\eta{}^j + \Pi_{2j}$$

It is clear that the condition for the achievement of an optimum in the simplex procedure, i.e., $Z_{\eta j} - C_{\eta j} \geqq 0$ for all η, j, is still applicable in the case the sets $\{E_j\}$ are no longer finite. To determine this, we solve m auxiliary divisional problems

$$\max C_j X'^j - \Pi_1 A_j X'^j$$

subject to

$$g_q{}^j(X^j) \leq R_q{}^j \qquad X^j = (x_1{}^j, \cdots, x_i{}^j)$$

$$X'^j \geq 0 \qquad q = 1, \cdots, m_j$$

The solution to this problem determines an extreme point $e_\eta{}^j \in E^j$ since the criterion function is linear.

In the case where an over-all maximum solution to the problem has not been achieved, we indicate the manner in which central staff utilizes the new information supplied by the divisions. Denote by q_{K*j} the column associated with the maximal solution to the jth subproblem. Thus

$$q_{K*j} = BZ^{K*j}$$

where Z^{K*j} is a column vector of so-called tableau elements. We define Z as the matrix $(Z^{K*1}, \cdots, Z^{K*m})$, $\Theta' = (\Theta_1, \cdots, \Theta_m)$ and $\hat{B} = [q_{K*1}, \cdots, q_{K*m}]$. Then we have

$$\hat{B}\Theta + B(\Lambda_B - Z\Theta) = b_0$$

where we must have $\Lambda_B - Z\Theta \geqq 0$

$$\Theta \geqq 0$$

Let C_ρ be the vector of elements $C_{\eta j}$ associated with Θ. The criterion function may be written

$$C_B(\Lambda_B - Z\Theta) + C_\rho\Theta = C_B\Lambda_B - (C_B Z - C_\rho)\Theta$$

Then we form the following linear programming problem

$$\max_{\Theta} - (C_B Z - C_\rho)\Theta$$

subject to

$$\Lambda_B - Z\Theta \geq 0$$

$$\Theta \geq 0$$

In this manner we may determine the greatest possible increase in the over-all criterion function by combining the divisional proposals with present tentative central staff plans.

Convergence of the algorithm, if a maximal value exists, can easily be demonstrated and we omit the details for lack of space. It suffices to note that boundedness of the criterion function implies that in the limit $Z_{\eta j} - C_{\eta j} \geq 0$, all η, j, for some basic feasible solution.

23

EXPERIMENTAL GAMING AND SOME ASPECTS OF COMPETITIVE BEHAVIOR

Martin Shubik

Introduction [1]

Today there are many hundreds of economic and military games in existence; these serve many quite different purposes. Some are for training, others for teaching, still others are operational and may be used for exploring plans and investigating alternative paths of action. Among them is a small group of games the major purpose of which is to serve as laboratory apparatus for the experimental investigation of different aspects of human behavior. The psychologist, social-psychologist, sociologist, psychiatrist, economist, and anthropologist have all been interested in games from very diverse viewpoints. Three broad areas can be usefully distinguished; they are: learning, organization, and competition. Each one of these can no doubt be approached from the special interests of the different disciplines noted above.

As our knowledge is limited, there is little doubt that a great number of fundamentally different approaches will all yield worthwhile and interesting results. They will contribute a few extra pieces to the intricate mosaic that makes up human behavior in any complex situation. The task of synthesizing the diverse results of investigations whose prime emphasis has been economics, psychology or sociology, etc., will have to be performed before we are able to obtain an understanding balanced both in depth and breadth.

[1] This research was supported in part by the Office of Naval Research under Contract No. Nonr 3775(00), NR 047040.

Having noted the scope of experimental gaming, the remainder of this chapter deals primarily with the problems of competition, and is approached with an emphasis on its economic and strategic aspects.

Some Theoretical Considerations

Even casual reflection will lead the reader to conclude that we do not possess clear or even adequate concepts of collusion, cooperation, competition, etc. To clarify our thoughts, we make distinctions in terms of environment, behavior, and action operators. We may be in a position to observe the environment and the behavior of the actors; we are not in a position to observe directly the action operators. Our theories for the solution to a game are usually of the form such that we postulate a set of action operators and predict that they will cause a certain behavior to be observed when they are applied to a specific environment. As will be noted below in further detail, there is no guarantee that different action operators will not cause the same behavior when applied to a given environment.

In constructing models for gaming investigation, formal game theory can be of considerable help if one realizes its methodological limitations and modifies or enlarges the methodology according to the needs at hand. For example, two areas where this is most necessary concern the termination rule of the gaming situation and the information conditions prevailing throughout the game. For the most part, behavioral scientists are interested in processes which have an uncertain termination date and about which the participants are usually poorly informed. The poker game, with a fixed number of players and a definite time for termination, is, for many purposes, a very poor analogue of human processes.

Much of the discussion of game theoretic concepts and many of the simple experiments in gaming have been based upon the representation of games by means of payoff matrices. An example of a pair of payoff matrices for a two-person nonconstant sum game, where each player has two strategies, is given below:

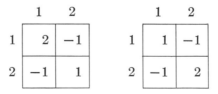

A strategy for each player consists of selecting either the number 1 or 2. If both, for example, select 1, then the first player obtains 2

and the second (or column) player obtains 1. In many experiments, simple games of this variety are repeated many times. Depending on how these one period games are put together, many importantly different "supergames" can be constructed. The difference in the games centers primarily upon information and communication conditions. For example, three different games may be described as "supersilent," "silent," and "noisy." In the first, the individual is informed only of the outcome of his own moves at the end of the game; he is not informed about the individual moves of his competitors or their payoffs until the termination of the supergame. In the second, the player may be supplied with information on the average performance and payoffs of his competitors; he may, for example, be informed of the average advertising budget in an industry but not know the breakdown. In the third case, all individuals are completely informed of the moves of their competitors at the end of each period as well as the resultant payoffs.

Although the various analyses of the theory of games have been based upon the assumption that players know the rules of the game, in many games the experimenter does not inform the players of the fine structure needed to give them this knowledge; thus, neither the parameters nor the functional form of, say, a demand equation may be known to the participants in a business game. Part of their problem will be to determine the unknown structure of their market.

The game tree diagrams on pp. 452–453 illustrate some of the more important possibilities in information conditions in repeated matrix games. They represent the simple game where two players each select an integer between 1 and 10. The individual who selects the smallest number wins that amount; the individual with the higher number obtains zero. If they select the same number, the referee randomizes to determine who is awarded the value of the bid. The matrix for the one-shot game is given on p. 452.

The tree for the noisy game, where players are completely informed after the play of each subgame, is indicated in Fig. 1.

For ease of exposition in the next two diagrams, assume that each player selects only one of three numbers in each period. In Fig. 1, as the players move simultaneously in each subgame, we note that player 2 is not aware of the choice of player 1, but is informed after he has moved; thus, at the end of each period, the information sets are one element sets. In the supersilent game illustrated in Fig. 2, the player does not obtain any information until the end of the game. In effect, he could be playing a set of simultaneous one move games.

In the silent game illustrated in Fig. 3, the player does not know

Payoff for Player 1

	1	2	3	4	5	6	7	8	9	10
1	0.5	1	1	1	1	1	1	1	1	1
2	0	1	2	2	2	2	2	2	2	2
3	0	0	1.5	3	3	3	3	3	3	3
4	0	0	0	2	4	4	4	4	4	4
5	0	0	0	0	2.5	5	5	5	5	5
6	0	0	0	0	0	3	6	6	6	6
7	0	0	0	0	0	0	3.5	7	7	7
8	0	0	0	0	0	0	0	4	8	8
9	0	0	0	0	0	0	0	0	4.5	9
10	0	0	0	0	0	0	0	0	0	5

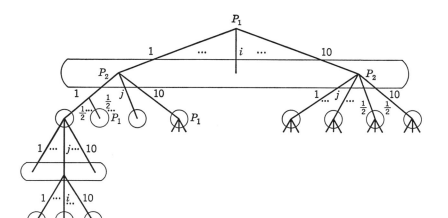

FIGURE 1

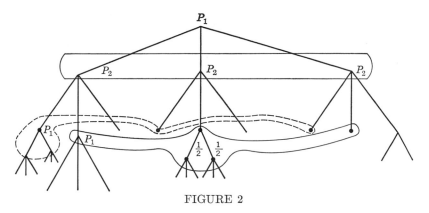

FIGURE 2

if a tie has occurred, if he won randomly, or if he won by under-cutting his competitor. Thus, we observe that after the second player has moved, the number of elements in the information sets of the first player will depend upon the move he had originally chosen. The difference in information sets has a great influence upon the possibilities for communication and coordination as is manifested in conditions for signaling.

In even relatively uncomplicated repeated matrix games, some of the solution concepts which may give rather simple unique predictions for the single period game, no longer do so. For example, the concept of a noncooperative equilibrium point is unambiguous in a matrix game, and if conditions are "nice," the equilibrium point may be unique; however, in iterated games there can be families of equilibrium points and different types may be distinguished and interpreted

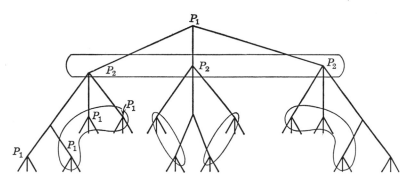

FIGURE 3

as state equilibria or threat equilibria ranging all the way from causing minimal to almost jointly maximal outcomes.[2] The degree of plausibility that one may wish to attach to these different equilibria calls for interpretations in terms of communication, belief in threats, and many problems of inference.

Both in gaming experiments and in much of the literature of game theory and the more popular semitechnical discussions of threats, bargaining, and competitive situations, two broad distinctions have been made; they are between cooperative and noncooperative solutions to games. The two best-known solution concepts which typify this distinction are the von-Neumann and Morgenstern stable-set solution to a game in which the players cooperate to jointly maximize and then divide the proceeds; and the Nash noncooperative equilibrium point (which is a generalization of the Cournot equilibrium point). Parenthetically, we must note at this point that one of the greatest stumbling blocks to the optimal usage of the theory of games has been some of its unfortunate terminology. The three words which have probably done the most damage have been "game, cooperative, and noncooperative." Mathematicians, when working with the mathematical theory of games, have not been impeded in their progress as the connotations of the words do not cause barriers in conceptualization in the formal manipulation of well-defined systems; they do, however, in model-building and application. Those interested in gaming have been most interested in the latter aspects and have been adversely affected.

The word game has unfortunate connotations in terms of play; lack of seriousness and enjoyment. The dropping of Hydrogen bombs is not part of a game in the parlance either of the man in the street or in the parlance of behavioral science. The words cooperative and noncooperative appear to present a dichotomy where none exists. The distinctions which are important for those who wish to apply the valuable concepts of game theory concern information, communication, signaling, learning, and so forth. Most of them refer to dynamic considerations as do most gaming experiments, whereas many (although not all) of the formal concepts of solution in the theory of games have been developed for static situations.

Three broad divisions of experimental gaming have been: 1. Gaming concerned primarily with learning, problem solving, and organization; these are modeled as one-person nonzero-sum games and are of prime concern to psychologists and sociologists. 2. Gaming involving two or

---

[2] See Griesmer and Shubik [235].

more teams in face-to-face communication where threats may be made and bargaining, haggling, ploying, etc., takes place. 3. Games with two or more teams where there is no direct communication. The communication that does exist takes place through a (usually) impersonal mechanism which indicates certain outcomes as a function of the actions of the teams. The second type of game is of most interest to those investigating negotiation, labor, or international bargaining, psychologists, sociologists, social-psychologists, political scientists and some economists. The third type of game is of considerable importance to the economist investigating the functioning of market mechanisms. Having observed the different types of games and noted some of the different interests, a few of the many concepts of solution are presented and discussed below.

Table 1 lists seven different solution concepts relevant to games played primarily under conditions where there is no face-to-face communication. Several of the solutions pertain only to economic market games. Four divisions are made in the headings, they are respectively into two-person games and into n-person games, where n is greater than two; each of these categories is split further into symmetric and nonsymmetric games. Formal analysis of many-person models is in general difficult. The mere task of calculating what outcome will be predicted by a given solution concept is onerous. In many cases, it is not known if certain solution concepts will lead to unique predictions. Symmetry is of considerable help in solving games. In general, in gaming, symmetry of varying degrees may be used for purposes of comparison and analysis. In general, nonsymmetric games are far more difficult to analyze than those which are symmetric (a possible exception to this rule is where one player is very different from the others). Although the qualitative effects of numbers of participants are most evident in games with face-to-face communication, even in games without this, the two-person games are somewhat special, both from the viewpoint of analysis and from the nature of the interaction of the players.

The entries in the table are by no means mathematically rigorous; there are many problems in modeling which have not been fully investigated and which must be solved before certain concepts of solution can be given meaning. Thus, for example, an eighth solution concept in addition to the seven given in Table 1 would be that economic organizations strive to maximize growth; however, growth is usually hard to define.

The sense of the statements in Table 1 is illustrated in a more detailed discussion of solution 1. It is noted that the two-person sym-

Table 1   Solution Concepts

(Games without Face-to-Face Communication)

	2-Person Games		n-Person Games $n > 2$	
	Symmetric	Nonsymmetric	Symmetric	Nonsymmetric
1. Noncooperative equilibrium	Generally solvable, often unique.	Often solvable unique?	Generally solvable often unique, otherwise usually finite	Solvable in special cases unique? finite?
2. Beat the average	Generally solvable, unique (except for degenerate cases). A two-person zero sum game	Not well defined	Generally solvable unique (except for degenerate cases)	Not well defined
3. Efficient point	Solvable provided that the model of market structure is sufficiently simple. With quadratic profits and capacity restraints, this leads to linear programming determination of solutions.			
4. Market share	Popular as a conjecture, but not always well defined; if reasonable limits on price paid for market share are introduced, this is equivalent to "beat the average" for symmetric cases.			
5. Price leader	Solvable and, in general, unique; equivalent to a game with perfect information for $n = 2$. Several problems of economic model building have not been settled.			
6. Aspiration level	A certain amount of theory developed in psychology and economics. Little known analytically or experimentally. Many problems of psychological, social, and economic model building have not been settled.			
7. Dynamic equilibria, games of economic survival	Solvable in special cases, rarely unique; usually families of equilibria with one or more parameters. Little known analytically or experimentally. Many problems of psychological, social, and economic model building have not been settled.			

metric game is "generally solvable" and that the equilibrium points are "often unique." In theory, all matrix games have equilibrium points; depending upon their size and entries, they may present computation problems. In general, little is known about the conditions for the existence of unique equilibrium points. In many cases, however, it is easy to construct games which are adequate for experimental purposes and which have unique equilibrium points.

We have noted above that the solution criteria may be regarded as operators operating upon the environment as reflected in the payoff functions; whereas, the solutions may be interpreted as the predicted behavior. The following three examples of 2 × 2 matrix games illustrate some of the problems concerning the multiplicity of solutions and the possibility that the same solution may be predicted by several different theories.

9, 11	7, 11
9, 13	7, 13

Matrix *A*

12, 12	10, 11
10, 11	9, 9

Matrix *B*

12, 12	8, 13
13, 8	9, 9

Matrix *C*

Matrix *A* provides an example of a game which has four equilibrium points out of four possible outcomes. If we were predicting that the players would jointly maximize, then the lower left-hand corner would be predicted. For matrix *B*, the entry in the upper left-hand corner is both jointly maximal and is the unique equilibrium point in this game. In matrix *C*, the beat the average and equilibrium point solutions are the same and are in the lower right-hand corner; the joint maximum is different and is in the upper left corner.

In the comments on the *n*-person games, it is noted that the solutions are "usually finite." By this we mean that, even when the payoffs are continuous, there are usually no areas or other continuous sets of solutions; this is not always the case as will be seen in Table 2 where solutions involving face-to-face communication are listed.

It can be seen in Table 2 that the predictive power of most of the cooperative solutions is not great and, hence, from the viewpoint of experimentation, several problems are posed. It is not difficult to construct games in which not only are there many solutions for some of the concepts; not only do these solutions each contain large sets of imputations but also the broad predictions of several different theories have large areas of overlap. The Shapley, Nash, and Harsanyi values appear to be the ones best suited for experimentation at this time.

The number of different solution concepts (many others have not been mentioned) and the broadness of their predictions stresses that we do not possess adequate characterizations of dynamic group processes. Game theory, which is primarily a methodology, cannot be expected to be a substitute for sociology, psychology, economics or organization theory. The various concepts of solution to *n*-person games with communication are of interest and of use in generating hypotheses and providing a certain amount of analysis to go along with these

Table 2   Solution Concepts [3]

(Games with Face-to-Face Communication)

	2-Person Games		n-Person Games	
	Symmetric	Nonsymmetric	Symmetry	Nonsymmetry
1. Von Neumann-Morgenstern stable sets	In general, these solutions are numerous and except for special cases, are difficult to compute. Given the multiplicity of solutions and the large number of imputations in each solution, these are difficult to investigate experimentally.			
2. Shapley value	These solutions are unique and are easy to compute for symmetric games; they are difficult to compute for nonsymmetric games. However, recently considerable progress has been made by Shapley. For games with ten or fewer players, computation presents no major difficulty.			
3. Nash cooperative game (i) with side payment (ii) without side payment	These solutions are unique and can be computed. They have been examined experimentally by Stone.		This solution is not well defined for games with more than two players.	
4. Harsanyi value	These solutions are unique and are easy to compute for symmetric games. For nonsymmetric games, they are difficult to calculate. They represent a generalization of the Shapley value and coincide with it when utilities are measurable and comparable.			
5. Aumann-Maschler bargaining sets	Although these solutions are numerous, they tend to be less than the von Neumann-Morgenstern solutions. For some very simple 3-person games, they have been investigated experimentally.			
6. Luce ψ stability	For this solution concept, a limitation is placed upon the formation of coalitions, beyond that side payments are permitted and individual and group rationality conditions are to be satisfied. Solutions are, in general, difficult to compute.			
7. Shubik $k - r$ stability	This is a partially "cooperative," partially "noncooperative" solution designed for games of indeterminate length, utilizing concepts of policing sets of players attempting to enforce a *status quo* by means of threats. Solutions tend to be many parameter sets of equilibrium points.			
8. Vickrey self-policing sets	Vickrey imposes added conditions on the von Neumann-Morgenstern concept of solution by introducing assumptions on the ability of conditions to be self-policing.			

hypotheses; however, in my estimation, it would be wise to consider them in the light of knowledge of limited areas of interest, to add more structure to the games under investigation, and to investigate and modify them as our substantive knowledge increases. For this reason, my own work has been restricted primarily to games with an

---

[3] For a discussion of solutions 1, 2, 3, and 6, see [356]; for 4, see [554a]; for 5, see [31]; for 7, see [492]; and for 8, see [554b].

economic background and with limited or no face-to-face communication between teams. There is an important class of situations which has this property and, furthermore, which provides many structural limitations which in turn cuts down the generality of the games to be considered.

In this section, we have attempted to stress the importance of game theory as an aid to gaming which is a tool of investigation in the behavioral sciences. Neither provides an alternative to substantive knowledge, both together provide additional methods for obtaining that knowledge.

Some Experimental Games

The remaining remarks are confined to gaming on competitive behavior with the prime interest being in market situations; there has been a great amount of work done recently with games of this type. Chamberlin, Hoggatt, Siegel, Fouraker, Shubik, Stern, and Stone, as well as many others, have examined and experimented with very simplified games based on economic considerations. Feeney, Hoggatt, Levitan, and Shubik have considered games which, although they are relatively simple in comparison to many of the large business games in existence, are considerably more complex than the preponderance of experimental games used in the study of bargaining, bidding, and simple competitive games without face-to-face communication. These latter games lie between the relatively austere and "environment-poor" laboratory experiments, as typified by Fouraker, Shubik, and Siegel [201], and the more or less "environment-rich" business and marketing games which have now been played at many business schools, corporations, and universities.

There is a fundamental difficulty in the use of gaming as an experimental device which has not yet been overcome. If the game is very simple, it is possible to exert considerable control over it experimentally and to utilize well-known procedures. Unfortunately, as the environment is "purified," it is quite possible that the effects of minor cues and noises become magnified. Kennedy has suggested that the briefing given to the participants at the start of the experiment may have considerable influence and this appears to be the case. Another way of considering some of the difficulties in performing "environment-poor" experiments on competition is that there is a considerable amount of sociological, psychological, and economic conditioning relevant to this type of activity, and that it is difficult to "dump memory" to understand the biases of the participants or to clear memory prior to the experiment. Thus, although one may randomize the selection of teams and exert a fair amount of control on initial conditions, it is necessary to be very careful in avoiding misinterpretations of the observations. For example, in bidding and oligopoly games, there appears to be an important difference between the performance of undergraduates and seasoned businessmen.

Another problem concerning the study of decision making is that it is possible that optimal performances are encountered when there is a certain noise level present in the environment; thus, the reduction of noise may actually adversely effect performance beyond a certain level.

The large-scale business games which have been built for many purposes, such as the teaching of facts, training in procedures as additional illustrative material to courses, etc., have the advantage of being complex and closer to the "real thing." They have the disadvantage that, in general, it is difficult to compute the outcomes that would be predicted by various theories of behavior. It is my belief that it is both feasible and fruitful to construct "simulation games" of the degree of complexity exhibited by the business games which are nevertheless amenable to analysis and experimentation. One of the properties that a game of this type must have is that by the appropriate selection of parameters it contains within its format the type of simple experimentation game that has already been investigated. The current work of R. Levitan and the author is directed at the construction of this type of game. A detailed description of the game, analysis, and data-reduction programs is available elsewhere [342] and [343].

The article by Anatol Rapoport and Carol Orwant [426] provides an excellent survey of much of the literature on experiments with experimental or "environment-poor" games. For games without communication, there appears to be a certain amount of evidence in favor of the "noncooperative equilibrium" and "beat the average" solutions. The work on experimental economic games is, unfortunately, scarcely dealt with and the comment on Hoggatt's game, "Although a simulation game, this situation does not lend itself to interpretations in terms of game theory. As a 3-person non-zero-sum game, it is extremely complex; and game theory to date is not adequate for analysis," is not completely justified. As a function of communication and payoffs, the works of Stern [521], Fouraker and Siegel [499], Hoggatt [278], Fouraker, Shubik, and Siegel [201], Shubik [496], and Feeney [187] have all obtained results which lend evidence to three different types of solution which can be interpreted in terms of economics or psychology or social psychology. They are respectively, joint maximization, the noncooperative equilibrium, and beat-the-average. If we denote the actual payoffs to the ith player by P_i, then if we consider an adjusted payoff denoted by π_i, where

$$\pi_i = \theta_{i1}p_1 + \theta_{i2}p_2 + \cdots + \theta_{in}p_n$$

then the three theories are characterized by:

Joint maximization $\qquad\qquad \theta_{i,j} = 1 \qquad\qquad$ for all i, j

Noncooperative equilibrium $\theta_{i,j} = 1 \qquad\qquad$ if $i = j$

$\qquad\qquad\qquad\qquad\qquad\quad = 0 \qquad\qquad$ if $i \neq j$

Beat-the-average $\qquad\qquad\quad \theta_{i,j} = 1 \qquad\qquad$ if $i = j$

$$= \frac{-1}{n-1} \qquad \text{if } i \neq j$$

The $\theta_{i,j}$ may be regarded as parameters of "cooperation."[4]

Some Observations and Results

R. Levitan and the author have recently constructed a business game which may be operated by as many as ten teams, with several members to a team, in which they can make decisions with respect to price, advertising, production, amount offered for sale, dividends, and investment. Five games each with five teams have been run. In the first three, competition was restricted to price, advertising, and production; and the information conditions were such that the players were not informed about the detailed structure of the game and at every quarter were only given market averages, not detailed breakdowns of the actions of their competitors. In the fourth game, the competitors were given detailed information concerning the moves of the others and the outcomes at the end of every simulated quarter; they did not, however, have any information concerning the structure of the market. They also were required to make a decision on dividend payments. In the fifth game, the players were given detailed information at the end of every quarter and were also completely informed about the structure of the game. Furthermore, in the fifth game, the players were selected from a group of mathematicians; they were requested to make decisions with respect to price, advertising, production, amount offered for sale, dividends, and investment (although as they all observed, optimal policy called for zero investment).

---

[4] The first use of this appears to have been by R. L. Bishop.

In spite of the relative complexity of the games, it was possible to solve for behavior predictions according to the three theories noted in the section starting on page 461. Although on each occasion in the briefing it had been stressed that the goal of each team was to maximize profits or (in the latter games) the expected discounted value of dividends and final assets, in all cases the best predictor of steady-state behavior was "beat-the-average" which is the solution which enables the players to transform the situation into one of a strictly competitive struggle for status. In some sense, this result is a negative result as it illustrates the difficulty in providing incentives to the players to prevent them from transforming the objectives of the game; on the other hand, it illustrated the possibility of being able to obtain results from a relatively complex game.

Although no numerical tests were made, or hypotheses advanced concerning the effect of increasing the amount of information about the moves of the opponents and the structure of the game, an examination of the graphs of price and advertising performances shows an increase in the speed of approach to beat-the-average levels as the amount of information was increased.

Even though the game was considerably more complex than most of the simple experimental games, on the whole, the players found it too simple and many became bored. As there was no product development or innovation and only one product under the control of each firm, they felt that their strategic freedom was too heavily constrained. As the experimenters, we tend to agree with the players; it is our intention to add more products, markets, and other features as long as we are able to add methods for calculating the outcomes predicted by various theories when applied to the more complex game, together with methods of data reduction and statistical analysis of the actual outcome of the game.

In the third game, which was played with teams of size four, three of the teams made their decisions by majority vote and two made their decisions by a general manager appointed by the experimenters. The managed teams were the second and fifth most profitable. It was not possible to deduce what was the effect of the organization on the play. The foregoing discussion and preliminary report on the five plays of the game is given more as evidence in support of my thesis concerning the need and potential of experimentation and development of this type of game rather than to stress the results concerning a type of competitive behavior.

There has been a growing recognition of the need for joint interdisciplinary work. There has also been a recognition of the need for the construction and examination of multivariate "environment-rich" situations. Our investigations have indicated to us that it is possible to construct games which may be regarded as apparatus for conducting several relatively few-variable experiments simultaneously on the same subjects but from different viewpoints. Thus, for example, the competitive prediction that we are willing to make is that, if there are not sufficient monetary stakes in the game, the average steady-state levels will be predicted by beat-the-average. It is consistent to test within the same experiment a hypothesis concerning the speed of approach to that level as a learning process differing with the information conditions. Furthermore, it is consistent with both of the above hypotheses and experimentally feasible to test for the effect on performance of different organization of the teams. By varying the parameters in a series of games, it is feasible to make these features of different sensitivity and importance; hence, although the over-all situation is multivariate, the importance of interaction between different aspects of the play can be controlled.

24

INFORMATION CONTROL IN
COMMAND-CONTROL SYSTEMS

Ruth M. Davis

Introduction

A command-control system is considered in this chapter as just one type of information system. As a subset of information systems, command-control systems include military control systems and military command systems; or, in other terminology, this subset includes military tactical systems and military strategic systems. No nonmilitary information system will be called a command-control system.

Within any military command staff a command-control system can be considered as the total of all the individual information systems which serves the staff division in its operational responsibilities. For example, the Operations Staff (J-3), the Logistics Staff (J-4), the Plans Staff (J-5), the Intelligence Staff (J-2), and the Communications Staff (J-6) all perform functions pertaining to the command and control of forces assigned to their command. Most of these functions involve the handling and/or processing of information, and it is for this latter set of tasks that command-control systems are being developed. Such systems are hybrid in nature in that their various subsystems present many aspects in common with nonmilitary systems. In some cases, real time processing of information is needed as is done in air traffic control systems or airline reservation systems. In other subsystems, inventory or allocation tasks are performed (say, for the logistics staff) which have much in common with marketing or manufacturing processes in industrial applications. Again, real time display may be called for in much the same sense as the Wall Street

Stock Exchange real-time displays are essential to the daily stock transactions.

Means of handling information in support of command-control functions have proceeded in parallel with the development of military capability. As such, no first command-control system can be cited. Again, the application of automated aids to command-control systems has paralleled the development of automatic devices. The first attempts to use electronic digital computers to assist military staffs appear to have occurred around 1952, within the first five years of development of digital computers. Since 1955 such efforts have mushroomed in all military departments and agencies in close correlation with the mushrooming of the electronic computer industry.

It should be noted, however, that command-control systems, as in the case with any information system, may be completely manual in nature or may be automated to the extent that only the final decisions are made by the users with all other operations being performed by automata. Command-control systems currently exist in all the various stages between these two extremes. The problems of information control discussed herein, however, are those arising through the use of electronic digital computers as aids to the system user as opposed to those existing whenever man manually uses information to make a decision or to form an opinion. To provide a more definitive background against which to discuss information control, the command-control system dealt with in this chapter is a system intended for use by a military staff headquarters. It is dependent upon the use of an electronic data-processing system. Its primary characteristics are:

1. It has several users of varying administrative levels.

2. The information within the system is of varying security classifications.

3. The information entering the system is both "raw" and "evaluated."

4. The user staffs are located both within the building which houses the computer systems and in remote sites.

In addition the term "electronic data-processing system" (EDPS) is used in the extended sense to include all input processing, data-processing and display equipment, as well as all personnel who operate equipment and manipulate data anywhere within the EDPS.

It should be noted here that there are two very interesting and significant differences between any military command-control system and any nonmilitary information system. The first of these is that justification of equipment or expenditures for an information system in a nonmilitary organization must be based on a predicted saving of money, on a full-shift (or two- or three-shift) operation of equipment, and/or on increasing the income of the organization. In a military command-control system, justification on the basis of increased efficiency or effectiveness of response to a given functional responsibility is sufficient. The second difference is that a command-control system must be operational at all times, whereas in a nonmilitary organization a failure of equipment—e.g., in the information system —although disruptive, is not normally catastrophic. As a result, in the military, great emphasis must be placed on reliability through redundancy and on multiple backups to the command-control system including capabilities for complete manual backup, so as to avoid any disruption in staff response.

The time frame considered in this chapter is the period from 1963–1970. Most of the discussion concerns techniques of information control as opposed to equipment to effect information control. This is not intended to imply that equipment technology as it currently exists is satisfactory. It is not and a great deal of effort is being placed on new data-processing organizations and on better techniques for processing nonnumerical data to meet better the needs of command-control system users. Rather, the emphasis here is being placed on an area long neglected and still not being subjected to the attention it must have before any command-control system becomes operational.

The remainder of this chapter is devoted to a classification of the essential types of information control, a discussion of each type, and the isolation of associated problem areas. Since this chapter is intended to be a survey report, no detailed solution to any of the problems will be presented. In addition, the section starting on p. 471 contains the foundation for one approach to a specific type of control, namely, security and data-access control. The chapter is based on investigations and work carried out by the author during the period 1957–1962, and is applicable to developments anticipated during the remainder of the 1960's.

The Background for Information Control in Automated Command-Control Systems

The introduction of computer systems into the command-control environment has removed the military commander three additional levels away from the information which he is asked to use in making decisions. The word "level" is used here in several contexts. First of all, it is intended to imply a "level of control" over the situation on the part of the commander. As he is removed a level from the information he feels that his control (i.e., understanding) of the information has been lessened. Secondly, it is intended to imply a "level of self-reliance" on the part of the commander. As he is removed a level from the information he feels an uneasy sort of dependency on the computer system with a correspondingly lower level of self-reliance on his part. Thirdly, his level of assuredness of the correctness of his decision decreases in direct proportion to the "levels" he is removed from the information.

These fears on the part of the commander are all currently justified. They can be allayed only through:

1. EDP system design techniques which incorporate all necessary information control procedures.

2. Familiarizing the commander's staff with the effectiveness of the information control procedures, with the reliability of the procedures and with their own ability to modify the procedures as dictated by experience.

3. Imparting understanding to the commander of the types of information control procedures incorporated into his command-control system and their effect on the resultant information available to him.

It is standard practice for anyone when justifying a decision either to themselves or to others to use such qualifying statements as:

This information was supplied by Mr. X who has invariably been right.

These data are a week-old, but they are the latest available.

My two sources of information were in agreement except for the fact that. . . .

The figures were averaged and the median rather than the mean was used because. . . .

The fact that the number of flights leaving National Airport was low has been traced to the poor weather rather than to poor maintenance practices.

The insertion of a computer system into a decision-making process must not remove the ability of the commander to make these same type of qualifying remarks. The introduction of information control procedures is done simply to ensure that this does not happen. The burden of establishing proper control procedures falls on the system designer who must in so doing use techniques of information theory, quality control, information redundancy control, error detection and correction, numerical analysis, queuing theory, sampling theory, statistical reliability, data reduction, cross correlation, display theory, decision processes, etc. The control procedures must be applied to the three areas within the computer system of:

1. Input processing.
2. Data processing.
3. Information display.

It is just these three functions which resulted in the previous statement that the commander has been removed from direct contact with his information base. That is, manipulations are performed on the data as they enter the system, as they are processed through the system, and as they are prepared for display. These manipulations must be carefully controlled and understood.

It is interesting to note that it is the speed of data handling and the flexibility of the interrelations of components of the electronic data-processing system which account both for the usefulness of the system for command-control and for its most serious faults.

General Discussion of Types of Information Control in Command-Control Systems

A major technical triumph was scored when it was recognized by system designers that the most important feature of a command-control system was the information it made available to the user. Another major technical triumph will be achieved when it is recognized that the effectiveness of a command-control system is measured directly in terms of its capability for providing the proper information to the appropriate user at the desired time. Furthermore, this measure of effectiveness is itself directly determined by the number of and degree of success of the types of information control procedures applied to the system. In any command-control system information entering the system (input) can be characterized in terms of its content, timeliness, accuracy, availability, and reliability. Information requested of the system (output) can be characterized by the same terms plus its completeness and accessibility. The measure of effectiveness of the system indicates how well the system design optimizes the characteristics of the output, assuming a given set of inputs with their accompanying characteristics.

Definitions and postulates can be established to point out the need for information control procedures and the types of control required.

DEFINITIONS

Item of information. The smallest unit of information which can exist within a command-control system and which can have informational attributes. It will not be separable into different subjects. Examples are: an individual's name, the course of a ship, the capacity of a storage tank, etc.

Information attributes. Qualities of a unit of information which affect its use within the system and to a system user. These qualities are timeliness, accuracy, availability and reliability.

System inputs, files and outputs. The basic system information units made up of items of information with their associated informational attributes. They will be commonly referred to as system reports for brevity.

Content. The substance of a report (input, output, file, etc.) separable by subject.

Timeliness

(a) The date (time) of preparation of the report (input, output, file, etc.).

(b) The date (time) of receipt of the report.

(c) The date (time) at which the information in the report was correct.

Accuracy. The known limits of correctness of the information in the report (input, output, file, etc.) usually expressed in terms of error bounds (e.g., $\pm 10\%$).

Availability. The allowable distribution of a report (input, output, file, etc.) expressed in terms of security classification, special information category, need-to-know, and administrative classification.

Reliability

(a) For a report, usually expressed in terms of reliability of the source.

(b) For information within the report, usually expressed in terms of the reliability of the data collection system (e.g., ± 10 miles, "probably a B-52," etc.).

Completeness. For a system output, a measure of the extent to which all pertinent information within the system has been utilized.

Accessibility. For a system output a measure of how readily the proper information was made available to the requesting user on the desired medium.

POSTULATES

1. The content, timeliness, availability, and reliability of inputs to a command-control system are invariants and, hence, are not subject to modification by the system.

2. The accuracy of an input to the system can be altered by system operations. Positive control procedures to improve the accuracy of inputs can be effected.

3. The timeliness, availability, and reliability of inputs and of information within the inputs are informational attributes which must be retained as the information flows through the system and must be reflected in any output produced by the system.

4. The completeness, accuracy, and accessibility of system outputs are each individually dependent upon system design and can be improved through improvement in system design.

5. The requirements as specified by the user staff for availability of information within the system and on system outputs determine, to a large extent, system design.

Using the above definitions and postulates as a basis, it is possible to state certain rules of system operation which must be effected through the application of information control procedures. Subsequent to the formulation of system rules, the required control procedures will be listed in outline form with summary comments only.[1] It should be noted here that the set of rules following is not complete but is internally consistent.

RULES

1. As information units are processed by the system, the informational attributes associated with them when they were entered into the system shall always be accessible to system users. This generally implies either carrying the attribute data along with the information items or designing attribute data tables for accession by system programs.

2. If the accuracy of information is changed by system processing, the changed accuracy limits should be known and/or available to system users. For example, analog data entering a digital system are quite frequently subjected to refining techniques which reduce their accuracy.

3. When information of different reliabilities, availabilities, and timeliness are combined into a single file or output, then the file or output can itself have only one over-all set of attributes. The rules for determining this single attribute set must be unambiguous, reproducible, and accessible to system users. Again, to reconstitute the units of information in different ways, the individual attributes for each unit must be retained within the system.

4. When a system is interrogated on any given subject, all available

---

[1] Additional details are available in Davis [441a]; Thompson [441c]; Bilden [55]; and Morgenstern [405].

(used in the sense of allowable distribution) data must be made accessible to the interrogator in the manner requested. In addition, if other information exists within the system but is not available to the individual requesting it, means should be provided for making this known to his superior or to another cognizant individual. In all cases, the interrogator should be able to determine (where availability exists) what sources were used to compile the system output along with all pertinent attribute data.

These rules, though compact, have not been adhered to in any substantial degree in any system existing or under development. They impose requirements on system analysis, system design, and basic system research not as yet initiated. However, it is felt that until these rules can be effected, proper system usage by user staffs cannot be accomplished and that reliance on the EDP system by a command staff cannot be justified.

To carry the discussion just one step further, a list of information controls to effect these rules is given in Table 1.

The Foundation for an Approach to Security Control of Information

This section illustrates the approach considered necessary for effecting a type of information control which has never been heretofore used either qualitatively or quantitatively. The discussion which follows lays down the general rules upon which very specific procedures have been formulated.

DEFINITION OF A SECURE COMPUTER SYSTEM

A secure computer system is one which permits the receipt, processing, display, and transmittal within the system of information of any required security classification with no unintentional disclosure to unauthorized personnel. A "computer system" in this context is defined in the extended sense to include all input processing (including receivers), data processing, and display equipment, as well as all personnel who operate equipment and manipulate data anywhere within the system. The equipment of the system is not assumed to be all collocated either in one room or in one building. If the system equipment and users are located in more than one building, then the linking communications lines are considered part of the extended system with respect to security requirements.

The security aspects of a computer system are not to be confused

Table 1   Information Controls

A. Information *Content* Controls
   1. Inputs
     (*a*) Error control through checks on quantitative data.
     (*b*) Correctness control through "common sense" or logical checks.
   2. System information (information flowing through the system or generated by the system)
     (*a*) Error control through parity checks, check sums, redundancy, etc.
     (*b*) Completeness control through use of associative techniques, cross correlation, multiple file query, etc.
     (*c*) Content currentness control through calculations of maximum useful information content life, of degradation decay, of maximum useful system life times, etc.
B. Information *Attribute* Controls
   1. Availability controls
     (*a*) Security controls and special information category controls.
     (*b*) Administrative controls.
       (1) Determination of need-to-know.
       (2) Determination of administrative availability criteria.
   2. Reliability controls through retention of input reliabilities and/or combinational techniques of melding reliabilities.
   3. Timeliness controls
     (*a*) Retention and/or calculation of date (time) of receipt of reports.
     (*b*) Retention and/or calculation of date (time) at which information was correct.
     (*c*) Retention and/or calculation of date (time) at which report was prepared.
   4. Accuracy control
     (*a*) Retention of input accuracy figures.
     (*b*) Calculations of errors generated by data manipulations.
       (1) Data reduction.
       (2) Numerical calculations.
       (3) Mechanical translation.
C. Information *Accessibility* Controls
   1. Priority control over output generation.
     (*a*) Queuing rules.
     (*b*) Programmed priority assignment.
   2. Control over information flow to remote user retrieval consoles.
   3. Dissemination control procedures over information flow within the system and to assist external dissemination.

---

with the physical security aspects of the facility in which the computer system is installed. Physical security measures are concerned with access to rooms, clearances of personnel, etc. The deliberate tapping of a computer cable by cleared personnel who thereby obtain access to computer data is a violation of physical security, *not* of the security of the computer system.

A DISCUSSION OF SECURITY CONTROL PROCEDURES

A computer system may have its operations and the data flowing through it subjected to four types of control. These are:

1. Program controls.
2. Mechanical controls.
3. Electronic controls.
4. Manual controls.

Representative *program controls* relevant to security measures include the following types:

1. A check on each message by message identifier to determine whether any given message is an allowable message for processing by the program currently in progress.

2. A check on each computer file by file identifier to determine whether an input of a given security classification can be inserted into the file by the program currently in progress.

3. A check on the contents of a given storage device to determine whether the information in storage must be erased prior to the initiation of a new program making use of that storage device so as to not violate security precautions.

Representative *mechanical controls* include the following types:

1. The use of a mechanical device to connect/disconnect a given set of equipment from the computer system. The mechanical device may be set manually.

2. The use of a mechanical device to block information of a given type from being displayed on an output device.

Representative *electronic controls* include the following types:

1. The use of an electronic circuit to identify electronically to a computer the display device requesting any display of information contained within the system.

2. The use of an electronic switching device to permit the flow of information from one equipment unit to another. This device may be under programmed or manual control.

Representative *manual controls* include the following types:

1. The control of information flow from one system unit to any other through visual inspection of the information to be transmitted.

2. The control of transfer of information from one system unit to another by manually transporting the information (e.g., the carrying of a magnetic tape reel, a punched paper tape, etc.).

Manual controls do *not* include control of information disseminated from the system to the external world. For example, information displayed on a visual display unit of the system is considered as subject to internal system checking procedures. On the other hand, the dissemination to headquarters personnel of a printed output produced by a system equipment unit is not considered as subject to internal system checks.

It is clear both from experience and logical considerations that a computer system may be made secure (see definition above) through the use of a combination of program, mechanical, electronic, and manual controls. In most, if not all, existing secure systems the security is provided completely through manual control procedures, supplemented occasionally by simple program controls. Such systems, although secure, may be awkward to use and may actually deprive certain staff groups of the use of the system. An objective of the author is to show that there is a given combination of system checks which affords to a given user the most satisfactory compromise between system complexity and system usability.

In a computer system serving a military commander, each piece of information being processed will have a classification c, where c may assume any of the values 1 through $N (1 \le c \le N)$. The most common classification situations in a military headquarters are depicted in Table 2:

Table 2   Standard Information Classification

Classification (C_s)	Description
1	Unclassified
2	Confidential
3	Secret
4	Top secret

For purposes of this chapter, standard classifications will be defined as those for which the following relationship exists: An individual having access to material of standard classification C_{s_j} has access to material of all standard classifications C_{s_i}, where $i = 1, 2, \cdots,$ $(j - 1)$.

We also distinguish between standard classifications, as in Table 2, and special categories, as in Table 3.

Table 3   Special Information Categories

Category (C_I)	Description
1	Special category A
2	Special category B
3	Special category C
.	. . .
.	
.	. . .
N	Special category N

No general relationship will be assumed between any two of the special information categories. The following relationship between special information categories and standard classifications are assumed:

Any individual having access to special information categories will be allowed to have access to information of all standard classifications. The administrative security classifications such as "For Army (or Navy, or Air Force) Eyes Only" will require separate treatment. Also, the "need-to-know" problem for all classifications c will be treated separately. Circumstances for which the above relationships for standard and special information categories do not hold simply require the substitution of the proper relationships and the corresponding modification of the rules presented later in this chapter.

The spaces in which the equipment units of the system are located may be cleared to any classification k, $1 \leqq k \leqq N$. Later, the situation will be considered in which system equipment is located in several spaces each having a different clearance.

A set of basic rules which must be adhered to in a secure system can be advanced in terms of the above assumptions and definitions. The rules are applied separately to the system tasks of input processing, data processing, data display, and data transmittal within the system. Each rule can be carried out through some combination of the four types of system control procedures discussed previously; i.e., program, mechanical, electronic, and manual controls. The possible control combinations are presented in tabular form wherever possible for ease of assimilation. The notation which will be used is as follows:

c = security classifications of data
  c_s = standard security classifications of data
  c_I = special categories of information
  c_H = highest required standard security classification of data
  $c_I{}^*$ = highest required special information category
k = security clearances of facility
  k_s = standard security clearances of facility
  k_I = clearance of facility processing special categories of data
P = security clearances of personnel
  P_s = standard security clearances of personnel
  P_I = access rights for personnel handling special categories of information

It is the various possible combinations of c, k and P which yield the allowable combinations of control procedures and which give a user staff the capability of choosing the type of secure system best suited for their purpose. The rules which can be presented indicate specifically how checking procedures will vary with varying relationships between c, k, and P. However, certain general statements can be made immediately which will be illustrative of the effects of the c-k-P relationships on checking procedures and ease of system usage. These are:

1. Completely manual control procedures are sufficient only if $k_s = P_s = c_H$ for a facility processing only standard information and $k_I = P_I = c_I{}^*$ for a facility processing either special categories of information only or a combination of standard classification and special category information. In such a situation, for example, the spaces and the personnel would all be cleared to Top Secret if this were the highest data classification to be encountered. Even here, however, program checks would have to be applied if system outputs [2] of lower classification, e.g., secret, were to be produced for display or distribution.

---

[2] "System output" is considered as being a preplanned output available under conditions of normal system operation. It is distinct from all outputs capable of being produced by the system equipment while not under system control. Such "nonnormal" operation would occur whenever system functions were stopped, the equipment "cleaned" of all system data and extraneous programs run on an *ad hoc* basis; after the extraneous outputs were produced, system data would be reinserted and system functions resumed. Such *ad hoc* procedures are always physically possible, but can never be considered as satisfying the requirements of a secure system.

2. The closer k_s approximates c_H and/or the more values of k_I which coincide with values of c_I^*, *then* the easier are the problems which must be faced by the system designers and system analyst/programmers. *Also* the use of the system may become correspondingly more awkward and the personnel clearance problem more acute. The display of outputs, for example, may either be more restricted (due to their universally higher security classification) or will require more clearances to be issued to staff personnel. As k_s and k_I increase, so must P_s and P_I and, as is well recognized, the granting of clearances, especially to nongovernment personnel, is expensive and sometimes impossible.

INTEGRATED SYSTEMS

One basic premise (which can be called the equality premise) attested to by experience is that k_s has always equaled c_H and k_I has always equaled c_I^* because of the inability of system designers to develop adequate program, mechanical, and electronic controls which would permit an inequality to exist. The alternative premise could be that it was the desire of the user staffs that the equality be maintained. This latter premise is denied both by experience and by the current vigorous rumblings of discontent on the part of user staffs who are beginning to see the problems besetting them as they plan the usage of such systems. A counter fact to the equality premise which should be recognized is that, even when $k_s = c_H$ and $k_I = c_I^*$ for all c_I, the existence of adequate program, mechanical, and electronic controls would still be advantageous to the user. The advantages would accrue primarily in the user's ability to obtain outputs of varying security classification for external distribution.

Certain specific characteristics of integrated systems are now apparent and can be discussed on the basis of ideas thus far developed. First of all an integrated system will be defined as one in which:

1. The data entering the system maintain their proper security or category throughout their existence within the system and are afforded the protection required by their security classification or category access.

2. Data of more than one classification or special category must be processed within the system.

3. Outputs of any of the classifications or special categories assigned to incoming data may be produced for display within the system or for external distribution with all the required security and special category access safeguards being maintained.

4. The set of allowable security classifications and special data

categories for system data is a known system parameter at all times where changes in this parameter are *not* precluded by system equipment design or program design.

An immediate outgrowth of the developments of this section are the facts that:

1. The relative values of k and c; i.e., of facility clearance and system data classification or category, do not determine whether or not the system is integrated.

2. A necessary condition for an integrated system is the existence of program and mechanical and/or electronic controls in addition to manual controls.

3. There is no unique sufficient condition for an integrated system in terms of security control procedures or special category access rights.

4. A system may be secure without being integrated.

Summary

During this first decade of development of automated command-control systems, emphasis has been placed on equipment development rather than on techniques of information handling, and of information control in particular. As a result there are many equipment systems in existence which are not satisfactorily meeting the needs of their users. However, remedies are being developed as problem areas are understood and isolated. Foremost among these problem areas is information control to which the preceding three sections have been devoted. With the current reorientation of effort on such areas, it is quite realistic to predict great advances in command-control system responsiveness and usefulness by 1970.

25

ENGINEERING SYSTEMS APPROACHES TO ORGANIZATIONS

George E. Briggs

Introduction

The goal of this chapter is to describe some of the working concepts and certain of the methods used in human factor engineering to provide information required in the design and management of complex multiman-machine systems. We will equate the terms "organization" and "system" in this presentation and introduce some of the concepts and research methodology being applied in an area of common interest.

Definitions and Concepts

A system is defined as an assemblage of components, each of which carries out assigned functions and all of which are intercoupled in such a way as to obtain a particular goal. There are three aspects of this definition: First, the goal of a system could be the provision of services as in a hospital system, the generation of research reports as in a laboratory, the manufacture of a product for marketing as in an industrial plant, etc. The important point here is that all components of the system are involved in some way with the generation of an output which attains the defined goal of the system.

Second, the hallmark of a system is the multiple interactions among its components. This concept of interaction takes two forms: (a) There exist sequential dependencies along a chain of system components such that activities carried on early in the chain affect those functions performed at a later stage in the system (for example, the efficiency of workers engaged in the final assembly of an automobile depends, in part, on the efficiency of workers back up the assembly line), and (b) control loops are present to regulate the functions being performed by the several components (for example, a slowdown in final assembly is perceived by a controller component in the system, and this component initiates action, first to slow down operations back up the assembly line and, then, to attempt a remedy of the bottleneck at final assembly).

Third, the functions performed by system components are diverse and get to the heart of internal system dynamics. Van Cott and Folley (Folley [567]) describe five common functions performed by systems. These include the following:

SENSING

Every system exists in a competitive and dynamic environment. To operate effectively, a system must have accurate and sensitive sensory equipment. There are three characteristics of the sensory function which are particularly relevant: (a) No sensor is capable of infinite resolution, and the detail of information that passes through the sensor may be rather gross. Other things being equal, the more sensitive a sensory device, the more quickly and effectively can the system respond. The dachshund, for example, has very poor far vision and, as such, he would never do as part of a game-retrieval system; however, he has an extremely sensitive olfactory or smell sense, and so he is an excellent system component for locating and ferreting out rabbits, ground hogs, rodents, and other animals who live underground. (b) Information sensed about an environment is always noisy to some extent. Noise, by the way, is defined as information which is irrelevant to and uncorrelated with the true signals in the environment. One of the most important requirements placed on the sensory function is that it filter out this noise. The most important implication of the filter function is that it implies some loss of relevant information due to an overlap of the characteristics of relevant and irrelevant (or noisy) information. An appropriate setting of the filter can minimize loss of relevant data, but some loss is to be expected. (c) Most systems have multiple sensors, and so it is necessary that a time-sharing function be present to permit efficient collation of information from these several input channels. It is important, also, that these several sensors have the appropriate filter bias so as to expedite the processing of and subsequent action on especially critical events in the environment of the system. A classic (and tragic) example of inappropriate bias in a sensor-filter component occurred on Sunday morning,

December 7, 1941, when a radar sensor faithfully reproduced relevant information on the Japanese attack aircraft north of Pearl Harbor, but the alarm was not sounded because a human filter had been biased to expect the arrival of friendly bombers from the mainland. Other sensors had not been biased, as intelligence reports were available suggesting Japanese attack as a real possibility. This latter information was not available to the abovementioned human filter who rejected the radar information; had it been, it is likely that he would have performed a rapid collation of information from the two sensors and alerted the defense forces.

MEASURING OR ENCODING

Sensed and filtered information must be encoded in a language which the system is capable of using. Inappropriate coding slows down the processing of information by the system and limits thereby the capacity of the system to deal efficiently with its environment. George Miller [402] cites some remarkable data on encoding: a human subject was able to more than *triple* his information-handling capacity when trained in the use of efficient coding schemes. Of course, we are all familiar with the fantastic capacities of modern digital computers, their power being due in part to the highly efficient binary coding scheme used.

Today, coding theory is one of the most active areas of research in communication engineering, and this is further testimony to its importance in complex systems (Reza [449]). Coding brings up two more concepts of importance—efficiency and redundancy. In information theory these concepts are related as follows:

$$\text{Redundancy} = 1 - \text{efficiency}$$

Thus, high efficiency is accompanied by low redundancy. However, redundancy is a desirable commodity in processing information from noisy sources or sensors, and it is desirable also when (a) the system is stressed by an overload of input information, (b) when one of several sensors is inappropriately biased and produces erroneous information, and (c) when the speed demands on the system exceed its capacity to handle information (Garner [211], pp. 301–304).

INFORMATION PROCESSING

Certainly the most intriguing aspect of system operations are those functions performed on sensed information in order to develop outputs which approximate the goals of the system. These information-processing functions must be intriguing because so many people have joined in the game of inference to describe them. Information processing is the antecedent of decision making, the latter being a readily observable act of choice among alternatives and thereby measurable behavior of a system. But information processing within the human components of a system is a private affair which can be specified only by inference or by analogy, the latter being a form of inference—thus the intrigue. Servo engineers have developed rather powerful tools for inference, by analogue, of the information-processing functions of human and of machine components. These techniques involve the derivation of what are called transfer functions, which specify a linear or quasi-linear relationship between the input to and the output from a system component or series of components. When one has developed a model which accurately describes a relationship between observable input and output, it is an almost irresistible next step to infer that the functions present in the model exist, at least by analogy, in the system component itself, especially when that component is a human operator. The most sophisticated work in deriving transfer functions for the human operator has occurred for the continuous case, i.e., controlling or tracking tasks (McRuer and Krendel [385]), although a strong beginning has occurred for the discrete case, i.e., problem solving (Newell, Shaw, and Simon [421]).

Actually, a taxonomy of information-processing functions is not readily available, and the three following classes are suggested as a starter: information *transmission, translation,* and *transformation.* These are listed in order of increasing complexity, and we will now try to illustrate these processes with reference to discrete information-processing tasks. In so doing, we will try to retain the same definitions that these terms have in the continuous case.

In simple transmission, the system component changes neither the content nor the form of the original message; instead, simply a reproduction of the information in the input to the component appears at the output. In the translation operation, the system component changes the *form* of the input information but (hopefully) not the content. And finally, in the transformation process, *both* the form and the content of the original message are changed when passed through the system component. The transmission function is self-evident, and, being the most simple of the three operations, one might assume it to be error-free. Unfortunately, this is not always true: teletype systems on occasion spew forth completely garbled messages, radio transmissions are plagued occasionally by static from atmospheric and solar noise sources, and the human operator is a consistent source of bias and distortion in transmission of information. The latter is the basis for a parlor game wherein a message is whispered from one person to another. The output of the last person, when compared to the original input message, usually reveals hilarious modifications including losses, distortions, and additions of information.

Donald Campbell [93] has catalogued a number of forms of biases which the human operator provides in simple transmission operations. These include (a) abbreviation and simplification of messages with an attendant loss of detail, (b) closure or a "filling in" of what the operator believes to be gaps in the original message, (c) symmetry or a "smoothing" operation whereby *apparent* irregularities or inconsistencies in the original message are smoothed out or are made more "consistent," and (d) contrast enhancement which can be achieved by the transmitter's tendency to emphasize certain portions of a message. An example of the latter bias from verbal communication is seen in the following simple statement: "The papers are burning" as compared to "*The* papers are burning." A simple speech inflection of one word biases the entire message.

Campbell [93] lists many other distortion and bias phenomena, and his paper makes excellent reading. Unfortunately, he does not recognize a distinction between translation and transformation operations, so we do not have the benefit of his insight on transformation distortions, although it is clear that they involve all those listed for transmission and translation biases.

To go on, translation operations change the form but (hopefully) not the content of input information. The encoding and recoding operations are obvious examples of the translation function. It is necessary to "use the language of the system," as has been pointed out previously, and so translation is required for most input information. It is also necessary to recode some information within a system, as when a human component passes on information to a machine component or as when a technician, engineer, or scientist attempts to communicate information to someone in the system not familiar with the technical jargon of the specialist.

An interesting and timely example of human error in the translation operation was reported by *Aviation Week* [33]. In regard to the autobiography of Major Gherman Titov, the Soviet Cosmonaut, an English translation reads, in part: "In order to 'quiet' my 'naughty' vestibular system, I cautiously found the most comfortable position in the chair and fainted." *Aviation Week* quotes the American publisher as saying that in the Russian version the last word in this quotation was "*zamer*" which should have been translated as "remained still" rather than "fainted" ([33], p. 35). Thus, a poor choice among alternative English "equivalents" changed drastically the content of the original information.

This example makes explicit a fundamental problem in translation operations: Seldom is there a one-to-one relationship between the original input code and the output code of a translator; either one has fewer output codes, in which case information may be lost in the process, or one has several code terms each suitable to some extent for each input term. The latter was the case in the above example, and to avoid a distortion of information, it is necessary either to examine the original context or to utilize sequential dependencies within the original message, or both.

Finally, the transformation operation is the most complex information-processing requirement of a system component. These operations consist of manipulations of input information to yield "new" information. For example, a market analyst examines sales records for Company A over the past 18 months (the original input information) and calculates the rate of change of sales over this time period (he transforms month-by-month sale quantities into average differences). From this transformation the analyst may note that whereas the sales of Company A increased over the 18 months, their rate of growth was less than that of a major competitor. From this he predicts that Company A will lose x percent of the market over the next 18 months (he generates "new" information in the form of a prediction based on transformations of "old" information).

Transformation operations are clearly apparent as antecedents to decision making: the decision is a result of fitting a complex weighting function to estimates of several characteristics of the input data. Thus, both the estimates of input characteristics and the weighting of these estimates are transformation operations. Also to be included as transformations are calculations of the reliability and the validity of information which one makes on his input data prior to a decision.

In addition to the human bias and distortion tendencies cited above for information transmission and translation, the transformation operations entail human error which results from the complexity of applying multiple criteria (the weighting function) to input information. One of the most significant advances in recent years has been the development of linear programming techniques which represent a machine aid to that class of human information transformations required to schedule sequences of system operations. Of even more recent vintage are the newly emerging techniques of using Bayesian statistical models for the appropriate weighting of information from transformed data in the decision process (Schlaifer [464]).

REGULATION AND CONTROL

Control over a dynamic process such as a multiman-machine system is attained by multiple feedback loops within the system. Under these conditions, the output of a component is compared with some standard (desired output) and the discrepancy, if any, is fed back to the component so as to correct for the discrepancy in future operations.

The feedback can take several forms which can be equated to levels of control sophistication. At the most elementary level, amplitude control is used: if production is five units per hour less than desired, a control signal to increase production by five units per hour would presumably correct the discrepancy. Unfortunately, so simple a level of control gives rise to marked oscillation in output quantity, i.e., during the next hour production might very well be two units, say, *over* the desired quantity. This could happen if the system, prior to the order to increase production by five units, was *increasing* its *rate* of production to make up an even earlier discrepancy. Thus, instantaneous amplitude of discrepancy (system error, as defined) is not as good a criterion for system control as is the rate at which the system error is changing since a rate control over system operations serves to dampen oscillations in output.

Now, rate control becomes inadequate when the desired output fluctuates periodically, as it does in most systems. Thus, if there is an increasing demand for output units, control over the system by a rate criterion will also result in oscillations around the (increasing) desired output quantities. In this case, acceleration control is needed to dampen out the oscillations and provide for more efficient system operations. From servo theory, the order of feedback control required in a system is one order greater than the highest derivative in the input (desired output). Thus, rate control is required when desired output is a fixed quantity, acceleration control is required when desired output is increasing or decreasing at a constant rate, and Δ acceleration control (the third derivative of system error) is required when the desired output changes by variable rates.

The complexity of the system dynamics themselves also influence the level of control required for system operations. In general, the more complex the system, the higher the order of control required. Since most multiman-machine systems exhibit complex dynamics with formidable lag times, the efficient control operations are (or should be) of high order. There are two feedback control techniques that psychologists and engineers have developed for these complex systems— quickening (Birmingham and Taylor [73]) and predictor solutions

(Kelley [310]). In the case of quickening, the actual output plus its rates, accelerations, etc., are fed back for control purposes. This provides for extremely simple moment-by-moment control, but does not necessarily permit the controller to modify his tactics or strategy. The predictor technique is ingenious: here a model of the system receives the same inputs as the real system but the model acts upon the inputs at many times the speed at which the real system responds and thereby generates predicted outputs. This fast-time solution is run repeatedly and, before each cycle, the model is readjusted in terms of the real system activity at that point in time, i.e., reality is used to weight the predictions repeatedly. The result is an accurate and sensitive extrapolation to future system output levels which prediction can extend over minutes, hours, or days, depending on the system lag times. It provides information which enables particularly massive and cumbersome systems to be controlled delicately by anticipating required changes in time to affect these through long lag-time constants.

Furthermore, since it displays the future system output in entirety, the predictor technique permits the controller to "experiment" with several control tactics and test out the more expedient—the controller may see whether a simple amplitude adjustment will solve a problem in system output by inserting the adjustment and observing the predicted outcome, and if it does not work (in the *predicted* outcome domain), he can quickly rescind the order and try another tack.

To date, the quickening and the predictor techniques have been thoroughly checked only in vehicular control tasks with a single operator, although preliminary work has been carried out in the Laboratory of Aviation Psychology at Ohio State by using the predictor technique in a simulated air traffic control system. The results were promising but only preliminary.

MAINTENANCE

Finally, a major function required in all systems is that of maintenance. This ranges from mundane janitorial service through preventative maintenance procedures, including refresher and retraining courses for personnel, to major replacement of system components. The care and feeding of systems is a major research area, but we will not devote more time to this topic since it is now appropriate to turn to research methods in human factor engineering.

Research Methodology

Let us assume that a group of human factor specialists were to assist in the design of a new system or were to recommend major modifications of an existing system. How would they go about this task? In general, there are two approaches that have been proved particularly useful—system or operational analysis and system synthesis.

This is a rational approach to system study whereby an analysis is made of the system and its environment which results in: (a) a specification of the several goals of the system; (b) an identification of the various components of the system; (c) a detailing of the several functions (as described above) performed by these components; (d) a description of information flow within the system together with a specification of the control loops and other types of interaction among components; and (e) details of the dynamics of the environment within which the system will operate, specifically in regard to the influence of the environment on the mission of the system. It may be seen that this effort is primarily *descriptive*. Indeed, system analysis is nothing more than a careful and complete description, since, like in any research area, an understanding of systems must be based on a sound description of phenomena.

Mission specifications—the goals of the system—usually are "givens," and the human-factor specialist may accept these specifications if they are sufficiently precise and "workable" or he may seek clarification through an examination of the influence of the expected environment of the system on system performance. This contingency analysis of the environment and the function analysis of the system permit the human-factor specialist to recommend allocation of function to the human and to the machine components of the system. It is then necessary to specify the exact nature of the tasks that will be handled by the human operators via task analysis procedures.

Task analyses provide information on three aspects: (a) The input variables defining the types of input information, the quantity of such inputs and the quality of information or display modes to be utilized; (b) the nature of the information-processing activities required of the human operator in dealing with input information; and (c) the characteristics of the output sinks (devices) to be utilized by the human operator. The characteristics of the controlling or feedback loops around the human operator must also be considered.

From the system and the environmental contingency analyses, one gains an understanding of system operations at a rather molar level. The task analysis results in an understanding of human functions in the system which, like system operations, must be at a fairly general level. The reason is that the task analysis is followed by *predictions* of human efficiency based on *reference* to human performance in similar tasks in other contexts (in other systems or in laboratory tasks requiring similar behavior).

Thus, the rational approach provides a method for understanding complex man-machine systems at a descriptive and rather molar level.

SYSTEM SYNTHESIS

In this approach, one starts with the same activities as those discussed above: the analysis of the system configuration and the environmental contingencies. However, rather than "stopping" at that point and inferring operational efficiency by reference to similar tasks and system operations, in the synthesis approach one proceeds to develop a test model of the system from the previously defined functional building blocks. Furthermore, the model is then exercised in a simulated environment by applying inputs to the model and observing the operation of the model (the rates and quality of information or process flow), and measuring the characteristics of the output.

Modern analogue and digital computers provide the basis for instrumenting the model and its environmental dynamics. This is much less expensive than the more traditional approach of building a "test plant," as in the chemical and petroleum industries, and simulation via computers provides for remarkable flexibility and efficiency, a point which will be illustrated later.

At this point, it is necessary to describe two variations of the system synthesis approach—fast-time versus real-time simulation.

Fast-time simulation. This approach has found favor with operations research personnel. Simply put, in this variation of system synthesis, the *entire* system, including both human and machine components, is simulated by expressing its real-life functions in computer language, by providing for the real-life links between components within the computer, and by expressing the environmental dynamics of the system in computer terms. Assuming that adequate expressions for the system components are employed, the synthesis approach provides a remarkably efficient method of studying complex systems because (a) modifications of the model (as in reallocating functions among the several components) can be effected very quickly, and (b) the exercise of the model can be carried out at computer speeds such that functions occur in milli- or microseconds rather than minutes or hours as in the real system. For example, Siegel et al. [498] were able to simulate in-flight refueling operations on a digital computer such that simulated operations took only 3.2 seconds as compared to 70 seconds in normal operations.

This rapid time exercise permits one to determine system efficiency rather quickly, especially when dealing with nondeterminant systems where efficiency will vary as a result of variability in component operations, the influence of nonstationary-state behavior of system components, and/or the presence of variable contingencies in the system environment.

The major limitation of this approach is that the model is a simulation of the human as well as the machine components, and we are a long way from a satisfactory analytic expression of human information-processing characteristics, especially in discrete information-processing tasks.

Real-time simulation. With this method, the human operator is not simulated as in the fast-time simulation approach, nor is the study of his effectiveness left to reference to behavior in similar tasks as in system analysis. Instead, he participates in real (or near-real) time in a simulated system. Thus, it is necessary first to determine those functions which are required of the human operator and which are provided by machine components in the reference system, to determine the contingencies present for each type of decision or the effects of system dynamics on each type of human control action. Second, it is necessary to determine how and when the effects of control actions or decisions will be fed back to the human operator and the nature of any distortions which may affect this feedback or display process. Thus, a system and task analysis is a part of the empirical approach just as it is for the synthesis approach.

Once this information is known, it remains only to provide the physical environment in which these factors will occur. This environment may be a scaled-down replica of the reference system, as in the test plant of a new petroleum plant or process, or it may be simulated entirely by analogue and/or digital computer instrumentation. In either case, the human operator carries out his assigned functions in real or near-real time, and, unlike the fast-time synthesis approach, rapid replication (at least at computer speeds) is not possible.

CRITERIA FOR SIMULATION

There are four major criteria which the human factor specialist applies to an evaluation of the synthesis approach in the study of complex systems. These are fidelity of simulation, performance measurement capability, flexibility, and control.

Fidelity of simulation. Fidelity of simulation means many things to different people. Those who are equipment-oriented tend to view the fidelity of the dynamics as all important; the layman tends to emphasize "face validity" or physical appearance; the human-factor specialist emphasizes fidelity of human functions and is willing to forego considerable face validity and fidelity of system dynamics, *provided* the requirements of the human operator in the simulator are nearly identical to those in the operational system and provided that the feedback of decision or control effects is accomplished on a realistic time base and determined by realistic contingencies or dynamic transformations.

Measurement of system performance. Measurement is an essential part of all research. Measurement is a critical requirement of training devices also, although in most applications it is ignored in these situations.

Thus, an important criterion for evaluating a simulator to be employed as a research tool is the extent to which measures of system performance are accurate and reliable. In this context, reliability is inversely related to variability. Thus, if a simulation run is measured repeatedly under the same or nearly identical conditions, the less variable the performance metrics the more reliable is the research vehicle.

Validity of system measures is another highly desirable characteristic. It is preferable to quantify system performance with metrics which have direct counterparts in the operational system. The program of air traffic control research at Ohio State (see below) illustrates this point. There a continuing effort involved the derivation of system measures such as separation errors, control time, and fuel usage which permit more or less direct reference to operational characteristics. Furthermore, an attempt was made to develop a set of semi-independent measures of system performance to assure adequate quantification of the total system.

Flexibility and control of system configuration. A good research tool is flexible in the sense that a variety of experimental conditions can be implemented without a major readjustment of the basic simulator. The advent of general-purpose analogue and digital computers has made such flexibility possible. However, flexibility must not be gained at a sacrifice of control. No research tool is adequate without provisions for experimenter control of the process under study. With modern large-scale computers there is a natural desire to "make the computer pay for itself" by developing complex simulation. One can easily sacrifice control in these situations and, perhaps, needlessly oversimulate.

It is interesting to note, on the matter of experimental control, that the real-time simulation technique is essentially a controlled field study conducted in the laboratory rather than in the field. The realism of the field is surprisingly easy to bring into the laboratory, as anyone will attest who has participated in a management game [1] or in a war game, the granddaddy of real-time (or near-real-time) simulation.

RECENT SIMULATION VEHICLES

Within the past decade, system simulation has been used increasingly for the purpose of evaluating human performance in complex multiman-machine systems. The human functions of interest have been information processing and decision making under realistic task demands and procedural constraints. Two groups have been particularly active in this research area—The RAND Corporation and the Laboratory of Aviation Psychology at Ohio State. More recently, other groups (at the University of Illinois, in Project Michigan, at Princeton, and at the System Development Corporation) have developed simulation vehicles and are now engaged in human factor research with these devices.

With the exception of the work at Princeton, all simulation has involved fairly large analogue and/or digital computers to supply system dynamics. Much has been said of the relative advantages of these two computer forms. Rather than continue a fruitless argument, it is best to recognize that both have unique advantages and that neither can serve as an all-purpose device.

The simulation research conducted in the Control Systems Laboratory at Illinois employed both analogue and digital components. At Ohio State the air traffic control simulator relied entirely on analogue devices, whereas the logistics simulator at RAND relies heavily on the manual mode but uses a digital computer for part of the operation.

THE OHIO STATE UNIVERSITY PROGRAM

Since 1953 the Laboratory of Aviation Psychology has contributed to empirical data and theory of systems research. From 1953 to 1959 this work centered around a simulation of a terminal area radar air traffic control (ATC) system. A brief description of this program follows:

A total of 20 systems studies were completed during the first 6 years of the program. Each study employed a total of from 300 to 3,000 simulated aircraft approaches. Each study examined system performance as a function of realistic variables and generated recom-

---

[1] See, for example, the description by Bass, Chapter 7, of this volume.

mendations of both a specific and a general level. To illustrate, a general conclusion, which emerged from several independent studies, held that procedural flexibility in systems operations was a desirable feature in that controllers given a wide range of alternative actions performed more efficiently and safely than when restrictions were placed on them, e.g., an unlimited number of alternative approaches versus relatively few approach paths.

It seemed reasonable that there would be limits to this conclusion, and system performance during emergency conditions was felt to provide such a limiting condition. It was predicted that, under emergency conditions, procedural flexibility might be less efficient and/or safe than constrained procedures. An emergency was simulated by blanking out the primary information display (a simulated plan-position indicator) during a normal run. The controller was required to process aircraft without this visual display under one of two conditions of constraint: he could use any of 17 flight paths or he was restricted to the use of only one of three. Again, the more flexible condition resulted in greater system efficiency; however, system safety was greater with the constrained condition (Howell, Christy, and Kinkade [285]).

It is apparent that such information is of value to system management, and it provides such information without requiring the considerable trial and error that would be necessary (with painful consequences) if operational systems were used.

26

AN AXIOMATIC APPROACH TO ORGANIZATIONS
FROM A GENERAL SYSTEMS VIEWPOINT

M. D. Mesarović, J. L. Sanders, C. F. Sprague

Introduction [1]

The principal objective of this chapter is to propose a formal conceptual framework for studies of organizations as systems and to review the results obtained so far which describe the behavior of such systems and shed light on the behavior of organizations.

There are three principal justifications for this attempt:

1. *A formal conceptual model of an organization will allow a more extensive use of formal concepts and analytical or quantitative techniques in studying the behavior of an organization.* This, in turn, will lead to an explanation of many phenomena present in a real-life organization which are as yet unexplainable without a proper framework. We shall touch on some of them in later sections.

2. Organizations are purposeful systems, the elements of which are essentially involved in a problem-solving activity. Now, by the very nature of the decision-making process a model or an image of the object of decision has to exist before a decision is made. (The cases where deliberate simplification of the image is introduced to facilitate the decision-making procedure or make it more economical are also included here.) *A person in an organization has to base his decisions on an image of the rest of the organization, its influence upon him, as*

[1] This chapter presents the results of research conducted by the Systems Theory Group of the Systems Research Center, Case Institute of Technology, which is supported in part by the ONR Contract No. 1141 (12).

well as his influence on the organization as a whole. In the absence
of a proper model, his recourse must be to very crude, often inadequate, descriptions.

It is important to emphasize that a formal model of an organization
should help an inside decision maker to properly take into account
the structure and functional pattern of the organization. It will not
necessarily remove the basic and essential uncertainties associated
with the current and future behavior of the environment and the rest
of the organization. The model will allow the decision maker to make
the decision with a higher likelihood of success but it will not readily
allow "mechanization" of that process. In other words, "intuition and
experience" of the decision maker will still be needed but the "logical
power" of decision makers will be "amplified."

3. *Concepts and methods developed for systems with a given structure cannot be adequately applied to the study of differently structured systems.* The particular case in point is the use of so-called
control and decision-making theory for providing an over-all model
of an organization. For example, occasional attempts have been made
to extend some of the concepts of feedback control systems to the
study of organizations. These attempts, however, cannot be successful
since they are developed for single-level–single-goal systems ($1l1g$
systems, as defined in the next section). They are, therefore, not directly applicable. The lack of an appropriate description of the structure
of an organization is a prime reason hindering direct application of
analytical and computational methods and techniques to the problems
of an organization.

For this reason, among others, an organization is defined in this
chapter as a multilevel-multigoal system. In this representation the
activities and functioning of the elements of an organization are described in an "objective" manner as they are seen or felt by the elements, the rest of the system, or the environment. Such an approach
does not exclude the role that human nature plays in an organization.
It only puts these effects into a proper perspective from which, hopefully, they can be resolved.

Multilevel-Multigoal System as a Model for an Organization

Organization is viewed here from a general systems theory standpoint. Some remarks on the general systems theory seem appropriate
(see also Mesarović and Eckman [397] and Mesarović [396]).

The general systems theory approaches the study of any system formally, on the basis of how it behaves, without inquiring why it behaves that way or from what fabrics it is made. It is therefore an abstract science.

General systems theory is concerned with abstract models as isomorphisms of systems in the sciences as well as with the classification of these systems with respect to structures, functionings, etc. It is only natural, therefore, that the human or social organizations find their place in such a development.

In general systems theory an organization is defined as a goal-seeking system which has interacting goal-seeking subsystems with different goals arranged in a hierarchy. The existence of a multiplicity of goals as a necessary characteristic for a system to be recognized as an organization is widely known and accepted.[2] General systems theory also holds that the existence of a multiplicity of goal-seeking subsystems hierarchically arranged is a sufficient characteristic for a system to represent an organization; that is, the existence of a multilevel-multigoal structure is the primary characteristic of an organization although its actual behavior is ultimately conditioned by the nature and behavior of the goal-seeking subsystem. For example, in the context of human organizations a goal-seeking subsystem in an $mlng$ (m-levels–n-goals) system might represent either a single human decision maker, a group of decision makers, a committee, etc.

After one accepts an $mlng$ system as a formal model of organization, the development of a new theory for the behavior of such systems as a prerequisite for understanding the behavior of human organizations becomes even more important. This can be illustrated by considering the classification of the goal-seeking systems in the general systems theory. This classification also indicates the relation of different fields concerned with the behavior of formal models of the goal-seeking systems.

Principal classification is in the following three categories:

SINGLE-LEVEL–SINGLE-GOAL, $1l1g$ SYSTEMS

A $1l1g$ system (Fig. 1) consists of a causal subsystem S and a goal-seeking subsystem G. The behavior of a $1l1g$ system can be completely described in terms of the pursuit of a goal which is either externally or internally generated. The basic features of $1l1g$ systems behavior are:

---

[2] See, for example, March and Simon [367], and Churchman, Ackoff, and Arnoff [126].

(a) Behavior of the *causal system* can be described completely in terms of its terminal behavior by means of an input-output transformation

$$y(t) = \Psi^* x(\tau) \tag{1}$$

where $y(t)$ = output of the causal system
$x(t)$ = input of the causal system
Ψ = systems operator

(b) Behavior of the *goal-seeking unit* can be described in terms of its activities in pursuing a given goal. In many cases this can be specified by means of an optimization problem: find $\mathbf{m}(t)$ so as to maximize

$$f^* = F\{\mathbf{y}(\tau), \mathbf{x}(\tau)\} \tag{2}$$

subject to equation 1, where $\mathbf{m}(\tau)$ represents the action of the goal-seeking unit on the causal system. In situations where uncertainties exist regarding the future behavior of the system or the environment, a "satisficing" procedure [3] might replace the optimization problem stated above.

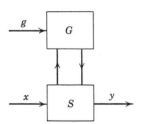

FIGURE 1 Single-level —single-goal system. *S*— system unit (causal part); *G* — goal-seeking unit; x—inputs; y—outputs; g—goals.

Equation 2 specifies the decision-making activity of the system. It is, of course, a very elaborate and complex activity. The functional F which is associated with the system's goal refers to the behavior of the system over a future period of time. This requires, in general, two additional activities which serve to provide the necessary conditions for decision making:

1. Prediction or generalization, in which subsystem G attempts to infer behavior of the system and environment in a future time interval.

2. Learning and adaption, in which, on the basis of the past experience, the subsystem G changes its behavior so as to improve the goal-seeking activity of the system in the future.

$1l1g$ systems offer a conceptual framework for many fields such as control theory, learning and adaptive systems, some self-organizing systems, sequential multistage decision making, etc.

---

[3] See March and Simon [367].

SINGLE-LEVEL–MULTIGOAL, $1l1g$, SYSTEMS

A set of interacting $1l1g$ systems represent a single-level–multigoal system (Fig. 2). Differences in the goals generate conflict and may cause the development of a competitive situation inside the system. The von Neumann-Morgenstern game theory deals with $1lng$ systems. The theory of behavior of $1lng$ systems is not in a wholly satisfactory state, but game theory at least indicates some of the more important modes of operation. The problems of complex systems in which every $1l1g$ system exhibits adaptation, learning, and prediction need further conceptual study.

MULTILEVEL–MULTIGOAL SYSTEMS, $mlng$ SYSTEMS

Systems of a still higher complexity are obtained by adding new goal-seeking subsystems which have goals encompassing different portions of the system and may influence the other goal-seeking units. For example, two $1l1g$ systems can be associated with an additional goal-seeking unit which is concerned with a goal common to both of the subsystems and, in fact, to the over-all system (see Fig. 3). In order to distinguish the new goal and the activities associated with it,

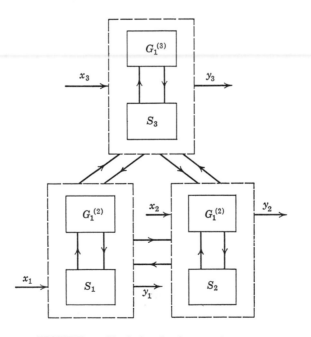

FIGURE 2   Single-level—three-goal system.

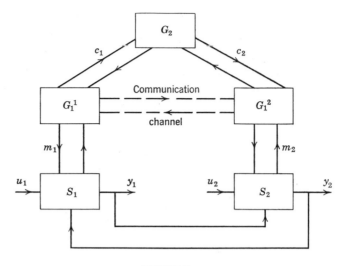

FIGURE 3

this is termed a "second-level" goal. This system is termed a two-level–three-goal ($2l3g$) system.

A two-level system may include any number of single-level systems so that, in general, one might have a $2lng$ system. Two second-level systems having one additional common goal with an associated goal-seeking unit represent a $3l5g$ system or, in general, a $3lng$ system if any of the two-level systems have more than two subsystems. In the same way one can now build a multilevel-multigoal $mlng$ system (Fig. 4).

There are advantages to defining more precisely what is meant by "level" in an $mlng$ system. Consider two goal-seeking units G_{ik} and G_{jl} in an $mlng$ system. The goal-seeking unit G_{ik} will be considered to be on a higher level than (have priority of action over) G_{jl}, $(i > j)$, if the decision made by G_{ik} directly affects the goal-seeking activity of G_{jl} while the decision made by G_{jl} might influence G_{ik} only indirectly via the performance of the over-all system. For example, a decision made by G_{ik} may influence the goal or objective functional of G_{jl} or it might change constraints and available resources allocated to G_{jl}, and it might even cause an alteration of the decision already made by G_{jl}.

The developments to date coming closest to studying $mlng$ systems are the areas called the theory of teams [4] and decentralized operations

---

[4] See Marschak [368].

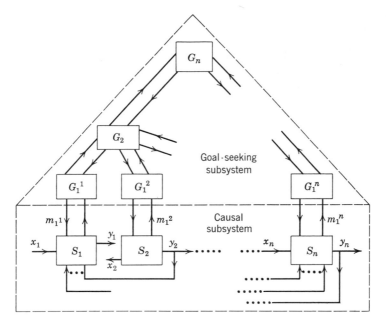

FIGURE 4

of a firm.[5] However, both of these developments are primarily concerned with the mutual relationship of the goal-seeking units on the
same level and in that sense address themselves to $1lng$ systems. Of
principal interest in the theory of $mlng$ system, however, are relationships between the units on different levels; i.e., "vertical relationships" in an organization.

We are making a concentrated effort to develop foundations for
a theory of $mlng$ systems. In this chapter we shall briefly outline some
of the results achieved so far in this direction.[6]

Structure of mlng System

Structure of $mlng$ systems can be characterized primarily by the
way the goals of different units depend upon each other and how the
decisions of a given unit influence the behavior of other units.

---

[5] See Arrow and Hurwicz [26].

[6] Detailed analytical considerations may be found in Mesarović [394], [395], and
[441b]; Sanders [458]; and Sprague [513].

Goals on different levels are, in general, interdependent in the sense that achievement of the ith goal on the jth level depends upon success in the achievement of goals on higher as well as lower levels. These goal interactions can be specified in general by the following set of relations:

$$\mathbf{g}_n = \mathbf{g}_n(\mathbf{g}_1, \cdots, \mathbf{g}_{n-1})$$

$$\vdots$$

$$\mathbf{g}_i = \mathbf{g}_i(\mathbf{g}_1, \cdots, \mathbf{g}_n) \tag{3}$$

$$\vdots$$

$$\mathbf{g}_1 = \mathbf{g}_1(\mathbf{g}_2, \cdots, \mathbf{g}_n)$$

where $\mathbf{g}_i = \{g_{ij}\}$ represents a set of goals on the ith level.

To facilitate the decision making associated with different units in a complex *mlng* system, the goal interaction of a goal-seeking unit is almost invariably restricted to the goals in neighboring levels. In the simplest case, the goal of each such unit depends only upon the goals of the first level above it and the first level below it. That is, in the simplest case, equation 3 becomes

$$\mathbf{g}_i = \mathbf{g}_i(\mathbf{g}_{i-1}, \mathbf{g}_{i+1}) \tag{4}$$

Goal interaction is of primary concern when constructing an *mlng* system. Goal-seeking units should interact in a fashion whereby the over-all goal ($\mathbf{g}_n$) is achieved with a reasonable degree of satisfaction. This might require us to specialize the functional $\mathbf{g}_i$ so that it monotonically increases with $\mathbf{g}_{i+1}$. This would ensure a motivation for lower level units to further higher level goals.

Two basic types of goal interdependence should be recognized:

Direct goal interdependence. Goals of the higher as well as the lower level units depend explicitly upon the outputs and behavior of the causal systems. The goals of higher level units, however, encompass larger portions of the causal system and, in dynamic situations, may extend over a longer period of time.

Consider for example a *2l3g* system (Fig. 2). Units G_{11} and G_{12} have goals defined in terms of respective subsets of outputs,

$$G_{11} = G_{11}(y_1, \cdots, y_j) \qquad G_{12} = G_{12}(y_{j+1}, \cdots, y_n)$$

The goal of the second level unit, however, depends upon all outputs of the causal system [7]

$$G_2 = G_2(y_1(t), \cdots, y_n(t))$$

Indirect goal interdependence. Goals of a given higher level unit may explicitly depend only upon the goals of the lower level units and implicitly upon the performance of the basic causal system. The relationships specifying the goal interdependence are of the form given in equations 3 and 4.

INTERVENTION

We now consider how a higher level unit uses its authority to influence the behavior of lower level units. Here we recognize two modes of operation:

Direct intervention. A higher level unit directly changes the decision made by the lower level unit unless the latter is found to be appropriate. "Management by exception" falls in this category. The principal feature of this mode of operation is that the controllability of the causal subsystem that the higher level units possess is often the same as that of the lower level units. However, when intervention is to be realized by changing the decisions at a lower level, the decision-making procedure may become quite complex.

Indirect intervention. A higher level unit cannot directly modify the decision already made by a lower level unit but can modify the goals and constraints of lower level units. For example, in a $2l3g$ system, G_2 may change the rules by which profits will be shared between G_{11} and G_{12} after an operation has been completed. Alternately, it might change the allocation of resources between them. Finally, it might inform G_{11} about the action of G_{12} in such a way that the former's image of the system's operation is changed or even distorted. Here a higher level unit does not have the same amount of controllability as in direct intervention, but the decision-making procedure involved in selecting the best method of modifying the behavior of the lower level unit might be considerably simpler. This mode of operation is found very often in human organizations.

From the brief discussion in this section it should become apparent that the behavior of a goal-seeking unit in an $mlng$ system should be different than the behavior of a unit in either $2l3g$ or $1lng$ systems.

---

[7] Notational convention: the first subscript indicates the level of the goal-seeking unit, and the second distinguishes the unit; thus, for the top level unit the second subscript is omitted.

Methodology of Presentation of the Results

To illustrate the nature of the results that can be obtained from the theory of *mlng* system, we give results of some typical studies.[8] These studies—or at least the aspects that are discussed here—all investigate the consequence of selecting a given goal-seeking structure on the behavior of the over-all *mlng* system.

A standard method is employed for presenting results. First, the conclusion regarding the behavior of the organization-like systems is given in the form of a general statement. Second, a specific class of *mlng* systems for which the stated conclusion has been rigorously proved is described. Finally, a basic justification is supplied for generalization from the results proved for a given class of systems into the context of a larger class of systems.

PLANNING AND PREDICTION IN AN ORGANIZATION

Among the most interesting *mlng* systems are those where indirect intervention is applied. In particular we shall confine our attention in this section to those systems in which a higher-level goal-seeking unit influences the goals of lower level units. We can now make the following statement about the behavior of such systems.

In an mlng system, the problem of internal planning (prediction) arises when indirect intervention is used. The extent of this internal planning as well as the time period in the immediate future to which the planning refers, depend upon the internal structure of the system or, more specifically, upon the method used by the higher level units in influencing the lower level goals.

First of all we need to specify more clearly what is meant by "internal planning." By assumption, the higher *j*th level unit influences the lower *i*th level by changing the values of a variable m_{ij} (possibly a vector) in the goal of the lower level unit.

$$g_i^*(t) = \min_{m_i} F_i[m_i(\tau), m_{ij}(\tau)] \qquad t \leq \tau \leq t + T \qquad (5)$$

where m_i is the decision variable of the unit G_i, and m_{ij} is the decision variable of a higher level unit G_j, expressing how it influences the goal of G_i; i.e., m_{ij} is an *intervention variable*. The decision problem for G_i is to solve equation 5 by optimization (taking into account the relevant con-

---

[8] Details are discussed in Mesarović [395] and [441b]; Sanders [458]; and Sprague [513].

straints) and to express m_i as a function of m_{ij}. When this has been done, we will have

$$m_i(t) = m_i[t, m_{ij}(\tau)] \qquad t \leq \tau \leq t + T \tag{6}$$

In equation 5, we view m_i as a functional of the intervention variable m_{ij}, i.e., the value of m_i at a given time t depends upon the complete function $m_{ij}(\tau)$ defined in a future period of time $t \leq \tau \leq (t + T)$. This dependence requires advance specification of the intervention variable and this is what, in the present study, is referred to as internal planning. Note, however, that to implement decision $m_i(t)$ at the time t, G_i has to be given $m_{ij}(\tau)$ for some value of τ in the intervals $t \leq \tau \leq t + T$. This requires G_j to decide in advance what m_{ij} will be used in the future. (Let us note in passing that F_i as well as m_i also depend upon many other variables of the system besides m_{ij}, but for the sake of simplicity this was not emphasized in equations 5 and 6.)

Let us now turn to a special case for which the statement on p. 502 was rigorously proved. Consider a system with the causal part (technological process) described by the discrete vector equation

$$\mathbf{y}_{t+1} = A\mathbf{y}_t + \mathbf{m}_{t+1} + \mathbf{u}_{t+1} \tag{7}$$

where $\mathbf{y} = $ output vector (random)

$\quad \mathbf{m} = $ input vector

$\quad \mathbf{u} = $ disturbance vector (random)

$\quad A = $ systems matrix, $A = \begin{bmatrix} A_{11} & A_{12} \\ A_{21} & A_{22} \end{bmatrix}$, the A_{ii} are square submatrices.

The subscripts indicate the relevant time period so that, for instance, $\mathbf{y}_t$ represents the output at time t.

The causal system is split into two parts which are directed by the two first-level goal-seeking units G_{11} and G_{12}. Goals of these units are defined in the following way:

$$g_1^* = \min_{m_{t1}} E\left[\sum_{t=1}^{n} (\mathbf{y}_{t1}{}^T B_{11} \mathbf{y}_{t1} + 2\mathbf{d}_{t1}{}^T \mathbf{m}_{t1}) \right] \tag{8}$$

where B_{11} is a submatrix of B and $\mathbf{d}_{t1}$ are decision variables of the second level unit. The latter can be viewed as "price" or "accounting" vectors which the second level charges to the first-level unit in accordance with resource usages contained in the vector of inputs $\mathbf{m}$. E means "expected value" with respect to $\mathbf{u}$ and the superscript, T, denotes transposition.

Unit G_{12} has, similarly,

$$g_2{}^* = \min_{m_{t2}} E\left[\sum_{t=1}^{n} (\mathbf{y}_{t2}B_{22}\mathbf{y}_{t2}{}^{t'} + 2\mathbf{d}_{t2}\mathbf{m}_{t2})\right] \tag{9}$$

Now we include B_{21} and B_{12} as submatrices in a matrix B which a second-level unit is to consider. The second-level unit is concerned with the activity of the entire system and has the goal

$$g^2{}^* = \min_{\mathbf{d}_{t1},\mathbf{d}_{t2}} E\left[\sum_{t=1}^{N} (\mathbf{y}_t{}^T B\mathbf{y}_t)\right] \tag{10}$$

That is, the second-level unit chooses $\mathbf{d}_{t1}$ and $\mathbf{d}_{t2}$ to obtain a minimum for $g^2{}^*$, where the $\mathbf{d}$ values serve, in turn, as prices applicable to their inputs $\mathbf{m}$. See equations 8 and 9.

The over-all operation of the system described here proceeds as follows:
Information
(a) Unit G_2 (second level) knows $E(\mathbf{u}_i) = \hat{\boldsymbol{\mu}}_i$.
(b) Unit G_2 knows B. $B = \begin{bmatrix} B_{11} & B_{12} \\ B_{21} & B_{22} \end{bmatrix}$, the B_{ii} are square sub-matrices.
(c) Unit G_2 knows the complete structure of first-level systems.
(d) First-level units know $\hat{\boldsymbol{\mu}}_i{}^1$ and $\hat{\boldsymbol{\mu}}_i{}^2$ respectively.
(e) First-level units know equations 8 and 9 respectively.
Operation
(a) First-level units optimize for arbitrary $\mathbf{d}_t$. $1 \leq t \leq n$.
(b) First-level units communicate $\mathbf{m}_t{}^{i*}\mathbf{d}_{ti}$ for system to G_2. $1 \leq t \leq n$.
(c) Second-level unit sets $\mathbf{d}_t$ to optimize over-all system performance relative to g^2.

Solution of the optimization problem of equations 9 and 10 gives the following expression for the decision variable of the subsystem G_{1i}:

$$\overset{*}{\mathbf{m}}_{N-k,i} = B^{-1}(A_i{}^T\mathbf{d}_{N-k+1,i} - \mathbf{d}_{N-k,i}) - (A_iC + \mathbf{m}_{N-k,i}) \tag{11}$$

$$A_1 = A_{11} \qquad A_2 = A_{22} \qquad A = \begin{bmatrix} A_{11} & A_{12} \\ A_{21} & A_{22} \end{bmatrix}$$

In order to make the decision at a given time $t = N - k$, the goal-seeking unit has to have information about the "price" variable $\mathbf{d}$ not only at the present time instant $t = N - k$ but also at the next time instant $t = N - k + 1$.

The difficulty is, however, that the second-level unit should use $\mathbf{m}_{N-k,i}$ in order to determine $\mathbf{d}_{N-k+1,i}$ in a truly optimal fashion. In the absence of this, G_2 has to select $\mathbf{d}_{N-k+1,i}$ on the basis of prediction.

In the context of the organizational systems, this result can be interpreted to mean that the planning function for the manager is the natural outgrowth of the organization structure.

Communication Problem in an Organization

When an organization is represented as an *mlng* system, existence of the communication channels becomes a property of the system which can be treated quantitatively as an aspect of optimal selection of a systems structure. Using this approach one can find out, for example, which "decision points" in the organization should be connected by the communication channels. In actual human organizations, these questions certainly depend upon the human element. However, it is of primary interest to know which communication channels could cause deterioration in the performance of the organization due to the structural properties of the system which are independent of the human elements.

Before proceeding further, we have to specify more clearly what is meant by a "communication pattern." For this we introduce a communication network which establishes exchanges of information among the units on the same or different levels. Furthermore, the type of information to be sent through the channels is specified in advance by explicitly given rules of operation. Then the communication network, together with the specification of the types of information that are allowed, specifies admissible communication patterns in the system. For example, unit G_i might have been told to send information regularly about the rate of change of its "goal-achieving" to unit G_j. Alternatively G_i may supply, perhaps, only a cumulative figure.

The problem to be considered is whether a given pattern of communication channels is advantageous in a given system. The cost of communication channels is not considered but only their effect on the over-all systems performance. Then on the basis of a specific study, the following general statement can be made:

From the standpoint of achieving the over-all goal for the entire system, there exists an optimal pattern composed of the communication channels of a given kind. Introduction of additional communication channels and the increased exchange of information that results cause deterioration in the performance of the over-all system. To be able to decide on the desirability of a given communication pattern it might be enough for the over-all manager to know only the types of the goals for all the units in the organization, and more specific knowledge about these goals is not required.

This property significantly simplifies synthesis of a communication network in an organization. It also allows the over-all manager to deal more successfully with the uncertainties and variations caused by lack of knowledge on human behavior in the system. As long as the uncertainties or variations in the individual behavior stay within a given class, they will not alter the desirability of a given type of the communication network.

We now consider a very special case. A production organization has two departments S_1 and S_2 with the respective department managers (first-level goal-seeking units) G_{11} and G_{12}. Let the production processes of the department be specified by the equations

$$\frac{dy_1(t)}{dt} = a_{11}y_1(t) + a_{12}y_2(t) + b_1m_1(t) + c_1(t) \qquad \text{for } S_1$$

$$\text{(12)}$$

$$\frac{dy_2(t)}{dt} = a_{21}y_1(t) + a_{22}y_2(t) + b_2m_2(t) + c_2(t) \qquad \text{for } S_2$$

where $y_1(t)$ and $y_2(t)$ are the outputs or finished products; $m_1(t)$ and $m_2(t)$ decision variables of the department managers G_{11} and G_{12}; $c_1(t)$ and $c_2(t)$ corrections by the over-all managers (second-level goal-seeking unit) G_2.

All decision variables are constrained in such a way that their amplitudes cannot exceed certain values at any time during the production process. It is required to produce certain quantities of products, and the goal of the over-all manager is to obtain these outputs in the shortest possible time.

The first-level managers G_{11} and G_{12} also are interested in producing their parts in a short time but not at "any cost," that is, they have a cost associated with the effort in producing the product. It is assumed in this study that this cost is linearly dependent upon the manipulated variables m_1 and m_2 used by the units G_{11} and G_{12} to speed up the process. Goals of the first-level managers are given now by the functionals

$$g_{11} = \min \int_0^{t_f} [1 + \alpha_1 m_1(t)] \, dt$$

$$\text{(13)}$$

$$g_{12} = \min \int_0^{t_f} [1 + \alpha_2 m_2(t)] \, dt$$

where t_f is the time when the process is completed.

Assume first that no communication between G_{11} and G_{12} exists so that neither manager is able to consider the influence of the other process on his own activity. Solution of the optimization problem then gives:

$$m_1(t) = - \operatorname{sign} M_1[z_1(t)]$$
$$m_2(t) = - \operatorname{sign} M_2[z_2(t)]$$

(14)

where M_1 and M_2 are constants, and $z_1(t)$ and $z_2(t)$ are solutions of the first-order differential equations. Since z_1 and z_2 are solutions of the first-order equations, they cannot change their signs so that solution of equation 13 becomes

$$m_1(t) = -M_1 \qquad m_2(t) = -M_2$$

(15)

Assume now that the communication channel between G_{11} and G_{12} is established and, furthermore, that the units are instructed to send information which enables each of them to know the entire process given in equation 12. Solution of the optimization problem is now

$$m_1(t) = -M_1 \operatorname{sign} [b_1 u_1(t) + \alpha_1 u_3(t)]$$
$$m_2(t) = -M_2 \operatorname{sign} [b_2 u_2(t) + \alpha_2 u_3(t)]$$

(16)

In the course of the production process, $m_1(t)$ and $m_2(t)$ can now change sign since a new variable $u_3(t)$ is added to the expression in parentheses. Solution of equation 13 is now

$$m_1(t) = M_1 \qquad 0 \le t \le \tau$$
$$m_1(t) = -M_1 \qquad \tau \le t \le t_f$$

(17)

where τ is the switching point, and similarly for G_{12}. The time for producing a given amount of output product is now longer than before the communication channels were established. This is true regardless of the values for α_1 and α_2. This leads to the following conclusion:

To shorten the production process, the over-all manager should not establish a communication channel between the production departments if they evaluate their efforts linearly or if they are charged for the resources used via a linear dependence. This conclusion does not depend upon the value of the per unit cost.

It is interesting to note that this conclusion changes when the cost function is quadratic. This shows that, to arrive at a decision regarding the establishing of the communication channels, the over-all manager has to estimate the class to which certain parameters belong.[9]

---

[9] See Mesarović [395].

Reorganization and Internal Image in an Organization

In a dynamic situation one might be able to measure the effectiveness of performance of an organization and to apply some changes in the organizational structure, if these changes appear promising. These changes can be carried out by any of the goal-seeking units and, in general, are applied to the respective lower levels. In exercising structural changes, however, a given goal-seeking unit might change the conditions under which some other units operate in a way that hinders successful operation of these units and, finally, causes disintegration of the organization. To avoid this, every goal-seeking unit has to obey certain rules while changing structure in its domain of organization. One such rule is given in form of the following principle:

Principle of Unique Image in an Organization: For proper functioning of an organization, activities of all the system units should be such that each and every unit, on the basis of the available information, has a unique image of the functioning of the rest of the organization.

The basis for this principle is obtained by considering the following system: *mlng* system under consideration has m levels. Goal interdependencies are such that the goal of a given decision maker G_{ij} depends upon some of the goals on one level above $(i + 1)$ and one level below $(i - 1)$.

$$g_{ij} = g_{ij}[g_{i-1}, R_{ij}^{(i+1)}(g_{i+1})]$$

The first level goals are then

$$\mathbf{g}_1 = \mathbf{g}_1[\mathbf{y}, \mathbf{m}, R^{(2)}(\mathbf{g}_2)]$$

and the over-all goal of the organization is

$$g_n = g_n(\mathbf{g}_{n-1}).$$

$\mathbf{y}$ and $\mathbf{m}$ are the output and input to the causal subsystem while $R_{ij}^{(i+1)}$ specifies the dependence of the decision maker G_{ij} upon the achievement of the goal on the higher $(i + 1)$ level. The reorganization activity consists in changing the functionals R.

For this type of organization the following theorem holds:

A sufficient condition for a unique behavior (unique solution of functional equations) of an mlng system is that all self-organizational transformations $R_{21}^{(1)}, \cdots, R_{n(n-1)}^{j}$ are contraction mappings.

It is understood here that $R(\mathbf{z})$ is a contraction mapping defined on the appropriate Euclidian space.

$$z = R(\mathbf{z}) \qquad z \in \Omega_z$$

The significance of this theorem for the structure-changing activity in an organization lies primarily in the fact that it specifies the conditions under which this activity can be localized. Namely, for harmonious operation of an organization in which goal conflicts exist, it is necessary that the organization evolve in a unique pattern. If the conditions of the theorem are satisfied every unit might change the organizational structure by replacing transformation $R_{j\mathrm{I}}$ with another $R_{j\mathrm{II}}$ but both transformations have to be contraction mappings.

On the other hand, if the conditions for the theorem are not satisfied, because of the action, say, of an external influence, various units in the organization might operate on the basis of different solutions which will definitely result in the breakdown of the entire organization.

Effect of Reorganization on the Performance of the System

mlng system models of an organization offer a particularly suitable framework for studying reorganizations aimed at improving the effectiveness of an organization. Basically, in the context of *mlng* systems, there are two types of structural changes, both initiated from higher level units: (1) Change in the causal system (change in the technological process used) or change in the subdivision of the process (change in the responsibility among the goal-seeking units). (2) Change in the number of the goal-seeking units, their hierarchical arrangement, or the types of goals to be followed: Change 1 is called *self-organizing activity* and change 2 *self-organizational activity*.

Systems with a self-organizing activity can develop new forms of organization while in operation. In particular, any delegation of authority might generate a new organizational problem if the goals of the subunits respond to the environment. This can generate conflict and irreversible changes in the organization.

We now consider more closely the self-organizing activity. There are many reasons for initiating self-organizing activity in an *mlng* system. In particular, the self-organization considered here is motivated by its relevance to problems in human organization and by possibilities for the use of simple computational and analytical apparatus.

One of the difficulties encountered in the study of self-organizing systems is the development of an ordering relation over the set of all possible structures of the system. Such an ordering relation is necessary if the goal-seeking units responsible for instituting structural alterations are to have a criterion for selecting a structure which will improve the performance of the system. In what follows, we will propose a basis for determining the "best" structure under which to operate.

The position of a structure in the ranking of a structure set under the ordering relation to be developed is determined by the efficiency of the lower level units in synthesizing the optimal policy when operating in that structure. In order to illustrate this, assume that in an *mlng* system:

1. The lower level goal-seeking elements are collectively exerting control by engaging in a temporal "action-counteraction" type of interplay in an attempt to arrive at a state of equilibrium, where the action of each unit is best under the conditions imposed by the other units.

2. The goal-seeking element at the apex has the ability to influence [10] these lower-level elements so that their collective *equilibrium* control actions coincide with the optimal control rule from the over-all viewpoint.

3. The rate at which the interplay described in (1) above approaches equilibrium is at least partially determined by the structure under which the lower level goal-seeking elements operate.

As long as the interplay described in (1) is in the "transient phase," because of (2), the over-all optimal control law is not being achieved. Because of (3), we can rank the structures according to how well this control law is approximated during the transient phase; a comparison of two structures would lead to a designation of the one with the higher rate of convergence as the better. For this would assure arrival at equilibrium, and hence optimal control, in lesser time.

Suppose we allow the highest level goal-seeking element in an *mlng* system the capability to change the existing structural arrangement of the lower level elements. With this capability and the method of ranking structures described above, this system displays behavior which we would classify as "self-organizing." The goal-seeking element at the highest level can alter the structure so as to "select" a structure from a set of different possible structures "below" it. This behavior is also purposeful, in that the criteria of choice assure the best approximation to the optimal control law.

---

[10] In order to maintain autonomy of the lower level goal-seeking elements, this will not be in the form of a "directive" as to what control action to apply.

Relation of the General Systems Organization to Social Organizations

It is apparent that, in general systems theory, an organization is defined on the basis of the system's functioning irrespective of the presence of the human elements. Two very pertinent questions immediately appear:

(1) In what sense is a general systems organization isomorphic to a social organization; and

(2) how can this isomorphism (if it exists) be used in improving their performance?

The key to answering these questions is, of course, contained in the role which humans play in an organization. Of particular importance are those aspects of its behavior which characterize goal-seeking units. For our purpose we shall classify behavior of a human in an organization in two categories: (1) Deductive reasoning; (2) inductive reasoning and chance behavior.

When confronted with a decision-making situation, a human proceeds in the following ways: (1) On the basis of inductive reasoning he builds the assumptions necessary for logical decision making; (2) on the basis of deductive reasoning he makes the choice which appears to be the proper one for the goal as he sees it.

The second aspect of human behavior can be definitely built into a general systems model. How much of the first kind of behavior can be built in is an open question. Some of the effects from the first kind of behavior can be described by means of random processes. Other effects, although present, are irrelevant to the functioning of the organization, or might be made to become irrelevant. Of course, much depends upon the delineation of the two kinds of reasoning or behavior. The limit that divides these two behavior patterns is, in fact, an operational one which moves steadily at the expense of inductive reasoning. Many aspects of human behavior, however, appear to be definitely beyond the limits of deductive contemplation. Such aspects, therefore, seem to remain outside a general systems approach. By the same token, however, those aspects will remain outside of the behavioral sciences and, in fact, any science whatsoever. Therefore, whatever is amenable to scientific method in the field of social studies can be put into a general systems model of an organization.

There is one important aspect of the multilevel systems structure which might help in this situation. Goal evaluation is, in most cases, expressed by functionals which represent many-to-one transformations. There might exist therefore an infinity of actions of the lower level units which, if they belong to a given class, will have the same influence on the goal-seeking. A proper use of such nonunique relationships might contribute to making the unknown activities irrelevant.

The second question, that involving the use of an isomorphism, has a more definite answer. Any decision maker involved in the functioning of an organization makes his decisions by using some image of the organization and its relation to the environment. In most cases it is a very much simplified model, and the logical rules which a human uses in decision making are correspondingly simple. A more detailed, even if incomplete, model can only help the decision maker if he is able to use it properly and focus his "intuition and experience" on the assumptions for this model rather than on the process of building the model itself. The examples discussed in the previous section provide evidence to this end. Built-in redundancy in an organization or in a formulation of the problem again offers great help. In the example studied, the communication channel should not be established for the linear first-level goal no matter what limits are imposed on the actions of first-level-goal units, and no matter how these units evaluate their effort in production processes. The optimal decision is, therefore, made with respect to the class of situations rather than with respect to any particular situation.

Finally, a general systems model should be used which is dynamic and adaptive in the sense that it is brought up to date as knowledge or experience increases. General systems models should, in any event, extend human ability to reason about organizations, just as, by analogy, digital computers extended the ability to calculate. Digital computers can be of significant help here also, but they should be used as logical systems rather than as extended "slide rules" or "calculating machines." The analysis and study of an organization may then be performed on a computer—possibly one of special design—which can perform the optimizations that might be needed when determining the *structure* of an organization.

PART FIVE

Conclusion: perspectives for further research

27

TOWARD A TAXONOMY OF ORGANIZATIONS

S. B. Sells

The Taxonomic Approach

Taxonomy has long been a special occupation of biologists, who have classified plants and animals according to their observed relationships and formulated principles underlying these classifications. The importance of the principles of taxonomic systems must be emphasized because classifications have little value in themselves, except as fascinating diversions for the idle and indigent. On the contrary, taxonomic models have served as a basic strategy for explanation and prediction of the behavior of organisms. Taxonomic characteristics are explanatory to the extent that they serve as indices to behavior traits (Cowles [140]).

TAXONOMIC PRINCIPLES

A useful taxonomy should be a theoretical model which orders empirical observations and also permits predictions guiding new observations, based on the developed network of relationships. In its fullest development the taxonomic approach should conform to the general systems approach; in any case, the two are compatible, and perhaps the salient strengths of each may contribute to the goals of the other. For example, the concern of the taxonomist with accounting systematically for extensive detail may enhance the systematist's analysis of complex systems, whereas the early appreciation of the characteristics of systems may orient the taxonomist to strategically significant interactions.

MODEL FOR A MULTIDIMENSIONAL ORGANIZATIONAL
TAXONOMY: ASSUMPTIONS

The multidimensional model for an organizational taxonomy presented here is based on the following assumptions:

1. Organizations are behaving organisms whose behavior is represented by the coordinated, composite action of their members functioning in their roles as organizational members.

2. The behavior of organizations with respect to any task or index is a predictable function of three major sources of variance, discussed below, which may be referred to as: (1) Characteristics of individuals participating (abilities, motivational and stylistic personality traits, background, past experience and training, ethnic factors, etc.); (2) organizational characteristics (goals, tasks, group structure, facilities, procedures, etc.); and (3) characteristics of the physical and social environment. It is assumed that significant portions of the variance of behavioral criteria will be accounted for by factors representing these separate sources as well as by other factors representing interactions of these sources.

3. The universes of variables representing persons, organizations, and external environment can be represented by factored dimensions (or common factors) which order the myriad of specific observable characteristics in terms of generalized composites that are both more stable and less redundant, for multivariate prediction, than the specifics by which they are defined.

4. The total variance of any criteria of organizational behavior can be accounted for by weighted combinations of the universe of dimensions of persons, organizations, and environment, within the limits of measurement error. Multiple-regression equations, discriminant functions, or other appropriate multivariate techniques are applicable to the prediction problem, but the development of predictor factors for each of the major sources of organizational behavior, and of suitable criteria, are issues of prior importance.

5. The dimensions of the taxonomy of organizations will be indicated by the differential patterns of predictive weights obtained for various combinations of factors.

INFORMATION AVAILABLE AND NEEDED RESEARCH

The research necessary to formulate even a tentative taxonomy of organizations in the present frame of reference has not yet been done, although the state of the scientific knowledge and measurement technology in the three major areas of concern is encouraging. These are commented upon in the appropriate sections to follow. It seems feasible to define the universes of variables with some expectation of agreement. However, progress toward dimensionalization has been meagre. This has been greatest in the area of individual differences; some impressive pioneering work (Hemphill [262]) has been published on dimensions of groups; dimensions of the physical and social environment appear to have received least attention. Finally, the criterion problem stands as a solid barrier that has defied solution almost from the beginning of behavioral science.

The program outlined here may appear impractical and, in fact, it may be impractical at this time, although I am not convinced of this. Developments in computer technology are moving so rapidly that new machines are obsolescent even before they appear on the market. However, it is hoped that the issues raised here will be judged on their scientific merit rather than on the basis of cost, equipment, or even time required. This problem offers great challenge. The question is, what steps are necessary to meet it?

The Universes of Variables Related to Organizational Behavior

CHARACTERISTICS OF INDIVIDUALS PARTICIPATING

In management terms, the characteristics of participating individuals are relevant in relation to the functions of organizational staffing, i.e., of obtaining qualified personnel for particular tasks and roles, including interrole coordination, when required. Personnel staffing is concerned primarily with fitting individuals to jobs, but the assumption is implicit that there is a relationship between characteristics of individuals and performance of groups composed of combinations of individuals. This relationship is, of course, not independent of other factors associated with group performance, such as organizational planning and management related to job definitions and procedures, compensation, working conditions, career plans, union-management relations, and numerous other internal and external factors.

PROBLEMS RELATED TO MEASUREMENT OF INDIVIDUAL DIFFERENCES

In the context of the present problem, there are three questions of interest concerning the measurement of individual differences among persons in the study of organizational behavior. These involve: (1) The extent of information available on the relation of individual qualifications to performance of various jobs or roles; (2) the relation of qualifications and/or performance of individuals to group or team performance; and (3) the state of knowledge concerning ability and personality organization and measurement technology regarding individual differences.

Relation of individual qualifications to performance. There is an extensive literature, in the field of personnel selection, on the correlation of various measures of individual differences with performance criteria of particular jobs. For the most part, however, the results reported are based on unsystematic, questionable instruments, confined to individual companies or organizations, or both, and the relevant conditions of organization and environmental setting have not been stated, thus limiting generalization. The latter difficulty might be reduced by randomization of uncontrolled factors through the use of large samples, but very few truly large-scale selection studies have been reported. The outstanding example is the U. S. Army Air Forces Aircrew Selection Program in World War II (Flanagan [198], Sells [471]), which included large enough numbers of employing organizations, so that the effects of internal factors were well randomized. As a result, the basic prediction formulas were successfully generalized to aircrew selection programs of other countries (France, Norway, West Germany), to postwar changes in aircraft equipment, when jets replaced piston-propeller types of aircraft, and to civilian airline selection. Information of this type is of great value for the present problem. However, there are only a few studies of this quality, mostly military, and even in these studies, the relations of individual to group proficiency are not clearly understood.

Aptitude, interest, and personality measures used in personnel selection have been of two types: special-purpose tests and scales, tailored to particular situations, and more general measures of primary traits in the ability and personality spheres, derived from factor analytic studies of responses to broad batteries of relevant variables. At best, the special-purpose selection devices have been difficult to interpret. Some have had utility in the limited circumstances for which they were designed, but have frequently lost validity when conditions changed. Development of composite validities for such measures from the published literature, by data-retrieval procedures, has generally been unproductive, for obvious reasons.

Theoretically, appropriately developed measures of common factors of ability and personality, which represent common sources of behavior variance, should fare better. Measurement, in such terms, is systematic and meaningful. It is comprehensively related to the entire spectrum of individual differences rather than to those particular behaviors assumed to be relevant to particular job samples. Then, when either job elements or job conditions change, it becomes necessary only to compute new regression equations based on the same predictors, but not to develop new predictors. Data retrieval of regression weights, based on a common taxonomy of human traits, is also a more reasonable prospect.

Relations of individual characteristics to group performance. Relationships between personal characteristics and performances of individuals and their composite performances when working together as teams have been studied in the field and in the laboratory. Haythorn [257] reviewed the research on group assembly, with particular reference to aircrew composition. He concluded that variations in crew effectiveness can be accounted for by variations in the particular combinations of individuals composing the groups, but also that self-selection methods of crew assembly were more successful than any rational methods that had been tried. Agreement on values relevant to group performance has been one of the most important determiners of compatibility among crew members and appears to be related to crew proficiency (Sells [472]).

Laboratory studies have not generally involved the interaction over time and standardization of roles characteristic of operational aircraft crews, but have achieved more accurate control of task and individual difference variables. In a number of such studies reviewed recently by Wiest, Porter, and Ghiselli [604], team proficiency depended on a variety of factors, including size of group, similarity of group members, type of task, and amount and type of interaction between members in performance of the task, as well as on the distribution of proficiencies among group members. Such research has usually concentrated on the relation of measures of individual members to criteria of composite performance and has noted only incidentally, if at all, the complex issues of group structure, norms, intergroup relations, and environmental factors. By the same token, group workers appear to be equally prone to overlook individual differences, although there is little doubt that these account for significant variance in group performance.

Status of scientific progress on identification and measurement of individual difference variables. At this time satisfactory measures of primary mental abilities (verbal comprehension, numerical facility, reasoning, spatial visualization, memory, word fluency, perceptual closure), perceptual abilities, sensory acuities, motor skills, and a number of aptitude clusters are available. But leading authorities, such as Thurstone [548] and Guilford [244], have expressed the belief that the range of significant primary human abilities includes areas additional to those thus far subjected to systematic study. In contrast to ability measurement, however, the classification and technology for measurement of motivational and personality traits are rudimentary. There is as yet no generally accepted taxonomy of motivational and stylistic personality traits, although developments in this field are progressing rapidly (Cattell [102], Guilford [244], Sells [473]). The best measures in this field today have limited validity for general use and require revalidation in specific situations. These limitations will be reflected in the schedule of measures of individual difference variables outlined below.

A detailed enumeration of the variables comprising the individual differences category is presented by Guilford [244]. Our purpose here is to outline the principal classes of such variables, from which further elaboration may be undertaken. These are:

1. Abilities (aptitudes and acquired skills).
2. Motivational traits.
3. Stylistic personality traits.
4. Biologic and constitutional factors: age; sex; height; weight; coloring; somatotype; appearance; ethnic origins; physical handicaps; genetic factors.
5. Social and demographic factors: education; social class; economic status; geographic-culture exposures; family background; siblings; family relations; marital status; citizenship; legal status (military service, voting, parole, etc.); occupational experience and status; responsibilities and dependencies; possessions; religious background and practice; linguistic background; group memberships; reference groups; roles.
6. Motivations related to participation in the situation: relations of individuals' goals to those of the organization; identification with the organization; identification with other organizations and groups; identification with role in organization, problem, or task with other participants; attitudes re locale, situation, and conditions of participation.
7. Relationships among participants: previous interactions among participants; role relationships in organization and their stability; dependencies among participants; social and cultural normative characteristics of participants (distribution).

This outline reflects the present imperfect state of the psychology of individual differences. If it were to be elaborated, at least 500 discrete variables would probably be required to represent all of the information implied. However, it is reasonable to expect that a considerably lower number will be found appropriate, even after further research on new abilities and personality traits, not yet isolated, upon factor-analytic reduction of the full range of variables. At present, a list of 35 to 45 variables representing factors most reliably measured and accounting for major segments of factor matrix variance could be realistically assembled. This might include a list such as the following:

Primary mental abilities (6 variables).
Motivational traits (10).
Stylistic traits (10).
Proficiency measures (3).
Age.
Sex.
Education.
Socioeconomic status.
Ethnic status.
Reference group indices (5).
Attitudes toward participation in organization (5).

Organizational characteristics. Despite the extensive activity in group behavior and management research, it is probably conservative to generalize that the state of rigorously demonstrated knowledge of organizational characteristics and behavior at this time approximates more closely that of personality measurement than ability measurement, commented on in the preceding section. A number of investigators, such as Cattell [101], [475*b*], Comrey, Pfiffner, and High [133], Hemphill [262], March and Simon [367], Stogdill [527], as well as others, have made significant theoretical and empirical contributions clarifying methodological problems and exploring major segments of the relevant universe of variables. But few would question that methodological difficulties have plagued this field, and what has been done, however fine, is scarcely more than a beginning.

Research problems. The difficulties inherent in both field and laboratory methods of organizational research are unquestionably frustrating and have given this field a "high risk" rating. We need not dwell on the familiar problems of criteria, control, data collection without disturbing on-going interactions, and the countless other barriers to effective field research, which have been surveyed recently by Adams and Preiss and their associates [7]. The issues are well known and will probably persist until more responsible management support, better financing, and closer integration of research with operations permit more effective planning and execution.

Laboratory approaches. These problems have led many investigators to simpler approaches, in the laboratory and through simulation. Although my own professional training and affiliations are experimental, I feel constrained to make a few methodological comments on the latter approaches. The interdependence of individual difference and environmental variables with those reflecting organizational characteristics has already been mentioned. Emphasis has also been placed, in the discussion of individual difference variables, on the importance of randomization of uncontrolled variance, preferably by very large samples, when significant sources of variance remain uncontrolled.

Many small group studies not only violate these principles but also, in the process, utilize conditions of interaction that could scarcely be called "group" and tasks that are unrealistic, even though often easier to control. An important condition of group formation is the awareness among several individuals of common motives shared, but incapable of separate attainment, which are conducive to interaction (Sherif and Sherif [489]). These practices greatly limit generalization of results.

An important aspect of group structure is the achievement of stable reciprocal expectations among members, as a result of cooperative interaction over a period of time. Group structure develops, as a reciprocal learning process, from incipient togetherness situations to highly stable organizations which reflect group norms, status, power, and specialized roles that exert significant effects on behavior of the participants. Laboratory groups, which consist of individuals given assigned roles on an *ad hoc* basis, without a developed structure, and which often perform tasks unrelated to their joint performance, often seem to lack the very characteristics of *groupness* that are critical to the research they are intended to implement.

Simulation approaches. Simulation techniques have attempted to provide more realism, and some, such as studies by Bass [475a] and by Haythorn [257], [258], have succeeded quite well in many respects. Critical appraisal of such studies will undoubtedly lead to further improvement, particularly with regard to issues of group stability, exploitation of more realistic common motives, and replication. The possibility of using full-time, paid participants in life-size, long-term simulations is a most engaging prospect.

Social situational (including organizational) variables. The following compressed list of variables does not fall into categories as neatly as those of the preceding section and is less specific. This probably reflects differences in methodology between psychometrics and group studies and perhaps also the limitations of the writer. It seems doubtful that organizations are more complex than the people who participate in them. However this may be, the following list of variables reflects types of information concerning organizations that have been found relevant to their behavior and that of their members. No claim of completeness can be made, but a wide range of organizational characteristics is outlined.

1. Characteristics of group task or problem, situation, and setting. Factors defined by the primary task (for each separate task group):

Area and level of knowledge and skills required.

Hazards and risks involved.

Novelty of situation to participants.

Procedures permitted.

Information required and available.

Number of participants, required, permitted, or available.

Material and facilities.

Degree of personal contact involved.

Role expectations regarding participants.

2. Group structure.

Stability of reciprocal expectations achieved by group; time in operation; reorganization, turnover.

Formal structure: intragroup patterns.

Group goals: definiteness; clarity; relation to basic objectives; relations to personnel capabilities and facilities; unusual aspects.

Membership patterns: requirements of experience; training; special qualifications; restrictive requirements (age, sex, race, religion, etc.); permeability of entrance and exit conditions; voluntary nature; time commitments.

Control of group members: freedom of movement, goals, expression, dress, schedules; regulations re conduct, work, living arrangements; rituals, ceremonies, standard operating procedures; regulation of group procedures; work controls; regulation of participation in activities; communication channels and practices.

Stratification; status hierarchy; power structure.

Modus operandi, including methods of communication, supervisory methods, procedures, decision-making, training.

Responsibility structure: organization and relationships of roles; departmentalization, division of labor among subgroups; role responsibilities (for what, to whom), power, privilege, prestige; requirements re individual qualifications; space and facility requirements; status mobility provisions.

Rewards; compensation; welfare; provision for individual and group satisfaction; incentives, recreation; benefits.

3. Formal structure: intergroup patterns.
Autonomy of organization and subgroups.
Pattern of centralization-decentralization.
Social status of organization and subgroups ("league standing").
Patterns of dependency, cooperation, competition in relation to other organizations.
Requirements concerning communication and transactions with other organizations.
Operating patterns, including conformity to formal patterns.
Goals.
Membership patterns.
Control.
Stratification, status hierarchy, power structure.
Modus operandi.
Responsibility structure.
Rewards, compensation, welfare, etc.
Intergroup patterns.
Superior-subordinate behavior patterns.

Research strategy. The strategy of the present approach is to reduce the specific variables, enumerated in relation to the universe suggested by the above outline, to a finite system of organizational factors comparable to those discussed under individual differences. A model for such a system is the set of organizational dimensions proposed by Hemphill [262], which is summarized below to illustrate the nature of the factors expected, although a more comprehensive set of factors should result from the systematic exploitation of this approach.

Using a questionnaire inquiry consisting of 150 items, Hemphill has developed measurement scales for the following 13 dimensions:

1. Autonomy: degree to which group functions independently of other groups and occupies an independent position in society. (Reflected by degree of self-determination of activities, absence of allegiance, deference, and/or dependence on other groups; 13 items.)

2. Control: degree of regulation of individuals while functioning as group members. (Reflected by modifications imposed on complete freedom of individual behavior and by intensity of group government; 12 items.)

3. Flexibility: degree of informality of group procedures, in contrast to adherence to established procedures. (Reflected by freedom of duties from formal specifications; 13 items.)

4. Hedonic tone: degree to which membership is accompanied by pleasant affect. (Reflected by frequency of laughter, conviviality, pleasant anticipation, etc.; 5 items.)

5. Homogeneity: degree to which members are similar with respect to socially relevant characteristics. (Reflected by relative uniformity of age, sex, race, socio-economic status, interest, attitudes, habits, etc.; 15 items.)

6. Intimacy: degree to which members are mutually acquainted and familiar with personal details of one another's lives. (Reflected by nature of topics discussed, modes of greeting, forms of address, and by interactions which presuppose a knowledge of the probable reactions of others under varying circumstances, as well as knowledge of members about each other; 13 items.)

7. Participation: degree to which members apply time and effort to group activities. (Reflected by number and kinds of duties performed, voluntary assumption of nonassigned duties, and amount of time spent in group activities; 10 items.)

8. Permeability: degree to which group permits ready access to membership. (Reflected by absence of entrance requirements and by degree to which membership is solicited; 13 items.)

9. Polarization: degree to which group is oriented and works toward a single goal which is clear and specific to all members (12 items).

10. Potency: degree to which group has primary significance to members. (Reflected by kinds of needs satisfied or potentially satisfied, by extent of individual readjustment implied should group fail, relation of group participation to central values of members; 15 items.)

11. Stability: degree of persistence over time with essentially unchanged characteristics. (Reflected by membership turnover rate, frequency of reorganization, constancy of group size; 5 items.)

12. Stratification: degree to which membership is ordered into status hierarchies. (Reflected by differential distribution of power, privileges, obligations, and duties, and by asymmetrical patterns of differential behavior among members; 12 items.)

13. Viscidity: degree to which members function as a unit. (Reflected by absence of dissension and personal conflict, self-aggrandizing behavior, resistance to disrupting forces, and by belief of members that they do function as a unit; 12 items.)

The interrelations of these 13 factors (plus size of group) are most readily shown by a rotated factor matrix published by Hemphill

[262], in which a major portion of the variance of the intercorrelations is accounted for by three group factors, which he named:

I. Behavior regulation appearing as social structure (with highest loadings on autonomy, low control, low stratification, permeability, low potency, and flexibility), which Hemphill characterized as "problem-induced" mobilization of behavior of individual members of the group.

II. Effective synergy (with highest loadings on polarization, viscidity, participation, and stability, which related to a similar factor reported by Cattell [101]), as referring to the total energy of group members, absorbed by group activity.

III. Primary personal interaction (with highest loadings on intimacy, size, homogeneity, stability, flexibility, hedonic tone, and low control), which is related to the concept of "primary" vs. "secondary" groups.

The rotated factor matrix for these three factors is as follows:

Table 1   Rotated Factor Loadings (Hemphill [262])

Dimension	I	II	III	h^2
1. Autonomy	0.78	0.14	0.11	0.64
2. Control (low)	0.69	−0.14	0.35	0.61
3. Flexibility	0.44	−0.12	0.37	0.34
4. Hedonic tone	0.15	0.17	0.37	0.19
5. Homogeneity	0.06	0.00	0.59	0.36
6. Intimacy	0.13	0.01	0.84	0.72
7. Participation	−0.29	0.69	−0.07	0.57
8. Permeability	0.62	−0.07	−0.18	0.42
9. Polarization	−0.08	0.76	−0.02	0.59
10. Potency (low)	0.60	−0.23	−0.16	0.43
11. Size (small)	0.01	0.17	0.74	0.57
12. Stability	0.02	0.40	0.41	0.33
13. Stratification (low)	0.64	0.22	0.15	0.48
14. Viscidity	0.17	0.72	0.23	0.60

This work of Hemphill's is a major contribution to organizational research. Yet it has been largely ignored since the monograph appeared. One possible reason for this is that the variables and factors have been somewhat disappointing as predictors of behavioral criteria. Whether this reflects defects in the scales or in the criteria employed, or other problems, remains to be settled. More particularly, however, the predictions of these and more extensive factors descriptive of organizations, developed along the lines pioneered by Hemphill, need to be investigated in combination with the other categories comprising the complete universe of organizational behavior.

ENVIRONMENTAL FACTORS

Of the three universes of variables, the preceding two have received most emphasis in relation to organizational behavior. This category includes the entire range of ecologic dependencies and relations among organizations. Although a related area involving studies of techniques and modes of organizational interaction appears to be an important area of organizational research, the effects of environmental factors on organizational behavior, although generally recognized as having significant effects on behavioral criteria, both directly and in interaction with other variables, have been largely neglected.

Ecologic dependencies of organizations. Ecologic dependencies include adaptations of organizations to conditions of both the physical and social environment. Recent emphasis on human ecology by behavioral scientists has focused attention on social dependencies, but the realities of adjustment of populations to the resources and physical conditions of the habitat have obvious implications for organizational behavior, which have received renewed prominence in view of current space explorations. The social aspects of human ecology have been represented by Hawley [254] as "an organization of interdependencies which constitute the population as a functional unity." Hawley regarded this as "an outcome of the adaptive strivings of aggregated individuals." The human community is thus viewed not only as dependent on the physical conditions specific to place and time but also as itself an adaptive mechanism in which the forms of communal structure in varying environmental contexts involve symbiotic relationships that influence behavior in many subtle and indirect as well as in obvious ways.

Limitations of the ecologic approach to organizational behavior. The ecologic approach to organizational behavior has certain limitations similar to those of the homeostatic concept as a basis for a psychological theory of motivation. Homeostatic functions are indeed observable in physiologic needs and tension reduction, but applied naively, this concept does not account for all motivated behavior. For example, the "wisdom of the body" appears to be vagrant in the behavior of people who overeat, overwork, and who frequently "bite their nose to spite their face." However, recent neurophysiologic theorizing (Pribram [440]) retains the basic equilibrative process in a more complex system that provides for variation and tuning of homeostats under central control. This new conception retains the principle of interaction of the organism and its environment, but also accounts for variation of adaptive patterns.

Similarly, at the level of populations, man has adapted in many ways to his environment, but he has also defied it in his frequently successful efforts to control and change it. He has learned how to purify sea water, to defy gravity, to inhabit uninhabitable places, and is now well on his way toward colonizing strange, new, extraterrestrial environments. These accomplishments, reflecting distinctively human intellectual capacities, have given man greater range and mobility, but have not, however, freed him from symbiotic dependencies on the physical and social environment. In many cases, they have created new problems, taxing his adjustive capacities. He may develop new sources of water, food, oxygen, and other needed supplies, but he still depends on these supplies. He may be able to generate thrusts to neutralize gravity, but cannot remain aloft otherwise. Conditioned living areas must be maintained within biological limits, and their utility for human activities depends on conditions of communication, mobility, and social support. These complex ecologic dependencies are well illustrated by the extensive changes observable in the behaviors of virtually identical air defense surveillance squadrons located in the environs of a large U. S. city, such as Fort Worth, in comparison with those stationed at remote Alaskan sites.

The methods of human ecology are primarily concerned with adaptive behavior of populations and are not suited to the study of ecologic problems of particular formal groups within populations. These important issues are better suited to the approaches of anthropology, sociology, psychology, and the behavioral science disciplines concerned with interactions of members of organizations and of actions reflecting the collective products of organizations.

Environmental variables. The variables in this category represent ecologic interactions with both the physical and social environment, by organizational members, their families, and associates, as well as by organizations. Extensive recognition of a wide range of social dependencies exists, even though not adequately reflected in research on organizational behavior. Comparable concern with physical aspects of the environment is unusual in organization research, but can be defended on both theoretical and practical grounds if it is granted that these aspects, too, account for significant criterion variance.

The following outline includes both aspects of the environment. Although an attempt has been made to be comprehensive, it is expected that some conspicuous hiatuses will be found.

1. Physical aspects of the environment:

Gravity.

Radiations and radioactive fallout.

Climate and weather: temperature; humidity; atmospheric pressure; oxygen tension; atmospheric changes (winds, storms); rainfall; snow; ice and related phenomena.

Terrain: rivers, lakes, mountains, valleys, deserts, forests, swamps, coastal plains; elevation, erosion; earthquakes, etc.

Natural resources: sources of food (fish, game, vegetation, crops), shelter, clothing; minerals; timber; water.

Culture products: facilities and technology related to transportation, power, communication, construction, manufacturing, distribution, agriculture, housing, habitability, warfare; characteristics and location of centers of population industry, government, education, research, entertainment, recreation, arts.

2. Social aspects of the environment:

Nonmaterial culture: ascriptive solidarities (family, kinship, relationship systems; ethnic solidarities; primary groups; territorial community); occupation and economy (economic institutions, organization of the economy, units of the economy, economic trends); stratification and mobility of the population (class, occupation, social stratification); political organization and authority (political power, political organizations); religion and society; linguistic patterns; education; law; the arts, recreation, and entertainment; technology; science, value systems, beliefs, symbolic systems, health and welfare.

Social and economic states: level of the economy, health, education, crime, morality, morale, intergroup tensions, cold war, strikes, disasters, etc.

Factors defined by locales and geographic setting of the organization: physical and social factors peculiar to locales, remoteness, physical restraints (communication, travel, mobility), parameters of nonmaterial culture, social and economic states applicable to sites and locales of operation.

Relations with other organizations: hierarchical relations with parent and subordinate organizations, sources of support, competitive organizations, sources of threat and conflict; relations with unions, clients, regulatory agencies, trade associations, community groups, eleemosynary agencies, etc.

Dimensions of the environmental variable universe. A modest research program designed to dimensionalize this universe has been undertaken by the author (Sells [474], [475]). The magnitude of this problem appeared discouraging to a number of the participants, but appropriate designs for both data collection and analysis are feasible, provided that the work can be undertaken on a large enough scale to reflect variations in significant dimensions that do not appear within the confines of a limited environmental situation.

Measurement of Organizational Behavior:
The Criterion Problem

By approaching the problem of organizational behavior in the frame of reference of a complete universe of relevant dimensions, the criterion problem is greatly simplified. Measures and indices of behavior that are inappropriate criterion measures in univariate prediction designs, because of differential effects of uncontrolled factors, become appropriate in what we may call, by contrast, the *omnivariate* approach, simply because this approach requires that all relevant factors be taken into account. It is therefore unnecessary to resort to indirect, substitute criterion measures, such as frequently questionable rating procedures, and more effective use can be made of objective indices of group performance, such as sales, production, and comparable information. The problem in the omnivariate model is not one of controlling disturbing factors, but only of distributing the criterion variance among a battery of predictors.

SELECTION OF CRITERIA

The determination of appropriate criteria for the aspects of group behavior relevant to the taxonomic study is an important feature of the research strategy. In view of the omnivariate approach, this may be guided by the research objectives, without undue concern about disturbance by issues of practical feasibility. Any reliable index of group behavior may be an eligible criterion measure, although factored composites of available performance indices have advantages of stability and generality. Multiple criteria, reflecting the range of meaningful behaviors of organizations in relation to their appropriate functions, are not only feasible but also essential to provide insights concerning the relative weights of various factors to significant aspects of organizational activity.

Mission-related criterion measures. Initially it would seem most profitable to focus attention on criteria related to organizational missions or objectives. The rationale for this position is related to the basic philosophy of organizational research, which is concerned with maximizing effectiveness of goal attainment. The mission is the *raison d'être* of an organization and if the mission fails, morale, welfare, and other desirable subgoals of its efforts are of little worth.

It is believed that satisfactory mission-related criterion measures are available for many kinds of organizations, particularly task-oriented organizations in industry and in the military services. A distinction must be made, in this connection, between what have been referred to as "can do" and "do do" criterion indices. The former refer to training, maintenance, proficiency up-grading, and the like, which serve the purpose of improving the posture of an organization with reference to mission performance, but do not actually reflect performance. In the present frame of reference such measures would be included among the dimensions of intraorganization description and would not be considered criteria. Similarly, proficiency tests on simulation tasks are not measures of actual performance, but belong properly in the "can do" category. The criteria must reflect the actual performance of the organization, with respect to desired aspects, over the entire period of time that such performance is subject to study.

Patterns of Interaction Related to Performance Criteria: Basis for a Taxonomy of Organizations

The programs of research outlined in the preceding sections are monumental. It is doubtful that they will ever be considered completed, but this is the nature of scientific progress. However, it is necessary to have some reasonably satisfactory inventory of factors to represent each of the three universes discussed in the foregoing, and measurement instruments for them, in order to undertake the taxonomic study. As indicated earlier, a reasonable battery of 35 to 45 dimensions of individual differences is available now. Dimensions of organizations and of environmental factors remain to be developed, although the organizational dimensions of Hemphill represent an important contribution in that area. For purposes of discussion, it is assumed that a battery of 100 dimensional variables will represent the three universes, of persons, organizations, and environment.

PROPOSED STUDY DESIGN

A preliminary study relating these variables to organizational criteria might be undertaken on a diverse sample of 250 organizations. Organizations, for this purpose, should be arbitrarily limited to organized, but not necessarily formal, groups of not over 150 persons, with reasonably specific over-all goals (as distinguished from multi-phase corporate operations), for which suitable criterion measures are available. The cooperation of their managements would, of course, be essential to complete the immense amount of individual measurement, observation, recording, and associated data collection. A period of observation of one year, common to all of the groups, would be ideal, but this would require a massive staff. As an alternative, data might be collected over a five-year period, taking 50 groups per year, still a gigantic undertaking, but closer to the limits of reality.

The analysis can be discussed in terms of a matrix of 100 independent (predictor) and perhaps 10 dependent (criterion) variables, for about 25,000 persons and 250 organizations scattered widely geographically. Electronic data processing equipment at a central location would handle scoring and computation. Standard multivariate methods would be used for multiple factor analyses of the intercorrelation matrices, including the criterion measures and discriminants predicting each of the criteria as well as combinations of criteria (Sells [470]). The results would indicate various patterns of variables related to patterns of organizational behavior. At this point the basis for taxonomy of organizations would be in view.

28

TOWARD A "THEORY OF METHOD" FOR RESEARCH ON ORGANIZATIONS

Joseph E. McGrath

Introduction

Organization research is a meeting ground (and, hopefully, a melting pot) for the sociologist, the economist, the political scientist, the operations researcher, the mathematician, the social psychologist, and the engineer. Men from each of these fields, and others, have contributed much to our current state of knowledge about the nature and dynamics of organizations.

But because the field of organization research is inherently as well as historically an interdisciplinary field, it is marked by great diversity in concepts, terms, and methods of study. Since the men who do organization research come from a variety of backgrounds, they tend to bring with them different tools, different concepts, and different methodological approaches. Consider, for example, the extreme differences in methodology between Mesarović, Sanders, and Sprague (Chapter 26) and Bass (Chapter 7) in this volume, and contrast them further with Seashore and Bowers [467] in their studies of organizational effectiveness; or consider the differences between Guetzkow's [243] and Jensen's [298] approaches to the study of internation tensions; similarly, notice the differences between Cyert and March's (Chapter 16, this volume), and Likert's [350] and Homan's [282] empirically derived organization theories. Even when these sets of studies deal with the "same" problem in the field of organization research, the methodological differences among them seem about as great as the differences between the methodologies of totally separate scientific disciplines.

Such diversity has both positive and negative effects on the field. On the plus side, diversity of concepts and methods insures a dynamic, searching, pluralistic growth for the field, which probably offers a substantial safeguard against conceptual stagnation. On the other hand, diversity of theoretical concepts—and above all, diversity in the use of methods—leads to considerable malcommunication within the field, which doubtless decreases the efficiency with which we can advance our knowledge.

Furthermore, it is apparent that every methodology has some limitations in terms of what it *cannot* do (or cannot do efficiently), as well as some advantages in terms of what it *can* do. Hence, methods are not totally interchangeable, and the choice of methodology in any given case should be made on the basis of the possibilities and limitations of that methodology *vis à vis* the research problem to which it is to be applied.

This chapter is written on the assumption that differences in research methodology *do* make a difference in the yield of research. In other words, when we choose one methodology over others in a study of organization, we are thereby affecting the kinds and amount of information which we can obtain from results of that study. If this assumption is true, it follows that we should choose the methodology that we will use in a given case on the basis of the kinds of information we are seeking (i.e., the nature of the problem we are studying), and we should choose so as to maximize the amount of information which we will gain about that problem. It also follows that when we choose our methodology for reasons of personal preference, familiarity, or operational expediency, we are changing the nature of the problem about which we will be gaining information, as well as altering the amount of information which we can gain from our study.

If we are to make "rational" choices of methodology, so as to maximize the amount of information relevant to our purposes, we must be able to do at least two things. First, we must be able to compare alternative approaches in terms of their relative effectiveness in providing the desired information. This, in turn, requires ability to specify what we mean by "research information," and how we will assess the efficiency of a research approach for generating such information. In short, if we are to make rational choices of method, we need a "theory of method" to guide us in those choices.

This chapter is an attempt to take some first steps toward the development of such a "theory of method" for the study of organizations. Our presentation falls naturally into three stages which constitute the three sections of the chapter. First, we will consider methodologies that have and/or can be applied to the study of organizations, and attempt to place them in a framework within which they can be related to one another. Secondly, we will attempt to define certain key concepts—"research information," "information potential" and "information yield"—and from them formulate what we mean by "comprehensiveness," "efficiency," and "effectiveness" of a study.[1] Then, in the final section, we will try to apply these concepts to compare and contrast different methodologies, and will consider some of the implications of these comparisons for programmatic planning of organization research.

It should be pointed out here that we doubt if any of the concepts presented in this chapter will in themselves be new or startling to the reader. Nor will our conclusions likely offer the reader profound new insights. The contribution which this chapter makes, if any, lies in its attempt to formulate some well-recognized concepts and distinctions in a fairly systematic and rigorous way. Hence, this chapter will not particularly add to "what we know," but, hopefully, it will add to our appreciation of the import of "what we know" for "what we do," when we set out to do research on organizations.

A Classification of Data-Collection Methods Used in Organization Research

Many streams of endeavor contribute to the current field of organization research, and studies based on many different methodological approaches form part of the body of knowledge of that field. The methodology used in studies of organizations range from carefully delimited, laboratory-controlled studies, such as those on communication networks by Bavelas [51], Leavitt [333], Guetzkow and Simon [242], and others, to broad and sweeping conceptual analyses of large organizations, and even total societies (e.g., Homans [282]; Merton [389]; Parsons [429]). Organization research includes intensive case studies of single organizations (e.g., W. F. Whyte [601]; Selznick [476]), broad surveys of many organizations of a single type,[2] journalistic analyses based on anecdotal evidence (e.g., W. H. Whyte [603]; Riesman [450]), true "field experiments" which involve experimental

---

[1] Many of the ideas presented in this chapter were developed in a research program designed to review and integrate research methodology used in studies of complex man-machine systems, sponsored by the Psychological Sciences Division, Office of Naval Research. See McGrath and Nordlie [378].

[2] For example, Comrey et al. [132] and Udy, Chapter 11, this volume.

manipulations of an entire large-scale organization (e.g., Morse and Reimer [407]; Seashore and Bowers [467]), man-computer simulation studies (e.g., Guetzkow [243]; Bass, Chapter 7, this volume; Rome and Rome [454]), all-computer simulations and use of formal mathematical models.[3] At a superficial glance, it would appear that the only common feature of all of these approaches is that they are—or are intended to be—applicable to the study of some aspect of organizations.

We can begin to see some common elements among these methodologies, however, when we consider each of them in terms of the nature of the setting within which data-collection takes place and in terms of the extent to which activities of the investigator intrude upon, or are responsible for, the nature of that setting. Viewed in these terms, in fact, most of the types of methodology used in organization research seem to fit within one of four major classes. We will label these four classes of research settings as field studies; experimental simulations; laboratory experiments; and computer simulations.

FIELD STUDIES

Field studies are those research investigations which take place within "natural" or "real-life" social situations. This category includes all types of empirical investigations which use data from real, existing organizations. Within this category we include a number of types of research which are heterogeneous in many respects. For example, one kind of "field study," as the term is used here, are those "studies" which consist only of casual or anecdotal observations. Another kind of field study would be the systematic and intensive case study of existing or past organizations, including those done primarily through analysis of records and documents (e.g., Selznick [476]; Alger [10]). Broad surveys are also included,[4] as are both the so-called natural experiments and the carefully planned, deliberately-executed field experiments (e.g., Seashore and Bowers [467]; Morse and Reimer [407]; Coch and French [129]).

The kinds of research here included within the over-all category of field studies show marked variations in method. They are listed here in a generally increasing order of rigor of procedure. At the same time, they are here classed together on the basis of one crucial common

---

[3] See, e.g., Chapter 15 by Bonini, Chapter 22 by Whinston, and Chapter 26 by Mesarović, Sanders, and Sprague, all in this volume.

[4] For example, Pepinski et al. [434] and Udy, Chapter 11, this volume.

feature. All of these types of field studies are investigations which obtain their data directly from real, existing organizations of the kind to which results are intended to apply. That is, all field studies are direct studies of (members of) the class of phenomena with which the investigation is concerned, namely, real "flesh-and-blood" organizations. One important feature of data obtained from a "real-life" situation is that the humans in that situation are operating under natural (not necessarily stronger) motivational forces, since the phenomena being studied are a part of their actual lives.

EXPERIMENTAL SIMULATIONS

The term "experimental simulations" is used here to refer to empirical investigations which attempt to create a relatively faithful representation of "an organization" under quasi-laboratory conditions, set that simulated organization "in motion," and study the operation of that organization as it is expressed in the behavior of humans who are assigned roles within it (e.g., Bass, Chapter 7, this volume; Guetzkow [243]; Rome and Rome [454]). This category is roughly equivalent to Guetzkow's category of "man-computer simulations" (Guetzkow [239]).

In such studies, many features of the structure and process of the organization are simulated, often by the use of computers, to study the process and consequences of behavior of human subjects who operate the simulated system. These studies are distinguished from laboratory experiments (Class 3 in our present classification) in several respects. First, the stimulus situation within which the individual is operating is more or less continuous in an experimental simulation, in contrast to the laboratory experiment which usually consists of a series of discrete trials. Secondly, as a part of the continuous nature of experimental simulations, participants' responses at any particular point in time partly determine (along with the "rules of the game") the stimulus situation in which they will be operating at subsequent points in time. Finally, experimental simulations differ from laboratory studies in that they attempt to simulate or model properties of "real-life" organizations, which is the key defining property of this class of methods in the present schema.

However, experimental simulations vary considerably in terms of the degree of fidelity of the simulation involved. They also vary in terms of the complexity of the simulation, and in terms of whether the particular simulation is intended to represent a generic type of organization or some particular type of organization. All three of these distinctions go together to determine whether the simulation presents the participants with a "bare-bones," fairly abstract representation of only the key processes felt to be important (e.g., Guetzkow's internation simulation [243]) or whether it attempts to provide them with a content-enriched stimulus situation which "seems" very similar to the "real" situation (e.g., see discussion on realism in Bass, Chapter 7, this volume). Experimental simulations also vary in terms of how "open" or "closed" they are; that is, in terms of how much of the total operation of the organization is simulated and how much is left to determination by the performance of the human participants.

LABORATORY EXPERIMENTS

Laboratory experiments are those studies in which the investigator does not attempt to recreate "reality" in his laboratory, but rather tries to abstract variables from real life situations and represent them in a more fundamental form. His purpose is to study the operation of these more fundamental processes under highly controlled conditions. He is not so much interested in making his laboratory situation a "greenhouse" for the study of some particular class of organizations. Rather, he is interested in studying fundamental processes which presumably underlie the behavior of humans in a broad range of organizational (and other) settings.[5]

Perhaps the essential features of laboratory experiments as they relate to the field of organization research can best be presented by using the studies of communication networks (Bavelas [51]; Christie, et al. [120]; Guetzkow and Simon [242]; Leavitt [333]; Shaw [480]; and others) as illustrations of this class of method. The communication net studies isolate one fundamental feature common to *all* organizations, namely, the pattern of communication linkages between organizational components and study the effects of variations in this pattern under laboratory conditions. Neither the specific nets studied (four and five node nets, of various patterns ranging from highly centralized to highly decentralized) nor the tasks being performed (symbol-identification problems, simple arithmetic problems, etc.) were meant to "simulate" real organizational structures or real organizational tasks. Rather, the purpose of the communication net studies was to determine

---

[5] In a sense, all laboratory experiments of human behavior, as individuals and as groups, are relevant to the field of organization research. A few of the many laboratory experiments which seem to have made important direct contributions to organization research, besides the communication net studies, include: studies on communication, development of norms, and pressures for conformity in informal groups [36], [192], [311], [460], [540]; and studies of cohesiveness and group pressures as they affect productivity [461], [64].

how variations in highly abstract and basic patterns of communication influenced certain basic kinds of human activities (e.g., transmission and reception of messages, deductive problem-solving, organizational planning) and certain classes of human reactions (felt satisfaction, attraction to the group, job satisfaction), which presumably operate in *all* human organizations.

This attempt to create and study generic structures or processes is one of several features which distinguish laboratory experiments from experimental simulations as discussed previously. Other distinguishing features are the frequent use of a series of discrete, independent "trials," for which the stimulus conditions are entirely preprogrammed by the investigator, rather than using a continuous stimulus situation which is partly determined by prior responses of participants. This pattern of procedure gives the laboratory experimenter greater control over the stimulus situation and reduces confounding between different stages of performance, although it also reduces the continuity and the "felt realness" of the situation for the participant.

COMPUTER SIMULATIONS

This class of methods should more properly be called "mathematical models." It is here referred to as computer simulations, both in order to contrast it with experimental simulations (Class 2 in the present schema) and because the special kind of logical or mathematical model which we call computer simulations is frequently used in the study of organizations. Guetzkow[6] designates this class of studies as "all-computer" studies. Computer simulations are also sometimes referred to as "Monte Carlo" studies, because they generally utilize the procedure of random selection from predetermined probability distributions as a means of "simulating" specific behaviors of parts of the system on specific occasions.

Computer simulations are distinguished from experimental simulations because they are closed or logically complete models of the class of phenomenon being simulated. *All* variables, including the "dependent variables" or "output variables" which result from operation of the system, are built into the formulation of the simulation model itself. Thus, the model does not involve or require performance by human participants. Performance or output variables are "contained" within the model, most often as stochastically determined consequences of the computerized "operation" of the simulated organization.[7]

---

[6] [239].

[7] See Bonini's Chapter 15 for an example.

Computer simulations can represent either a generic class or a particular class of organizations. Computer simulations vary considerably in the "richness" and complexity with which they simulate the (class of) organizations being studied. They vary, in particular, in the extent to which the simulation tries to represent "depth" characteristics of the human components of the organization (e.g., values, attitudes, norms, conformity pressures) as well as their superficial "output" characteristics. They also vary, of course, in the "validity" or "reasonableness" of the assumptions by means of which such representations of human behavior are inserted into the model.

Models do not necessarily have to make use of computers to belong in the computer simulation class as here defined. In fact, an interesting example of a simple and low-cost model, which "runs" without the use of any major computational aids but which nevertheless has all of the essential characteristics of this class of research methods, is presented in Guetzkow [239]. The essential feature of this class of research is that *all* structures and processes which are to be dealt with in the investigation are represented in the simulation model itself either as parameters, as operating rules, or as stochastic processes.

RELATIONS BETWEEN THE FOUR CLASSES OF METHODS

These four classes of methods appear to be more or less ordered along a continuum which has several facets. The ordering continuum can be thought of as proceeding from concrete (at the field study end) to abstract (at the computer simulation end). Alternatively, we can label the ends of the continuum as realism versus artificiality, or we can label them as going from "open" to "closed" settings, or from "loose" to "controlled" conditions.[8]

Regardless of how we designated the underlying continuum, the four different classes of methods which we have identified along that continuum differ markedly from one another in terms of the advantages which they offer the researcher and in terms of the limitations which they impose upon him. At the field study end of the continuum, for example, the investigator has the substantial advantages of "felt realism" and of the operation of inherent motivational forces. As

---

[8] It is obvious from the prior discussion that the methodologies being considered vary along a continuum rather than in a categorical manner. For example, the "field experiment," which is here classified as a field study, often shades into the experimental simulation class. Similarly, experimental simulations which are highly abstract representations of generic classes of organizations may become nearly indistinguishable from the laboratory experiment. The four-category classification of methods is used for convenience and clarity of presentation.

pointed out previously, this does not necessarily mean that human participants are operating at higher levels of motivation. Rather, it means that they are operating under more "natural" kinds of motivations, since the study itself is an integral part of their lives. These advantages of the field study are gained at the cost of less precision, less control, and less freedom to manipulate variables whose effects may be of central concern. Research methods at the other end of the continuum—laboratory experiments and computer simulations—have as their major advantages precisely those characteristics which are the major disadvantages of the field study: precision, control of variables, and considerable freedom to manipulate variables of central concern. However, they also have the complementing disadvantage of lack of realism.

These and many other advantages and disadvantages of various research settings make it very clear that the four classes of methods are not at all interchangeable. Rather, they seem to offer complementary approaches, and the choice of the best approach in a given case must reckon with the *relative* importance of realism, precision of measurement, opportunities to manipulate variables, and many other features of the research situation. Our purpose here is to work toward development of some guide rules for making these comparisons, hence for making our choices of method more nearly "rational."

Development of such guide rules requires that we establish a network of basic methodological concepts—a theory of method—in terms of which we will "calculate" the relative efficiency, comprehensiveness, and effectiveness of various research approaches, so that their relative usefulness to us in a given case can be determined with some rigor. Accordingly, we will interrupt our consideration of different classes of research methods temporarily to establish some basic tools for methodological comparisons in the next section of this presentation. Then, in the final section of the chapter, we will return to a comparison of advantages and disadvantages of different research settings armed with more adequate tools for making such comparisons.

Some Concepts for Assessing the Adequacy of Research Methods

THE NATURE OF A RESEARCH PROBLEM

Research has to do with identification and measurement of variables thought to be relevant to a certain problem or phenomenon and determination of the interrelationships among those variables. When we do research, we ask three basic questions: (*a*) What are the important or relevant variables (conditions, parameters, properties, etc.) of the phenomenon I wish to study? (*b*) How does each of them vary (in nature); what range of values can each of them assume? (*c*) How do they covary; is the value of one variable predictable from (or predictive of) the value of one or more other variables?

Let us consider a "research problem" as a set of variables, descriptive of some phenomenon which is of interest to us, whose covariations we are going to attempt to describe. The variables in such a set include: (*a*) properties of the class of object or entity being studied (e.g., individuals, organizations, etc.), including properties that have to do with relations between parts; (*b*) properties of the environment, situation, or setting within which that class of objects exists (including suprasystems to which the objects are organic, their physical environments, their tasks); and (*c*) properties of the action or behavior of the objects in relation to the environment.

A variable of any of the above types is *relevant* to the research problem if its variation has an (appreciable) effect on, or is (detectably) affected by, variations in one or more of the other variables of the set.

We will assume that, in any given case, there are a *finite* number of relevant variables in the set to be studied. (Variables which are determinable mathematical functions of one another—such as the radii and diameters of a given set of circles—are considered collectively as a unitary variable.) *All* of the relevant variables are always present at *some* value (including "zero" or "absent") in a research situation, whether their presence is recognized by the researcher or not. Hence, the research problem always concerns the total set of variables V. We cannot reduce the number of relevant variables in the situation; we can only limit the scope of our study by restricting variation of some of them, or reduce the precision of our study by ignoring variation of some of them.

ALTERNATIVE TREATMENTS OF VARIABLES

We must do something about each of the relevant variables in a research problem. Basically, any one variable can be treated in one of four mutually exclusive ways:

Treatment W. We can *control* a certain variable V_j so that all of its values except one, k_i, are *prevented* from occurring. We can do this in several ways: by selective sampling of cases, by arrangement of conditions, etc.

Treatment X. We can *manipulate* a certain variable V_j so that a certain value k_i is *required* to occur. This operation can also be performed by a number of techniques, including design or assembly of parts, induction of conditions, and so forth.[9]

Treatment Y. We can deal with a given variable V_j by *permitting it to vary freely and measuring* the values of it which do occur. Such measurement can take various forms, including the use of physical instruments, the use of human observers, the use of self-reports by the objects of study.

Treatment Z. We can *ignore* a variable V_j by permitting it to vary freely, but failing to determine what values *do* occur. This treatment is applied to all variables which are *in* the relevant set V, but which are not dealt with by Treatments X, Y, or Z.

In any given research situation, *every* relevant variable is handled by one and only one of these four treatments. These four ways of treating variables are used with differential frequency in studies conducted in different types of research settings. For example, Treatments W and X are the hallmarks of laboratory studies and are used seldom or not at all in field studies. The use of Treatment Z is more or less inevitable in field studies, but its use can be minimized in the laboratory.

These four ways of treating variables have different implications for the scope, precision, and effectiveness of study design, because they have different effects on the amount of research information which inheres in a study design and the amount of information which can be extracted from that study. So, before returning to a discussion of research settings and their uses, let us consider the concepts of research information, information potential and information yield within a research design.

RESEARCH INFORMATION, INFORMATION POTENTIAL, AND INFORMATION YIELD

Research information has to do with the specification of relationships between variables. We have gained research information when we ascertain *whether or not* the occurrence of a particular value of a variable V_1 is predictive of (or predictable from) the value(s) which obtain for variable V_2 ($V_3, \cdots, V_N$). As a convention, we will say that

---

[9] There are several important special cases of Treatment X. One of the more interesting ones, which is widely used under the name of "Monte Carlo technique," is the random selection of a value k_i for a given variable V_j on a given "trial," out of a predetermined probability distribution of values for V_j. Here, although there is some indeterminancy for any given trial, the distribution of values over a series of trials is predictable in advance, the accuracy of the prediction being a function of the number of trials in the series.

we gain research information from determination of *whether or not* two (or more) variables vary together, while we will say that we gain *positive research information* when we discover that two such variables *do*, in fact, vary together predictably.

The amount of information which *can* be gained about any given situation is a function of the amount of "uncertainty," or *potential information*, which is inherent in that situation. The *potential information* contained in a situation depends on the number of (relevant) variables and the number of values which each variable can assume. If there are V variables relevant to a situation, and each has k values, then for *any given instance* (trial, event, etc.) of that situation there are k^v possible combinations of values of the variables involved. That term k^v represents the *total information potential* of a situation.[10]

We gain *positive research information* to the extent that we reduce the number of possible combinations of values of variables k^v by ascertaining that two or more variables vary concomitantly. That is, we gain *positive research information* when we can predict that the occurrence of a certain value k_1 of variable V_1 will be accompanied by the occurrence of a certain value k_i (or a *restricted* range of values, less than the total range) of another variable V_2, *under conditions where values of V_2 other than the predicted value(s) are free to occur* (insofar as the study operations are concerned). Hence, we gain positive research information *when and only when* something that is *free to happen* predictably *does not*.

On the other hand, when we *reduce the potential information* of a situation by deliberately precluding the occurrence of certain values of a variable (as we do when we "experimentally control" a variable, as in Treatment W), we have not gained any research information by so doing. Rather, when we *alter* what values of a variable can occur— either by preventing some values from occurring (as in experimental control of a variable, Treatment W), or by insuring that a certain value of the variable does occur (as in experimental manipulation, Treatment X)—we *reduce* the potential information which our study situation contains below that which is contained in the "real-world" situation. For example, if one variable is controlled at a single value, its range of occurrence is reduced from k to 1 value, and the total information potential is reduced from k^v to k^{v-1}. If there are five variables, each with ten possible values, $k^v = 100,000$, $k^{v-1} = 10,000$, a reduction by $\frac{9}{10}$ in this particular case.

---

[10] This formulation assumes that there are a *finite* number of relevant variables in a situation, and that each has a *finite* range and a *finite* number of possible alternative values.

This reduction of potential information represents a restriction of the scope of our study and a limitation on the generality of our findings. We can represent the scope or generality of a given study in terms of the ratio of the information potential of the study to the information potential of the "real-world" situation to which it refers (and to which its results are intended to apply) k^{v-w}/k^v, where w refers to the number of variables which were *made to occur* at one particular value.

The total potential information in a study situation sets the upper limit for the total research information which that study *can* yield, just as the amount of uncertainty associated with a message limits the amount of information which the message can convey. Within this limit, study procedures affect the extent to which that potential information is realized as research information. By definition, research information involves statements about the covariation (or lack of it) between two or more variables, at least one of which is free to vary "at will." Determination of such covariation, or its absence, requires: (*a*) that at least one of the variables being related be free (insofar as our study procedures are concerned) to take on any of a range of values, *and* (*b*) that we identify (measure) what value of all of the variables being related *actually obtained* in each of a given set of instances. When we permit a variable V_j to vary freely, but do not determine what values it assumes (Treatment Z), we do *not* reduce the information potential inherent in the situation (i.e., the number of alternative combinations of values of variables which can occur), but we greatly reduce the information which we can *extract* from the situation (i.e., the *information yield* of our study). Variables which are uncontrolled but unmeasured (Treatment Z) generate *noise* in our data. Extending the previous illustration: If we have five variables, each with ten values, $k^v = 100,000$. If one of the five variables is controlled at a single value, but a second variable is ignored, the total information potential of the *study* remains $k^{v-1} = 10,000$; but the accountable or specifiable information is reduced to k^{v-2}, which equals 1,000. If *accountable* information is considered *information yield*, and effects of variables which are uncontrolled but ignored are considered *noise*, the ratio $k^{v-(w+z)}/k^{v-w}$ expresses the *precision* of a study in terms of the ratio of *accountable information* (*information yield*) to *potential information*.[11]

---

[11] This is equivalent to the ratio of "signal" to "signal-plus-noise." It is an expression of the effects of unsystematic confounding of a variable.

One might consider that the *efficiency* of a study is reflected in its precision as defined above; that is, the ratio of accountable information to potential information, $k^{v-(w+z)}/k^{v-w}$. One might further view the *comprehensiveness* of a study in terms of its scope or generality, expressed as the relation between information potential of the study and information potential of the referent situation, k^{v-w}/k^{v}, as previously discussed. However, we should probably view the *over-all effectiveness* of a study by comparing its *information yield* to the *total potential information of the referent situation*. Hence, effectiveness of a study can be expressed as $k^{v-(w+z)}/k^{v}$. In this view, we lose "comprehensiveness" when we control variables (i.e., restrict their range of values, by Treatments W or X); we lose "efficiency" when we ignore variables (i.e., let them vary but fail to measure them, Treatment Z); and we lose "effectiveness" when we do *either* of these.

Since different types of research settings vary in their relative uses of Treatments W, X, Y, and Z, as previously noted, these settings also differ, in an orderly way, in the extent to which they are limited in comprehensiveness, efficiency, and effectiveness. We shall examine these differences in the next section.

Comparison of Research Methods

Let us return now to consideration of the four classes of research settings previously described. As already noted, these four classes of research settings differ in the extent to which they utilize the four treatments of variables (see Table 1). Hence, they differ in their potential information and their information yield. Let us consider the four classes of methods comparatively, in terms of the way they use the four different treatments of variables, and the consequences of that use.

The use of Treatment W, control of a variable by experimental means, tends to increase as we move along the continuum of methods from field studies to computer simulations. This occurs in two ways. First, the laboratory or computer investigator uses Treatment W deliberately to hold certain of the relevant variables in the problem at a single, constant value so that they will not confound effects of other variables which are of more central concern to him. In doing so, he deliberately reduces the scope or comprehensiveness of his study—he

Table 1   Relative Frequency of Use of Different Treatments
of Variables in the Four Classes of Research Settings

Classes of Research Settings	Alternative Treatments of Variables			
	Treatment W Excluded by Control	Treatment X Made to Occur by Experimental Manipulation	Treatment Y Varying Freely and Measured	Treatment Z Varying Freely but Ignored
Field studies	Low or no use	Low or no use	High or low use, gross measurement	Very high use
Experimental simulations	Medium to high use	Moderate use	High or low use, moderately precise measurement	High use
Laboratory experiments	High use	High use	High or low use, precise measurement	Low use
Computer simulations	Very high use	Very high use	Not possible	Not possible

cuts down the potential information in it—as a price for excluding "noise" from it. However, the laboratory or simulation investigator also often uses Treatment W *unwittingly*. That is, in the process of simulating or recreating the class of phenomena being studied, he is likely to overlook important features of the real life situation which he is modeling. Hence, he applies Treatment W to these variables by holding them at a single constant value ("zero" or "excluded"). These exclusions also reduce the information potential of the study, even though they are not done on the basis of deliberate choice by the investigator. In the field study, the investigator usually does not have an opportunity to control variables, either deliberately or unwittingly. Hence he avoids both the problems and the advantages involved in use of Treatment W.

The use of Treatment W has positive and negative effects on a study design. On the positive side, to control a variable (Treatment W), rather than permitting it to vary freely without measuring it (Treatment Z), prevents a loss of efficiency in the study by reducing the "noise." On the other hand, to control a variable at a single value (Treatment W), rather than making it occur at each of a series of specific values (Treatment X) or letting it vary but measuring its variation (Treatment Y), reduces the information potential of the study below the information potential of the referent situation and thus reduces the scope or comprehensiveness of the study.

Results of a study only refer to the specific combinations of conditions used. They might or might not hold if one or more of those variables to which Treatment W has been applied had been held at some *different* value. Such a situation would occur in all cases where a variable that is held constant has *interactive* effects with other variables in the problem. It is often said that systems in general, and organizations in particular, are complexes of *interactive* variables. If so, then we need to be very careful not to violate that concept of organizations by choosing to control key *interactive* variables at a single value in order to make our study design more feasible.

We should also be concerned, it would seem, about selection of the *particular value* at which we will control a variable to which we have decided to apply Treatment W. If we *must* limit a relevant variable to a single value, hence limit the applicability of our results to combinations of conditions which include that value, we probably ought to choose the natural modal value of that variable as it occurs in the referent situation rather than some value which gives us "baseline" information, or a "cleaner" (looking) design, or a study plan that is easy to implement.

As a rather simple illustration, suppose we wish to simulate or do experiments pertaining to an organization whose subsystems have a mixture of male and female members. We might want to do a laboratory study of the effects of group communication processes on the performance effectiveness of such groups. A study using uniformly male groups (or uniformly female groups), or using a constant ratio of males and females in each group, would seem on the surface to offer a "cleaner" design (and perhaps a design that is easier to implement). However, such designs may very well not be as useful as a design which determines male-female composition of groups on a random basis. Sex differences (and especially *sex composition* differences) may very well *interact with* communication patterns in affecting task performance. That is, the "best" communication pattern for task effectiveness may be quite different in all-male, all-female, and mixed-sex groups.

If this were true, results obtained from study of all-male groups just simply would not apply to mixed-sex groups even if all other features of the study were well executed. In fact, trying to apply results of such a study to real life organizations which have mixed-sex work groups would *systematically* lead us to the *wrong* answer (i.e., we would be led to select as optimal a communication pattern which was definitely *not* optimal for task effectiveness).

If we found it necessary to do our experiment with groups of only one sex composition, we would be better off using the composition pattern that is modal for those groups (or organizations) to which we want to apply our findings. If we used randomly composed groups, or groups with the male-female proportion which was most predominant in the referent organizations, we still would not gain information about other sex composition patterns, of course. Nor would we avoid the problems posed by the interaction effects of the variable we chose to control. But at least we would obtain results which, when applied, would lead us to be *systematically right* in our choice of optimal communication patterns.

TREATMENT X: EXPERIMENTAL MANIPULATION

In Treatment X, we use experimental manipulation to insure that a certain value k_i of variable V_j will occur on a certain occasion (or trial). Most often, we are manipulating circumstances so that different values of V_j occur on different trials according to a predetermined schedule. If only one value of a variable is used for *all* trials, Treatment X becomes identical with Treatment W, and has the same restrictive effects on the study design. If the variable is manipulated so that every one of its possible values occur on some trials, then Treatment X does not place any limitation on the information potential of the study. In most cases, however, experimental manipulations use more than one, but less than all values of the variable; hence they lead to some restriction in scope.

The use of Treatment X tends to increase as we go from field studies to computer simulations. Furthermore, there tends to be an increase in the number of values of a variable which are utilized when a variable is manipulated. For example, when a field study does manage to include an experimentally manipulated variable it is almost always necessary to limit the manipulation to two, or at the most, three, levels of the variable (including control groups) (e.g., Seashore and Bowers [467]; Morse and Reimer [407]). In laboratory experiments, on the other hand, it is often possible to vary systematically one or more variables at each of a series of values. To the extent that this can be done, we can then determine the functional relationships between the manipulated variables and other "free-but-measured" variables (Treatment Y).

On the other hand, while the field study is seldom able to manipulate any variables, or to manipulate them at many levels, the manipulations which sometimes can be achieved in field settings are often very powerful. Partly, this power comes from the fact that manipulations of conditions in a field study—whether due to "natural" causes or to experimental plan—affect the very lives of the participants in the study. Manipulations in the laboratory, on the other hand, are often relatively weak, both for ethical reasons and because of the inherent artificiality of the motivational conditions under which participants are operating.

One of the special advantages of the computer simulation lies in the facility which it provides for systematic manipulation of many variables at each of many values. In fact, the computer simulation can generate combinations of conditions which do not exist in the real world, but whose effects may be of vital importance for theoretical development. For example, a computer simulation might be developed to represent an organization whose "human components" perform with perfect efficiency and rationality—a situation not found in nature—to study upper limit conditions for performance of that organization. (Sometimes, computer simulations seem to build such assumptions about human perfection into their models, without recognizing that they are dealing with hypothetical upper limits.)

TREATMENT Z: UNCONTROLLED VARIABLES

The uncontrolled and unmeasured operation of a variable (Treatment Z) generates "noise" within a study design. All variables which are neither controlled, manipulated, nor measured are, necessarily, noise-producing variables. The "use" of Treatment Z in a study is always more or less unwitting, either as a result of lack of knowledge about the phenomena being studied or as a result of lack of knowledge about appropriate scientific procedures.

By their very nature, field studies are likely to contain variables handled by Treatment Z (i.e., variables which have been ignored), because field study situations preclude much use of control (W) and manipulation (X), and are likely to contain more variables than can be measured effectively (Y). The major advantage of laboratory studies is their ability to minimize uncontrolled variables (i.e., minimize use of Treatment Z). They do so by applying Treatments W and X, and sometimes Y, to variables which might have received Treatment Z

in a field setting. Experimental simulations also share this advantage with the laboratory setting, but to a lesser degree because of the greater complexity and the continuity-of-situation which they contain. Computer simulations essentially eliminate Treatment Z. They have no "noise." [12]

TREATMENT Y: A NECESSARY CONDITION
FOR OBTAINING RESEARCH INFORMATION

The number of variables handled by Treatment Y does not necessarily increase or decrease as we proceed along the continuum of methods from field studies to the laboratory situation. However, the precision with which variables can be measured tends to increase. Precision of measurement is used here to refer both to sensitivity (the number of values of a variable which can be distinguished) and to reliability (the stability of results from independent measures) of the measurement process.

Treatment Y does not exist in the computer situation, for the same reason that Treatment Z is not a part of that class of research settings. Treatment Y refers to permitting a variable to vary freely and measuring its variation; Treatment Z refers to permitting a variable to vary freely but not measuring it. Since no variable is operating outside the control of the investigator in a "closed model" such as a computer simulation, neither Treatment Y nor Treatment Z are possible within it. Even the "output" variables of a computer simulation do not vary freely, but rather are *wholly determined* by the values and relationships built into the model. Thus, even though the complexity of the model and the stochastic nature of some of the variables in it may prevent us from clearly specifying the output of its "operation" in advance, that output is nevertheless determined fully, albeit in a complex manner.

Hence, while the computer simulation entirely eliminates "noise" because it does not permit Treatment Z, it also entirely eliminates *information*, in the sense in which that term is here defined, because it does not permit Treatment Y. Returning to our earlier definition, we can gain research information when and only when something that is

---

[12] One might argue that computer simulations contain "noise" because they deliberately introduce random variation by the use of stochastic processes. Such variation is noise of a different sort than meant here. Although it produces indeterminancy for a given trial, the distribution of values for the total set of trials is predictable in advance. As noted previously (see footnote 9), these "Monte Carlo" procedures are really a special case of Treatment X.

free to happen does not happen. That condition is never met by a computer simulation or any logically closed formal model.

Since the presence of Treatment Y is a necessary condition for obtaining research information, maximizing its use would seem to be an unqualified desideratum. However, such a generalization could lead to substantial inefficiency in the collection of empirical data. For example, there may be a particular value of a variable which seldom occurs in nature but which is of key theoretical significance. To obtain information on how that value affects other variables by use of an "all-Treatment Y" approach might be prohibitively costly. We would need to obtain a rather large sample of data for all frequently occurring values in order to obtain even a meager sample of cases which include the value of particular concern. The substitution of Treatment X in such a situation greatly increases efficiency by controlling the rate at which we sample values of (independent) variables. It permits us to substitute *systematic* for *representative* sampling, hence to provide an adequate amount of data for all values of concern within a minimum total amount of data.

COMPREHENSIVENESS, EFFICIENCY, AND EFFECTIVENESS

Comparisons of the research methods in terms of their comprehensiveness, efficiency, and effectiveness are implicit in the foregoing discussion. Any procedure which reduces the number of combinations of values of variables which can occur in the study situation reduces the comprehensiveness of that study. Use of Treatment W, and use of Treatment X so that only a small number of values of a variable occur during the study, both lead to a reduction of information potential and hence to a reduction of comprehensiveness. Since the use of both W and X increases as we move from field study to experimental simulation to laboratory study, comprehensiveness decreases at the same time. Generally, comprehensiveness decreases still further in the computer simulations because of the extensive use of Treatment W (often in the form of simplifying assumptions designed to make the model feasible for computer programming). But it is *possible* for a computer simulation to offset the reduction of comprehensiveness somewhat by systematically "playing" many values of many variables (i.e., using Treatment X rather than Treatment W).

At the same time, permitting a variable to go unmeasured and uncontrolled (Treatment Z) introduces noise into the design, which will tend to confound information from other variables, and hence reduce the efficiency of the study. Since the use of Treatment Z decreases as we move from the field study to other settings, it follows that field studies are generally less efficient than experimental simulations, which in turn are less efficient than laboratory experiments. Computer simulations eliminate noise in the present sense of the term, but they do so in a manner which also eliminates information. Hence, no meaningful statement of efficiency, in the present sense, can be made about the computer simulation.

Thus, within the framework of the present set of concepts, field studies are relatively comprehensive but inefficient. As study designs they retain almost all of the potential information which exists in the real life situation, but they also contain much noise which reduces the effective information yield. Laboratory experiments, on the other hand, are relatively efficient but low in comprehensiveness. They minimize noise, and hence convert much of the potential information in the study design into information yield. But they do so by restricting the information potential of the study design far below the information potential of the real-world situation to which the study is related. Experimental simulations seem to lie between field studies and laboratory experiments in both comprehensiveness and efficiency. Computer simulations are often relatively low in comprehensiveness, while the concept of efficiency does not apply since they yield no research information in the present use of that term.

We might summarize these comparisons by commenting that field studies may learn a little about a lot, whereas laboratory experiments may learn a lot about a little. In the same vein, computer simulations may learn "everything" about nothing.

But we have not yet commented on the relative *effectiveness* of these four classes of methods. Previously, we defined effectiveness of a research setting such that a loss in *either* scope or efficiency constitutes a loss in effectiveness. No over-all comparison of these four classes of methods in terms of their relative effectiveness can be made from the present context, since methods high in efficiency tend to be low in comprehensiveness and *vice versa*.

It might be argued that experimental simulations provide the most effective setting since they offer an optimal balance of scope and efficiency. To make such a conclusion, however, we would need to be able to formulate the metric properties of our continuum of methods, and accurately place the four classes of methods along that continuum; and this we clearly cannot do with our present "weak" model. Thus, we cannot reasonably conclude that experimental simulations are inherently more effective research settings than other methods.

However, they do seem to provide a research context which lets us avoid an extreme loss of *either* scope or efficiency.

Ultimately, effectiveness depends in a large measure on the specific research procedures which we use in a given case and the rigor with which we apply them. Hence, we can assess the relative effectiveness of specific studies, rather than of classes of study settings, because studies using any of the four types of settings can be executed well or poorly in terms of the rigor of procedures. However, the type of study setting used does place *limits* on the comprehensiveness and efficiency of *any* study done in that kind of setting, hence, effectiveness of a study is not entirely independent of the type of research setting by means of which it is done.

IMPLICATIONS FOR PROGRAMMATIC RESEARCH

It should be pointed out that use of the different classes of research settings imply different levels of prior knowledge about the problem to be studied. The investigator needs to know a lot more (or assume he knows a lot more) about the phenomena he is studying in order to work with the methods at the laboratory and computer end of the continuum. As we proceed down the continuum from field studies to laboratory and computer studies, our results become more and more a function of the structure which we impose on the situation (by our Treatment W and Treatment X operations). Consequently, the empirical "truth" of the results which we obtain (as they apply to the real-life phenomena which we are studying) becomes more and more dependent upon the empirical "truth" of the structure which we have imposed.

On the field study end of the continuum, however, the investigator needs to know (or assume) less about the phenomena before he starts. He imposes less of a structure or a theory upon the situation. However, it should never be assumed that the field investigator does not also impose some theory as he selects and measures variables. Furthermore, although in one sense the data from the field study is necessarily "true," the investigator needs to know (or assume) a lot about what was and was not operating in his field situation in order for his *interpretations* to be "true." Hence, the field study investigator imposes a "strong" structure *after*, rather than before, he collects his data.

Obviously, then, the choice of methods along this continuum is not to be done in a haphazard way, on the basis of personal preference, or on the basis of mere expediency. We might view the continuum of

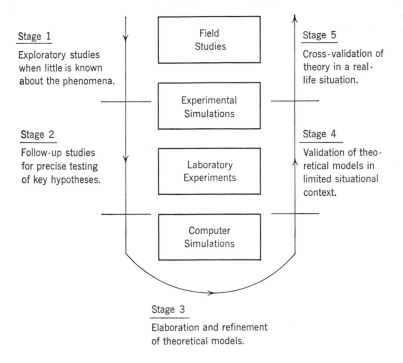

FIGURE 1   Diagram of a five-stage logical path for programmatic research.

methods as a two-way street.[13] If we are starting research on a relatively unexplored phenomenon, it would seem to be best to start far over at the field study end of the continuum. As we learn more about the problem, we can then work with methods further along the continuum, with which we can gain more precise information. Then, having explored the problem with precision and in depth, and perhaps having formulated and thoroughly manipulated a formal model, we can return toward the field study end of the street to find out how closely our representations fit the phenomena of the real world. This "path" of programmatic research is illustrated in Fig. 1.

This is, of course, an idealized description of what everyone knows

---

[13] To extend the analogy of the "two-way street," our prior discussion of variations within each class of methods (see footnote 4) suggests that the four classes of methods here defined are *neighborhoods,* rather than specific addresses, along that street. Within each neighborhood, the specific methods range so that some (such as field experiments) are on the borderline between adjacent neighborhoods.

to be the best way to do programmatic research. What is not specified here, and perhaps cannot be answered in the general case, is how to allocate time and effort among the various classes of methods, both on the "way down" and on the "way back" on this two-way street. In any actual case, for example, choice of methods must be determined on the basis of available resources, as well as on the basis of our present stage of knowledge about the problem. Methods differ considerably in the cost of running a given number of "cases." The more artificial and more abstract methods of the laboratory and computer generally have a far lower cost per case.

But the ever present need to compromise our idealized research plans on pragmatic grounds does not in any way lessen the need for a full and careful reckoning of the advantages and limitations of methodological alternatives. Only by such a reckoning of the relative information which can be derived from different approaches to a given problem can we possibly be in a position to know how "costly" a given compromise would be. It must be recognized, of course, that the present formulation of a "theory of method" for the study of organizations is only a first step toward that aim. A much more thorough and precise formulation will be needed before we can truly "calculate" the relative losses and gains to be achieved by the choice of one approach over another. Still, it is hoped that this partial and tentative formulation may take us closer to the point where our choices of method for organization research can be done more often in a rational and efficient manner.

29

ORGANIZATIONAL DESIGN

R. M. Cyert and J. G. March

Organizational Design and Theory

Organizational engineering is an ancient calling. Aristotle, Machiavelli, Bentham, and Madison devoted considerable energies to the design of purposive organizations. In more recent times, Urwick, Taylor, Fayol, Mooney, Gulick, and Davis focused on the problems associated with engineering joint human effort through complex organizational systems. Out of this work has come a relatively distinctive vocabulary and some principles of design. The dimensions of organizational anatomy have been reduced to a few simple canonical symbols. In the purest form of descriptive anatomy we require only two symbols: a rectangle (representing a basic element of the organization —a position) and a directed line (representing a relationship between two positions). The relationship is normally defined in terms of such expressions as "reports to," "has authority over," "is the boss of." By using these two symbols, we can construct a schematic representation of an organization—the familiar organization chart. Alternatively, we can translate the basic notation into one appropriate for graph theory or matrix manipulation. In any case, much of the basic material of classical organizational engineering represents constraints imposed on this simple chart.

Conventional practice requires that each position should "report to" one and only one other position (scalar principle); conventional practice places some constraints on the number of positions that should "report to" any given position (the span of control); conventional practice distinguishes among positions on the basis of the pattern of "reports to" relationships (e.g., the distinction between "line" and "staff"). Usual organizational engineering goes well beyond these simple relations and elementary principles. We consider the design of a reward system, communication system, work flow system, etc., against the background of the organization chart (e.g., an ordering of positions according to salary is ordinarily required to be consistent with an ordering of positions according to the "reports to" relationship). Or we elaborate the chart to include additional symbols (e.g., most charts now contain at least one kind of dotted line representing some kind of relation other than the strict "reports to" relation). Or we suggest an alternative form of anatomy altogether (e.g., a sociometric chart, a means-end tree, an information processing diagram).

In the last decade, however, developments in organization design and organization theory have been remarkably independent. Except in the area of interpersonal and intergroup relations in organizations— where the research has been considerably influenced by applied problems—attempts to develop the engineering implications of modern theories of organizational decision making have been modest. Possibly this is because the engineering implications are themselves meager. Neither the professional journals nor the folktales of the culture report any spectacular successes; few responsible organization theorists would be enthusiastic about a major leap into the problems of design, although there are some obvious possibilities for using parts of recent work to design decision systems.

As we consider these possibilities, it should be clear that we approach the problem of design in a manner that is somewhat different from the manner characteristic of many conventional treatments of management theory. We cannot distinguish between "good" and "bad" organizations without a criterion, and we know of no general criterion function which can be used. Nor do we think it particularly useful for organizational engineers to devote their energies to looking for such a criterion. The function of the engineer, as we see it, is to design a system that will perform to certain specifications, to provide information on potential inconsistencies among specifications, or to evaluate the probable consequences of specified changes in design. Given existing knowledge and given some specifications of the kind of organization desired, we may be able to design an organization that will come tolerably close to the specifications. At least, we may be able to do this occasionally for some kinds of specifications.

In the next two sections we consider some possible directions for considering design problems. We reconsider a model that we first presented in the context of duopoly theory, and we examine some recent attempts to develop models of organizational decision making.

Organizational Structure and Behavior
in a Model of Duopoly

In 1955 we suggested that "it should be possible to develop a model that specifies a meaningful relationship between significant characteristics of organizational structure and some important attributes of organizational behavior." [1] We then proceeded to outline four propositions about the effect of organizational structure on decision behavior, specify two ideal-type firms exhibiting extreme organizational structures, and describe the impact on the conventional Cournot duopoly analysis of having decision making systems such as we specified. The models were naive in a number of ways. We have not found them particularly useful in subsequent research; but they illustrate one kind of approach that might be feasible and fruitful.

Consider the two firms we described: In Firm 1, the decision-making unit consists in a committee of equals and does not have responsibility for establishing the criteria for pricing decisions (i.e., the unit is decentralized and is subject to dicta from above with respect to price policy). At the same time, communication chains between the decision-making unit and the primary sources of information are long; and information on demand, competitor's behavior, and official firm policy are all channeled through a relay point (e.g., an accounting department) that emphasizes the importance of costs and cost conservatism. In Firm 2, the decision-making unit is an individual and he has responsibility both for the specific decisions and for the criteria for pricing (i.e., the unit is centralized). Communication chains tend to be short, and information on demand, competitor's behavior, and firm policy are channeled through a relay point (e.g., a sales department) that emphasizes demand and the importance of sales.

It seemed reasonable to argue that Firm 1 would be a firm in which price changes tend to be infrequent and reaction to competitors primarily passive; conversely it seemed reasonable to expect Firm 2 to exhibit frequent price changes and price leadership with respect to competitors. We then explored a modified Cournot analysis to determine the effects of these structural characteristics on market equilibrium.

Let there be two duopolists in the market (Firm 1 and Firm 2). Following Cournot, let there be no costs, let the market demand function be:

---

[1] See [141], p. 129.

$$p = 25 - \frac{x_1 + x_2}{3}$$

where p = price
  x_1 = output of Firm 1
  x_2 = output of Firm 2

and assume that each duopolist expects no reaction on the part of the other in response to a change in output:

$$\frac{dx_1}{dx_2} = \frac{dx_2}{dx_1} = 0 \text{ (conjectural variation terms)}$$

The Cournot market solution is reached by setting marginal revenue for each duopolist equal to zero (i.e., the point of optimal production under the assumption of no costs) and solving the resulting equations. In this case, an equilibrium is reached at

$$x_1 = 25$$

$$x_2 = 25$$

$$p = 8.33$$

To explore some of the implications of the organizational models, we assumed that in the market specified above, Firm 1 and Firm 2 had reached the Cournot equilibrium point. We then postulated a shift in market demand, such that

$$p = 30 - \frac{x_1 + x_2}{3}$$

Under the assumptions previously outlined, it can be predicted that Firm 1 will tend to: (a) be slow in changing its perception of the market demand; (b) underestimate demand when its perception does change; and (c) give a positive value to the conjectural variation term.[2] To provide a specific solution, we argued that Firm 1 might have expectations with regard to the market demand function and the conjectural variation term as follows:

$$p = 25 - \frac{x_1 + x_2}{3}$$

$$\frac{dx_2}{dx_1} = 1$$

Similarly, it can be predicted that Firm 2 will tend to: (a) change its

---

[2] A more complete development of these predictions will be found in [141], p. 132 ff. See also the related report by Cyert, March, and Starbuck [145].

perception of market demand quickly; (b) overestimate demand; (c) give a value of zero to the conjectural variation term.[3] Thus, we asserted that Firm 2 might have the following estimates of key information:

$$p = 100 - x_1 - x_2$$

$$\frac{dx_1}{dx_2} = 0$$

Under these conditions, the market solution obviously deviates significantly from the standard Cournot solution.

$$x_1 = 10$$

$$x_2 = 45$$

$$p = 11.67$$

The effect is to make Firm 2 dominant in the market.

In our original paper [141] we argued that the solution derived above would be stable only if the new production level and the resultant profits were acceptable to the dominant control groups of the two firms. Otherwise, some reaction—in the form of a reorganization —might reasonably be expected. Such a reorganization would have obvious consequences for the model. In point of fact, it is possible to specify a set of values for organizational structure and the aspiration level of control groups such that a market which has, under standard economic analysis, a given equilibrium point has, with the addition of the organizational factors, either a different equilibrium point or no stable equilibrium at all. Thus, under the postulated conditions, the design of organizational structure is critical to decision-making behavior; and decision behavior is critical to the outcome in the market.

The paper [141] from which we have borrowed considerably was not intended as a contribution to organizational engineering. Quite to the contrary, we were exclusively concerned with the development of a positive theory of oligopoly. Nevertheless, it is clear that, if the positive theory is correct in this case, the design implications are direct and obvious. A firm organized according to the Firm 1 structure will follow a pricing policy quite different from that followed by a firm organized along the lines of Firm 2, and the relative positions of the two firms will depend on the interaction between their organizational structure and the characteristics of the market. The attributes of organizational structure specified in the model are attributes that can

---

[3] *Ibid.*

be manipulated deliberately in the real world; the predictions of consequences are relatively straightforward.

Organizational Structure and Decision Making: Goals and Search

In the eight years that have passed since the publication of the duopoly model, we have learned some things about organizational decision making. At least we have learned enough to suggest that the approach taken in that model was at best incomplete, certainly over simple, and quite possibly fundamentally wrong. The simplicity of the ideas in the model permits us to illustrate the way in which organizational design is implicit in parts of organization theory, but for substantively more promising work we need to turn to developments that are largely subsequent to 1955.

In general, recent studies of organizational decision making suggest two things: First, they seem to confirm our earlier argument that the major impact of organizational structure on decision making occurs when feasible solutions to organizational problems are nonunique. The action of an organization is constrained by external (e.g., market, governmental) forces, but at many points in a decision sequence there is more than one feasible solution. Organizational design is primarily relevant in determining what potentially feasible solutions will be discovered and how they will be evaluated. Where the external constraints are severe and feasible solutions scarce, we would not expect organizational structure to play as important a role. Second, the studies picture an organization as an adaptive, incompletely rational, political coalition. It is a political coalition in the sense that it consists of a number of individuals and groups making demands which are only partially consistent and which lead to imperfectly rationalized goals within the organization. It is incompletely rational in the sense that it acts upon imperfect and incomplete information about alternatives and the consequences of alternatives. It is adaptive in the sense that it modifies its behavior on the basis of experience.

Since our purpose is hortatory and suggestive rather than exhaustive, we do not propose to elaborate greatly the description of organizational decision making that we think is consistent with recent work. It will suffice to outline a quite simple framework in which the process of decision is viewed as a series of conditional steps.

1. The organization first considers whether performance is satisfactory on a particular goal.

2. If it is, the system "learns" that the procedures used were effective—thus becomes more likely to use them in future situations and the goal is modified to reflect experience.

3. If performance has been unsatisfactory, the organization searches for a solution to the problem. The search involves first defining what class of problem exists and then following a search procedure learned from previous experience with problems of that class.

4. If the search is successful, the organization "learns" to search in the same way in future cases and to be relatively sanguine about future goal failure.

5. If the search is unsuccessful, the organization learns to prefer other search rules. It also modifies its goals. Thus, search rules, decision rules, and goals adapt to experience.

It is clear from this simple framework that two of the key concepts are "goals" and "search." If the theory is correct, organizational factors that affect either organizational goals or the procedures for search will affect organizational decisions. If the theory can be elaborated to show in more detail how goals or search procedures (and their development with experience) are influenced by organizational factors, we would have the basis for some propositions in organizational design.

Consider first the process of goal formation within an organization. One theory (our own) of organizational objectives describes goals as the result of a continuous bargaining-learning process. The bargaining is among the members of the organizational coalition and particularly among the more active members of that coalition. It is primarily through bargaining within this active group that the basic outline of what we call organizational objectives arise. Side payments among coalition members are not exclusively the distribution of a fixed, transferable booty. On the contrary, since a significant number of these payments are in the form of basic policy commitments, they represent the central process of goal specification.

These commitments are elaborated in the sense that subunits develop specific subgoals through three internal processes:

1. A problem-solving process by which subgoals and specific performance criteria are associated with higher level goals. The organization finds over time that a certain level of attainment with respect to some subgoal (e.g., share of market volume of sales) is apparently consistent with satisfactory performance on some nonoperational, widely shared goal (e.g., maximum profit). The subunits then tend to take these subgoals as their own specific goals.

2. A learning process by which subgoals and specific performance criteria are selected by subunits in terms of their attractiveness to the subunits involved and converted into their own goals. The criteria of performance selected tend to be those that are rewarding either in terms of their relative ease of achievement, or in terms of their side effects.

3. A subunit identification process by which subgoals and specific performance criteria are linked to specific subgroups. This identification process is reinforced by the internal interaction of the members of the subunit. Thus, the volume of sales may become the subgoal of the sales department and its importance reinforced among the members of the sales department by their constant references to it.

These three internal processes are of particular significance because operative subgoals determine the behavior of the organization. Thus it is not enough to design an organization to achieve some broad nonoperative higher level goal. The critical question for behavior is how the subunits will convert the higher level goal into operative subgoals and the nature of the subgoals.

How can organizational design affect the development of goals in such a process? In classical treatments of organizational design, decisions on how to organize major subunits (e.g., whether to organize by purpose or process) are usually described as affecting primarily the problems of efficiency in coordination and communication. However, if the above theory of organizational goals is roughly correct, departmental structure should have a number of important effects on operative goals. First, the structure identifies a conspicuous solution to the coalition problem. If a coalition focusing on the major subunits of the organization is a viable coalition, it is likely to be considered before other alternative viable coalitions that cut across or outside major subunits. Second, the structure influences the interaction among members of the organization and thus the development of subunit identification with subgoals. Thus, one important way of influencing the development of goals is to modify the organizational structure. At the same time, the theory suggests that modifications in reports (i.e., operational criteria) made available to the organization will—under appropriate conditions—lead to shifts in goals.

Similarly, if we examine the nature of organizational search, we can identify some ways in which organizational design can affect the decisions of the organization. We generally refer to organizational search as problemistic search. By problemistic search we mean search that is stimulated by a problem (usually a rather specific one) and is directed toward finding a solution to that problem. A problem is recognized when the organization either fails to satisfy one of its goals or when such a failure can be anticipated in the immediate future. So long as the problem is not solved, search will continue. The problem is solved either by discovering an alternative that satisfies the goals or by revising the goals to levels that make an available alternative acceptable.

We assume that rules for search are simple-minded in the sense that they reflect simple concepts of causality. Subject to learning, search is assumed to be concentrated in the "neighborhood" of the problem symptom and in the "neighborhood" of the current alternative. These two constraints reflect different dimensions of the basic causal notions that a cause will be found "near" its effect and that a new solution will be found "near" an old one. "Nearness," thus, refers (among other things) to organizational associations (e.g., search in the department in which the symptom was discovered), means-ends associations (e.g., search in links on the means-end chain that are adjacent to the symptom), or temporal associations (e.g., search in a time period near to the time of the symptom).

What does all this say for the effect of organizational design on search behavior? There are at least three relevant points: First, the problems the organization attends to are partly a function of organizational design. "Gresham's law of planning" says that routine or structured activity drives out the nonroutine or nonstructured. Thus, for example, if planning is a desirable activity of the organization, the design has to take account of Gresham's law (e.g., by isolating planning from more programmed activity) or there will be no planning, and no planning problems on which search activity is expended. Second, organizational structure is an important device for associating search behavior with particular problems. In effect, the structure is a surrogate for a learned, causal map of problems. It serves as one important kind of memory for the organization. We can destroy or modify the organization's memory by altering the structure. Third, the problem solution discovered by the search activity will depend upon the organizational locus of the group doing the search. Differences in training, information sources, and subgoals assure quite different search procedures by different groups. The problem of organizational design is to construct an organization such that the search stimulated by a particular problem takes place in the "right" locale.

Methodological Problems and Research Strategy

It is hardly necessary to dwell upon the methodological problems involved in translating research on organizational decision making into useful precepts for organizational design. They are large and they are obvious. We do not know much about the functional forms describing the behavior of organizations. We have at best only crude guesses or broad bounds for the parameters of imperfectly identified functions. We know rather little about second- or third-order side effects. Although the availability of computer simulation as a technique permits us to relax some of the constraints we have traditionally faced with respect to allowable complexity, we still require some meaningful inputs in order to generate much in the way of meaningful outputs.

These problems or their natural progeny will be with us indefinitely. They are annoying, and hopefully they will be solved. But there are two compelling reasons for proceeding with the study of organizational design without awaiting a complete tidying of the methodological mess. First, however incomplete and inaccurate the present models of organizations may be, they seem to have both some validity and some possible relevance to design problems. The risks of using them for design purposes seem modest; the potential gains somewhat larger. Second, organization theory will develop faster if it is built on an engineering model of research as much as on a "pure science" model. This is not simply a plea for methodological permissiveness. Many problems in complex systems are likely to be more amenable to an approach that emphasizes the design of a system to meet certain specifications than to an approach seeking a complete mapping of causal connections. It seems quite likely that such a situation holds in many areas of organizational analysis.

BIBLIOGRAPHY

[1] "A List of Bibliographies on Industrial Engineering and Management," *Society of Industrial Engineers,* **III,** No. 6, 1920.

[2] Abegglen, J. C., *The Japanese Factory; Aspects of Its Social Organization* (Glencoe, Ill.: The Free Press, 1958).

[3] Abel, N. H., *Oeuvres complètes,* new edition published at the cost of the State of Norway by L. Sylow et S. Lie (Christiania: Grøndahl & Søn, 1881).

[4] Aczel, J., *Vorlesungen über Funktionalgleichungen und ihre Andwendungen* (Basel: Birkhäuser Verlag, 1961).

[5] Adams, J. S., "Toward an Understanding of Inequity," *Journal of Abnormal and Social Psychology,* **67,** 1963, pp. 422–436.

[6] ———, and W. B. Rosenbaum, "The Relationship of Workers Productivity to Cognitive Dissonance about Wage Inequities," *Journal of Applied Psychology,* **46,** 1962, pp. 161–164.

[7] Adams, R. N., and J. J. Preiss (eds.), *Human Organization Research: Field Relations and Techniques* (Homewood, Ill.: The Dorsey Press, 1960).

[8] *Addresses and Discussions at the Conference on Scientific Management Held October 12, 13, 14 Nineteen Hundred and Eleven,* The Amos Tuck School of Administration and Finance, Dartmouth College, Hanover, New Hampshire (Norwood, Mass.: The Plimpton Press, 1912).

[9] Alford, L. P., and H. R. Beatty, *Principles of Industrial Management,* rev. ed. (New York: The Ronald Press Co., 1951).

[10] Alger, C. F., "The External Bureaucracy in U. S. Foreign Affairs," *Administrative Science Quarterly,* **7,** 1962, pp. 50–78.

[11] Allee, W. C., A. E. Emerson, O. Park, T. Park, and K. P. Schmidt, *Principles of Animal Ecology* (Philadelphia: W. B. Saunders Co., 1949).

[12] Allen, A. H., " 'Automation'—A Magic Word Which May Spell Lower Production Costs for You," *Steel,* April 3, 1950.

[13] Allen, L. A., *Management and Organization* (New York: McGraw-Hill Book Co., 1958).

[14] Allport, G. W., *Personality: A Psychological Interpretation* (New York: H. Holt and Co., 1937).

[15] ———, "Scientific Models and Human Morals," *Psychological Review,* **54,** 1947, pp. 182–192.

[16] Anderson, L. F., "Beginnings in Industrial Education," *School and Society,* **13,** 1921, pp. 518–523.

[17] Anderson, M., and O. J. Sizelove (eds.), *Fifty Years Progress in Management, 1910–1960* (New York: The American Society of Mechanical Engineers, 1960).

[18] Anderson, W., and J. M. Gaus, *Research in Public Administration* (Chicago: Committee on Public Administration of the Social Science Research Council, 1945).
   a. Gaus, J. M., "Changes in the Setting, 1930–1944."

[19] Anshen, M., and G. L. Bach (eds.), *Management and Corporations, 1985* (New York: McGraw-Hill Book Co., 1960).

[20] Argyle, M., "The Concepts of Role and Status," *Sociological Review,* **44,** 1952, pp. 39–52.

[21] Argyris, C., "The Impact of Budgets on People," prepared for Controllership Foundation, Inc. (Ithaca, N. Y.: Cornell University, The School of Business and Public Administration, 1952).

[22] ———, *Personality and Organization* (New York: Harper, 1957).

[23] ———, *Understanding Organizational Behavior* (Homewood, Ill.: The Dorsey Press, 1960).

[24] Arrow, K. J., *Social Choice and Individual Values* (New York: John Wiley & Sons, 1951).

[25] ———, "Optimization, Decentralization and Internal Pricing in Business Firms," in *Contributions to Scientific Research in Management* (Los Angeles: University of California Press, 1959).

[26] ———, and L. Hurwicz, "Decentralization and Computation in Resource Allocation," in R. W. Pfouts (ed.), *Essays on Economics and Econometrics* (Chapel Hill, N. C.: University of North Carolina Press, 1960).

[27] Asch, S. E., "Effects of Group Pressure Upon the Modification and Distortion of Judgments," in H. Guetzkow (ed.), *Groups, Leadership and Men* (Pittsburgh: Carnegie Press, 1951).

[28] ———, *Social Psychology* (New York: Prentice-Hall, 1952).

[29] Atkinson, J. W. (ed.), *Motives in Fantasy, Action and Society* (Princeton, N. J.: Van Nostrand, 1958).
   a. Atkinson, J. W., "Towards Experimental Analysis of Human Motivation in Terms of Motives, Expectancies and Incentives."

[30] ———, and W. R. Reitman, "Performance as a Function of Motive Strength and Expectancy of Goal Attainment," *Journal of Abnormal and Social Psychology,* **53,** 1956, pp. 361–366.

[31] Aumann, R., and M. Maschler, "The Bargaining Set for Cooperative Games," in M. Dresher, L. S. Shapley, and A. W. Tucker (eds.), *Advances in Game Theory,* Annals of Mathematical Studies No. 52 (Princeton, N. J.: Princeton University Press, 1963).

[32] ———, and J. B. Kruskal, "Assigning Quantitative Values to Qualitative Factors in the Naval Electronics Problem," *Naval Research Logistics Quarterly,* **6,** 1959, pp. 1–16.

[33] *Aviation Week and Space Technology,* **76** (19), 1962, p. 35.

[34] Babbage, C., *On the Economy of Machinery and Manufactures* (London: Charles Knight, 1832).

[35] ———, *The Exposition of 1851; or Views of the Industry, the Science, and the Government of England* (London: John Murray, 1851).

[36] Back, K. W., "Influence Through Social Communication," *Journal of Abnormal and Social Psychology,* **46,** 1951, pp. 9–23.

[37] Baker, H., and R. R. France, *Centralization and Decentralization in Industrial Relations* (Princeton, N. J.: Princeton University, Industrial Relations Section, 1954).

[38] Baldamus, W., *Efficiency and Effort: An Analysis of Industrial Administration* (London: Tavistock Publications, 1961).

[39] Balderston, C. C., R. T. Brecht, V. S. Karabasz, and R. J. Riddle, *Management of an Enterprise,* 2nd ed. (New York: Prentice-Hall, 1949).

[40] Bales, R. F., *Interaction Process Analysis: A Method for the Study of Small Groups* (Cambridge, Mass.: Addison-Wesley Press, 1950).

[41] ———, and P. E. Slater, "Role Differentiation in Small Decision-Making Groups," in T. Parsons, and R. F. Bales (eds.), *Family, Socialization and Interaction Process* (Glencoe, Ill.: The Free Press, 1955).

[42] Baritz, L., *The Servants of Power* (Middletown, Conn.: Wesleyan University Press, 1960).

[43] Barker, R. G., and H. F. Wright, *Midwest and Its Children: The Psychological Ecology of an American Town* (Evanston, Ill.: Row, Peterson, 1954).

[44] Barnard, C. I., *The Functions of the Executive* (Cambridge, Mass.: Harvard University Press, 1938).

[45] Barnes, R. M., and N. A. Englert, *Bibliography of Industrial Engineering and Management Literature* (Dubuque, Iowa: Wm. C. Brown Co., 1945).

[46] Barr, S., *Purely Academic* (New York: Simon and Schuster, 1958).

[47] Bass, B. M., *Leadership, Psychology and Organizational Behavior* (New York: Harper & Row, Publishers, 1960).

[48] ———, and J. A. Vaughan, "Experimenting with the Man in the Middle of the Organization," presented at the First Seminar on the Social Science of Organizations, University of Pittsburgh, June 10–22, 1962.

[49] Batchelder, R. C., *The Irreversible Decision, 1939–1950* (Boston: Houghton Mifflin, 1962).

[50] Baum, B. H., *Decentralization of Authority in a Bureaucracy* (Englewood Cliffs, N. J.: Prentice-Hall, 1961).

[51] Bavelas, A., "Communication Patterns in Task Oriented Groups," *Journal of the Acoustical Society of America,* **22,** 1950, pp. 725–730.

[52] ———, "Communication Patterns in Task-Oriented Groups," in D. Lerner, and H. D. Lasswell (eds.), *The Policy Sciences* (Stanford, Calif.: Stanford University Press, 1951).

[53] Becker, S., and L. Parsons, "Subjective Probabilities and Level of Aspiration," Unpublished Manuscript, 1961.

[54] ———, and S. Siegel, "Utility of Grades: Level of Aspiration in a Decision Theory Context," *Journal of Experimental Psychology,* **55,** 1958, pp. 81–85.

[55] Belden, T. G., "The Language of Command," *Studies of Command and Control, Study No. 2* (Princeton, N. J.: Institute for Defense Analysis, 1962).

[56] Belousov, V. V., "Experimental Geology," *Scientific American,* **204,** 1961, pp. 96–107.

[57] Bendix, R., *Work and Authority in Industry* (New York: John Wiley & Sons, 1956).

[58] Benne, K., and P. Sheats, "Functional Roles of Group Members," *Journal of Social Issues,* **4,** 1948, pp. 41–49.

[59] Bennis, W. G., K. D. Benne, and R. Chin (eds.), *The Planning of Change* (New York: Holt, Rinehart and Winston, 1961).
    a. Bennis, W. G., and H. A. Shepard, "A Theory of Group Development."

[60] Benoit-Smullyan, E., "Status, Status Types, and Status Interrelations," *American Sociological Review,* **9,** 1944, pp. 151–161.

[61] Berg, I. A., and B. M. Bass (eds.), *Conformity and Deviation* (New York: Harper, 1961).
    a. Asch, S. E., "Issues in the Study of Social Influences on Judgment."
    b. Blake, R. R., and J. S. Mouton, "Competition, Communication and Conformity."

[62] Berg, R. M., *Bibliography of Management Literature Including An Author Index* (New York: The American Society of Mechanical Engineers, 1931).

[63] Berge, C., *Theorie des Graphes et ses Applications* (*Theory of Graphs and Their Applications*) translated by A. Doig (New York: John Wiley & Sons, 1962).

[64] Berkowitz, L., "Group Standards, Cohesiveness and Productivity," *Human Relations,* **7,** 1954, pp. 509–519.

[65] Bethel, L. L., F. S. Atwater, G. H. E. Smith, and H. A. Stackman, *Industrial Organization and Management,* 2nd ed. (New York: McGraw-Hill Book Co., Inc., 1950).

[66] Bhattacharyya, A., "On a Measure of Divergence Between Two Statistical Populations Defined by Their Probability Distribution," *Bulletin of the Calcutta Mathematical Society,* **35,** 1943, pp. 99–109.

[67] Biddle, B. J., *The Present Status of Role Theory* (Columbia, Mo.: University of Missouri Press, 1961).

[68] ———, and J. P. Twyman, "Concepts of Role and Role Conflict," *Human Relations,* forthcoming.

[69] ———, H. A. Rosencranz, and E. F. Rankin, Jr., *Studies in the Role of the Public School Teacher* (Columbia, Mo.: University of Missouri Press, 1961).
    Vol. 1, *Orientation, Methods and Materials.*
    Vol. 2, *General Characteristics of the School Teacher's Role.*
    Vol. 3, *Positional Differences in Teacher Role.*
    Vol. 4, *Role of the Teacher and Occupational Choice.*
    Vol. 5, *Own and Attributed Cognitions for the Teacher.*

[70] ———, ———, E. Tomick and J. P. Twyman, "Pluralistic Ignorance in the Role of the Teacher," in B. J. Biddle, and E. J. Thomas (eds.), *The Role Orientation* (New York: John Wiley & Sons, 1963).

[71] Bierstedt, R., "An Analysis of Social Power," *American Sociological Review,* **15,** 1950, pp. 730–738.

[72] Bindra, D., *Motivation: A Systematic Reinterpretation* (New York: The Ronald Press, 1959).

[73] Birmingham, H. P., and F. V. Taylor, "A Human Engineering Approach to the Design of Man-Operated Continuous Control Systems," *USN Research Laboratory Report No. 4333,* 1954.

[74] Blackwell, D., and M. A. Girshick, *Theory of Games and Statistical Decisions* (New York: John Wiley & Sons, 1954).

[75] Blau, P. M., *The Dynamics of Bureaucracy* (Chicago: University of Chicago Press, 1955).

[76] ———, and W. R. Scott, *Formal Organizations: A Comparative Approach* (San Francisco: Chandler Publishing Co., 1962).

[77] Boalt, G., *Arbetsgruppen (The Work Group)* (Stockholm: Tiden, 1954).

[78] Bonini, C. P., "Accounting—Information Systems in the Firm," *ONR Memorandum No. 59* (Pittsburgh: Carnegie Institute of Technology, Graduate School of Industrial Administration, 1958).

[79] ———, *Simulation of Information and Decision Systems in the Firm* (Englewood Cliffs, N. J.: Prentice-Hall, 1963).

[80] Boulding, K. E., *The Skills of the Economist* (Cleveland: Howard Allen, 1958).

[81] Bouriel, and Leroy, Th., "L'évolution de l'Organization Scientific en France," *Methodes,* November 1938, p. 324.

[82] Bowman, M. J., "A Graphical Analysis of Personal Income Distribution in the United States," *American Economic Review,* **35,** No. 1, 1945, pp. 607–628.

[83] ———, "The Analysis of Inequality Patterns: A Methodological Contribution," *Metron,* **18,** N. 1–2, 1956, pp. 189–206.

[84] Briggs, G. E., "Engineering Systems Approaches," *ONR Seminar on Research in Organization* (Columbus: The Ohio State University, Laboratory of Aviation Psychology, 1962).

[85] Brookings Institution, "Report to the Senate Select Committee to Investigate Executive Agencies of the Government with a View to Coordination," in *Investigation of Executive Agencies of the Government,* Senate Report 1275, 75th Congress, 1st Session, 1937 (Washington, D. C.: Superintendent of Documents, U. S. Government Printing Office).

[86] Brown, A., *Organization. A Formulation of Principle* (New York: Hibbert Printing Co., 1945).

[87] Brown, W. B., *Exploration in Management* (New York: John Wiley & Sons, 1960).

[88] Brown, W. V., *Scientific Management. A List of References in the New York Public Library* (New York: New York Public Library, 1917).

[89] Brzezinski, Z., "Deviation Control: A Study in the Dynamics of Doctrinal Conflict," *American Political Science Review,* **56,** 1962, pp. 5–22.

[90] Buck, P. H., O. Handlin, F. Merk, S. E. Morison, A. M. Schlesinger, and A. M. Schlesinger, Jr., *Harvard Guide to American History* (Cambridge, Mass.: Belknap Press of Harvard University Press, 1954).

[91] Burns, T., "The Directions of Activity and Communication in a Departmental Executive Group," *Human Relations,* **7,** 1954, pp. 73–97.

[92] Bury, J. B., *The Idea of Progress; An Inquiry into Its Origin and Growth* (New York: Dover Publications, 1932).

[93] Campbell, D. T., "Systematic Error on the Part of Human Links in Communication Systems," *Information and Control,* **1,** 1958, pp. 334–369.

[94] Cannons, H. G., *Bibliography of Industrial Efficiencies and Factory Management* (London: George Routledge and Sons, 1920).

[95] Caplow, T., and R. J. McGee, *The Academic Marketplace* (New York: Basic Books, 1958).

[96] Cardullo, F. E., "Industrial Administration and Scientific Management," in

C. B. Thompson (ed.), *Scientific Management* (Cambridge, Mass.: Harvard University Press, 1914).

[97] Carlson, S., *Executive Behaviour* (Stockholm: Strömberg, 1951).

[98] Carnegie, Dale, *How to Win Friends and Influence People* (New York: Simon and Schuster, 1936).

[99] Cartwright, D., "A Field Theoretical Conception of Power," in D. Cartwright (ed.), *Studies in Social Power* (Ann Arbor: The University of Michigan Press, 1959).

[100] ——, and A. Zander (eds.), *Group Dynamics, Research and Theory,* 2nd ed. (Evanston, Ill.: Row, Peterson, 1960).

   a. Bales, R. F., "A Theoretical Framework for Interaction Process Analysis." First ed. only.

   b. French, J. R. P., Jr., and B. Raven, "The Bases of Social Power."

   c. Kahn, R. L., and D. Katz, "Leadership Practices in Relation to Productivity and Morale."

[101] Cattell, R. B., "New Concepts for Measuring Leadership in Terms of Group Syntality," *Human Relations,* **4,** 1951, pp. 161–184.

[102] ——, *Personality and Motivation Structure and Measurement* (Yonkers-on-Hudson, N. Y.: World Book Co., 1957).

[103] Chandler, A. D., *Henry Varnum Poor, Business Editor, Analyst, and Reformer* (Cambridge, Mass.: Harvard University Press, 1956).

[104] Chapman, D. W., and J. Volkmann, "A Social Determinant of the Level of Aspiration," *Journal of Abnormal Psychology,* **34,** 1939, pp. 225–238.

[105] Chapman, R. L., J. L. Kennedy, A. Newell, and W. C. Biel, "The Systems Research Laboratory's Air Defense Experiments," *Management Science,* **5,** 1959, pp. 250–269.

[106] Chapple, E. D., and C. Arensberg, "Measuring Human Relations," *Genetic Psychology Monographs,* **22,** No. 1, 1940, pp. 3–147.

[107] ——, and L. R. Sayles, *The Measure of Management* (New York: The Macmillan Co., 1961).

[108] Charnes, A., "Future of Mathematics in Management Science," *Management Science,* **1,** 1955, pp. 180–182.

[109] ——, and W. W. Cooper, "Management Models and Industrial Applications of Linear Programming," *Management Science,* **4,** 1957, pp. 38–91.

[110] ——, and ——, "The Theory of Search: Optimum Distribution of Search Effort," *Management Science,* **5,** 1958, pp. 44–50.

[111] ——, and ——, "On Some Theorems of L. V. Kantorovich, J. R. Isbell and W. H. Marlow," *ONR Research Memorandum No. 9* (Evanston: Northwestern University, The Technological Institute, and Pittsburgh: Carnegie Institute of Technology, Graduate School of Industrial Administration, 1958).

[112] ——, and ——, "Chance Constrained Programming," *Management Science,* **6,** 1959, pp. 73–79.

[113] ——, and ——, *Management Models and Industrial Applications of Linear Programming,* Vols. I and II (New York: John Wiley & Sons, 1961).

[114] ——, and ——, "Management Science and Managing," *The Quarterly Review of Economics and Business,* **2,** 1962, pp. 7–19.

[115] ——, and ——, "Deterministic Equivalents for Optimizing and Satisficing Under Chance Constraints," *Operations Research,* **11,** No. 1, 1963, pp. 18–39.

[116] Charnes, A., W. W. Cooper, and Y. Ijiri, "Breakeven Budgeting and Programming to Goal's," *Journal of Accounting Research,* **1,** No. 1, 1963, pp. 16–43.

[117] ——, ——, and K. Kortanek, "Duality in Semi-Infinite Programs," *Management Science,* **9,** No. 4, 1963, pp. 209–228.

[118] ——, ——, and M. H. Miller, "Application of Linear Programming to Financial Budgeting and the Costing of Funds," *Journal of Business of the University of Chicago,* **32,** No. 1, 1959, pp. 20–46.

[119] ——, ——, and G. H. Symonds, "Cost Horizons and Certainty Equivalents: An Approach to the Stochastic Programming of Heating Oil," *Management Science,* **4,** 1958, pp. 235–263.

[120] Christie, L. A., et al., *Communication and Learning in Task Oriented Groups* (Cambridge, Mass.: Research Laboratory of Electronics, 1952).

[121] Churchill, N. C., "Behavioral Effects Of An Audit," Ph.D. thesis (Ann Arbor, Mich.: University of Michigan, School of Business Administration, 1962).

[122] ——, and W. W. Cooper, "An Experimental Approach to Ascertaining the Effects of an Audit," for the Project NR-047011, Planning and Control of Industrial Operations, ONR Contract Nonr-760(01) (Pittsburgh: Carnegie Institute of Technology, Graduate School of Industrial Administration, 1960).

[123] ——, and L. N. Teitelbaum, "The Effects of an Audit. A Statement of the Problem and a Program for Research," for the Project NR-047011, Planning and Control of Industrial Operations, ONR Contract Nonr-760-(01) (Pittsburgh: Carnegie Institute of Technology, Graduate School of Industrial Administration, 1960).

[124] Churchman, C. W., *Prediction and Optimal Decision* (Englewood Cliffs, N. J.: Prentice-Hall, 1961).

[125] ——, "Decision and Value Theory," in R. L. Ackoff (ed.), *Progress in Operations Research* (New York: John Wiley & Sons, 1961).

[126] ——, R. L. Ackoff, and E. L. Arnoff, *An Introduction to Operations Research* (New York: John Wiley & Sons, 1957).

[127] Clarkson, G. P. E., *Portfolio Selection: A Simulation of Trust Investment* (Englewood Cliffs, N. J.: Prentice-Hall, 1962).

[128] Clements, R. V., *The Managers: A Study of Their Careers in Industry* (London: George Allen & Unwin, Ltd., 1958).

[129] Coch, L., and J. R. P. French, "Overcoming Resistance to Change," *Human Relations,* **1,** No. 4, 1948, pp. 512–532.

[130] Cohen, K. J., "Simulation of the Firm," *American Economic Review,* **50,** 1960, pp. 534–540.

[131] ——, W. R. Dill, A. Kuehn, and P. R. Winters, *The Carnegie Tech Management Game: An Experiment in Business Education* (Homewood, Ill.: Richard D. Irwin, 1964).

[132] Comrey, A. L., J. M. Pfiffner, and H. P. Beem, "Factors Influencing Organizational Effectiveness I: The U. S. Forest Survey," *Personnel Psychology,* **5,** 1952, pp. 307–325.

[133] ——, ——, and W. S. High, *Factors Influencing Organizational Effectiveness,* Final report of Contract N6-ONR-23815 (Los Angeles: University of Southern California, 1954).

[134] Cooper, W. W., "Some Implications of the Newer Analytic Approaches to Management," *California Management Review,* **4,** 1961, pp. 51–64.

[135] Cooper, W. W., and J. D. Savvas, "Transient Patterns in Budgeting Costs and Aspirations," *ONR Memorandum No. 83* (Pittsburgh: Carnegie Institute of Technology, Graduate School of Industrial Administration, 1960).

[136] Copley, F. B., *Frederick W. Taylor* (New York: Harper and Brothers, 1923).

[137] Cordiner, R. J., *New Frontiers for Professional Managers* (New York: McGraw-Hill Book Co., 1956).

[138] Coulomb, C. A., "Resultat de plusiers experiences destinées a determiner la quantité d'action que les hommes peuvent fournir par leur travail journalier, suivant les differentes manières dont ils emploient leur forces," from *Memoires de l'Académie des Sciences,* pp. 255–297. Printed with *Theorie des machines simples, en ayant egard au frottement de leurs parties et a la roideur des cordages* (Paris: Nouvelle Edition, 1821).

[139] Coutu, W., "Role-Playing Versus Role-Taking: An Appeal for Clarification," *American Sociological Review,* **16,** 1951, pp. 180–187.

[140] Cowles, H. C., "An Ecological Aspect of the Conception of Species," *The American Naturalist,* **42,** 1905, pp. 265–271.

[141] Cyert, R. M., and J. G. March, "Organizational Structure and Pricing Behavior in an Oligopolistic Market," *American Economic Review,* **45,** 1955, pp. 129–139.

[142] ———, and ———, "Organizational Factors in the Theory of Oligopoly," *Quarterly Journal of Economics,* **70,** 1956, pp. 44–64.

[143] ———, and ———, *A Behavioral Theory of the Firm* (Englewood Cliffs, N. J.: Prentice-Hall, 1963).

[144] ———, E. A. Feigenbaum, and J. G. March, "Models of a Behavioral Theory of the Firm," *Behavioral Science,* **4,** 1959, pp. 81–95.

[145] ———, J. G. March, and W. H. Starbuck, "Two Experiments on Bias and Conflict in Organizational Estimation," *Management Science,* **7,** 1961, pp. 254–264.

[146] Dahl, R. A., "Hierarchy, Democracy and Bargaining in Politics and Economics," in Brookings Lecture, *Research Frontiers in Politics and Government* (Washington, D. C., Brookings Institution, 1955).

[147] ———, "The Concept of Power," *Behavioral Science,* **2,** 1957, pp. 201–215.

[148] ———, and C. E. Lindblom, *Politics, Economics and Welfare* (New York: Harper & Row, 1953).

[149] Dahlström, E., *Information på Arbetsplatsen (Internal Communication),* (Stockholm: Studieförbundet Näringsliv och Samhälle, 1956).

[150] Dale, E., *Planning and Developing the Company Organization Structure* (New York: American Management Association, Research Report No. 20, 1952).

[151] ———, *The Great Organizers* (New York: McGraw-Hill Book Co., 1960).

[152] Dalton, M., *Men Who Manage* (New York: John Wiley & Sons, 1959).

[153] Dantzig, G. B., and P. Wolfe, "Decomposition Principle for Linear Programs," *Operations Research,* **8,** No. 1, 1960, pp. 101–111.

[154] Davidson, D., P. Suppes, and S. Siegel, *Decision Making: An Experimental Approach* (Stanford, Calif.: Stanford University Press, 1957).

[155] Davies, O. L. (ed.), *The Design and Analysis of Industrial Experiments* (New York: Hafner Publishing Co., 1956).

[156] Davis, O. A., and A. Whinston, "Externalities, Welfare and the Theory of Games," *Journal of Political Economy,* **70,** 1962, pp. 241–262.

[157] Davis, R. L., "Structures of Dominance Relations," *Bulletin of Mathematical Biophysics,* **16,** 1954, pp. 131–140.

[158] Dean, J., *Managerial Economics* (New York: Prentice-Hall, 1951).

[159] ———, "Decentralization and Intracompany Pricing," *Harvard Business Review,* **33,** 1955, pp. 65–74.

[160] de Gerstner, F. A. C. (ed.), *A Treatise on Mechanics* (Vienna: 1831–1832).

[161] de la Hire, P., "Examen de la force de l'homme pour mouvoir des fardeaux, tant en levant, qu'en portant et en tirant, laquelle est considerée absolument et par comparison à celle des animaux qui portent et qui tirent comme les chevaux," *Histoire de l'Academie Royale des Sciences,* anné M.DC.XCIX, avec les *Memoires de Mathematique et de Physique* pour la même anné (Paris: Chez Jean Boudot, 1702), pp. 153–162.

[162] de Roover, R., "The Development of Accounting Prior to Luca Pacioli According to the Account Books of Medieval Merchants," in A. C. Littleton, and B. S. Yamey (eds.), *Studies in the History of Accounting* (Homewood, Ill.: R. D. Irwin, 1956).

[163] *Descriptions des arts et metiers faites ou approuvées par Messieurs de l'Academie Royale des Sciences, avec figures en taille-douce* (Paris: Chez Desaint & Saillant, Libraires, 1761).
  a. de Resumur, M., "'Art de l'Epinglier,' avec des additions de M. Du-Hamel du Moncesu, des remarques estraites des memoires de M. Perronet, Inspecteur General des Ponts et Chaussées."

[164] Dethier, V. G., and E. Stellar, *Animal Behavior* (Englewood Cliffs, N. J.: Prentice-Hall, 1961).

[165] Dewey, J., *The School and Society* (*1900*) (Chicago: University of Chicago Press, 1950).

[166] Diebold, J., *Automation: The Advent of the Automatic Factory* (New York: D. Van Nostrand Co., 1952).

[167] Diemer, H., "A Bibliography of Works Management," *Engineering Magazine,* **27,** 1904, pp. 626–642.

[168] Dill, W. R., "Environment as an Influence on Managerial Autonomy," *Administrative Science Quarterly,* **2,** 1958, pp. 409–443.

[169] Drucker, P. F., *Concept of the Corporation* (Boston: Beacon Press, 1960).

[170] Drury, H. B., "Scientific Management, A History and Criticism" in *Studies in History, Economics and Public Law,* **LXC,** No. 2 (New York: Columbia University, 1918).

[171] Dubin, R., "Industrial Workers' Worlds: A Study of the Central Life Interests of Industrial Workers," *Social Problems,* **5,** 1956, pp. 131–142.

[172] Du Bois, H. M., S.J., *Monographie des Betsileo* (Paris: Institut d'Ethnologie, 1938).

[173] Dunford, N., and J. T. Schwartz, *Linear Operators,* Part I (New York: Interscience Publishers, 1958).

[174] Dupin, Baron Charles, *Géométrie et mechaniques des arts et metiers et des beaux-arts* (Paris: Bachelier, 1826).

[175] Durand, W. F., *Robert Henry Thurston* (New York: The American Society of Mechanical Engineers, 1929).

[176] Durkheim, E., *The Division of Labor in Society* (1893), translated by G. Simpson (New York: The Macmillan Co., 1947).

[177] Edwards, R. S., and H. Townsend, *Business Enterprise* (London: Macmillan & Co., Ltd., New York: St. Martin's Press, 1958).

[178] Eisenstadt, S. N., "Primitive Political Systems: A Preliminary Comparative Analysis," *American Anthropologist*, **61**, No. 2, 1959, pp. 200–220.

[179] Elkin, A. P., *The Australian Aborigines* (London: Argus & Robertson, 1948).

[180] Emerson, R. M., "Power-Dependence Relationships," *American Sociological Review*, **27**, 1962, pp. 31–41.

[181] Emmet, Dorothy, *Function, Purpose and Powers* (London: Macmillan & Co., Ltd., 1958).

[182] Enke, S., "On the Economic Management of Large Organizations: A Laboratory Study," *Journal of Business*, **31**, 1958, pp. 280–292.

[183] Etzioni, A., "Two Approaches to Organizational Analysis: A Critique and a Suggestion," *Administrative Science Quarterly*, **5**, 1960, pp. 257–278.

[184] ———, *A Comparative Analysis of Complex Organizations* (Glencoe, Ill.: The Free Press, 1961).

[184a] ——— (ed.), *Complex Organizations: A Sociological Reader* (New York: Holt, Rinehart, and Winston, 1961).

[185] Fältström, E., *Administration i Teori och Tillämpning* (*Study of Administrative Structure in Theory and Practice*) (Stockholm: Foretagsekonomiska Förskningsinstitutet, 1959).

[186] Fayol, H., *General and Industrial Management*, translated by C. Storrs (London: Sir Isaac Pitman & Sons, Ltd., 1949).

[187] Feeney, G. J., "Simulating Marketing Strategy Problems," *Marketing Times*, **2**, 1, Jan., 1959.

[188] Ferguson, A. (ed.), *Natural Philosophy Through the Eighteenth Century and Allied Topics* (London: Taylor & Francis, Ltd., 1948).

[189] Ferguson, L. W., "The Development of Industrial Psychology," in B. Von Haller Gilmer, *Industrial Psychology* (New York: McGraw-Hill Book Co., 1961).

[190] Festinger, L., *A Theory of Cognitive Dissonance* (Evanston, Ill.: Row, Peterson, 1957).

[191] ———, K. Back, S. Schachter, H. H. Kelley, and J. Thibaut, *Theory and Experiment in Social Communication* (Ann Arbor, Mich.: Research Center for Group Dynamics, University of Michigan, 1950).

[192] ———, H. B. Gerard, B. Hymovitch, H. H. Kelley, and B. Raven, "The Influence Process in the Presence of Extreme Deviates," *Human Relations*, **5**, 1952, pp. 327–346.

[193] Fiedler, F. E., *Leader Attitudes and Group Effectiveness* (Urbana, Ill.: University of Illinois Press, 1958).

[194] Filipetti, G., *Industrial Management in Transition*, rev. ed. (Chicago: Richard D. Irwin, 1953).

[195] Fingarette, H., *The Self in Transformation* (New York: Basic Books, 1963).

[196] Fisch, G. G., "Line-Staff is Obsolete," *Harvard Business Review*, **39**, 1961, pp. 67–79.

[197] Fisher, R. A., "Statistical Methods and Scientific Induction," *Journal of the Royal Statistical Society*, Series B (Methodological), **17**, 1955, pp. 69–77.

[198] Flanagan, J. C., *The Aviation Psychology Program in the Army Air Forces*, A.A.F. Aviation Psychology Research Reports, No. 1 (Washington, D. C.: Superintendent of Documents, U. S. Government Printing Office, 1948).

[199] Folley, J. D., Jr., "A Study of Strategies in Procedural Task Performance," Ph.D. thesis (Pittsburgh: Carnegie Institute of Technology, Department of Psychology, 1961).

[200] Forrester, J. W., *Industrial Dynamics* (New York: John Wiley & Sons, 1961).

[201] Fouraker, L. E., M. Shubik, and S. Siegel, "Oligopoly Bargaining: The Quantity Adjuster Models," Pennsylvania State University, *Research Bulletin, No. 20,* July 1961.

[202] Frank, A. G., "Goal Ambiguity and Conflicting Standards: An Approach to the Study of Organizations," *Human Organization,* **17,** 1959, pp. 8–13.

[203] Frank, J. D., "Individual Differences in Certain Aspects of the Level of Aspiration," *American Journal of Psychology,* **47,** 1935, pp. 119–128.

[204] Frank, R. E., A. A. Kuehn, and W. F. Massy, *Quantitative Techniques in Marketing Analysis: Text and Readings* (Homewood, Ill.: R. D. Irwin, 1962).

[205] Freedman, R., A. H. Hawley, W. S. Landecker, and H. M. Miner, *Principles of Sociology* (New York: Henry Holt and Co., 1952).

[206] French, E. G., "Some Characteristics of Achievement Motivation," *Journal of Experimental Psychology,* **50,** 1955, pp. 232–236.

[207] French, J. R. P., J. Israel, and D. Ås, "An Experiment on Participation in a Norwegian Factory," *Human Relations,* **13,** 1960, pp. 3–19.

[208] French, R. L., "Sociometric Measures in Relation to Individual Adjustment and Group Performance Among Naval Recruits," *American Psychologist* (abstract), **4,** 1949, p. 262.

[209] Friedman, M., and L. Savage, "The Utility Analysis of Choices Involving Risk," *Journal of Political Economy,* **56,** 1948, pp. 279–304.

[210] Galanter, E., and G. A. Miller, "Some Comments on Stochastic Models and Psychological Theories," in K. J. Arrow, S. Karlin, and P. Suppes (eds.), *Mathematical Methods in the Social Sciences, 1959,* Stanford Mathematical Studies in the Social Sciences, IV (Stanford, Calif.: Stanford University Press, 1960).

[211] Garner, W. R., *Uncertainty and Structure as Psychological Concepts* (New York: John Wiley & Sons, 1962).

[212] Geisler, M. A., "Integration of Modeling and Simulation in Organization Studies," *Report P-1634* (Santa Monica: The RAND Corporation, March 1959).

[213] Georgopoulos, B., G. Mahoney, and N. Jones, Jr., "A Path-Goal Approach to Productivity," *Journal of Applied Psychology,* **41,** 1957, pp. 345–353.

[214] Getzels, J. W., and E. G. Guba, "Social Behavior and the Administrative Process," *School Review,* **65,** 1957, pp. 423–441.

[215] Gilman, G., "An Inquiry into the Nature and Use of Authority," in M. Haire (ed.), *Organization Theory in Industrial Practice* (New York: John Wiley & Sons, 1962).

[216] Ginzberg, E., and E. Reilley, *Effecting Change in Large Organizations* (New York: Columbia University Press, 1957).

[217] Glanzer, M., and R. Glaser, "Techniques for the Study of Group Structure and Behavior," *Psychological Bulletin,* **58,** No. 1, January 1961, pp. 1–27.

[218] Goffman, E., *The Presentation of Self in Everyday Life* (New York: Doubleday and Co., 1959).

[219] ———, *Encounters* (Indianapolis, Ind.: Bobbs-Merrill Co., 1961).

[220] Goldbeck, R. A., B. B. Bernstein, W. A. Hillex, and M. H. Marx, "Application of the Half-Split Techniques to Problem-Solving Tasks," *Journal of Experimental Psychology*, **53**, 1957, pp. 330–338.

[221] Good, I. J., *Probability and the Weighing of Evidence* (London: Griffin, Ltd., 1950).

[222] ———, "Rational Decisions," *Journal of the Royal Statistical Society*, Ser. B, **14**, 1952, pp. 107–114.

[222a] ———, "How Much Science Can You Have at Your Fingertips," *IBM Journal of Research and Development*, **2**, 1958, pp. 282–288.

[223] ———, "Kinds of Probability," *Science*, **129**, 1959, pp. 443–447.

[224] ———, "Subjective Probability as the Measure of a Non-Measurable Set," *International Congress for Logic, Methodology, and Philosophy of Science*, Stanford University, 1960.

[225] ———, "Weight of Evidence, Corroboration, Explanatory Power, Information, and the Utility of Experiments," *Journal of the Royal Statistical Society*, Ser. B, **22**, 1960, pp. 319–331.

[226] ———, "A Causal Calculus," *British Journal of the Philosophy of Science*, **11**, 1961, pp. 305–318.

[227] ———, *ibid.*, **12**, 1961, pp. 43–51; **13**, 1962, p. 88.

[228] ———, "Amount of Deciding and Decisionary Effort," *Information and Control*, **4**, 1961, pp. 271–281.

[229] ———, "How Rational Should a Manager Be?," *Management Science*, **8**, 1962, pp. 383–393.

[230] Gordon, R. A., *Business Leadership in the Large Corporation* (Washington, D. C.: The Brookings Institution, 1945).

[231] Gore, W. J., and F. S. Silander, "A Bibliographical Essay on Decision Making," *Administrative Science Quarterly*, **4**, 1959, pp. 97–121.

[232] Gouldner, A. W., *Patterns of Industrial Bureaucracy* (Glencoe, Ill.: The Free Press, 1954).

[233] Greenberger, M. (ed.), *Management and the Computer of the Future* (Published jointly by the M.I.T. Press, Cambridge, Mass., and John Wiley & Sons, New York, 1962).
 a. Forrester, J. W., "Managerial Decision Making."
 b. Holt, C. C., "Comments in Response to a Paper by J. W. Forrester."
 c. Miller, G. A., "Comments in Respone to a Paper by H. A. Simon."
 d. Simon, H. A., "Simulation of Human Thinking."

[234] Gregory, O., *Mathematics for Practical Men* (Philadelphia: E. L. Carey and A. Hart, 1834).

[235] Griesmer, J. H., and M. Shubik, "The Theory of Bidding II," *IBM Research Report, RC-688*, May 1962.

[236] Gross, N. C., W. S. Mason, and A. W. McEachern, *Explorations in Role Analysis: Studies of the School Superintendency Role* (New York: John Wiley & Sons, 1958).

[237] Gruchy, A. G., *Modern Economic Thought; The American Contribution* (New York: Prentice-Hall, 1947).

[238] Guest, R. H., *Organizational Change: The Effect of Successful Leadership* (Homewood, Ill.: The Dorsey Press, 1962).

[239] Guetzkow, H., *Simulation in Social Science* (Englewood Cliffs, N. J.: Prentice-Hall, 1962).

[240] Guetzkow, H., and A. E. Bowes, "The Development of Organizations in a Laboratory," *Management Science, 3,* 1957, pp. 380–402.

[241] ———, and W. R. Dill, "Factors in the Organizational Development of Task-Oriented Groups," *Sociometry, 20,* 1957, pp. 175–204.

[242] ———, and H. A. Simon, "The Impact of Certain Communication Nets Upon Organization and Performance in Task-Oriented Groups," *Management Science, 1,* 1955, pp. 233–250.

[243] ———, R. A. Brody, and M. J. Driver, *An Experimental Approach to the n-Country Problem* (St. Louis, Mo.: Washington University, 1961).

[244] Guilford, J. P., *Personality* (New York: McGraw-Hill Book Co., 1959).

[245] Gurin, G., J. Veroff, and S. Feld, *Americans View Their Mental Health* (New York: Basic Books, 1960).

[246] Haberstroh, C. J., "Administration of Safety in the Steel Industry," *Management Science, 7,* 1961, pp. 436–444.

[247] Haire, M. (ed.), *Modern Organization Theory* (New York: John Wiley & Sons, 1959).
   a. Bakke, E. W., "Concept of the Social Organization."
   b. Cyert, R. M., and J. G. March, "A Behavioral Theory of Organizational Objectives."
   c. Marschak, J., "Efficient and Viable Organizational Forms."

[248] Haley, B. F. (ed.), *A Survey of Contemporary Economics,* Vol. II (Homewood, Ill.: Richard D. Irwin, 1952).

[249] Halmos, P. R., "The Basic Concepts of Algebraic Logic," *American Mathematical Monthly, 63,* 1956, pp. 363–387.

[250] Halpin, A. W., and B. J. Winer, "A Factorial Study of the Leader Behavior Descriptions," in R. M. Stogdill, and A. E. Coons (eds.), *Leader Behavior: Its Description and Measurement* (Columbus: The Ohio State University, Bureau of Business Research, Research Monograph No. 88, 1957).

[251] Harberger, A. C., "Monopoly and Resource Allocation," *American Economic Review, 44,* No. 2, 1954, pp. 77–87.

[252] Harbison, F. H., and C. A. Myers, *Management in the Industrial World; An International Analysis* (New York: McGraw-Hill Book Co., 1959).

[253] Harlow, H. F., and C. N. Woolsey (eds.), *Biological and Biochemical Bases of Behavior* (Madison, Wis.: University of Wisconsin Press, 1958).

[254] Hawley, A. H., "Ecology and Human Ecology," *Social Forces, 22,* 1944, pp. 398–405.

[255] Hayek, F., *The Road to Serfdom* (Chicago: University of Chicago Press, 1944).

[256] Haynes, W. W., and J. L. Massie, *Management Analysis, Concepts and Cases* (Englewood Cliffs, N. J.: Prentice-Hall, 1961).

[257] Haythorn, W. W., *Simulation in RAND's Logistics Systems Laboratory* (Santa Monica, Calif.: The RAND Corporation, Report P-1075, 1957).

[258] ———, *ibid.* (Report P-1456, 1958).

[259] Hayward, E. G., *A Classified Guide to the Frederick Winslow Taylor Collection* (Hoboken, N. J.: Stevens Institute of Technology, 1951).

[260] Hebb, D. O., *The Organization of Behavior* (New York: John Wiley & Sons, 1949).

[261] Heider, F., *The Psychology of Interpersonal Relations* (New York: John Wiley & Sons, 1958).

580 BIBLIOGRAPHY

[262] Hemphill, J. K., *Group Dimensions. A Manual for Their Measurement* (Columbus, Ohio: Bureau of Business Research, The Ohio State University, Research Monograph No. 87, 1956).

[263] ———, P. N. Pepinsky, et al., *Leadership Acts: III. The Effects Upon Attempts to Lead of Task Motivation and the Expectancy of Accomplishment of the Task* (Columbus, Ohio: The Ohio State University Research Foundation, 1955).

[264] Henneman, H. G., Jr., *Manpower Management: New Wrapping on Old Merchandise* (Minneapolis, Minn.: Industrial Relations Center, University of Minnesota, 1960).

[265] Henriksson, E., *Frånvaro Från Arbetet (Absence from Work)* (Stockholm: Foretagsekonomiska Förskningsinstitutet, 1954).

[266] Hepburn, W. M., *A Manual of the William Freeman Myrick Goss Library of the History of Engineering and Associated Collection* (Lafayette, Ind.: Purdue University Engineering Experiment Station, 1947).

[267] Herzberg, F., B. Mausner, and B. B. Snyderman, *The Motivation to Work* (New York: John Wiley & Sons, 1959).

[268] Hickey, Carole B., "The Utility of Outcomes as a Function of the Characteristics of the Distribution of Outcomes: The Influence of Extreme End Anchors," Master's thesis (Chapel Hill, N. C.: University of North Carolina, 1962).

[269] Hickman, C. A., and M. H. Kuhn, *Individuals, Groups and Economic Behavior* (New York: The Dryden Press, 1956).

[270] Hill, T. M., and M. J. Gordon, *Accounting: A Management Approach,* rev. ed. (Homewood, Ill.: Richard D. Irwin, 1959).

[271] Hill, W. W., *The Agricultural and Hunting Methods of the Navaho Indians* (New Haven: Yale University Press, 1938).

[272] Hirshleifer, J., "On the Economics of Transfer Pricing," *Journal of Business,* **29,** 1956, pp. 172–184.

[273] Hoagland, J. H., "Charles Babbage—His Life and Works in the Historical Evolution of Management Concepts," Ph.D. thesis (Columbus, Ohio: The Ohio State University, 1954).

[274] ———, "Management Before Frederick Taylor," *Proceedings of the Academy of Management,* December 1955.

[275] ———, "Management Before Frederick Taylor," in P. M. Dauten, Jr. (ed.), *Current Issues and Emerging Concepts in Management* (Boston: Houghton-Mifflin Co., 1962).

[276] Hocking, J. G., and G. S. Young, *Topology* (Reading, Mass.: Addison-Wesley Publishing Co., 1961).

[277] Hoffman, L. R., and N. R. F. Maier, "Quality and Acceptance of Problem Solutions by Members of Homogeneous and Heterogeneous Groups," *Journal of Abnormal and Social Psychology,* **62,** 1961, pp. 401–407.

[278] Hoggatt, A. C., "An Experimental Business Game," *Behavioral Science,* **4,** 1959, pp. 192–203.

[279] Höglund, R., *Företaget i Samhället (The Enterprise in Society)* (Stockholm: Foretagsekonomiska Förskningsinstitutet, 1953).

[280] Holden, P. E., L. S. Fish, and H. L. Smith, *Top Management Organization and Control* (Stanford, Calif.: Stanford University Press, 1941).

[281] Holt, C. C., F. Modigliani, J. F. Muth, and H. A. Simon, *Planning Production, Inventories and Work Force* (Englewood Cliffs, N. J.: Prentice-Hall, 1960).

[282] Homans, G. C., *The Human Group* (New York: Harcourt, Brace, 1950).

[283] ——, *Social Behavior: Its Elementary Forms* (New York: Harcourt, Brace & World, 1961).

[284] Hovland, C. E., I. L. Janis, and H. H. Kelley, *Communication and Persuasion* (New Haven: Yale University Press, 1953).

[285] Howell, W. C., R. T. Christy, and R. G. Kinkade, *System Performance Following Radar Failure in a Simulated Air Traffic Control Situation*, USAF, WADC Technical Report No. 59-573, September 1959.

[286] Hudson, J. W., *The History of Adult Education* (London: Longmen, Brown, Green, Longmans, 1851).

[287] Hughes, E. C., "Institutional Office and the Person," *American Journal of Sociology,* **43,** 1937, pp. 404–413.

[288] Hull, C. L., *Essentials of Behavior* (New Haven: Yale University Press, 1951).

[289] Hunt, E. E. (ed.), *Scientific Management Since Taylor* (New York: McGraw-Hill Book Co., 1924).

[290] Hutchins, J. G. B., "Education for Business Administration," *Administrative Science Quarterly,* **5,** 1960, pp. 279–295.

[291] Ijiri, Y., "Goal Oriented Models for Accounting and Control," Ph.D. thesis (Pittsburgh: Carnegie Institute of Technology, Graduate School of Industrial Administration, 1963).

[292] Jackson, J. M., "Structural Characteristics of Norms," in *The Dynamics of Instructional Groups*, The Fifty-ninth Yearbook of the National Society for the Study of Education, Part II (Chicago: University of Chicago Press, 1960).

[293] Jaques, E., *The Changing Culture of a Factory* (London: Tavistock, 1951).

[294] ——, *The Measurement of Responsibility: A Study of Work, Payment and Individual Capacity* (London: Tavistock Publications, Ltd., 1956, also Cambridge, Mass.: Harvard University Press, 1956).

[295] Jasinski, F. J., "Adapting Organization to New Technology," in E. A. Fleishman (ed.), *Studies in Personnel and Industrial Psychology* (Homewood, Ill.: The Dorsey Press, 1961).

[296] Jenks, L. H., "Early History of a Railway Organization," *Business History Review,* **35,** 1961, pp. 153–179.

[297] Jensen, J., "The Use of Mean Values in Stochastic Linear Programming," Master's thesis (Philadelphia: University of Pennsylvania, 1959).

[298] Jenson, L., *The Postwar Disarmament Negotiations: A Study in American-Soviet Bargaining Behavior* (Ann Arbor, Mich.: University of Michigan, 1962).

[299] Jevons, W. S., *The Theory of Political Economy,* 2nd ed. (London: Macmillan and Co., 1879).

[300] *Journal de l'Ecole Polytechnique* (Paris: l'Imprimerie de la Republique, II).

[301] Kahn, R. L., "The Prediction of Productivity," *Journal of Social Issues,* **12,** 1956, pp. 41–49.

[302] ——, "Human Relations on the Shop Floor," in E. M. Hugh-Jones (ed.), *Human Relations and Modern Management* (Amsterdam, Netherlands: North Holland, 1958).

[303] Kaldor, N., "The Equilibrium of the Firm," *Economic Journal,* **44,** 1934, pp. 60–76.

[304] Kalecki, M., "The Principle of Increasing Risk," *Economica,* **4** (New Series), 1937, pp. 440–447.

[305] Katz, D., N. Maccoby, and N. C. Morse, "Productivity, Supervision and Morale in an Office Situation," *SRC Monograph Series, No. 2* (Ann Arbor, Mich.: Institute for Social Research, University of Michigan, 1950).

[306] ———, ———, G. Gurin, and L. G. Floor, "Productivity, Supervision and Morale Among Railroad Workers," *SRC Monograph Series, No. 5* (Ann Arbor, Mich.: Institute for Social Research, University of Michigan, 1951).

[307] Katzell, R. A., "Contrasting Systems of Work Organization," *American Psychologist,* **17,** 1962, pp. 102–108.

[308] Kaufmann, H., "Task Performance and Responses to Failure as Functions of Imbalance in the Self-Concept," *Psychological Monographs,* **77,** No. 6, 1963.

[309] Kausler, D. H., "A Study of the Relationship between Ego-Involvement and Learning," *Journal of Psychology,* **32,** 1951, pp. 225–230.

[310] Kelley, C. R., *Further Research on the "Predictor Instrument,"* Dunlap & Associates Technical Report No. 252-60-2, Final Report, Contract Nonr-2822(00), 1960.

[311] Kelley, H. H., "Communication in Experimentally Created Hierarchies," *Human Relations,* **4,** 1951, pp. 39–56.

[312] ———, and A. J. Arrowood, "Coalitions in the Triad: Critique and Experiment," *Sociometry,* **23,** 1960, pp. 231–244.

[313] Kemeny, J. G., and J. L. Snell, *Finite Markov Chains* (Princeton, N. J.: D. Van Nostrand Co., 1960).

[314] ———, ———, and G. L. Thompson, *Introduction to Finite Mathematics* (Englewood Cliffs, N. J.: Prentice-Hall, 1957).

[315] Khaldûn, Ibn, *The Muqaddimah,* translated by Franz Rosenthal (New York: Pantheon Books, 1958).

[316] Kimball, D. S., and D. S. Kimball, Jr., *Principles of Industrial Organization,* 6th ed. (New York: McGraw-Hill Book Co., 1947).

[317] Kirby, R. S., and P. G. Laurson, *The Early Years of Modern Civil Engineering* (New Haven, Conn.: Yale University Press, 1932).

[318] Knight, F. H., *Risk, Uncertainty and Profit* (London: The London School of Economics and Political Science, No. 16 in a Series of Reprints of Scarce Tracts in Economic and Political Science, 1946).

[319] ———, *The Economic Organization* (New York: A. M. Kelley, 1951).

[320] Kohler, E. L., *A Dictionary for Accountants,* 2nd ed. (New York: Prentice-Hall, 1957).

[321] Kolmogorov, A. N., *Foundations of the Theory of Probability* (New York: Chelsea Publishing Co., 1950).

[322] Koopman, B. O., "The Theory of Search II: Target Detection," *Operations Research,* **4,** 1956, pp. 503–531.

[323] Koopmans, T. C., "Analysis of Production as an Efficient Combination of Activities," in T. C. Koopmans (ed.), *Activity Analysis of Production and Allocation,* Cowles Commission Monograph No. 13 (New York: John Wiley & Sons, 1951).

[324] Kruisinga, H. J. (ed.), *The Balance Between Centralization and Decentralization in Managerial Control* (Leiden: H. E. Stenfert Kroese, 1954).

[325] Kuehn, A. A., "An Analysis of the Dynamics of Consumer Behavior and Its Implications for Marketing Management," Ph.D. thesis (Pittsburgh: Carnegie Institute of Technology, Graduate School of Industrial Administration, 1958).

[326] Kuhn, H. W., and A. W. Tucker, "Nonlinear Programming," in J. Neyman (ed.), *Proceedings of the Second Berkeley Symposium on Mathematical Statistics and Probability* (Berkeley, Calif.: University of California Press, 1951).

[327] Kullback, S., *Information Theory and Statistics* (New York: John Wiley & Sons, 1959).

[328] Kyle, J. E., "Personnel Administration Must Embark on a Program of Rigorous Self-Development," *Personnel and Industrial Relations Journal,* **8,** 1961, pp. 9–17.

[329] L'Abbe, M., "Structures algebrique suggerées par la logic mathematique," *Bulletin Soc. Math. France,* **86,** pp. 299–314.

[330] Lardner, D., *Railway Economy: A Treatise on the New Art of Transport, Its Management, Prospects and Relations* (London: Taylor, Walton and Maberly, 1850).

[331] Larson, H. M., *Guide to Business History* (Cambridge, Mass.: Harvard University Press, 1950).

[332] Lawrence, P. R., *The Changing of Organizational Behavior Patterns* (Boston: Harvard University, Graduate School of Business Administration, Division of Research, 1958).

[332a] Leacock, S., "A, B, and C: The Human Element in Mathematics," *Literary Lapses* (New York: Dodd, Mead, 1944). Reprinted in *Laugh with Leacock* (New York: Apollo Editions, 1961).

[333] Leavitt, H. J., "Some Effects of Certain Communication Patterns on Group Performance," *Journal of Abnormal and Social Psychology,* **46,** 1951, pp. 38–50.

[334] ———, *Managerial Psychology* (Chicago: Phoenix Books, The University of Chicago Press, 1962).

[335] ———, "Management According to Task: Organizational Differentiation," *Management International,* **1,** 1962, pp. 13–34.

[336] ———, "Unhuman Organizations," *Harvard Business Review,* **40,** July–August 1962, pp. 90–98.

[336a] ——— (ed.), *The Social Science of Organizations: Four Perspectives* (Englewood Cliffs, N. J.: Prentice-Hall, 1963).

[337] ———, and T. L. Whisler, "Management in the 1980's," *Harvard Business Review,* **36,** November–December 1958, pp. 41–48.

[338] Le Bon, G., *The Crowd* (London: Ernest Benn, Ltd., 1938).

[339] Lenin, N., *What Is to be Done?* (c 1929) (New York: International Publisher, 1947).

[340] Lepawsky, A., *Administration* (New York: Alfred A. Knopf, 1949).

[341] Levine, S., and P. E. White, "Exchange as a Conceptual Framework for the Study of Interorganizational Relationships," *Administrative Science Quarterly,* **5,** 1961, pp. 583–601.

[342] Levitan, R., and M. Shubik, "A Business Game for Teaching and Research Purposes: Part I, A General Description of the Game," *IBM Research Report No. RC-730,* July 1962.

584   BIBLIOGRAPHY

[343] Levitan, R., and M. Shubik, "A Business Game for Teaching and Research Purposes: Part II, A Theory and Mathematical Structure of the Game," *IBM Research Report No. RC-731*, July 1962.

[344] Lewin, Kurt, *Field Theory in Social Science* (New York: Harper, 1951).

[345] ———, R. Lippitt, and R. K. White, "Patterns of Aggressive Behavior in Experimentally Created 'Social Climates'," *Journal of Social Psychology*, **10**, 1939, pp. 271–299.

[346] ———, T. Dembo, L. Festinger, and P. S. Sears, "Level of Aspiration," in J. McV. Hunt (ed.), *Personality and the Behavior Disorders* (New York: The Ronald Press Company, 1944).

[347] Lewis, J. S., *The Commercial Organization of Factories* (London: E. & F. N. Spon, 1896).

[348] Likert, R., "Measuring Organizational Performance," in E. A. Fleishman (ed.), *Studies in Personnel and Industrial Psychology* (Homewood, Ill.: The Dorsey Press, 1961).

[349] ———, "An Emerging Theory of Organization, Leadership and Management," in L. Petrullo, and B. M. Bass (eds.), *Leadership and Interpersonal Behavior* (New York: Holt, Rinehart & Winston, 1961).

[350] ———, *New Patterns of Management* (New York: McGraw-Hill Book Co., 1961).

[351] Linton, R., *The Study of Man* (New York: Appleton-Century-Crofts, 1936).

[352] ———, *The Cultural Background of Personality* (New York: Appleton-Century-Crofts, 1945).

[353] Lippitt, R., J. Watson, and B. Westley, *The Dynamics of Planned Change* (New York: Harcourt, Brace, 1958).

[354] Lomont, J. S., *Applications of Finite Groups* (New York: Academic Press, 1959).

[355] Lowell, E. L., "The Effect of Need for Achievement on Learning and Speed of Performance," *Journal of Psychology*, **33**, 1952, pp. 31–40.

[356] Luce, R. D., and H. Raiffa, *Games and Decisions: Introduction and Critical Survey* (New York: John Wiley & Sons, 1957).

[357] Lyons, Sir Henry, *The Royal Society, 1660–1940* (Cambridge: The University Press, 1944).

[358] Maccoby, E. E., T. M. Newcomb, and E. L. Hartley (eds.), *Readings in Social Psychology* (New York: Holt, 1958).
  a. Leavitt, H. J., "Some Effects of Certain Communication Patterns on Group Performance."
  b. Lippitt, R., and R. K. Whyte, "An Experimental Study of Leadership and Group Life."

[359] MacDonald, D., *The Ford Foundation* (New York: Reynal & Co., 1956).

[360] Machiavelli, N., *The Prince* (1640) (New York: Random House, Modern Library College Edition, 1950).

[361] ———, *The Discourses* (New York: Random House, Modern Library Edition, 1950).

[362] Mahdi, Muhsin, *Ibn Khaldûn's Philosophy of History* (London: George Allen and Unwin, Ltd., 1957).

[363] Maher, J. E., "Union, Nonunion Wage Differentials," *American Economic Review*, **46**, No. 3, 1956, pp. 336–352.

[364] Mannheim, Karl, *Ideology and Utopia* (New York: Harcourt, Brace and Co., 1936).

[365] March, J. G., "An Introduction to the Theory and Measurement of Influence," *The American Political Science Review*, **49**, 1955, pp. 431–451.

[366] ———(ed.), *Handbook of Organizations* (Chicago: Rand-McNally, 1964).

[367] ———, and H. A. Simon, *Organizations* (New York: John Wiley & Sons, 1958).

[368] Marschak, J., "Elements for a Theory of Teams," *Management Science*, I, No. 2, January 1955, pp. 127–137.

[369] ———, "Problems in Management Economics," Working Paper No. 24 (Los Angeles: Western Management Sciences Institute, University of California, 1962).

[370] Marschak, T., "Centralization and Decentralization in Economic Organizations," *Econometrica*, **27**, No. 3, 1959, pp. 399–430.

[371] Martin, N. H., and J. R. Sims, "The Problem of Power," in W. L. Warner, and N. H. Martin (eds.), *Industrial Man* (New York: Harper, 1959).

[372] Marx, M. H., R. A. Goldbeck, and B. B. Bernstein, "An Apparatus for Investigating the Methods Humans Use in Solving Complex Problems," *The American Journal of Psychology*, **69**, 1956, pp. 462–465.

[373] Maunier, Rene, *La construction collective de la maison en Kabylie* (Paris: Institut d'Ethnologie, 1926).

[374] Mautz, R. K., and H. A. Sharaf, *The Philosophy of Auditing, American Accounting Association Monograph, No. 6* (Menasha, Wisconsin: George Banta Publishing Co., 1961).

[375] McClelland, D. C., *The Achieving Society* (Princeton, N. J.: Van Nostrand, 1961).

[376] ———, J. W. Atkinson, R. A. Clark, and E. L. Lowell, *The Achievement Motive* (New York: Appleton-Century-Crofts, 1953).

[377] McGehee, W., and P. W. Thayer, *Training in Business and Industry* (New York: John Wiley & Sons, 1961).

[378] McGrath, J. E., P. G. Nordlie, and W. S. Vaughan, *A Systematic Framework for Comparison of System Research Methods* (Arlington, Va.: Human Sciences Research, Technical Note HSR-59/7, Contract No. Nonr 2525-(00), 1960).

[379] McGregor, D., "Getting Effective Leadership in the Industrial Organization," *Advanced Management*, **9**, 1944, pp. 148–153.

[380] ———, *The Human Side of Enterprise* (New York: McGraw-Hill Book Co., 1960).

[381] McKeon, R. P. (ed.), *The Basic Works of Aristotle* (New York: Random House, 1941).

[382] McMurry, R. N., "The Case for Benevolent Autocracy," *Harvard Business Review*, **36**, No. 1, 1958, pp. 82–90.

[383] McNulty, J. E., *Some Economic Aspects of Business Organization* (Philadelphia: University of Pennsylvania Press, 1964).

[384] ———, "Organizational Change in Growing Enterprises," *Administrative Science Quarterly*, **7**, 1962, pp. 1–21.

[385] McRuer, D. T., and E. S. Krendel, *Dynamic Response of Human Operators*, USAF, WADC Technical Report No. 56-524, 1957.

[386] McWhinney, W. H., "A Study of Self-Organization in the Communications Network Experiments," Ph.D. thesis (Pittsburgh: Carnegie Institute of Technology, Graduate School of Industrial Administration, 1964).

[387] Meier, R. L., "Explorations in the Realm of Organization Theory IV: The Simulation of Social Organization," *Behavioral Science,* **6,** 1961, pp. 232–248.

[388] Meriam, L., and L. F. Schmeckebier, *Reorganization of the National Government* (Washington, D. C.: The Brookings Institution, 1939).

[389] Merton, R. K., "Bureaucratic Structure and Personality," *Social Forces,* **18,** 1940, pp. 560–568.

[390] ———, "The Role-Set: Problems in Sociological Theory," *British Journal of Sociology,* **8,** 1957, pp. 106–120.

[391] ———, *Social Theory and Social Structure,* rev. ed. (Glencoe, Ill.: The Free Press, 1957).

[392] ———, "Social Problems and Sociological Theory," in R. K. Merton and R. A. Nisbet (eds.), *Contemporary Social Problems* (New York: Harcourt, Brace and World, 1961).

[393] ———, A. Gray, B. Hockey, and H. C. Selvin (eds.), *Reader in Bureaucracy* (Glencoe, Ill.: The Free Press, 1952).
   a. Davis, A. K., "Bureaucratic Patterns in the Navy Officer Corps."
   b. Weber, Max, "The Essentials of Bureaucratic Organization: An Ideal-Type Construction."

[394] Mesarović, M. D., "On Self-Organizing Control Systems," *Proceedings of the Third Symposium on Discrete Adaptive Systems,* AIEE, 1962.

[395] ———, "On Self-Organizational Systems," *Proceedings of the Third Conference on Self-Organizing Systems,* in M. C. Yovits, G. T. Jacobi, and G. D. Goldstein (eds.) (Washington, D. C.: Spartan Press, 1962).

[396] ———, "Foundations for a General Systems Theory," in *General Systems Theory* (New York: John Wiley & Sons, 1963).

[397] ———, and D. P. Eckman, "On Some Basic Concepts of the General Systems Theory," *Proceedings of the Third International Congress on Cybernetics,* Namur, Belgium, August 1961.

[398] Michels, R., *Political Parties* (New York: Dover Publications, 1959).

[399] Miles, M. B., *Learning to Work in Groups* (New York: Bureau of Publications, Teachers College, Columbia University, 1959).

[400] Milgram, S., "Nationality and Conformity," *Scientific American,* **205,** December 1961, pp. 45–51.

[401] Miller, A. L., "Evaluation of Prospective Social Relationships: A Function of Comparison Level and Estimated Reward Level," *Journal of Abnormal and Social Psychology,* **67,** No. 5, 1963, pp. 437–445.

[402] Miller, G. A., "The Magical Number Seven, Plus or Minus Two: Some Limits on Our Capacity for Processing Information," *Psychological Review,* **63,** 1956, pp. 81–97.

[403] Mooney, J. D., *The Principles of Organization,* rev. ed. (New York: Harper & Row, 1947).

[404] Moore, W. E., and A. S. Feldman (eds.), *Labor-Commitment and Social Change in Developing Areas* (New York: Social Science Research Council, 1960).

[405] Morgenstern, O., "The Command and Control Structure," *Econometric Research Program, Research Memo. No. 47,* Princeton University, Princeton, New Jersey, 1962.

[406] Morse, N. C., *Satisfactions in the White-Collar Job* (Ann Arbor, Mich.: Institute for Social Research, University of Michigan, 1953).

[407] Morse, N. C., and E. Reimer, "The Experimental Change of a Major Organizational Variable," *Journal of Abnormal and Social Psychology,* **52,** 1956, pp. 120–129.

[408] Mott, F. L., *A History of American Magazines, 1741–1850* (Cambridge, Mass.: Harvard University Press, 1938).

[409] Mulder, M., "Power and Satisfaction in Task-Oriented Groups," *Acta Psychologica,* **16,** 1959, pp. 178–225.

[410] Münsterburg, H., *Psychology, General and Applied* (New York: D. Appleton, 1914).

[411] Murdock, G. P., *Outline of Cultural Materials* (New Haven, Conn.: Human Relations Area Files, 1954).

[412] ———, "World Ethnographic Sample," *American Anthropologist,* **59,** August 1957, pp. 664–687.

[413] ———, C. J. Ford, A. E. Hudson, et al., *Outline of Cultural Materials* (New Haven, Conn.: Human Relations Area Files, 1950).

[414] National Association of Accountants, "Current Applications of Direct Costing," *Research Report No. 37* (New York: National Association of Accountants, 1961).

[415] Neiman, L. J., and J. W. Hughes, "The Problem of the Concept of Role: A Re-Survey of the Literature," *Social Forces,* **30,** 1951, pp. 141–149.

[416] Newcomb, T. M., "Social Psychological Theory: Integrating Individual and Social Approaches," in J. H. Rohrer, and M. Sherif (eds.), *Social Psychology at the Crossroads* (New York: Harper, 1951).

[417] ———, "An Approach to the Study of Communicative Acts," *Psychological Review,* **60,** 1953, pp. 393–404.

[418] Newcomer, M., *The Big Business Executive* (New York: Columbia University Press, 1955).

[419] Newell, A., and H. A. Simon, "What Have Computers to Do with Management?" in G. P. Shultz and T. L. Whisler (eds.), *Management Organization and the Computer* (Glencoe, Ill.: The Free Press, 1960).

[420] ———, and ———, "Computer Simulation of Human Thinking," *Science,* **134,** 1961, pp. 2011–2017.

[421] ———, J. C. Shaw, and H. A. Simon, "Elements of a Theory of Human Problem Solving," *Psychological Review,* **65,** 1958, pp. 151–166.

[422] Nicholson, J., *The Operative Mechanic and British Machinist: Being a Practical Display of the Manufactories and Mechanical Arts of The United Kingdom* (Philadelphia: H. C. Carey and I. Lee, 1826).

[423] Odiorne, G. S., "Company Growth and Personnel Administration," *Personnel,* **37,** 1960, pp. 32–41.

[424] Oeser, D. A., and F. Harary, "A Mathematical Model for Structural Role Theory I," *Human Relations,* **15,** 1962, pp. 89–109.

[425] Ore, Ø., *Theory of Graphs* (Providence, R. I.: American Mathematical Society, 1962).

[426] Orwant, C., and A. Rapoport, "Experimental Games: A Review," *Behavioral Science,* **7,** 1962, pp. 1–37.

[427] Park, R. E., and W. Burgess, *Introduction to the Science of Sociology* (Chicago: The University of Chicago Press, 1936).

[428] Parsons, T., *The Structure of Social Action* (Glencoe, Ill.: The Free Press, 1949).

[429] Parsons, T., *Structure and Process in Modern Society* (Glencoe, Ill.: The Free Press, 1960).

[430] ——, E. A. Shils (eds.), *Toward a General Theory of Action* (Cambridge: Harvard University Press, 1951).

[431] Paulsson Frenckner, T., *Internprestationer Som Företagsekonomiskt Bedömningsproblem (Intra-Company Pricing)* (Stockholm: Foretagsekonomiska Förskningsinstitutet, 1954).

[432] ——, *Bestimmung des Produktionsprogramms (Economic Production Planning and Linear Programming)* (Stockholm: Foretagsekonomiska Förskningsinstitutet, 1958).

[433] Penrose, E. T., *The Theory of the Growth of the Firm* (New York: John Wiley & Sons, 1959).

[434] Pepinsky, Pauline N., et al., "The Research Team and Its Organizational Environment," Paper presented at AFSDR Conference on Research on Organization Behavior, Athens, Ga., May 1962.

[435] ——, J. K. Hemphill, and R. N. Shevitz, *Leadership Acts:* II. The Relationship Between Need for Achievement and Affiliation and Attempts to Lead Under Conditions of Acceptance and Rejection (Columbus: The Ohio State University Research Foundation, 1955).

[436] Pepinsky, H. B., P. N. Pepinsky, and W. P. Pavlik, *Motivational Factors in Individual and Group Productivity,* I. Successful Task Accomplishment as Related to Task Relevant Personal Beliefs (Columbus: The Ohio State University Research Foundation, 1956).

[437] Person, H. S. (ed.), *Scientific Management* (New York: Harper and Brothers, 1947).

[438] Petersen, E., and E. G. Plowman, *Business Organization and Management,* rev. ed. (Chicago: Richard D. Irwin, 1948).

[439] Pribram, Karl, "Comparative Neurology and the Evolution of Behavior," in A. Roe, and G. G. Simpson (eds.), *Behavior and Evolution* (New Haven: Yale University Press, 1958).

[440] ——, "A Review of Theory in Physiological Psychology," *Annual Review of Psychology,* **11** (Palo Alto, Calif.: Annual Reviews, 1960).

[441] *Proceedings of the 1st Congress on the Information System Sciences* (Bedford, Mass.: Mitre Corp., 1962).
   a. Davis, R. M., "Techniques of Information System Design."
   b. Mesarović, M. D., "Multi-Level Systems and Information Processing."
   c. Thompson, F. B., "Fundamentals Underlying Military Information System Design Techniques."

[442] Prosser, C. L., and F. A. Brown, Jr., *Comparative Animal Physiology* (Philadelphia: W. B. Saunders Co., 1961).

[443] Quandt, R., "Probabilistic Errors in the Leontief System," *Naval Research Logistics Quarterly,* **5**, No. 2, 1958, pp. 155–171.

[444] Ramfalk, C. W., *Top Management Selection* (Stockholm: Swedish Council for Personnel Administration, 1957).

[445] Rämstrom, D., *Försaljningsorganisatoriska Problem: (Problems of Sales Organization)* (Stockholm: Foretagsekonomiska Förskningsinstitutet, 1959).

[446] Remitz, U., *Professional Satisfaction Among Swedish Bank Employees* (Copenhagen: Ejnar Munksgaard, 1960).

[447] *Report of the Commissioner of Education for the Year 1899–1900* (Washington: U. S. Government Printing Office, 1901).

[448] *Report of the President's Committee on Administrative Management in the Government of the United States* (Washington, D. C.: U. S. Government Printing Office, 1937).

[449] Reza, F. M., *An Introduction to Information Theory* (New York: McGraw-Hill Book Co., 1961).

[450] Riesman, D., *The Lonely Crowd* (New Haven, Conn.: Yale University Press, 1950).

[451] Riordan, J., *An Introduction to Combinatorial Analysis* (New York: John Wiley & Sons, 1958).

[452] Roethlisberger, F. J., and W. J. Dickson, *Management and the Worker* (Cambridge, Mass.: Harvard University Press, 1941).

[453] Rogers, C. R., *Counseling and Psychotherapy* (Boston: Houghton Mifflin Co., 1942).

[454] Rome, S. C., and B. K. Rome, *The Leviathan Technique for Large-Group Analysis* (Santa Monica, Calif.: System Development Corp., 1960).

[455] Ross, A. M., "The Influence of Unionism on Earnings," *Quarterly Journal of Economics,* **62,** No. 2, 1948, pp. 263–286.

[456] ———, *Business Concentration and Price Policy* (Princeton, N. J.: Princeton University Press, 1955).

[457] Rubenstein, A. H., and C. J. Haberstroh (eds.), *Some Theories of Organization* (Homewood, Ill.: Richard D. Irwin, 1960).
   a. Chowdhry, K., and A. K. Pal, "Production Planning and Organization Morale."
   b. Haberstroh, C. J., "Control as an Organizational Process."
   c. McGregor, D. M., "The Human Side of Enterprise."
   d. Rubenstein, A. H., "Setting Criteria for R and D."
   e. Simon, H. A., "Comments on the Theory of Organizations."

[458] Sanders, J. L., "The Application of a Theory of Multi-Level Systems to Optimization Problems," Ph.D. thesis (Cleveland: Case Institute of Technology, 1963).

[459] Sarbin, T. R., "Role Theory," in G. Lindzey (ed.), *Handbook of Social Psychology,* Vol. I (Cambridge: Addison-Wesley Publishing Co., 1954).

[460] Schachter, S., "Deviation, Rejection, and Communication," *Journal of Abnormal and Social Psychology,* **46,** 1951, pp. 190–207.

[461] ———, N. Ellertson, D. McBride, and D. Gregory, "An Experimental Study of Cohesiveness and Productivity," *Human Relations,* **4,** 1951, pp. 229–238.

[462] Schanck, R. L., "A Study of a Community and Its Groups and Institutions Conceived of as Behaviors of Individuals," *Psychological Monographs,* **43,** No. 2, 1932, pp. 1–133.

[463] Scheff, T. J., "Control Over Policy by Attendants in a Mental Hospital," *Journal of Health and Human Behavior,* **2,** 1961, pp. 93–105.

[464] Schlaifer, R., *Probability and Statistics for Business Decisions* (New York: McGraw-Hill Book Co., 1959).

[465] Scott, W. A., "Personal Values and Group Interaction," in D. Willner (ed.), *Decisions, Values and Groups* (New York: Pergamon Press, 1960).

[466] Seashore, S. E., *Group Cohesiveness in the Industrial Work Group* (Ann Arbor, Mich.: Institute for Social Research, University of Michigan, 1954).

[467] Seashore, S. E., and D. G. Bowers, *Communications and Decision Processes as Determinants of Organizational Effectiveness,* AFOSR Contract No. AF 49 (638)-1032 (Ann Arbor, Mich.: Institute for Social Research, University of Michigan, 1962).

[468] Segerstedt, T. T., and A. Lundquist, *Människan i Industrisamhället: Arbetslivet (Man in Industrialized Society: Life Within the Plant)* (Stockholm: Studieförbundet Näringsliv och Samhälle, 1952).

[469] ———, *Människan i Industrisamhället: Fritidsliv Samhällsliv (Man in Industrialized Society: Leisure Time and Community Life)* (Stockholm: Studieförbundet Näringsliv och Samhälle, 1955).

[470] Sells, S. B. (ed.), *Symposium on Pattern Analysis* (Randolph AFB, Texas: Air University, USAF School of Aviation Medicine, 1955).

[471] ———, "Psychological Methods of Aircrew Selection," in H. G. Armstrong (ed.), *Aerospace Medicine* (Baltimore: Williams and Wilkens Co., 1960).

[472] ———, "Group Behavior Problems in Flight," in S. B. Sells, and C. A. Berry (eds.), *Human Factors in Jet and Space Travel* (New York: Williams and Wilkins, 1961).

[473] ———, *Essentials of Psychology* (New York: The Ronald Press Co., 1962).

[474] ——— (ed.), *Symposium on Dimensions of Stimulus Situations Which Account for Behavior Variance* (Fort Worth, Texas: Texas Christian University, Contract Nonr-3436(00), Technical Report No. 1, 1962).

[475] ——— (ed.), *Stimulus Determinants of Behavior* (New York: The Ronald Press Co., 1963).
   a. Bass, B. M., "Experimenting with Simulated Manufacturing Organizations."
   b. Cattell, R. B., "Formulating the Environmental Situation, and Its Perception, in Behavior Theory."

[476] Selznick, P., *TVA and the Grass Roots* (Berkeley: University of California Press, 1949).

[477] ———, *Leadership in Administration* (Evanston, Ill.: Row, Peterson, 1957).

[478] Sengupta, S. S., and G. H. Symonds, *A Model of Competitive Business Behavior* (Cleveland, O.: Case Institute of Technology, 1963).

[479] Shaw, M. E., "Some Effects of Unequal Distribution of Information Upon Group Performance in Various Communication Nets," *Journal of Abnormal and Social Psychology,* **49,** 1954, pp. 547–553.

[480] ———, "Communication Patterns in Small Groups," *Research Review,* 1955, pp. 11–12.

[481] Shelly, M. W., "A Topological Approach to the Measurement of Social Phenomena," in J. Griswell, H. Solomon, and P. Suppes (eds.), *Mathematical Methods in Small Group Processes* (Stanford, Calif.: Stanford University Press, 1962).

[482] ———, "Personal Structures I: A Basis for Personal Structures," *Psychological Reports,* **13,** 1963, pp. 3–17.

[483] ———, "Personal Structures II: Personal Substructures," *Psychological Reports,* **13,** 1963, pp. 935–949.

[484] ———, "The Response in Personal Structures," *Psychological Reports,* **14,** 1964 (forthcoming).

[485] ———, "Personal Structures III: The Structure of Their Variety" (in preparation, 1963).

[486] Shelly, M. W., and G. L. Bryan (eds.), *Human Judgments and Optimality* (New York: John Wiley & Sons, 1964).
  a. Anscombe, F. J., "Some Remarks on Bayesian Statistics."
  b. Aumann, R. J., "Subjective Programming."
  c. Churchman, C. W., and H. Eisenberg, "Deliberation and Judgment."
  d. Radner, R., "Practical Mathematical Specification of Goals for Decision Problems."
  e. Reitman, W. R., "Hueristic Decision Procedures, Open Constraints and the Structure of Ill-Defined Problems."
  f. Shelly, M. W., "Intensional Optimization and a 'Psychotherapeutic' Situation."
  g. Shepard, R. N., "On Subjectively Optimum Selection Among Multi-Attribute Alternatives."

[487] ———, and J. C. Gilchrist, "Some Effects of Communication Requirements in Group Structures," *Journal of Social Psychology,* **48,** 1958, pp. 37–44.

[488] Sherif, M., *The Psychology of Social Norms* (New York: Harper and Bros., 1936).

[489] ———, and C. W. Sherif, *An Outline of Social Psychology* (New York: Harper, 1956).

[490] Shubik, M. (ed.), *Readings in Game Theory and Political Behavior* (New York: Doubleday and Co., 1954).

[491] ———, "Economics, Management Science and Operations Research," *The Review of Economics and Statistics,* **40,** 1958, pp. 214–220.

[492] ———, *Strategy and Market Structure: Competition, Oligopoly, and the Theory of Games* (New York: John Wiley & Sons, 1959).

[493] ———, "Games, Decisions and Industrial Organization," *Management Science,* **6,** 1960, pp. 455–474.

[494] ———, "Approaches to the Study of Decision-Making Relevant to the Firm," *The Journal of Business,* **34,** 1961, pp. 101–118.

[495] ———, "Incentives, Decentralized Control, the Assignment of Joint Costs and Internal Pricing," *Management Science,* **8,** 1962, pp. 325–343.

[496] ———, "Some Experimental Non-Zero Sum Games with Lack of Information About the Rules," *Management Science,* **8,** 1962, pp. 215–234.

[496a] Shultz, G. P., and T. L. Whister (eds.), *Management Organization and the Computer* (Glencoe, Ill.: The Free Press, 1960).

[497] Shure, G. H., M. S. Rogers, I. M. Larsen, and J. Tassone, "Group Planning and Task Effectiveness," *Sociometry,* **25,** 1962, pp. 263–282.

[498] Siegel, A. I., J. J. Wolf, and K. Crain, *Techniques for Evaluating Operator Loading in Man-Machine Systems. A Model for Digital Simulation of One- and Two-Operator Man-Machine Systems,* Applied Psychological Services, ONR Contract No. Nonr-2492(00), March 1961.

[499] Siegel, S., and L. E. Fouraker, *Bargaining and Group Decision-Making: Experiments in Bilateral Monopoly* (New York: McGraw-Hill Book Co., 1960).

[500] Simon, H. A., *Administrative Behavior* (New York: The Macmillan Co., 1957).

[501] ———, *Models of Man* (New York: John Wiley & Sons, 1957).

[502] ———, *The New Science of Management Decision* (New York: Harper and Bros., 1960).

[503] Simon, H. A., H. Guetzkow, G. Kozmetsky, and G. Tyndall, *Centraliza-tion vs. Decentralization in Organizing the Controller's Department* (New York: The Controllership Foundation, 1954).

[504] Simons, H. C., *Economic Policy for a Free Society* (Chicago: University of Chicago Press, 1948).

[505] Skinner, B. F., *Walden Two* (New York: The Macmillan Co., 1948).

[506] Small, A. W., "Fifty Years of Sociology in the United States (1865–1915)," *The American Journal of Sociology,* **21,** No. 6, 1916, pp. 721–864.

[507] ———, *Origins of Sociology* (Chicago: The University of Chicago Press, 1924).

[508] Smith, C. A. B., "Consistency in Statistical Inference and Decision," *Journal of the Royal Statistical Society,* B, **23,** 1961, pp. 1–37.

[509] Smuts, J. C., *Holism and Evolution* (New York: The Macmillan Co., 1926).

[510] Snyder, R. C., and G. D. Paige, "The United States Decision to Resist Aggression in Korea," *Administrative Science Quarterly,* **3,** 1958, pp. 341–378.

[511] Sorel, G., *Reflections on Violence* (Glencoe, Ill.: The Free Press, 1950).

[512] Sotheby, Wilkinson, and Hodge, *Mathematical and Scientific Library of the Late Charles Babbage* (London: C. F. Hodgson and Son, 1872).

[513] Sprague, C. F., "Self-Organizational Aspects in General Systems Theory Models of Organizations," Ph.D. thesis (Cleveland: Case Institute of Tech-nology, 1963).

[514] Spriegel, W. R., *Industrial Management,* 4th ed. (New York: John Wiley & Sons, 1947).

[515] Sprowls, R. C., and M. Asimow, "A Model of Customer Behavior for the Task Manufacturing Corporation," *Management Science,* **8,** 1962, pp. 311–324.

[516] Stedry, A., *Budget Control and Cost Behavior* (Englewood Cliffs, N. J.: Prentice-Hall, 1960).

[517] ———, "Aspiration Levels, Attitudes and Performance in a Goal-Oriented Situation," *Industrial Management Review,* **3,** No. 2, 1962, pp. 60–76.

[518] ———, and A. Charnes, "Exploratory Models in the Theory of Budget Control," ONR Research Memo No. 43 for the Project, Temporal Plan-ning and Management Decision Under Risk and Uncertainty (Evanston, Ill.: The Technological Institute, Northwestern University, 1962).

[519] Stene, E. O., "An Approach to a Science of Administration," *American Political Science Review,* **34,** 1940, pp. 1124–1137.

[520] Stephan, F. F., and E. G. Mishler, "The Distribution of Participation in Small Groups: An Exponential Approximation," *American Sociological Review,* **17,** 1952, pp. 598–608.

[521] Stern, D. H., "Some Notes on Oligopoly Theory and Experiments," West-ern Management Science Institute, *Research Report 75,* May 1962.

[522] Steuart, Sir James, *An Inquiry into the Principles of Political Economy* (London: A. Millar and T. Cadell, 1767).

[523] Stewart, L., "Management Games Today," in J. M. Kibbee, C. J. Craft, and B. Nanus (eds.), *Management Games: A New Technique for Execu-tive Development* (New York: Reinhold Publishing Corp., 1961).

[524] Stigler, G. J., *The Theory of Price* (New York: The Macmillan Co., 1947).

[525] Stinchcombe, A. L., "Comment on S. H. Udy's 'Technical and Institutional Factors in Production Organization: A Preliminary Model,'" *American Journal of Sociology*, **67**, November 1961, pp. 255–259.

[526] Stogdill, R. M., *Leadership and Structures of Personal Interaction* (Columbus: The Ohio State University, Bureau of Business Research, Research Monograph No. 84, 1957).

[527] ——, *Individual Behavior and Group Achievement* (Fair Lawn, N. J.: Oxford University Press, 1959).

[528] Strauss, G., "Tactics of Lateral Relationship: The Purchasing Agent," *Administrative Science Quarterly*, **7**, 1962, pp. 161–186.

[529] Strother, G. B. (ed.), *Social Science Approaches to Business Behavior* (Homewood, Ill.: The Dorsey Press, and Richard D. Irwin, 1962).
   a. Argyris, C., "The Integration of the Individual and the Organization."
   b. Haire, M., "The Concept of Power and the Concept of Man."

[530] Sun Tzu, "The Art of War," in Brig. Gen. T. R. Philips (ed.), *Roots of Strategy* (Harrisburg, Pa.: The Military Service Publishing Co., 1940).

[531] Swanson, G. E., T. M. Newcomb, and E. L. Hartley (eds.), *Readings in Social Psychology*, 2nd ed. (New York: Holt, 1952).
   a. Hammond, S., "Stratification in an Australian City."
   b. Lewin, K., "Group Decision and Social Change."

[532] Sykes, C., *Orde Wingate* (London: Collins, 1959).

[533] Sykes, G. M., "The Corruption of Authority and Rehabilitation," in A. Etzioni (ed.), *Complex Organizations: A Sociological Reader* (New York: Holt, Rinehart, and Winston, 1961).

[534] Tannenbaum, A. S., "The Concept of Organizational Control," *The Journal of Social Issues*, **12**, 1956, pp. 50–60.

[535] ——, "Control and Effectiveness in a Voluntary Organization," *American Journal of Sociology*, **67**, 1961, pp. 33–46.

[536] Tannenbaum, R., I. R. Weschler, and F. Massarik, *Leadership and Organization* (New York: McGraw-Hill Book Co., 1961).

[537] Taussig, F. W., and C. S. Joslyn, *American Business Leaders* (New York: The Macmillan Co., 1932).

[538] Taylor, F. W., *The Principles of Scientific Management* (New York: Harper and Bros., 1911).

[539] ——, *Scientific Management* (New York: Harper, 1947).

[540] Thibaut, J. W., "An Experimental Study of the Cohesiveness of Underprivileged Groups," *Human Relations*, **3**, 1950, pp. 251–278.

[541] ——, and H. H. Kelley, *The Social Psychology of Groups* (New York: John Wiley & Sons, 1959).

[542] Thompson, J. D., et al. (eds.), *Comparative Studies in Administration* (Pittsburgh: University of Pittsburgh Press, 1959).
   a. Thompson, J. D., and A. Tuden, "Strategies, Structures and Processes of Organizational Decision."

[543] ——, and W. J. McEwen, "Organizational Goals and Environment: Goal-Setting as an Interaction Process," *American Sociological Review*, **23**, 1958, pp. 23–31.

[544] Thompson, V. A., *Modern Organization* (New York: Knopf, 1961).

[545] Thorndike, E. L., *Animal Intelligence: Experimental Studies* (New York: The Macmillan Co., 1911).

594 BIBLIOGRAPHY

[546] Thurston, R. H., "Instruction in Mechanical Engineering," *The Journal of the Franklin Institute,* **118,** 1884, pp. 188–196.

[547] ——, *The Animal as a Machine and a Prime Mover, and the Laws of Energetics* (New York: John Wiley & Sons, 1894).

[548] Thurstone, L. L., "Testing Intelligence and Aptitudes," *Hygeia,* **23,** 1945, pp. 32–36, 50–52, 54.

[549] Tolman, E. C., "Purpose and Cognition: The Determiners of Animal Learning," *Psychological Review,* **32,** 1925, pp. 285–297.

[550] Trow, D. B., "Autonomy and Job Satisfaction in Task-Oriented Groups," *Journal of Abnormal and Social Psychology,* **54,** 1957, pp. 204–209.

[551] Trueblood, R. M., "Internal Control," internal memorandum (mimeo) (Chicago: Touche, Ross, Bailey and Smart, Certified Public Accountants).

[552] ——, and R. M. Cyert, *Sampling Techniques in Accounting* (Englewood Cliffs, N. J.: Prentice-Hall, 1957).

[553] Truman, D. B., *Administrative Decentralization* (Chicago: The University of Chicago Press, 1940).

[554] Tucker, A. W., and R. D. Luce (eds.), *Contributions to the Theory of Games, IV,* Annals of Mathematical Studies No. 40 (Princeton: Princeton University Press, 1959).
   a. Harsanyi, J. C., "A Bargaining Model for the Cooperative n-Person Game."
   b. Vickrey, W., "Self-Policing Properties of Certain Imputation Sets."

[555] Tukey, J. W., "Conclusions vs. Decision," *Technometrics,* **2,** 1960, pp. 423–433.

[556] Udy, S. H., Jr., " 'Bureaucratic' Elements in Organizations," *American Sociological Review,* **23,** 1958, pp. 415–418.

[557] ——, *Organization of Work: A Comparative Analysis of Production Among Nonindustrial Peoples* (New Haven: Human Relations Area Files Press, 1959).

[558] ——, " 'Bureaucracy' and 'Rationality' in Weber's Organization Theory," *American Sociological Review,* **24,** 1959, pp. 791–795.

[559] ——, "Technical and Institutional Factors in Production Organization: A Preliminary Model," *American Journal of Sociology,* **67,** 1961, pp. 247–260.

[560] ——, "Rejoinder to A. L. Stinchcombe's 'Comment,' " *American Journal of Sociology,* **67,** 1961, pp. 259–260.

[561] ——, "Administrative Rationality, Social Setting and Organizational Development," *American Journal of Sociology,* **68,** 1962, pp. 299–308.

[562] United States Government, NAVEXOS P-2426B (Washington, D. C.: Department of the Navy, 1962).
   a. Vol. 1, "Review of Management of the Department of the Navy," Advisory Committee J. H. Dillon, Adm. C. U. Ricketts, Vice Adm. G. F. Beardsley, Lt. Gen. J. C. Munn, and J. J. Corson.
   b. Vol. 2, Study 1, "External Environmental Influences Study," Study Director Rear Adm. J. U. Smith.
   c. Vol. 2, Study 2, "Planning, Programming, Budgeting, and Appraising Study," Study Director Rear Adm. H. A. Renken.
   d. Vol. 2, Study 3, "Research and Development Management Study," Study Director Rear Adm. R. Bennett (Ret.).
   e. Vol. 2, Study 4, "Material Management Study," Study Director Rear Adm. R. E. M. Ward.

f. Vol. 2, Study 5, "Manpower Management Study," Study Director Rear Adm. H. J. Kossler.

g. Vol. 2, Study 6, "Facilities Management Study," Study Director Capt. Madison Hall, Jr.

h. Vol. 2, Study 7, "Financial Management Study," Study Director Capt. S. H. Ivison, Jr.

[563] Urwick, L., "The Function of Administration," in L. Gulick, and L. Urwick, *Papers on the Science of Administration* (New York: Columbia University Institute of Public Administration, 1937).

[564] ———, *The Elements of Administration* (New York: Harper, 1943).

[565] Uzawa, H., "On the Stability of Dynamic Processes," *Technical Report No. 61* (Stanford, Calif.: Stanford University, Department of Economics, 1958).

[566] Vallentin, A., *Leonardo da Vinci,* translated by E. W. Dickes (New York: The Viking Press, 1938).

[567] VanCott, H. P., and J. D. Folley, Jr., "Concepts and Approach to Human Factors in Systems Design," in J. D. Folley, Jr. (ed.), *Human Factors Methods for Systems Design,* Research Report No. AIR-290-60-FR-225, ONR Contract No. Nonr-2700(00) (Pittsburgh: American Institute for Research, 1960).

[568] Van Riper, P. P., "A Survey of Materials for the Study of Military Management," *The American Political Science Review,* **49,** 1955, pp. 828–850.

[569] ———, "Public Personnel Literature: The Last Decade," *Public Personnel Review,* **22,** October 1961, pp. 226–231.

[570] Vazsonyi, A., *Gaming Techniques for Management Planning and Control,* Foundation for Instrumentation Education and Research, Oct. 1960.

[570a] Vegetius, "De Re Militari," in Major T. R. Phillips (ed.), *Roots of Strategy* (Harrisburg, Pa.: The Military Service Publishing Co., 1940).

[571] Videbeck, R., and A. P. Bates, "An Experimental Study of Conformity to Role Expectations," *Sociometry,* **22,** 1959, pp. 1–11.

[572] Viteles, M., *Motivation and Morale in Industry* (New York: Norton, 1953).

[573] Von Bertalanffy, L., "An Outline of General System Theory," *The British Journal for the Philosophy of Science,* **1,** No. 2, 1950.

[574] ———, "General Systems Theory," in L. Von Bertalanffy and A. Rapaport (eds.), *General Systems* (Ann Arbor, Mich.: Society for General Systems Research, Vol. I, 1957).

[575] Von Mises, L., *Bureaucracy* (New Haven: Yale University Press, 1944).

[576] Von Neumann, J., and O. Morgenstern, *The Theory of Games and Economic Behavior* (Princeton: Princeton University Press, 1947).

[577] Vroom, V. H., *Some Personality Determinants of the Effects of Participation* (Englewood Cliffs, N. J.: Prentice-Hall, 1960).

[578] ———, and N. F. R. Maier, "Industrial Social Psychology," *Annual Review of Psychology* (Palo Alto, Calif.: Annual Reviews, Inc., 1961).

[579] ———, "The Self Concept: A Balance Theoretical Treatment," unpublished manuscript (Philadelphia: University of Pennsylvania, 1961).

[580] ———, *Work and Motivation* (New York: John Wiley & Sons, 1964).

[581] Waldo, D., *The Administrative State* (New York: The Ronald Press Co., 1948).

[582] Waldo, D., *Ideas and Issues in Public Administration* (New York: Mc-Graw-Hill Book Co., 1953).

[583] Wallace, A. D., "Separation Spaces," *Annals of Mathematics,* **42**, 1941, pp. 687–697.

[584] Warner, W. L., and J. C. Abegglen, *Occupational Mobility in American Business and Industry, 1928–1952* (Minneapolis: University of Minnesota Press, 1955).

[585] ———, and J. O. Low, *The Social System of the Modern Factory* (New Haven, Conn.: Yale University Press, 1947).

[586] ———, P. P. Van Riper, N. H. Martin, and O. F. Collins, *The American Federal Executive* (New Haven, Conn.: Yale University Press, 1962).

[587] Wärneryd, K. E., *Motiv och Beslut i Företagsledningens Marknadspolitik* (*Motives and Decisions in Management's Marketing Policy*) (Stockholm: Företagsekonomiska Förskningsinstitutet, 1956).

[588] Watts, G. B., "The Encyclopedia and the Descriptions des Arts et Métiers," *The French Review,* **25**, No. 6, 1952, pp. 444–454.

[589] Weber, Max, *From Max Weber: Essays in Sociology,* translated by H. H. Gerth and C. Wright Mills (New York: Oxford University Press, 1946).

[590] ———, *The Theory of Social and Economic Organization,* translated by A. M. Henderson and T. Parsons (New York: Oxford University Press, and Glencoe, Ill.: The Free Press, 1947).

[591] ———, *General Economic History* (Glencoe, Ill.: The Free Press, 1950).

[592] Weingartner, H. M., *Mathematical Programming and the Analysis of Capitol Budgets* (Englewood Cliffs, N. J.: Prentice-Hall, 1963).

[593] Weiss, R. S., *Processes of Organization* (Ann Arbor, Mich.: Institute for Social Research, University of Michigan, 1956).

[594] Weld, C. R., *The History of the Royal Society, with Memoirs of the Presidents* (London: John W. Parker, 1848).

[595] Wendt, H. W., "Motivation, Effort, and Performance," in D. C. McClelland (ed.), *Studies in Motivation* (New York: Appleton-Century-Crofts, 1955).

[596] Westerlund, G., *Group Leadership* (Stockholm: Nordisk Rotogravyr, 1952).

[597] Whinston, A., "Price Guides in Decentralized Institutions," Ph.D. thesis (Pittsburgh: Carnegie Institute of Technology, Graduate School of Industrial Administration, 1962).

[598] White, H., "Uses of Mathematics in Sociology," in J. C. Charlesworth (ed.), *Mathematics and the Social Sciences* (Philadelphia: American Academy of Political and Social Science, 1963).

[599] ———, *An Anatomy of Kinship* (Englewood Cliffs, N. J.: Prentice-Hall, 1963).

[600] White, L. D., *Trends in Public Administration* (New York: McGraw-Hill Book Co., 1933).

[601] Whyte, W. F., *Human Relations in the Restaurant Industry* (New York: McGraw-Hill Book Co., 1948).

[602] ———, "Social Structure of the Restaurant," *American Journal of Sociology,* **54**, 1949, pp. 302–310.

[603] Whyte, W. H., Jr., *The Organization Man* (New York: Simon and Schuster, 1956).

[604] Wiest, W. M., L. W. Porter, and E. E. Ghiselli, "Relationships Between Individual Proficiency and Team Performance and Proficiency," *Journal of Applied Psychology,* **45,** 1961, pp. 435–440.

[605] Wilson, Erle, *Adams of the Bounty* (New York: Popular Library, 1959).

[605a] Wirdenius, H., *Supervisors at Work* (Stockholm: Swedish Council for Personnel Administration, 1958).

[606] Wolf, A., *A History of Science Technology and Philosophy in the Sixteenth and Seventeenth Centuries,* 2nd ed. (London: George Allen & Unwin, Ltd., 1950).

[607] ———, *A History of Science Technology and Philosophy in the Eighteenth Century,* 2nd ed. revised by D. McKie (London: George Allen & Unwin, Ltd., 1952).

[608] Wolf, W. B., *The Management of Personnel* (Belmont, Calif.: Wadsworth Publishing Co., Inc., 1961).

[609] Woodger, J. H., *The Axiomatic Method in Biology* (London: Cambridge University Press, 1937).

[610] Woodward, Joan, *Management and Technology* (London: Her Majesty's Stationery Office, 1958).

[611] Wright, S. L., *The Story of the Franklin Institute* (Philadelphia: The Franklin Institute, 1938).

[612] Wyatt, S., F. G. L. Stock, and L. Frost, "Incentives in Repetitive Work: A Practical Experiment in a Factory," *Industrial Health Research Board, Report No. 69* (London: His Majesty's Stationery Office, 1934).

[613] Yost, E., *Partners for Life* (New York: The American Society of Mechanical Engineers, 1949).

[614] Young, P. T., *Motivation and Emotion: A Survey of the Determinants of Human and Animal Activity* (New York: John Wiley & Sons, 1961).

[615] Young, T., *A Course of Lectures on Natural Philosophy and the Mechanical Arts* (London: Porter and Walton, 1845).

[616] Yovits, M. C., and S. Cameron (eds.), *Self-Organizing Systems* (New York: Pergamon Press, 1960).
    a. Campbell, D. T., "Blind Variation and Selective Survival as a General Strategy in Knowledge-Processes."
    b. Newell, A., "Comments in Response to a Paper by D. T. Campbell."
    c. ———, J. C. Shaw, and H. A. Simon, "A Variety of Intelligent Learning in a General Problem Solver."

[617] Zander, A., *Effects of Group Goals Upon Personal Goals,* Technical Report No. 12, Nonr. Contracts 1147(03), 2285(01), 3088(00), 1961.

ALTERNATE AUTHOR DESIGNATIONS

Abegglen, J. C. [584]
Ackoff, R. L. [125], [126]
Anscombe, F. J. [486a]
Arensberg, C. [106]
Argyris, C. [529a]
Armstrong, H. G. [471]
Arnoff, E. L. [126]
Arrow, K. J. [210]
Arrowood, A. J. [312]
Ås, D. [207]
Asch, S. E. [61a]
Asimow, M. [515]
Atkinson, J. W. [376]
Atwater, F. S. [65]
Aumann, R. J. [486b]

Bach, G. L. [19]
Back, K. [191]
Bakke, E. W. [247a]
Bales, R. F. [41], [100a]
Bass, B. M. [61], [349], [475a]
Bates, A. P. [571]
Beardsley, G. F. [562a]
Beatty, H. R. [9]
Beem, H. P. [132]
Benne, K. D. [59]
Bennett, R. [562d]
Bernstein, B. B. [220], [372]
Berry, C. A. [472]
Biddle, B. J. [70]
Biel, W. C. [105]
Blake, R. R. [61b]
Bowers, D. G. [467]
Bowes, A. E. [240]

Fish, L. S. [280]
Fleishman, E. A. [295], [348]
Floor, L. G. [306]
Folley, J. D., Jr. [567]
Ford, C. J. [413]
Forrester, J. W. [233a]
Fouraker, L. E. [499]
France, R. R. [37]
French, J. R. P. [100b], [129]
Frost, L. [612]

Gaus, J. M. [18]
Gerard, H. B. [192]
Gerth, H. H. [589]
Ghisell, E. E. [604]
Gilchrist, J. C. [487]
Girshick, M. A. [74]
Glaser, R. [217]
Goldbeck, R. A. [372]
Goldstein, G. D. [395]
Gordon, M. J. [270]
Gray, A. [393]
Gregory, D. [461]
Griswell, J. [481]
Guba, E. G. [214]
Guetzkow, H. [27], [502]
Gulick, L. [563]
Gurin, G. [306]

Haberstroh, C. J. [457]
Haire, M. [215], [529b]
Hall, Madison, Jr. [562g]
Hammond, S. [531a]
Handlin, O. [90]
Harary, F. [424]
Harsanyi, J. C. [554a]
Hartley, E. L. [358], [531]
Hawley, A. H. [205]
Henderson, A. M. [590]
Hemphill, J. K. [435]
High, W. A. [133]
Hockey, B. [393]
Holt, C. C. [233b]
Hudson, A. E. [413]
Hughes, J. W. [415]
Hugh-Jones, E. M. [302]
Hunt, J. McV. [346]
Hurwicz, L. [26]
Hymovitch, B. [192]

Mason, W. S. [236]
Massarik, F. [536]
Massie, J. L. [256]
Massy, W. F. [204]
Mausner, B. [267]
McBride, D. [461]
McClelland, D. C. [595]
McEachern, A. W. [236]
McEwen, W. J. [543]
McGee, R. J. [95]
McGregor, D. M. [457c]
McKie, D. [607]
Merk, F. [90]
Mesarović, M. D. [441b]
Miller, G. A. [210], [233c]
Miller, M. H. [118]
Mills, C. Wright [589]
Miner, H. M. [205]
Mishler, E. G. [520]
Modigliani, F. [281]
Morgenstern, O. [576]
Morison, S. E. [90]
Morse, N. C. [305]
Mouton, J. S. [61b]
Munn, J. C. [562a]
Muth, J. F. [281]
Myers, C. A. [252]

Nanus, B. [523]
Newcomb, T. M. [358], [531]
Newell, A. [105], [616b], [616c]
Nisbet, R. A. [392]
Nordlie, P. G. [378]

Paige, G. D. [510]
Pal, A. K. [457a]
Park, O. [11]
Park, T. [11]
Parsons, L. [53]
Parsons, T. [41], [590]
Pavlik, W. P. [436]
Pepinsky, P. N. [263], [436]
Petrullo, L. [349]
Pfiffner, J. M. [132]
Pfouts, R. W. [26]
Philips, T. R. [530], [570a]
Plowman, E. G. [438]
Porter, L. W. [604]
Preiss, J. J. [7]

Radner, R. [486*d*]
Raiffa, H. [356]
Rapaport, A. [126], [574]
Rankin, E. F., Jr. [69]
Raven, B. [100*b*], [192]
Reilley, E. [216]
Reimer, E. [407]
Reitman, W. R. [30], [486*e*]
Renken, H. A. [562*c*]
Ricketts, C. U. [562*a*]
Riddle, R. J. [39]
Roe, A. [439]
Rogers, M. S. [497]
Rohrer, J. H. [416]
Rome, B. K. [454]
Rosenbaum, W. B. [6]
Rosencranz, H. A. [69], [70]
Rosenthal, Franz [315]

Savvas, J. D. [135]
Savage, L. [209]
Sayles, L. R. [107]
Schachter, S. [191]
Schlesinger, A. M. [90]
Schlesinger, A. M., Jr. [90]
Schmeckebier, L. F. [388]
Schmidt, K. P. [11]
Schwartz, J. T. [173]
Scott, W. R. [76]
Sears, P. S. [346]
Selvin, H. C. [393]
Shapley, L. S. [31]
Sharaf, H. A. [374]
Shaw, J. C. [421], [616*c*]
Sheats, P. [58]
Shepard, H. A. [59*a*]
Shepard, R. N. [486*g*]
Sherif, M. [416]
Sherif, C. W. [489]
Shevitz, R. N. [435]
Shils, E. A. [430]
Shubik, M. [201], [235], [342]
Shultz, G. P. [419]
Siegel, S. [54], [154], [201]
Silander, F. S. [231]
Simon, H. A. [233*d*], [242], [281], [367], [419], [421], [457*e*], [616*c*]
Simpson, G. G. [439]
Sims, J. R. [371]
Sizelove, O. J. [17]
Slater, P. E. [41]

Smith, G. H. E. [65]
Smith, H. L. [280]
Smith, J. U. [562*b*]
Snell, J. L. [313]
Solomon, H. [481]
Stackman, H. A. [65]
Starbuck, W. H. [145]
Stellar, E. [164]
Stock, G. L. [612]
Stogdill, R. M. [250]
Storrs, C. [186]
Suppes, P. [154], [210], [481]
Symonds, G. H. [119], [478]
Synderman, B. B. [267]

Tassone, J. [497]
Taylor, F. V. [73]
Teitelbaum, L. N. [123]
Thayer, P. W. [377]
Thibaut, J. [191]
Thomas, E. J. [70]
Thompson, C. B. [96]
Thompson, F. B. [441*c*]
Thompson, G. L. [314]
Tomick, E. [70]
Townsend, H. [177]
Tucker, A. W. [31], [326]
Tuden, A. [542*a*]
Twyman, J. P. [68], [70]
Tyndall, G. [503]

VanRiper, P. P. [586]
Vaughn, J. A. [48]
Vaughan, W. S. [378]
Veroff, J. [245]
Vickrey, W. [554*b*]
Volkmann, J. [104]
Von Haller Gilmer, B. [189]

Ward, R. E. M. [562*e*]
Warner, W. L. [371]
Watson, J. [353]
Weber, Max [393*b*]
Weschler, I. R. [536]
Westley, B. [353]
Whinston, A. [156]
Whisler, T. L. [337], [419], [496*a*]
White, P. E. [341]
White, R. K. [345]
Whyte, R. K. [358*b*]

Willner, D. [465]
Winer, B. J. [250]
Winters, P. R. [131]
Wolf, J. J. [498]
Wolfe, P. [153]
Woolsey, C. N. [253]
Wright, H. F. [43]

Yamey, B. S. [162]
Young, G. S. [276]
Yovits, M. C. [395]

Zander, A. [100]